**SAP PRESS e-books**

Print or e-book, Kindle or iPad, workplace or airplane: Choose where and how to read your SAP PRESS books! You can now get all our titles as e-books, too:

- By download and online access
- For all popular devices
- And, of course, DRM-free

Convinced? Then go to www.sap-press.com and get your e-book today.

Sourcing and Procurement with SAP S/4HANA®

PRESS

SAP PRESS is a joint initiative of SAP and Rheinwerk Publishing. The know-how offered by SAP specialists combined with the expertise of Rheinwerk Publishing offers the reader expert books in the field. SAP PRESS features first-hand information and expert advice, and provides useful skills for professional decision-making.

SAP PRESS offers a variety of books on technical and business-related topics for the SAP user. For further information, please visit our website: *www.sap-press.com*.

Jawad Akhtar
Production Planning with SAP S/4HANA
2019, 1010 pages, hardcover and e-book
www.sap-press.com/4821

Mahesh Babu MG
PP-DS with SAP S/4HANA
2020, 476 pages, hardcover and e-book
www.sap-press.com/4951

Namita Sachan, Aman Jain
Warehouse Management with SAP S/4HANA (2nd Edition)
2020, 909 pages, hardcover and e-book
www.sap-press.com/5005

Jawad Akhtar, Martin Murray
Materials Management with SAP S/4HANA: Business Processes and Configuration
2018, 946 pages, hardcover and e-book
www.sap-press.com/4711

Justin Ashlock

Sourcing and Procurement with SAP S/4HANA®

Rheinwerk
Publishing

Editor Will Jobst
Acquisitions Editor Emily Nicholls
Copyeditor Melinda Rankin
Cover Design Graham Geary
Photo Credit Shutterstock.com/1162492597/© Barry Neal
Layout Design Vera Brauner
Production Hannah Lane
Typesetting III-satz, Husby (Germany)
Printed and bound in the United States of America, on paper from sustainable sources

ISBN 978-1-4932-1911-7
© 2020 by Rheinwerk Publishing, Inc., Boston (MA)
2nd edition 2020

Library of Congress Cataloging-in-Publication Data
Names: Ashlock, Justin, author.
Title: Sourcing and procurement with SAP S/4HANA / Justin Ashlock.
Description: 2nd edition. | Bonn ; Boston : Rheinwerk Publishing, 2020. |
  Includes index.
Identifiers: LCCN 2019052882 (print) | LCCN 2019052883 (ebook) | ISBN
  9781493219117 (hardcover) | ISBN 9781493219124 (ebook)
Subjects: LCSH: Industrial procurement--Data processing. | Management
  information systems. | SAP HANA (Electronic resource)
Classification: LCC HD39.5 .A844 2020 (print) | LCC HD39.5 (ebook) | DDC
  658.70285/53--dc23
LC record available at https://lccn.loc.gov/2019052882
LC ebook record available at https://lccn.loc.gov/2019052883

Contents at a Glance

Dear Reader,

You're pretty good at getting the things you need.

How do I know? Well, in front of you you've got the key to sourcing and procurement with SAP S/4HANA. But then again—for you, acquiring the right tools is a professional concern. If you're a logistics consultant, an implementation lead, or a team member, then your project's success depends on getting the right information you need to set up the system. Or perhaps you're a process owner, manager, buyer, or analyst, in which case your day-to-day productivity hinges on making sure the right items get to the right places.

SAP PRESS authors get the things they need, too. For example, logistics star Justin Ashlock has compiled years of consulting experience, fine-tuned SAP acumen and best practices, and plain old hard work into this new edition on SAP S/4HANA Sourcing and Procurement. Justin has gone to great lengths to make sure that all the S&P information you need-to-know are bought to one place: this book.

What did you think about *Sourcing and Procurement with SAP S/4HANA*? Your comments and suggestions are the most useful tools to help us make our books the best they can be. Please feel free to contact me and share any praise or criticism you may have.

Thank you for purchasing a book from SAP PRESS!

Will Jobst
Editor, SAP PRESS

willj@rheinwerk-publishing.com
www.sap-press.com
Rheinwerk Publishing · Boston, MA

Contents

1   Introduction to Sourcing and Procurement   31

2   Implementation Options   51

3   Organizational Structure

4   Master Data

5   Operational Procurement

6   Automated and Direct Procurement

7   Inventory Management

8   Contracts Management

9   Enterprise Contract Management and Assembly   393

10   External Sourcing   425

11 Invoice and Payables Management   455

12   Supplier Management

13   Centralized Procurement   557

14   Sourcing and Procurement Analytics   599

15   Integrating SAP S/4HANA with SAP Ariba and SAP Fieldglass

619

16   Customizing the UI

669

Foreword

The very positive reception of the first edition of this book revealed to us that it provides invaluable support for anyone interested in SAP S/4HANA Sourcing and Procurement. I'm very excited about this interest and look forward to illuminating numerous compelling innovations in this second edition.

In the first edition of this book, we described core functionalities across indirect and direct procurement; how to configure purchasing, sourcing, and invoicing; and how to benefit from real-time analytics. Now, with the second edition, we not only present functional enhancements across all areas, but also introduce new innovations for central procurement and the intelligent enterprise.

Let me briefly emphasize the importance and significance of these two themes.

Whether through the acquisition of another company with unconsolidated systems or because one or several divisions have created their own systems, distributed procurement landscapes with numerous backend systems are quite common across larger companies.

Procurement is particularly impacted by this lack of centralization in an ERP landscape. As a business function, procurement benefits from scale and volume: the more volume you put through a supplier or in purchasing an item, the greater the cost savings and the more efficient the process becomes. Thus, the business advantages of centrally managing local procurement entities are evident.

In this book, you'll learn not only how SAP supports you in achieving and hitting these business needs and advantages, but also how a transformation to central procurement leads to a lower total cost of ownership by consolidating your landscape into a smaller number of backend systems.

Along similar lines, we continue our tremendous investment in realizing SAP's corporate strategy of the intelligent enterprise for the entire line of business in procurement.

The intelligent suite as one component of the intelligent enterprise features integrated business scenarios across SAP S/4HANA, SAP Ariba, and SAP Fieldglass. It produces operational data to automate day-to-day business processes, share insights across functions, and better interact with customers, suppliers, employees, and partners. Intelligent technologies embedded in the intelligent suite, such as machine learning and real-time analytics, deliver additional business value.

How does SAP's procurement line of business put this strategy into practice? You will find many examples in this book, but allow me to emphasize two here. First, SAP's procurement solutions increase your automation rate for business documents across functions by connecting your systems and your buyers with your sellers and trading partners, leveraging the combined power of SAP S/4HANA and the Ariba Network. Second, SAP's procurement solutions allow you to take advantage of discovering, visualizing, and predicting purchasing spend with thanks to SAP Analytics Cloud integrated with SAP S/4HANA to uncover saving opportunities.

We hope you enjoy exploring in this second edition how the power of SAP S/4HANA Sourcing and Procurement delivers a tangible step up in performance, speed, agility, visibility, and control.

Salvatore Lombardo
Head of SAP S/4HANA Source-to-Pay and Order-to-Cash

Preface

This is the second edition of *Sourcing and Procurement with SAP S/4HANA*, a book devoted to procurement topics in SAP's flagship enterprise resource planning (ERP) solution. Once more of a chapter within books on materials management, the second edition you hold in your hands (or on your tablet) now has quite a large size and scope. This shouldn't come as a surprise, as SAP has been a leader in the procurement space for several decades now, having pioneered the first integrated ERP systems to run in real time in an integrated fashion. With the advent of the cloud, SAP has also built out cloud areas for procurement that will be further illuminated in this book, such as SAP Cloud Platform, supporting augmented decision-making functionality in both SAP S/4HANA Sourcing and Procurement and SAP S/4HANA Cloud for enterprise contract assembly. SAP has also pursued an acquisition strategy to further extend its leadership in the areas of procurement and sourcing, most notably with the acquisitions of SAP Ariba, SAP Fieldglass, and SAP Concur.

With SAP S/4HANA Enterprise Management, SAP has moved the needle in regard to speed and simplicity to such a degree that it also creates an array of new features and functionality on the procurement side of the ledger. No longer do users need to conduct transactions in an ERP environment and then swivel their chairs over to another system to conduct after-the-fact analysis. The tables overhaul and in-memory data design in SAP S/4HANA mean that both transactions and analysis can be conducted directly in a single system, at exponentially faster speeds. Combine this with SAP Cloud Platform for supplier collaboration on contracts and augmented decision-making, along with industry-leading cloud solutions from SAP Ariba and SAP Fieldglass, and you have SAP S/4HANA as the digital core, with SAP Ariba and SAP Fieldglass covering procurement transformation at all levels of an organization.

This book covers SAP S/4HANA Sourcing and Procurement in detail and lays out functionality, configuration, and guidelines for running successful implementations in each of its areas. We provide you with a comprehensive guide to implementing SAP S/4HANA Sourcing and Procurement, as well as key integration points in leveraging the cloud solutions from SAP Ariba and SAP Fieldglass.

Target Audience

This book should be of interest for anyone working with SAP S/4HANA Enterprise Management and SAP Ariba and/or SAP Fieldglass, or anyone looking to roll out procurement solutions in either an on-premise or cloud environment. Business users, procurement managers, and consultants are the primary target audience of this type of book. This book assumes a familiarity with and interest in procurement solutions and terminology, as well as project management and delivery topics around these solutions. Finally, critical reasoning skills for understanding just where these solutions will provide your organization the most value individually and in concert will serve you in good stead in this journey.

Objective

This book's focus is on implementing SAP S/4HANA Sourcing and Procurement, in conjunction with key SAP cloud solutions for procurement, principally SAP Ariba and SAP Fieldglass. Together, SAP S/4HANA, as well as SAP Ariba's solutions and SAP Fieldglass, cover a vast area of collaboration and processes between an organization and its suppliers. Although it's not possible to cover every permutation of configuration in these solutions, this book will provide an in-depth look at each of the SAP S/4HANA solution areas for procurement and furnish system-specific guidelines, methodologies, and functionality, as well as provide guidance for integrating SAP S/4HANA with select SAP Ariba solutions.

Structure of This Book

Organized into seventeen chapters, the first four chapters cover a general SAP S/4HANA overview, implementation options, organization structure, and master data setup. The remaining chapters cover the major procurement solution areas in SAP S/4HANA, beginning with operational procurement and concluding with the SAP Fiori user interface topics.

This book is a comprehensive guide to setting up and using SAP S/4HANA Sourcing and Procurement. After Chapters 1–4, each chapter describes the features and post-go-live use of key functionality for a given procurement topic, teaches how to configure it, and explains how to integrate it with relevant applications using system screenshots and detailed, step-by-step instructions.

As a feature, the book uses text boxes to show readers where SAP S/4HANA functionality overlaps with SAP Ariba, or where an SAP Ariba application (e.g., the Ariba Network) can be used to optimize a particular task.

- **Chapter 1: Introduction to Sourcing and Procurement**
  This chapter explains the software-agnostic procurement business process for today's enterprises, the boundaries between operational procurement with an ERP system and strategic procurement with an SAP Cloud solution such as SAP Ariba or SAP Fieldglass, and the key simplifications that have arrived with SAP S/4HANA.

- **Chapter 2: Implementation Options**
  SAP customers can choose from on-premise or cloud versions of SAP S/4HANA implementations, which have slightly different functional scopes and IT project requirements and therefore have their own pros and cons. This chapter defines processes covered by each product and the relative merits of each SAP S/4HANA implementation approach. The chapter closes with a description of the SAP Activate methodology and the project setup for each implementation scenario.

- **Chapter 3: Organizational Structure**
  As with previous versions of SAP ERP, defining a core organizational structure foundation for SAP S/4HANA Sourcing and Procurement is a key step for a successful implementation and system adoption. This chapter will cover that organizational structure, much of which is similar to previous iterations of SAP.

- **Chapter 4: Master Data**
  Master data for supporting procurement and sourcing activities also remains similar to previous versions of SAP ERP. Material masters, material groups, units of measure, and other familiar objects remain central. One significant change with SAP S/4HANA, however, centers on the consolidation of both customer and supplier master records into a single business partner record in SAP S/4HANA. This chapter will review these objects and lay out in detail what is required to convert supplier masters in SAP ERP to the new business partner model in SAP S/4HANA.

- **Chapter 5: Operational Procurement**
  What we think of as operational procurement happens between the creation of a purchase order and the delivery of an invoice. This chapter covers the actions that occur among the purchase order, goods receipt, and invoicing for day-to-day purchasing of indirect materials and services.

- **Chapter 6: Automated and Direct Procurement**
  Much of direct procurement and other reoccurring types of procurement can be

automated in SAP S/4HANA, leveraging tried-and-true approaches such as source lists, reorder points, information records, and scheduling agreements. materials requirement planning (MRP) ties all of this together and creates requisitions as in previous SAP ERP editions. However, MRP has also changed significantly from previous versions of SAP ERP, with the new MRP Live transaction. MRP Live enables users to leverage the speed of SAP S/4HANA to run in-system modeling of requirements. This chapter outlines the approaches and configuration steps for setting up direct procurement and automating this and other types of reoccurring procurement.

- **Chapter 7: Inventory Management**
  Inventory management is fully integrated with SAP S/4HANA Sourcing and Procurement and supports many procurement activities and processes. This chapter will outline the various processes in procurement that integrate with inventory management, such as reservations, stock transfer postings (STPs), and special stocks, as well as how to configure inventory management to support these processes in SAP S/4HANA.

- **Chapter 8: Contracts Management**
  Contracts solidify pricing and volumes with suppliers, as well as terms and conditions, making contracts a must-have for orderly procurement operations. ERP systems have traditionally focused upon the operational aspects of contracts, integrating the negotiated terms into transactions. SAP S/4HANA continues this tradition while adding some nuances on the integration side with SAP Ariba and embracing a robust contract creation with enterprise contract management, explained in Chapter 9. This chapter outlines contract functionality and usage in SAP S/4HANA Sourcing and Procurement, configuration, and integration with SAP Ariba Contracts.

- **Chapter 9: Enterprise Contract Management and Assembly**
  In the interim between the last edition and the current edition of this book, a name change and further build out of the offering has occurred for Legal Content Management and Assembly, which is now called Enterprise Contract Management and Assembly. There are three new names and acronyms, as well as updated functionality:

  - Enterprise contract management
  - Enterprise contract assembly
  - Enterprise contract management and assembly

This chapter outlines contract functionality and the use of enterprise contract management and assembly in SAP S/4HANA Sourcing and Procurement, as well as configuration and integration with general contract business processes.

- **Chapter 10: External Sourcing**
  In the source-to-pay process, external sourcing can occur after forecasting and planning have been completed, but prior to any transactions in the system; for a purchase requisition or order for which a source of supply has not been defined; or simply at the whim of a purchasing agent planning ahead. Sourcing in SAP S/4HANA leverages the sourcing cockpit available in previous versions of SAP ERP, along with native integration with SAP Ariba Sourcing. This chapter will outline the various areas in a procurement process in which sourcing can be inserted, configuration of sourcing in SAP S/4HANA, and the integration activation and setup for SAP Ariba Strategic Sourcing.

- **Chapter 11: Invoice and Payables Management**
  Once a good or service has been requested, approved, ordered, and received, it's time for payment. This chapter covers the invoicing/accounts functionality in SAP S/4HANA from a process and configuration standpoint, as well as integration with OpenText and SAP Ariba.

- **Chapter 12: Supplier Management**
  The final step in the procurement process is to evaluate a supplier to determine whether it's wise to continue partnering with them. This chapter examines supplier management and evaluation topics, providing step-by-step instructions for setup and use of key SAP S/4HANA functionality.

- **Chapter 13: Centralized Procurement**
  Large and small SAP customers often have multiple ERP environments, either from acquisitions, from different businesses, or for other reasons that seemed like a good idea at the time. When it comes to procurement, centralizing your procurement activities allows for economies of scale, which in turn translates into better spending and larger savings advantages. SAP S/4HANA for central procurement has been around for several iterations of SAP S/4HANA, but it has increased in importance for customers moving off of SAP Supplier Relationship Management (SAP SRM) with multiple backend systems under management, as well as SAP Ariba implementations that need to interface with multiple backend systems for document management. This chapter outlines the core functionality of SAP S/4HANA for central procurement, as well as its integration capabilities with SAP Ariba guided buying.

- **Chapter 14: Sourcing and Procurement Analytics**
  This chapter teaches readers how to use existing SAP S/4HANA reports to analyze their sourcing and procurement processes in real time. It highlights key reports for spend analysis, contract expiration, sourcing, and supplier performance that are common to many organizations, teaches how to configure those reports, and shows where they supply/receive data to or from peripheral cloud applications.

- **Chapter 15: Integrating SAP S/4HANA with SAP Ariba and SAP Fieldglass**
  Integration of cloud solutions, such as SAP Ariba and SAP Fieldglass, with the digital core ERP system remains a key topic for SAP S/4HANA Sourcing and Procurement. This chapter outlines the main integration areas for these applications with SAP S/4HANA and provides high-level approaches.

- **Chapter 16: Customizing the UI**
  If business users prefer to update or fine-tune the user interface for organization-specific roles or user access, they can! This chapter teaches readers how to define roles, configure the UI, and set up the project.

- **Chapter 17: Conclusion**
  This chapter summarizes the preceding chapters, reiterates the implementation options for SAP customers, and considers how upcoming procurement topics like automation, big data, the Internet of Things, and artificial intelligence will impact the SAP procurement portfolio.

References and Resources

The following resources were used as references by the authors in the course of writing this book and should be consulted for continued learning:

- **SAP Help**
  http://help.sap.com
- **SAP Product Documentation, Downloads, Service, and RDS Content (Integration)**
  http://service.sap.com

Acknowledgments

Many colleagues and friends made significant contributions to this second edition. In particular, I would like to thank our editors, Emily Nicholls and Will Jobst of SAP Press; contributing authors Bob Gotschall, independent SAP expert and former long-time consultant at SAP, and Chelliah Soundar, principal consultant and member of the SAP Regional Implementation Group (RIG) for SAP S/4HANA; Salvatore Lombardo, SVP head of SAP S/4HANA source-to-pay and order-to-cash; Christine Hoffman, area engineering lead for SAP Sourcing and Analytics; Dennis Bruder, VP head of engineering for SAP S/4HANA source-to-pay; Peter Paschert, head of product for SAP S/4HANA for central procurement; Frank Suetterlin, head of product for enterprise contract management and assembly; Ingrid Nikkels, solution manager for SAP S/4HANA enterprise contract management and assembly; my mentor for all things IT and career—John Leslie King, William Warner Bishop Collegiate Professor of Information and professor of information at the School of Information, University of Michigan; Katrin Guenther, SVP and head of CX Success and Services Organization; Kristie Collins, global VP for CX Success and Services Delivery; Dr. Jochen Hoeffner, MEE Head of Practice PTP; Oleg Sokolov, CIS Head of Practice PTP; Kenneth Pechous, VP SAP Ariba Cloud Services Delivery NA; and our procure-to-pay practice colleagues, Anil Punjala, Paul Bibb, Matthew Cauthen, John Corcoran, Lora Holst, Workman Meeks, Amar Neburi, Tuan Pham, Alan Salgado, Rachith Srinivas, Ramesh Vasudevan, Joe Wolff, Kannan Krishnan, Tushar Ganguly, Tania DeRoche, Othon Roitman, Noel Nera, Mohit Kumar, Sanjay Panday, Mario Ponce, Viet Le, and Brendan MacBride. Finally, special thanks and love to my wonderful wife and sons for supporting my long weekends and writing sessions.

Justin Ashlock
Chicago, IL
January 2020

Chapter 1

Introduction to Sourcing and Procurement

At its core, procurement is simply the purchase of a good or service by one organization or individual from another organization or individual. Companies and governments require both direct and indirect inputs of this nature to deliver the goods and services they in turn seek to deliver to the marketplace or directly to their customer base.

This chapter explains the software-agnostic procurement business process for today's enterprises, the boundaries between operational procurement with an SAP ERP system and strategic sourcing with an SAP Cloud system such as SAP Ariba or SAP Fieldglass, and the key innovations and simplifications introduced with SAP S/4HANA.

1.1 Sourcing and Procurement Basics

Sourcing is a process of matching requirements and needs originating from an organization with a supplier to provide these goods and/or services, preferably under a negotiated price and set of conditions. Sourcing entails identifying and understanding the requirements, identifying the most viable set of suppliers, requesting information and bids from the suppliers, awarding the purchase to a supplier, and creating the follow-on documents via the procurement process.

Procurement often takes up where sourcing leaves off, issuing purchase requisitions and purchase orders for goods and/or services with the supplier identified during the sourcing process as the source of supply and then receiving and processing the receipts and invoices in the follow-on processes of a procure-to-pay process.

Sourcing and procurement are essential, core processes in enterprise resource planning (ERP). Without sourcing and procurement, production of a good or service isn't possible, and without production no goods/services are produced. Without goods/services to provide, no spending justification can be made by a government entity, nor can sales/revenues be obtained by a firm. Following this logic to its conclusion, without input, a government or enterprise can't deliver its goods and services, and without sourcing and procurement, you can't obtain input. Without sourcing and procurement, therefore, you can't run a firm or government.

1.1.1   Sourcing

Sourcing of goods and services is critical for an organization to meet its objectives and obligations in the marketplace and/or for its stakeholders. An example of a direct input driving strategic sourcing can be found in the airline industry. Airlines provide a service that is heavily dependent on fuel and its costs. The price of fuel can change daily, with airlines not always able to pass the costs (or, more recently, the savings) directly to their end customers. Fuel can comprise up to one-third of an airline's operating costs. At this level, fuel easily qualifies as a strategic sourcing area for an airline.

Unlike one-off items ordered by employees in the office or on the shop floor, strategic sourcing items have more predictable and sizeable quantity requirements and anticipated costs. If an organization fails to adequately estimate its needs in the strategic sourcing area, the consequences can be severe. Securing too little fuel at an airline can mean having to buy fuel on the spot market at much higher costs or even grounding flights. Sourcing from untested or appropriately vetted suppliers for strategic input can undermine the brand image, as products are shipped with a built-in point of failure. In severe cases, some organizations may not get a second chance to "make it right" and may be immediately cast into the dustbin of history. Quality control begins at the supplier level for any organization, especially if your products and services are the sum of your suppliers' inputs.

From a systems standpoint, strategic procurement requires three things from SAP ERP: First, you must have robust forecasting to accurately estimate supply needs. Some companies and organizations run forecasting for their business in Excel sheets and rely on historical experience. This is a 1.0 approach and doesn't scale well for larger enterprises. Second, strategic sourcing requires an understanding of inventory and supply chains. If you have supply requirements from end customers forecasted at a certain level, what does this mean at all levels of your production? Do the suppliers have enough lead time to provide the input required? Do the areas of production have the adequate inventory and quality-management processes in place to fulfill these requirements within the timeline required? Third, do you have the right suppliers for this undertaking at the optimal price? This is perhaps the most challenging area for SAP ERP because it requires collaboration, a weak point for the system.

The supplier collaboration area is a weak point for SAP ERP because, by definition, SAP ERP can't connect to the outside world unencumbered by security requirements and concerns. Yet SAP ERP forms the basis for forecasting and the interconnected production planning areas in the strategic procurement equation. SAP ERP is tightly integrated with inventory management and planning modules, which can be used to drive strategic purchasing automatically for purchases, issuing POs based on stock levels and forecast models. Collaboration with suppliers is best conducted in a demilitarized zone, in which the organization doesn't have to risk its crown jewels regularly to trade simple and complex pieces of information at a system level. This is why SAP Ariba is the go-to solution for strategic sourcing execution, especially when it's time to collaborate with suppliers. Basic supplier collaboration capabilities are also available in SAP S/4HANA.

In summary, strategic sourcing is central to an organization and spans many core areas, from finance to inventory and quality management to product development and production to sourcing. From a systems standpoint, both SAP ERP systems and supplier collaboration platforms/solutions are required to cover this area.

The supplier collaboration platform from an SAP solutions standpoint is SAP Ariba. To cover all strategic sourcing, using SAP Ariba alone isn't feasible because it would only be able to cover parts of the process and would need to integrate with the SAP ERP backend for others. However, handing this process entirely in SAP ERP creates its own challenges: supplier collaboration areas, from request for quotation/purchase/information (RFX) scenarios to contract negotiation to network-enabled suppliers for document exchange, are not as robust as in SAP Ariba or aren't available at all in SAP ERP, as in the case of network-enabled supplier collaboration.

1.1.2 Operational Procurement

Operational procurement keeps the lights on and the office supplies stocked for an organization. Much of this type of procurement can be driven directly at the employee level, rather than by a designated buyer aggregating demand and then placing larger orders. Depending on the industry and the process and system maturity of an organization, operational procurement is pushed all the way down to the requesting employee, centralized at a buyer level, often at the site, company division, or a centralized buying group for the entire company.

Operational procurement is transactional and conducted on a day-to-day basis to support the ongoing operations of the firm or government entity. Some direct procurement may be included in this designation, which usually is defined along the lines of cost, type, and volume. If any of these three characteristics is relatively high or classified as a direct, mission-critical input to an end product or successful execution of a service, the procurement of this good/service may be deemed strategic. By and large, strategic procurement usually centers on strategic sourcing for direct procurement activities, but an indirect product or service that has particularly high volume or cost relative to the operating costs of a company may also qualify.

Pushing procurement down to the employee level requires system support and capabilities. Employees must be able to quickly, intuitively find what they are looking for in the system, order it and have it approved by the corresponding manager with adequate approval authority, and then have the order either routed for sourcing and processing by a buyer or, if already sourced, sent directly to the designated supplier for fulfilment.

In a buyer-brokered model, employees on a shop floor, for example, go to their point of contact for purchasing and place orders and requests. These are then routed for approval and sourced either by the designated buyer or by a buyer group once approved. Many times, this model is positioned as the only way, due to system limitations or the inability of the general staff to create coherent orders in a system. The designated shopper and/or buyer model is seen as a way to get all orders into the system cleanly and with minimal issues. However, this puts the onus on and creates a bottleneck with the designated buyers: the employees have to explain to an individual what they need purchased, and the buyer needs to translate this to an order, source it, and process the shipment or have the supplier deliver to the original requestor. Issues around transcription errors (if the supplier has questions, the buyer is caught in the middle on every order), receiving (who handles the goods receipt—the buyer or the requestor), and invoice processing (who approves payment for the order having been fulfilled) all can detract from the centralization model's strengths.

Another factor to consider is the aspect of relevance to total spend. Indirect spend usually comprises no more than 17 to 20 percent of total spend, which may be too small an amount to prioritize from a systems standpoint or procurement standpoint in general. Each dollar of savings is essentially profit, however. Many large companies and organizations ignore potential savings of millions in operational procurement, not realizing that they will have to sell the equivalent of hundreds of millions of dollars of additional goods and services to realize the corresponding amount they just passed up by neglecting this area of their operations.

For operational procurement, it is preferable from a systems and process standpoint to push the procurement decision-making and ordering out to the point of need—

that is, the employee with job responsibilities that require this good or service. This requires enablement of the procurement process and simplification, to ensure that a casual user with a minimal amount of training can walk up, log in, and order an item in a small amount of time in an intuitive manner, providing the eventual supplier with a clear understanding of the product required, quantity with unit of measure, terms and conditions, expected delivery date, delivery address, any discounting, and a host of other information a typical casual user may not be able to provide or be interested in providing. Much of the information provided in this order to the supplier needs to be automatically generated, so as to not risk burdening the casual user with unnecessary steps and requirements to complete an order.

Finally, operational procurement done correctly requires, like most iterative processes, a phase of analysis and application of lessons learned, to make the process and the procurement activities iteratively more effective at an individual and an aggregate level. The aggregate analysis, in particular, needs to be conducted by someone tasked with understanding things at this level, usually a procurement specialist.

In summary, operational procurement is best initiated at the employee level, supported by adequate system and data processes, such as intuitive UIs, approval workflows, and minimal steps, as well as clean master data, contracts, and catalog items to populate the order with all of the required information for the supplier, purchasing, and accounts payable, while minimizing manual entry on the part of the employee. Finally, each iteration needs to be examined at the process and data level to make the next time the process is conducted more efficient and cost-effective. The next section looks at the holistic processes around sourcing and procurement.

1.2   Sourcing and Procurement from End to End

As with all core processes within an organization, sourcing and procurement can be competitive differentiators and sources of strength. An organization that understands its supply base thoroughly and collaborates with its suppliers in an efficient manner can bring more innovation, lower prices, and quality to its customers than an organization that doesn't manage these processes and relationships. A company that fails to obtain effective pricing on its inputs usually begins to lose to a competitor that does. In certain scenarios in which much of the supply chain is vertically integrated into one company or entity, external procurement may not be as big a factor as other core processes in the success or failure of the firm. A vertically integrated firm would not have too much to procure from outside suppliers for its direct inputs, by virtue of owning the input production upstream. Most entities today, however, are not vertically integrated like automakers of yore, which owned the rubber plantations, oil fields, iron ore, components manufacturing, and so on required for making their products. Vertical integration often is the most compelling in an undeveloped market, where suppliers don't exist or are unreliable partners. Even in a vertically integrated organization, the process of procurement doesn't go away, but rather becomes an intercompany purchasing activity, an activity with its own set of internal procurement intricacies and cost accounting decisions.

1.2.1 Ideal Procurement

Ideally, sourcing and procurement operations want to understand demand down to the lowest detail level possible as far out as possible, in order to focus its activities and discussions with the appropriate suppliers, discussing the appropriate quantities, pricing, and timelines. Foresight usually equals cost savings, and cost savings is one of the key value adds of procurement. Foresight can also bring the added benefit of building the appropriate level of relationship and understanding with a supplier prior to needing a product or service in a rush. The other value generator within sourcing and procurement is obtaining the right product or service from the right supplier.

Too often, sourcing and procurement are reduced to a tactical exercise of obtaining the lowest cost, but cost savings isn't the only goal. Lowest cost doesn't always equal optimal procurement for an organization, as the lowest cost can bring a host of trade-offs, such as lower quality and lower supplier reliability. Some commodity businesses value cost savings over many other aspects, whereas businesses competing in areas of innovation and quality value these characteristics in their supply base over cost and can be quite *cost-insensitive*, so to speak.

From luxury goods to mobile phones to fast food, examples abound of companies working tightly with suppliers to ensure the best quality possible or impactful innovation or other drivers beyond cost to move the needle for their businesses. Government has countless examples as well, even in situations in which corruption or ineptitude is not the driving force behind choosing a supplier with higher prices. In fairness, it should be noted that government entities do not have a monopoly in this area. There is plenty of ineptitude in the corporate world in procurement as well, especially in industries with oligopolies or competitive moats. As with economics, our models and processes for procurement assume rational actors operating with near-perfect information, which is rarely the case.

1.2.2   Source-to-Pay and Procure-to-Pay

Procure-to-pay processes in an enterprise often are extended to encompass the planning, forecasting, sourcing, and analytics steps that surround this process. This is called *source-to-pay*, but the term is somewhat misleading, as finding a source of supply may not be the first step in the procurement process every time. Sometimes the sourcing happens prior to the requisition being created and approved, but many times it happens after a requisition has been approved with no source of supply. Other times sourcing is triggered by strategic planning or even buyer hunches for upcoming demand. Regardless of how the process is organized sequentially, there are two components to procurement: a cerebral, planning- and analysis-based side; and a transactional component of creating and issuing agreements, whether sourcing and contracts or actual purchase orders, then receiving and paying for these purchase orders via an invoice process in accounts payable.

1.2.3   Key Process Areas

There is no catch-all process flow for sourcing and procurement; some individual activities can move in sequence, depending on the type of sourcing and procurement, as well as the organization's and/or industry's norms for procurement processes. It's easier to break up procurement into some general areas and categories, as in Table 1.1.

Procurement Process Area	Description	Occurrence in Source-to-Pay Process	Main SAP S/4HANA Integration Points with Other Areas
Operational Purchasing	Transactional procurement, core purchase order, goods/service receipt, invoice (PO-GR/SES-IV)	Before invoice and payables management	Finance, inventory management, Production Planning
Collaborative Sourcing and Contract Management	Request for quote, purchase, information process, source selection via bidding or single source, and contract definition	Either after or before operational purchasing	Finance, Inventory Management, Production Planning

Table 1.1 Procurement Process Areas

Procurement Process Area	Description	Occurrence in Source-to-Pay Process	Main SAP S/4HANA Integration Points with Other Areas
Invoice and Payables Management	Invoice submission by supplier, verification, and payment by accounts payable (AP)	After operational purchasing	Finance
Supplier Management	Supplier designation, master data and performance management	Run in parallel to the other process steps and/or end of the procurement process	SAP ERP master data
Procurement Analytics	Analysis of core, key performance indicators (KPIs), such as spend analysis, demand/forecast planning, as well as supplier performance and consolidation	Run in parallel to other process steps and/or the end of the procurement process	Finance, inventory management

Table 1.1 Procurement Process Areas (Cont.)

One of the challenges ERP systems face within sourcing and procurement is with supplier collaboration. The more tightly integrated sourcing and procurement are with the organization's ERP system, the more real-time information is available for analysis and the more that ERP areas such as finance and inventory management can support the procurement process seamlessly. However, supplier processes may differ from your internal processes, and supplier systems will differ from your internal systems. Herein lies the issue with an ERP system's architecture. The supplier cannot be given access to everything in an organization's ERP system, and in many instances a firewall blocks access even to relevant information and functionality the supplier could leverage. System-to-system communication has to be negotiated on a one-to-one or one-to-network basis in ERP systems, between customer and supplier. This is costly, time-consuming to set up, and often still limits the interaction.

Areas such as request for information/proposal/quote/bid (collectively RFx) processes/bidding, contract negotiation, and supplier portals remain challenges for an

ERP-only approach to procurement as these areas often require iterative collaboration with suppliers. SAP ERP is a transactional, command-and-control environment with high security requirements due to the sensitive data contained in many SAP ERP modules. Financial, Human Resources, and other data mandates stricter firewall requirements than needed in a collaborative environment, and if one has to preclude the other, security will almost always carry the day. This has led to earlier iterations of purchasing systems, such as SAP Supplier Relationship Management (SAP SRM), branching off from SAP ERP but remaining integrated with the backend SAP ERP system and still installed on-premise, albeit on a separate client/server. Although this allows for focused purchasing activities, organization structures, and the support of casual users, actual supplier collaboration is limited and still requires a one-to-one negotiated setup for the supplier to access the customer's portal or receive electronically transmitted purchasing documents beyond fax/email.

The next wave of purchasing systems embraces the cloud/software as a service (SaaS) model. SAP Ariba was at the forefront of this shift, taking indirect procurement transactions into a focused, multitenant, cloud-based environment in which a much greater degree of collaboration with suppliers, improved ease of use, and richness of content are available. Most customers still need to connect to a backend SAP ERP environment, at least for financials. Many customers run a split environment, sourcing and purchasing indirect items in their SAP Ariba environments while covering their direct procurement—direct procurement meaning the purchasing of input related directly to the end products and services produced by the firm or government entity—directly out of SAP ERP.

Direct procurement and capital purchasing are particularly integrated with other modules in SAP ERP, such as Inventory Management and Warehouse Management, as well as Asset Management and Finance. For most firms, procurement is a vital aspect of their operations and their strategy, often with direct procurement deemed strategic and indirect deemed operational. This can reinforce boundaries at a system level further, as direct procurement is typically conducted out of SAP ERP and indirect out of SAP Ariba. Yet strategic sourcing for direct procurement activities often requires more supplier collaboration during the RFx process than sourcing for operational procurement.

Now that we've covered SAP ERP processes, let's explore the innovations offered by SAP S/4HANA with regard to sourcing and procurement. The following section will introduce SAP S/4HANA and look further into these integration areas with cloud-based solutions.

1.3   Procurement with SAP S/4HANA

SAP sees the procurement line of business (LoB) through the lens of its overarching intelligent enterprise initiative. SAP's strategy is to become an experience company powered by the intelligent enterprise. With a focus on the three pillars of experience, operations, and intelligence, the intelligent enterprise leverages emerging technologies such as artificial intelligence (AI), Internet of Things (IoT), and analytics to allow users to focus on higher-value outcomes and automate repetitive tasks.

Rather than having to choose either on-premise or cloud for procurement activities, there is an SAP procurement strategy to fit every organization's size and needs. The core SAP procurement solution strategy today leverages SAP S/4HANA Enterprise Management as the digital core, with SAP Ariba as the go-to solution portfolio for procurement transformation. This combination of SAP S/4HANA Enterprise Management and SAP Ariba allows you to take control in the following areas:

- **Transform procurement**
  Savings from strategic sourcing, scaling supplier management, and efficient operational procurement can be found in SAP Ariba procurement solutions.

- **Achieve digital IT transformation**
  Next-gen SAP ERP solutions for IT transformation, procurement in the digital core, and a simplified digital landscape can be found in SAP S/4HANA and Ariba Network.

- **Realize digital IT transformation with procurement**
  Next-gen digital landscape procurement savings and engagement at scale across the enterprise can be found in SAP S/4HANA, SAP Ariba procurement solutions, and Ariba Network.

The three main paths for procurement transformation with SAP all include Ariba Network. There is no substitute or on-premise alternative for Ariba Network, and the power of the network for supplier collaboration at every step of the procurement process can be leveraged by small and large organizations alike.

Regardless of your choice of ERP system, you can run SAP Ariba in the cloud with Ariba Network to transform your procurement operations. Smaller businesses with less than $1 billion in revenue annually can run their procurement operations directly in SAP S/4HANA, with supplier collaboration supported by Ariba Network and SAP Ariba Catalog. For larger enterprises, SAP recommends running SAP Ariba solutions and Ariba Network for all source-to-pay business processes integrated into SAP S/4HANA as the digital core.

1.3.1   Cloud versus On-Premise ERP Systems

SAP S/4HANA Enterprise Management is the latest ERP platform from SAP. SAP S/4HANA Enterprise Management is a new, separate product line completely rearchitected to run natively on the SAP HANA in-memory computing platform and operational database system (ODS) pioneered in-house at SAP. SAP S/4HANA is therefore not a legal successor version to the SAP Business Suite or SAP ERP; SAP ERP and SAP Business Suite products will still be available as separate product lines. SAP S/4HANA Enterprise Management thus charts a new path, but it isn't a complete break with the previous SAP ERP product lines. Much of the functionality offered in SAP S/4HANA and even the on-premise configuration approaches remain the same or similar. There is also an upgrade path on offer from SAP ERP and SAP Business Suite powered by SAP HANA to SAP S/4HANA.

Digital Core

SAP is pursuing a digital core strategy from its traditional position of strength in ERP systems. SAP S/4HANA serves as the core, and the cloud solutions in the SAP portfolio then integrate with and augment the core. For sourcing and procurement topics, SAP S/4HANA is the logical area to support procurement processes with heavy cross-module dependencies, such as direct procurement, inventory management, and accounts payable.

The digital core does not mean on premise, necessarily. SAP S/4HANA has two deployment options or editions: on-premise SAP S/4HANA and SAP S/4HANA Cloud. Similar to the SAP Business Suite products, the on-premise edition supports over 30 languages, over 60 country versions, and over 20 industry solutions. SAP S/4HANA Cloud has a more restricted scope of supported languages and industry solutions to date, with the goal of adding further supported areas in the coming quarters. SAP S/4HANA Cloud covers specific business scenarios for the marketing line of business and for the professional services industry, as well as the most essential scenarios to run an entire enterprise in the cloud with a digital core, including finance, accounting, controlling, procurement, sales, manufacturing, plant maintenance, project system, and product lifecycle management. Marketing, professional services, and enterprise are the three main SAP S/4HANA Cloud options currently available. The complete universe of the digital core and the associated SAP Cloud solutions is shown in Figure 1.1.

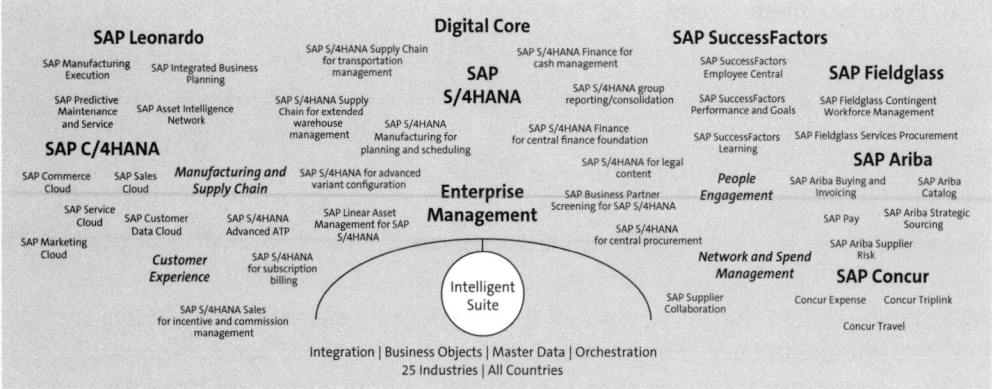

Figure 1.1 Intelligent Suite with Digital Core: SAP S/4HANA

The most obvious differences from previous iterations of SAP ERP and SAP S/4HANA, for either cloud or on-premise editions, are threefold. First, the improvements in speed are breathtaking, especially in the areas of in-system analytics. Second, the UI is completely reengineered for SAP Fiori. Third, the extensibility via native and almost native integrations with SAP Cloud solutions like SAP Ariba and SAP Fieldglass, as well as the optimizations and consolidations of areas requiring separate clients and interface layers, serves to further boost performance of the system and streamline the system landscape requirements.

The table structures and SAP ERP applications themselves have been completely overhauled to run optimally in an in-memory database environment. In the past, multiple indices and tables were prebuilt to minimize the impacts of calculations on system performance. These tables created inflexibility and complexity challenges of their own, however.

Cloud Procurement

SAP Ariba has cloud-based solutions for all of the major and minor areas of procurement. The most straightforward approach to understanding where SAP Ariba fits with SAP S/4HANA in your overall solution landscape is to look at your organization's requirements and size, as well as your in-scope business processes.

Supplier management and risk, strategic sourcing, and contract negotiations are driven through SAP Ariba. The result is negotiated savings, which now need to be realized. To drive that price and contract compliance, there are two main buying channels: direct procurement, which happens in SAP S/4HANA and is plan-, replenishment-, or materials requirement planning (MRP)-driven; and plant maintenance in SAP S/4HANA, accessing the SAP Ariba Catalog to find materials and services. End-user-driven indirect procurement of maintenance, repair, and operating (MRO) supply, services, and indirect materials happens in SAP Ariba through an intuitive, policy-driven, guided buying experience to drive ease of use for all employees of a company. Supplier collaboration for all procurement scenarios coming from SAP S/4HANA or SAP Ariba will occur via the Ariba Network. This recommendation drives simplicity and fast speed to value. Cost savings from the SAP Ariba business case can self-fund digital transformation or other customer initiatives.

SAP Ariba is the go-to solution for strategic procurement requirements going beyond the traditional capabilities in SAP ERP, and this will continue to be the case in SAP S/4HANA. With the Ariba Network, SAP Ariba is also the main solution for network-supported transactions and collaboration, and the SAP Ariba Catalog is the main solution for content management. In this hybrid approach, SAP S/4HANA supports the operational procurement side, including the full purchase order management process, as well as supplier management, with tight integration into other logistics areas.

Figure 1.2 details the areas covered by SAP S/4HANA Sourcing and Procurement and shows where cloud solutions from SAP Ariba, SAP Fieldglass, and SAP Concur are recommended.

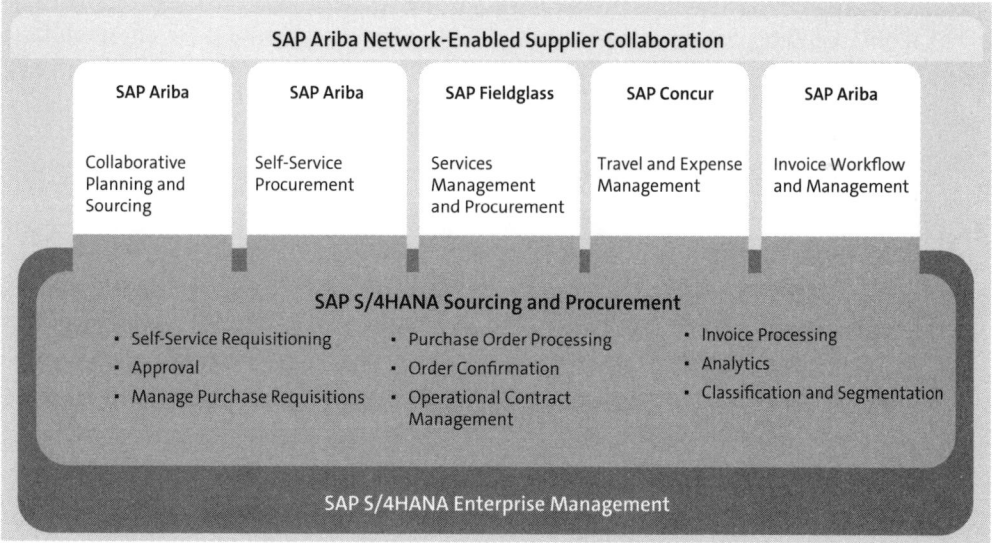

Figure 1.2 SAP S/4HANA Sourcing and Procurement Integration with SAP Ariba, SAP Fieldglass, and SAP Concur

You can run self-service procurement, for example, in either SAP S/4HANA or SAP Ariba Supply Chain Collaboration for Buyers, or in both, depending on the type of procurement. Where it makes sense, cloud options should always be evaluated, and between SAP Ariba and SAP Fieldglass, there is a cloud procurement solution for almost every scenario available. Although the focus of this book is on SAP S/4HANA, we will highlight integration opportunities in various procurement scenarios, with SAP Cloud solution counterparts noted where applicable. The next section focuses on strategic procurement in the cloud, for which the emphasis is still on cost savings and efficiencies, with the buying group often playing with much larger stakes.

1.3.2 Strategic Sourcing

One of the areas with clear advantages for the cloud is strategic sourcing. Here, a buyer needs to interact and collaborate with multiple suppliers, many of whom may not be onboarded yet. The buyer needs a platform from which to establish sourcing strategies and publish requests for pricing, quotes, information, and bid responses. Auctions and other activities also need to be supported. At the end of the sourcing event, a contract and/or purchase order (PO) is typically generated, confirming the supplier and price. For contracts, the handoff from the bidding process to contract negotiation and finalization ideally should be seamless. As per Figure 1.3, the recommended approach from SAP is to leverage SAP Ariba for project/category management, sourcing, contracts, and catalogs while operationalizing the contract in SAP S/4HANA to have a source of supply for any purchasing activities initiated in the core, such as plan-driven direct procurement.

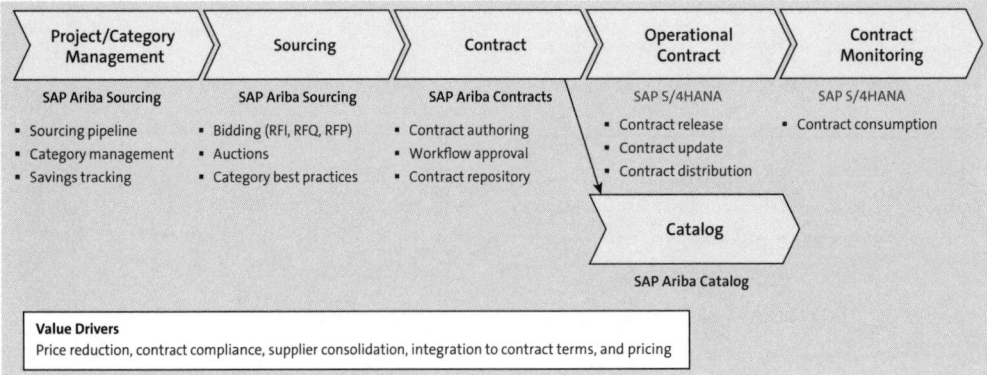

Figure 1.3 SAP Ariba and SAP S/4HANA Strategic Sourcing

1.3.3   Procurement

For the procurement of MRO, indirect, and services, the SAP Ariba guided buying capability provides a consumer-grade guided buying experience leveraging negotiated contract pricing, company policies, and a spot marketplace for longtail spend, and it drives easy, effortless employee requisitioning through the shopping cart process using SAP Ariba Supply Chain Collaboration for Buyers and the SAP Ariba Catalog. This process then integrates with the SAP S/4HANA environment for PO execution and inventory management, backs up to the Ariba Network for purchase order and invoice (PO/IV) collaboration, and finally to SAP S/4HANA for accounts payable processing (see Figure 1.4).

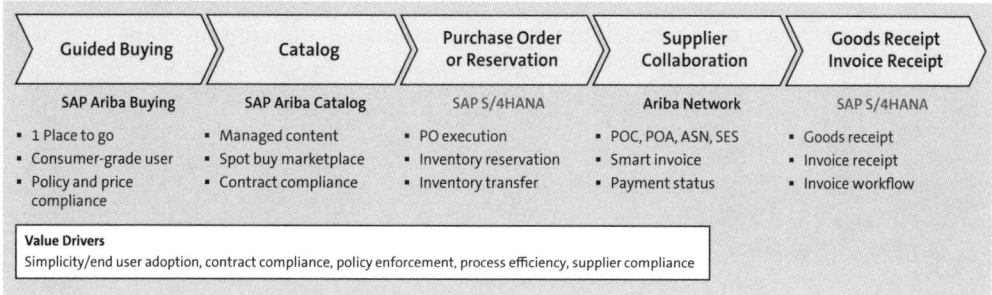

Figure 1.4 Procurement of Indirect, MRO, and Services

SAP Ariba guided buying is a key solution of SAP Ariba; end users require easy and simple user experiences combined with rich catalog content, which is managed and requires no maintenance from buyers. All of this is combined with deep integration with core processes in SAP S/4HANA, including operational transactions, inventory management, and plan-driven procurement. This makes the process a strong one to take advantage of the cloud.

On the direct procurement side, things are somewhat flip-flopped between SAP Ariba and SAP S/4HANA. Here, the trigger for the procurement proposal occurs during an MRP run or is created manually in response to a need in production and planning. These processes take place in SAP S/4HANA, and the requisition, source determination, and purchase order can follow in SAP S/4HANA. All supplier collaboration for direct materials happens over the Ariba Network. With SAP Ariba Supply Chain Collaboration for Buyers, you now have the capability to support the more complex types of ordering such as scheduling agreements, forecasting, and contract manufacturing found in direct procurement seamlessly at the collaboration point in the transaction in the Ariba Network, as shown in Figure 1.5.

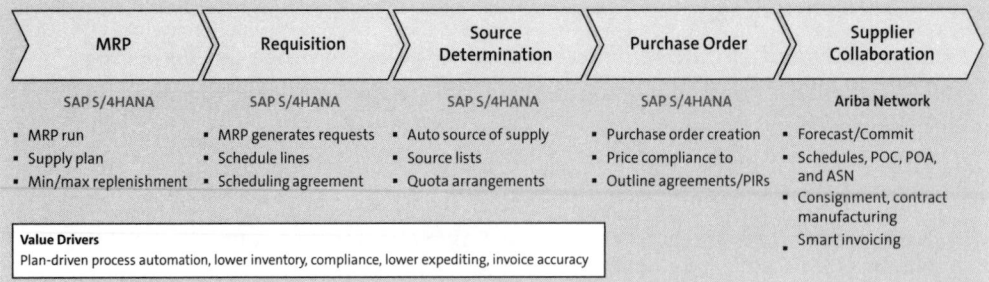

Figure 1.5 SAP Ariba and SAP S/4HANA Plan-Driven Procurement

For procurement activities originating in plant maintenance or in project management, as shown in Figure 1.6, more dynamic sourcing and content management is typically required. Here, the transaction originates in SAP S/4HANA but is then sourced by leveraging the SAP Ariba Catalog. The SAP Ariba Catalog in turn can host large MRO supplier catalogs and apply contract pricing to these items for plant maintenance requestors. Once the PO is created, the PO/IV collaboration process is supported in SAP S/4HANA via the Ariba Network as in the other scenarios, returning finally for goods receipt and invoice processing to SAP S/4HANA.

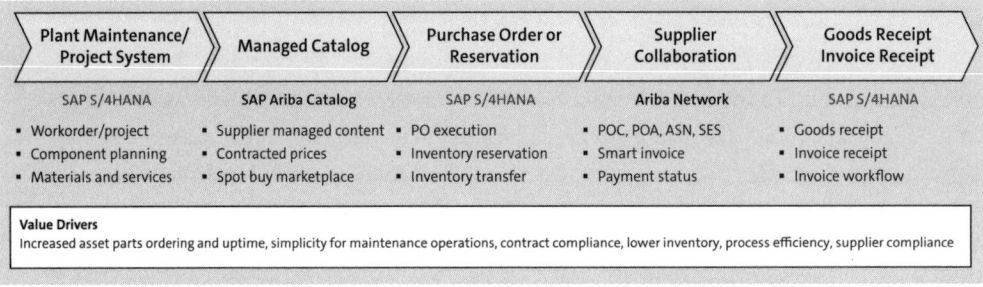

Figure 1.6 SAP S/4HANA and SAP Ariba Workorder and Project-Driven Procurement

1.3.4   Accounts Payable and Invoicing

Finally, for accounts payable and invoicing, SAP Ariba offers an array of solutions that go well beyond the simple transfer and processing of invoice documents. SAP Ariba allows all sizes of suppliers to create electronic invoices, email-based smart invoices, or business-to-business connections to buyers. SAP Ariba Invoice Management leverages smart invoice rules and invoices based on contracts (rate sheets) to reduce invoice errors, drive price and tax regulatory compliance, and ultimately allow buyers to receive a clean, error-free, 98 percent touchless invoice in SAP S/4HANA or SAP ERP, all to help drive automation and close the financial books faster. In addition to supporting collaboration between supplier and buyer and allowing for rules-based invoice submission, SAP Ariba also offers dynamic and self-service discounting for the suppliers and supply chain financing in SAP Pay, as shown in Figure 1.7. SAP S/4HANA serves as the digital core for accounts payable transactions, receiving an invoice and creating payment runs, but the frontend collaboration with the supplier can be significantly augmented from efficiency and discount standpoints via the inclusion of the Ariba Network and the SAP Pay solution.

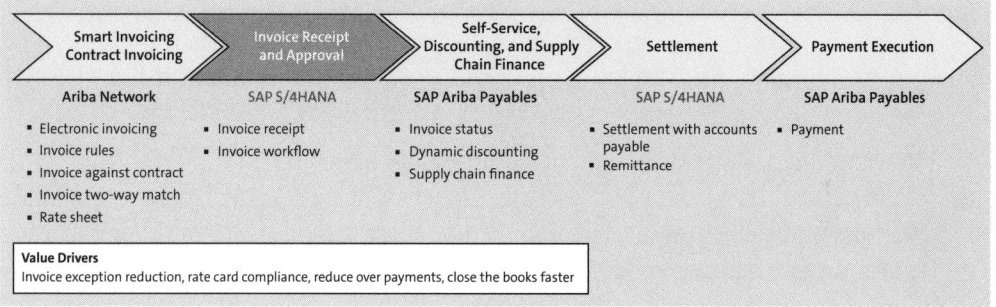

Figure 1.7 SAP Ariba and SAP S/4HANA Smart Invoicing and Contract Invoicing

SAP has embraced a cloud strategy that spans its entire solution portfolio. When assessing any SAP solution area, including procurement, you should aim to understand your options in the cloud, as well as the SAP roadmap and investment plans, from a product standpoint.

1.3.5   SAP Fiori Roles and Applications

As with previous UIs, the concept of roles is central to SAP S/4HANA Sourcing and Procurement. The principal roles are listed in Table 1.2.

SAP S/4HANA Sourcing and Procurement Role	Description
Employee procurement—R0056-12	Manages purchase requisitions: creates purchase requisitions, confirms goods receipt and/or services performed, returns deliveries, approves supplier invoices, and evaluates suppliers

Table 1.2 SAP S/4HANA Sourcing and Procurement Roles

SAP S/4HANA Sourcing and Procurement Role	Description
Manager procurement—R0091	Approves purchasing documents: requisitions, contracts and purchase orders
Operational purchaser—R0128	Manages purchase orders, including the creation and tracking of these documents, and monitors requisitions and contracts
Strategic buyer—R0153	Manages sourcing, including supplier evaluation, manages purchase contracts and purchase orders, and monitors requisitions
Accounts payable accountant—R0005-12	Manages supplier invoices, including the creation of supplier invoices and release of blocked invoices

Table 1.2 SAP S/4HANA Sourcing and Procurement Roles (Cont.)

Perhaps equally important, several procurement apps are available for SAP Fiori in SAP S/4HANA. These apps fall into transactional, analytical, and navigational categories.

All told, there are over 500 SAP Fiori apps already available for SAP S/4HANA Enterprise Management and over 100 roles. This provides a customer with a wide array of prebuilt options with which to tailor the user experience and process optimization. For further requirements beyond the prebuilt roles and apps, customizing apps and roles further to the customer's needs has never been easier and more mobile-ready than with the SAP Fiori–based UI.

This book's focus is on the SAP S/4HANA Sourcing and Procurement capabilities and SAP Ariba's business scenarios integrated with SAP S/4HANA. For an in-depth look at the functionality and implementation approaches for SAP Ariba, there is a dedicated title available from SAP PRESS: *SAP Ariba: Business Processes, Functionality and Implementation* (2019, *www.sap-press.com/4769*).

1.4   Summary

As a business computing concept, ERP has been around since the inception of computing itself. Up until recently, analytics and transactions had to run in separate environments because of computing constraints. Over time, computing became faster, but complexity, requirements, and data loads grew at a similar pace, moving in lock-step with the improvements in computing hardware and software speed and necessitating further separation. Now, we're at an inflection point with SAP S/4HANA Enterprise Management, in which both software and hardware advances are able to support the reunification of analytics and transactions into one unified platform.

SAP S/4HANA Enterprise Management achieves this breakthrough by leveraging simplification of the ERP data model, making quantum leaps in in-memory database technology, adding the flexibility of SAP Fiori to underpin a mobile-centric UI, and engaging in rationalization of what SAP ERP processes constitute the SAP S/4HANA core versus a separate client module requiring an interface. The platform also requires customers to reevaluate their existing SAP ERP system footprints, architectures, and processes to take full advantage of these considerable advances in ERP and business computing as a whole. Each process area will require a level of effort and strategy to achieve a comprehensive implementation of SAP S/4HANA Enterprise Management. With SAP S/4HANA Sourcing and Procurement, the procurement processes are a core part of this new platform and the focus of this book. In the following chapters, we'll attempt to provide a roadmap towards realizing a successful, comprehensive implementation of SAP S/4HANA Sourcing and Procurement.

Chapter 2
Implementation Options

SAP S/4HANA Enterprise Management is a new ERP product line from SAP, but not all upgrade paths from existing ERP systems have to be built from scratch. When embarking on a journey to SAP S/4HANA Enterprise Management, there are a number of questions to answer and areas to analyze prior to deciding on the best route.

SAP customers can choose from on-premise or cloud versions of SAP S/4HANA implementations, which have slightly different functional scopes and IT project requirements and therefore have their own pros and cons. This chapter defines processes covered by each product and the relative merits of each SAP S/4HANA implementation approach. The chapter closes with a description of the SAP Activate methodology and model company approaches and covers the project setup for each implementation scenario.

2.1 Implementation Overview

First, what does your current ERP system look like? If you're running SAP ERP, what version is it on? Are there multiple instances? A lot of custom code and processes or a pretty vanilla implementation using the standard processes of the system? Second, what are the goals of this implementation? Are you looking to upgrade on a technical level or is the mandate to reengineer processes *and* upgrade the current environment to the latest stack? Third, what areas are to be covered in this upgrade by SAP S/4HANA Enterprise Management, and what add-on solutions and interfaces are required? Can all of the business processes, transactions, and analytics run from SAP ERP, or do you need to factor in additional modules and cloud solutions to address all of your requirements? Finally, are your design requirements or corporate initiatives such that SAP S/4HANA Enterprise Management could be deployed in the cloud?

2.1.1   Deployment Options

There are five main deployment options:

- SAP S/4HANA or SAP HANA Enterprise Cloud
- SAP S/4HANA Cloud, single tenant edition
- SAP S/4HANA Cloud
- SAP Marketing Cloud

The implementation options for on-premise systems fall largely into four primary types, as outlined in Table 2.1.

SAP S/4HANA Transformation Type	Example/Benefits
System conversion	*Example:* Complete conversion of an existing SAP Business Suite system to SAP S/4HANA *Benefits:* Reevaluation of customization and existing process flows, transformation over time
Landscape transformation	*Example:* Consolidation of current regional SAP Business Suite landscape into one global SAP S/4HANA system *Benefits:* Stay with current business processes and move gradually to SAP S/4HANA innovations
New implementation	*Example:* New or existing SAP customer implementing a new or *greenfield* SAP S/4HANA system *Benefits:* Reengineering and process simplifications based on ready-to-run business processes
SAP S/4HANA for central procurement	*Example:* Three ERP systems (SAP ERP 6.0 EHP 6 or higher and/or SAP S/4HANA) connected to SAP S/4HANA for central procurement, or SAP S/4HANA for central finance foundation connected in this manner to a distributed SAP ERP environment to centralize financial management *Benefits:* Specific for a multi-ERP landscape, SAP S/4HANA for central procurement enables buyers to manage purchasing in multiple systems without having to consolidate the ERP systems into one ERP.

Table 2.1 SAP S/4HANA Transformation Options

A customer can convert an existing SAP ERP 6.0 EHP 7 or higher instance by following the conversion steps to on-premise SAP S/4HANA, consolidate one or multiple ERP systems into an on-premise SAP S/4HANA or SAP S/4HANA Cloud system, or create a new implementation of an on-premise SAP S/4HANA or SAP S/4HANA Cloud system. A customer can also "land" an SAP S/4HANA for central procurement instance on top of several existing SAP ERP and/or SAP S/4HANA systems and manage procurement activities centrally in a distributed environment.

With each option, there are both benefits and trade-offs. An organization with a lot of unnecessary processes and legacy data could elect to convert an existing system to SAP S/4HANA, but it may benefit more from rearchitecting its processes and system from the ground up in a new implementation. A relatively modern implementation on SAP ERP 6.0 with a later enhancement pack may be able to simply convert, but this is also an opportunity to evaluate a new implementation in SAP S/4HANA Cloud, if this is the direction the organization is moving in general. An organization with multiple ERP systems to upgrade may run the analysis and decide that consolidation or reimplementation is too complex/costly and instead bypass this by implementing SAP S/4HANA for central procurement. In short, deciding on a path for SAP S/4HANA involves comparing internal architecture and goals with the external options on deck and arriving at the approach that best fits the organization.

2.1.2 Cloud

Cloud computing is a general (and popular) term to describe the delivery of services hosted by a third-party cloud provider on the internet. This option enables a customer to consume a computing resource by paying a subscription fee, versus using a traditional perpetual license and annual maintenance fees. The cloud options offer less flexibility in processes, configuration, access (web only), and governance versus on-premise implementations. However, in exchange for this, the customer also receives quarterly updates to the system, little to no internal IT overhead, and core processes on a subscription basis.

The cloud model leverages several acronym-laden concepts, including software as a service (SaaS), platform as a service (PaaS), integration platform as a service (IPaaS), and infrastructure as a service (IaaS). A PaaS provides a cloud platform and tools to help developers build and deploy cloud applications. An IPaaS is a suite of cloud services enabling development, execution, and governance of integration flows connecting any combination of on-premise and cloud-based processes, services, applications, and data within an individual organization or across multiple organizations. An IaaS lets companies "rent" computing resources such as servers, networks, storage, and operating systems on a pay-per-use basis. IaaS providers host the infrastructure and handle tasks like allocation of physical computing resources, data partitioning, security, and backup. Users can access all of these services from a web browser and pick and choose options on a subscription basis. SAP's cloud offerings include SaaS (application offerings in the cloud), IaaS (infrastructure via application and database services), IPaaS (integration platform options for integration of multiple cloud services and apps), and PaaS (platform for the services under the SAP Cloud Platform) options.

The main models for cloud computing are described in Table 2.2.

Cloud Computing Type	Description
Private cloud	System hosted by provider solely for a single customer. Customer accesses the system over a virtual private network (VPN).
Public	System hosted by the provider for multiple customers (tenants).
Hybrid	Combines two or more distinct public cloud environments and/or on-premise providers. Integrated by standardized or proprietary technology enabling data and application portability.

Table 2.2 Cloud Computing Types

SAP S/4HANA Cloud falls into the public cloud type of service—that is, a true multitenant service model that includes quarterly innovation cycles and updates. SAP S/4HANA Cloud comes in several different flavors:

- *SAP S/4HANA Cloud, single tenant edition*, a bring-your-own-license (BYOL) option and therefore essentially a hosted version of an on-premise system
- *SAP S/4HANA Cloud*, the general SAP S/4HANA ERP edition for the cloud
- *SAP Marketing Cloud*, tailored for the marketing area of an organization or for a marketing-centric organization in general

A decision matrix can be laid out for the five deployment options—on-premise, private cloud, or the three cloud variations—as in Table 2.3.

2

Scenario/ Deployment Option	On-Premise SAP S/4HANA	SAP S/4HANA Cloud, Single Tenant Edition	SAP S/4HANA Cloud	SAP Marketing Cloud
Customer needs full control of system and functionality with ability to customize and even potentially modify.	Best option for scenario, as the full functionality is available on-premise and customer owns governance of system and can customize and even modify if absolutely required.	Second-best option, as some customization and full functionality is available in a private cloud. No modification permissible, however, and system governance shared between SAP and customer.	Not an option as system governance is owned by SAP and only limited customizations are allowed.	Not an option due to specific functionality focus of system and cloud restriction on governance/ AMS/mods.
Customer requires a subscription-based deployment option but wants full functionality and to retain some influence over governance and release updates.	Not an option, as on-premise is not a subscription.	Best option as SAP S/4HANA private cloud allows the customer subscription model to deploy updates at its own pace and comanage governance.	Not an option as system governance/ AMS is owned by SAP and only limited customizations are allowed.	Not an option due to specific functionality focus of system and cloud restriction on governance/ AMS/mods.
Customer requires quarterly updates in a pure cloud environment with order-to-cash and plan-to-produce.	On-premise not an option as updates are not quarterly and by definition it is not cloud-based.	Private cloud not an option as it does not provide quarterly updates.	Best option as SAP S/4HANA Cloud provides quarterly updates and also supports order-to-cash and plan-to-produce.	Not an option as it doesn't support order-to-cash and plan-to-produce.

Table 2.3 Decision Matrix: Deployment Options

Scenario/ Deployment Option	On-Premise SAP S/4HANA	SAP S/4HANA Cloud, Single Tenant Edition	SAP S/4HANA Cloud	SAP Marketing Cloud
Requires professional services and a focused ERP system in the cloud with quarterly updates.	On-premise not an option as updates are not quarterly and by definition it is not cloud-based.	Private cloud not an option as it does not provide quarterly updates.	Best option: has professional services focus and is cloud-based.	Not an option as it has a marketing focus and no professional services focus.
Customer requires cloud-based ERP system with marketing focus, including executive dashboard for customer analysis and planning.	On-premise not an option as updates are not quarterly and by definition it is not cloud-based.	Private cloud not an option as it does not provide quarterly updates.	Second-best option: is cloud-based but doesn't have professional services focus.	Best option: has marketing focus in the cloud, with an executive dashboard for marketing analysis and planning.

Table 2.3 Decision Matrix: Deployment Options (Cont.)

Sometimes, the decision comes down to the on-premise option and one of the cloud editions from a functionality standpoint. Other times, both the on-premise option and the main cloud option are further joined by one of the specialized cloud editions; for example, if you are in a professional services company evaluating options, you might end up with three SAP S/4HANA options from which to choose.

Understanding your long-term plans for the system and your long-term approach to cloud can help balance the decision-making process with the short-term cost and effort considerations. One thing always to keep in mind is that ERP implementations are usually not something you "set and forget." An ERP platform forms the backbone of most organizations, and the decision and path to take on this upgrade journey should warrant thought and consideration.

2.1.3   On-Premise

The main options for on-premise systems moving to SAP S/4HANA are to convert to on-premise SAP S/4HANA or to set up a new implementation of either on-premise SAP S/4HANA or SAP S/4HANA Cloud. You can't convert an on-premise system directly to SAP S/4HANA Cloud.

If you're already running SAP ERP and need to figure out whether to migrate or reimplement, it helps to understand the options you have available for migration before deciding on one. If your SAP ERP level is at SAP ERP 6.0 EHP 7 or higher, you likely can upgrade to SAP S/4HANA Enterprise Management at a technical level rather than reimplementing (for a full compatibility scope to support system conversion, see SAP Note 2269324). However, this only makes sense if you aren't trying to reduce your data footprint substantially and can leverage the new SAP S/4HANA processes with your previous SAP ERP system as a template for the new system. You'll also need to convert your existing database to the SAP HANA database and model as per Figure 2.1.

There are underpinning themes and infrastructure along the upgrade path from SAP ERP to SAP S/4HANA, mainly in the form of SAP NetWeaver, which remains a core infrastructure component regardless of whether you are running SAP ERP or SAP S/4HANA. Other aspects, such as SAP S/4HANA Finance, were among the first to be available on an SAP S/4HANA architecture and thus can be upgraded at an earlier enhancement pack level than some of the other components, including the sourcing and procurement functionality.

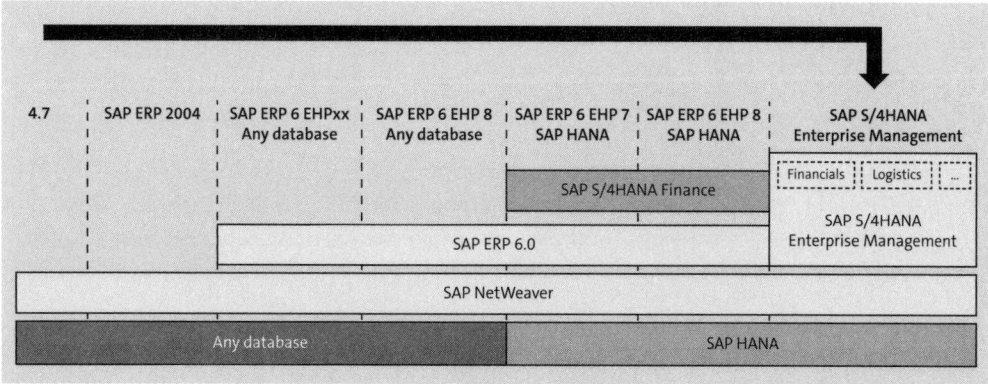

Figure 2.1 Upgrade Paths to SAP S/4HANA Enterprise Management

2.1.4   New Implementation versus System Conversion

Many customers choose the route of new implementation when moving to SAP S/4HANA from SAP ERP. ERP systems get cluttered with data and customizations over time and may carry layers of such data sediment and legacy processes from previous upgrades. SAP S/4HANA, while heavily based on SAP ERP, is a separate product and code base, built with the holistic intent of simplification and speed. Some customers are able to take their footprint from terabytes of data to double- or even single-digit gigabytes. The speed and optimization benefits from such housecleaning can be quite substantial. However, the additional time/effort investment required for a new implementation versus an upgrade cannot be ignored.

One way of assessing the pros and cons of reimplementing versus converting to get to SAP S/4HANA is to build a decision matrix for the conversion and cloud decisions and weigh each category's pros and cons.

Conversion or Reimplementation Decision Matrix

In Table 2.4, some general pros and cons are detailed for typical SAP ERP assessment findings.

SAP ERP Analysis Finding	Reimplementation Pros	Conversion Pros
Heavily customized SAP ERP environment with large amounts of these customizations and legacy data no longer in used in production.	Strong opportunity to streamline SAP ERP and simplify processes based on SAP S/4HANA standards.	If some customizations and data are still required/ necessary and archiving of legacy data can be performed prior to conversion, converting versus reimplementing may save on costs and effort.
Current processes in SAP ERP are mostly standard with little customization and legacy/unarchived data.	If the implementation is simple to the point at which conversion and reimplementation entail similar efforts, it may be an option to reimplement and start fresh on SAP S/4HANA.	Because less effort is required and results will be similar, conversion is a good option for implementations in SAP ERP that were already streamlined and using standard processes.

Table 2.4 SAP S/4HANA Conversion versus Reimplementation Decision Matrix

SAP ERP Analysis Finding	Reimplementation Pros	Conversion Pros
The customer business/government model has changed significantly since SAP ERP was implemented. The system no longer supports many of the required processes.	Reimplementation provides an opportunity to build system processes to match new operating processes and conditions not reflected in the current environment.	Feasibility assessment needs to be conducted to see if conversion and then addition of new processes is possible and more cost- and effort-effective versus re-implementation.
Not all modules can be moved at once to SAP S/4HANA, but a conversion approach nonetheless makes sense for a business transformation and investment approach.	Reimplementation may be too costly or disruptive if a gradual migration option is feasible.	Gradual conversion/migration possible using the landscape consolidation approach discussed in the following section. Would provide managed migration versus the "big bang" cutover of SAP ERP to SAP S/4HANA.

Table 2.4 SAP S/4HANA Conversion versus Reimplementation Decision Matrix (Cont.)

System Conversion

A system conversion to SAP S/4HANA can be done all at once, but it also can allow for evaluation of existing customizations and a gradual transformation of existing process flows over time versus a new implementation. This is also an opportunity to consolidate multiple SAP ERP instances into one instance of SAP S/4HANA.

If your analysis points toward reimplementation, you can always start fresh with a new SAP S/4HANA environment. Doing so is obviously more work and investment up front, but you can still do an initial conversion/load of your legacy data, and this approach allows you take full advantage of the SAP S/4HANA functionality up front and start with a data foundation and set of processes that have been built for and on SAP S/4HANA's data/process model and architecture. There are three options in this area:

- **System conversion**
  An ERP system to an on-premise SAP S/4HANA system—for example, a complete conversion of an existing SAP Business Suite system to SAP S/4HANA. This allows for a reevaluation of customization and existing process flows, as well as transformation over time.

- **Landscape transformation**

  Hybrid scenario in which several ERP systems are moved on premise, and some into the cloud—for example, the consolidation of a current regional SAP Business Suite landscape into one global SAP S/4HANA system. This allows you to retain current business processes and move gradually to SAP S/4HANA innovations.

- **New implementation**

  An SAP ERP system or a non-SAP system to a new SAP S/4HANA system—for example, a new or existing SAP customer implementing a new SAP S/4HANA system. This allows you to reengineer and simplify based on ready-to-run business processes.

New Implementation

For a new implementation, there are two main steps: first, install SAP S/4HANA Enterprise Management using SAP's software provisioning manager; then, load your ERP data in from either SAP ERP or a third-party ERP system as part of the initial data load, as detailed in Figure 2.2.

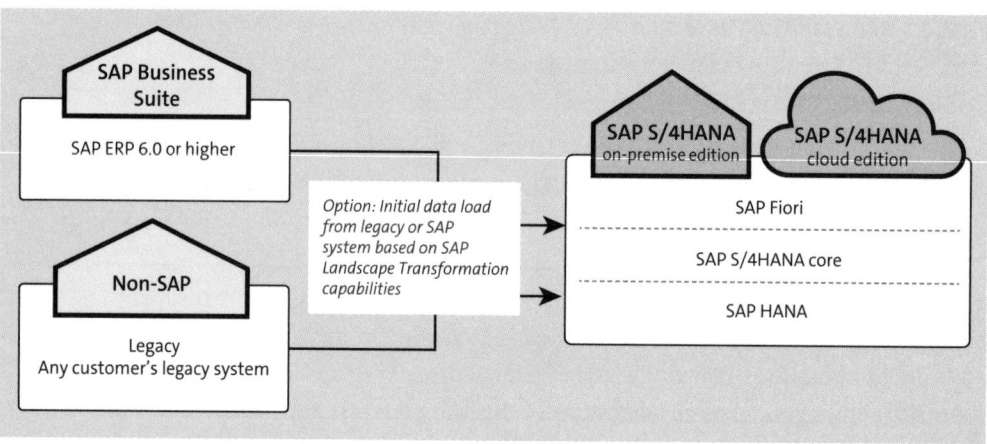

Figure 2.2 Scenario 1: New Installation of SAP S/4HANA Enterprise Management

New implementations are undertaken if there is no core ERP system to begin with or the core, underlying business processes have shifted over the years, to the point to which upgrading the SAP ERP environment brings in too many legacy processes and data to be useful and/or to take full advantage of SAP S/4HANA's architecture and simplifications.

Full Conversion

Another route to SAP S/4HANA is to convert an existing SAP ERP environment into SAP S/4HANA Enterprise Management. This entails three main steps: checking add-ons and business functions and industry-specific functionality using maintenance planner, executing pretransition checks to validate conversion viability to SAP S/4HANA, and executing the conversion using the Software Update Manager (SUM) with the data migration option (DMO), as shown in Figure 2.3. It's important to note that the DMO is only available as of SAP ERP 6 EHP 7. If you're running an earlier release of SAP ERP or even SAP R/3, you must upgrade the SAP ERP environment to 6.0 EHP 7 via SUM and then use the DMO to convert the SAP ERP 6.0 EHP 7 environment to SAP S/4HANA Enterprise Management.

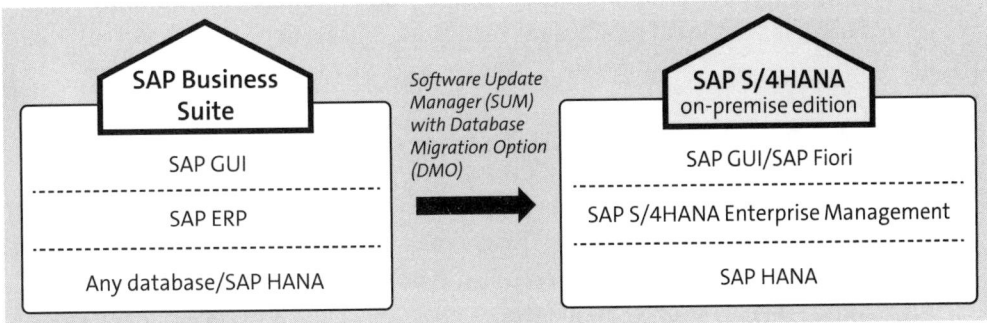

Figure 2.3 Scenario 2: System Conversion

In a full conversion to SAP S/4HANA, there may be some SAP solutions from SAP ERP that haven't been simplified in SAP S/4HANA but are still required by the customer in the new environment. Compatibility packages enable a customer to run certain classic SAP solutions on SAP S/4HANA installations in which no application simplification has been done. In many cases, SAP S/4HANA may offer a functional equivalent (reflecting the SAP S/4HANA target architecture), or the corresponding application simplification may be planned for a future SAP S/4HANA release. Compatibility packages are part of the SAP S/4HANA shipment and are supported by SAP through 2025 at this time.

Some conversions may require multiple phases and steps to reach SAP S/4HANA in the most cost-effective and least disruptive manner possible. Scenario 3 supports the consolidation of multiple legacy systems into one ERP system prior to converting to SAP S/4HANA. This can also refer to a phased migration whereby certain company codes, business units, and/or modules are migrated individually, depending on their total cost of ownership (TCO) and total cost of investment (TCI) to migrate. This way, an upgrade and a landscape consolidation can be achieved in consideration of business drivers gradually, allowing the business and IT to move areas strategically into SAP S/4HANA in a sequence rather than performing the entire migration at once.

In addition to consolidation of multiple SAP ERP systems into one SAP S/4HANA platform or a selective data transformation as necessary for company codes and business units, you also have the option to consolidate financials alone into SAP S/4HANA for central finance foundation. SAP S/4HANA for central finance foundation allows you to move multiple FI-CO modules into one SAP S/4HANA system and centralize financial postings. There is also an option to central purchasing activities from multiple ERP environments into a single SAP S/4HANA instance, leveraging SAP S/4HANA for central procurement. SAP S/4HANA for central procurement is outlined in a later section of this chapter Section 2.4, and again later in Chapter 13.

2.2   On-Premise SAP S/4HANA

Users can access SAP S/4HANA Enterprise Management on premise via either SAP GUI or using a supported web browser. This means using either a web dispatcher or load-balanced web dispatchers to frontend clients, or both an SAP Fiori and SAP S/4HANA application client with an SAP S/4HANA database client and Adobe Document Services for the SAP NetWeaver Application Server in the backend, as shown in Figure 2.4.

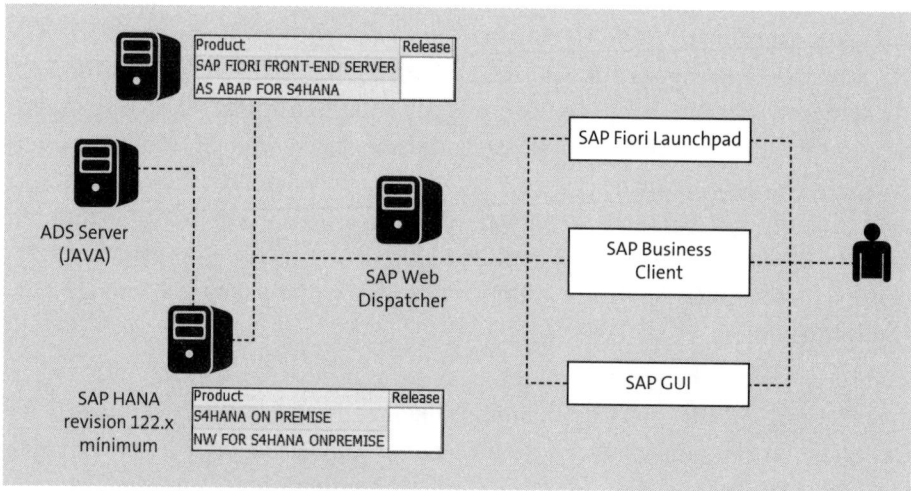

Figure 2.4 SAP S/4HANA Standard On-Premise Landscape

2.2.1   Complete Functional Scope

For organizations across industries and government sectors that need a deep and broad level of functionality combined with a high degree of flexibility in customization and system maintenance and backups, SAP S/4HANA Enterprise Management on-premise fits the bill. The functional scope of a typical implementation project either leverages an existing or includes a finance implementation. Without finance and controlling, few other lines of business can be managed successfully in the system. Once this is established, other areas, including sourcing and procurement, can be added to cover business processes and needs.

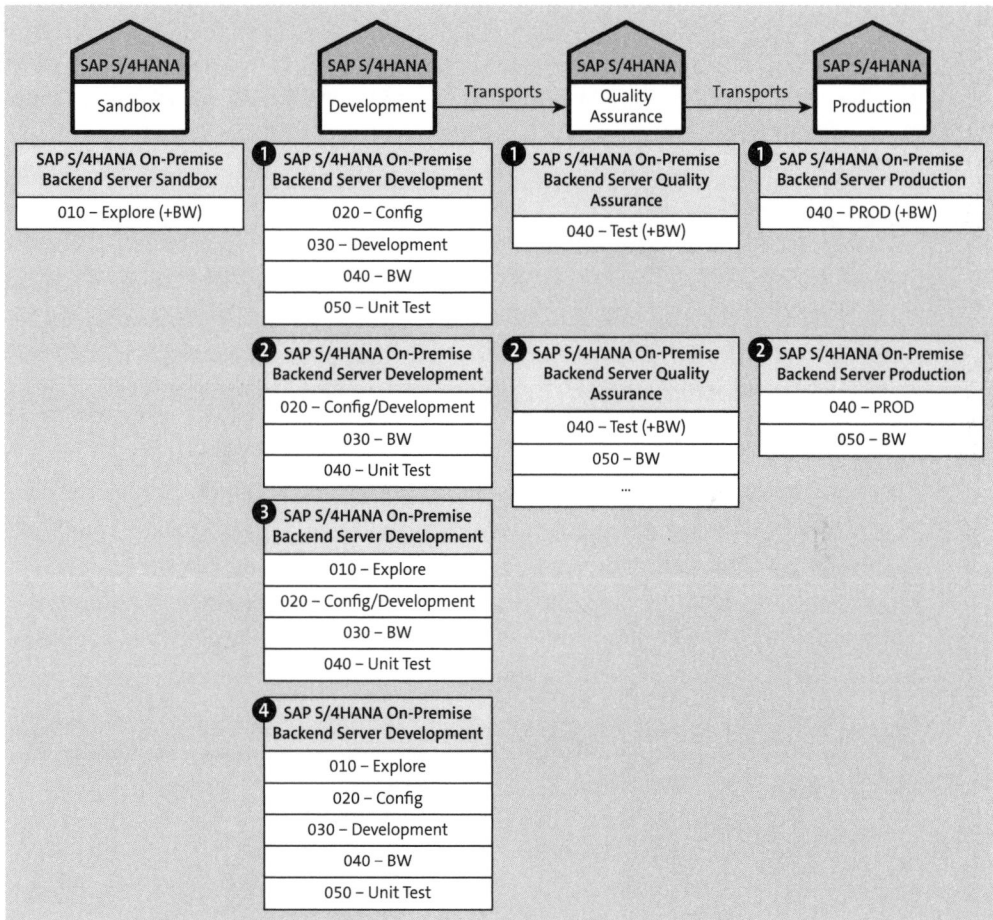

Figure 2.5 SAP S/4HANA Four-Tier Landscape

For sourcing and procurement, self-service procurement and operational procurement, direct procurement, sourcing, contract management, supplier management, and purchasing analytics comprise the core scope for a comprehensive project in this area. Many projects focus on a more reduced scope, targeting self-service procurement for Phase 1 and then analytics during a follow-on phase.

From a development standpoint, SAP S/4HANA Enterprise Management leverages a model similar to that of previous SAP ERP platforms, with sandbox, development, quality assurance, and production environments. The development environment is further delineated with configuration and explore environments, as shown in Figure 2.5.

2.2.2   Installation

For the actual install of the SAP S/4HANA environment, SAP Basis resources follow these general steps:

1. Logon to maintenance planner (available on the SAP Portal at
   http://s-prs.co/500300).
2. Select the backend system.
3. Select additional systems.
4. Define changes on servers.
5. Select OS/DB-dependent files.
6. Download selected files and install.

There are two options to cover at this point in the install. One option, called the *activated appliance* option, will accelerate your installation of the software; the other, called *SAP Best Practices*, is the consequent implementation. SAP Best Practices will be discussed in detail in the next section of this chapter, along with some other options, like SAP Model Company. For the install, however, the activated appliance option would apply, as detailed in Table 2.5.

Fully Activated SAP S/4HANA Enterprise Management Appliance			
SAP S/4HANA	SAP NetWeaver for Java/Adobe Documents Service	Remote desktop (option/available via SAP Cloud Appliance Library)	SAP BusinessObjects BI platform (option/available via SAP Cloud Appliance Library)

Table 2.5 SAP S/4HANA Appliance Packages

Fully Activated SAP S/4HANA Enterprise Management Appliance			
ABAP server: with SAP S/4HANA, SAP Gateway/SAP Fiori, SAP NetWeaver, SAP Best Practices	Java server: Adobe Document Services, SAP NetWeaver Java	Windows Remote Desktop: Mozilla Firefox, SAP GUI 7.40, ABAP developer tools/SAP HANA Studio, SAP Lumira, SAP Lumira, designer edition	SAP BusinessObjects Explorer: SAP BusinessObjects BI platform, SAP Lumira, designer edition, SAP BusinessObjects BI best practices content
SAP HANA 1.0	SAP Adaptive Server Enterprise		

Table 2.5 SAP S/4HANA Appliance Packages (Cont.)

2.2.3   Activated Appliance

The activated appliance option includes the software to download or ship to you, provided you already have licenses for the products ordered and hardware with Linux installed (see SAP Note 2041140). This option is exclusive to SAP customers with enabled partners or SAP Services engaged. You can also go to SAP Cloud Appliance Library at *http://cal.sap.com* and enable a hosted solution with Amazon Web Services (AWS) or Microsoft Azure. For this approach, you need valid credentials for using AWS/Azure, as depicted in Figure 2.6.

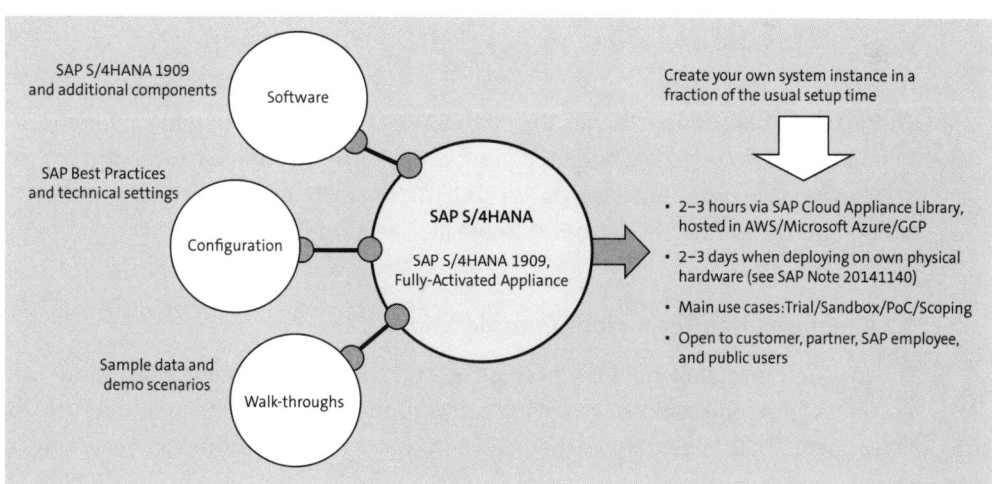

Figure 2.6 SAP S/4HANA 1909 Fully Activated Appliance

The SAP S/4HANA appliance includes the clients described in Table 2.6.

ABAP Client	Description
Client 100—trial client	■ Preactivated SAP Best Practices configuration and sample master data (Germany, United States). ■ Additional configuration for end-to-end sample business process. ■ Transactional data and demo scenarios in US company code.
Client 200—ready-to-activate client	■ Technical preparation activities prior to SAP Best Practices content activation. ■ Whitelist copy of Client 000 customizing with SAP S/4HANA Best Practices activation on top. *Whitelist* refers to a select set of tables and configuration from Client 000 needed to complement SAP Best Practices configuration in the development client. ■ This is the standard delivery state for SAP Best Practices (no additional configuration, no corrections applied).
Client 400—SAP BW client	■ For SAP Integrated Business Planning for Supply Chain.
Client 500—SAP Best Practices reference client	■ Full copy of client 000 customizing with SAP S/4HANA. ■ This is the standard delivery state of SAP Best Practices (no additional configuration, no corrections applied).

Table 2.6 SAP S/4HANA Appliance Package Clients

There are numerous approaches to install SAP S/4HANA both in a hosted environment and in your own data center. If you have determined that a conversion to SAP S/4HANA is the most preferred route, this path also includes some options and decision points to consider, as discussed in the next section.

2.2.4   Information Technology Considerations

For procurement stakeholders, evaluating the current state, objectives, and SAP S/4HANA and cloud options is a key step toward successful realization and return on investment (ROI). What moves the needle in the organization from a procurement standpoint? Does the organization manufacture product and rely on a broad base of suppliers to source inputs and develop better ones? Perhaps a sourcing focus will drive the best outcomes from an impact standpoint. Are these sourcing processes largely defined, but general employees are buying things off contract and out of catalog with no approval?

Choose Your Own Procurement Adventure

Self-service procurement in SAP S/4HANA or SAP Ariba Buying can reign in this maverick spending and cut costs, as more spend moves to negotiated agreements and volumes are brought to bear. Are account payable processes out of sync with the rest of the procurement organization, leading to missed early-payment discounts and long lead times on matching POs to invoices? PO/invoice integration with the Ariba Network may offer an elegant solution for cleaning this up. In short, as with many things in life, the procurement solution you craft with SAP S/4HANA and its cloud portfolio of products is what you make of it, and you will want to set directions and priorities to align with your biggest areas of opportunity.

System Administration

When choosing your implementation approach and path, understanding the system administration implications is also important. If your IT organization is running very lean, you may not have the resources onsite to support an onsite implementation of a heavy-duty ERP system such as SAP S/4HANA. On-premise SAP S/4HANA requires, at minimum, an SAP Basis team to support day-to-day operations, to keep the hardware and software humming, and to implement upgrades and maintenance items for the software. You may not have enough business users in the purchasing department to support a "big bang" roll out of SAP S/4HANA functionality to suppliers. Without this helpdesk, running a bidding exercise or skills assessment may quickly overwhelm the group. These considerations will allow you to choose between cloud and on-premise approaches or hybrid versions of these approaches.

SaaS means less maintenance and administration, but you will still need technically savvy colleagues to maintain data and support issue resolution jointly with SAP. Also, in integration and platform areas, technical system administration doesn't completely go away just because you're running in the cloud. However, these areas should be much lighter; hardware-wise, though you still have to worry about maintaining and supporting the devices connecting to the cloud services, you no longer have to worry about hardware itself.

2.2.5   Integration Options

For both SAP S/4HANA Cloud and on-premise, there are a multitude of SAP and non-SAP solutions with which you can integrate, as shown in Figure 2.7.

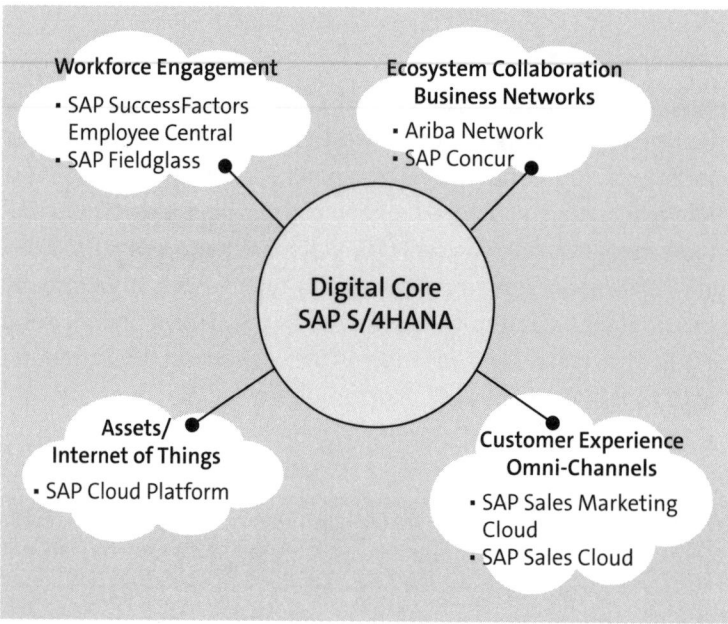

Figure 2.7 Integration Options for SAP S/4HANA

These integration areas break down into the following categories:

- *People:* SAP SuccessFactors Employee Central; SAP Human Capital Management for SAP S/4HANA, on-premise
- *Customer management:* SAP Marketing, SAP Cloud for Customer
- *Finance:* SAP Multi-Bank Connectivity
- *Procurement:* SAP Ariba
- *Contingent workforce:* SAP Fieldglass
- *Travel:* SAP Concur
- *Extensions, integrations, and custom application development:* SAP Cloud Platform

For both cloud and on-premise options, SAP S/4HANA offers prebuilt integrations, out-of-the-box integrations for areas like PO/IV collaboration between SAP S/4HANA and the Ariba Network, and extensions, integrations, and custom application development.

2.2.6   SAP S/4HANA System Conversion

For a system conversion, there is more preparation required up front and more vetting of the existing system to be converted. The main tools leveraged for a conversion are as follows:

- SUM: Allows you to update the software version or support package to the level supported for conversion.
- DMO of SUM: Upgrade an existing SAP NetWeaver–based system, perform Unicode conversion (single code page), and migrate to SAP S/4HANA in one step as part of the SUM tool.
- Software provisioning manager: This tool is used both to install a new SAP S/4HANA system and to migrate a system to the required software level for an SAP S/4HANA conversion. This tool can also be used to perform Unicode conversions.

The conversion process for SAP S/4HANA relies on two main phases: a preparation phase and a realization phase. Without a well-thought-out and well-executed preparation phase, a conversion incurs unnecessary risk that the conversion will produce a corrupted instance of SAP S/4HANA, missing key data, components, or both. The software provisioning manager and SUM tools are used right from the beginning in this preparation, whereas the DMO is used during the realization phase to activate the conversion.

Maintenance Planner

Once the system requirements and approach have been defined, the preparation steps begin in maintenance planner in the **Plan for SAP S/4HANA** tile, as with the install of a new environment. Here, after selecting **Plan an SAP S/4HANA Conversion of an Existing System**, define the changes based on your landscape data in your customer profile, select the files, and push all required tools, archives, and stack.xml data to the download.

Prechecks

The stack.xml file is recommended to be used during the prechecks, as shown in Figure 2.8.

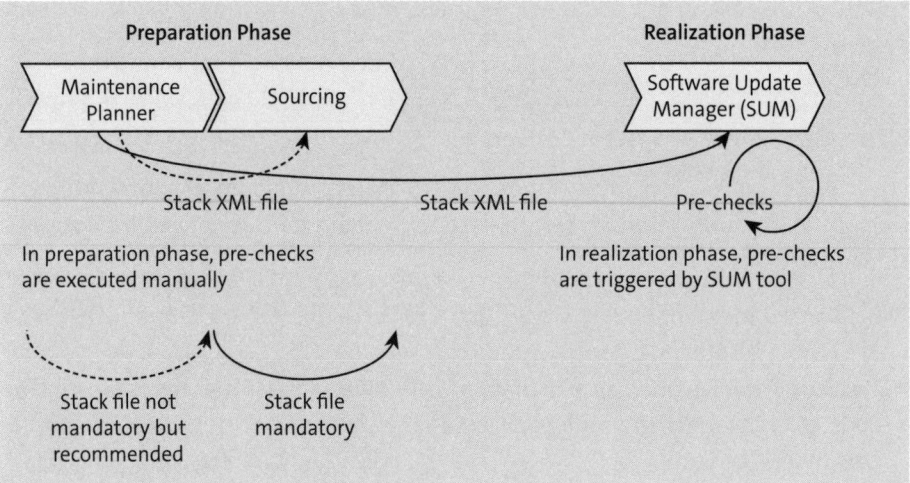

Figure 2.8 Stack XML File-Based Prechecks

Prechecks are completed as the first step in maintenance planner as part of the conversion process. Prechecks are available as SAP Notes for customers that want to convert to SAP S/4HANA. These prechecks are executed on the SAP Business Suite system targeted for conversion. The precheck results list details the mandatory items to address prior to upgrading. These checks are run twice again during the conversion process in SUM, and the conversion is stopped if errors are found, as illustrated in Figure 2.9.

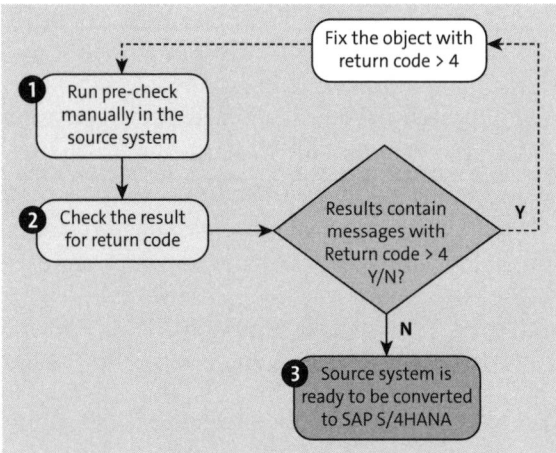

Figure 2.9 Manual Precheck before Start of System Conversion Process

During the prechecks, any objects with a return code greater than 4 must be fixed prior to starting the conversion (see Figure 2.9).

To perform prechecks, you must implement the reports from SAP Note 2502552. Ensure that you are using the most current SAP Note with the updated reports prior to installing it on your clients. The reports need to be run on all of the systems in scope for conversion, starting with the sandbox/development environments and then working up to quality and production. Report R_S4_PRE_TRANSITION_CHECKS should be run in the core Client 000 using Transaction SE38/SA38 with the stack XML file generated in maintenance planner, as per Figure 2.8. Note that though general ledger prechecks are included in the report, to check asset accounting you'll need to implement all of the SAP Notes listed in SAP Note 2333236.

Even though you can technically move through warning messages with return code 4, these messages shouldn't be ignored entirely; they highlight issues that can cause data loss during conversion if not addressed up front.

If during the prechecks a return code of 8 or higher is issued, this is a hard-stop error; you won't be able to continue with the conversion until it's addressed.

These hard-stop error messages often refer to components that aren't supported and will need to be removed prior to conversion. Other hard-stop errors will point to SAP Notes to help address the issue identified.

During its first set of prechecks, maintenance planner will identify which business functions can and can't be converted and which ones will be turned off or converted in always-off mode. Likewise, strategies of business functions can change in between feature package releases. Use SAP Note 2240359 (SAP S/4HANA: Always-Off Business Functions) and the attachment contained in this note to determine the strategy changes.

If you have SAP-delivered or third-party add-ons installed on your existing system, these also will be checked. SAP Note 2214409 (SAP S/4HANA: Compatible Add-Ons) lists the compatible ones delivered by SAP for SAP S/4HANA.

Custom Code Review

With the prechecks concluded, the next step is to review the custom code in the system to be converted. For SAP NetWeaver 7.50, this involves applying SAP Notes as per Figure 2.10.

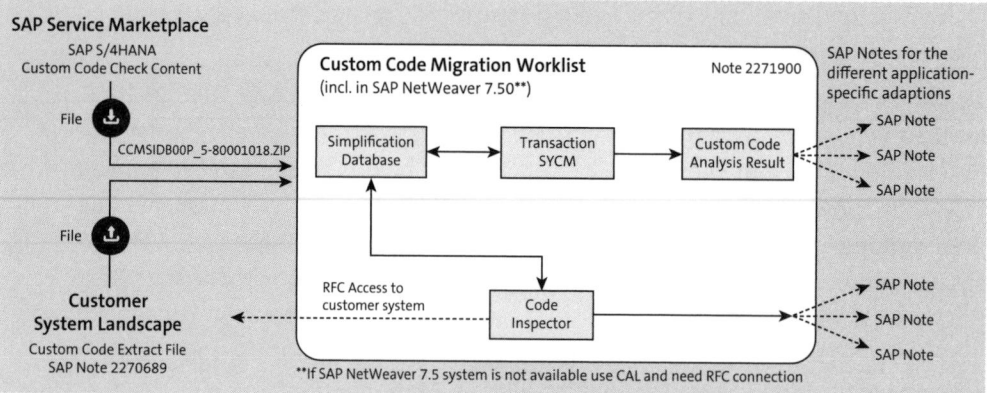

Figure 2.10 Custom Code Checks for SAP NetWeaver 7.50

The main difference between the approaches for SAP NetWeaver 7.50 and 7.51 is the custom code analysis report. This isn't required in 7.51, as shown in Figure 2.11.

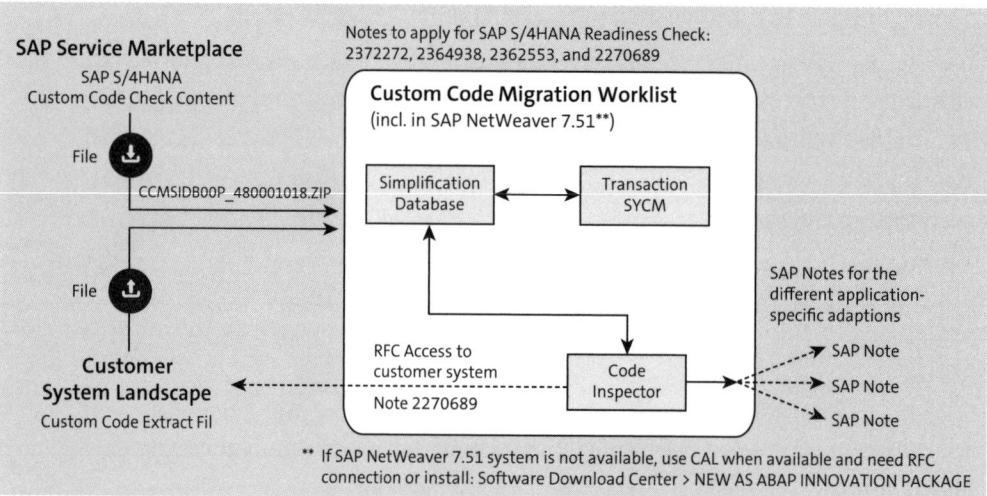

Figure 2.11 Evolution of Custom Code Checks: SAP NetWeaver 7.51

The main steps remain the same in both versions:

1. Download custom code check content.

2. Start the Code Inspector (Transaction SCI).

3. Use check variant **S4HANA Readiness**.

4. Specify objects to be checked.

5. Start inspection run.

6. Analyze check results.

Once the prechecks are complete, you are ready to run the conversion in the realization phase.

The conversion of a four-tier landscape, as shown in Figure 2.12, starts with copying the production instance back to the sandbox and running the conversion of this environment. Once the sandbox has been converted, you'll have a pretty good feel for how production will stand up to the conversion process, as you have essentially just converted it.

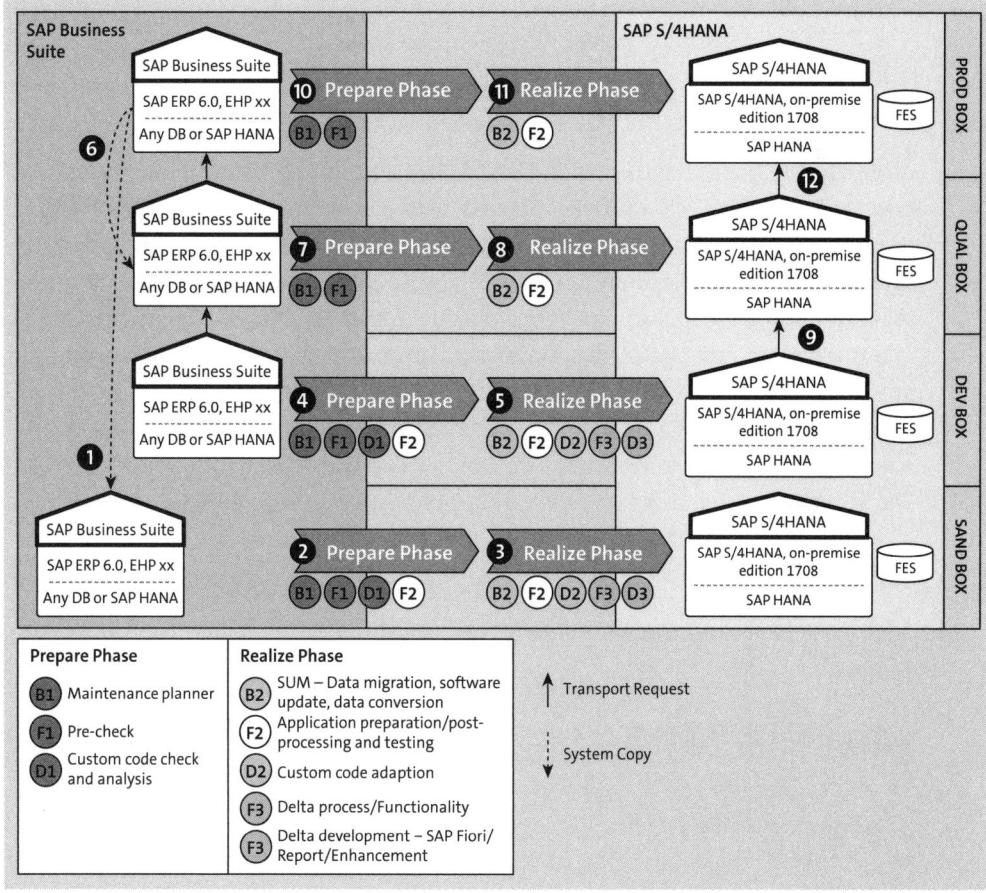

Figure 2.12 Four-Tier Landscape Conversion Overview

Next, the instances on the transport bath, beginning with the development environment, are converted. For both the sandbox and the development environment conversion, delta processes and functionality, as well as enhancements and SAP Fiori adjustments, are implemented. These changes are then promoted forward on the transport path from development, once the other instances in the landscape have been converted to SAP S/4HANA.

Once the install or conversion to SAP S/4HANA is complete, you're ready to proceed with the implementation project. Traditional plan, design, realize, test, and go-live approaches are still used on occasion to implement SAP S/4HANA. However, there are a number of methodologies and tools that you can use to both accelerate and enhance your implementation, as detailed in the next section.

2.3   SAP S/4HANA Cloud

As detailed in the previous sections, SAP S/4HANA Cloud is a multitenant SaaS solution that provides a cloud-based ERP environment running on SAP HANA. Implementing SAP S/4HANA Cloud is different than implementing the on-premise version in several respects. First, there are fewer IT considerations, as the baseline equipment requirements can be as straightforward as having a device and a browser to log in. The integration approaches are more straightforward, as many of the integrations are prebuilt for other SAP solutions and cloud services; those that require customization and buildouts typically have reduced options for integrating with a cloud environment, leading to less complex decision trees and design and development cycles. The scope is reduced from that for the on-premise version, as detailed in the Hybrid Implementation box in Section 2.3.3.

2.3.1   SAP Best Practices Scope

The SAP S/4HANA Cloud scope includes the elements shown in Table 2.7.

Streamlined Procure-to-Pay	Core Finance
■ Sourcing and contract management ■ Operational procurement ■ Inventory management ■ Invoice and payables management	■ Accounting and closing operations ■ Cost management and profitability analysis ■ Treasury and financial risk management ■ Finance operations into receivables management

Table 2.7 SAP S/4HANA Cloud Options

Accelerated Plan-to-Product	Project Services
■ Basic production planning ■ Basic production processing ■ Inventory management ■ Maintenance management	■ Contract-to-cash ■ Project management ■ Time and expense management
Optimized Order-to-Cash	HR Connectivity
■ Order and contract management ■ Inventory management ■ Receivables processing	■ SAP SuccessFactors Employee Central

Table 2.7 SAP S/4HANA Cloud Options (Cont.)

The principal area of concern for a sourcing and procurement project is the streamlined procure-to-pay process area. However, other considerations and integration points arise with core finance and HR connectivity.

2.3.2   Information Technology Considerations

Many information technology (IT) departments today face ever-increasing demands from business, as well as fragmentations of their once-centralized budgets to respond. The cloud approach has provided business decision-makers with direct access to business applications, a domain that was once brokered by, and often controlled entirely by, IT. However, just because a business unit chooses to buy a service does not mean that integration and landscape decisions, in addition to the inevitable cost and TCO decisions, shouldn't be factored in. IT needs to stay involved, even if its decision-making authority has somewhat devolved to that of an influencer rather than a driver. In purchasing SAP S/4HANA Sourcing and Procurement, a purchasing department may ignore the overall landscape of its organization from an IT standpoint, choosing an on-premise approach when core line of business processes are in the cloud, or cloud when a group such as finance has already built finance on-premise. Just as having IT make all of the business decisions in a company rarely leads to business user satisfaction, so too do business units ignore IT implications at their own peril. There are sufficient options to support a plethora of landscapes, directives, and needs from an IT standpoint in SAP S/4HANA. Inclusion of both IT and business stakeholders during the design and decision process is essential for realizing the best outcomes and ROI.

Multitenant Environment

A multitenant environment means less customization and more adoption of best practices and existing system processes by necessity. If a system is running a common code base, it can't follow the whims of every individual customer, just like a tenant living in an apartment building can't decide to remove a load-bearing wall in the building or rearchitect the plumbing without extreme consequences. Unlike in a building, in a multitenant environment you aren't at liberty to try and hack the system in this manner; the options simply aren't available. Just as living in an apartment building is not for everyone and doesn't cover everyone's needs, so too may a multitenant environment prove to be too restrictive for very large enterprises with competitive differentiation built into their systems and processes. Then again, a large enterprise may prefer a multitenant environment for the cost savings and discipline it brings in providing best practices without allowing the organization to indulge in its own unmanageable sprawl.

Automatic Upgrades

One benefit that most cloud environments have, including SAP S/4HANA Cloud, is a more frequent cadence for upgrades. Some of these upgrades may be mandatory, though most new functionality can be left turned off if required. The point is that the upgrades allow for more frequent updates to the system and are not managed directly by your organization, both saving money and preventing the familiar predicament in the on-premise world of fewer and fewer upgrades due to the effort involved as the system ages and the customization increases.

2.3.3   Standard Integration and Customization

SAP S/4HANA Cloud provides standard integration via its IPaaS approach with the SAP Cloud portfolio of products, as well as with other on-premise instances of SAP ERP. Despite having customization limitations, some customization and configuration is still quite possible in an SAP S/4HANA Cloud implementation, so it should not be interpreted as being entirely locked down to meeting business requirements that may adjust the existing processes to a degree.

Hybrid Implementation

As described in Table 2.3, a hybrid implementation combines two or more distinct public cloud environments and/or on-premise providers. This in turn is integrated by standardized or proprietary technology, enabling data and application portability. A hybrid option using the SAP S/4HANA portfolio leverages and integrates the options outlined in Section 2.2.5. For procurement, a typical hybrid implementation would include SAP Ariba solutions for procurement transformation areas connected to SAP S/4HANA (either cloud or on-premise), alongside SAP Fieldglass for contingent labor and SAP Concur for travel and expense. From an implementation standpoint, these are multiple cloud and/or on-premise deployments connected via an integration phase and emphasis of the project, which potentially entails more interfaces and cross-system coordination but can realize further efficiency gains and business process optimization/user satisfaction as a result of using the optimal solution and environment for individual business processes and areas.

2.4   SAP S/4HANA for Central Procurement

Some customers, especially large customers that grew through acquisition or had disparate business units and businesses to manage as a conglomerate, have multiple instances of SAP ERP. These instances may be in different versions and have altogether different processes. It may not be feasible to consolidate these instances into a single SAP S/4HANA environment. A previous solution used to consolidate multiple ERPs into a single environment for purchasing was called SAP Supplier Relationship Management (SAP SRM). However, SAP SRM will go out of maintenance in 2025. The need for a solution to manage purchasing centrally for multiple ERP systems is still there, and this is where SAP S/4HANA for central procurement is now the go-to solution.

SAP S/4HANA for central procurement enables an SAP customer to centralize procurement activities in requisitioning, purchasing, contracts, analytics, and (eventually) invoicing. The process flow covered by central procurement is shown in Figure 2.13.

SAP Ariba guided buying can also be integrated on top of SAP S/4HANA for central procurement to provide users with a consumer-grade purchasing experience before transferring the requisition to SAP S/4HANA for central procurement. SAP S/4HANA for central pocurement has planned integrations with SAP Ariba Contracts and SAP Analytics Cloud as well.

SAP S/4HANA for central procurement greatly enhances SAP S/4HANA for Sourcing and Procurement's options for managing a complex ERP landscape. An SAP customer looking to deploy SAP S/4HANA procurement functionality doesn't necessarily have to upgrade and consolidate every one of their ERP systems into a single SAP S/4HANA instance. Instead, they can deploy a single instance of SAP S/4HANA for central procurement in the cloud or on premise and connect all of their SAP ERP 6.0 EHP 6 and above environments. Future support is planned for non-SAP ERP systems and older versions of SAP ERP. With these connections set up, central procurement enables purchasing professionals to manage their purchasing operations centrally, calling directly to the individual ERP systems to validate master data and purchasing documents. The documents and master data continue to reside in the respective ERP systems, allowing for central management of purchasing in a distributed landscape, without heavy investment in integration and consolidation.

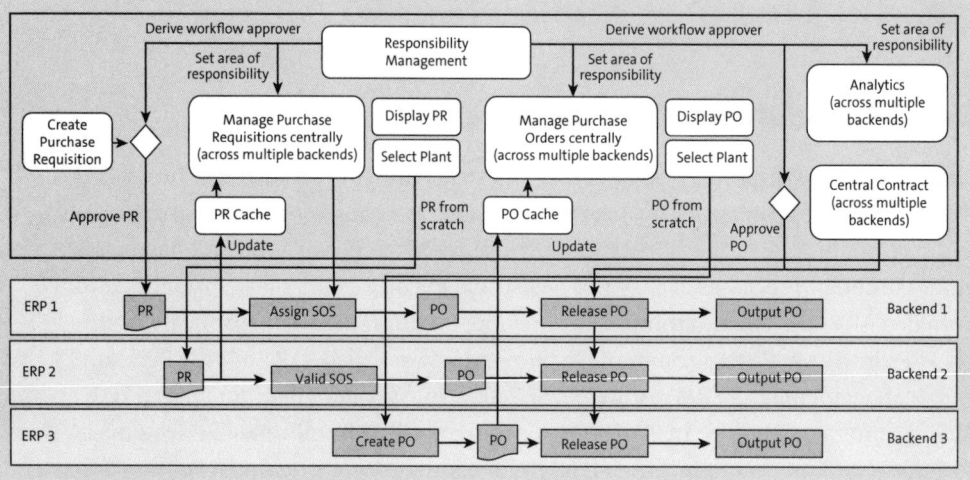

Figure 2.13 Central Procurement Process Flow

SAP S/4HANA for central procurement can be used to facilitate deployments in a phased consolidation approach, whereby an SAP customer decides to consolidate some of their ERP systems during the initial phase but leave others as is. Conceivably, you could also leverage SAP S/4HANA for central procurement to avoid upgrading to SAP S/4HANA for the time being while still creating a centralized procurement area in SAP S/4HANA for your purchasing department. However, as SAP S/4HANA for central procurement leverages the data and customizations native to each ERP system, there are limits to how much SAP S/4HANA functionality you can use in this approach:

- The central requisitioning scenario enables a buyer to centrally create and manage requisitions within Central Procurement and the connected ERPs.

- The central purchasing scenario expands upon central requisitioning to include centralized creation and management of purchase orders with central procurement and the connected ERP systems.

- The central contracts scenario enables a buyer to create and manage contracts within central procurement and the connected ERP systems.

- The central analytics scenario allows a buyer to centrally analyze purchasing activities across the ERP landscape from central procurement.

- The central invoicing scenario allows for central coordination and processing of invoices via central procurement and the connected ERP systems. Note that central invoicing is still on the roadmap and not available as of the 2019 SAP S/4HANA releases.

2.5   Quick Start Approaches and Materials for SAP S/4HANA

Traditional approaches to ERP entail five to six distinct phases. First, a preparation phase needs to be conducted to align all of the stakeholders, goals, and materials. Second, a design phase should cover all of the design considerations with the various stakeholders and juxtapose these with the system capabilities and constraints. Third, a realization phase kicks off where the system is built. A test and deploy phase (sometimes split into two separate phases) is instituted to ensure the system works as built and meets the stakeholder requirements; during deployment, users are trained and the system is put into production. Finally, a run phase is used to delineate continual improvements in production. Needless to say, many of these steps can take up cycles, and these cycles are expensive from time and investment standpoints.

In recent years, many firms and government entities have begun rethinking and refocusing system implementations. Some of these tuning exercises have yielded whole new approaches toward software development, such as *agile methodology*, which relies on *sprints* and *scrums* to iteratively improve upon the end product of the project, combining many mini projects within phases rather than using a formalized, linear realization phase. SAP provides its own version of this approach in its latest project methodology, called *SAP Activate*, which will be detailed further in Section 2.5.4. SAP Activate leverages prebuilt materials and models to further jumpstart the implementation process and focus the resources and timeline on getting to value versus reinventing the basics.

2.5.1   Prebuilt Content and Templates

There are numerous assets available to make SAP S/4HANA implementation projects more efficient. Most implementations are for entities that share many processes in common with other entities in their industry, and general processes for manufacturing and other areas have a high degree of similarity. You don't need to reinvent the wheel for every project and create a bespoke implementation for every entity; some uniformity is necessary and even desirable—desirable because it allows implementation projects to move quickly through the commodity processes with best practice approaches and focus on the areas that truly differentiate the firm or government entity, allowing for condensed timeframes for implementations and more impactful results. These savings can amount to as much as 30 percent of the total implementation timeframe and costs. In areas like the blueprint phase, the reduction in time and investment can be as high as 90 percent.

For quick-start materials to aid in the implementation, SAP offers an SAP S/4HANA appliance option and SAP Best Practices, in addition to project methodologies in SAP Activate and SAP Model Company.

2.5.2   SAP Best Practices

The SAP S/4HANA appliance option relates more to the technical software package side of the equation on a new install approach, whereas the SAP Best Practices simplify the functional SAP S/4HANA business processes by providing core elements of each business process area and removing less common ones. SAP Best Practices are installed during the system setup. Once you have reviewed the and selected the SAP Best Practices content for your project, you build the client system and download and activate the content, which functional consultants then use as a springboard for further tailoring of the system to the customer's requirements.

SAP Best Practices content covers all of the major areas of SAP S/4HANA. The sourcing and procurement areas covered are as follows:

- Supplier classification and segmentation
- Supplier activity management
- SAP Ariba Sourcing integration
- Purchase contract
- Requisitioning
- Procurement and consumption of consigned inventory

- Procurement of direct materials
- Serial number management
- Consumables purchasing
- Real-time reporting and monitoring of procurement
- SAP Ariba Network integration

2.5.3   SAP Model Company

Another accelerator approach for implementing SAP S/4HANA is the SAP Model Company approach. This approach is provided as an engineered service by SAP consulting/delivery groups as a preconfigured solution, supported by handover and enablement workshops conducted by SAP consultants to jumpstart the discovery, exploration, and realization phases of the SAP S/4HANA project.

The SAP Model Company includes a business process hierarchy, end-to-end scenarios, and process diagrams sorted by role, as well as materials about configuration, test and demo scripts, and implementation tools. There are over 20 individual model company packages available for different industries and processes.

Once you've evaluated these models and tools for laying a foundation of prebuilt content to support your project, it's time to move into the SAP S/4HANA implementation. For this task, SAP has introduced a tailored project management approach for SAP ERP implementations called SAP Activate.

2.5.4   SAP Activate

SAP Activate is the successor to the AcceleratedSAP (ASAP) and SAP Launch methodologies. Based on a six-phase package with agile approaches to implementation, SAP Activate leverages guided configuration, as well digital business and technology processes. The main phases of SAP Activate are discover, prepare, explore, realize, deploy, and run. As a simple, modular methodology, SAP Activate has broad coverage of SAP solutions, beginning with on-premise SAP S/4HANA and SAP S/4HANA Cloud, as well as hybrid deployments.

Discover Phase

In the *discover* phase, customers familiarize themselves with the solution to be implemented and the value it can bring their business or government entity. One of the outputs of this phase is to design an overall digital transformation strategy and an implementation approach that can realize and leverage the solution to create value for the company or government entity.

Prepare Phase

The *prepare* phase in an SAP Activate project provides for the project organization and governance planning and formation, including project schedule, budget, and project management plans. Once the prepare phase is complete, you begin the explore phase.

Explore Phase

The main goal of the *explore* phase is to map out the requirements for the implementation and the gaps using a sandbox environment; optionally, you can use this phase to design thinking workshops and prototyping, to do a hands-on validation rather than a conceptual one.

Realize Phase

In the *realize* phase, unlike in previous methodologies, both the realization of the business requirements resulting from the validation in the explore phase and the testing are combined.

Deploy Phase

Some of the final testing, such as system testing, is conducted in the *deploy* phase, in which the readiness of the solution is finalized, including end-user training, system management, and cutover activities/planning.

Run Phase

Finally, during the *run* phase, the solution is further optimized to meet the business and technical objectives of the implementation. The phases are outlined in Table 2.8.

SAP Activate Project Phase	Deliverables
Discover	Strategic planning, application value and scoping, trial system provisioning

Table 2.8 SAP Activate Phases for SAP S/4HANA Cloud and On-Premise

SAP Activate Project Phase	Deliverables
Prepare	Project organization and governance, schedule, budget, management plans, project standards and policies, organizational change management roadmap and training strategy, project team onboarding, project team infrastructure, solution scope and value determination, technical infrastructure requirements and sizing, data migration approach strategy, sandbox environment
Explore (used only in on-premise SAP S/4HANA deployments)	Project management execution, results management, results controlling, change impact analysis, communication plan, baseline build, validation workshops, gap validation, backlog prioritization, gaps and deltas design, legacy data migration design and plan, technology design and setup of DEV environment, test strategy and plan, release and sprint plan
Realize	Project management execution, management and controlling of results, organizational alignment and user enablement, technology setup for quality assurance (QA) and production environments with security and authorizations, spring execution, integrated solution and user acceptance testing, legacy data migration, value audits, technical operations setup plan including SAP Operations Control Center for premium engagements, cutover and transition plan
Deploy	Project management execution, management and controlling of results, organizational and production support readiness check, pre-go-live end user training and delivery, technical and system testing, setup operational support, cutover to production, production support post go-live
Run	Value management, application lifecycle management, PE: operations control center, operation solution, improve and innovate solution

Table 2.8 SAP Activate Phases for SAP S/4HANA Cloud and On-Premise (Cont.)

SAP Activate in SAP S/4HANA Cloud

For SAP S/4HANA Cloud, SAP Activate's discover phase provides a preconfigured solution, value assessment, and roadmap service, as shown in Figure 2.14. With SAP S/4HANA Cloud, there is less customization possible, but business process optimization is still very much part of the implementation to take advantage of the SAP Best Practices offered for various industries.

Unlike most of the on-premise SAP S/4HANA options, licensing for SAP S/4HANA Cloud is on a subscription basis and includes infrastructure. The infrastructure preparation and customization are two areas that don't need to be covered or can be covered less extensively than with an on-premise installation. Because there's less room to address gaps between your business processes and the underlying cloud solution, SAP S/4HANA Cloud implementations seek to verify in the discover and prepare phases whether there are any impediments to implementing in the cloud. Gaps constituting showstoppers and must-haves that can't be addressed in SAP S/4HANA Cloud may prompt evaluation of on-premise SAP S/4HANA, with which you would have greater flexibility to address these gaps.

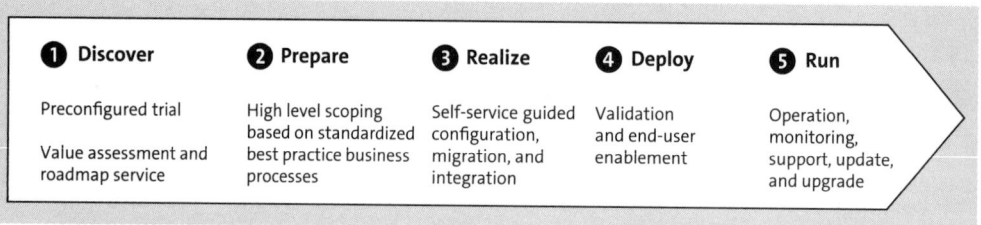

Figure 2.14 SAP S/4HANA Cloud Edition

SAP Activate Workflows

With the discover and run phases bookending, SAP Activate can be run repetitively to reach the desired outcome of the project, stringing together a number of mini projects, as shown in Figure 2.15.

Further iterations are built into the SAP Activate methodology in the individual phases via the agile-driven sprints, as shown in Figure 2.16. These sprints use the pre-built content and configuration from SAP Best Practices and SAP Model Company.

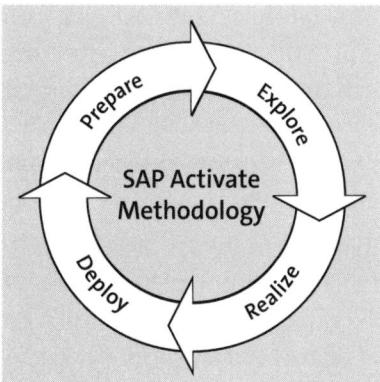

Figure 2.15 SAP Activate Methodology: Prepare, Explore, Realize, and Deploy

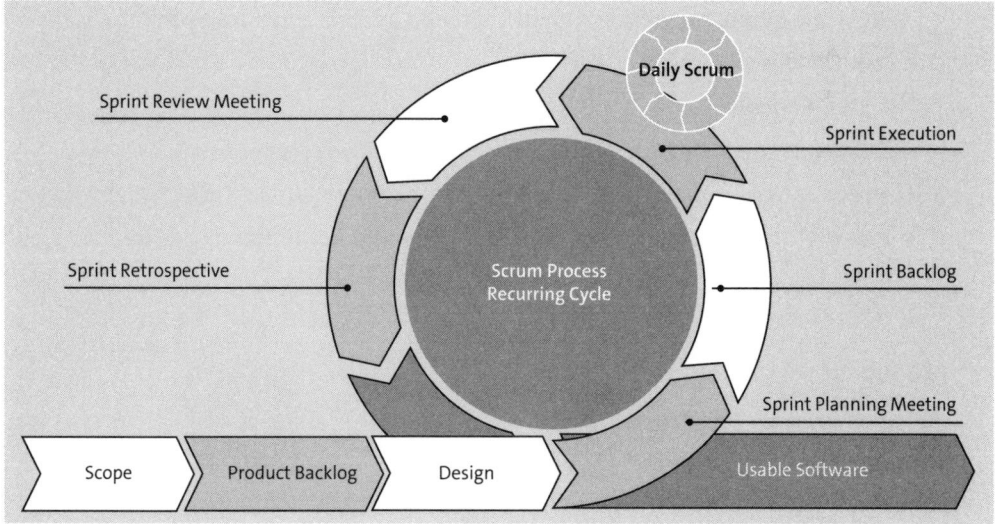

Figure 2.16 Agile Build: Use of Scrum-Based Approach in SAP Activate

Scrum approaches work to create individual and solution elements in parallel, itemizing, prioritizing, designing, building, and validating these various product configurations and customizations as part of the scrum process during the explore and realization phases of SAP Activate. Further augmenting the agile approach in SAP Activate is the use of prebuilt content to provide modular building blocks and a platform from which to begin the explore and realize phases.

Preassembly packages available via the SAP S/4HANA appliance, SAP Best Practices, and SAP Model Company are deployed during the prepare phase to jump-start the explore phase and enable project participants to focus on validating the solution and identifying requirements and gaps that require a process adjustment and/or customization within the system. These configurations and customizations in turn are built out, validated, and tested in parallel during the realization phase.

Within an agile-based approach in SAP Activate, there are two types of workshops. The first kind are solution validation workshops, in which the group validates the SAP solution and identifies and prioritizes any gaps. The gap output of this workshop is then prioritized with the other identified areas, and then a second type of workshop focused on the delta design is initiated in sequence, or sometimes in parallel, resources and scheduling permitting. During the delta design workshop, the business models and processes, as well as potential solution customizations, are reworked to address the identified gaps and then validated and accepted following the steps of solution validation and delta design.

The solution validation steps are as follows:

1. Reference value: Provide process, value, and strategic context.
2. Validation of SAP solution: Show and tell of SAP standard key design elements.
3. Identify delta and gaps: Identify delta scope and requirements, as well as document gaps.
4. Prioritize scope (delta).

The delta design steps are as follows:

1. Delta design: Update business models and process design, as well as solution visualization/user experience (UX).
2. Verify and accept: Verify process and solution design; design acceptance.
3. Document product backlog: Divide priority categories into must, should, could, and would, in order of severity.
4. Release and plan the next sprints.

During the explore and realize phases, when many of these workshops take place, there is a constant working of the product backlog, which prioritizes the work efforts and consequent workshops based on what is a must-have versus a nice-to-have. In this way, the project continually focuses on the most important and valuable items for the implementation. If the project at any time needs to move on to the next phase without addressing further log items, you can be assured that the items addressed up to this point were the most pressing, meaning the project has delivered the most value possible given resource and time constraints.

In Figure 2.17, *epic* refers to a large user story that may take multiple sprints to build out completely. For an SAP S/4HANA project, an epic is basically a larger set of related requirements around a particular business process. The business priority product backlog is created during the explore phase to prioritize and sequence the different epics and their corresponding sprints. As an iterative process, multiple epics can run simultaneously or sequentially, drawing off the product backlog list. Finally, these epics are then validated and tested at the user level (during user acceptance testing [UAT]) while gating out of the realize phase.

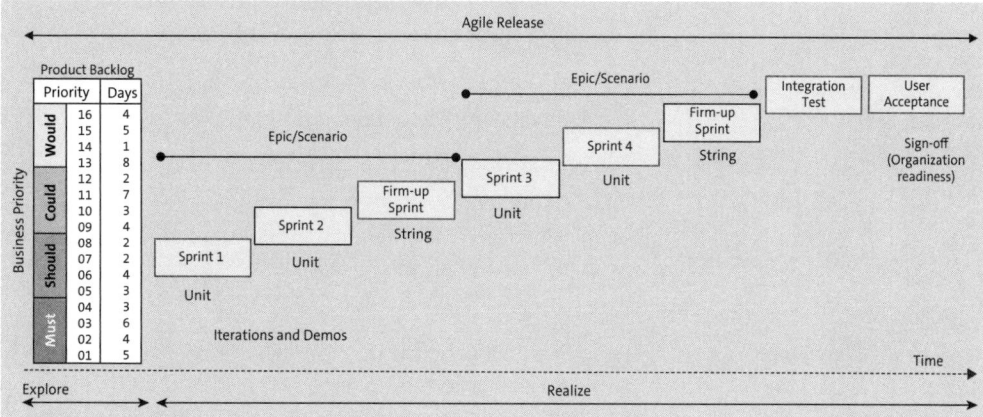

Figure 2.17 Agile Build: Iterative Realize Phase

Quality Gates

Another safeguard in SAP Activate are *quality gates*. Quality gates ensure that a proper review and sign-off takes place prior to passing to the next phase. In a quality gate, you verify that acceptance is met for the deliverables during the phase prior to gating out of the phase. For the aforementioned scenario, during the realize phase after UAT, the project would arrive at a quality gate prior to moving on to the next phase. Quality gates provide a formalized approach toward project alignment and memorialize the acceptance and understanding of participants and sponsors prior to rushing into the next phase of the project and potentially leaving critical elements of the previous phase unaddressed.

2.5.5   SAP Activate Roles

For the project team and roles involved in an SAP S/4HANA implementation, the main roles for both a migration and a new implementation of SAP S/4HANA are similar to SAP ERP role requirements in previous project scenarios, as described in Table 2.9. The main difference here is that these participants in the project team will be working within different structures and cycles than before.

Roles	Tasks and Skillsets
Project management	Align resources across various work streams and drive project to achieve milestones.
Functional expert	Determine the functional transformation capabilities enabled by SAP S/4HANA. Prioritize adoption of refined business processes to achieve and enhance business outcomes.
Technical architect	Determine the technical architecture, including security and UX requirements needed to support the target solution.
Operating system (OS)/ database lead	Perform the technical migration of the transactional system information to the new SAP S/4HANA system. The migration approach utilized will determine the skillsets required. For a new implementation, this role focuses on structuring converted data to be loaded into the new system for optimal usage.
Development lead	Perform an evaluation of the existing system for an SAP S/4HANA conversion and/or proposed customizations for a new implementation of SAP S/4HANA and determine the effort required to revert to standard and/or remediate code for SAP S/4HANA migration, or the effort required to realize the customization requirements in a new implementation.
Change management lead	Build and execute the strategy to lead the organization through the transformation underpinned by SAP S/4HANA.
End users	Perform system testing required to confirm proper operation of a migrated or newly implemented SAP S/4HANA system.
Analytics	Develop analytic requirements and determine how to utilize the transformative capabilities of SAP S/4HANA, in which transactional and analytical processes are combined to accelerate business processes and empower end users.

Table 2.9 Project Roles: SAP S/4HANA Conversions and New Implementations

Each project may have specific role requirements that join the basic ones outlined in Table 2.9. Having the right individuals and roles on a project is as critical as it's been in previous methodologies.

2.6   Summary

Before diving deep into SAP S/4HANA Sourcing and Procurement, an SAP S/4HANA edition and implementation approach needs to be selected. The decision of on-premise or cloud is binary, but further decisions have to be made, such as which cloud edition to choose, which prebuilt solutions will be leveraged, and how to structure the actual implementation project. At all steps of this process, SAP provides tools, processes, and methodologies, as well as solutions. Now that we've reviewed the implementation options, we'll drill deeper in the next chapter into the SAP organizational structure model.

Chapter 3
Organizational Structure

As with previous SAP ERP releases, the organizational structure and master data in SAP S/4HANA are fundamental elements for structured reporting, financial postings, and automating the procurement process in general. These topics warrant their own chapter and discussion.

An ill-defined organizational structure can have far-reaching ramifications for procurement operations and transactions, as can poorly defined and maintained master data. Each element, whether organizational structure or master data, carries maintenance efforts and potential trade-offs. This chapter will provide an overview of organizational structure and master data and how they relate to sourcing and procurement in SAP S/4HANA.

3.1 SAP S/4HANA Enterprise Management Organization Objects

The SAP organizational structure hierarchy is the underpinning of an SAP ERP system, and SAP S/4HANA Enterprise Management leverages this framework as well. The hierarchy supports every transaction and forms the main relationships with the master data elements in the system. As such, the SAP hierarchy comprises the management structures, markets, operational environment, geographic structures, and reporting requirements. Once established with master data and transactions associated within the system, the organizational structure is difficult to remove or rework. Therefore, special cross-module care must be taken in defining the organizational structure, beyond just sourcing and procurement, and the design must have the flexibility to add more organization units as the organization grows and/or changes.

An organizational structure can refer to the configuration of an organization's human resources and not just the corporate entities. Essentially, the organizational structure created in the form of company codes and plants forms the backbone for the HR organizational structure. These employees can be managed directly in SAP S/4HANA's HR functions or in a cloud solution connected to SAP S/4HANA, such as

SAP SuccessFactors. These employees also can be material to the previous Business Rule Framework (BRF)–based workflows and the new flexible workflow and purchasing approval capabilities available as early as SAP S/4HANA on-premise release 1709. For more information on workflow configuration, see Chapter 5.

Figure 3.1 outlines the three main areas for system design and configuration. First, the organization structure has to be defined. Next, master data, such as material masters and material groups, must be defined. The master data and the organization structure have dependencies and linkages with one another in most cases. General ledger accounts, for example, are typically mapped to material groups for spend capture and analysis. Finally, transaction data is generated using the system processes and the master and organizational data.

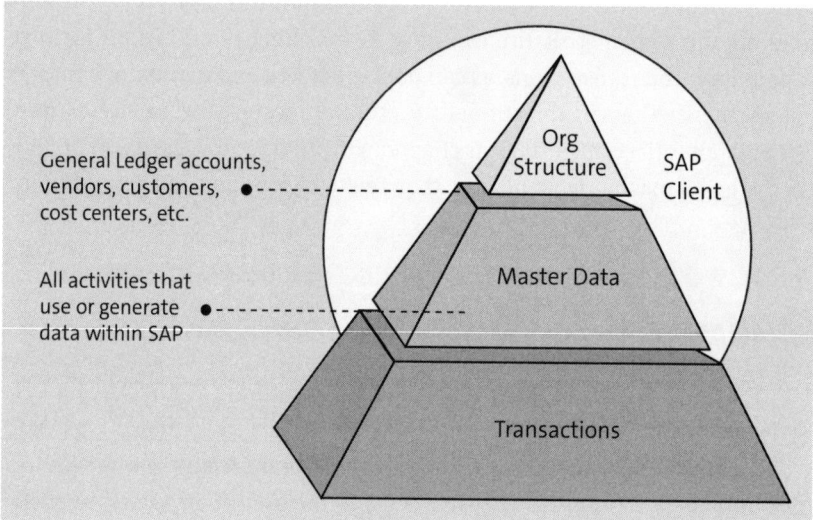

Figure 3.1 SAP Data and Organizational Hierarchy

Many terms are used during these SAP design phases that mean something particular in SAP. Often, consultants and long-time SAP users can sound like they're speaking their own special language. These next sections lay out the core objects that you use to build the organizational structure in SAP S/4HANA. Some of these objects may well be defined in the system by finance and other stakeholders by the time procurement kicks off its project phase. Other times, you will have the opportunity to influence these structures during a greenfield or new implementation. In any event, procurement should always be involved in the definition and design of purchasing organizations and groups; these are completely procurement-focused entities in the system.

This section outlines the finance-related objects that are material for SAP S/4HANA Sourcing and Procurement. Many of these areas need to be defined prior to rolling out core areas in SAP S/4HANA, including materials management. Without a financial structure to underpin procurement, there is little value in setting up procurement processes and activities in the system, as the system is not yet capable of making financial sense of procurement. However, projects can design these areas in tandem or even sequence procurement design first, so long as finance is there to support the procurement piece when the system goes into production.

The main organizational building blocks in an SAP ERP system, including the latest versions of SAP S/4HANA, are as follows:

- **Client**
  The *client* is the highest level in the SAP system hierarchy, and the specifications and data that you enter cascade down the organization structure for all company codes and other objects in the organization. You make these settings at the beginning of the system setup to ensure data consistency.

- **Controlling area**
  The *controlling area* represents a closed system used for cost accounting purposes and may contain one or more company codes operating in different countries and regions if required.

- **Company**
  A *company* is the smallest organizational unit for which individual financial statements are created according to the relevant legal requirements. A company can include multiple company codes; here, the company code would represent a division for the general company.

- **Business area**
  A *business area* is an internal management reporting area within the company. A business area is used for additional reporting that subdivides a company code. Business areas are similar to profit center functionality.

- **Operating concern**
  The *operating concern* represents the highest reporting level in profitability analysis. An operating concern defines the product/market structure in an organizational unit in your company.

- **Credit control**
  The *credit control area* is an internal hierarchy element addressing the processes of credit control and credit management.

- **Chart of accounts**

  The *chart of accounts* is a list of all of the general ledger accounts used by one or multiple company codes.

- **Operating chart of accounts**

  The *operating chart of accounts* contains the general ledger accounts that are used for posting in your company code during daily activities. Financial accounting and controlling both use the operating chart of accounts.

- **Group chart of accounts**

  The *group chart of accounts* contains the general ledger accounts for the entire corporate group. The group chart of accounts enables reporting on the entire corporate group.

- **Country-specific chart of accounts**

  The *country-specific chart of accounts* contains the general ledger accounts required to meet a country's legal requirements. This allows you to provide statements for the country's legal requirements.

- **Profit center**

  The *profit center* in controlling represents an area of responsibility within a company, typically a business unit that monitors both costs and revenues. The profit center behaves as an independent operating unit for which a separate operating statement can be calculated.

- **Cost center**

  The *cost center* is the smallest area of responsibility in which budget control is required. The cost center is used to collect expenses and is frequently used in procurement processes.

- **Cost element**

  The *cost element* is used to classify the organization's valuated consumption within a controlling area.

- **Activity types**

  Activity types classify the activities performed within a cost center.

- **Fiscal year and currencies**

  The *fiscal year* is typically a 12-month period that is either a calendar year or defined by the company; regular financial statements and other process cadences are defined for the fiscal year. *Currencies* are the monetary units defined at the country or currency union level.

3.2 SAP S/4HANA Sourcing and Procurement-Specific Organization Structure Objects

Once the general organization structure and financials have been defined and designed for SAP S/4HANA Enterprise Management, you will need to further define the purchasing-specific areas for the organization structure and master data for SAP S/4HANA Sourcing and Procurement.

SAP S/4HANA Sourcing and Procurement leverages an organization structure beginning with the system client, controlling area, and company code and moving on through the plant and down to the storage location. In the case of an SAP Extended Warehouse Management (SAP EWM) implementation, you can take this one step further to the bin level.

Using this terminology and hierarchy, a company or government entity can eventually tailor the organizational structure in the system to reflect its own organization, such as in Figure 3.2. Although this organization structure may appear to be quite complex, examples from actual customers are often far more variegated.

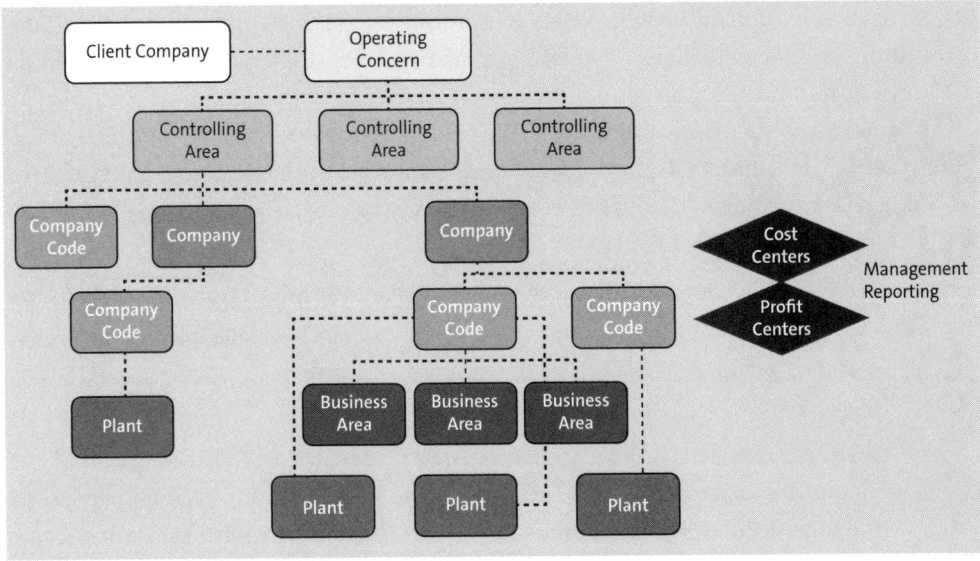

Figure 3.2 SAP Organization Structure Example

Underneath several of the company codes in Figure 3.2, there are plants. These plants are key to purchasing activities, as are several other linkages further down from the plant level, such as storage locations.

There are several organizational structure objects in SAP S/4HANA that are either shared, such as plants and storage locations, or used solely for procurement activities, such as purchasing organizations and buyer groups.

3.3 Company Code

The *company code* is the smallest organizational unit of external accounting for which a complete, self-contained set of accounts can be created. This includes the entry of all posted transactions and the creation of individual financial statements, such as the balance sheet and the profit and loss statement. In other words, the entity typically entering into an agreement with a supplier, from both an organizational structure and a legal standpoint, is usually a company code. Purchase orders must have a company code referenced in order to be created in SAP.

Creating a company code in SAP S/4HANA is the same as in previous SAP ERP iterations, and the guidelines for creating company codes still apply as well. You should try to minimize org structure levels and hierarchies whenever possible. Creating a large number of company codes will create system overhead. In a complex enterprise, this is sometimes unavoidable, and finance usually has a larger say in this area than procurement. The steps involved for creating a one-to-one company linked to a company code are as follows:

1. To create the company, follow IMG menu path **Enterprise Structure • Definition • Financial Accounting • Maintain Company**, or run Transaction OX15.

2. Select **New Entries**, then enter your company name and address information (see Figure 3.3).

3. Next, you need to create a company code and enter address information. To create a company code in SAP S/4HANA, first enter Transaction OX02 or follow IMG menu path **Enterprise Structure • Definition • Financial Accounting • Define, Copy, Delete, Check Company Code**. Maintain the company code data at a high level as shown in Figure 3.4.

On this screen, you define the number (**Company Code**), **Company Name**, **City**, **Country**, **Currency**, and **Language** for the company code. You'll define the full address in the accounting data in the next step.

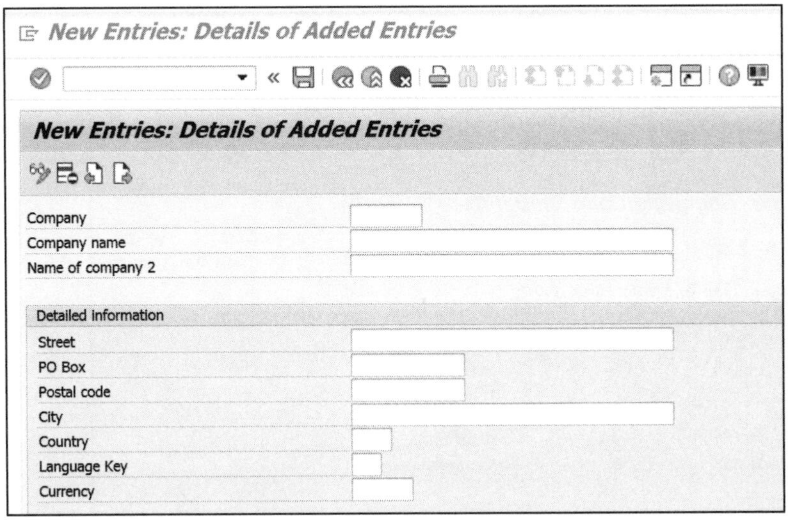

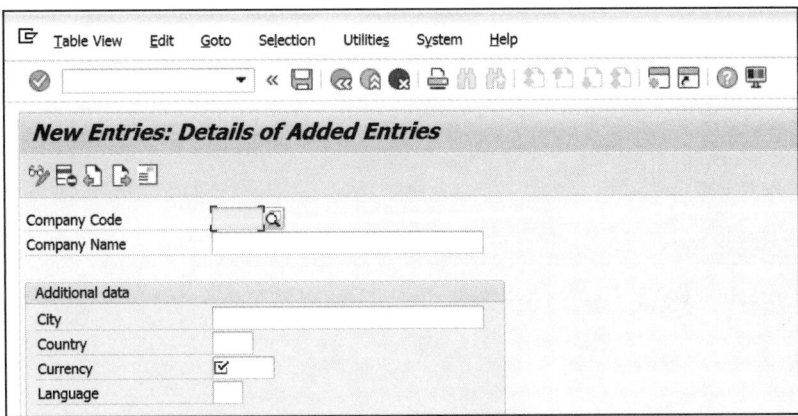

Figure 3.3 Company Creation in SAP S/4HANA

Figure 3.4 New Company Code Entry Screen

4. Once you've created the company code, maintain the company code address and key accounting data in Transaction OBY6. After you create a company code, it can be assigned to a company, controlling area, and/or a financial management area, as shown in Figure 3.5. Here you can also update key areas like the chart of

accounts, tax data, fiscal year reporting settings, and other finance-driven data. Note that this is not for procurement to define in a vacuum; procurement should be working in full conjunction with finance. Just as finance shouldn't drive the purchasing org discussion, neither should procurement drive the company code definition at this level.

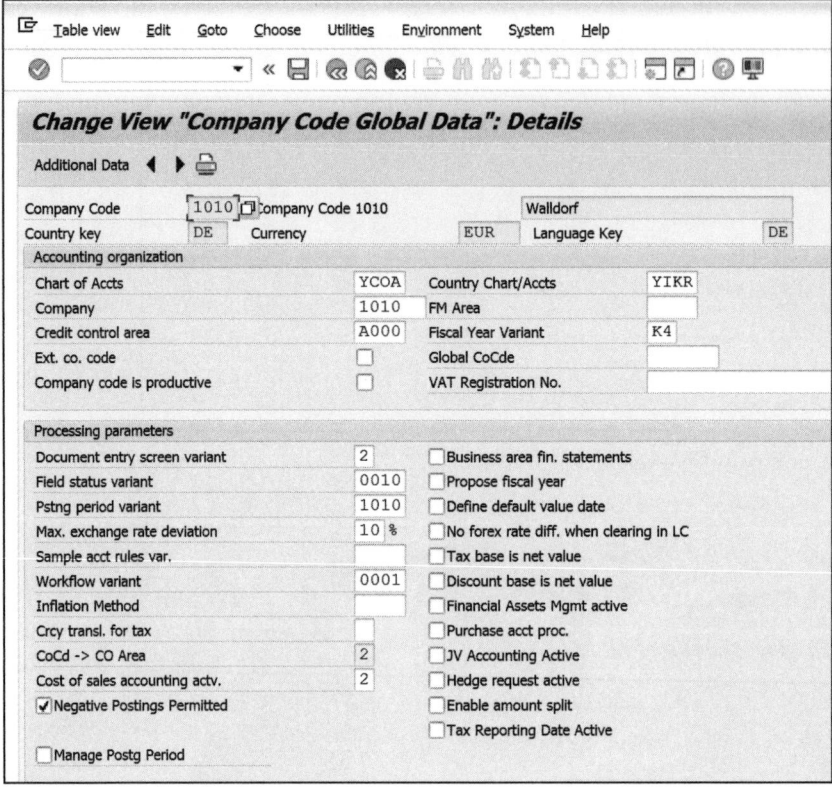

Figure 3.5 Transaction OBY6: Change Address

3.4   Plants

A plant is always assigned to a company code and can be a manufacturing facility, a warehouse distribution center, a corporate or government headquarters, or a sales office. A plant is also, and this is important for procurement processes, where valued goods and services are produced, stored, consumed, and/or distributed. The plant allows for flexibility in the system to define procurement items at the plant level. You can assign a different price or valuation and run planning activities at the plant level. For inventory management at the plant level, you assign what are called *storage locations* to the plant, then locate the inventory from the plant in these storage location areas.

Plant in SAP refers to a number of different things, such as a location with valuated inventory, an organization unit central in planning and production, an office, or another location type applicable to the system owner's business and activities. To create a plant, enter Transaction OX10 or follow IMG menu path **Enterprise Structure • Definition • Logistics • General • Define, Copy, Delete, Check Plant**. Here you define the **Plant**, **Name**, and address information, as well as **Factory Calendar** settings (see Figure 3.6). Different countries use different factory calendars for production, which can be very important for accurately estimating lead times in production and other areas. If the factory workers are on holiday during a time you've anticipated they would be working based on your own schedule, your supply chain calculations will be impacted.

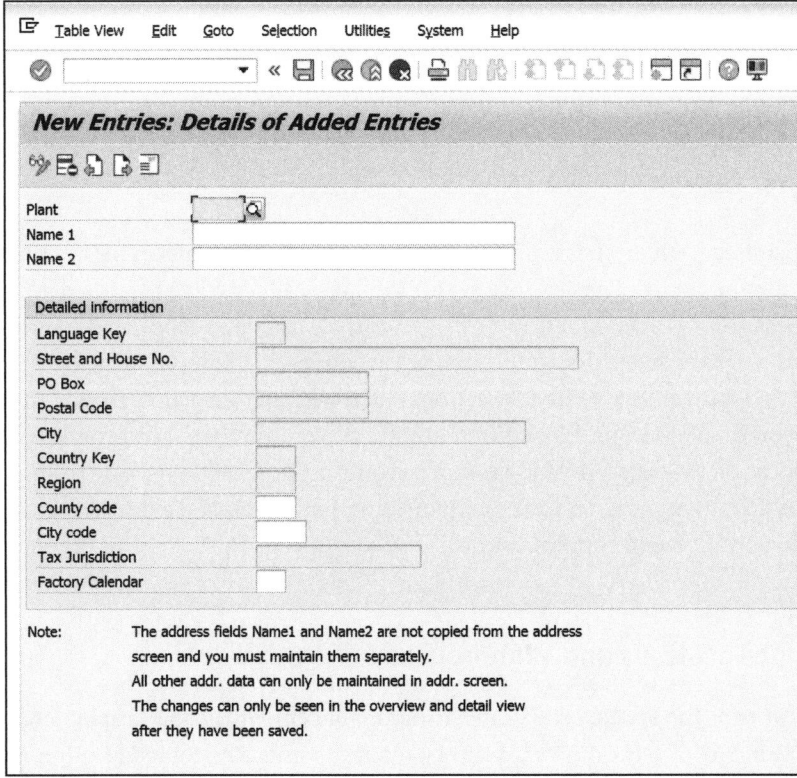

Figure 3.6 Plant Definition

A plant needs to be assigned to a company code to form part of the organization structure. A plant can't be used in the system without a company code relationship, as the key accounting settings inherited from the company code wouldn't be available. To assign a plant to a company code, enter Transaction OX18 or follow IMG path **Enterprise Structure • Assignment • Logistics—General • Assign Plant to Company Code**.

As shown in Figure 3.7, the assignment process simply consists of entering a company code number (**CoCd**) and a plant (**Plnt**) and clicking the **Save** button. A plant can be assigned to only one company code, but a company code can have many plants.

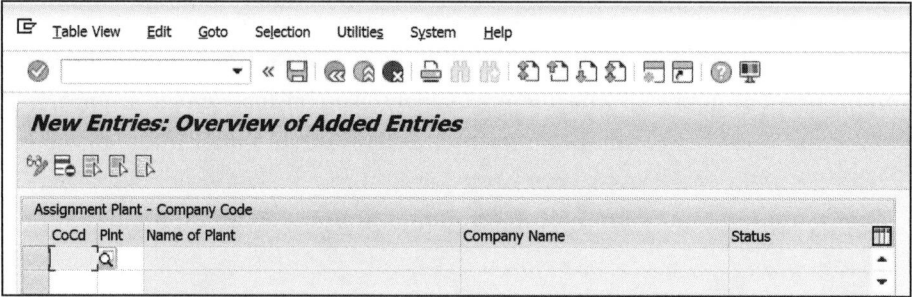

Figure 3.7 Assigning Plants to Company Code

To set up a plant, the valuation level for the system needs to be defined. This is a setting that cannot be changed easily once set and will typically involve finance determining how stock is to be valued in SAP. You can set the valuation level at the company code or plant level. If set at the company code level, a material will have the same valuation for inventory value calculations and the like across plants. If set at the plant level, you can value a material differently from plant to plant. For instance, if you have a location that is particularly remote, requiring large delivery costs to ship items there, you may want to value these items differently than at a plant with economical transportation and supply options.

3.5   Storage Locations and Warehouses

A *storage location* is the lowest level of inventory management without implementing SAP EWM in SAP S/4HANA. For inventory management, the storage location is defined as the physical location of the stock in the plant. If you aren't using SAP EWM, it's possible to assign multiple storage locations to one plant.

For SAP EWM, the rule is generally to use only one storage location per plant, and then allow for the creation of multiple warehouses underneath the storage location.

Individual *warehouses* (high-rack storage, block storage, picking area, etc.) are defined as storage types within a warehouse complex and are grouped together under a warehouse number. This warehouse number is then assigned to the storage location from inventory management. For each of these individual warehouses/storage types, you then define the bin levels for the warehouse location, creating a further level of inventory management at the warehouse level. The SAP Fiori-based frontend of SAP EWM has also changed significantly, as shown in Figure 3.8.

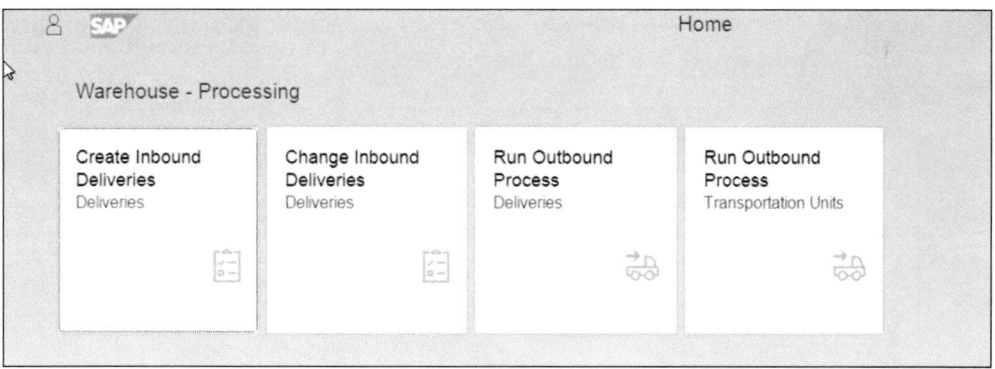

Figure 3.8 SAP EWM in SAP S/4HANA

From an organization structure standpoint, the setup of SAP EWM in SAP S/4HANA is similar to its setup in other SAP ERP versions. However, from a technical standpoint, running warehouse management as part of the core SAP S/4HANA Enterprise Management system clears out a lot of redundant configuration and data loads as the two systems become one. However, not all functionality available in previous versions of SAP EWM are available in the embedded version in SAP S/4HANA. Careful analysis needs to be conducted to determine your requirements for warehouse management and the capabilities of the current SAP S/4HANA release prior to embracing the embedded approach. More information about the inventory management aspects of SAP EWM and its setup will follow in Chapter 7.

3.5.1   Storage Location and Warehouse Creation

In SAP, *storage locations* allow for differentiation of the location of a material item or stock in a plant. A plant can have one or several storage locations assigned to it. Storage locations are the next level down from plant, allowing plants to have multiple storage locations for inventory management functions. Storage locations are the lowest level in materials management. The next level down in the organization structure after storage location is the warehouse, which is managed by the SAP EWM module in SAP S/4HANA (either embedded directly in the SAP S/4HANA system or as a sidecar module, depending on your landscape and warehouse functionality requirements). A *warehouse* is a building or location devoted to housing inventory, whereas a plant may have multiple functions, such as production, in addition to managing inventory.

Storage locations can be linked with warehouses via IMG menu path **Enterprise Structure • Assignment • Logistics Execution • Assign Warehouse Number to Plant/Storage Location**. Here you assign the plant (**Plnt**), storage location (**SLoc**), and warehouse number (**WhN**) on one line, as shown in Figure 3.9.

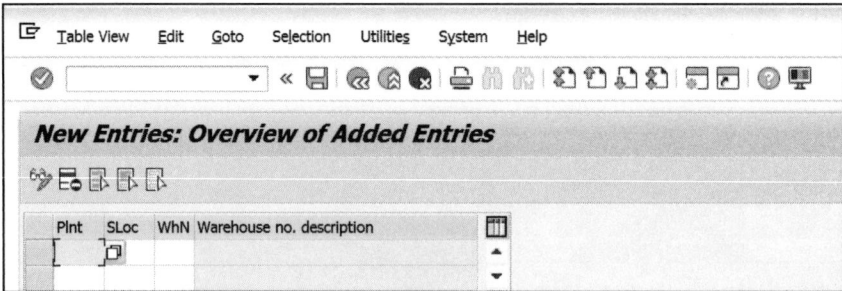

Figure 3.9 Assigning Storage Location to Warehouse

You can manage inventory directly in the storage locations without going down to a bin-level scenario necessitating a warehouse layer. Once linked, a storage location is in a parent-child relationship with SAP EWM, inheriting its settings and processes to a degree.

To create a storage location, enter Transaction OX09 or follow IMG menu path **Enterprise Structure • Definition • Materials Management • Maintain Storage Location**. Enter the plant to which the new storage location is to be assigned, as shown in Figure 3.10.

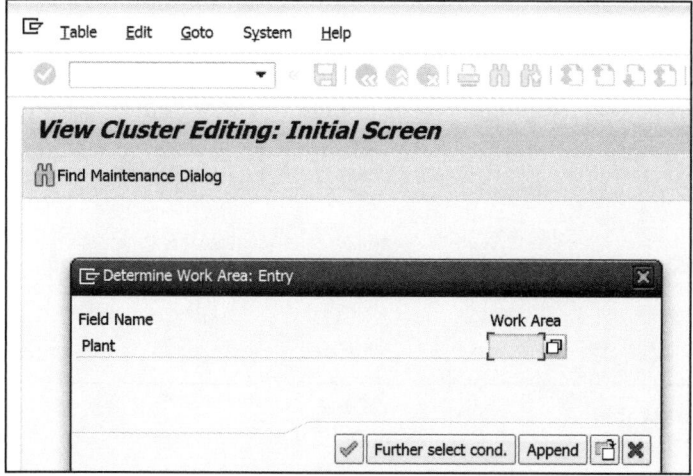

Figure 3.10 Create Storage Location in SAP S/4HANA

Once you have selected the plant, select **New Entries** to create a storage location (see Figure 3.11).

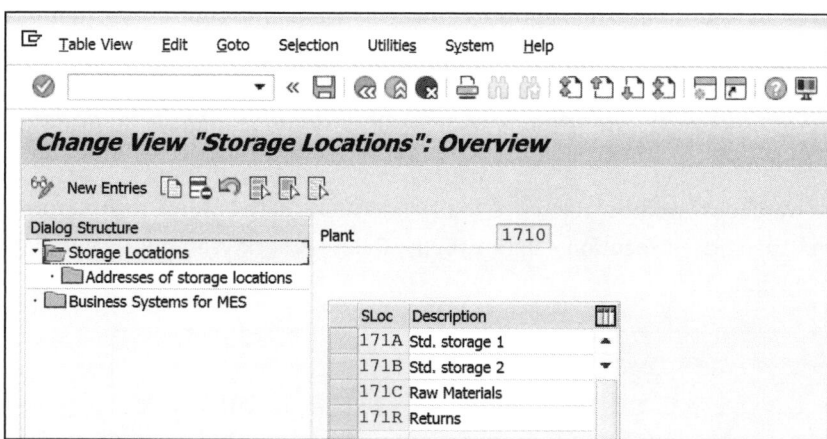

Figure 3.11 Storage Location: New Entries

Next, enter the storage location (**SLoc**) and **Description** in the fields shown in Figure 3.12 and click **Save**.

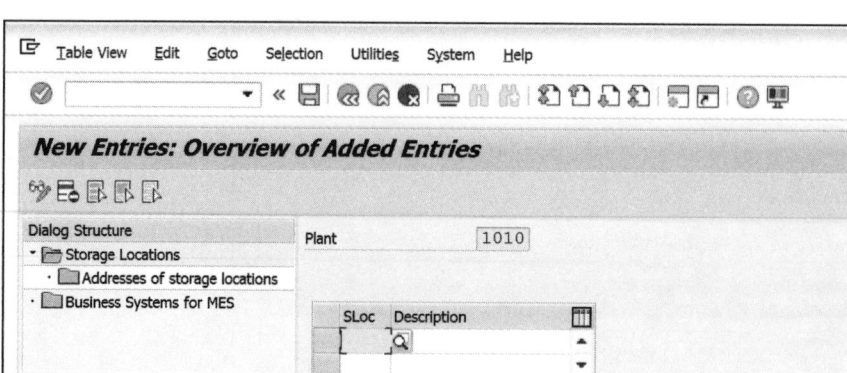

Figure 3.12 New Storage Location

3.5.2   Warehouse Creation

If you have a requirement to manage items beyond just a general area in the plant or to maintain a physical warehouse operation that supports your plants, you'll need to evaluate SAP EWM as an option for integrating your warehouse management operations with SAP S/4HANA and managing them outright. SAP EWM allows you to manage stocks at a bin level within the warehouse, providing a much more granular level of detail. This is particularly useful when manufacturing is using a large set of parts and needs to know exactly where items are in the facility and to manage them at this level in the system.

To create a warehouse number reference, follow IMG menu path **Enterprise Structure • Definition • Logistics—Execution • Define, Copy, Delete, Check Warehouse Number**, as shown in Figure 3.13.

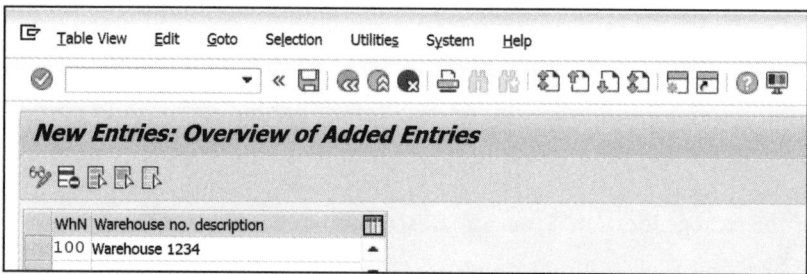

Figure 3.13 Creating Warehouse Number in SAP S/4HANA

3.6 Purchasing Organizations

Once you've defined your organization structure objects down to at least the plant level, you're ready to create your purchasing organization structure. A *purchasing organization* is responsible for procuring materials or services for one or more plants and for negotiating general conditions of purchase with suppliers. The purchasing organization is a required field and assignment for all main purchasing documents. If a plant needs to be able to procure items, it must be assigned to one or more purchasing organizations. So long as the plants are assigned a purchasing organization, the company code is optional for assignment of a purchasing organization. Assigning a company code to the purchasing organization limits the purchasing organization to the plants of the company code to which it has been assigned. Therefore, if the purchasing organization is intended to cover plants in multiple company codes, you would assign the purchasing organization at the plant level.

Purchasing organizations can be assigned as one to many, one to one, or even many to one for organization structure areas such as company codes and plants, as shown in Figure 3.14.

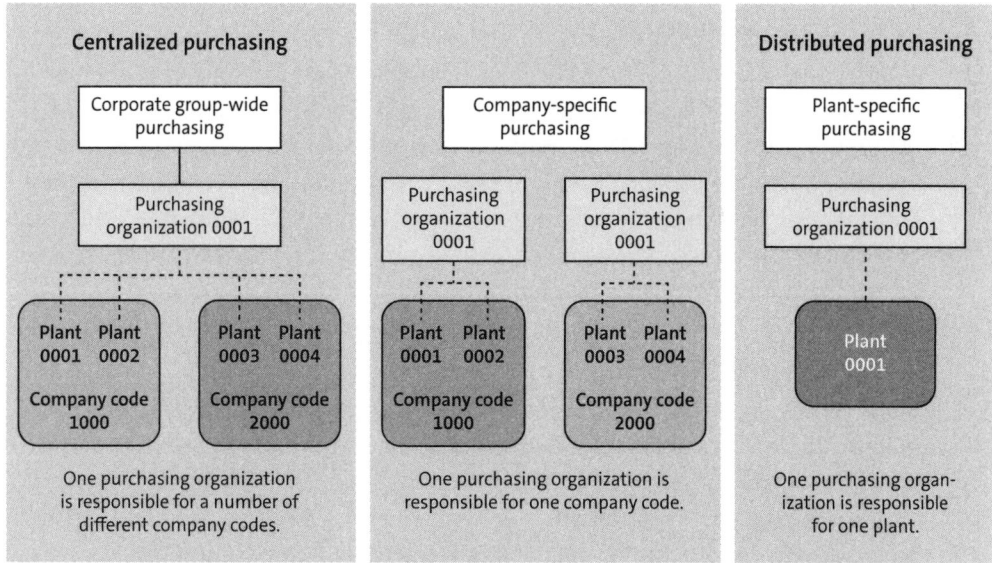

Figure 3.14 Purchasing Organization Assignments in SAP: Centralized versus Distributed

Although purchasing organization structures can be expanded or distilled to a central organization responsible for many company codes, the general rule is that there needs to be justification for expanding the number of purchasing organizations, as these create overhead in the system. Each contact and supplier will require a reference to the purchasing organizations that use these in the system. If you create a number of unnecessary purchasing organizations, you will quickly find yourself handling a lot of unnecessary setup each time you create a new organization structure element and/or related master data item.

Similar to purchasing groups in SAP, there are setup approaches that help minimize painting yourself into a corner later on from a system standpoint. SAP purchasing groups aren't assigned to purchasing organizations in SAP S/4HANA and SAP ERP contexts, although they are set up this way in SAP SRM. Purchasing groups are named with three-character (number or letter) combinations. This format can be quite accommodating if the purchasing group is defined as a group and reassigned to new buyers coming on board. However, if you assign each purchasing group to an individual, each time a buyer leaves or changes organizations within the company, a new purchasing group code must be created to accommodate the new buyer replacement. This can lead to consuming the viable purchasing group codes in long term. It is also unwieldy as the purchasing documents associated with the previous purchasing group and buyer will need to be reassigned manually, rather than having a new buyer simply take over the group and the documents already in flight.

A *purchasing organization* in SAP is an organizational unit responsible for procuring materials or services for one or more plants and for negotiating general conditions of purchase with suppliers. The purchasing organization assumes legal responsibility for these transactions. A plant must always have at minimum one purchasing organization assigned to it and must always in turn be assigned to a company code. A purchasing organization can be assigned at the company code level. If not assigned to individual company codes, a purchasing organization can lead transactions across company codes for your system. Assignment of the purchasing organization to the plant level is then required.

A purchasing organization can be assigned either centrally or in distributed fashion to individual plants. As with other organization structure elements, adding purchasing organizations means adding overhead in the system and in general. A centralized purchasing organization structure is preferable, unless there are requirements that drive a distributed purchasing organization structure in which one or more purchasing organizations are assigned at the plant level. Note that in a distributed model, in addition to creating multiple purchasing organizations, not only must these organizations be assigned to plants, but supplier records will need to be extended for each individual purchasing organization. This is where a simple master data update or change can begin to require multiple steps to assign and extend these connections to suppliers, contracts, purchase orders, and other documents. Having a single purchasing organization or a limited number for clarity and delineation is the recommended position for design.

To create a purchasing organization, use Transaction OX08 or navigate to IMG menu path **Enterprise Structure • Definition • Materials Management • Maintain Purchasing Organization**, and enter the purchasing organization (**Purch. Organization**) as shown in Figure 3.15.

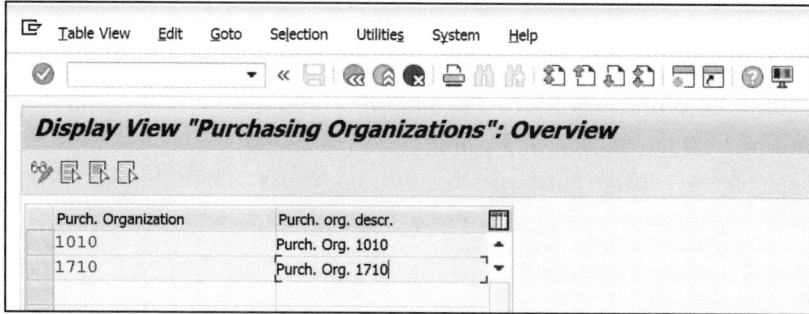

Figure 3.15 Create Purchasing Organization

Creating a purchasing organization requires simply defining a number and a description. Once you've entered this information, you can save your entries and move to the next step.

Note

Although creation of a purchasing organization is quite straightforward, remember that purchasing organizations can cover multiple countries and company codes when required and should not be created on a whim without accounting for design and maintenance considerations. As with other objects, a purchasing organization will create additional maintenance overhead in the system, so covering your requirements with the minimal amount of purchasing organizations will serve you well down the road.

The next step is to assign the purchasing organization to a company code using Transaction OX01 or by following IMG menu path **Enterprise Structure • Assignment • Materials Management • Assign Purchasing Organization to Company Code**, as shown in Figure 3.16.

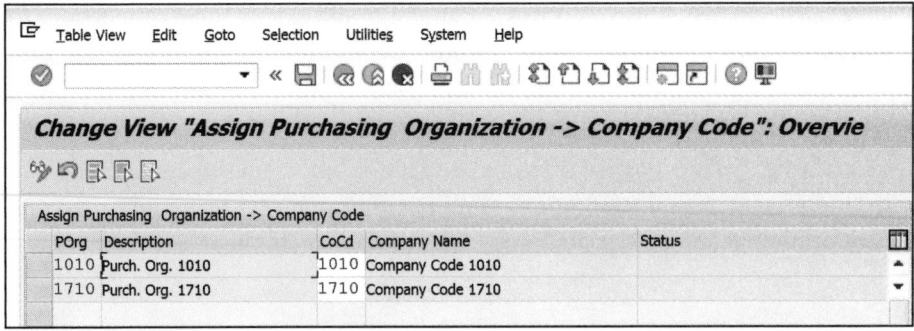

Figure 3.16 Assign Purchasing Organization to Company Code

To assign a purchasing organization to a plant, use Transaction OX17 or menu path **SAP Customizing Implementation Guide (IMG) • Enterprise Structure • Assignment • Material Management • Assign Purchase Organization to Plant**. Enter the plant (**Plnt**) and purchasing organization (**POrg**) as shown in Figure 3.17.

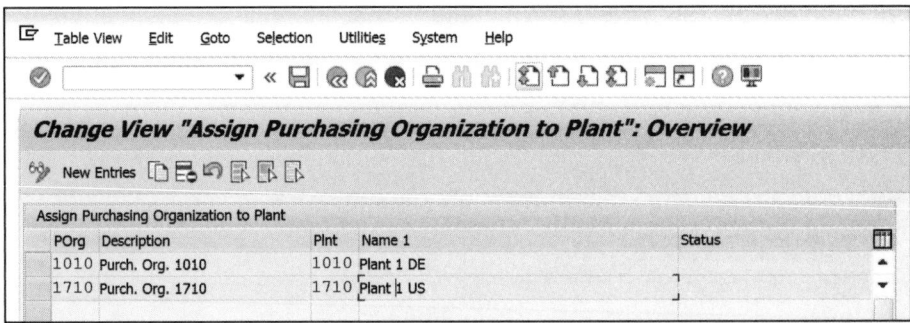

Figure 3.17 Assign Purchasing Organization to Plant

Purchasing organizations are not the only grouping and assignment available for procurement activities. You also have a further level called purchasing groups, discussed next.

3.7 Purchasing Group Creation

Purchasing groups are responsible for day-to-day buying activities and need not be assigned to a single purchasing organization. Purchasing groups also shouldn't be assigned to an individual buyer directly, but instead should be kept generic enough to be reassigned if a new buyer or group joins the organization to cover the purchasing group in question. Once you have designed, created, and assigned your purchasing organization entities/structure, you create these buyer groups, called *purchasing groups*. To create purchasing groups, follow IMG menu path **Materials Management • Purchasing • Define Purchasing Groups** (see Figure 3.18).

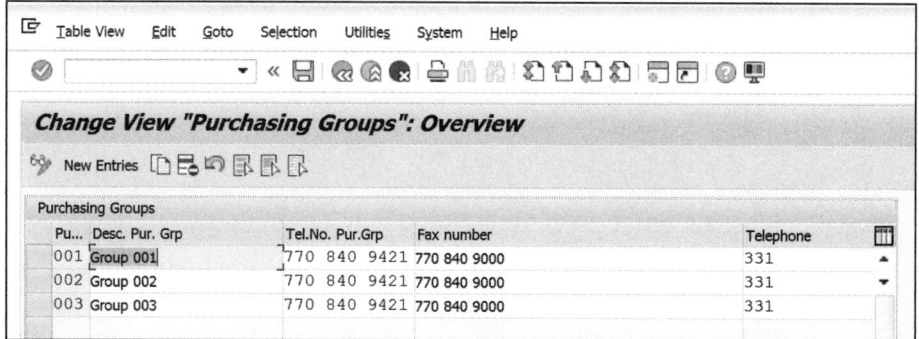

Figure 3.18 Create Purchasing Group

Enter a purchasing group number (**Pu...**), description (**Desc. Pur. Grp**), phone number (**Tel.No. Pur.Grp**), and **Fax Number**, and **Save**.

You now have configured the baseline objects for an organization structure for purchasing in SAP S/4HANA.

3.8   Summary

The organization structure, master data, and transactional data designs underpin and simplify system usage in SAP ERP environments when implemented in a thoughtful manner. In all three areas, finding the optimal balance between the level of detail required and a level of simplicity to support the UX and overall volumes/ footprint is paramount. Creating too many organization structures leads to redundancies and maintenance work, such as having a purchasing organization created for each company code when an overarching purchasing organization would do. Driving a level of granularity in the material masters that is not required for the business leads to user frustration in trying to find the appropriate material master to use in a transaction, as well as additional maintenance to enact any changes to the material masters.

In addition, SAP S/4HANA introduces a significant change to how supplier and customer masters are managed in the system. These two types of partner functions in SAP S/4HANA are unified into a business partner concept, which has ramifications on conversions and upgrades from previous versions of SAP ERP, as well as usage of the master record in purchasing transactions in SAP S/4HANA. With organizational structure elements covered, the next chapter shifts focus to master data.

Chapter 4
Master Data

Master data is defined at a system level as reusable data records supporting transactions and processes. Practically every business solution from SAP makes use of some form of master data.

For SAP S/4HANA, master data continues to play the pivotal role it has over the years in other SAP ERP environments, providing semistatic data records for suppliers, materials, material groups, units of measure, incoterms, and other data highly relevant for procurement transactions. Master data represents the building blocks of a transaction in SAP, and this data can save a significant amount of effort duplication and effort in general when built and maintained correctly. Rather than having to create each transaction from scratch and enter in each detail, a user or automated procurement process can leverage the existing master data in SAP to create comprehensive orders using a few premaintained elements, as indicated in Figure 4.1.

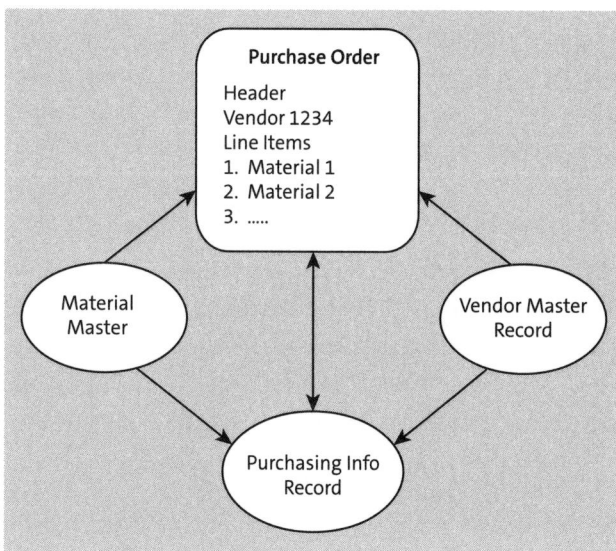

Figure 4.1 SAP Master Data

Master data in SAP refers to data that remains relatively static and is used often in transactions. Rather than recreating this data each time or storing it throughout the system in multiple records, master data is stored centrally and reused throughout the system. This makes it important to govern the creation and management of this type of data to avoid duplicate records and data redundancy.

A best practice is typically to have one group responsible for master data, rather than allowing everyone in the system to create multiple, and invariably duplicate, master data records for procurement areas such as material masters, suppliers, material groups, and purchasing info records (PIRs). Other approaches include allowing different groups to "own" different master data or even parts of the master data record. This happens frequently for payment information on a vendor master. Purchasing needs to update some areas, but payment information and verification is often the responsibility of accounting and accounts payable (AP).

4.1   Material Masters and Material Groups

A *material master record* stores a company's or government entity's material-specific data, allowing for this record to be used in all areas of logistics within the SAP ERP environment.

The information contained in a material master record may be used in a variety of activities and processes, including warehouse management, purchasing, inventory management, and/or planning. As such, a centralized group often coordinates the creation of the master data "shell" and the entry of area-specific data for purchasing, warehouse management, and other groups as part of this record. Allowing a single group to create and manage the entire record leads to duplicate entries, with each duplicate material master containing a piece of the complete data picture.

As with previous versions of SAP ERP, you can control the user views in SAP S/4HANA to allow different departments to update only the areas pertinent to their parts of the process or business activity. You can also deputize a master data group to own the entire record and enter information centrally via a request process. Both approaches have their advantages and disadvantages. The least advantageous approach, however, is to allow for anarchy to reign in the material masters, as different groups will quickly fragment the material master records into duplicates and records with inconsistent and divergent information. Once these fragmented material masters are used in a transaction, they become very difficult to remove from an SAP ERP system. The main point of creating and maintaining master data is to standardize and simplify usage of the system, and this discipline needs to guide the governing approach.

There are both main data and additional data screens in a material master record. Data can be maintained for the entire organization, at the plant level, or down to the storage location.

Several fields and tabs have been updated in SAP S/4HANA's material master. Some of the changes to fields in Transactions MM01, MM02, and MM03 are as follows:

- **Unit of Measure Group** is considered retail-only in SAP S/4HANA, and it isn't required to switch it on in **Lot Size Data1** of the **MRP1** tab.

- You don't have to switch on **Quota Arrangements** in the **MRP2** tab in SAP S/4HANA's material master, as quota arrangements are always considered.

- **BOM Explosion/Dependent Requirement** isn't required in **MRP4 Selection Method**. Nor are **Action Control, Fair Share Rule, Push Distribution**, and **Deployment Horizon** in **MRP4**.

- **MRP4** also no longer has settings for the **Storage Location MRP indicator, Spec. Procurement Type SLoc, Reorder Point**, or **Replenishment Quantity**.

4.1.1   Activating a Material Master Field

Material master functionality and fields are numerous in SAP, as the material master has been built out over multiple decades of use in SAP ERP platforms and modules. Not all fields will be required for your implementation, and you may find that a custom field is required if the functionality requested cannot be met in the standard fields and functionality. In these cases, you have the option to activate a field or create a custom one. To activate a field, follow **Logistics General • Material Master • Maintain Field Selection for Data Screens** or enter Transaction OMS9, as in Figure 4.2.

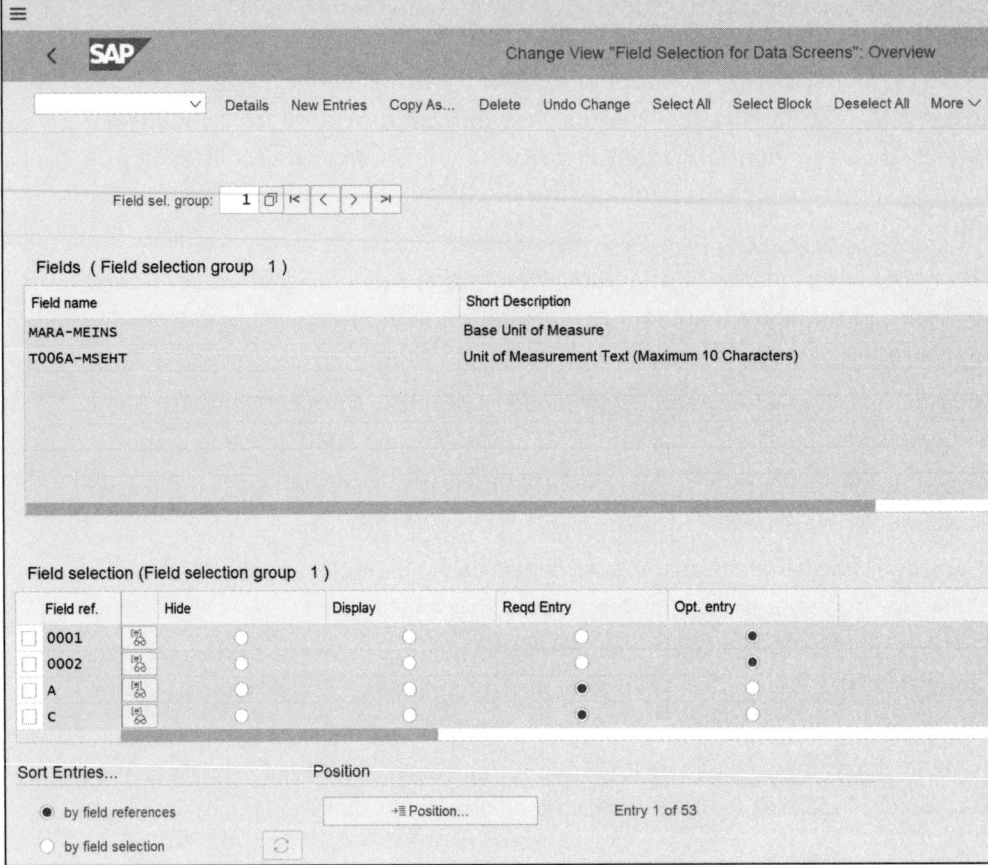

Figure 4.2 Transaction OMS9: Changing Material Master Fields

In Transaction OMS9, you can drill into individual material master fields by their groups and make changes. If you wish to make changes at the material master field group level, follow **Logistics General • Material Master • Assign Fields to Field Selection Groups** or enter Transaction OMSR Figure 4.3.

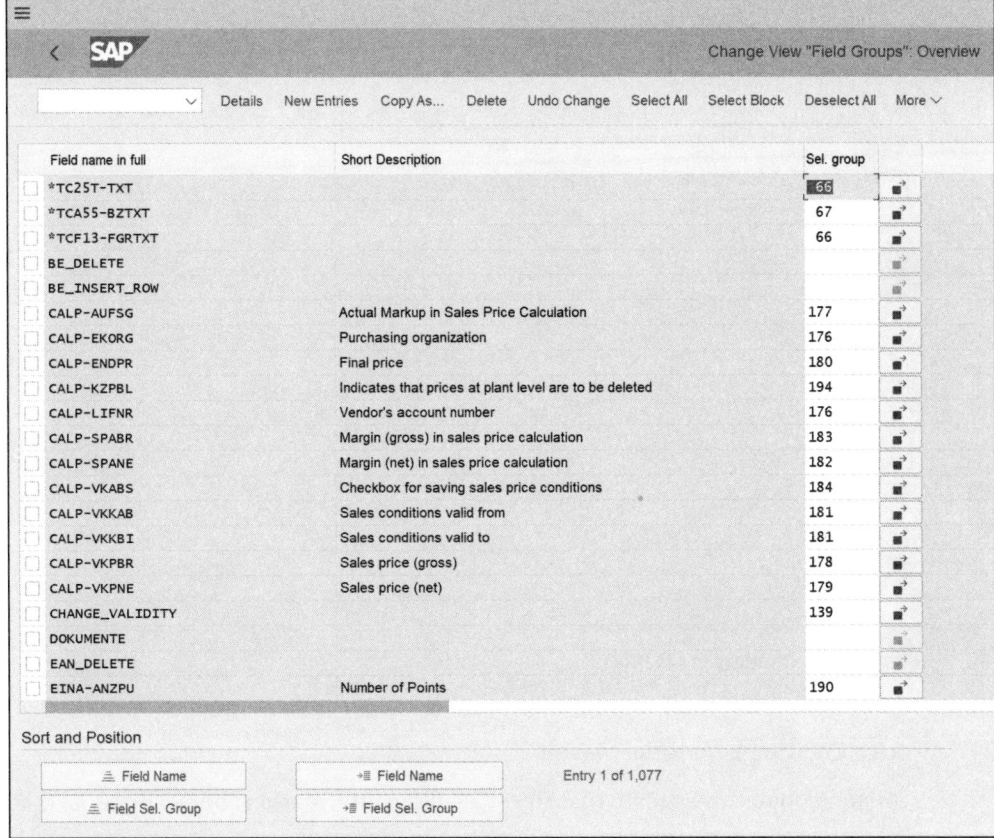

Figure 4.3 Changing Material Master Field Groups

Via menu path **Logistics General • Material Master • Assign Fields to Field Selection Groups** or Transaction OMSR, you can reassign material fields to different groups and drill into fields at the detail level to maintain visibility and Application Link Enabling (ALE) settings at the field level, as in Figure 4.4.

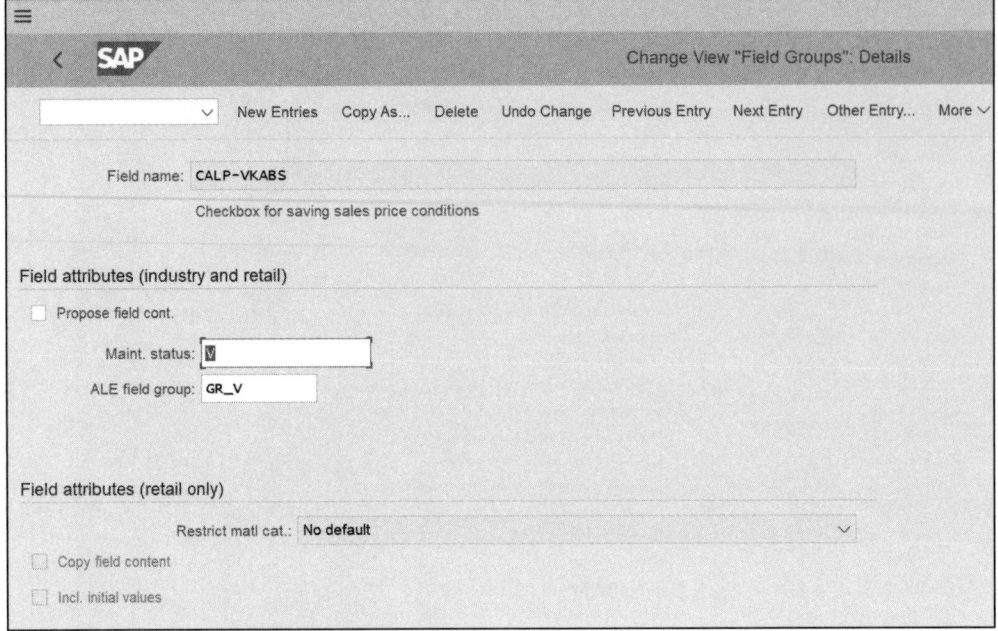

Figure 4.4 Change View Details

4.1.2 Creating a Material Master

A material master is a record that stores all of the information about a material that an organization procures, stores, and sells. These records can be created in SAP GUI in SAP S/4HANA via Transaction MM01 (Create), MM02 (Change), or MM03 (View), as shown in Figure 4.5, or in the SAP S/4HANA Create Material SAP Fiori app (see Figure 4.6).

When you create a material master, you must define a **Material Type** and assign an industry sector. Material types include **Operating Supplies**, **Semifinished Product**, **Raw materials**, **Services**, and **Finished Product**. The material type controls whether the product is produced in house or can be procured externally and controls account postings upon receipt.

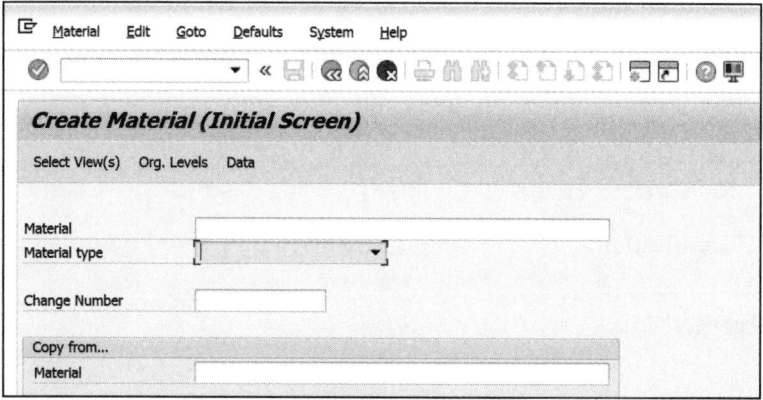

Figure 4.5 Create Material Master, SAP GUI

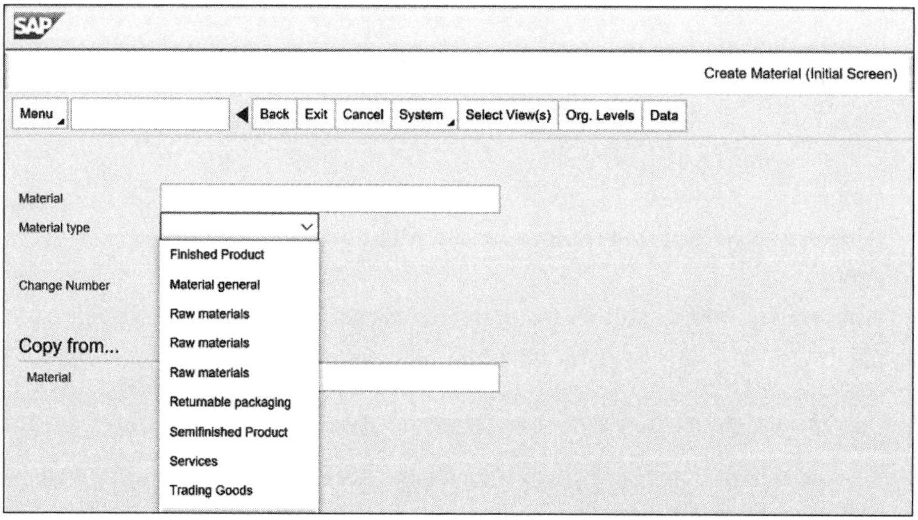

Figure 4.6 Material Master Type, SAP S/4HANA Create Material App

The industry sector type controls the screens and the order in which they can be accessed/displayed. Additional industry sector types can be configured depending upon the requirements. Once you set the industry sector type, it can't be changed by a normal user in the system.

Once you're in the material master record, there are numerous tabs available to define data for the various processes involving a material master. The main tabs are as follows:

- **Basic Data**
  Material, plant, general data, number of periods required, control data

- **Basic Data 2**
  Other data, environment, design documents assigned, design drawing, client-specific configuration

- **Classification**
  Material type classification

- **Sales Org**
  Material and general data

- **Sales Org 2**
  Material and grouping items

- **Sales General Plant**
  General data, shipping data, packaging material data, general plant parameters

- **Foreign Trade**
  Foreign trade data, origin

- **Sales Text**
  Text set at organizational level

- **MRP 1**
  General data, MRP procedure, lot size data, MRP areas

- **MRP 2**
  Procurement, scheduling, net requirements calculation

- **MRP 3**
  Forecast requirements, planning, availability check, plant-specific configuration

- **MRP 4**
  Bill of materials explosion, discontinued parts, repetitive manufacturing/assembly/deployment strategy

- **Work Scheduling**
  General data, tolerance data, in-house production time in days

- **Plant Data/Storage Area 1**
  General data, shelf life criteria

- **Plant Data/Storage Area 2**
  Weight/volume, general plant parameters

- **Accounting 1**
  Periods, future costing run, current costing run, previous costing run

- **Accounting 2**
  Determination of lowest value; last-in, first-out (LIFO) data

- **Costing 1**
  General data, quantity structure data

- **Costing 2**
  Standard cost estimate, planned prices, valuation data

- **General data**
  General data, plant stocks in current period, plant stocks in previous period

- **Storage Location Stock**
  General data, storage location stock in current period, storage location stock in previous period

The main tabs for procurement are the **Basic Data** and **General** tabs, **Procurement** tabs, and **MRP** tabs. The **MRP** tabs allow for controlling the MRP process used with the material. MRP replenishments typically run, at some point, through SAP S/4HANA Sourcing and Procurement, which makes these material master tabs particularly relevant. Once you have defined these areas, you save or update the record. The record can now be used in transactions involving materials.

4.1.3   Creating a Material Group

A material group is used to categorize items being procured, stored, and sold for reporting, taxation, and classification purposes. Via Transaction OMSF or IMG menu path **Logistics General • Material Master • Settings for Key Fields • Define Material Groups**, you define these categories as shown in Figure 4.7, maintaining a material group code (**Matl Group**), description (**Material Group Desc.**), account group (**AGrp**), default unit of weight (**DUW**), and a second description (**Description 2**) if required.

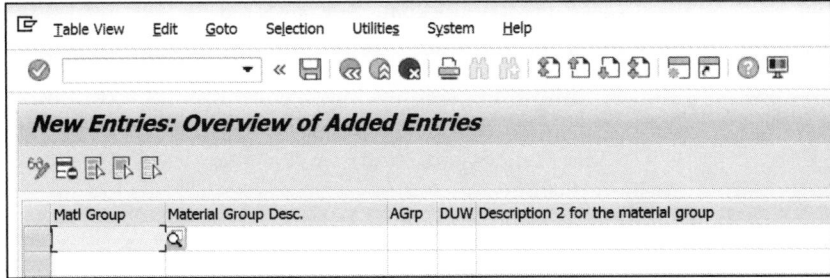

Figure 4.7 Define Material Group: SAP GUI

The material group format usually derives from an overall set of material groups selected by your organization to form the structure for managing this type of classification. United Nations Standard Product and Service Codes (UNSPSC) are popular in private sector companies, whereas federal, state, and local entities in the United States often use Federal Supply Class (FSC) codes. With any material group definition, you need to limit access to this area to avoid duplication of codes and dilution of the overall structure. Especially when it comes time to report, having a tight foundation for categorizing your purchasing spend aids enormously in reporting and analytics, not to mention in correctly classifying items during transactions.

4.1.4   Creating a New Product Services Type (SERV)

During the initial creation of a material master, selecting **SERV** under **Product Type** classifies an item as a service material, removing several tabs and fields in the process, as noted in Table 4.1, per SAP Notes 2224251 and 2224371. These fields/tabs remain in the system tables but aren't visible to the user.

Material Master Tab in SERV Record	Fields Impacted
Basic Data 2	All
Accounting 2	All
Basic Data 1	EAN/UPC, EAN Category, Product Allocation, Assigned vs. Effected Vals, Material Group Package Materials
Purchasing	Fields Material Group Freight, Other data
Sales General/Plant	Replacement Part, Availability Check, Material Freight Group, Shipping Data, Packaging Material Data, and General Plant
Accounting 1	VC: Sales Order stk, Price Control—Value 5, Moving Price, Total Stock, Proj. Stk Value Class, Total Value, Valuated Un, Accounting Previous Year (Button), Std. cost estimate (Button)
Sales/Sales Org 1	Extended Distribution Chain Status, Valid from, Distribution Chain-Specification status, Valid from, Minimum Delivery Quantity, Delivery Unit
Sales/Sales Org 2	Material statistics group product attributes

Table 4.1 Fields and Tabs Not Available in SERV Product Type Material Master

To activate **SERV** as a product type, you need to verify that delivery class G is set in table T133K for **Material Type SERV** and in the **Screen Sequence Control** (Transaction OMT3E). Note that **SERV** does not replace the **Service Master DIEN**; it augments it so that items used directly with a service can be classified as such.

4.1.5 Select Material Master Configuration Options

For configuration options in purchasing, you can define the view of the material master (what tabs the user can and can't access), as well as the following:

- **Define shipping instructions**
  Here, you can detail instructions for the supplier, which can then be assigned for one or more material masters.
- **Define purchasing value keys**
  These value keys establish rules for the issue of reminders and letters (expediters) with respect to nearly due and overdue deliveries, the admissibility of over- and under deliveries (overages and underages), the order acknowledgment requirements for PO items, and general shipping/packaging instructions.
- **Define the manufacturer part number (MPN)**
  This is a larger topic and needs design thought prior to activation. Essentially, if you have multiple suppliers for a particular material, you can activate MPN and retain one material master with multiple suppliers. These MPNs can be further managed using source lists, PIRs, and outline agreements to provide the plant-specific logic for which ones can be ordered.
- **Define reasons for blocking approved MPN**
  Defining reasons for blocking approved MPNs allows a user to select a valid reason from a drop-down menu.
- **Entry aids for items without a material master**
  This configuration allows you to assign default purchasing values via a value key for PO items without a material master and info record. A valuation class assignment allows the system to determine different accounts for individual material groups.

4.1.6 Material Master Field Character Expansion in SAP S/4HANA

One significant update to the material master in SAP S/4HANA is that the maximum field length of the material number has been extended to 40 characters from 18 in the

MATNR field. The expansion to 40 characters applies for all fields and tables in SAP S/4HANA in which the material master can be stored. This means that a larger range is now available to use for material masters, but, as discussed in this section, this doesn't mean that you should necessarily use all of these numbers just because you now have them available. The character expansion also means that conversion from earlier systems will need to be analyzed for enhancements and interfaces that reference the old field length or expand the field length to ensure orderly conversion of these material masters into SAP S/4HANA. For interfaces, the material field with the new length has been added to the table or appended as a new parameter. The new 40-character-field functionality for the material master must be switched on explicitly in the system to avoid inadvertent disruptions to interfaces and previous versions and their compatibility with SAP S/4HANA material master functionality. Web services already had a 60-character length for material masters and so are not impacted. Industry solutions in SAP ERP, such as discrete industries and mill products (DIMP), which had their own character-extension add-ons for material masters, will see these replaced with the standard extension now available in SAP S/4HANA.

To activate the extended material number functionality (after completing analysis of conversion impacts and interface impacts with older versions of SAP ERP or otherwise), complete the following steps:

1. First, ensure that your configuration role contains table maintenance authorization group FLE (authorization S_TABU_DIS), using Transaction FLETS or IMG menu path **Cross Application Components • General Application Functions • Field Length Extension • Activate Extended Fields**.

2. Change the material master number format using Transaction OMSL or via menu path **Logistics General • Material Master • Basic Settings**.

4.2   Batch Management and Serialization

Organizations produce in a variety of ways, but each production method can be grouped largely into two categories: a company manufactures products continuously or in batches. When purchasing an item, especially one taken into inventory, understanding the batch number of the product allows for a better understanding of the product and facilitates communication with the supplier in the event a recall occurs or a follow-up issue arises with a particular batch of product. Serialization plays a similar role in making the tracking of particular products and items back to their origins easier for the end user or buyer. On the production side, batch management can be set at the client, plant (default), or material level. A serial number is given to a unique item, rather than being set at an organization level or material master level. Serial numbers are used to manage warranties on individual equipment and items in plant maintenance scenarios.

4.2.1   Configuring Batch Numbers

Batch and serial numbers are typically set up in conjunction with the other stake-holders of this functionality (production planning and logistics/supply chain groups) during the initial configuration of an SAP ERP environment. To configure a batch number, follow these directions: First, navigate to the **Activate Internal Batch Number Assignment** screen by following menu path **Logistics General • Batch Management • Batch Number Assignment • Activate Internal Batch Number Assignment • Activate Batch Number Assignment**, or entering Transaction OMCZ (see Figure 4.8).

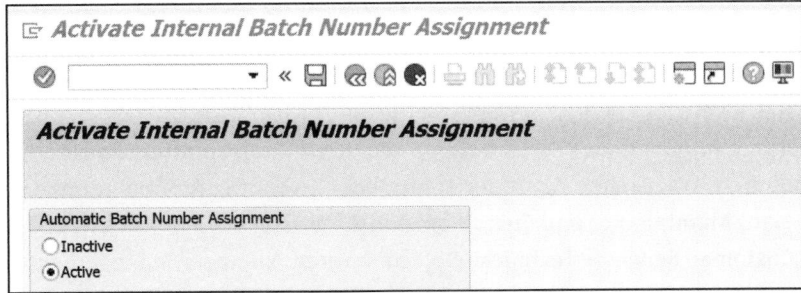

Figure 4.8 Activate Internal Batch Number Assignment

If you set the batch number assignment to **Active**, you have the ability to classify your materials by batch number, allowing for tracking at the batch level. This is use-ful for procurement, in that you can track incoming batches in shipments. If there is a recall or an issue, you don't have to throw out or return the entire set of materials but can have control of the batch to compartmentalize the issue, creating a kind of firebreak.

Next, if you need the system to automatically number batches on a goods receipt with an account assignment, follow IMG menu path **Logistics General • Batch Management • Batch Number Settings • Activate Internal Batch Number Assignment • Internal Batch Number Assignment for Assigned Goods Receipt**, as shown in Figure 4.9. On this screen, you can select the batch checkbox **Batch Number Automatic For Goods Receipt with Account Assignment** to create and assign an internal batch number upon goods receipt automatically. If this shipment proves defective or otherwise different, you can use this batch number to quickly address the issue in your production and storage areas.

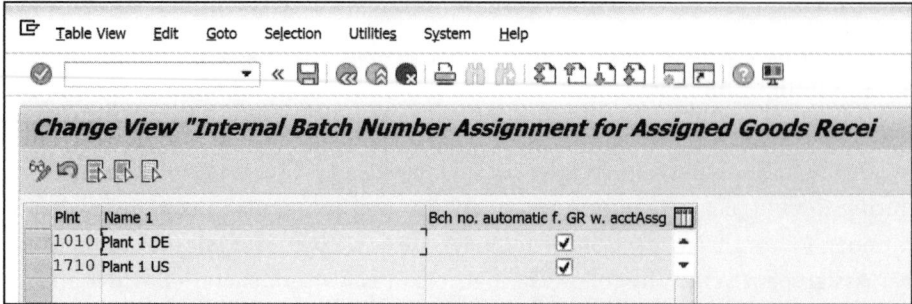

Figure 4.9 Internal Batch Number Assignment for Goods Receipts

4.2.2   Configuring Serial Numbers

Next up is the serial number. Generic material masters identify a product type, but not at the batch level or individual item in stock level. The batch identifies a group of materials coming in on a goods receipt. If you require material master items to be identified uniquely, you can configure serial numbers. To configure serial numbers, navigate to **Plant Maintenance and Customer Service • Master Data in Plant Mainte-nance and Customer Service • Technical Objects • Serial Numbers Management • Define Serial Number Profiles • Serial Number Profile**, or use Transaction OIS2 (see Figure 4.10).

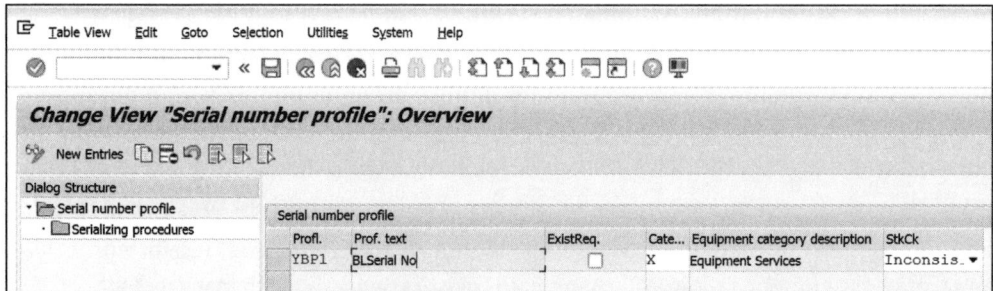

Figure 4.10 Serial Number Profile

Setting up the serial number profile and assigning it to the material master allows for a serial number to be created upon goods receipt of that particular material.

To define where serial numbers are to be used, you can use Transaction OIS2 again or follow IMG menu path **Plant Maintenance and Customer Service • Master Data in Plant Maintenance and Customer Service • Technical Objects • Serial Numbers Management • Define Serial Number Profiles • Serializing Procedures**.

The different usages for serialization are provided in the procedure codes and descriptions shown in Figure 4.11. Serialization is used in a number of areas, for which corresponding types of usage are defined (none, obligatory, automatic, optional), as well as whether or not equipment creation is required in line with the serialization.

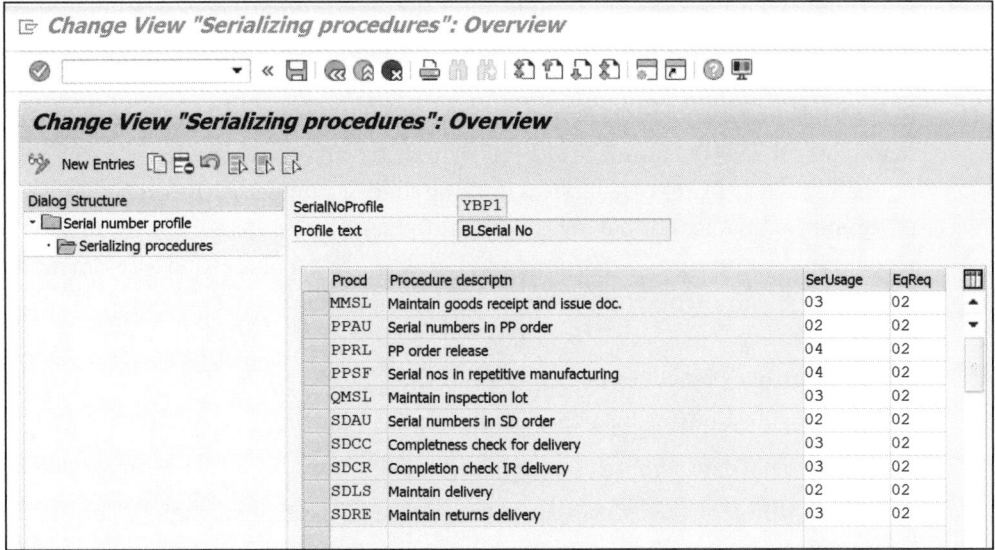

Figure 4.11 Serializing Procedures

4.3   SAP S/4HANA Business Partner Model

In SAP S/4HANA, the supplier or vendor master that was once the core master data object for procurement activities in SAP ERP becomes part of the business partner record. The business partner is the new approach going forward for SAP S/4HANA and can be backported to SAP ERP environments above SAP ERP 6.0 EHP 6. This is important for SAP Ariba Supplier Lifecycle Performance as well. SAP Ariba Supplier Lifecycle and Performance manages supplier identification, onboarding, and maintenance, which often requires or benefits from integration with SAP ERP environments. To integrate SAP Ariba Supplier Lifecycle and Performance with an SAP ERP environment, the SAP ERP system must have the business partner model implemented. This means that customers need to convert an existing SAP ERP supplier master model to the SAP S/4HANA business partner one if they wish to integrate SAP Ariba Supplier Lifecycle and Performance, even if the customer does not intend to upgrade to SAP S/4HANA in the near future.

4.3.1   Suppliers as Business Partners

Business partners in an SAP ERP environment, including SAP S/4HANA, are entities that transact with the SAP ERP system and your organization. Loosely defined, business partners can be suppliers who sell something to your organization, employees, and/or customers. Sometimes, an individual can represent all three categories. For example, some state and local government entities employ an individual who is maintained in the HR module of SAP ERP. This individual may sell services to the government, such as foster care services, making them a supplier in the system capable of submitting invoices or having checks cut for services rendered. Finally, this individual could be set up as a customer in the system when requesting assessment or other state government–provided services requiring a fee.

Business Partner Objectives

The SAP S/4HANA business partner model has the following strategic objectives:

- Share general data across different roles.
- Support different business partner categories, such as organization, person, or group.
- Allow for role versatility; one business partner can perform multiple roles, such as customer and vendor (supplier).
- Support multiple addresses for one business partner.
- Support time dependency on different subentities, such as roles, addresses, relationships, bank data, and so on.
- Support relationship flexibility, such as a supplier having a contact person.
- Provide harmonized architecture.

There were reasons for creating separate records for each of these relationships in previous versions, a principal one being that sidecar systems such as SAP SRM or SAP Customer Relationship Management (SAP CRM) only needed a certain type of relationship record to support their dependent transactions—a supplier record or a customer record, respectively. The SAP S/4HANA business partner approach leverages Customer/Vendor Integration (CVI) to do this translation and delineation for dependent systems while synchronizing changes with the business partner in SAP S/4HANA.

Business Partner Creation Workflow

Per Figure 4.12, a business partner is created whenever a customer or supplier is created in SAP S/4HANA. The CVI contains the business partner-specific data, as well as customer and supplier data. Upon commit, the customer and/or vendor data is routed through the CVI and combined with business partner data, and the CVI link tables are maintained. Some of the vendor and customer data overlaps; for example, name and address are contained in both the customer and the vendor record and can be the same for a business partner.

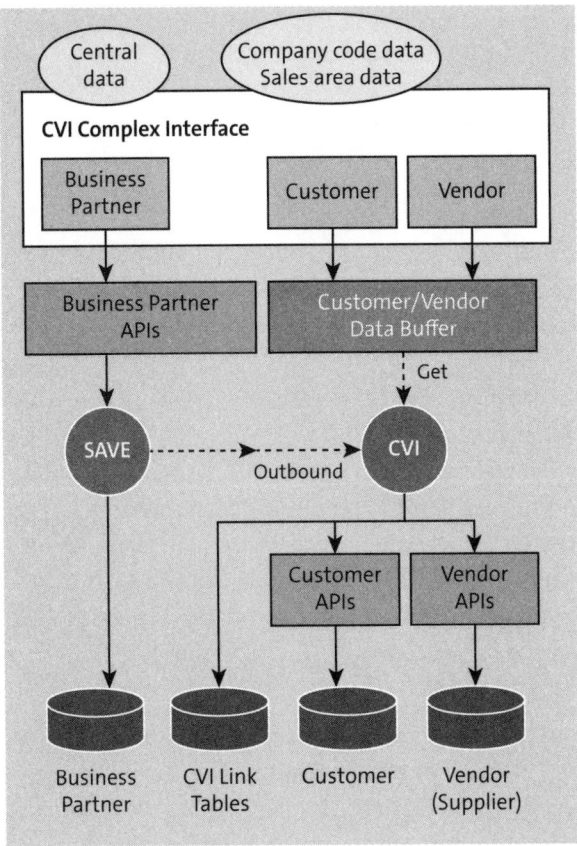

Figure 4.12 Integrated Object Model: Business Partner Customer/Vendor Integration

Business Partners in SAP S/4HANA

Changing the business partner design impacts the upgrade path from SAP ERP to SAP S/4HANA. If you're looking to move suppliers and/or customers to SAP S/4HANA from a previous SAP ERP instance, you must have CVI in place to move to on-premise SAP S/4HANA. All customers, suppliers, and their contacts need to be converted to business partners. Also, whereas before in SAP ERP a user might access a supplier using Transaction XK03, this transaction—along with the others listed in Table 4.2— no longer exist in SAP S/4HANA. In the best case, if you input a transaction code listed in the following table, you will be redirected to Transaction BP, which is the main transaction for all business partner–related transactions, including supplier and customer records.

Transaction Codes						
FD01	FK05	MK05	V-06	VAP1	XD01	XK03
FD02	FK06	MK06	V-07	VAP2	XD02	XK05
FD03	MAP1	MK12	V-08	VAP3	XD03	XK06
FD05	MAP2	MK18	V-09	VD01	XD05	XK07
FD06	MAP3	MK19	V-11	VD02	XD06	
FK01	MK01	V-03	V+21	VD03	XD07	
FK02	MK02	V-04	V+22	VD05	XK01	
FK03	MK03	V-05	V+23	VD06	XK02	

Table 4.2 Supplier and Customer Transaction Codes No Longer Used in SAP S/4HANA

Transaction BP is thus the single point of entry to create, edit, and display master data for business partners, customers, and vendors in SAP S/4HANA. The business partner number also replaces the supplier and customer numbers. This has further implications for an upgrade and/or data conversion. However, this doesn't mean that you should collapse all of the existing customer/vendor transactions in SAP ERP into Transaction BP; there is functionality in SAP ERP transactions not available in Transaction BP, and the SAP ERP help documents refer users to a variety of transactions, which could confuse users if you were to centralize business partner functions in a single transaction in older versions of SAP ERP.

In SAP S/4HANA, all of the previous SAP ERP transactions, reports, condition records, and forms that use the customer or vendor number as input fields require the customer or vendor number, not the BP number. Even if a new BP number has been assigned to the customer or vendor, the former customer or vendor number is required.

4.3.2 Loading Supplier Records in SAP S/4HANA

For previous versions of SAP ERP, the standard data migration loading tool used most frequently was the Legacy System Migration Workbench (LSMW). Per SAP Note 2287723, LSMW is not the recommended option for SAP S/4HANA on-premise implementations, however, and not even available as an option for SAP S/4HANA Cloud. The recommended options are listed in Table 4.3.

Source System	SAP S/4HANA On-Premise	SAP S/4HANA Cloud
SAP R/3 SAP ERP Third-party ERP system	▪ SAP Data Services ▪ SAP Information Steward ▪ SAP Rapid Data Migration content ▪ SAP S/4HANA migration cockpit and SAP S/4HANA migration object modeler	▪ SAP S/4HANA Migration Cockpit ▪ For SAP S/4HANA Cloud, single tenant edition, the migration object modeler is also available

Table 4.3 Data Migration Tool Options for SAP S/4HANA

For more information on migration and data loading approaches for SAP S/4HANA on-premise, visit *https://rapid.sap.com/bp/RDM_S4H_OP*.

4.3.3 Setting Up the Supplier Master

Also known as the vendor master in previous versions of SAP ERP, the *supplier master* contains the core data about the supplier used to conduct transactions. The supplier master contains the following information:

- General data, such as name, address, and bank information, as shown in Figure 4.13.
- *Purchasing data*, such as the type of products supplied, the assigned purchasing organization, tax ID, incoterms/terms of payment, and several other related fields.
- *Accounting data*, such as reconciliation account, creditor number, and payment methods. The reconciliation account number is for a general ledger account depicting the liabilities with regards to several vendors. The creditor number is assigned either automatically by the system or manually upon creation of the vendor master and is used as the subsidiary ledger number in financial accounting. In subledger accounting, total liabilities are calculated by vendor, rather than the process in general ledger accounting in which the liabilities are calculated for a group of vendors in that particular general ledger account. The reconciliation account is derived from the vendor master record upon entry of an invoice during the payment process.

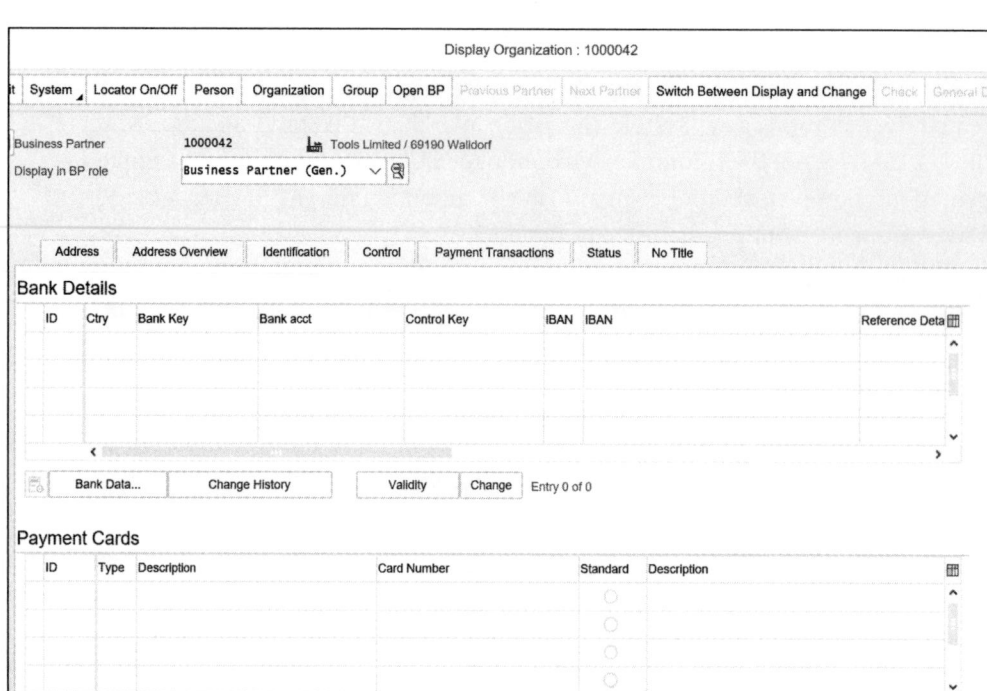

Figure 4.13 Bank Information Tab in SAP S/4HANA, Transaction BP

The supplier master record in SAP S/4HANA includes a customer master component now that the supplier master and customer master are unified in Transaction BP. There is some baseline configuration required to set up the supplier master in the system. The updated business partner configuration guides and steps are available at *service.sap.com*. These steps should be completed prior to loading and/or entering supplier masters into the SAP S/4HANA environment. These configuration steps for customer/vendor setup are general guidelines for an on-premise implementation; you should always check online for the latest updates to any configuration steps and view recommendations for the version of SAP S/4HANA you're implementing. Your project should determine customer-specific entries and steps in conjunction with sales and distribution stakeholders and owners in that project stream.

Substantial configuration is required for business partner setup in SAP S/4HANA, as well as the follow-on conversion scenarios for CVI. The next section outlines the business partner conversion steps in more detail, as well as the business partner setup required in each phase of the project.

4.3.4   Performing Customer/Vendor Integration

The supplier master is arguably the most vital master data for procurement. Suppliers are the core of a purchasing document; without a source of supply defined, no purchasing document can be generated. This area has also changed significantly in SAP S/4HANA. This section will both cover the initial configuration and then provide a brief tutorial on creating suppliers.

Little has changed from previous versions of SAP ERP in how you set up the organization structure in SAP S/4HANA. However, in master data there is a significant change in how vendors are set up in SAP S/4HANA Enterprise Management versus previous versions of SAP ERP. The first change is that vendors are now definitively referred to as *suppliers* in SAP S/4HANA, but not in the naming convention for customer/vendor integration (CVI). In SAP S/4HANA, customers and vendors are now centralized into a single business partner concept. The conversion process and nuances of CVI are further explained in the next sections.

In previous versions of SAP ERP, a supplier and a customer could be the same company, but they could not share the same master data element. You had to create a supplier record and a customer record. Here, the system constraints were not reflecting the reality for many companies and government entities. A citizen today may provide the local government with services such as foster care services, submit invoices to the government, and also be a "customer" in the sense that they pay their street cleaning fees or water delivery services directly to the local government. Many companies today interact both as suppliers and customers with their business partners. A large manufacturer and an MRO distributor, for example, may buy from and sell to each other in large volumes as the manufacturer leverages the MRO distributor for plant maintenance product orders and sells to the distributor many of the items the manufacturer produces. In previous versions of SAP, both a customer and a supplier record needed to be created to represent these relationships. In SAP S/4HANA Enterprise Management, only one business partner record is needed.

Keeping all of these data elements in sync for both the customer and the supplier falls on CVI. CVI ensures that customer and vendor master data tables, such as the core tables KN and LF, are updated automatically after a business partner is created/changed. Tables KN and LF are still populated in SAP S/4HANA as they are in SAP ERP.

Some other caveats of CVI and business partner design in SAP S/4HANA are as follows:

- The customer/vendor hierarchy remains the same as in SAP ERP.
- To create a customer or supplier record in SAP S/4HANA via an interface, the interface must call the customer/vendor creation BAPI `CVI_EI_INBOUND_MAIN`.
- Business partner data for retail systems such as SAP Fashion Management and customer as consumer, as used in retail industry solution versions, are not part of the conversion at this point.
- CVI is not mandatory for SAP S/4HANA Finance, on-premise.
- Mass maintenance is possible for customers and vendors via Transaction BP. Transactions XD99, XK99, and MASS are available in Transaction BP. For SAP S/4HANA 1511, implementation of SAP Note 2346269 (Mass Maintenance Functionality of Customers/Suppliers using XD99 and XK99) is required.
- DEBMAS, an IDoc used for updating customer information, and CREMAS, an IDoc used for updating supplier information, can be used in SAP S/4HANA on premise 1610 and in 1511 if you implement SAP Note 2312529.
- To get nine additional customer/vendor data structures, you need to implement SAP Notes 2324208 and 2331298, then run Reports NOTE_2324208_DDIC and NOTE_2331298 to activate the DDIC structure changes. Program LSMW will need to be modified to include the input data structure.
- Custom code calls to old transactions are automatically redirected to the new versions. You don't need to change the custom code for this area. However, interfaces creating customer or vendor master data have to call the `CVI_EI_INBOUND_MAIN` or `BusinessPartnerSUITEBulkReplicateRequest` or `BusinessPartnerRelationshipSUITEBulkReplicateRequest` webservice rather than a previous function module and/or webservice. If you have interfaces that rely on previous function modules from SAP ERP, the code will need to be changed to call `CVI_EI_INBOUND_MAIN` or the aforementioned webservice, and mapping logic to new and/or custom fields may be required. To activate `CVI_EI_INBOUND_MAIN`, implement SAP Note 2405714 for `RFC_CVI_EI_INBOUND_MAIN` enhancements. You can also navigate to Transaction BP in SAP S/4HANA by calling `BUP_PARTNER_MAINTAIN` from an external application.
- If you're running SAP S/4HANA alongside SAP ERP environments in your landscape, CIF interfaces to and from SAP S/4HANA for business partners are still supported, as are middleware for business partner synchronization and SAP BW reporting on customers and vendors.

- For converting credit management data, go to IMG path **Migration to SAP S/4HANA Finance • Data Migration • Credit Management Migration**.

- For converting employees to business partners, see SAP Note 2340095 (S4TWL—Conversion of Employees to Business Partners).

Implementing CVI

The implementation process with regards to vendors and CVI is outlined in Figure 4.14. During a greenfield implementation, in which no legacy ERP system is being converted directly to SAP S/4HANA, a data conversion nonetheless would take place if you are loading supplier or customer records into SAP S/4HANA. You need to upload these supplier records via CVI if this is the case. For conversion of an existing SAP ERP environment running SAP Business Suite on SAP HANA, you need to convert the suppliers and customer records in the system to business partners first, then initiate the overall conversion to SAP S/4HANA.

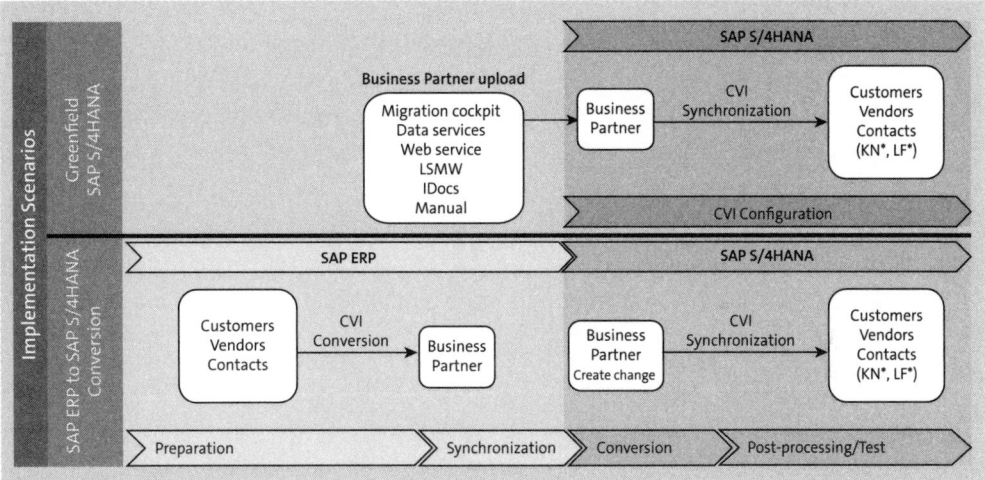

Figure 4.14 Customer/Vendor Interface: Process Scenarios

Here you verify the configuration detailed at *support.sap.com* under **Best Practice Building Block J61 for CVI Conversion** (see *https://support.sap.com/content/dam/SAAP/Sol_Pack/Library/Configuration/J61_S4HANAX_BB_ConfigGuide_EN_XX.docx*), or the corresponding version of these steps for your on-premise version of SAP S/4HANA. For SAP S/4HANA Cloud, the implementation team does not perform these steps.

CVI Conversion of SAP ERP Customers and Vendors to SAP S/4HANA Business Partners

This section covers the conversion steps for SAP S/4HANA business partners. Both vendor and customer steps are included in this section. The customer record is required when initiating returns to a supplier in SAP S/4HANA. Therefore, you can't ignore the customer records in the SAP ERP environment during a conversion process to SAP S/4HANA and CVI, and some cross-business collaboration with other stakeholders on the project and in the system outside of procurement (sales and distribution typically owns the customer master) must take place to ensure that full master data to support certain areas, including those required for returns, is in the new SAP S/4HANA environment on go-live.

To initiate the conversion process with CVI from SAP ERP to on-premise SAP S/4HANA, there are a couple of key items to keep in mind. First, we recommend archiving the business partners (customers and vendors) marked with the **Deletion** flag. Number ranges and numbering should also remain the same in the new system, if possible, to avoid confusion and mapping exercises (note that number ranges are a non-transportable configuration item, as in previous releases of SAP ERP; you'll need to perform manual configuration in each client, including production, to set the number ranges). SAP ERP must be at version 6.0 with enhancement pack levels of 0 to 7 to begin a conversion. If you have SAP ERP 6.0 EHP 0 to 4, you'll need to apply SAP Note 2383051 if you have vendor contacts that need to be converted. For lower releases, EHP 1 to 3, you may either want to upgrade the EHP prior to conversion or create an incident message to obtain more guidance on conversion of vendor contacts.

The CVI conversion steps from SAP ERP to SAP S/4HANA will be described in further detail ahead, beginning with the preparation phase.

CVI Preparation Phase: SAP S/4HANA Vendor/Customer Conversion to Business Partners

The first phase of a CVI conversion is *preparation*, as shown in Figure 4.15. The following tasks must be completed, many in conjunction with your technical team. As with the baseline configuration, we recommend that you check the latest conversion steps at *support.sap.com* based on the version of SAP S/4HANA to be implemented prior to proceeding with a CVI conversion.

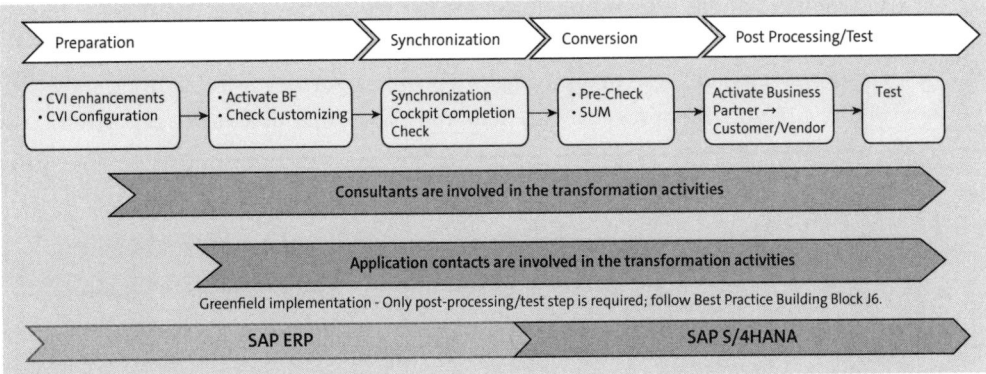

Figure 4.15 CVI Conversion for On-Premise SAP S/4HANA and Greenfield Implementations

In general, here are the steps you will follow:

1. Check and integrate customer/vendor enhancements. If you have any enhancements in the SAP ERP system being converted or planned in the SAP S/4HANA system that would normally call an individual customer or vendor function module and/or transaction, these enhancement objects will need to be rewritten for the new business partner concept and functionality.

2. Activate business function CA_BP_SOA. This is typically done by your technical team via Transaction SW05, as shown in Figure 4.16.

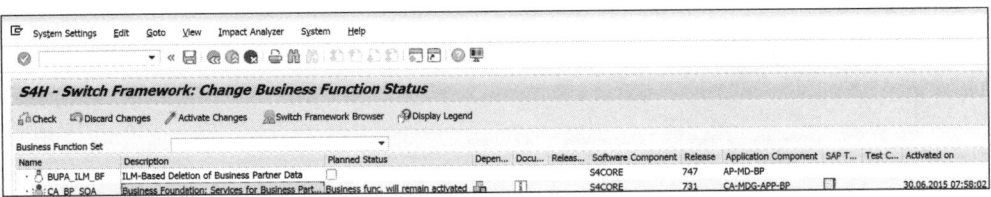

Figure 4.16 Activate CA_BP_SOA in Transaction SW05

3. Perform CVI customizing, check customizing, and trigger necessary changes as per the guides at *support.sap.com*.

4. Define number assignments according to the SAP S/4HANA conversion guide provided at *support.sap.com*.

5. Maintain business partner mapping customizing and run the check report. In this step, you'll map all of the business partner elements to their CVI counterparts. Follow menu path **Cross-Application Components • Master Data Synchronization •**

Customer • Vendor Integration • Business Partner Settings • Settings for Customer Integration • Field Assignment for Customer Integration • Assign Attributes. After the number assignment mapping from a business partner to a customer, shown in Figure 4.17, you then proceed with mapping a customer to a business partner.

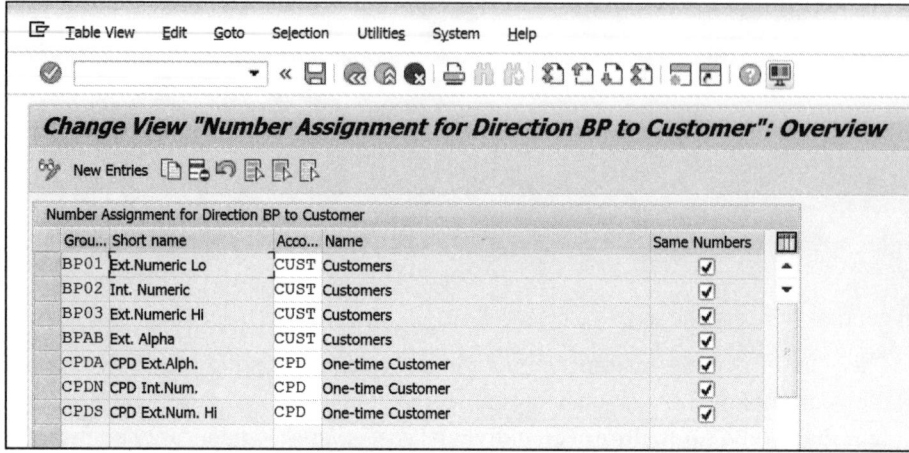

Figure 4.17 Number Assignment Direction to Customer

Finally, you map the attributes for a contact person, as shown in Figure 4.18, so that data such as legal form and legal status carry over seamlessly.

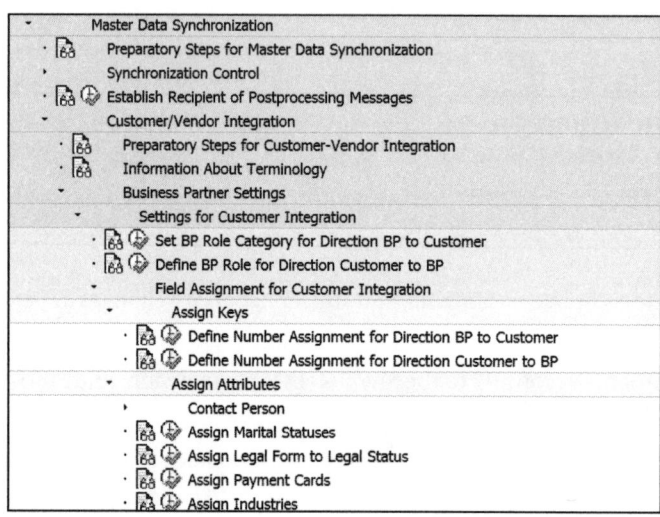

Figure 4.18 Assign Attributes Mapping for CVI to Customer

Attribute Value Mapping

Attribute value mapping must be maintained and must be equal for every existing customer instance, as in Figure 4.18. The IMG menu path is **Cross-Application Components • Master Data Synchronization • Customer/Vendor Integration • Business Partner Settings • Settings for Customer Integration • Field Assignment for Customer Integration • Assign Attributes • Contact Person**, followed by one of the following options.

For the contact person:

- **Activate Assignment of Contact Persons**
- **Assign Department Numbers for Contact Person**
- **Assign Functions of Contact Person**
- **Assign Authority of Contact Person**
- **Assign VIP Indicator for Contact Person**

For the customer attributes:

- **Assign Marital Statuses**
- **Assign Legal Form to Legal Status**
- **Assign Payment Cards**
- **Assign Industries**

For the assign industries option, the industry value mapping must be maintained and should be equal for every existing vendor instance; the industry assignment for the vendor and customer shares the same configuration table. Outbound industry mapping maps the business partner to the customer/vendor, and inbound mapping maps the customer/vendor to the business partner.

Now, check and clean up customer/vendor data. Prior to initiating the conversion, this is an excellent time to tidy your supplier master records and customer records to provide the new system with clean data. Follow these steps:

1. Archive vendors marked with the **Deletion** flag (optional; you can also convert these into the new system if preferred).

2. Download the following check reports:
   - 2216176: Pre- and postconversion check report
     Report PRECHECK_UPGRADATION_REPORT
   - 1623677: CVI customizing check report
     Report CVI_FS_CHECK_CUSTOMIZING

- 974504: Inconsistencies in link tables of master data sync check report
- 2399368: Excel upload option in MDS_LOAD_COCKPIT (allow for customer/ vendor selection upload from Excel for business partner conversion)

3. Check and integrate customer/vendor enhancements (see SAP Notes 2309153 and 1623809). The SAP Notes explain how to make customer enhancements to the customer/vendor integration (integrating additional customer/vendor fields in the business partner and using CVI synchronization to update them in the customer/ vendor).

4. Activate business function CA_SUPPLIER_SOA, again using Transaction SFW5.

5. Switch to active status using the **VENDOR_SFWS_SC1** and **VENDOR_SFWS_SC2** options in Transaction SW05, as shown in Figure 4.19, to allow the vendor contact person data to be synchronized with the business partner contact person data, and ensure that they have **Global Status** set to **On**. Also, you will need to verify SAP Note 1454441 (Development of Contact Person for Vendors).

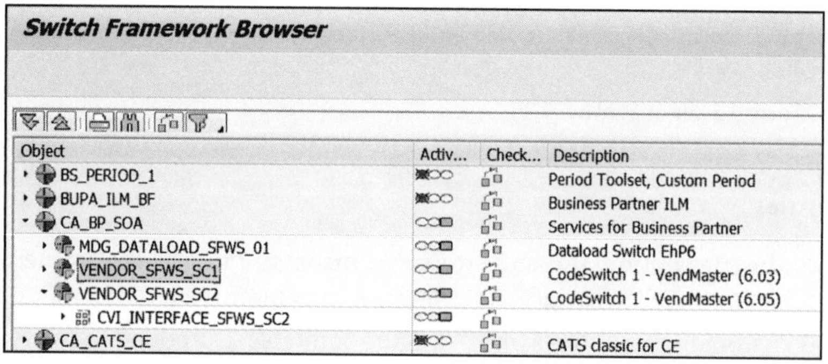

Switch Framework Browser

Object	Activ...	Check...	Description
▸ BS_PERIOD_1			Period Toolset, Custom Period
▸ BUPA_ILM_BF			Business Partner ILM
▾ CA_BP_SOA			Services for Business Partner
▸ MDG_DATALOAD_SFWS_01			Dataload Switch EhP6
▸ VENDOR_SFWS_SC1			CodeSwitch 1 - VendMaster (6.03)
▾ VENDOR_SFWS_SC2			CodeSwitch 1 - VendMaster (6.05)
▸ CVI_INTERFACE_SFWS_SC2			
▸ CA_CATS_CE			CATS classic for CE

Figure 4.19 Vendor Sync Switches

Preparation Phase Customizing Tasks

Next, perform the following customizing tasks:

1. Activate the postprocessing order request for the business partner synchronization object in IMG menu path **Cross-Application Components • Master Data Synchronization • Synchronization Control • Synchronization Control • Activate PPO Requests for Platform Objects in the Dialog**.

2. Activate the sync of the vendor, customer, and business partner under IMG menu path **Cross-Application Components • Master Data Synchronization • Synchronization Control • Synchronization Control • Activate Synchronization Options**, as shown in Figure 4.20.

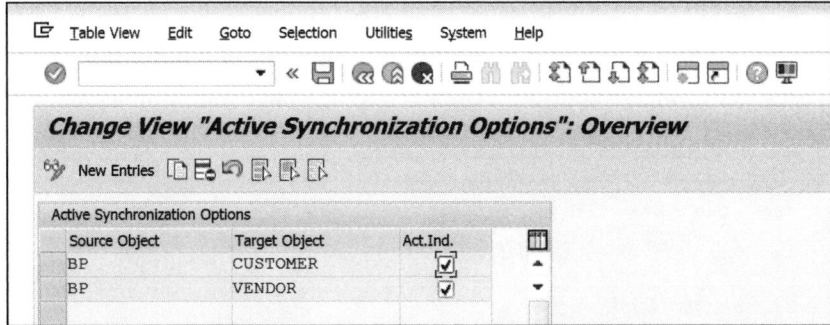

Figure 4.20 Activate Synchronization Options

3. Activate creation of postprocessing orders for component AP-MD in IMG menu path **Cross-Application Components • General Application Functions • Postprocessing Office • Business Processes • Activate Creation of Postprocessing Orders**, as shown in Figure 4.21.

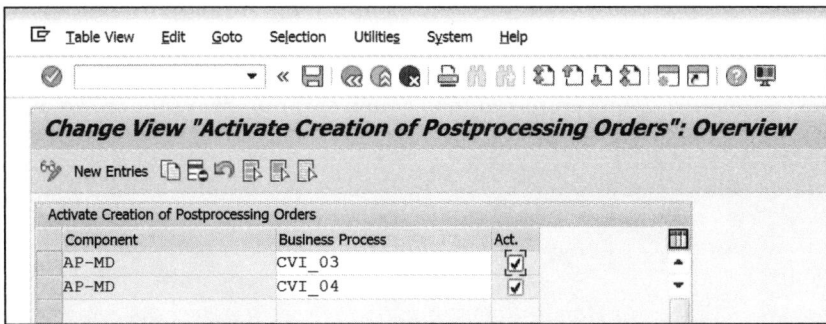

Figure 4.21 Activate Creation of Postprocessing Orders

4. Verify that the customer and vendor number ranges from the system to be converted do not overlap. If the number range settings do not overlap, they should be mirrored in the receiving system. If the number ranges do overlap, the number ranges in the receiving SAP S/4HANA system should be set so that most vendor and customer numbers can be reused.

5. If the numbers for customers and vendors should be taken into SAP S/4HANA business partner records, the number ranges in SAP S/4HANA for business partner, vendor, and customer must be set to **External** during the conversion and then set back to **Internal** upon completion of the conversion.

The three IMG menu paths for locating the applicable number ranges are as follows:

1. Define number ranges for customers at IMG menu path **Logistics—General • Business Partner • Customers • Control • Define and Assign Customer Number Ranges** (see Figure 4.22).

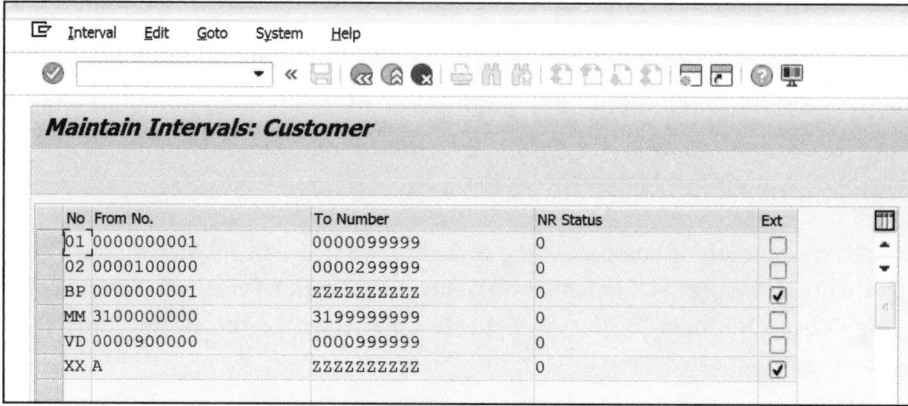

Figure 4.22 Define Customer Number Range Intervals

Once you've defined the interval, you then assign this number range to the customer records as shown in Figure 4.23.

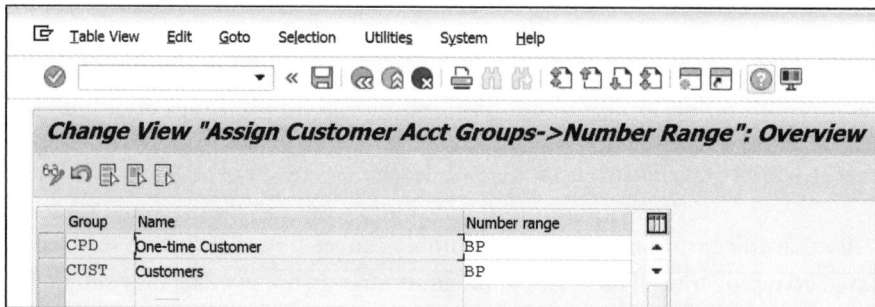

Figure 4.23 Assign Customer Account Groups to Number Range

2. Follow the same steps for vendors by defining and then assigning number ranges via vendor IMG menu path **Logistics—General • Business Partner • Vendor • Control • Define Number Ranges for Vendor Master Records**.

3. Define number range groupings via IMG menu path **Cross-Application Components • SAP Business Partner • Business Partner • Basic Settings • Number Ranges**

and Groupings • Define Number Ranges/Define Groupings and Assign Number Ranges (see Figure 4.24).

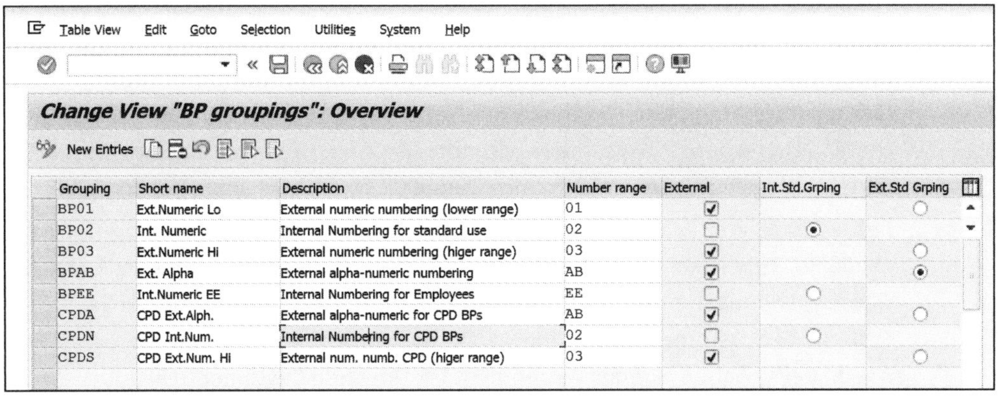

Grouping	Short name	Description	Number range	External	Int.Std.Grping	Ext.Std Grping
BP01	Ext.Numeric Lo	External numeric numbering (lower range)	01	☑		○
BP02	Int. Numeric	Internal Numbering for standard use	02	☐	◉	
BP03	Ext.Numeric Hi	External numeric numbering (higer range)	03	☑		○
BPAB	Ext. Alpha	External alpha-numeric numbering	AB	☑		◉
BPEE	Int.Numeric EE	Internal Numbering for Employees	EE	☐	○	
CPDA	CPD Ext.Alph.	External alpha-numeric for CPD BPs	AB	☑		○
CPDN	CPD Int.Num.	Internal Numbering for CPD BPs	02	☐	○	
CPDS	CPD Ext.Num. Hi	External num. numb. CPD (higer range)	03	☑		○

Figure 4.24 Business Partner Groupings Overview Settings for Customer/Vendor Conversion to Business Partner

Finally, you define the contact person business partner number range. This step is very important if you wish to maintain/convert contact persons successfully. The CVI conversion Report MDS_LOAD_COCKPIT assigns an internal business partner number to each contact person during conversion. The internal number range is the number range assigned to the internal standard grouping (see Figure 4.24). If the assigned internal number range conflicts with the targeted customer or vendor number ranges, the number range for the contact person will need to be changed to a new range that doesn't overlap with the range targeted for business partner numbers. Failure to set these number ranges correctly can result in GUID error R1124: **Business Partner with GUID Number X Does Not Exist**.

Customizing CVI Behavior with BAdIs

In the event that you need to customize the CVI behavior, there are several SAP Business Add-ins (BAdIs) provided for data assignment. Access them via IMG menu path **Cross-Application Components • Master Data Synchronization • Customer/Vendor Integration • Business Partner Settings • Business Add-Ins (BAdIs)**. For business partner/customer/vendor table field extension, see SAP Note 2309153 (BP_CVI: Guide for Customer Enhancements in CVI (Customer/Vendor Integration) in S4HANA Releases), as well as SAP Note 2295823 (BP_CVI: Transfer of Customer/Vendor Fields to the Business Partner-Template Source Code).

Mapping is the next step in the preparation phase. The following steps need to be completed and validated prior to gating out of the preparation phase:

1. For a customer, enter business partner roles FLCU00 (company data) and FLCU01 (sales data) under IMG menu path **Cross-Application Components • Master Data Synchronization • Customer/Vendor Integration • Business Partner Settings • Settings for Customer Integration • Define BP Role for Direction Customer to BP**. For vendors, the IMG menu path is the same as path for customers, but add the following at the end: **• Settings for Vendor Integration • Define BP Role for Direction Vendor to BP**.

2. For every customer and vendor account, a business partner grouping must be available. This is set using menu path **Cross-Application Components • Master Data Synchronization • Customer/Vendor Integration • Business Partner Settings • Settings for Customer Integration • Field Assignment for Customer Integration • Assign Keys • Define Number Assignment for Direction Customer to BP** for customers, and the same path plus **• Settings for Vendor Integration • Field Assignment for Vendor Integration • Assign Keys • Define Number Assignment for Direction Vendor to BP** for vendors.

Running Final Reports

You are now ready to run the reports prior to completing the preparation phase steps for the conversion:

1. The first report can be accessed via Transaction CVI_FS_CHECK_CUST and is used to check the customizing or in SAP Note 1623677 (BP_CVI: Check Report for Checking CVI Customizing).
   As with the mapping step, this report checks the customizing in both directions: customer/vendor to business partner and business partner to customer/vendor. This is done in SAP S/4HANA in postprocessing or a in greenfield implementation.

2. Report FSBP_IND_SECTOR_MAPPING_CHECK is optional; it checks and creates industry mapping entries for industry assignment in the context of CVI while evaluating existing or missing assignment entries. If the number of industry values is low, this report is not required.

3. Report PRECHECK_UPGRADATION_REPORT, provided in SAP Note 2216176, is a precheck report to check if all the mappings have been completed correctly. This report can be accessed via Transaction CVI_PRECHECK_UPGRADE.

Note that the **CVI Mapping** and **Contact Person Mapping** checkboxes are checked by default in Report PRECHECK_UPGRADATION_REPORT. They are used after business partner conversion to check if all customers/vendors/contact persons are converted. The report also checks whether business partner roles are assigned to account groups, whether the account groups are available, and the customer/vendor value mapping.

The following SAP Notes can be used to automate the configuration steps and suppress the mandatory business partner field groups check during CVI conversion. All three SAP Notes have to be applied, even if you only need part of the functions (e.g., you need to suppress the mandatory business partner field groups check during CVI conversion but don't need to use the automation feature):

- 2336018—BP S4HANA: Suppress Mandatory BP Field Groups Checks via MDS_ LOAD_COCKPIT Transaction
- 2345087—BP_BAP: Missing Values in Required Entry Fields Cause Posting Termination in Mass Processing
- 2344034—S/4HANA: Automation for Master Data Migration

If you want mandatory fields to throw error messages during migration, disable the mandatory field suppression feature. To do so, deactivate the CVI_MIGRATION_SUPPRESS_CHK implementation of BAdI definition CVI_CUSTOM_MAPPER.

Once all of the red light error messages have been resolved from the report and the yellow error messages are reviewed, you can proceed to the CVI synchronization phase of the conversion to SAP S/4HANA Enterprise Management.

Synchronization

Once you've completed and/or verified the preparation steps, you're ready for the *synchronization* phase, as illustrated in Figure 4.25.

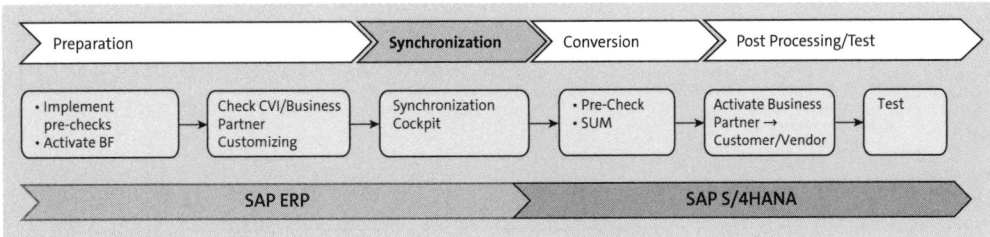

Figure 4.25 Synchronization Phase

During this phase, you will perform the following tasks:

1. Synchronize the data load according to the SAP S/4HANA Conversion Guide.

2. Review and resolve any errors due to data/customizing found in the **Monitor** tab.

3. Run postprocessing orders in the synchronization cockpit and verify the results with Report PRECHECK_UPGRADATION_REPORT.

To begin, run Report MDS_LOAD_COCKPIT, which creates a corresponding SAP business partner for the customer, vendor, and contact data for general data, addresses, role data, and bank details. In this report, you have the option to choose a customer and/or vendor conversion to a business partner or to filter by criteria such as account group and customer/vendor numbers. To expedite error analysis, we recommend running this report as a small batch initially in blocks of 10 to 50 customers/vendors.

To resolve errors, click the postprocessing object (**PPO**) icon.

This displays a master data error list. You can resolve these errors within the postprocessing object screen or outside it, but the errors must be corrected to complete the conversion of the customer/vendor and contact person. For more information on this and the synchronization cockpit, be sure to check *http://s-prs.co/500323* for the latest information and guidance.

Once you've resolved the errors, you're ready to review the conversion using the CVI_PRECHECK_UPGRADE report and the PRECHECK_UPGRADATION_REPORT. Execute these reports using the default selections, with the **CVI Mapping** and **Contact Person Mapping** boxes checked as shown in Figure 4.26.

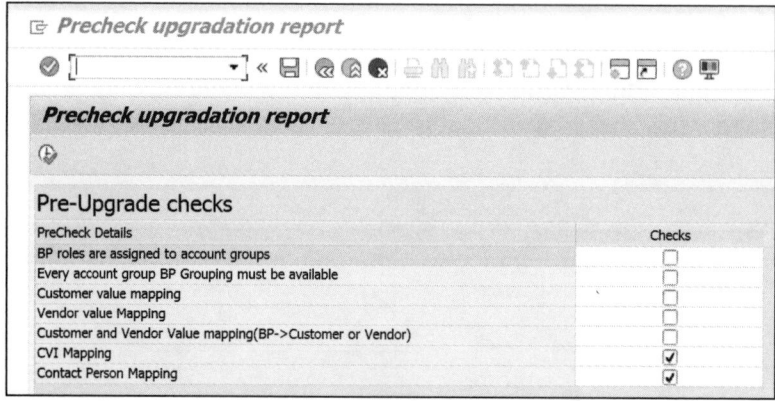

Figure 4.26 Preupgrade Checks: Default Settings

The CVI mapping checks whether all customers and vendors were mapped to a business partner, and the contact person mapping checks whether the contact persons have been converted to business partners. If you find inconsistencies, check SAP

Note 974504 (Inconsistencies in Link Tables of Master Data Sync). Once you've resolved any errors, run Report MDS_LOAD_COCKPIT to complete the synchronization, then move on to the conversion phase.

Conversion Phase

The conversion phase (see Figure 4.27) is executed by the project's technical team as part of the overall conversion from SAP ERP to SAP S/4HANA. No CVI activities are required during this phase.

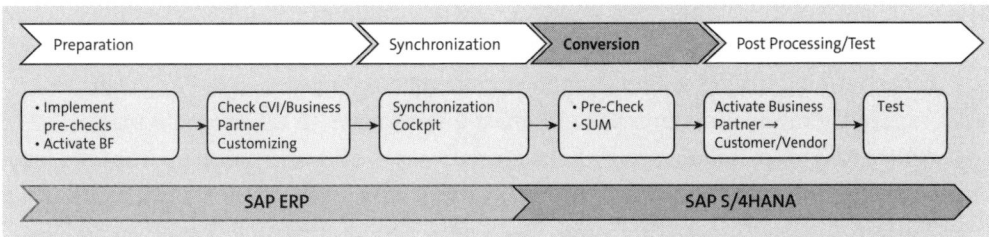

Figure 4.27 CVI Conversion Phase

Postprocessing/Test Phase

Once the technical team has completed the overall upgrade, the processing/test phase is all that remains (see Figure 4.28). In this phase, you verify the configuration detailed in the Best Practice Building Block for CVI Conversion, which can be found at *support.sap.com* under **Central Configuration of Business Partners (J61)** (see *https://s-prs.co/500324*). Ensure that these configuration settings have been made prior to testing. If your project is not based on Best Practice Building Blocks, then this guide should be used as a general reference only. Actual configuration may be determined based on your project design considerations.

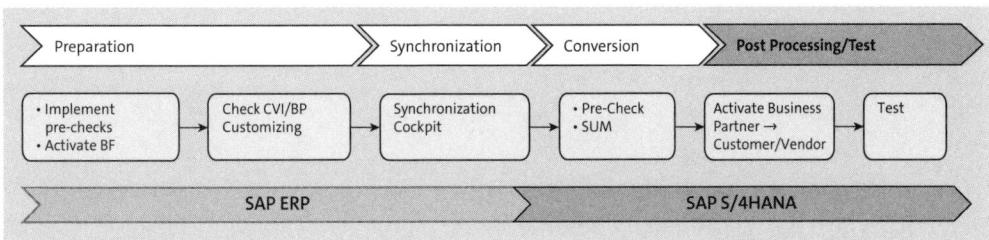

Figure 4.28 CVI Conversion: Postprocessing/Test

Once your testing is complete, you've completed the CVI conversion, which is one of the major steps in moving from SAP ERP to SAP S/4HANA Sourcing and Procurement, both from a design standpoint and in terms of conversion effort. Other master data setup/conversion, such as for material masters, isn't nearly as involved.

4.4   Summary

Master data and transactional data designs underpin and simplify system usage in SAP ERP environments when implemented in a thoughtful manner. Driving a level of granularity in the material masters that is not required for the business leads to user frustration in trying to find the appropriate material master to use in a transaction, as well additional maintenance to enact any changes to the material masters. For material groups, not designing a structured system of classification up front can lead to reporting challenges down the line as users misclassify materials and purchasing departments lack clear views into what types of items are being consumed and used in production activities.

These were all key areas in previous iterations of SAP ERP. One area that differs in SAP S/4HANA is the business partner record. SAP S/4HANA introduces a significant change to how supplier and customer masters are managed in the system. These two types of partner functions in SAP S/4HANA are unified into a business partner concept, which has ramifications for conversions and upgrades from previous versions of SAP ERP and for usage of the master record in purchasing transactions in SAP S/4HANA. With master data addressed, the next chapter shifts focus to operational procurement and the base-level types of transactions in purchasing.

Chapter 5
Operational Procurement

Operational procurement concerns the day-to-day buying activities of a business or government entity. Much of operational procurement is unplanned or partially planned, low-value, high-volume activity. Operational procurement therefore comprises the procurement activities that keep an organization running.

Unlike in other procurement activities, which typically include a trained buyer using a tool with some degree of familiarity and training, many organizations permit any employee to create a requisition for an operational or indirect procurement item. This poses a challenge for the solution used, as the baseline training for the solution and familiarity with any process may be next to nil for the average user in operational procurement. Previous versions of SAP ERP, such as SAP ERP 6.0, supported operational procurement by leveraging existing document frameworks designed for heavy-duty buying activities between suppliers and the firm or government entity.

5.1 What Is Operational Procurement?

Operational procurement supports the day-to-day processes of an organization via tactical procurement of services and materials, often by a casual user purchasing for a department's needs or even their own role-specific ones. For example, a casual user may need to order a new laptop or IT equipment in order to perform their job. An office manager may need to order office supplies to keep an office stocked with paper, toner, and other supplies. These types of purchases can be driven by various parts of the organization in high-frequency, low-value orders.

From the onset, the mismatch of a complex solution designed to support complex purchasing for direct procurement and the casual, untrained user looking to conduct operational procurement was sure to cause issues. There is nothing inherently wrong with having large amounts of detail in a **Purchase Order** or **Requisitioning** screen in a system used for heavy-duty industrial manufacturing. Often, this level of functionality is quite necessary—say, for Electronic Data Interchange (EDI) activities with a supplier or for complex items vital to the production process. Having complex, professional, buyer- and engineer-centric screens makes purchasing for the casual user a bit more cumbersome than optimal. Many of these screens can make it downright frustrating for an untrained user trying to order mundane supply items like pens and paper, as each field can issue a hard-to-understand warning message or hard-stop error, incorrect entries quickly negate the entire document's validity, and multiple tabs and steps have to be completed—all this for a simple order that costs perhaps $10. Using SAP ERP for this kind of procurement often is akin to having to use an airplane cockpit and all of its controls to steer a bicycle, and a casual user accustomed to sleek, online shopping experiences will quickly tire of trying to navigate a corporate procurement system designed to support direct procurement.

One approach to operational procurement is to take the process out of ERP systems. Cloud solutions such as SAP Ariba Buying and on-premise solutions such as SAP Supplier Relationship Management (SAP SRM) are examples of this approach. This allows a system to mask all of the complexity and the procurement options that aren't applicable to a simple transaction, distilling for the user what is necessary to find items and create orders with the fewest clicks, entries, and headaches possible. This approach, especially in cloud-based applications, works very well for simplifying the UX and allowing even the most casual and untrained user to find what he's looking for and order it, without calls to the helpdesk or frustration. However, early in the transaction, these operational procurement systems are already dependent upon ERP, even if their UIs appear independent.

First, calls need to be made from the procurement system back to the "mothership" ERP system to find out if the user is purchasing via a correct financial object in the finance and controlling system. Finance has to support a number of functions in SAP ERP, so it can't be moved into a standalone procurement solution without bringing all the other dependent modules with it or leading to an expensive, "interface spaghetti" scenario. The users themselves need to be managed in real time; terminated employees can't be allowed to continue to make purchases on behalf of a company or government entity. For this, the purchasing system requires real-time updates from the HR system or a user-management system that deactivates users throughout the landscape immediately when they leave the company or government entity.

There also is the question of efficiency and avoiding unnecessary stock to consider. What if the user is looking for an item already held and available in a company or government entity warehouse? If the operational procurement system and/or buyer cannot check this prior to assigning a source of supply and issuing a PO, excess stock may be purchased instead of consuming existing stock. Excess stock causes waste, inefficiency, and, most alarmingly for a business, expense. If checking for existing stock needs to be a manual process step in a procurement system, buyers are focusing on performing manual tasks that could be automated in an integrated system, rather than strategic procurement activities that generate exponentially more savings and value for the firm or government entity. These issues pose a conundrum for operational procurement in SAP ERP: running operational procurement directly in SAP ERP can be quite difficult for casual users and from an IT landscape perspective, but it's also the ideal place for it in many cases because all of the dependent modules and integration topics are already covered.

The main stumbling block to operational procurement in SAP ERP has always been usability and UI issues, as well as transactional volumes. An ERP system supporting operational procurement needs to be intuitive to use, minimize transaction steps while remaining flexible and capable of handling a diverse set of transactions, support catalog content, and support heavy volumes of low-dollar transactions, all while making the most of an ERP system's native integrations with associated modules. Incidentally, these are the driving forces behind SAP S/4HANA Sourcing and Procurement's embrace of operational procurement as a core ERP process. SAP S/4HANA Sourcing and Procurement supports the operational purchaser across self-service requisitioning, requirement processing, PO processing, service purchasing and entry, and purchase order collaboration.

Requisitions can be created directly by a user via a self-service procurement process or from a system/business process occurring in a module in SAP ERP, such as an MRP run in which defined reorder points trigger the creation of a requisition—a bill of materials (BOM)—that requires an additional item be ordered as part of the materials list or a project systems requirement generated from what's called a *network* in project system. A network in project system tells the user what tasks need to be performed in sequence by a certain time. Automated procurement processes typically used in the procurement of items needed in production, known as *direct procurement*, will be discussed in Chapter 6. The focus in self-service requisitioning is on user-driven requisitioning, which is more typically found in indirect procurement.

As illustrated in Figure 5.1, self-service procurement is part of the requisition-to-pay process flow. The requisition is the first document in the procurement chain that eventually leads to a purchase order and/or contract, as well as follow-on documents, such as order confirmations, advanced shipping notifications (ASNs), goods/service receipts (GRs), and invoices (IVs).

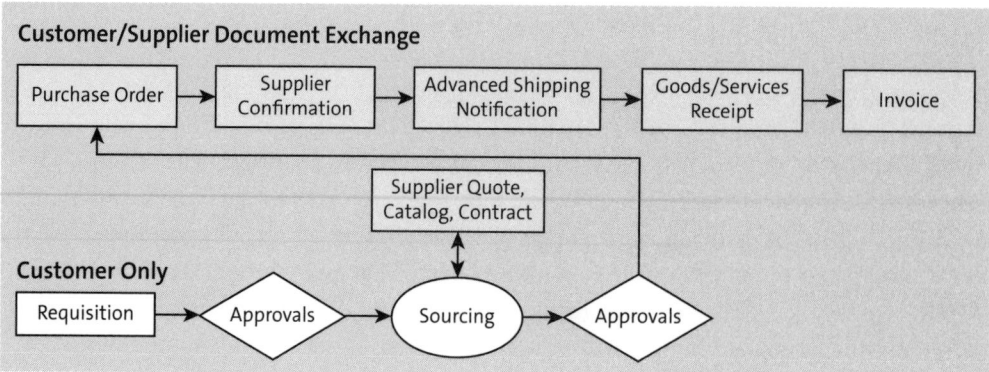

Figure 5.1 Operational Procurement: Requisition-to-Pay Process Flow

There are three main types of procurement conducted in operational procurement: stock, consumables, and external services. All of these types of procurement can be used in other procurement scenarios. Stock procurement is typically used for direct procurement activities, such as the ones discussed in the next chapter, but you can purchase and take into inventory items such as office supplies and equipment that qualify as operational indirect items as well. Consumable items are directly in the wheelhouse of operational procurement. A *consumable item* is typically an indirect item that is consumed and replenished on an ongoing basis, often by the consumers themselves. Pens, paper, coffee for the office kitchen, and other types of consumables may be ordered by the office manager or directly by an employee who notices that the office needs more of a consumable good. Consumables often do not require a goods receipt or a valuated goods receipt used primarily for inventory management processes and valuations, as these consumable purchases are petty at an individual level. In aggregate, however, consumable purchasing can be quite significant for an organization, and a level of management in the system may thus be desirable, if not a necessity.

External services procurement is the procurement of services to be delivered by individuals or groups who are not employees of the organization, but only involved to deliver that particular scope of work. These services can support the direct side of the equation, but they can also comprise cleaning or gardening services for the grounds of the office, for example, making these external services indirect. Although an office manager may set up the purchasing documentation for external services relating to the office, a project manager may need to directly set up the purchasing framework for consultants being hired to support a project.

The defining feature for operational procurement and for stock, consumable, and external procurement is that these types of procurement do not necessarily require a trained, dedicated buyer to initiate the requisition. The demand and consequent requesting in the system may come from the employee directly. When it does, this type of procurement is squarely in the category of operational procurement, and it follows that the solution provided in system to support this activity must support its untrained and barely trained users in a way that makes self-service procurement possible and even enjoyable. This is the goal of SAP S/4HANA with self-service procurement.

5.2   Self-Service Procurement

In SAP S/4HANA Sourcing and Procurement, users can create a requisition and identify appropriate sources of supply via a consumer-grade UX; that is, a UX like that users would find in their personal online shopping experiences (Figure 5.2). Self-service requisitioning is completely supported with a UI built on SAP Fiori, with tiles and step simplification to enable a completely different UX from that found in traditional ERP requisitioning.

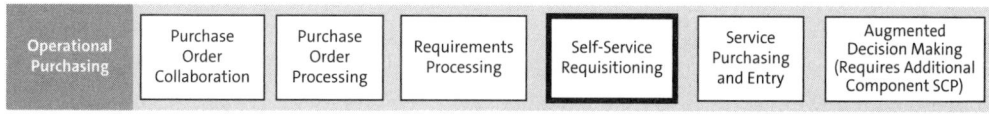

Figure 5.2 Self-Service Requisitioning in SAP S/4HANA Sourcing and Procurement

Requisitions are internal documents a corporation or government entity uses to lay claim to a service or material—essentially, a formalized request for a supply or service. Requisitions can be created with or without a source of supply and with or without a material master or service master number.

There are a number of key innovations around simplification and speed for self-service procurement in SAP S/4HANA. Most importantly, one-click ordering is the predominant concept in this area, as personified in the new UI. The content search and dynamic filtering is built on SAP S/4HANA, allowing for vast performance improvements and usability over traditional ERP-based requisitioning. Catalog content is accessed like a punchout catalog in the SAP Ariba Catalog area and/or loaded directly into SAP S/4HANA in the case of internally built catalogs. Loading and indexing catalogs in SAP S/4HANA allows for cross-catalog search directly in SAP S/4HANA.

As of SAP S/4HANA Sourcing and Procurement on-premise 1909, you also have increased flexibility for *shop-on-behalf*, where a user can select from a group of users when creating a requisition and order something on behalf of a colleague as shown in Figure 5.3.

Figure 5.3 Shop on Behalf of Requisition Functionality

5.2.1   Creating a Requisition or Shopping Cart in SAP S/4HANA

In Figure 5.4, the screen is simplified down to the bare essentials for creating a requisition. Either a user elects to use a catalog to find the item or, if the item isn't found in a catalog, the user can describe it. Note that the SAP Ariba Catalog solution can be embedded in this view, creating a seamless catalog experience even when the user is punching out to a catalog area.

To create a requisition for an operational procurement item or service, a user logs into the Purchase Requisition app and types in the item in the search bar, as shown in Figure 5.5. If the desired item doesn't appear in the search results, the user can search using a different term or create a descriptive item by selecting the **Create Own Item** option (see Figure 5.5).

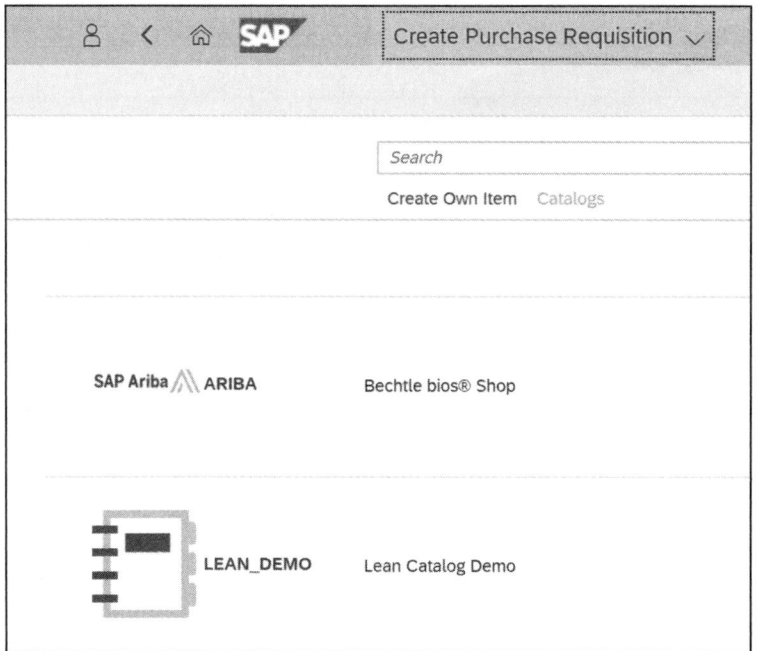

Figure 5.4 SAP S/4HANA Sourcing and Procurement: Create Requisition App

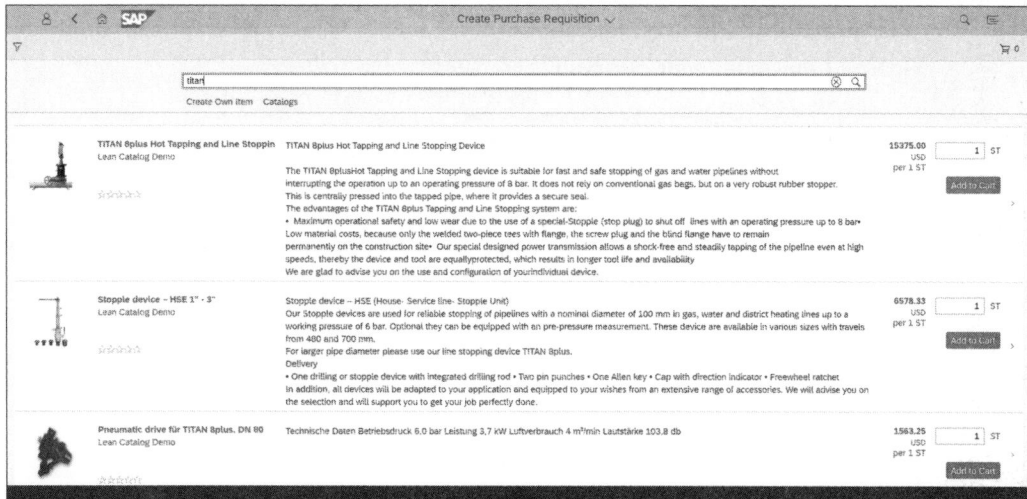

Figure 5.5 Selecting Item in Create Purchase Requisition

Once the user has selected or described an item, she is ready to order the items in the shopping cart (see Figure 5.6).

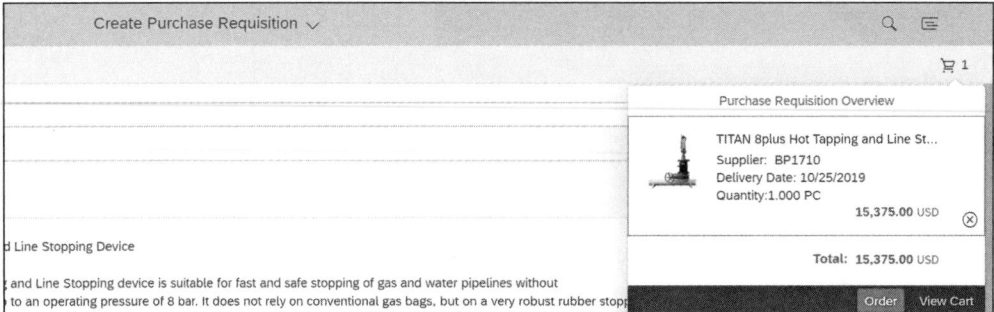

Figure 5.6 Shopping Cart Ready to Order in Purchase Requisition Create App

After clicking **Order**, the user receives confirmation and a requisition number (see Figure 5.7).

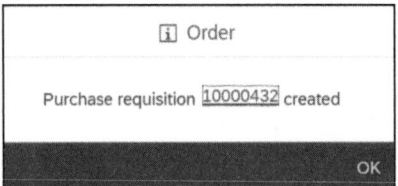

Figure 5.7 Purchase Requisition Number Created

Note

This requisition creation process went from a multistep, data-entry-intense process in SAP ERP to a couple of steps, with one data entry step to define the item required and pointing to and clicking the corresponding item in the catalog—in essence achieving or exceeding parity with a consumer shopping experience online (here, the user didn't have to enter credit card information or define a shipping address).

5.2.2   Confirmation and Return Delivery

After a PO has been issued to the supplier and the goods/services have been delivered to the customer, a goods and/or services receipt often is required by the customer to process an invoice. During the goods receipt process, the customer verifies whether the correct goods/services have been delivered and whether the right quantity has been delivered, and also defines the good for inventory management if flagging, such as perishable/nonperishable, is required.

To create a goods receipt entry that can be used for a three-way match with the PO and invoice documents (see Figure 5.8), you need to reference the PO number on your goods receipt. There are two key apps in SAP S/4HANA to support goods receipts:

- Post Goods Receipt for Purchase Order
- Post Goods Movement

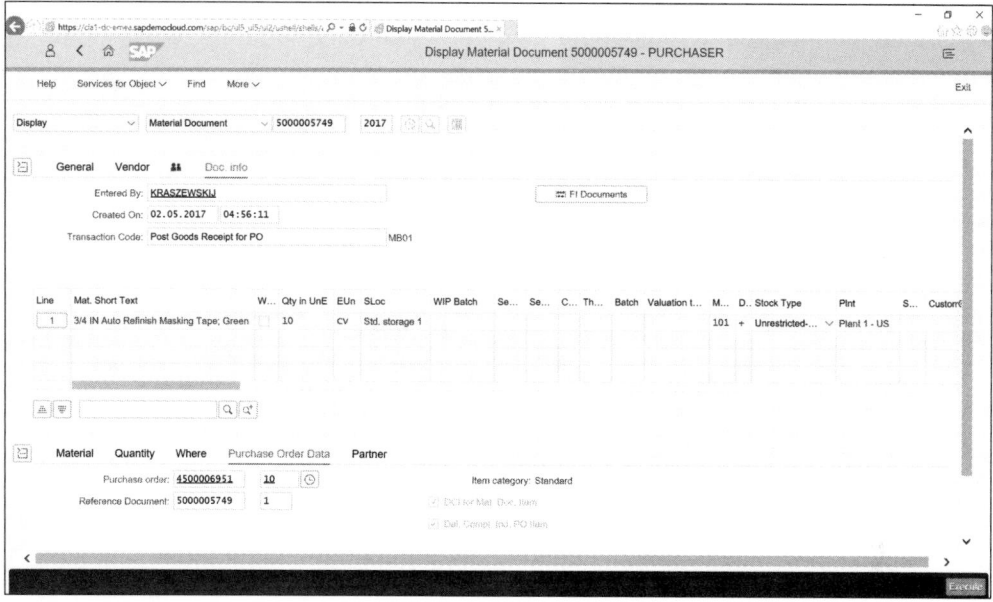

Figure 5.8 Create Goods Receipt

Goods receipts can be created in the Post Goods Receipt for Purchase Order app by searching for the PO, selecting the goods/quantity received, defining the receipt type, and then clicking **Post**, as shown in Figure 5.9.

Multiple goods receipts can be entered against a single PO or even a single line item. This is typically done when items are being distributed among several plants and storage locations or items are being received into different classifications, such as in a quarantine or quality review status.

The *movement type* is a three-character key in SAP used to differentiate between goods movements, including transfer orders and issues between plants and storage locations. The most prevalent movement type is *101*, which is a basic goods receipt for a purchase order. Movement types thus play an important role in inventory management and automatic account determination/posting. Goods receipts can be both valuated, generating accounting documents and postings, or nonvaluated, merely confirming that an item was received but not generating accounting documents/postings.

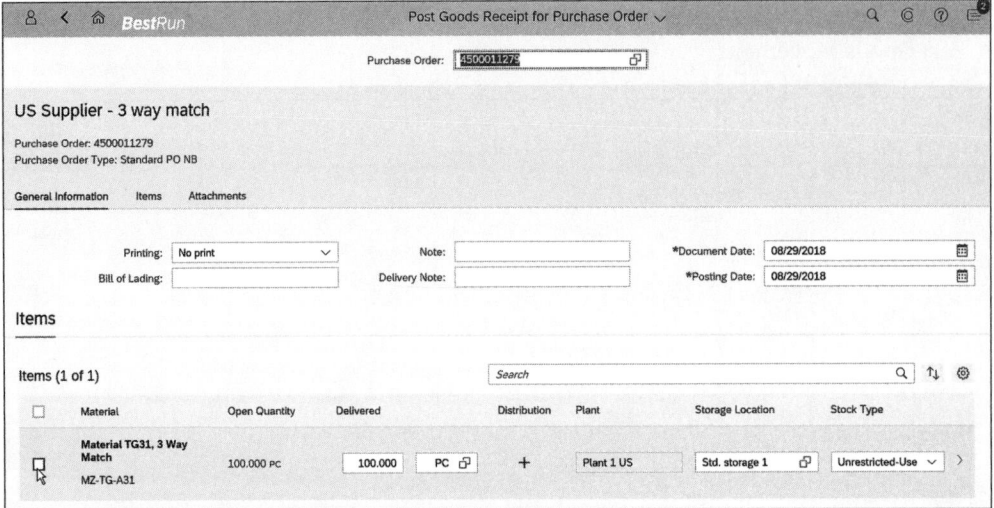

Figure 5.9 Post Goods Receipt for Purchase Order

Valuated goods receipts are particularly relevant when purchasing assets, when depreciation runs in asset management sometimes can start the minute the good is taken into receipt. Using a valuated goods receipt approach allows for finance to realize the tax savings of depreciation in a more efficient manner, rather than waiting for the invoice posting to occur. Valuation defaults are often set at the vendor master level or for the PO type. If valuation is required—that is, if the PO is flagged for valuated goods receipt—then the goods receipt will generate an accounting document in addition to the material document (see Figure 5.10).

Creation of a goods receipt can initiate the following documents and updates in SAP ERP:

- **Update of PO and PO history**
  The goods receipt updates both the open quantities in the PO and the **PO History** tab with a **Goods Receipt Document** link.

- **Update of inventory and value**
  The goods receipt updates the stock quantities in inventory management areas, as well as any changes in valuation of said stock.

- **Update of stock and consumption accounts**
  The goods receipt triggers accounting updates.

- **Notification of goods receipt to the supplier**
  You can send an (optional) notification to the person ordering and/or the supplier upon goods receipt via the system.

- **Printing of a goods receipt slip**
  In some paper-oriented receiving operations, a further hard copy of the receipt is required.

- **Transfer requirement sent to warehouse management**
  If warehouse management is active, a goods receipt can also trigger a transfer request to move the newly received item into the warehouse.

- **Quality inspection**
  If the item received first needs to be inspected, prior to being placed into general availability stock, a goods receipt can trigger these activities in quality management.

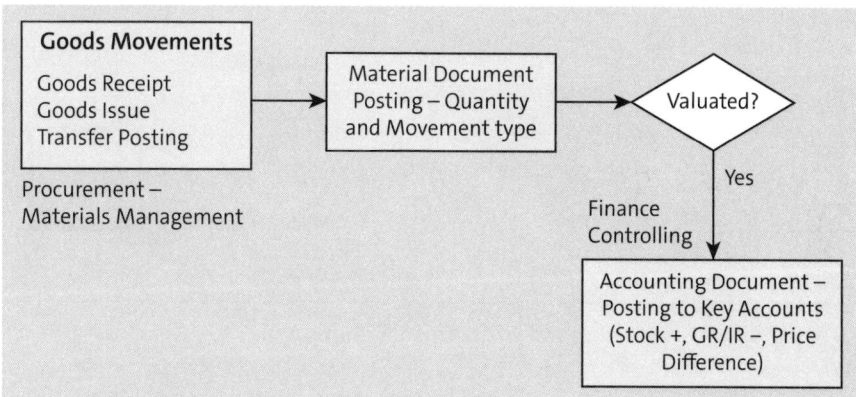

Figure 5.10 Goods Receipt: Document Postings

Return delivery can also be initiated directly in the Return Delivery app (Figure 5.11). The self-service requisitioning functionality supports return deliveries for employees via the **My Purchase Requisitions** app, in which you select **Return**. It will then show you the return reasons.

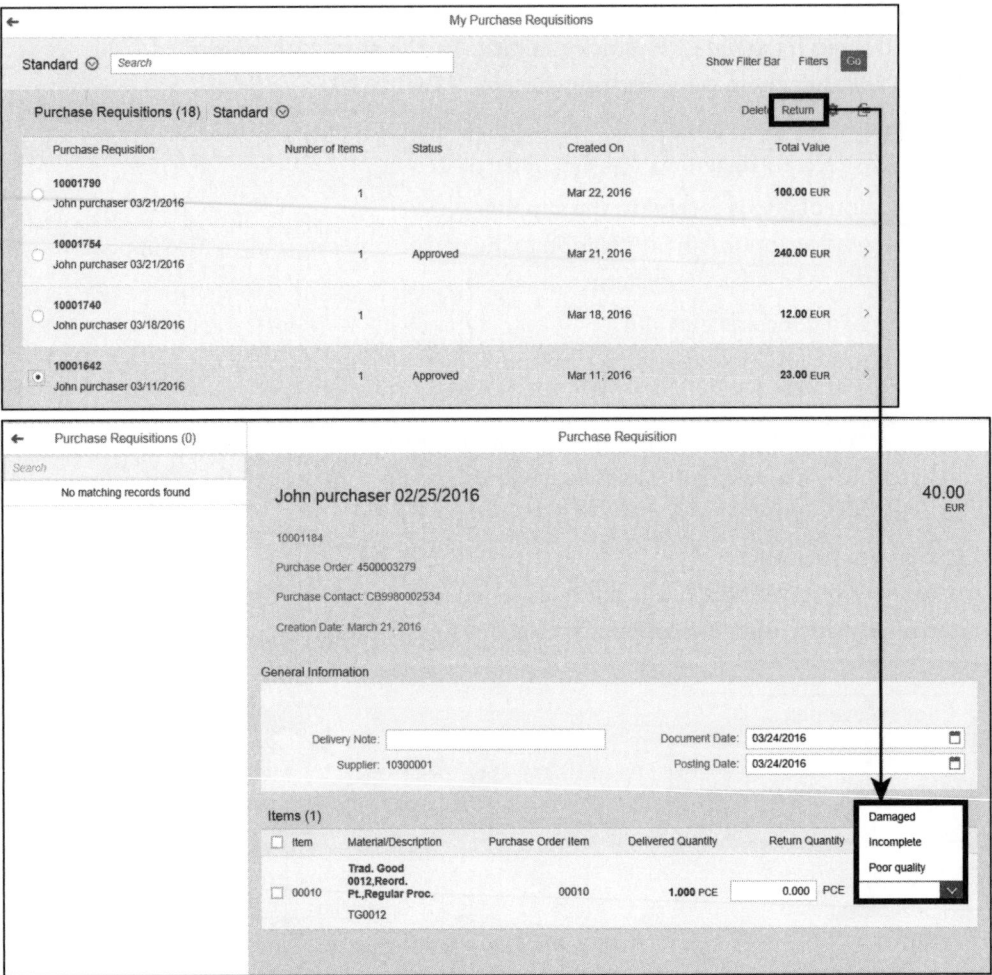

Figure 5.11 SAP S/4HANA Sourcing and Procurement Returns App

Self-service requisitioning in SAP S/4HANA provides an integrated UX for requesting, reviewing, receiving, and returning. If you lose the session during the transaction, a draft of the document you were working on when you lost connectivity is created automatically and retrieved automatically upon return. This proactive connectivity extends to other parts of the process in SAP S/4HANA as well. Instead of having to click the **Refresh** button on a list or grouping, SAP S/4HANA updates these dynamically.

5.2.3   Shopping Cart versus Requisition-to-Pay and Migrating SAP SRM Shopping Carts

Shopping carts are essentially requisitions with a more user-friendly name and, hopefully, UI. The term was first used at SAP for SAP SRM, but it's now used in SAP S/4HANA requisitions, as outlined earlier. Any requisition processes that begin to rival a consumer UX in their simplicity and usability will typically take the label *shopping cart processes*.

5.2.4   Migrating SAP SRM Shopping Carts to SAP S/4HANA

We reviewed the shopping cart/requisitioning process in SAP S/4HANA at the beginning of this chapter, but there's also a shopping cart concept in SAP SRM. Much of SAP SRM's shopping cart functionality and simplification has been replicated in SAP S/4HANA. Many SAP customers are evaluating their SAP SRM implementations during the move to SAP S/4HANA and finding this to be an opportune time to migrate from SAP SRM, given the new, streamlined functionality available in the SAP S/4HANA core and in the SAP Cloud solutions available today. This section covers the conversion process at a high level from SAP SRM shopping carts to SAP S/4HANA.

SAP SRM functionality has been built out substantially in SAP S/4HANA Sourcing and Procurement for the self-service procurement scenario. In addition, running SAP SRM in the one-client scenario embedded within SAP S/4HANA is not an option like it was with SAP ERP. In a one-client SAP SRM scenario, your options for moving to SAP S/4HANA are to reimplement SAP SRM and connect it to SAP S/4HANA either in the classic or extended classic scenario (see Table 5.1). You can also reimplement in a standalone scenario, but this isn't typical if you already have finance running in SAP ERP.

SAP SRM Deployment Option	Classic	Extended Classic
Multiple SAP backends	Migration optional (restrictions apply)	Migration optional (restrictions apply)
Single SAP ERP backend	Migration optional	Migration optional (restrictions apply)
One client	Migration (or reimplementation on different SAP SRM scenario, such as classic) mandatory	N/A

Table 5.1 SAP SRM Deployment Scenarios and SAP S/4HANA

The other option is to use this SAP S/4HANA transition to migrate your SAP SRM users and open documents into SAP S/4HANA. SAP provides informational SAP Note 225146 for this approach.

The first step is to complete your configuration and the setup of the self-service procurement scenario in SAP S/4HANA Sourcing and Procurement (as we'll discuss in Section 5.5). Prior to shutting down your SAP SRM environment, you would then run Report BBP_SC_MIGRATE_TO_PR in SAP SRM. You can migrate shopping carts prior to your system conversion to SAP S/4HANA, during the conversion, or before *and* during the conversion. However, the shopping cart migration report can be run multiple times as needed, so long as SAP SRM is still up and running. This means that for a one-client SAP SRM scenario with SAP ERP, the report has to run before the conversion, because SAP SRM won't be available once the conversion begins. You can define which migration scenario you'll use during system conversion from SAP ERP/SAP SRM to SAP S/4HANA by using Report BBP_MIGRATE_SCEN in SAP SRM.

After running the report, run follow-on Report MMPUR_MIGR_EBAN in SAP S/4HANA. After this step, you can access a former SAP SRM shopping cart in SAP S/4HANA as a requisition in the self-service procurement process you have established in SAP S/4HANA and process this item further. Associated purchase orders in SAP S/4HANA also will have a linkage to the requisition created during the conversion of the shopping cart. Any PO information that wasn't transmitted to SAP ERP by the time of conversion will be unavailable in the new environment. Errors in processing shopping carts, for example, which failed to create a follow-on PO in SAP ERP, won't convert without the error being resolved first. These reports don't convert any of the SAP SRM workflows and customizations surrounding these shopping carts, and there may be manual steps to perform once the conversion is complete to process these shopping carts in SAP S/4HANA. Currently, these migration reports and approaches only apply to shopping carts. Any documents created in SAP SRM such as contracts, purchase orders, or receipts that haven't been transferred to SAP ERP at the time of conversion won't migrate automatically to SAP S/4HANA during the conversion. As with all conversions, the best approach is to close out as many open documents as possible prior to the conversion so as to convert the smallest number of open documents possible.

5.2.5   Workflow

SAP S/4HANA offers individual approval workflow apps for various procurement objects. These workflow apps rely on preconfigured release strategy procedures and business workflows. However, SAP S/4HANA also offers a generic workflow inbox that provides a holistic view across all workflow items. This inbox can be accessed in an application directly or via a mobile app and filtered/sorted to prioritize workflow items. Individual workflow items can be sorted and worked on in one screen while viewing the queue (see Figure 5.12). The SAP S/4HANA workflow introduces the following improvements from previous SAP ERP versions:

- Execute all tasks in one screen
- Keep work items list while processing single work item
- Mobile approval possible
- Filter and sort list of work items
- Edit requisitions during approval (on-premise 1909)

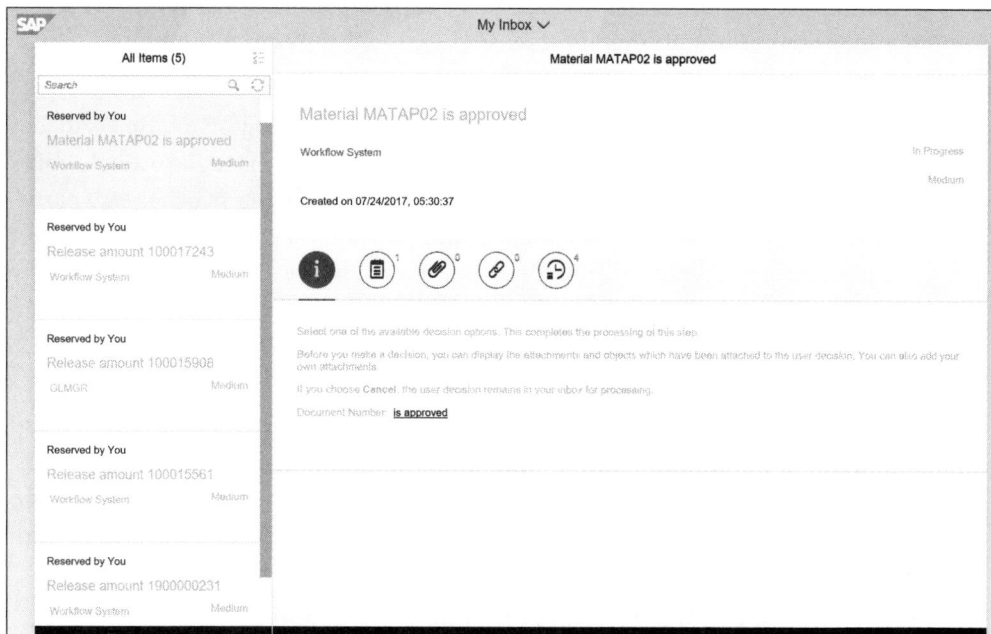

Figure 5.12 Workflow Inbox in SAP S/4HANA

As of SAP S/4HANA on-premise 1909, there is also a new app called **Manage Workflow for Purchase Requisitions—New**. This app enables the user to simulate workflow for purchase requisitions, as well as add deadlines and identify workflows that are past due.

5.2.6   Machine Learning-Based Purchasing Functionality via SAP Cloud Platform and SAP Leonardo

Machine learning has been described as a data-driven process of discovery, where instead of forming a hypothesis and then examining the data to find supporting patterns, a machine analyzes the data first and derives patterns and, ultimately, hypotheses from this data organically. One of the most exciting areas of innovation for SAP S/4HANA Sourcing and Procurement is driven by machine-learning capabilities in SAP Leonardo on the SAP Cloud Platform. SAP Leonardo is an integrated system of software and services focused on intelligent technologies, with SAP Cloud Platform providing the PaaS infrastructure foundation. The next sections will detail these machine-learning, SAP Leonardo-based capabilities in SAP S/4HANA, with further configuration steps outlined in Section 5.7. Now we'll discuss some of the key machine-learning functionality supported by SAP Leonardo in SAP S/4HANA Sourcing and Procurement via this approach:

- **Image-based buying**
  Image based buying identifies related images in a catalog or multiple catalogs linked via cross-catalog search to provide recommendations to the user of similar items based on the current selection. For example, if the user searches for a particular part, provided there is an image of this part, another similar or identical part can be displayed in the recommendations. At its most evolved, this functionality could allow for a scan of an image to then locate similar items in the catalog, without the user having to enter the metadata (name, description, etc.) in the search.

- **Intelligent approval workflow**
  An intelligent approval workflow analyzes approval pattern history for requisitions based on price, source of supply, material group, approvers, value thresholds, and other data points, identifying requisitions en mass, meaning the approver can approve a group of suggested requisitions without individual review, and/or automated approval, whereby approvals occur without human intervention.

- **Predictive analytics for contract consumption in procurement**
  A purchaser can train a predictive model using this functionality to review purchase orders, expiring contracts, historical purchasing data, and contract consumption based on historical contract usage to derive a more accurate picture for advanced planning and contract negotiations.

- **Proposal of new catalog item or material group**
  During creation of a free text item in a requisition, the system can propose a catalog item and/or a material group based on previous system usage.

For any of these machine-learning features, you'll need to configure the connections to SAP Cloud Platform and SAP Leonardo and subscribe to the procurement assistant. This functionality also requires SAP S/4HANA batch processes to load data into SAP Leonardo for analysis, with the insights then being sent back to SAP S/4HANA via the procurement assistant functionality.

5.3   Requirements Processing in SAP S/4HANA Sourcing and Procurement

Requirements processing (Figure 5.13) refers to the buyer activity of sorting through various requirements in need of adjustments and/or sources of supply. The main thrust in most procurement organizations is to focus requirements-processing activities on the more strategic procurement items and to automate, using intuitive designs, workflows, and catalog content, to create touchless, issue-ready purchase orders.

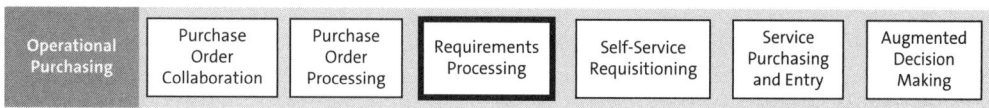

Figure 5.13 Requirements Processing

Once a requisition is created, depending upon the workflow settings in the system, the requisition either is sent for approval or, if under the workflow thresholds for a given value, can be converted directly to a PO. The requisition then goes into a buyer's queue for sourcing if it contains a descriptive item or is converted to a PO directly by the buyer or automatically via a batch process if it contains only catalog items. A buyer typically takes the order from here, using one of the following SAP S/4HANA apps (see Figure 5.14) to convert the requisition to a PO:

- Automatic Creation of Purchase Orders from Requisition
- Assign and Process Purchase Requisition
- Create Purchase Order via Purchase Requisition
- Release Reminder Purchase Requisition
- Manage Purchase Requisitions—Professional

With the Automatic Creation of Purchase Orders from Requisitions app (see Figure 5.15), the buyer can begin converting sourced requisitions en masse to POs.

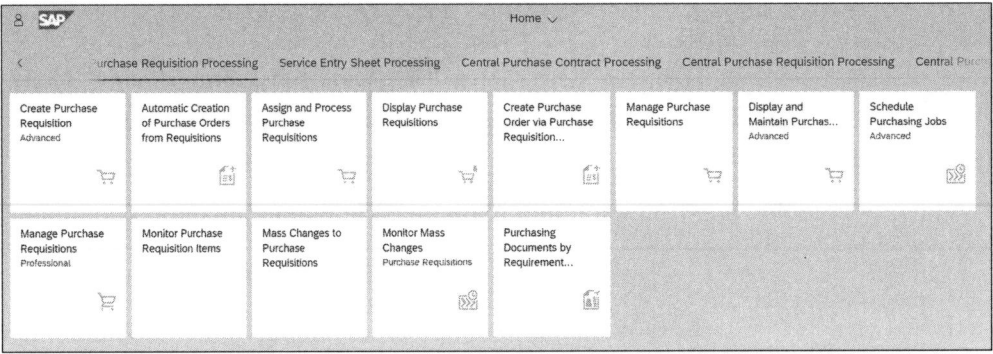

Figure 5.14 Purchase Requisition Processing

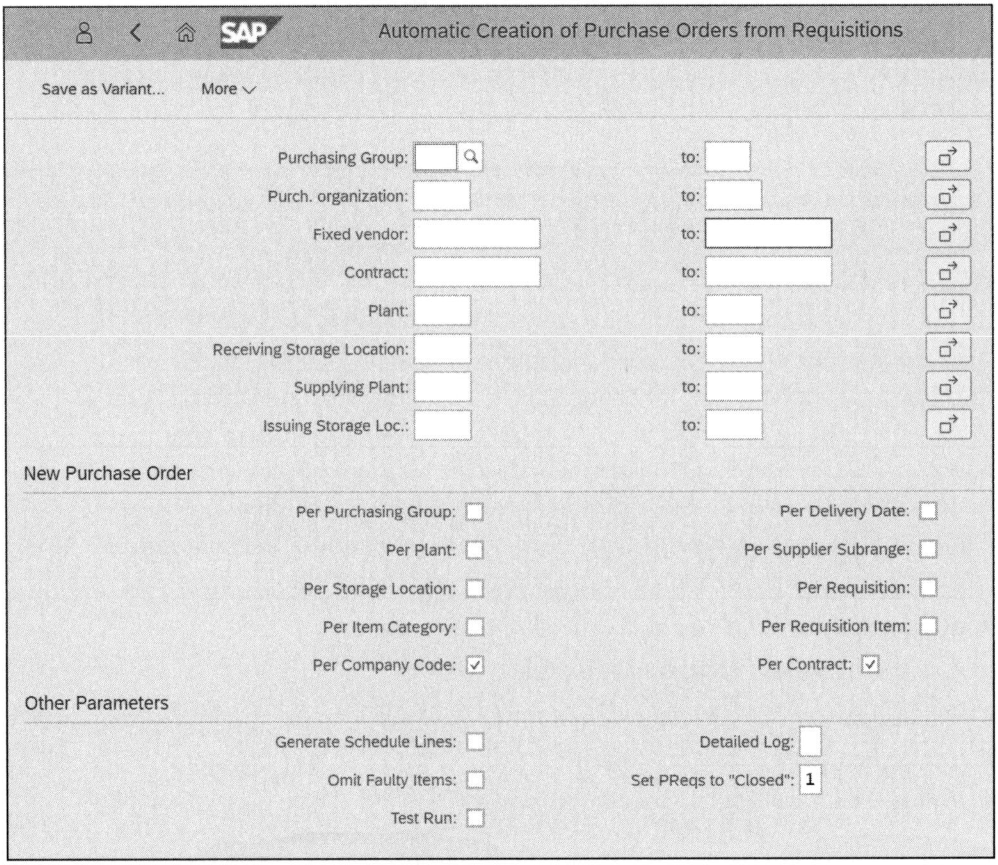

Figure 5.15 Automatic Creation of Purchase Orders from Requisitions

After selecting various criteria (here, **Per Company Code** and **Per Contract**), the buyer then executes the job to create purchase orders from all the available and completed requisitions matching the chosen criteria.

Traditionally in SAP ERP, a buyer has to run a search using selection criteria, review the list and manually check for sources, assign the supplier, and then move the order into a batch queue. The batch job is then run either at a set interval or manually to create an actual purchase order. The requirements processing area is streamlined in SAP S/4HANA to one screen, with prebuilt search criteria that pull in all requisitions. The options allow the buyer to dynamically change the search criteria; generate proposed sources of supply automatically based on PIRs, source lists, or contracts/agreements; and then enter direct creation of the purchase order once the source of supply has been defined—all from one screen, as shown in Figure 5.16.

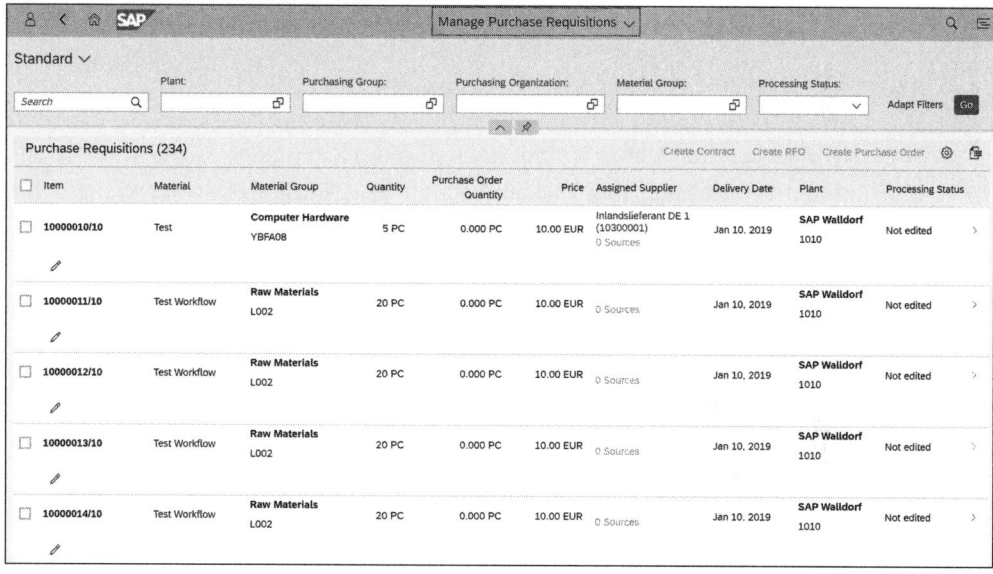

Figure 5.16 Manage Purchase Requisitions

Requirements processing in SAP S/4HANA has the following improvements compared to previous versions of SAP ERP:

- Dynamic search and filtering and automatic proposal of search help values
- Ability to change search parameters easily in the same screen
- Automatic proposal of available info records or agreements
- Direct creation of purchase orders

If a buyer wishes to drill into any particular requisition, simply clicking a link takes him into the header of the requisition. Rather than inundating the user with a bunch of tabs and tangential information, the revised screen focuses on the essentials of item, quantity, price, material group, plant, and delivery date. If further information is required, the user can drill further into the line-item levels (see Figure 5.17). Here, **General Information**, **Quantity Date**, **Valuation**, **Account Assignment**, **Source of Supply**, **Status**, **Contact Person**, **Notes**, and **Delivery Address** links move you down the page to the applicable information area without needing to open a new tab.

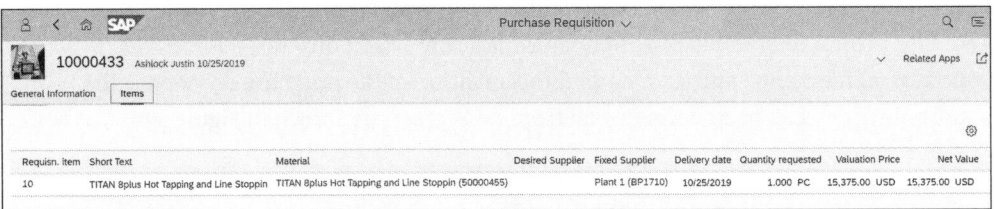

Figure 5.17 Line-Item Details in SAP S/4HANA Requisition

A buyer also has the option to create an additional purchase requisition in the Requirements Processing app. This allows a buyer to jump from the Requirements Processing app to create a new requisition and then resume work in the Requirements Processing app seamlessly.

Next, let's discuss processing purchase orders directly in SAP S/4HANA.

5.4   Purchase Order Processing

Traditionally, purchase order creation and processing in SAP ERP (see Figure 5.18) involves entering numerous data points in the purchase order form, checking the document, identifying errors and further required data, tracking this missing data down, entering it and then checking again, and finally, when the document shows no further error messages, ordering. Another approach is to convert a requisition or use an existing purchase order as a template. Here too, any errors identified have to be researched and corrected prior to issuing the purchase order.

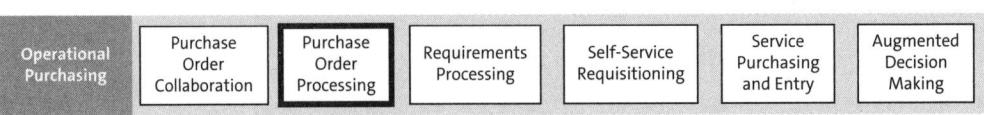

Figure 5.18 SAP S/4HANA Sourcing and Procurement Purchase Order Processing

Purchase order processing in SAP S/4HANA has been updated: there's now a centralized screen that allows for drilling down into further detail of items sequenced based on data relevance, as well as automatic population of required fields based on the materials, suppliers, and templates selected. Possible field entries are also restricted in SAP S/4HANA during the PO process. This reduces the time spent chasing down errors and entering associated data and ultimately accelerates the timeline from initiation to completion. As Figure 5.19 shows, the Create Purchase Order app in SAP S/4HANA allows the user to focus on the important and mandatory fields in the purchase order while providing tabs for the more detailed areas of the document. The top part of the screen provides the PO header information, the middle shows the items, and the bottom shows the item details.

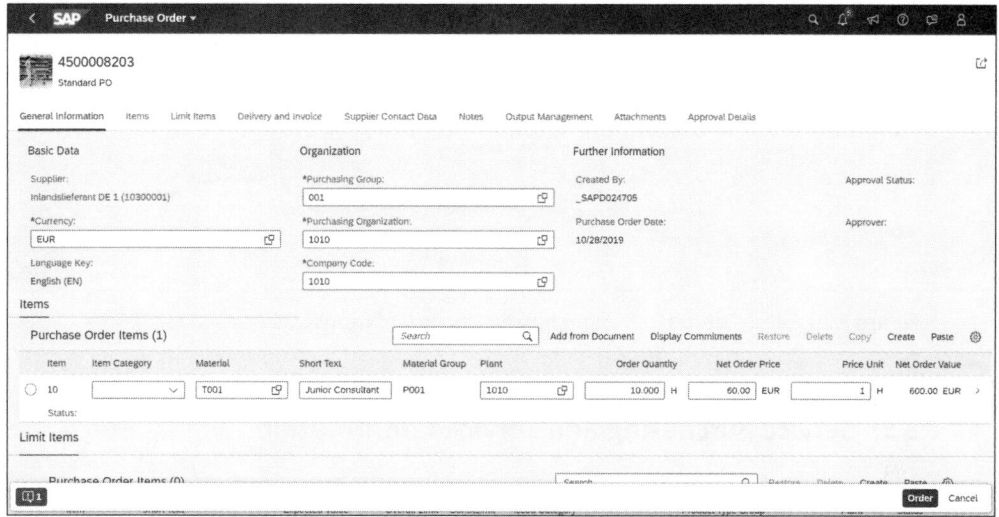

Figure 5.19 Purchase Order Header in SAP S/4HANA Sourcing and Procurement

Additional filter criteria are available in **Procurement Overview**, allowing for specifying **Purchasing Organization**, **Material**, **Material Group**, **Display Currency**, **Supplier**, **Purchasing Category,** and **Purchasing Group** as shown in Figure 5.20.

Other feature updates to the PO processing area of SAP S/4HANA Sourcing and Procurement include incoterms, short text change options, and attachments. *Incoterms* refers to payment, delivery, and other terms that define when the obligation and risk shift from supplier to customer during the transfer of goods/services. Incoterm specifications are now available at both the header and the item level. This means that if one item in a purchase order should require different incoterms than the rest, you can set this at the item level. You can also change the short text on a PO, which was previously not an option. Attachments to an SAP S/4HANA purchase order can be accessed from all of the purchase order apps in SAP S/4HANA Sourcing and Procurement.

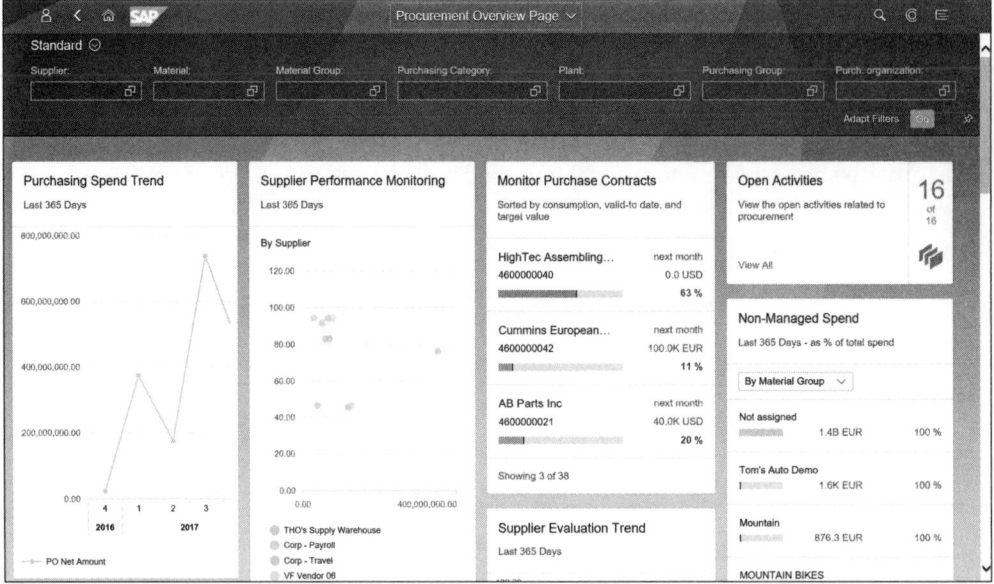

Figure 5.20 Filter Criteria in My Purchasing Document Items

5.5   Service Purchasing and Service Confirmation

Service purchasing in Figure 5.21 doesn't refer solely to SAP S/4HANA Sourcing and Procurement functionality in this process. Although the user still has services procurement capabilities similar to those used when purchasing a material in SAP S/4HANA Sourcing and Procurement, there is also SAP Fieldglass integration. SAP Fieldglass is a cloud-based vendor-management system (VMS) used to manage services procurement and external workforce programs. For external service procurement and service-supplier management, SAP Fieldglass invoices are integrated as of SAP S/4HANA 1610, and further integration is planned in later releases of SAP S/4HANA.

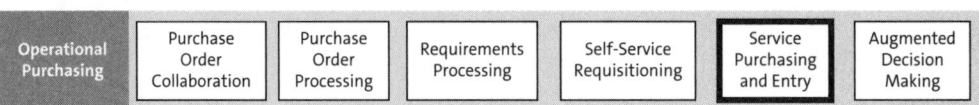

Figure 5.21 Service Purchasing and Entry

As of SAP S/4HANA 1709, further improvements to the service procurement capabilities within the SAP S/4HANA core include simplified service procurement, with SAP Fiori apps for Service Entry Sheet and Service Confirmation (see Figure 5.22).

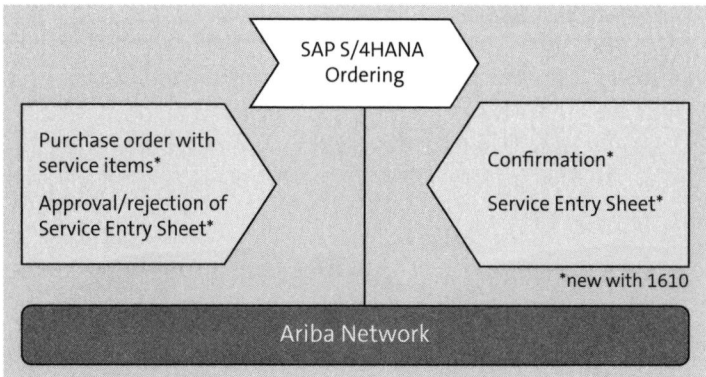

Figure 5.22 Ariba Network Integration with SAP S/4HANA Sourcing and Procurement: Services

5.6 Purchase Order Collaboration

Upon creation of a PO, the PO can be issued to a supplier via the Ariba Network and/or via EDI, email, fax, or other transmission methods supported in SAP S/4HANA. Suppliers often connect to the Ariba Network and use this as an integration layer to receive their purchase orders directly into their systems via their EDI linkage, rather than setting up a point-to-point EDI integration going out to the network to process these orders.

As mentioned in Chapter 1, PO collaboration is not something that can be done adequately in SAP ERP or even in SAP S/4HANA alone; an interaction between supplier and buyer needs to take place, and documents need to be exchanged without compromising the security of the core SAP ERP environment. Point-to-point solutions such as supplier self-services suffer from the maintenance aspects and training/change management required for the supplier base. The point-to-point model doesn't scale well, as each additional supplier represents additional calls and emails to the help desk, all of which are the onus of the buyer's organization. And yet, for a point-to-point solution to be economical, it has to scale to encompass many suppliers and high spending. This is where a network like the Ariba Network can take over the heavy lifting aspects of infrastructure, supplier onboarding, and support and allow the buyer to focus on the value-added activities within collaboration.

The Ariba Network is the main approach for true PO collaboration, as it allows the supplier to receive and work with the purchase order, confirming items or proposing changes to delivery dates and potential quantities. SAP S/4HANA provides out-of-the-box integration with the Ariba Network. The Ariba Network handles well over $1 trillion in annual transactions among millions of participants. Invoicing will be covered in Chapter 11, but for now note that PO collaboration is covered with this integration to the Ariba Network, as well via traditional processes of document exchange such as email, fax, and EDI.

Note

SAP S/4HANA Cloud offers best practices for integration with the Ariba Network, which differs slightly from the on-premise standard integration and includes more documents from the invoice/payment part of the process. There are also further best practice integration points with SAP Ariba Strategic Sourcing, which will be detailed further in Chapter 9.

This best practice approach for SAP S/4HANA Cloud integrations also includes invoice documents from SAP Fieldglass.

5.7   Configuring Operational Procurement

This section outlines the general configuration steps required to set up self-service operational procurement processes in SAP S/4HANA Sourcing and Procurement. As discussed earlier, self-service procurement can be used for stock items, consumables, and or external services. For stock items and services, this same baseline configuration for self-service procurement can support these scenarios to a degree. Stock items also require a material master, which is discussed in more detail in Chapter 4 and Chapter 6.

5.7.1   Self-Service Procurement Requisitioning

As with all configuration guides, this section is to be used as a reference to support your particular requirements and project. Prior to beginning configuration, you should always ensure you have researched the latest configuration and version-level guidance online and verified that you have met the requirements to begin configuration.

Also, note that traditional workflow, report, interface, conversion, enhancement, and form (WRICEF) objects are beyond the scope of this configuration section and book in general; these are project-specific and typically require some development to realize. For the baseline configuration of the self-service procurement scenario, the steps are as follows in SAP S/4HANA:

1. Create employee data. For a user to access the appropriate areas of the organization structure and system functionality for self-service procurement, you must first create an employee record and assign it in the organization structure.

   In SAP Human Capital Management for SAP S/4HANA, an employee record is comprised of *infotypes*, information units used to store specific employee master data. To create an employee, use Transaction PA30. For procurement activities, Infotypes 0001 (organizational assignment) and 0105 (system user name and communication information, such as email and address) are mandatory.

2. Create an assignment (position) for the employee in the organization structure via Transaction PPOMA.

3. Assign a business partner to the position. BP BUP003 is the employee business partner role.

4. Maintain attributes mandatory for procurement activities as per Table 5.2.

Mandatory Attributes	Default Value
Document Type: Can be configured in customizing under IMG menu path **Materials Management • Purchasing • Purchase Requisition • Define Document Types**	BSART
Company Code	BURKS
Cost Center	COSTCENTER
Catalog: Allows the employee to access predefined catalogs	CATALOG
Purchasing Organization	EKORG
Purchasing Group	RESPPGRP
Account Assignment Category: Asset, Cost Center, Sales Order, Order and **Network** are supported	KNTTP
Material Group	MATKL

Table 5.2 Mandatory Procurement Activity Attributes

Mandatory Attributes	Default Value
Currency	WAERS
Plant	WERKS

Table 5.2 Mandatory Procurement Activity Attributes (Cont.)

Catalogs

Catalog options in SAP S/4HANA include punchout catalogs, in which a user clicks on the catalog link and accesses a catalog outside of the SAP S/4HANA system, selects an item or items, and then returns with the items to the shopping cart. There is also an internal search bar within the SAP S/4HANA requisitioning app, which allows for searching for available internal catalog items within SAP S/4HANA. A user can also search across catalog data in this search bar from multiple catalogs, provided the catalog data has been loaded in the SAP S/4HANA system. Finally, there is a consulting solution from SAP Consulting Delivery called the *lean catalog*, which enables a more extensive internal catalog.

Punchout Catalogs

To set up a punchout catalog, you need to configure the webservice to access the catalog. To create a catalog link (webservice), go to **Materials Management • Purchasing • Environment Data • Web Services: ID and Description**. For typical webservice configuration values, see Table 5.3.

Sequence Number	Name of Parameter for Webservice	Value of Parameter for Webservice
10		https://s1.ariba.com/Buyer/Main/ad/contentPunchin/OCIPunchinDirectAction
20	PunchinId	NAME/USER ID
30	PunchinPassword	PASSWORD
40	Realm	APCProduction-T
50	Full Name	S4 HANA Catalog
50	UniqueName	S4HANA
	EmailAddress	EMAIL ADDRESS

Table 5.3 Webservice Configuration Values

Sequence Number	Name of Parameter for Webservice	Value of Parameter for Webservice
60	DefaultCurrency	USD
70	UserLocate	US
80	ModifyURL	FALSE
90	User.Address.UniqueN	OCI_DEFAULT
100	Hook_URL	Return URL

Table 5.3 Webservice Configuration Values (Cont.)

SAP S/4HANA requires a *hook URL* to be maintained with the type set as Return URL. If you wish to keep some parameters secure from catalog vendors, you can leverage the MMPUR_OCI_PARAMETERS BAdI.

Internal Catalog

To create and/or manage items in the internal catalog within SAP S/4HANA, go to the Manage Catalog Items app, select **+**, and enter the item data as in Figure 5.23.

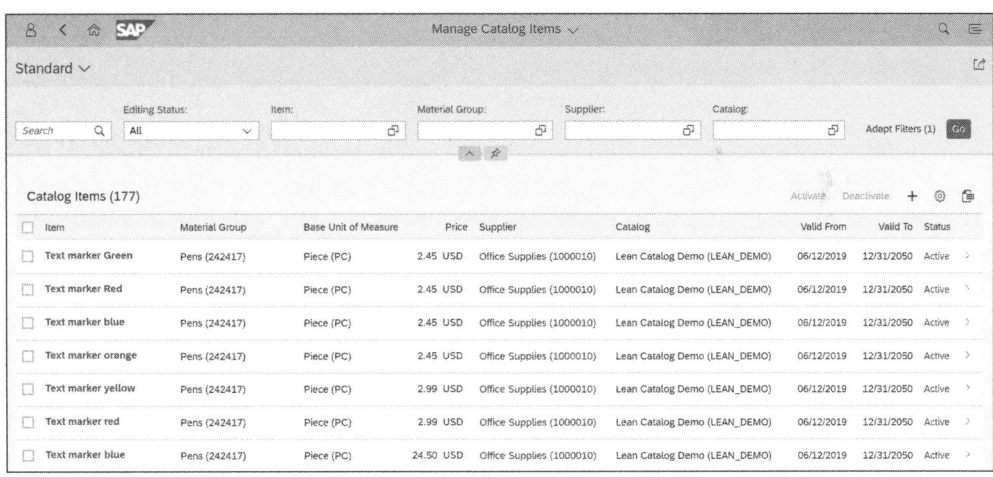

Figure 5.23 Manage Catalog Items

As in the new item screen in Figure 5.24, you can then enter detailed information on the item, including organization structure and lead times, as well as reference an image.

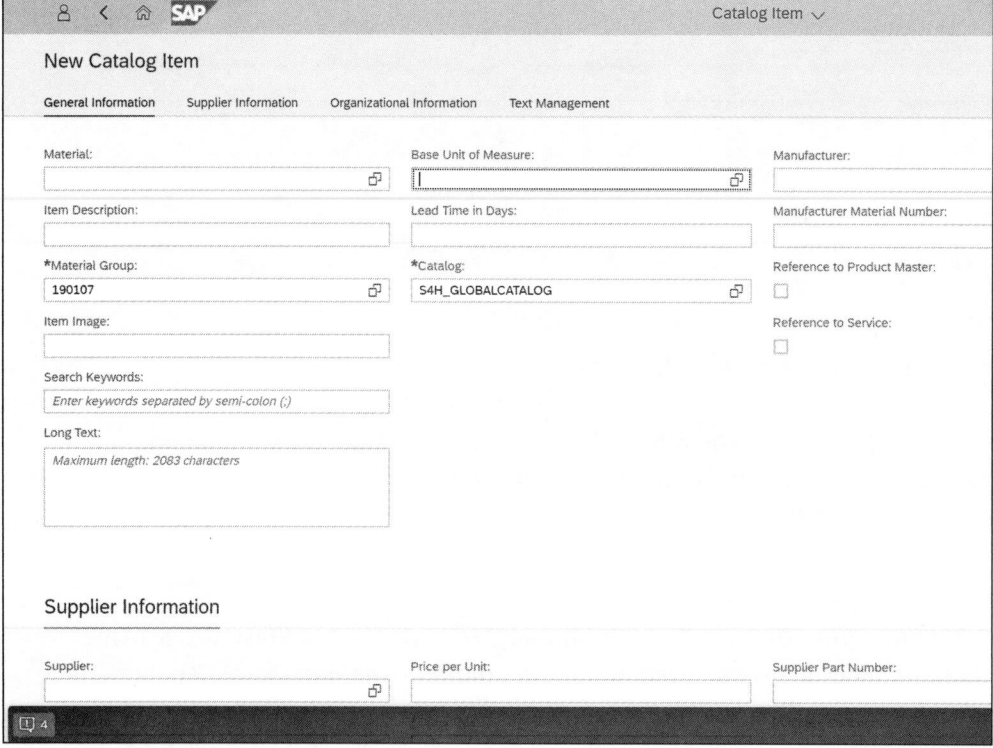

Figure 5.24 New Catalog Item

Lean Catalog

The lean catalog is a consulting solution from SAP Delivery that consists of the following:

- A web application for product searches and selection
- An editing cockpit for creating your catalog product range
- Supplier material as a new business object to store supplier content
- An import manager for importing catalog items from files delivered by your suppliers
- A product relation tool to manage any kind of linkages between your SAP materials, supplier materials, or a mixture of both

The lean catalog leverages Open Catalog Interface (OCI) or the cross-catalog search capabilities in SAP S/4HANA, detailed in the next section, to allow for detailed search and selection of catalog items. You can search for products using a keyword search, a hierarchical search, or an advanced search as in Figure 5.25.

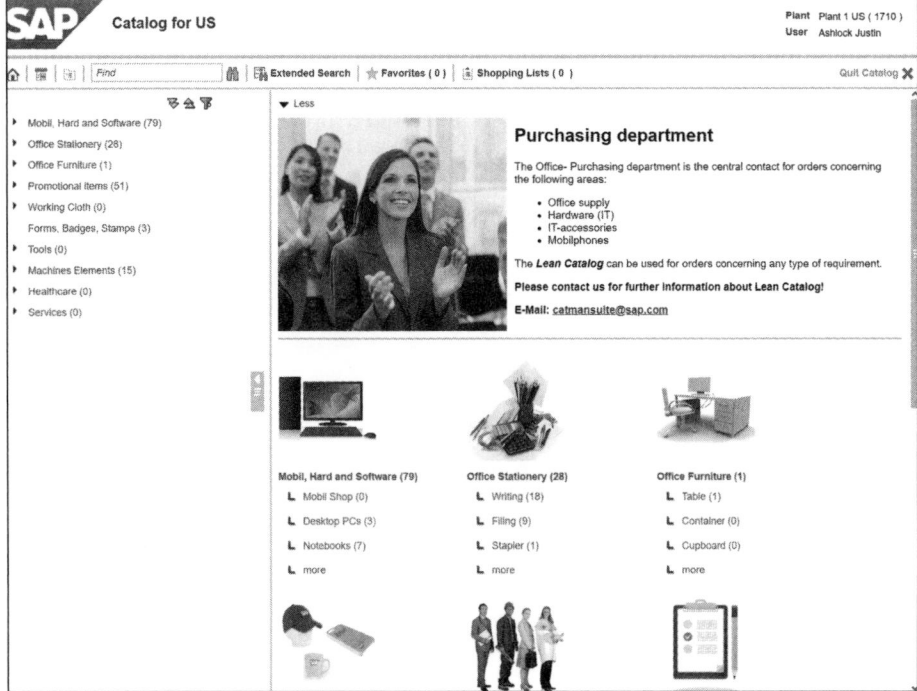

Figure 5.25 Lean Catalog

Cross-Catalog Search

SAP S/4HANA now allows for cross-catalog search in the **Search** bar of the Create Requisitions app without going into each individual catalog. If you plan to use this functionality, there are some setup steps required.

As prerequisites, verify that catalog data is available in OCI 5.0 format and that your catalog suppliers can provide this as a JSON file or through an HTTP service. Catalogs and their corresponding webservice IDs, as well as content management services (CMSs; for loading images and attachments), must be set up and configured in the system.

To set up cross-catalog search, complete the following steps:

1. Replicate catalog data and any required material master data to materials management staging tables.

2. Index the data for cross-catalog search.

3. Define number ranges for catalog items by entering "01" as the catalog item number range. Follow IMG menu path **Materials Management • Purchasing • Purchase Requisition • Self Service Procurement • Define Number Ranges for Catalog Items**.

4. Enter a number range for search items. Follow IMG menu path **Materials Management • Purchasing • Purchase Requisition • Self Service Procurement • Define Number Ranges for Search Items**. Enter "01" as the attachment key number range for MMPUR_ATT.

5. Maintain a common **Currency** to enable a price filter on items. Follow IMG menu path **Materials Management • Purchasing • Purchase Requisition • Self Service Procurement • Define Settings for Cross Catalog Search** as per Figure 5.26.

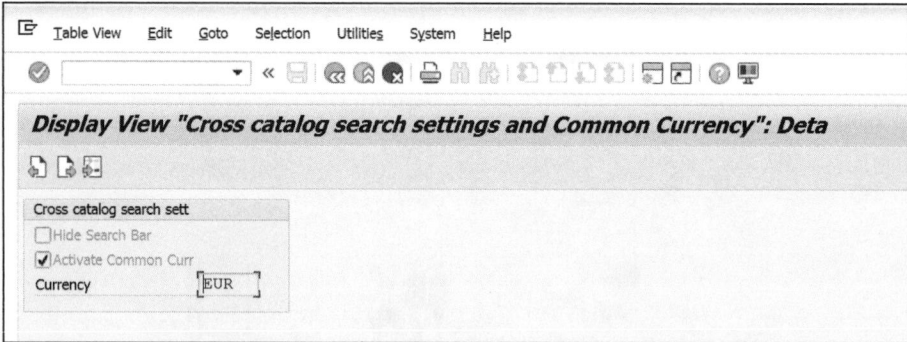

Figure 5.26 Cross-Catalog Search Settings

> **Note**
>
> After the data is extracted, if you change this setting to another common currency, you'll need to re-index and run Program MM_PUR_CTLG_EXT_COM_CUR_UPD. Also, if you elect to hide the search bar, you will prevent users from accessing the internal SAP S/4HANA catalog in the Create Requisition App, as they will not be able to search.

6. If you've enabled catalogs using OCI 4.0, you'll have to activate the ICF service OCI_ CATALOG using Transaction SICF. To do so, first select menu option **Service • Host**, then select **Activate Service**. Second, ensure that every node path is set to active in /SAP/BC/REST/SAP/OCI_CATALOG. For more information, check SAP Note 2376996.

7. Maintain additional attributes for catalogs. You can control whether a catalog is visible and whether it is used for OCI 5.0 extraction by following IMG menu path

Materials Management • Purchasing • Purchase Requisition • Self Service Procurement • Define Additional Attributes for Product Catalog Categories. Enter a webservice and maintain the attributes. Select the **Don't Show** checkbox if you don't wish to display the catalog. Select the **OCI Extraction** checkbox if you want to import data from this catalog using the catalog data import (see Figure 5.27).

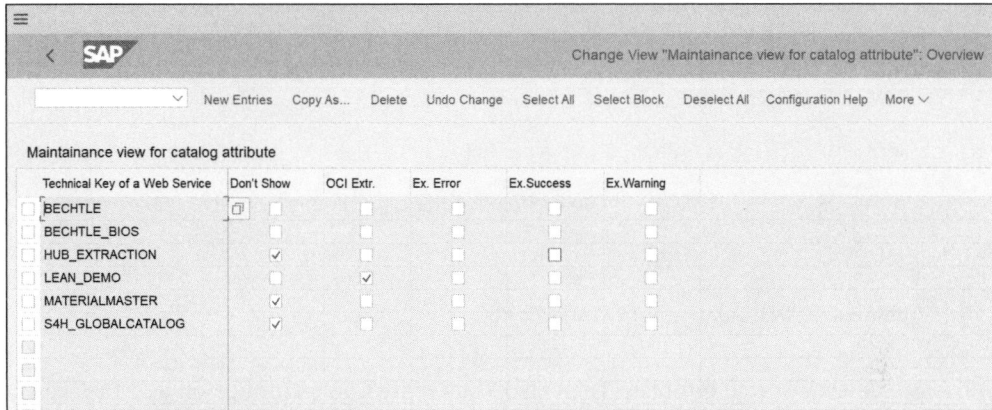

Figure 5.27 Maintaining Catalog Attributes for Display and OCI Extraction

8. Indexing and embedded search configuration is typically conducted by a technical resource with SAP Basis–level access to the system. Embedded search in SAP S/4HANA Sourcing and Procurement leverages SAP NetWeaver Enterprise Search, a search solution providing unified and secure real-time access to enterprise data and data from within and outside of an organization. SAP NetWeaver Enterprise Search returns data from SAP systems and other search providers and allows direct access to the associated applications and actions. Embedded search is the Enterprise Search component for SAP NetWeaver Application Server (AS) ABAP and serves as the search platform using the SAP HANA engine, connecting via RFC destinations, URLs, and/or repository addresses to outside search providers and data sources. Refer to SAP Note 1164979 and *help.sap.com* for configuration guidelines. For selfservice requisitioning, SAP NetWeaver Enterprise Search includes business templates and indexes via search object connectors to enable search and access of both supplier catalogs and material master data from materials management.

9. For search templates, the SAP S/4HANA administrator needs to create one search template for each business connector, which then delivers the result data in a predefined form as per the attributes in the template. These templates are not delivered by default in an SAP S/4HANA environment and require activation on the

admin's part. You can mass-activate search templates using Transaction ESH_ COCKPIT. To do so, select **Switch to Modeler** and go to the software component MM-PUR-REQ. Under this component you will find the templates listed in Table 5.4.

Search Template	Description
MM_PUR_CTLG_SRH	Search results model (catalog item data)
MM_PUR_CTLG_ATTCH	Images and attachments
MM_PUR_CTLG_ATTRB	Attributes
MM_PUR_CTLG_CUST_FLD	Customer fields
MM_PUR_CTLG_PRC_CON	Converted price data (prices in different exchange rates)
MM_PUR_CTLG_SRCHTRM	Search terms

Table 5.4 Search Templates in MM-PUR-REQ

10. Select a search template, then click the **Create Connector** button and the search object connector will be created.

Importing Catalog Data and Images

Cross-catalog search is enabled in SAP S/4HANA by importing and syndicating data from catalog items and material masters into a single repository of SAP S/4HANA tables for search, indexing the data, and then leveraging embedded search APIs to drive the item search queries. For more information on the tables, see package VDM_ MM_PUR_CATALOG. Table 5.5 lists the associated key tables.

Table	Description
MMPUR_CAT_ITM	Main data for catalog items
MMPUR_CAT_PRCONV	Price converted to common currency
MMPUR_CAT_LNGTXT	Long text
MMPUR_CAT_DSCTXT	Description
MMPUR_CAT_PRCSCL	Price scales
MMPUR_CAT_ITM_SRH	Search items description

Table 5.5 MMPUR_CAT Tables

Table	Description
MMPUR_CAT_MGPTXT	Material group text
MMPUR_CAT_ATMAIN	Attachments main
MMPUR_CAT_ATTCHM	Attachments
MMPUR_CAT_ATTHMB	Thumbnail attachment
MMPUR_CAT_ATHTXT	Attachment text
MMPUR_CAT_ATTRB	Attributes for catalog items

Table 5.5 MMPUR_CAT Tables (Cont.)

Figure 5.28 shows the steps involved in preparing data for cross-catalog search.

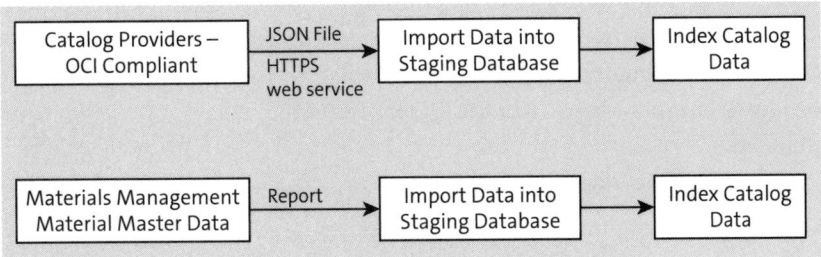

Figure 5.28 Preparation for Cross-Catalog Search in SAP S/4HANA

Open catalog interface-compliant (OCI) data maintained by catalog providers can be imported as a Java Script Object Notation (JSON) file or HTTPS webservice, while material master data can be extracted using reports. Starting with OCI 5.0, multiple customer fields are supported for import. You can maintain the customer fields in INCLUDE structure MMPUR_CA_INCL_CAT_ITM of table MMPUR_CAT_ITM.

The CMS must be configured to extract and store images in an SAP S/4HANA catalog scenario. This is cross-client configuration and requires appropriate authorization. The content management repository is MMPUR_CAT_CONTENT and the contents are maintained in table MMPUR_CAT_CNTNT. Follow these steps to maintain a physical storage path and the HTTPS requirement for loading images:

1. Follow IMG menu path **SAP NetWeaver • Knowledge Management • Settings in Knowledge Warehouse System • Content Management Service • Define Content Repositories**.

2. In the **Content Repository** field, select **MMPUR_CAT_CONTENT** and click **Edit**.

3. In the **Phys. Path** field, enter the physical path determined for storing the files in your system landscape, then select the HTTPS requirement in the fields for both the frontend and backend.

4. The ABAP server or other servers hosting images need to be configured in the web dispatcher. The system administrator needs to configure the system in such a way that any URL containing the term *imageloader* should be redirected to where the images are loaded. For importing OCI 5.0–compliant catalogs via JSON or a report/ webservice approach, you must have the MMPUR_CAT_CONTENT_MGMT role assigned.

Import JSON File

To import a file via JSON, follow these steps:

1. Add the catalog webservice ID or existing catalog webservice ID and select **Import Action Applicable File**. In the **Import File/URL** field, provide the path of the file to be imported. Select the **Import Image** checkbox if images are to be imported. In the **Image Folder** field, enter the path for the folder containing images. Click the **Schedule Job** button.

2. Define the start time for the load to begin, then execute it.

Import Catalog via Webservice

To import a catalog via a webservice, follow these steps:

1. Enter Transaction MMPUR_CAT_EXT or the Schedule Import of Catalog Data app and click **Add a New Job**. A new job screen appears as in Figure 5.29.

2. Add the catalog webservice ID or existing catalog webservice ID and select **Import Action Applicable HTTP/HTTPS**. Provide the **URL**, **User Name**, and **Password** to be imported. You can also provide a transaction ID and requested page if you want to resume a stalled transaction.

3. Select the **Import Image** checkbox if you want to import images, and provide the folder path to the folder containing the images. If using a proxy server, BAdI MMPUR_CAT_PROXY_INFO needs to be implemented.

4. Click the **Schedule Job** button. Define the start time for the load to begin, and execute it.

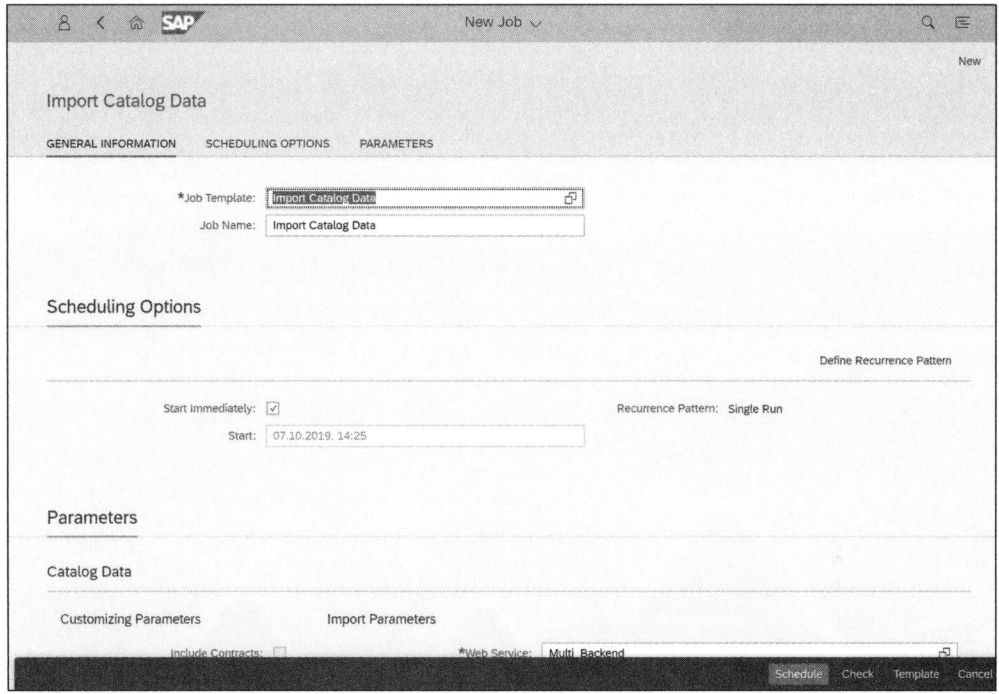

Figure 5.29 Import Catalog Data Job

5. Select the **Reschedule Delta** indicator for activating a delta import. The indicators are described further in Table 5.6.

Importing Type	Value of Indicator	Remarks
Full or initial load	**Reschedule Delta: OFF**	Use when you're importing data into a catalog the first time. All catalog items are added to tables.
Delta load	**Reschedule Delta: ON**	Use when you want to change data or add additional items to an already imported catalog.

Table 5.6 Reschedule Delta Indicators

6. Table 5.7 contains some user-exit BAdI options to support meeting requirements outside of the standard content-management capabilities in SAP S/4HANA.

SAP S/4HANA BAdI (Enhancement)	Description
MMPUR_CATALOG_ENRICH_DATA	The ENRICH_ITEM_DATA enhancement spot provides access to catalog item data, search terms, attributes, price scales, images, and customer fields.
MM_PUR_CTLG_BDI_SRH	Influence search behavior using this BAdI. Standard search behavior searches more relevant columns first and then organizes these in the results.
MMPUR_CATALOG_ENRICH_DATA	The MMPUR_CATALOG_TRANSFER enhancement spot allows items selected in a catalog to be enriched when transferring to the user's requisition in SAP S/4HANA Sourcing and Procurement.
MMPUR_CAT_PROXY_INFO	You can use the MM_PUR_CAT_PROXY_INFO enhancement spot to specify proxy server settings to access the internet.
MMPUR_CAT_CLL_ENRICH	You can use the MMPUR_CAT_CLL_ENRICH enhancement spot to transfer additional parameters to a webservice, such as a product catalog or a vendor list.
BD_MMPUR_REQ_APPR_PRV	You can use the ES_MMPUR_REQ_APPR_PRV enhancement spot to modify the approver data, such as displaying the approver name on the user interface of the My Purchase Requisition app.

Table 5.7 Available BAdIs for Influencing Purchasing in SAP S/4HANA Sourcing and Procurement

5.7.2 Machine Learning-Based Procurement Functionality

The first step in setting up machine-learning functionalities is establishing a connection to SAP Cloud Platform and SAP Leonardo from your SAP S/4HANA environment and subscribing to the procurement assistant application. For the initial steps and set up, you will require an SAP S/4HANA on-premise system (1909—or a cloud version in the 1900s or higher), system details, a system ID, a username, and a password. On the SAP Leonardo side, you will need URLs, a username and password, and a host name. You will also need the role SAP_BR_BPC_EXPERT assigned to your user to make the necessary configurations.

Enabling the Procurement Assistant in SAP Leonardo

Before obtaining the OAuth access credentials, you must enable the procurement assistant in the SAP Leonardo environment. If you have SAP S/4HANA intelligent insights procurement service already enabled in SAP Cloud Platform, you essentially have this covered. Within the SAP Cloud Platform Marketplace, find the procurement assistant (ID code `intg-pa`) and request/create a new instance of the service (standard instance). Request the service keys and note the content.

In the **Enable Communication System** section, you'll need the content of the service key and the mappings provided in Table 5.8.

Communication Settings	Location of the Service Key JSON
Host Name	serviceurls
OAuth 2.0 Endpoint	url
OAuth 2.0 Token Endpoint	url + "/oauth/token"
Username	Clientid
Password	clientsecret

Table 5.8 Enable Communication System Settings

Remote Function Call Definition

After activation of the service, the remote function call (RFC) destination needs to be created and configured in the SAP S/4HANA environment via the following steps:

1. Log on to the required SAP S/4HANA system.
2. Go to Transaction SM59 and click the **Create** button.
3. Fill in the **RFC Destination Name**, **Connection Type** (enter "G"), and **Description**.
4. Name the RFC—for example, "SCP RFC".
5. In the **Technical Settings** tab, fill the **Host** field with the URL from the machine learning service name and set the **Port** as 443 and **Path Prefix** as *ia*.
6. In the **Logon & Security** tab, select the **Do Not Use a User** option under **Logon Procedure Logon with User**.
7. In the same tab, under **Security Option Status of Secure Protocol**, select **Active** for **SSL** and **ANONYM** (anonymous) **SSL Client** for **SSL Certificate**.
8. Choose **Save**.

Create and Configure the New OAuth 2.0 Client

If you have the OAuth client 2.0 profile S4ML_PROCURE already created in the system, you can skip these steps. Otherwise, verify that your user that has the following authorizations:

- S_TCODE:TCODE = OA2C_CONFIG
- S_OA2C_ADM:ACTVT = *
- S_OA2C_USE:PROFILE = *
- ACTVT = *
- S_OA2C_USE:PROFILE = *;ACTVT = *

Then complete the following steps:

1. Open the following URL: *https://ml-us.authentication.sap.hana.ondemand.com.*
2. Press F12 and open security tab **View Certificate**. Here, click on details, copy to file, and save.
3. Download the trusted root certificate from the token endpoint.
4. Go to *https://mlus.authentication.sap.hana.ondemand.com/oauth/token.*
5. Select the trusted root certificate, such as **DigiCert Global Root CA**.
6. Export the trusted root certificate into a file.
7. Enter Transaction STRUST in the SAP S/4HANA system.
8. Choose the **Anonymous** SSL client.
9. In the **Certificate** section, choose **Import**.
10. Import the certificate file saved in the second step.
11. The certificate will be displayed. Choose the change mode.
12. In the **Certificate** section, choose **Add to certificate** to the list.
13. Choose **Save**.

Now you can begin the OAuth 2.0 configuration. This configuration ensures that SAP users can access external apps:

1. Enter Transaction OA2C_CONFIG.
2. Choose **Create** and a new pop-up will open.
3. Choose **S4ML_FREETEXT** for the **OAuth 2.0 Client Profile** and enter "any" for the **Configuration Name**.
4. Enter the OAuth 2.0 **Client ID** as provided by SAP Cloud Platform and choose **OK**.

5. In the **Details • Administration** section, make entries in the **Client Secret, Authori-zation Endpoint**, and **Token Endpoint** fields with the information provided by SAP Cloud Platform.

6. In the **Access Settings** section, select the values in Table 5.9 and save.

Field	Value
Client Authentication	Basic
Resource Access Authentication	Header field
Selected Grant Type	Client Credentials

Table 5.9 Access Settings

Once you have the baseline setup complete for SAP Leonardo connecting to SAP S/4HANA, you can activate individual functionality in SAP S/4HANA. The next sections will detail the steps required to set up the configuration in SAP S/4HANA on-premise.

Image-Based Buying

For image-based buying, first ensure that the prerequisite steps for the SAP Cloud Platform Purchasing Assistant and the RFC connection have been completed. Next, log in to the SAP S/4HANA Configuration GUI and go to **SPRO • Materials Management • Purchasing • Self-Service Procurement • Define Machine Learning Scenarios**.

1. Choose **New Entries**, select **Image-Based Buying**, and ensure the **Activate the Scenario** checkbox is checked. Save your changes.

2. Next, map the RFC destination to the machine-learning scenarios by entering Transaction SM30 in SAP S/4HANA. Choose table view MMPUR_MLFND_CNF and add the entry as follows:
   - **Outbound Service ID**: Image-based Buying
   - **Activate**: Yes
   - **RFC Destination:** Enter the RFC destination created in the previous steps

3. Choose **Save**.

Next, make the search bar available in the cross-catalog search settings by following **SPRO • Materials Management • Purchasing • Purchase Requsition • Define Cross Catalog Search** and uncheck the checkbox for **Hide Cross Catalog Search Bar**.

Finally, schedule the job to upload data for machine learning.

Next, schedule the jobs to upload/export data to SAP Cloud Platform, ensuring the user running the job has authorization SAP_BR_BPC_EXPERT:

1. Log on to your SAP S/4HANA web UI.

2. Choose the **Schedule Export of Catalog Item Images For Machine Learning** app tile under **Job Scheduling for Purchasing**.

3. Choose **New**. Under **Job Template**, choose **Training Data for Image-Based Buying**, and select the corresponding catalog containing these images. Enable fine-tuning if the catalog has clean data for training.

4. Set **Start Immediately** in **Scheduling Options** according to your requirements.

5. Choose **Schedule**.

6. Monitor the application log on the **Application Jobs** page to check the status of the training job.

For more on setting up and tuning this functionality, review the SAP Best Practices at *https://s-prs.co/500324*.

Intelligent Approval Workflow

In these steps, you activate the intelligent approval workflow:

1. Follow **SPRO • Materials Management • Purchasing • Purchase Requisition • Flexible Workflow • Activate Intelligent Approval of Purchase Requisitions**.

2. In **Machine Learning Configurations** select **Change View** then **New Entries**. Choose **Scenario 1 Intelligent Approval for Purchase Requisitions** and enter the values as follows:
   - **Activate**: Yes
   - **Number of Attempts**: 3
   - **Calculation Currency**: Your Preferred Currency or USD

Next, map the RFC destination to the machine-learning scenarios by following path **SPRO • Materials Management • Purchasing • Intelligent Insights for Procurement**. Select **Edit** to change the **Maintain RFC Destination for Machine Learning Services** details screen. Add the values as follows:

- **Outbound Service ID:** Intelligent Approval for Purchase Requisition
- **Activate:** Yes
- **RFC Destination:** Enter the RFC destination created in the previous steps.

Next, schedule the jobs to upload/export data to SAP Cloud Platform, ensuring the user running the job has authorization SAP_BR_BPC_EXPERT:

1. Log on to your SAP S/4HANA web UI.
2. Choose the **Schedule Transfer of Purchase Requisitions for Intelligent Approval** app tile under **Job Scheduling for Purchasing**.
3. Choose **New**. Under **Job Template**, choose **Upload Records for Purchase Requisition Intelligent Approval**.
4. Set **Start Immediately** in **Scheduling Options** according to your requirements.
5. Choose **Schedule**.
6. Monitor the application log on the **Application Jobs** page to check the status of the training job.

Create a second job for **Upload Records (Failed during Inference) for PR Intelligent Approval**.

If you encounter issues during configuration, you can create a ticket referencing component MM-FIO-PUR-REL.

For more on setting up and tuning this functionality, review the SAP Best Practices at *https://s-prs.co/500326*.

Predictive Analytics for Contract Consumption in Procurement

In this machine-learning functionality, the setup steps are different from the others. An analytics specialist conducts the predictive model training leveraging the Quantity Contract Consumption app (F2012), with either the SAP_BR_BUYER or the SAP_MM_BC_PUR_STRATEGY and SAP_BR_BUYER authorizations assigned. Once you have activated the predictive model, you will need to schedule the SAP_MM_PUR_PAI_CTR_CONSUMP job to consume the predictions in the frontend app in SAP S/4HANA 1909. In cloud versions with this functionality, this SAP_MM_PUR_PAI_CTR_CONSUMP job runs weekly and does not require scheduling.

For more on setting up and tuning this functionality, review the SAP Best Practices at *https://s-prs.co/500327*.

Proposal of New Catalog Item or Material Group

SAP S/4HANA will also make recommendations for adding items to the catalog based on ordering trends in the system. If an item is ordered repeatedly as a free text item, you will see a recommendation in the Manage Catalog Item Recommendations app to create a catalog item for this order. This functionality leverages SAP Leonardo for making recommendations. To activate this in SAP S/4HANA, your SAP Basis team will need to connect to the SAP Leonardo environment, request the procurement assistant, and connect and map an RFC. Follow path **SPRO • Materials Management • Purchasing • Self-Service Procurement • Define Machine Learning Scenarios** to reach the screen shown in Figure 5.30.

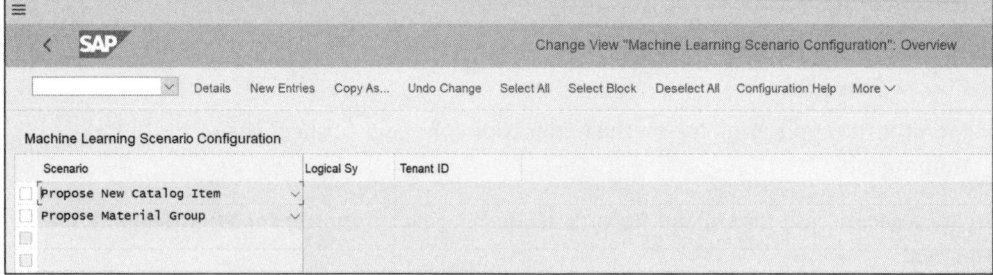

Figure 5.30 Define Machine Learning Scenarios

Here you can activate either recommendations by item or by material group, or both, by clicking **New Entries** and maintaining the packet size, checking the **Activation** checkbox, and setting the historical data period to use in days as in Figure 5.31.

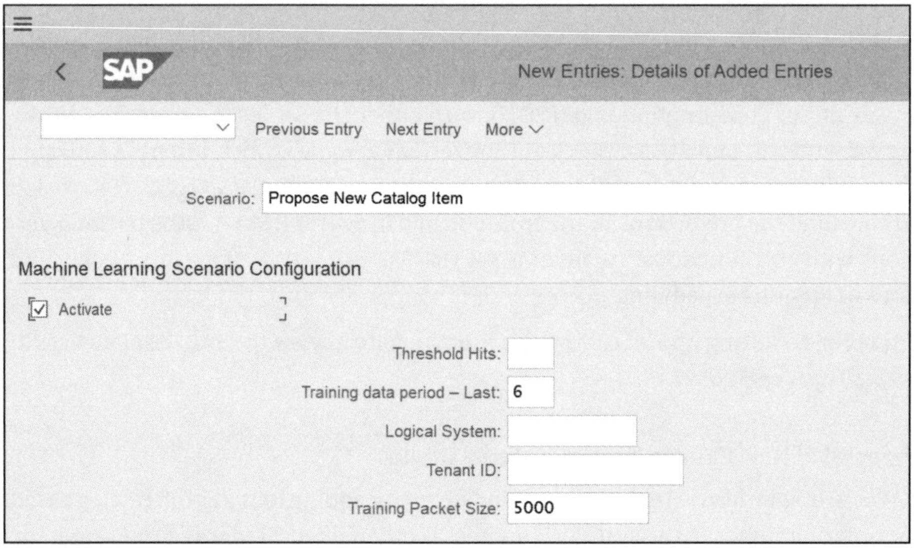

Figure 5.31 Propose New Catalog Item

After activating the scenario in SAP S/4HANA and having SAP Basis create and configure an OAuth 2.0 client, you then need to schedule jobs to export the data and train the model.

To schedule the export job, use the following steps:

1. Log on to your SAP S/4HANA system web UI.

2. Under **Purchasing Configuration**, choose the **Schedule Export of Purchase Orders** tile as in Figure 5.32.

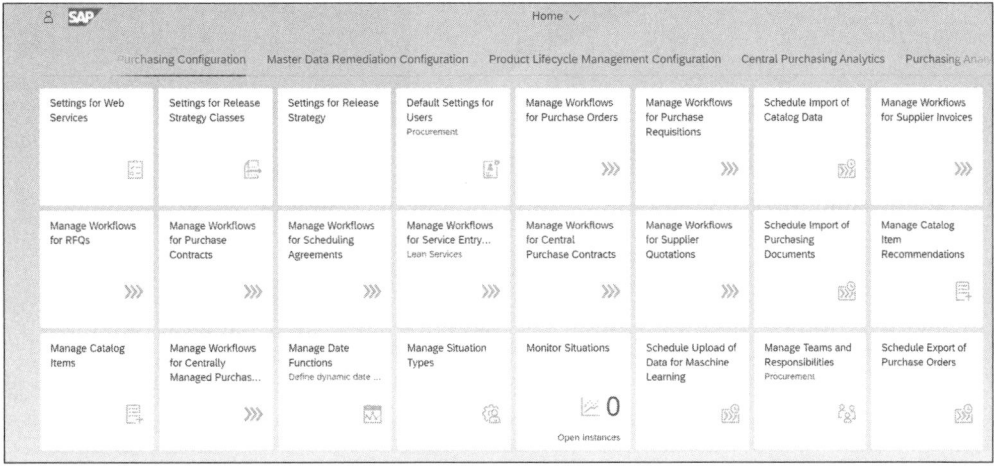

Figure 5.32 Schedule Export of Purchase Orders

3. Choose New (**+**).

4. Under **Job Template**, choose **Training Data for Free Text** as in Figure 5.33.

5. Set **Start Immediately** in **Scheduling Options** according to your requirements.

6. You can choose **Define Recurrence Pattern** if you want to schedule job frequency.

7. Enter a **Company Code** and **Plant**.

8. Choose a **Schedule**.

9. Monitor the background job on the **Application Jobs** page.

Next, schedule job SAP_MM_REDUCE_FTXT_ML_JOB_STATUS using Transaction SM36 in the SAP GUI to update the status of the training job training the model executed in SAP S/4HANA.

Finally, have your security team assign the standard template PROC_CATALOGITEM-PROPOSAL to the designated procurement users who will access the functionality.

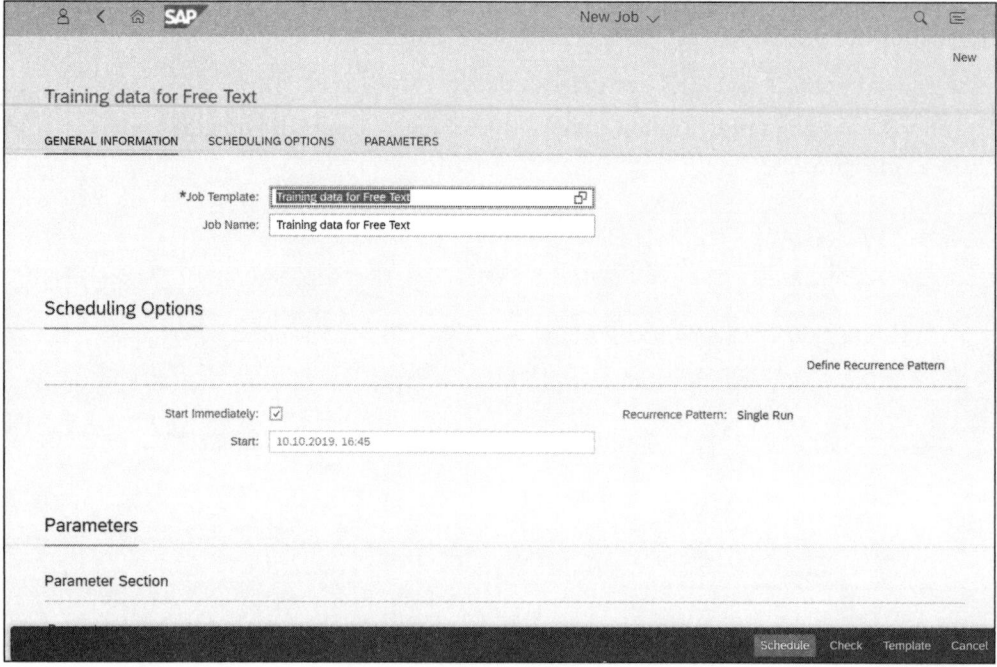

Figure 5.33 Training Data for Free Text Job

For more on setting up and tuning this functionality, review the SAP Best Practices at *https://s-prs.co/500328*.

5.7.3   Requirements Processing

To set up requisitions for requirements processing, you will need to set up the document type(s) and number range(s). First, you will need to define number ranges to which to tie the document types by following **SPRO • Materials Management • Purchasing • Purchase Requisition • Define Number Ranges** as in Figure 5.34.

After maintaining your number range, or multiple number ranges if you intend to have multiple types of requisitions, maintain the requisition document types by following **SPRO • Materials Management • Purchasing • Purchase Requisition • Define Document Types** as in Figure 5.35.

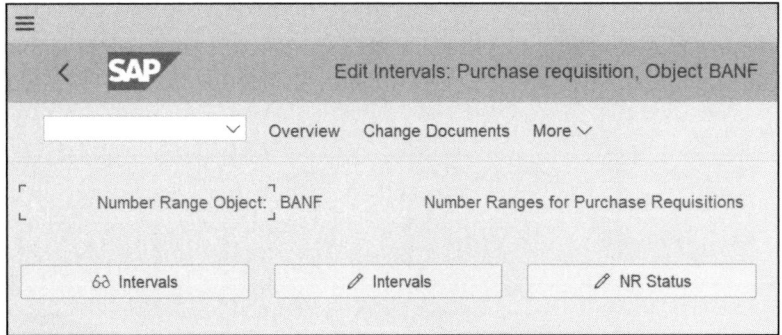

Figure 5.34 Define Requisition Number Ranges

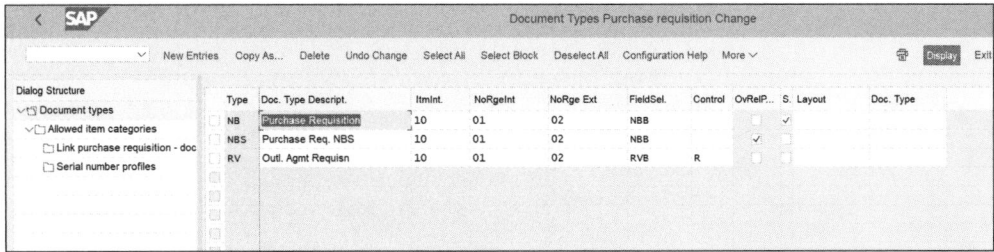

Figure 5.35 Document Types Purchase Requisition Change

In this transaction, you maintain the document type and assign it to a number range, as well as define whether the requisition doc type is an external one (originating from outside the SAP S/4HANA system—in SAP Ariba, say) or an internally generated requisition, created directly in SAP S/4HANA.

5.7.4   Purchase Order Processing

Similar to requisition configuration, in order to create and process purchase orders, you must maintain the number ranges and document types by following **SPRO • Materials Management • Purchasing • Purchase Order • Define Number Ranges** and **SPRO • Materials Management • Purchasing • Purchase Requisition • Define Document Types**. There are several additional configuration options available, such as tolerance definition for price variance. Here, you can set thresholds for price variance by following **SPRO • Materials Management • Purchasing • Purchase Order Requisition • Set Tolerance Limits for Price Variance**, as in Figure 5.36.

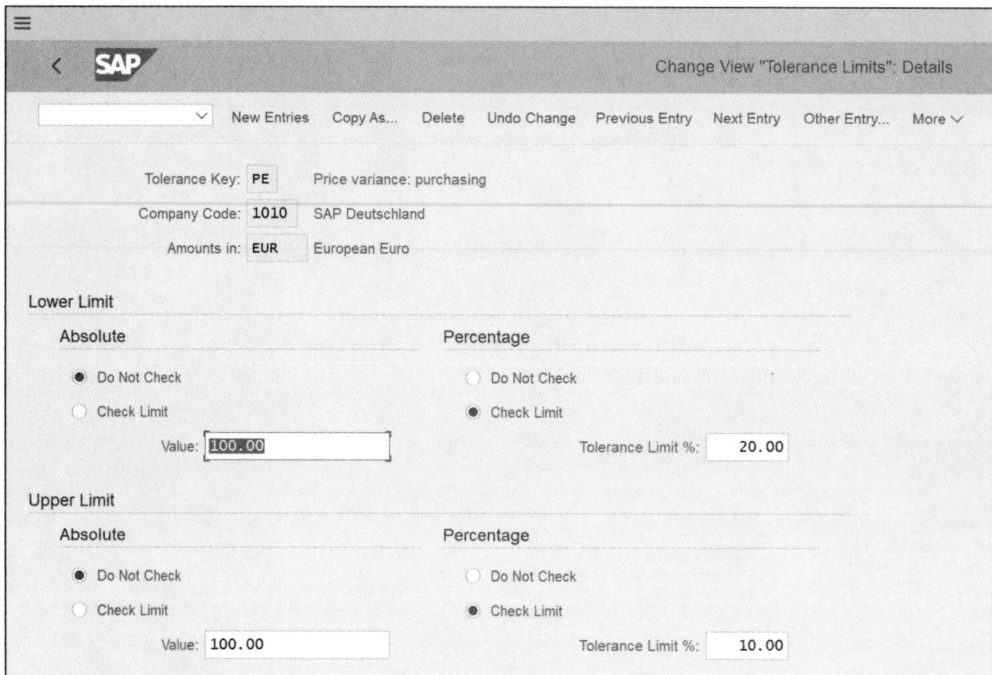

Figure 5.36 Setting Purchase Order Tolerance Limits for Price Variance

Note that the tolerance settings are typically made at the company code level and include both a lower and an upper limit.

5.7.5   Service Order Processing

SAP S/4HANA Cloud is a natural integration candidate for SAP Fieldglass. As shown in Figure 5.37, SAP S/4HANA Cloud leverages best practices integration approaches to integrate and extend SAP S/4HANA Cloud with the Ariba Network and SAP Fieldglass, primarily on the invoicing side for SAP Fieldglass for now and the significant documents in a P2P process for the Ariba Network (PO, confirmation, ship notice, goods receipt, and invoice). Future releases of SAP S/4HANA and SAP S/4HANA Cloud are expected to build on the standard integration of document types for SAP Fieldglass.

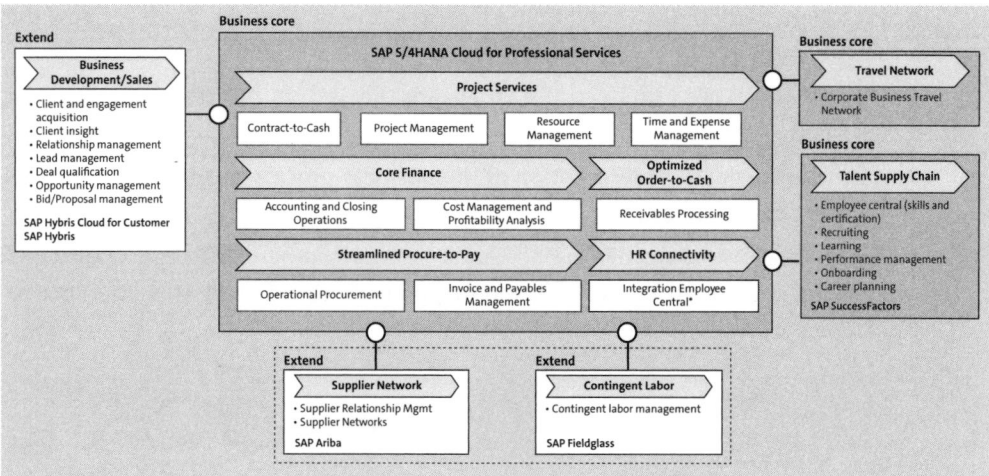

Figure 5.37 SAP Fieldglass and SAP Ariba Integration with SAP S/4HANA Cloud for Professional Services

5.7.6 Purchase Order Collaboration

Purchase order collaboration, whereby the supplier logs into a supplier portal, reviews the purchase order, confirms the order, and moves on to processing/delivering the requested quantities, is facilitated via the Ariba Network. For SAP S/4HANA operational procurement integration with SAP Ariba, the main applicable scenario is the natively supported purchase order/invoice integration with the Ariba Network. There are a number of resources available to support you with the install and deployment of this integration for SAP S/4HANA Cloud and on-premise.

The process flow in Figure 5.38 details the integration elements between SAP S/4HANA and the Ariba Network.

The integration is native within SAP S/4HANA and can be established using guided configuration within SAP Activate or via the SAP Ariba account settings. These best practices are available at *https://rapid.sap.com/bp/#/BP_OP_ENTPR*. The building block to implement for the self-service procurement scenario in SAP S/4HANA is Ariba—Purchase Order to Invoice Integration with Procurement (J82). This building block contains the following:

- Scope item simulation, with which you can test-run the scope to understand where the configuration guide steps will cover your requirements or leave gaps

- Process model BPMN2, providing a business process representation of how the software works, which you can use in process-modeling applications
- Prebuilt test scripts you can use to ensure the system has been integrated as designed
- A process model, a representation of the business process to show how the software works as standard
- The Ariba Network Configuration Guide (J81), providing configuration of logon credentials to the Ariba Network and mapping of org structure elements such as company codes to Ariba Network IDs

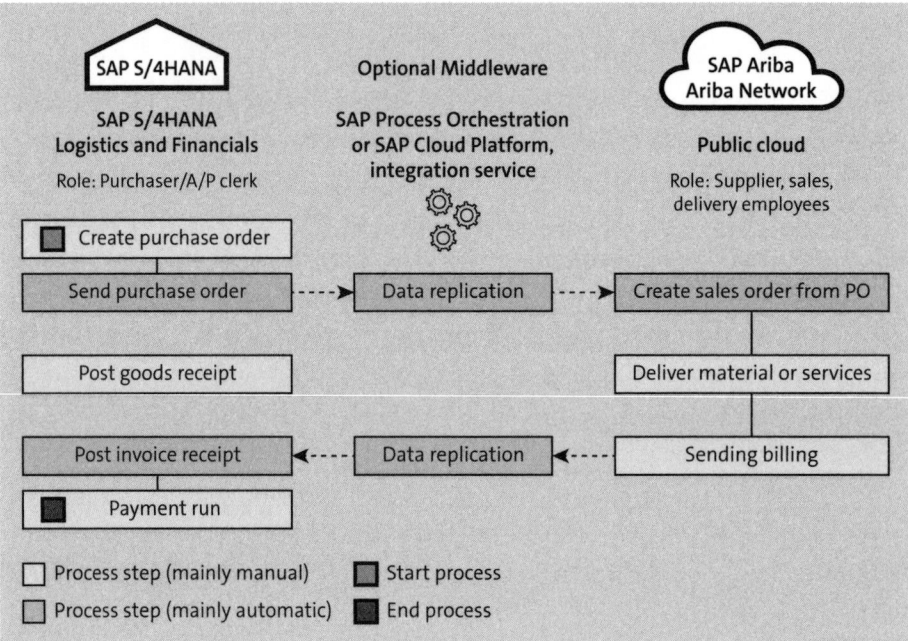

Figure 5.38 Process Flow: Purchase Order Invoice Integration with Ariba Network

Once you've configured the logon credentials and mappings from SAP S/4HANA to your Ariba Network (J81) subscription, you'll invite and (in the event that they aren't already transacting on the network) onboard your suppliers in the Ariba Network to begin transacting in your SAP S/4HANA instance.

You can also integrate SAP S/4HANA Cloud editions with the Ariba Network. As with the SAP S/4HANA integration with the Ariba Network, this integration leverages

guided configuration, best practices, and SAP Activate to support the solution depicted in Figure 5.39. For SAP S/4HANA Cloud, the solution approach uses native direct webservices for integrating to and from the Ariba Network. The J82 building
block materials include the following:

- A process model, outlining the process between SAP S/4HANA Cloud and Ariba
  Network
- A test script, for validation for integration implementation
- A configuration guide, for step-by-step instructions on implementation

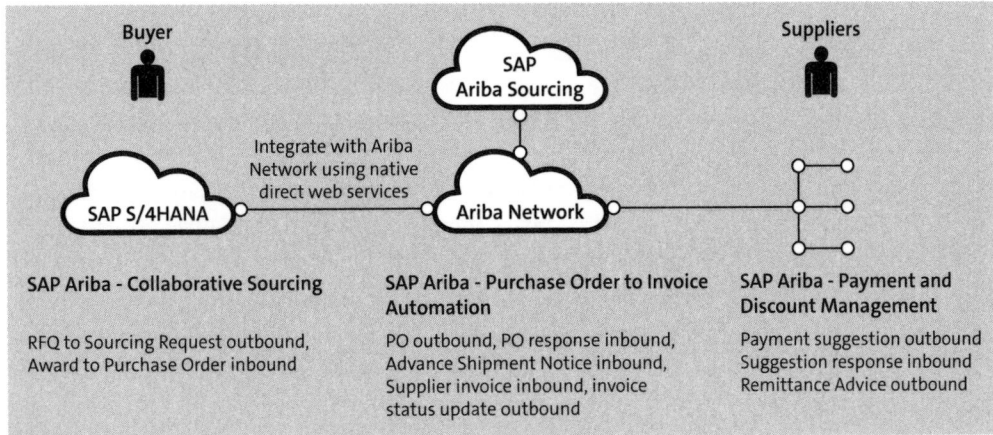

Figure 5.39 SAP S/4HANA Cloud Integration with SAP Ariba

5.7.7 SAP SuccessFactors

SAP SuccessFactors integration with both SAP S/4HANA and SAP S/4HANA Cloud has
a similar integration framework and approach as that for SAP Ariba, based on predefined integration scenarios that you evaluate, activate, and deploy in your environment.

SAP S/4HANA, On-Premise Edition Integration with SAP SuccessFactors
Employee Central

SAP S/4HANA integrates with SAP SuccessFactors by leveraging predefined configuration and integration scenarios (see Figure 5.40). This integration is webservice-
based and can be scheduled as a middleware job.

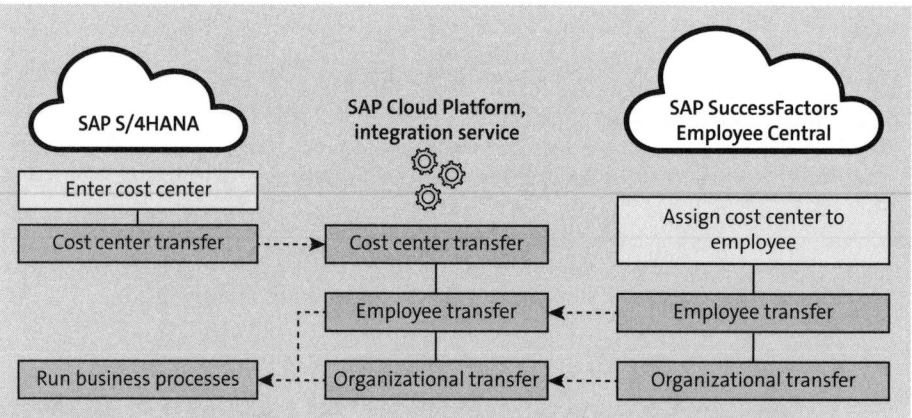

Figure 5.40 Integrating SAP S/4HANA with SAP SuccessFactors Employee Central

The manual process entails creating or identifying a cost center first in SAP S/4HANA. This is a manual step. The cost center is then transferred to SAP SuccessFactors and assigned to the employee. The employee and/or organizational data is transferred back to SAP S/4HANA automatically via batch processing. The configuration is available at *https://rapid.sap.com/bp/#/RDS_EC_S4*. This includes overview documentation, scope documentation, and the following accelerators:

- A sales supplement, an overview of the package and business value
- A customer presentation, slides on the scope of integration
- A demo script, for communicating the scope and functionality
- A delivery supplement, providing important information about the delivery of the solution
- Service and one-page slides, slides defining the solution and scope (one-pagers)
- Software and delivery requirements, a list of prerequisites for the deployment of the solution
- The solution scope and scope documents
- A project schedule, a schedule for the project including roles/skills required
- SAP Notes, providing additional documentation for package and implementation

SAP S/4HANA Cloud Integration with SAP SuccessFactors Employee Central

SAP SuccessFactors can also integrate with SAP S/4HANA Cloud using the same approach of best practices, building blocks, and SAP Activate. The required efforts are slightly more varied, and therefore involved, than with the Ariba Network packages. Upon completion of the integration, an employee from SAP SuccessFactors is realized as a business partner in SAP S/4HANA. Data from SAP SuccessFactors can be used to populate the employee data in SAP S/4HANA, such as the following:

- Basic employee information (person, name, employee)
- Communication information, such as email, phone, and fax
- Payment information with payment method and bank account
- Employee status
- Employment percentage
- Working hours per week
- Job title
- Job information, business unit, division, and department
- Cost center assignment

As with on-premise SAP S/4HANA integrations, from a process standpoint, you first establish or identify the cost center in SAP S/4HANA, then transfer this cost center to SAP SuccessFactors Employee Central and assign an employee, and then transfer the employee record back over to SAP S/4HANA (see Figure 5.41). The transfer processes are automated process steps, whereas the cost center assignment is manual.

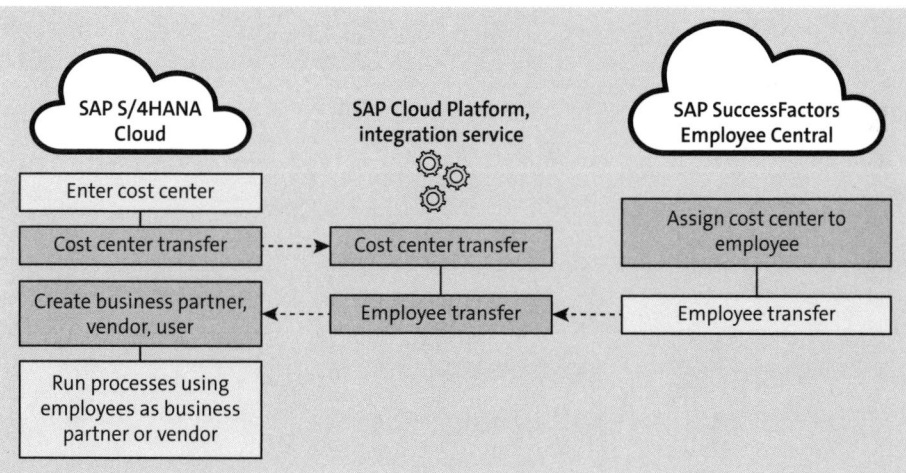

Figure 5.41 Integrating SAP S/4HANA Cloud with SAP SuccessFactors Employee Central

More on SAP SuccessFactors Employee Central integration building blocks and integration information is available at *http://s-prs.co/500301*, where you'll find the latest integration information, as well as the following:

- A process diagram, which outlines the integration approach
- A test script, for verification of implementation
- Process model BPMN2

5.8   Summary

Operational procurement has been updated in SAP S/4HANA Sourcing and Procurement, both at the UI level with the SAP Fiori app-based approach for key transactions and views, and in terms of internal catalog emphasis. Although many of the core requisitioning transactions are simplified for the casual user, SAP S/4HANA Sourcing and Procurement retains some of the old favorites for PO creation in the advanced options of the apps to support complex ordering processes created by professional buyers with multiple data points and references. Many of these processes and options are required by direct procurement for their types of purchase orders. Now, the next chapter will dive deeper into automated and direct procurement topics.

Chapter 6
Automated and Direct Procurement

This chapter outlines direct and automated procurement approaches and simplifications/changes in SAP S/4HANA, providing an overview of the main processes and related solution areas, configuration steps, and design considerations.

SAP S/4HANA thoroughly supports automated and direct procurement. Perhaps more than any other procurement area, automated and direct procurement are dependent upon the cross-functional capabilities and depth of an ERP system. To automate a procurement process, you must first understand the demand for your products, how you produce your products, and what your inventory levels are. This knowledge base resides in multiple areas of an organization and multiple areas of SAP S/4HANA.

6.1 What Is Automated and Direct Procurement?

In manufacturing, it's easier to make a clear distinction between indirect procurement of office supplies supporting day-to-day business operations and direct procurement of parts and items going into the end product(s) produced by the organization. Direct procurement need not only apply to manufacturing verticals, however. Government organizations purchase services and materials that go directly into their end products as well. For example, a government organization tasked with building and managing infrastructure will purchase direct materials and construction services that create and maintain these infrastructure assets. Direct procurement is often separated into its own area from an organizational standpoint. Direct procurement also is a leading candidate for automation in procurement operations due to its high volumes, predictability, and longer lead times.

One main thrust of automating procurement is to identify sources of supply up front for materials. Once sources of supply have been identified, you then allow for the forecasting processes and approaches in material requirements planning (MRP) to generate sourced requisitions. The requisitions are converted via batch jobs in an ERP system to purchase orders or updates to scheduling agreements and transmitted, without employee intervention, to suppliers.

Once the source of supply is assigned automatically for a particular material, automation of the entire transaction, from demand generation to proposal to purchasing document to transmission, is possible. Much of direct procurement and other reoccurring types of procurement can be automated in SAP S/4HANA, leveraging tried-and-true, ERP-based approaches such as MRP, source lists, reorder points, information records, and scheduling agreements. However, in SAP S/4HANA, not all direct procurement processes and functionality is like-for-like with previous versions of SAP ERP.

Automated procurement in traditional ERP scenarios is typically procurement that is repetitive. In SAP environments, the direct procurement department often operates autonomously or only loosely aligned with the rest of the procurement organization. Direct procurement may only have a few buyers working directly with the product teams to procure the desired mix of products and raw materials from the optimal mix of suppliers. Direct buyers may be "embedded" with product groups or a company's plants, with razor-sharp focus on their particular areas of procurement to ensure proper cost-effective supply at all times and avoid disruption to the business. Products and goods purchased as direct procurement items by an organization may have long lead times, require special handling, and involve deep partnerships with the suppliers.

Indirect procurement items are typically more straightforward; where indirect procurement flips to direct procurement is on the user side. User management and workflows are typically more complex on the indirect side than the direct side. Direct buyers may number in the single digits and be responsible for an enormous amount of spend. The job of these buyers is to know and understand their procurement systems and tools so they can create optimal orders based on demand and forecasts from the areas they cover. Indirect buyers may push most of the up-front ordering process via self-service requisitioning onto lightly trained employees ordering items for themselves or their offices. Indirect procurement users, therefore, may number in the thousands and have little to no training, purchasing once every quarter rather than every day or week.

SAP S/4HANA Enterprise Management, like its predecessor SAP ERP platforms, offers a wide array of functionality and processes to support and automate direct procurement processes (*automated procurement*). Some of these automation techniques are also applicable to frequently bought indirect items and/or indirect items with longer lead times and a regular purchasing cadence. There are two main planning approaches for these procurement scenarios: consumption-based planning and materials requirements planning (MRP). *Consumption-based planning* is driven by previous material consumption. As in Figure 6.1, consumption-based planning leverages reorder point, forecast-based, and time-phased planning, which can be defined as follows:

- **Reorder point planning**
  Sets a stock threshold; if the planned available stock falls below this point, an order is issued. The reorder point is set to cover average material requirements during the replenishment lead time. Manual reorder point planning entails the MRP controller, an employee tasked with optimizing MRP processes and order volumes, creating the reorder point manually. In automatic planning, the system determines the reorder point using the forecast.

- **Forecast-based planning**
  Creates forecast requirements at regular intervals using the historical values in the material forecast.

- **Time-phased planning**
  Also uses historical values in the material forecast and uses predefined intervals in a particular cadence.

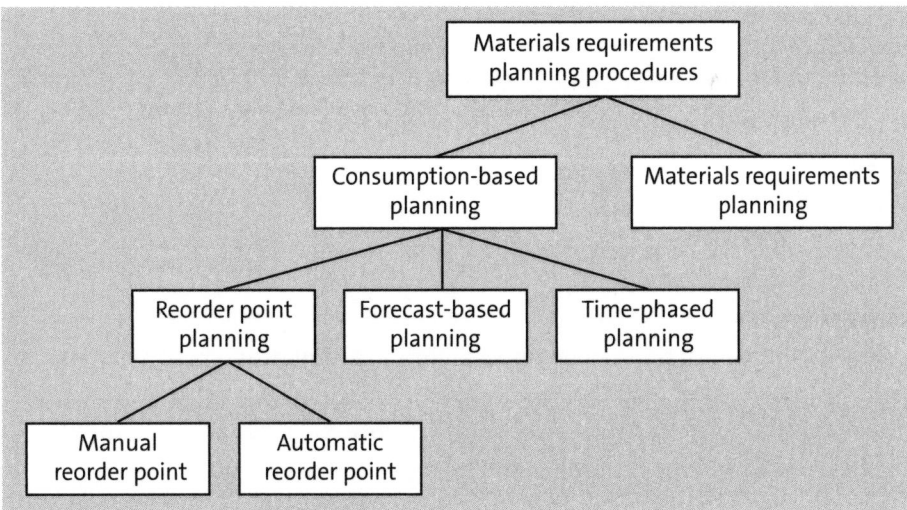

Figure 6.1 Overview of MRP Procedures

Current demand drivers for materials, such as sales orders and dependent and manual reservations, display in the current stock requirements list to help consumption-based planning approaches take these elements into account, in addition to the historical consumption patterns. If the demand for materials in production is relatively static, then low-value-item, consumption-based planning approaches may suffice for creating sufficient stock on hand. If the item is high value with fluctuating demand, then MRP provides more accurate provisioning of materials than consumption-based planning. In the next section, we'll review MRP as it relates to procurement activities, as well as the changes to MRP in SAP S/4HANA.

6.2   Materials Requirements Planning

MRP aggregates the demand from various production, inventory, and forecast processes to secure and/or procure materials and have them available when needed for the production process. These materials can be in inventory at the plant/storage/warehouse level. If sufficient materials are not in stock or certain reorder point thresholds are crossed by drawing down the stock, the MRP run can generate procurement proposals, such as planned orders, requisitions, or scheduling agreement line items. A planned order is reviewed first by the MRP controller and then converted into a requisition, whereas a requisition is immediately available for purchasing to review and source. Some organizations prefer to review the requisition and designate MRP run requisitions for a review step prior to having purchasing convert them. Other organizations prefer a more formal process whereby the MRP run creates a planned order, the MRP controller reviews and converts to a requisition, and only then does purchasing get involved.

As illustrated in Figure 6.2, once the MRP controller and the other stakeholders in this process, including purchasing, have reviewed the proposed items/orders for procurement, these internal planning documents are converted to reservations or stock transfers if the stock is on hand or, if not, to actual purchase orders and releases them to the suppliers. MRP thus generates the internal planning and proposed procurement line items automatically, which are then typically reviewed and adjusted (if required) by the MRP controller and other employees involved in the process and then released for ordering and fulfillment.

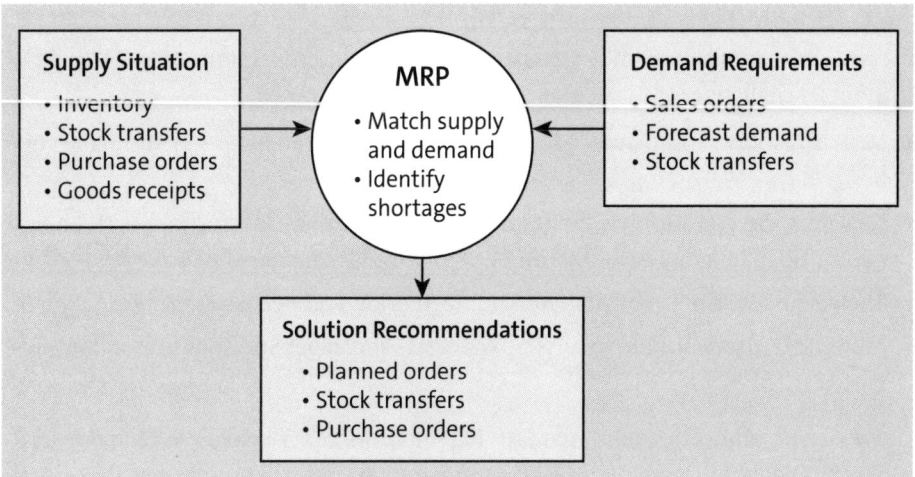

Figure 6.2 MRP General Flow

MRP-specific information is maintained in the material master, and it follows that MRP approaches require material masters as a core master data element in this process. Material masters have multiple tabs for maintaining MRP information, including the following:

- General data that must be defined for a planning material
- Data dependent on the MRP procedure
- Data requirement scheduling
- Data required for lot-size calculation

The material type defined in the material master also controls the types of procurement that are permissible for the material master, whether in-house only, external procurement only, or both. Defining the material types and understanding the procurement ramifications for a particular material type is thus key to establishing a coherent MRP strategy and procurement strategy in general. For example, if your material master type defines the material as requiring in-house-only procurement and you occasionally need to source it from an external supplier, then you'll need to create a duplicate material with a material type that allows for external procurement. In addition to nuances of material settings and MRP, there are significant changes between SAP ERP and SAP S/4HANA when it comes to MRP. We'll cover these differences ahead and outline both MRP improvements and limitations in SAP S/4HANA.

6.2.1   MRP in SAP ERP versus SAP S/4HANA

Executing the traditional MRP run transaction in previous versions of SAP ERP is not without its challenges:

- MRP is resource-intensive and sometimes requires batch runs spanning several hours/days.
- New demand and supply changes impact the MRP plan, leaving you with an outdated MRP plan or a need to rerun MRP to take the changes into account.
- There's no real-time view of material information and needs across sites.
- Multiple transactions are required to navigate shortages and solutions in MRP scenarios.

These shortcomings in traditional SAP ERP environments impact MRP and lead to suboptimal decision-making, as well as unnecessary efforts to arrive at these decisions. Fortunately, SAP S/4HANA is well-positioned to address shortcomings in MRP in traditional ERP systems by leveraging significant improvements in speed and simplifications. The SAP S/4HANA-specific transaction *MRP Live* is the new version for MRP Run, used in previous ERP versions. Some of the key advantages of and advances in MRP Live include the following:

- MRP runs are exponentially faster—up to 10 times faster—in SAP S/4HANA, which leads to MRP controllers having more timely and accurate information.
- There's a single, real-time view of material shortages across sites.
- You have the ability to pinpoint critical demands and supplies, such as overdue orders, in SAP S/4HANA.
- You can simulate a solution's viability in real time and then implement it in an expedient manner.
- The MRP planning scope has been expanded in SAP S/4HANA, allowing for planning sets of materials with all components, materials for which a certain production planner is responsible for one material across all plants.
- The main transaction for the MRP run in previous SAP ERP versions was MD01 (see Figure 6.3).

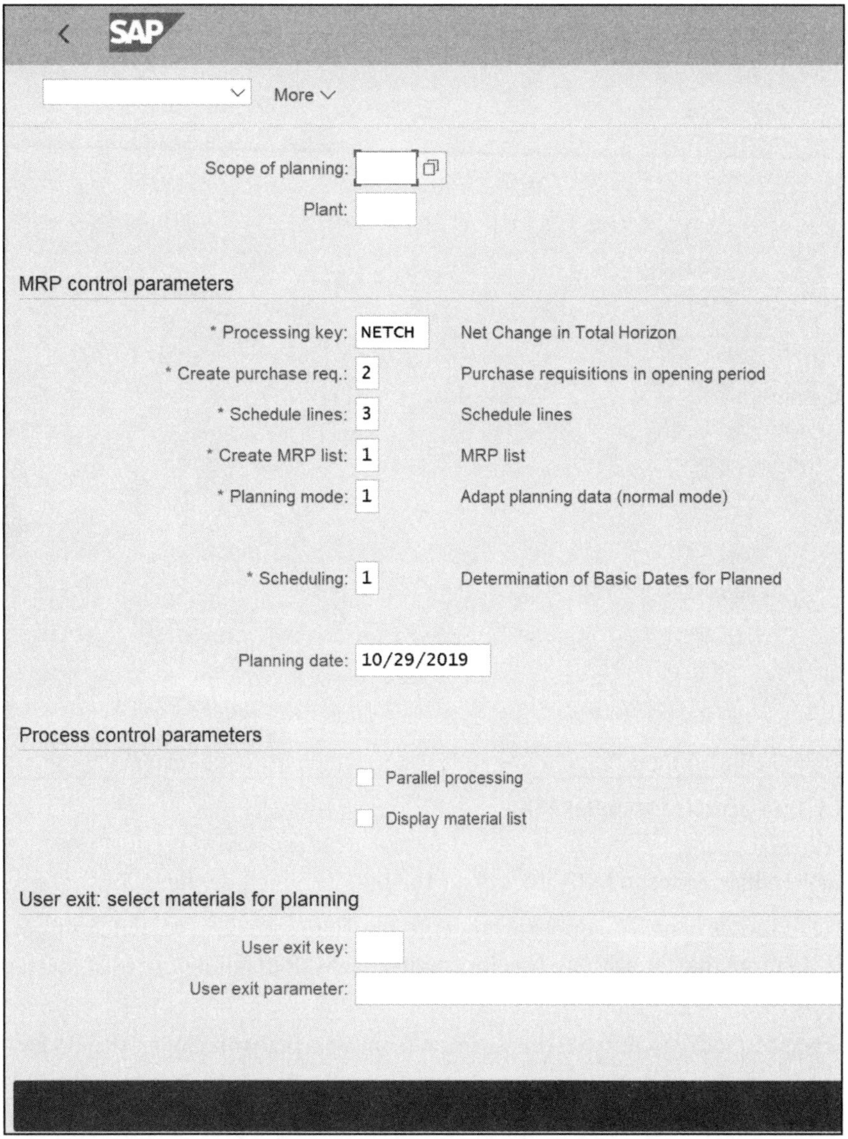

Figure 6.3 Transaction MD01 MRP Run

The new transaction in SAP S/4HANA MRP Live (Transaction **MD01N**) is shown in Figure 6.4.

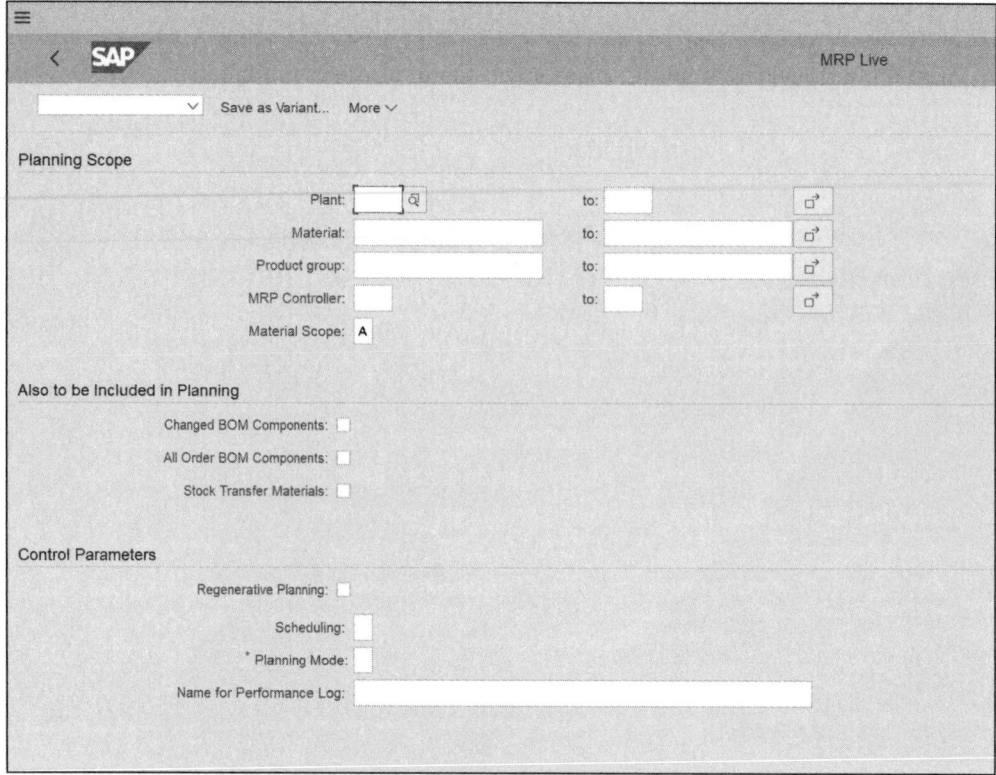

Figure 6.4 Transaction MD01N: MRP Live

Some further differences in MRP Live versus the MRP run include the following:

- MRP Live always considers quota arrangements; there's no need to switch this on in the material master as there was for traditional MRP (flagging material master attribute MARC-USEQU).

- If you want to source a purchase requisition from a particular supplier, you no longer need to define a source list entry. It's sufficient to flag **Auto Source** in the PIR. Flagging an item for automatic sourcing in the PIR allows MRP Live to automatically assign the supplier as the source of supply.

- Production versions are the main source of supply for MRP Live. If you want a BOM, phantom assembly, subcontracting, or routing item to be considered by MRP Live, you need to create a production version.

- Forecast-based planning and planned independent requirements are not differentiated in the SAP Fiori UI in SAP S/4HANA for MRP.

- Report PPH_SETUP_MRPRECORDS (shown in Figure 6.5) replaces Reports RMMD-VM10 and RMMDVM20; to display variants for the new report, use Transaction PPH_MDAB instead of Transactions MDAB and MDRE. The long-term planning report is now Report PPH_SETUP_MRPRECORDS_SIMU rather than Reports RMMD-VM10 and RMMDVM20. However, Transaction MD21 is still used to display planning file entries.

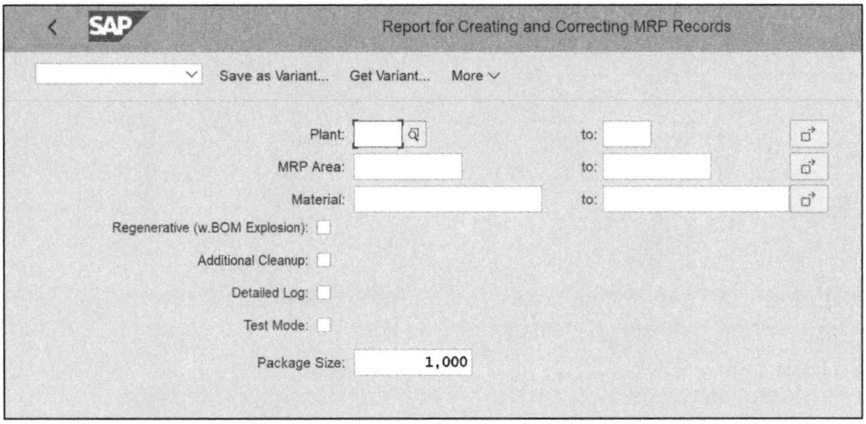

Figure 6.5 Report PPH_SETUP_MRPRECORDS

- The original planning files MDVM/MDVL and DBVM/DBVL are no longer available in SAP S/4HANA. They were replaced by the new planning file PPH_DBVM.
- SAP S/4HANA MRP plans for the plant and MRP area. Planning at the storage location level isn't possible.

MRP areas define where the product is to be stored, whereas MRP groups define parameters for MRP. MRP groups are discussed in more detail in Section 6.4.4. Note that once an MRP area is created in the system via **Production • Materials Requirements Planning (MRP) • Master Data • MRP Areas • Define MRP Areas**, it can't be undone easily. Careful consideration and coordination with production planning and stakeholders of MRP is thus required prior to implementing MRP areas.

6.2.2   SAP Fiori Apps for MRP

There are many available apps for monitoring and working with MRP in SAP S/4HANA. Two of these apps, Monitor Production Orders (Figure 6.6) and Picking Components for Process Orders (Figure 6.7), are assigned to the production planning users of the system.

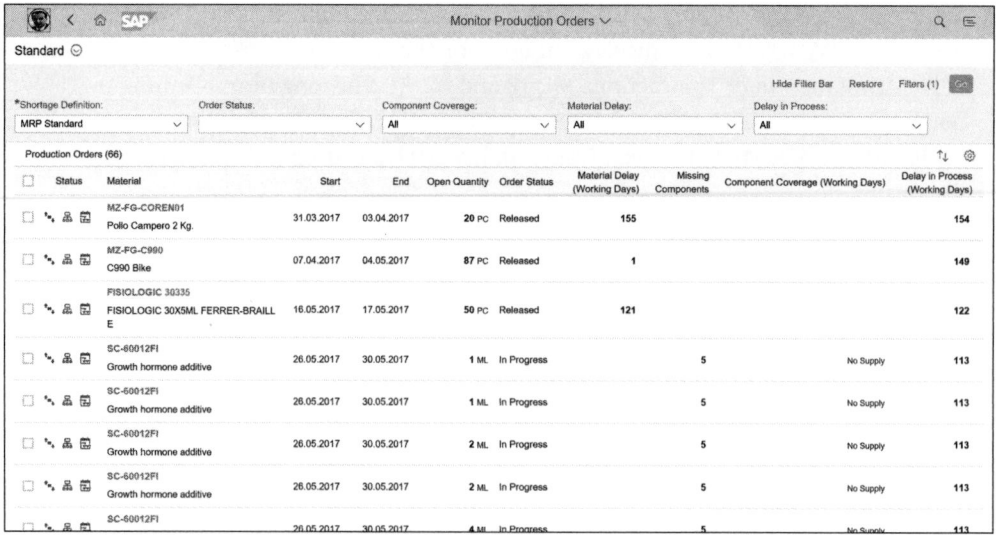

Figure 6.6 Monitor Production Orders App

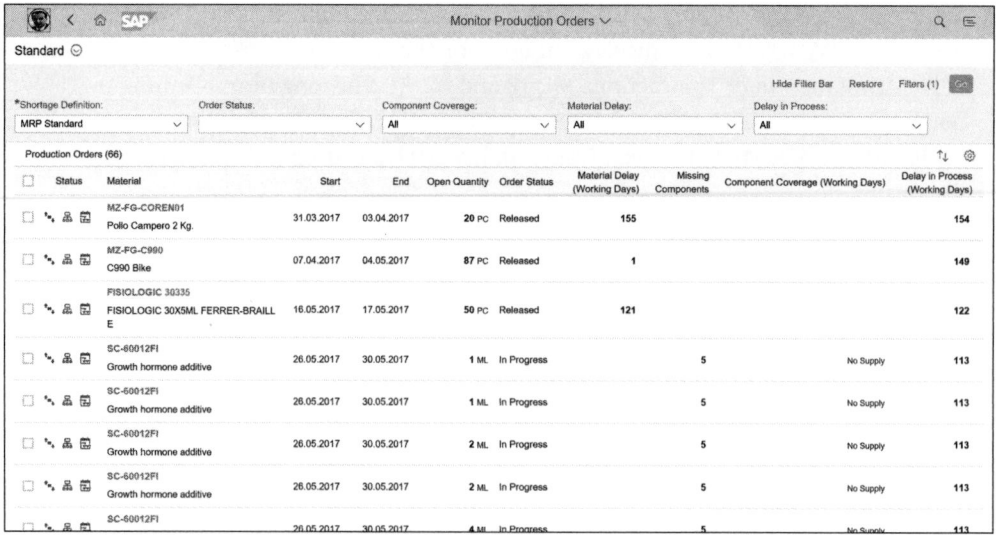

Figure 6.7 Picking Components for Process Order App

To navigate the production orders area, first define your MRP controllers by using the Maintain MRP Controllers app (see Figure 6.8).

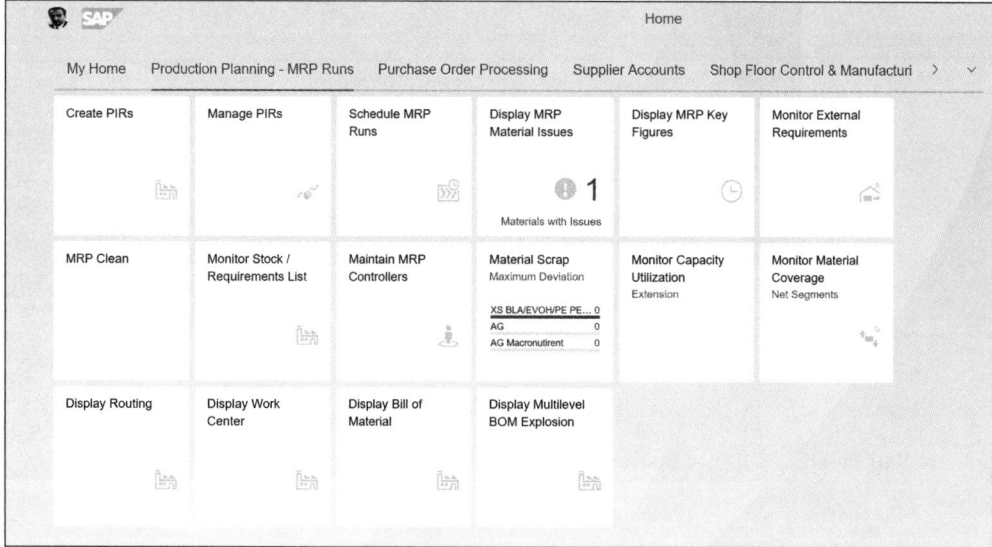

Figure 6.8 MRP Production Orders Apps

Once you've defined the individual plants for the MRP controller, continue on to the other apps shown in Figure 6.8. These apps are not part of the procurement area and apply mainly to production planning roles. If you have a buyer role/SAP Fiori UI, you'll need to request these tiles if you don't have them on your screen. Additional SAP Fiori apps used in MRP and SAP S/4HANA Sourcing and Procurement in general are outlined in Table 6.1 and can also be further augmented by searching the SAP Fiori app library at *http://s-prs.co/500302*.

The SAP Fiori apps for MRP in SAP S/4HANA can be categorized into transactional apps, object page apps, and analytical apps. The transactional apps allow a user to conduct transactions in and around MRP processes (see Table 6.1).

Role Name	SAP Fiori App Name	UI Technology
Material planner	Monitor External Requirements	SAPUI5
Material planner	Monitor Material Coverage	SAPUI5
Material planner	Manage External Requirements	SAPUI5

Table 6.1 MRP SAP Fiori Apps: Transactional

Role Name	SAP Fiori App Name	UI Technology
Material planner	Manage Material Coverage	SAPUI5
Material planner	Monitor Internal Requirements	SAPUI5
Material planner	Monitor Production Orders or Process Orders	SAPUI5
Material planner	Manage Internal Requirements	SAPUI5
Material planner	Manage Production Orders or Process Orders	SAPUI5
Purchaser	My Inbox—Approve POs	SAPUI5: Smart Template
Purchaser	My Purchasing Document Items	SAPUI5
Material planner	Manage Change Requests	SAPUI5
Purchaser	Manage Sources of Supply	SAPUI5
Purchaser	Manage POs	SAPUI5
Material planner	MRP Cockpit Reuse Component	SAPUI5
Purchaser	Manage Purchase Requisitions	SAPUI5
Inventory manager	Manage Stock	SAP Fiori UI5
Material planner	Manage PIRs	SAPUI5
Material planner	Schedule MRP Runs	Generic SAPUI5 Job Scheduling Framework
Material planner	Maintain MRP Controllers	Generic SAPUI5 Config. Framework
Material planner	Display MRP Material Issues	Generic SAPUI5 Config. Framework
Material planner	Display MRP Key Figures	Generic SAPUI5 Config. Framework
Purchaser	Manage Purchase Contracts	SAPUI5
Purchaser	Schedule Purchasing Jobs (cloud only)	Generic SAPUI5 Job Scheduling Framework

Table 6.1 MRP SAP Fiori Apps: Transactional (Cont.)

Role Name	SAP Fiori App Name	UI Technology
Production planner	Schedule Order Conversion Runs	Generic SAPUI5 Job Scheduling Framework
Purchaser	Manage Source Lists (cloud only)	SAPUI5
Purchaser	Manage Purchasing Info Records	SAPUI5: Smart Template
Purchaser	Procurement Overview Page (cloud only)	SAPUI5: Overview Page
Purchaser	Manage Supplier Quotation (cloud only)	SAPUI5: Smart Template

Table 6.1 MRP SAP Fiori Apps: Transactional (Cont.)

The object page apps in SAP for MRP are listed in Table 6.2.

Role Name	SAP Fiori App Name	UI Technology
Purchaser	Purchase Order	SAPUI5: Smart Template
Purchaser	Purchase Requisition Item	SAPUI5: Smart Template
Purchaser	Purchase Contract	SAPUI5: Smart Template
Purchaser	Purchasing Info Record	SAPUI5: Smart Template
Purchaser	Supplier	SAPUI5: Smart Template
Purchaser	Purchase Requisition (Cloud only)	SAPUI5: Smart Template
Purchaser	Purchase Contract Item	SAPUI5: Smart Template
Inventory manager	Material Document	SAPUI5: Smart Template

Table 6.2 MRP SAP Fiori Apps: Object Pages

The SAP S/4HANA analytical apps for MRP are listed in Table 6.3.

Role Name	SAP Fiori App Name	UI Technology
Inventory manager	Stock—Single Material	SAPUI5
Inventory manager	Material Inventory Values—Balance Summary	Web Dynpro
Inventory manager	Material Inventory Values—Line Items	Web Dynpro

Table 6.3 MRP SAP Fiori Apps: Analytical

Role Name	SAP Fiori App Name	UI Technology
Inventory manager	Stock—Multiple Materials (cloud only)	SAPUI5
Material planner	Analyze PIR Quality (on-premise)	Web Dynpro
Inventory manager	Inventory Turnover Analysis (cloud only)	SAPUI5

Table 6.3 MRP SAP Fiori Apps: Analytical (Cont.)

Rather than digging through transaction codes or finding the correct IMG menu path, an SAP S/4HANA MRP controller simply needs to be assigned the aforementioned apps to do her work, accessing these apps via the tiles in a dashboard-like setting. To make settings for an MRP controller to manage material shortages in the MRP apps, follow IMG menu path **Production • Material Requirements Planning • Apps for Material Requirements Planning • General Settings • Define Material Shortage Profiles**. Here, you define what constitutes a material shortage via assigning a profile, as in Figure 6.9.

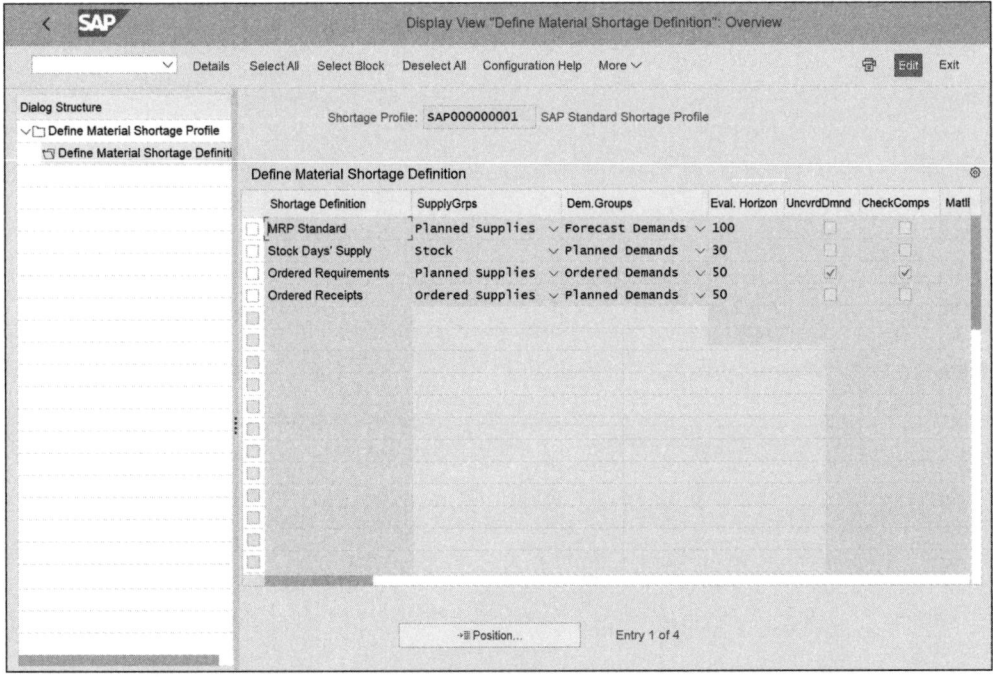

Figure 6.9 Define Material Shortage

In tandem with MRP, you typically need some approach to estimate future requirements. Setting a reorder point is useful in some instances, but knowing what future demand for a component or material will be with some degree of accuracy may provide a better understanding of the sourcing and ordering requirements, ultimately achieving greater efficiencies in direct procurement operations. Fortunately, SAP S/4HANA MRP combines reflexive demand indicators such as reorder points with proactive forecasting approaches and historical analysis to drive precision and alignment in the material quantities ultimately ordered.

SAP S/4HANA provides an app view in the Monitor Material Coverage app. Once in the app, you have an overview of the coverage with availability details, as in Figure 6.10, where you see the net and individual segments of materials with the MRP analysis of supply.

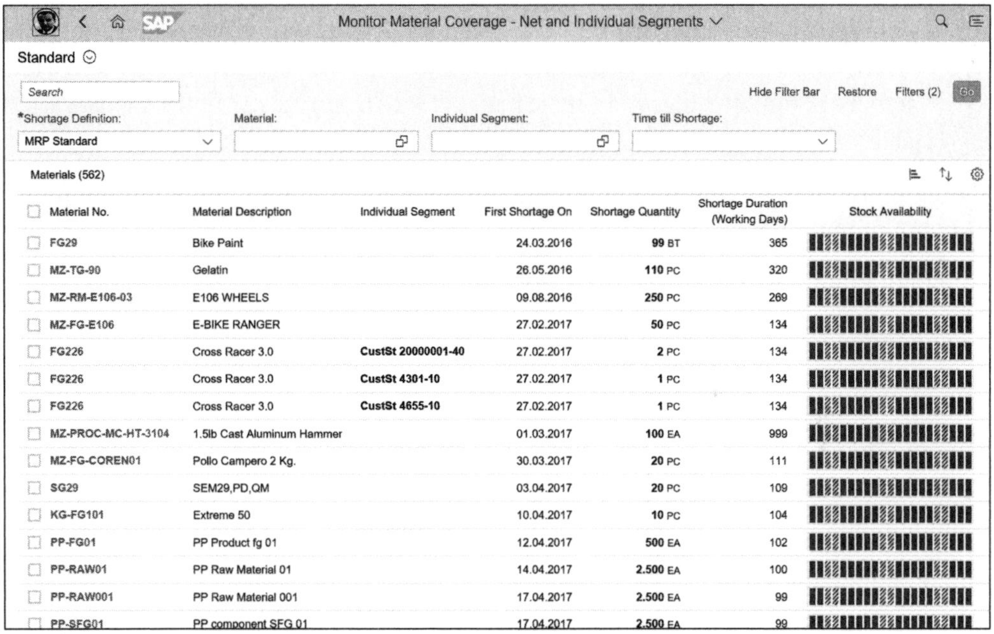
Monitor Material Coverage - Net and Individual Segments
Standard
Search
Hide Filter Bar Restore Filters (2) Go
*Shortage Definition: MRP Standard
Material:
Individual Segment:
Time till Shortage:
Materials (562)
Material No. Material Description Individual Segment First Shortage On Shortage Quantity Shortage Duration (Working Days) Stock Availability
FG29 Bike Paint 24.03.2016 99 BT 365
MZ-TG-90 Gelatin 26.05.2016 110 PC 320
MZ-RM-E106-03 E106 WHEELS 09.08.2016 250 PC 269
MZ-FG-E106 E-BIKE RANGER 27.02.2017 50 PC 134
FG226 Cross Racer 3.0 CustSt 20000001-40 27.02.2017 2 PC 134
FG226 Cross Racer 3.0 CustSt 4301-10 27.02.2017 1 PC 134
FG226 Cross Racer 3.0 CustSt 4655-10 27.02.2017 1 PC 134
MZ-PROC-MC-HT-3104 1.5lb Cast Aluminum Hammer 01.03.2017 100 EA 999
MZ-FG-COREN01 Pollo Campero 2 Kg. 30.03.2017 20 PC 111
SG29 SEM29,PD,QM 03.04.2017 20 PC 109
KG-FG101 Extreme 50 10.04.2017 10 PC 104
PP-FG01 PP Product fg 01 12.04.2017 500 EA 102
PP-RAW01 PP Raw Material 01 14.04.2017 2.500 EA 100
PP-RAW001 PP Raw Material 001 17.04.2017 2.500 EA 99
PP-SFG01 PP component SFG 01 17.04.2017 2.500 EA 99

Figure 6.10 Monitor Material Coverage: Net and Individual Segments

This section outlined the tools available for understanding MRP requirements in SAP S/4HANA from a materials-on-hand standpoint. The next section will cover augmenting this planning understanding with further forecasting and predictive capabilities in SAP S/4HANA to drive a comprehensive picture of historical consumption, existing stocks, and future predictive consumption for MRP controllers.

6.3   Forecasting and Planning

At its core, MRP is a prediction of upcoming needs and requirements. To drive accuracy in this prediction, forecasting and planning for future demand is required. There are several different forecasting scenarios to consider, such as forecasting for ongoing production operations, for which you have history and current stock counts; expansions of production areas, for which you are making changes to existing products that may require additional components and stock, but the overall product line is established and has historical data and some of the stock to support the forecast; and new product and production areas, for which you don't have history or existing stock upon which to base your forecast.

With regards to stock counts, having real-time analysis in SAP S/4HANA provides tactical information on potential supply shortages for materials. If consumption history for an item exists in the system, you can also carry out a forecast process. Alternatively, if you don't have consumption data for a particular item, you can carry out forecast planning using an alternate material with historical consumption data available. You also can enter historical consumption data for a material manually. This section covers forecasting and planning in SAP S/4HANA MRP, beginning with forecasting.

Note

MRP Live on SAP S/4HANA doesn't perform forecast-based planning, so this type of planning reverts to the classic MRP run transaction.

6.3.1   Forecast Planning

Forecast planning uses material consumption patterns, both planned and unplanned, to derive future requirements and align stocks and orders with anticipated demand. Forecast planning can't be planned in the new MRP Live transaction in SAP S/4HANA (Transaction MD01N). To execute forecast planning, forecast parameters must be maintained in the material record under the **Forecast** tab and the **MRP3** tab, under **Forecast Requirements**, as shown in Figure 6.11.

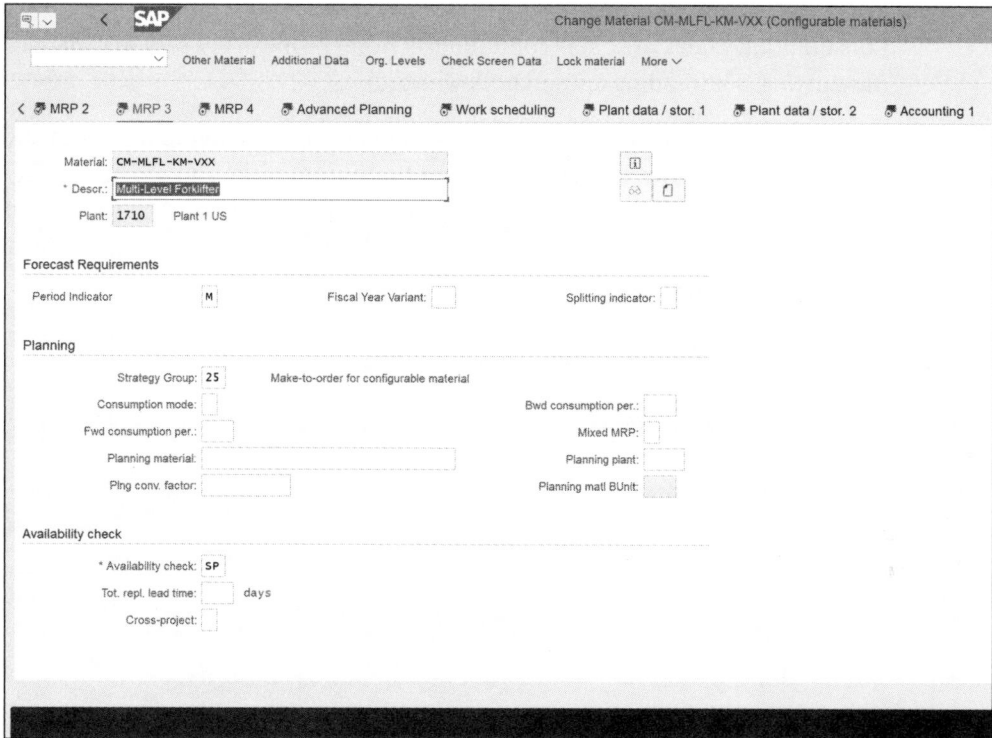

Figure 6.11 Forecast Planning Parameters

You can execute a forecast at the at the plant level via Transaction MP30. You can also select **MP38** (foreground) or **MPBT** (background) as an option on this menu path, for forecasting at the MRP area total level.

To carry out the forecast, you must first select a model to be applied. General patterns typically can be discerned by analyzing the historical consumption of a material. The main models in SAP forecasting are as follows:

- **Constant model**
  Consumption values vary statistically over time by a mean value.

- **Trend model**
  Consumption values rise or fall over a period of time with only minor fluctuations.

- **Seasonal model**
  Consumption values rise and fall according to time period or events occurring annually.

- **Seasonal trend model**
  Consumption values rise or fall continuously from the mean in a seasonal manner (fluctuating, but trending upward or downward).

The MRP controller can choose one of these models in the material master in the **Forecasting** tab, as shown in Figure 6.12; have the system make an automatic selection; or select one manually and have the system verify the selection. The system will automatically apply the constant model if it's unable to discern another model pattern while analyzing the data.

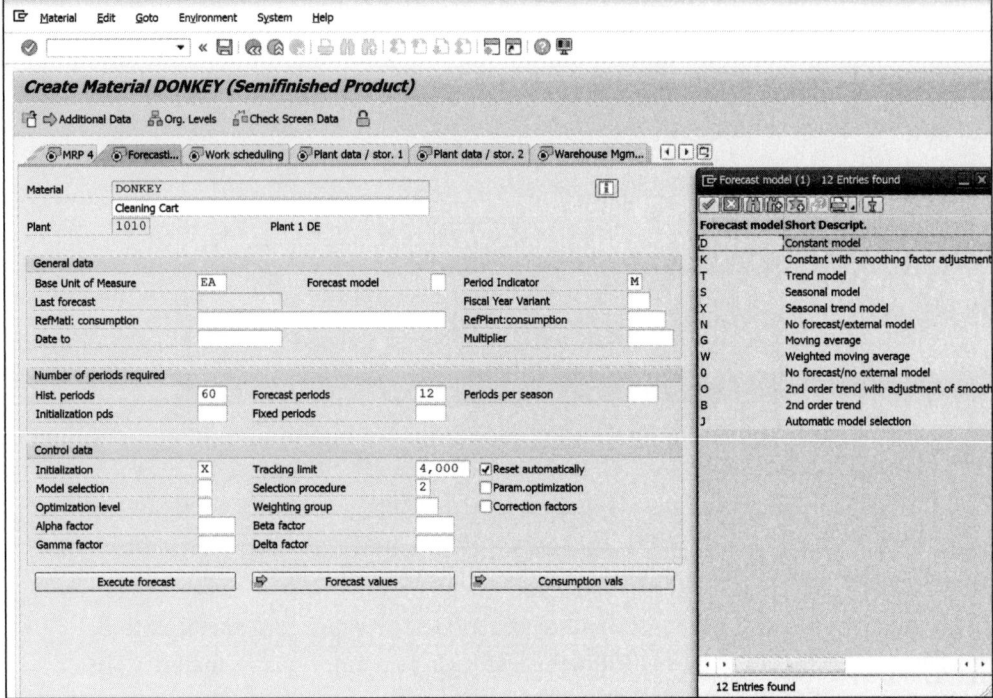

Figure 6.12 Forecast Model Selection: Forecasting Tab in Material Master

You can set the forecast model to be used directly in the material master or via a forecast profile in Transaction MP80. Here, you define the defaults and settings for the forecast profile, including the model, as shown in Figure 6.13.

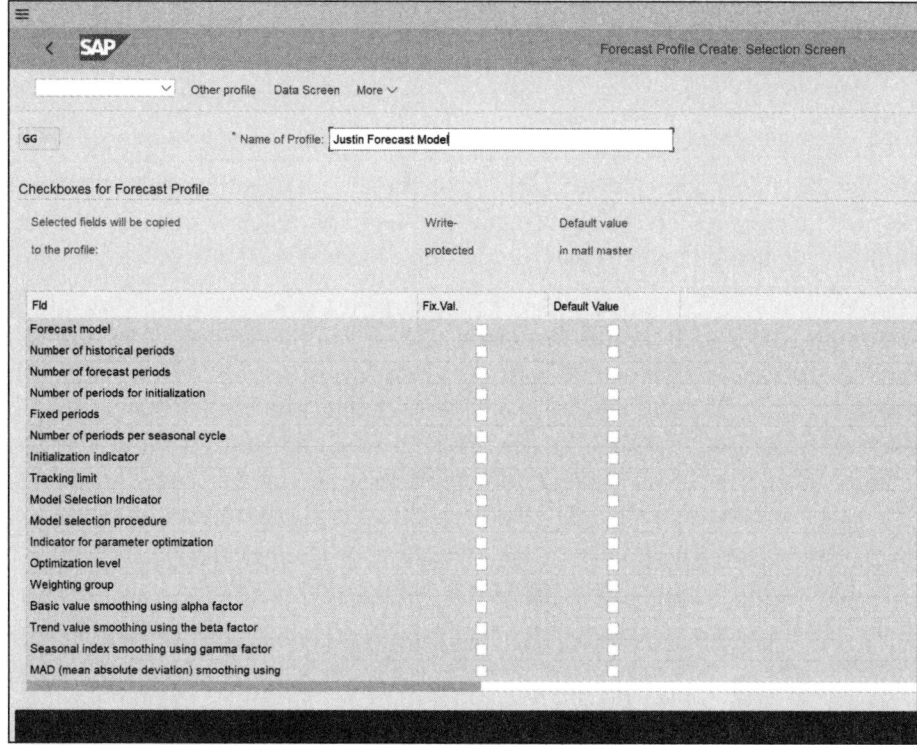

Figure 6.13 Forecast Profile Settings

The forecast requirements calculation then compares the existing stock and orders outstanding for a material with the amounts required per the forecast and creates purchasing proposals to cover any deltas/shortages, as shown in Figure 6.14.

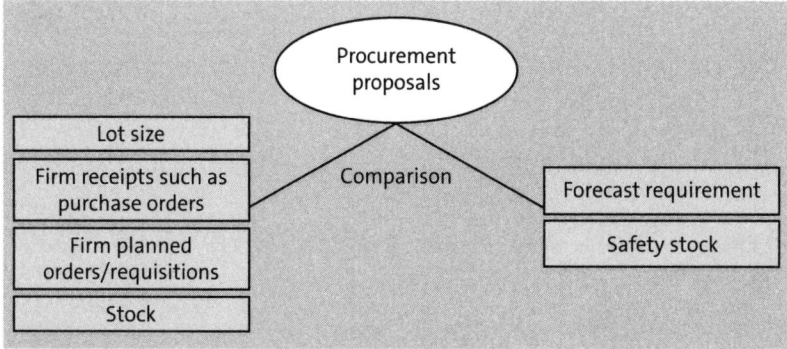

Figure 6.14 Forecast-Based Planning: Net Requirements Calculation

Forecasting relies heavily on planning data to derive forecast estimates in SAP. Next, we'll discuss two types of planning: reorder point planning and time-phased planning.

6.3.2   Reorder Point Planning

For manual reorder point planning, you can make settings directly in the **MRP 1** tab of the material master. Here, you can set the **MRP Type/controller**, as well as maximum stock permissible in the **MRP Procedure** section, as shown in Figure 6.15.

You can also have the system calculate reorder points in an automated fashion by selecting the MRP type **VM** for **Automatic Reorder Point Planning**. The system will then calculate the reorder point based on historical consumption and select the optimal reorder point level for you. Reorder point planning is most effective when there is a clear historical dataset and future forecast of requirements, or when a certain amount of material always needs to be on hand, regardless of material requirements. The system calculates the reorder point by adding the safety stock with the average usage of the product multiplied by the lead time. If lead times are high, the reorder point and commensurate inventory carry adjusts upward as well.

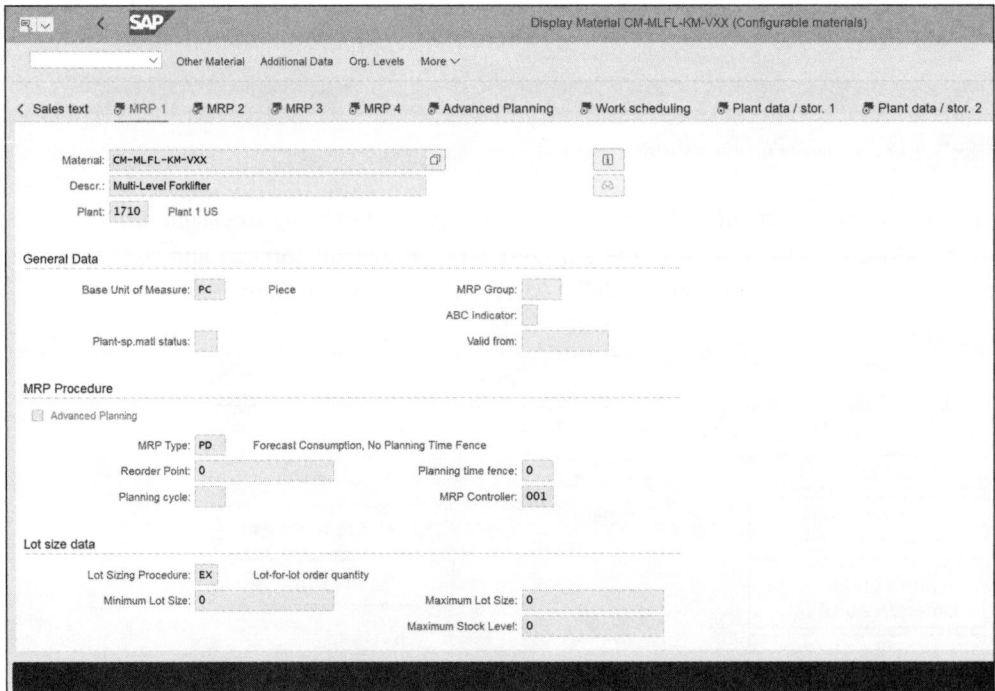

Figure 6.15 MRP 1 Tab: Reorder Point

6.3.3   Time-Phased Planning

Time-phased planning (TPP) is based on a specific time interval, often based on the supplier delivery schedule to align the orders better with the delivery time. Time-phased planning can be combined with reorder point planning. If a reorder point is crossed, the material is planned from the point of shortage to the next MRP run, and for this time interval the ordered quantity must cover the shortage. Beginning with the next MRP run, time-phased planning again plans the material at the regular intervals.

To leverage time phased planning, you can create a custom MRP Type "Y1" for time-phased planning as shown in Figure 6.16 and then select **New Entries** as in Figure 6.17. You can access these transactions via menu path **Production • Master Data • Check MRP Types** or via Transaction OMDQ.

Once you've configured a time-phased planning option, you can use it in the **MRP** tab of your materials in conjunction with your planning cycles as in Figure 6.17. Here you see the custom type "Y1" has been set up for **Time-Phased Materials Planning**. Further general MRP settings can be made in this screen for the **Firming Type**, which allows the MRP user to define what type of follow-on activity/order is to occur. The options are automatic firming and order proposals rescheduled out, automatic firming without order proposals, manual firming and order proposals scheduled out, and manual firming without order proposals. The MRP user can also define the degree to which the forecast is used in MRP and whether safety stock or a reorder point is to be calculated.

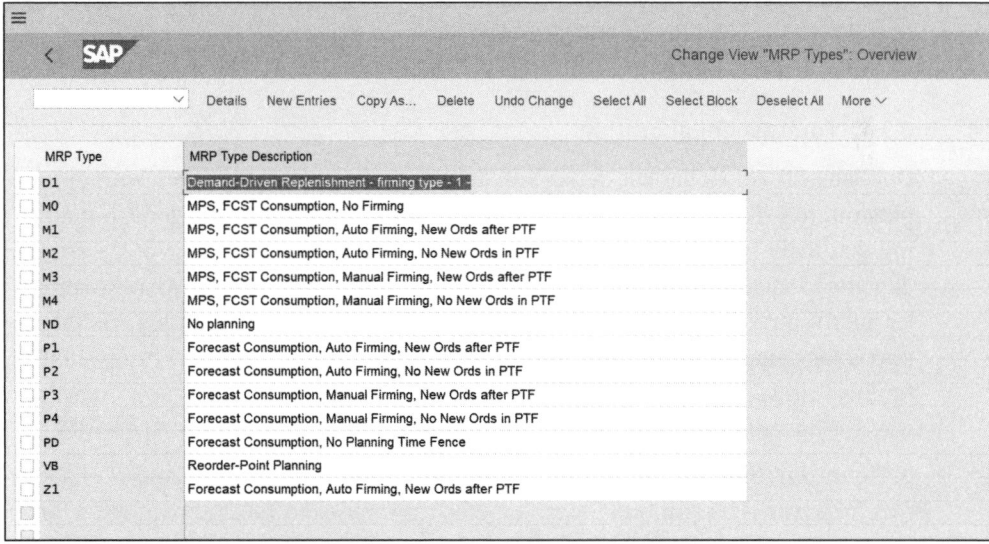

Figure 6.16 Change View "MRP Types"

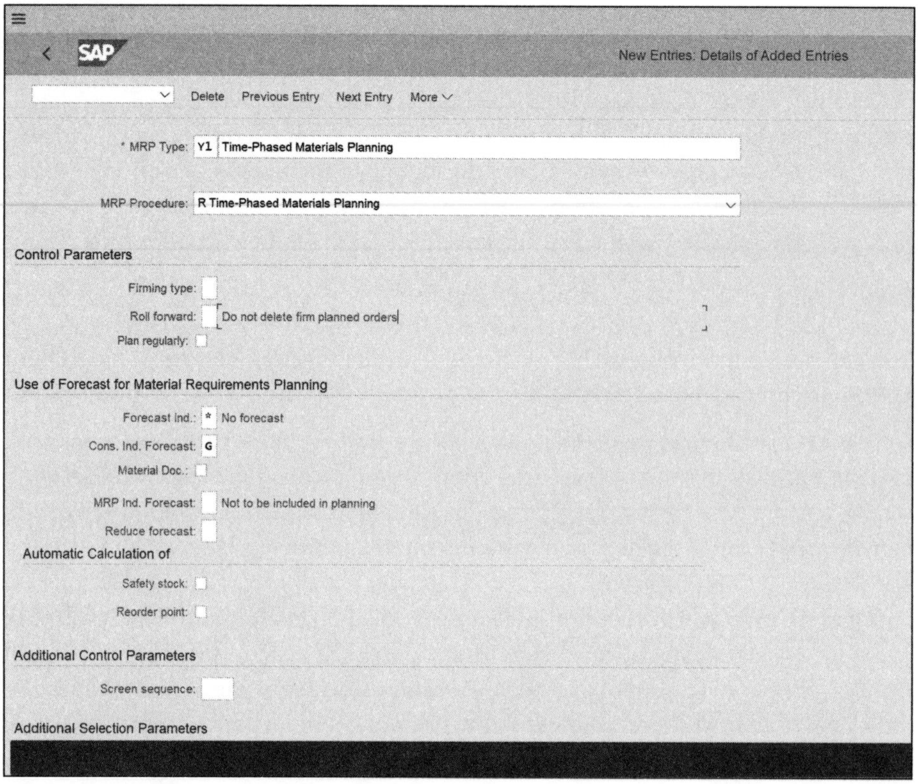

Figure 6.17 Time-Phased Planning MRP Type

6.3.4   Forecast Collaboration

Once an MRP controller has derived an internal forecast, a reality check with the supplier often is required. Determining requirements far in advance is good, but ensuring that there is a supply base with contracts in place and knowledge of the coming demand to adequately fulfill the orders in the expected time is better. An MRP controller and/or buyer can always reach out to suppliers to confirm readiness and discuss upcoming demand outside of the system. Using SAP Ariba Supply Chain Collaboration for Buyers, a supplier can also review and commit materials forecasts and share them with the buyer in system, as shown in Figure 6.18.

In Figure 6.19, the supplier commits an amount in SAP Ariba Supply Chain Collaboration for Buyers. If the amount doesn't match the forecasted amount required, a buyer knows to begin looking at alternate sources of supply for the remainder or all of his order.

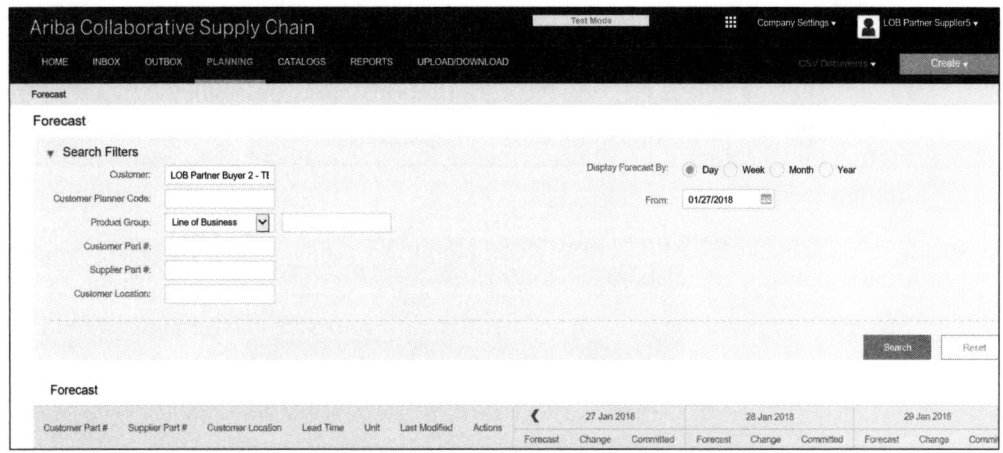

Figure 6.18 Forecast Review in SAP Ariba Supply Chain Collaboration for Buyers

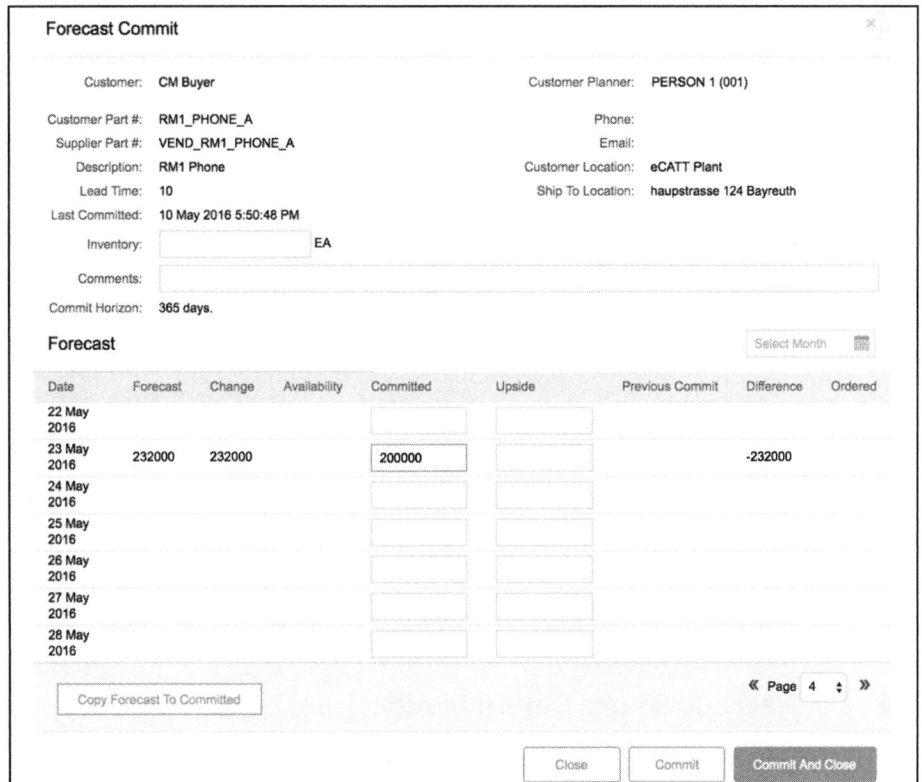

Figure 6.19 Forecast Commit in SAP Ariba Supply Chain Collaboration for Buyers

221

In addition to forecast commit on the supplier side, the buyer also has a forecast dashboard at her disposal (see Figure 6.20), which allows the buyer to view what was shared with the supplier for the forecast, not just what currently exists in the SAP S/4HANA planning areas. Leveraging this dashboard, the buyer is able to obtain real-time status information, measure supplier performance, and prevent potential supply chain disruptions.

Via the Supply Chain Monitor, further alerts and overview analysis is possible in SAP Ariba Supply Chain Collaboration for Buyers.

Once you've created the forecast and verified with your supply base that it should be possible on both sides to realize, the next step is to underpin the MRP requirements with agreements and suppliers, which is the topic of the next section.

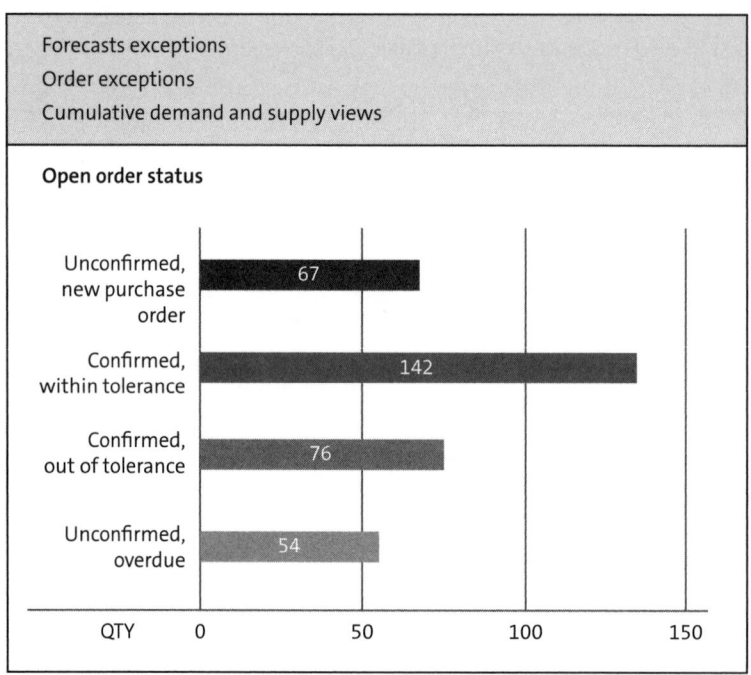

Figure 6.20 Forecast Dashboard in SAP Ariba Supply Chain Collaboration for Buyers

6.4   Contract and Source Determination

Once the material requirements have been determined in an MRP run, the source of supply needs to be identified to determine whether a procurement proposal is to be generated or a reservation or other in-house transaction made to secure the material. SAP S/4HANA supports the following sources of supply, prioritizing these options in descending order:

1. Production versions (in-house)
2. Delivery schedules (external)
3. Purchasing contracts (external)
4. Purchasing info records (external)
5. Source list (available as of SAP S/4HANA on-premise 1709; previous versions do not support source lists)

Once a source of supply has been identified and assigned, or it's determined that no source of supply is available for automatic assignment, the MRP run then generates a schedule line in a scheduling agreement, a sourced requisition, or an unsourced requisition (see Figure 6.21). Upon review of the requisitions, the source of supply is confirmed, and these requisitions are then converted to purchase orders and transmitted to the suppliers.

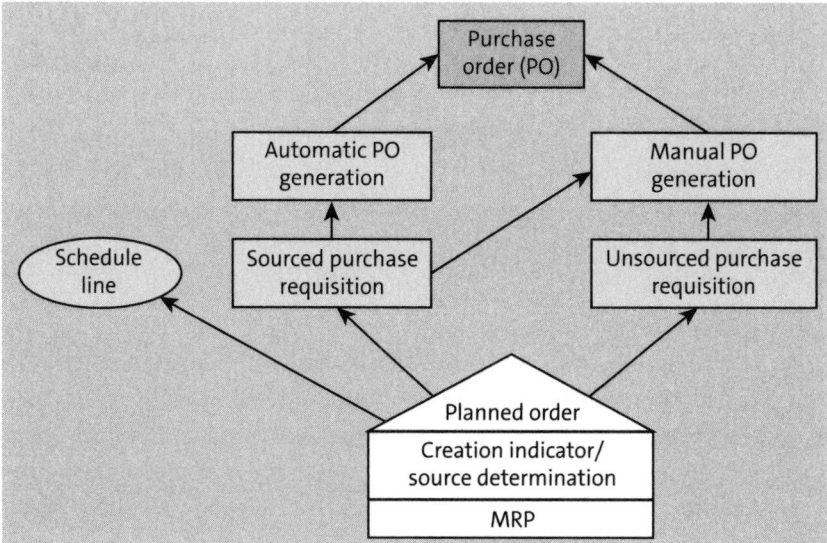

Figure 6.21 Planned Orders: Sources of Supply

Now, let's discuss the ways in which you can assign a source of supply (or multiple sources) up front.

6.4.1   Purchasing Information Record

The PIR contains additional information for a material purchased from a specific supplier and can apply either at the purchasing organization or plant level. The PIR contains a source of supply for the material, as well as a purchasing group, invoice verification indicators, net price, delivery tolerances, and other purchasing-specific data. The pipeline and consignment PIRs can store prices for different validity periods to assist in purchasing planning. There are four main PIR categories:

- **Standard PIR**
  Used for standard purchase orders, the standard PIR can be used for materials and services with and without master records.

- **Pipeline PIR**
  Used for purchasing liquids that are delivered via a pipeline from supplier.

- **Consignment PIR**
  Used for consignment, in which the supplier maintains stock on your premises at their cost, only billing after consumption.

- **Subcontracting PIR**
  Used for subcontract orders and can contain information on component assembly prices from the supplier.

In SAP S/4HANA, numerous apps support PIR transactions and analysis, including the following:

- **Purchasing Info Record**
  Displays individual PIRs.

- **Create Purchasing Info Record**
  App version of Transaction ME11.

- **Manage Purchasing Info Records**
  You can view, manage, change, and create PIRs using this app, as shown in Figure 6.22. Here, you can create a PIR, which includes tabs for **General Information, Conditions, Invoice, Delivery and Quantity**, and **Supplier**. As of SAP S/4HANA Sourcing and Procurement on-premise 1909, you can also create and manage category-specific info records for consignment, subcontracting, and pipeline, in addition to the standard categories.

- **Mass Change to Purchasing Info Records**
  You can change multiple fields in multiple records simultaneously using this app.

- **Monitor Purchasing Info Records Price History**
  Allows for monitoring price history and details (date, price, and units), based on filter criteria you set.

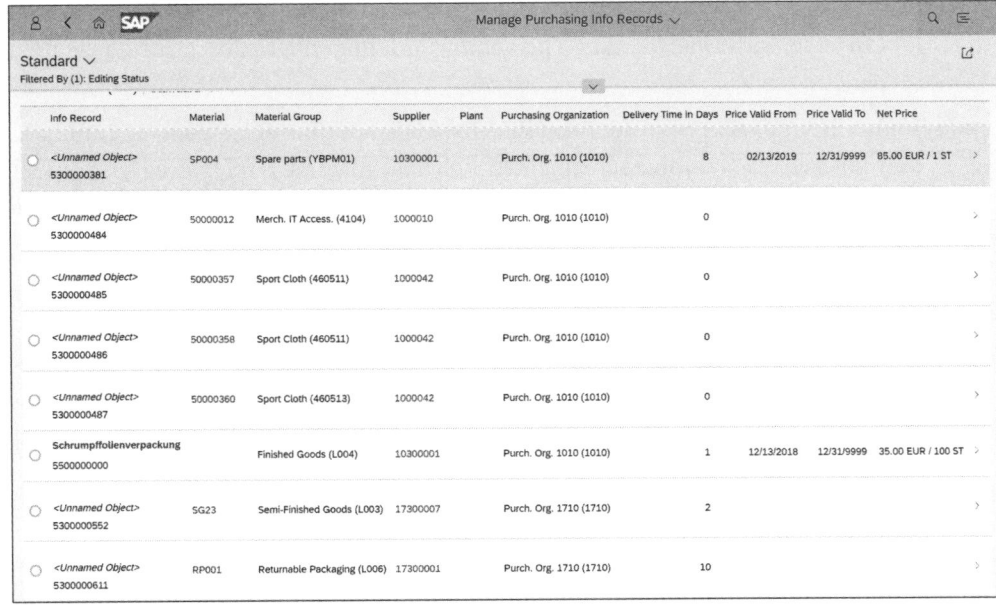

Figure 6.22 Manage Purchasing Info Records: Create PIR

If going directly to SAP GUI, the main PIR transaction codes are listed in Table 6.4.

Transaction Code	Description
ANZE	Display Purchasing Info Record
ME11	Create Purchasing Info Record
ME12	Change Purchasing Info Record
ME13	Display Purchasing Info Record

Table 6.4 Purchasing Info Record Transaction Codes

6.4.2 Source List

The source list specifies suppliers for a material by time period. You can create an entry in a source list directly from the PIR and define a source of supply as fixed (preferred), planning (used for MRP), or blocked. For the planning indicator, in SAP S/4HANA 1709 and beyond, if you set the source of supply with the MRP 1 indicator, this source of supply is automatically assigned to purchase requisitions and planned orders in MRP. If you set MRP 2 for the scheduling agreement, scheduling agreement lines created to order the material will contain the supplier as the source of supply. The blocked indicator can be set with a validity range, preventing ordering with a particular supplier for a set period of time.

Source lists can also be maintained directly, via an outline agreement, or automatically for each PIR or outline agreement in which the material is referenced. You can set a source list requirement for a plant, which requires each material procured for the plant to have a source list entry. You can also set a source list requirement at the material master level, requiring the material to have a source list entry prior to ordering.

Although source lists are integral to many plant-specific direct procurement activities, they aren't supported in SAP S/4HANA versions 1511 and 1610 for MRP. Later versions beginning with SAP S/4HANA 1709 will take source lists into account during MRP runs. For older versions of SAP S/4HANA, quota agreements are recommended as a workaround. MRP in SAP S/4HANA considers quota arrangements automatically; no switch activations are required in the material master.

6.4.3   Quota Arrangement

Quota arrangements are used in MRP processes to allocate purchasing between two or more suppliers. Quota arrangements are used to hedge supply chain risks and ensure purchasing allocation in a formalized manner. Quota arrangements are often used in MRP scenarios and allow for an automated procurement proposal generation to allocate procurement proposals among designated suppliers in a defined fashion. In SAP S/4HANA Sourcing and Procurement, quotas can be managed in the **Manage Quota Arrangements** app, shown in Figure 6.23.

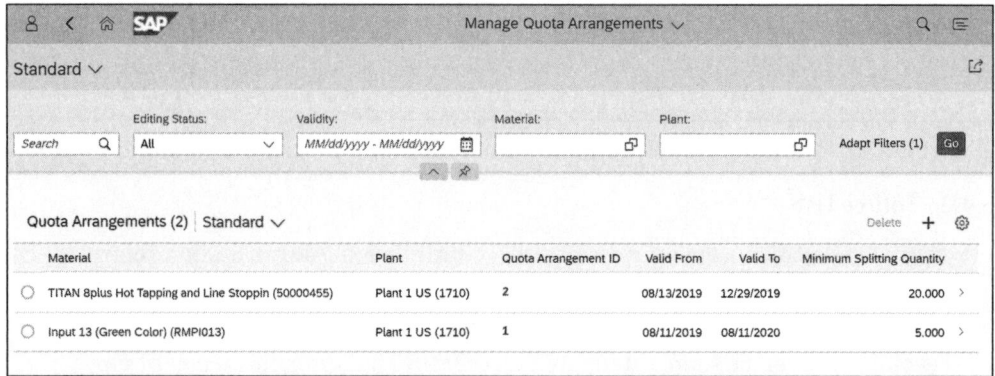

Figure 6.23 Manage Quota Arrangements App

Here, you can search for quota arrangements and create, maintain, analyze, and view them, as well as maintain base quantities so that a minimum quantity is assigned even if further suppliers are added. You also can navigate to a supplier/material fact sheet to further inform the settings of the quota arrangement.

For MRP, you can use allocation quota arrangements and splitting quota arrangements. *Allocation quota arrangements* allocate the entire lot to a particular supplier, whereas *splitting arrangements* allow for lots to be split between suppliers.

If you wish to analyze quota arrangements, use Transaction MEQ6 in the SAP GUI, as in Figure 6.24.

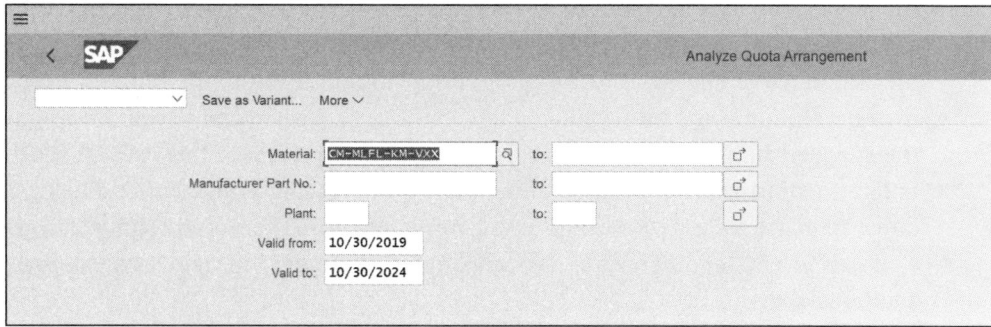

Figure 6.24 Analyze Quota Arrangement

6.4.4   Scheduling Agreement

A *scheduling agreement* is an outline agreement with a supplier defining the time-frame and delivery dates when certain materials and services are to be delivered over a period of time. Quantities to be delivered can be divided among schedule lines to feed production appropriately and optimize inventory during the process. Rather than carry all the inventory up front for the production process, the materials can be planned and ordered in the appropriate quantities at the applicable times.

One scheduling agreement can replace a significant number of purchase orders and the administrative overhead associated with managing each of these PO document flows to invoice in the system. In SAP S/4HANA, the following SAP Fiori apps are available for scheduling agreement creation and management:

- Manage Scheduling Agreements
- Mass Changes to Scheduling Agreements (As of SAP S/4HANA 1909, enhanced grouping of header and item fields from multiple scheduling agreements is possible, further enabling mass changes.)
- Manage Workflows for Scheduling Agreements

As of SAP S/4HANA On Premise 1909, you can also view scheduling agreement confirmations in the **Monitor Supplier Confirmations App**. Previously, only supplier confirmations of standard POs were visible.

A scheduling agreement can have an additional release step prior to being issued to the supplier (document type LPA), or a scheduling agreement can be issued directly to the supplier (document type LP). Using scheduling agreements without release documentation requirements, as in the latter option, in conjunction with MRP, allows for material requirements for scheduling line items to be created and issued directly to the supplier during the MRP run. A scheduling line agreement thus can be fixed, unlike a requisition or a planned order, making scheduling agreement line items a direct approach toward procuring items from an MRP run. There is no second conversion step to a PO, in other words; the scheduling agreement line item constitutes an additional order.

Scheduling agreements cover the following procurement types:

- Standard, which covers most general scenarios.
- Subcontracting, which can specify when components are to be delivered to the subcontractor for assembly/work for each scheduled line item
- Consignment, for scenarios in which the supplier only invoices after consumption of provided stock on-premise at customer
- Stock transfer, for internal orders of items from other plants/warehouses

The creation of scheduling agreement lines during MRP runs can be assigned in the MRP group and plant parameters. To maintain parameters either by plant or by MRP group, follow IMG menu path **Materials Management • Consumption Based Planning**, then either **Plant Parameters • Carry Out Overall Maintenance of Plant Parameters**, or **MRP Groups • Carry Out Overall Maintenance on MRP Groups** (see Figure 6.25 and Figure 6.26).

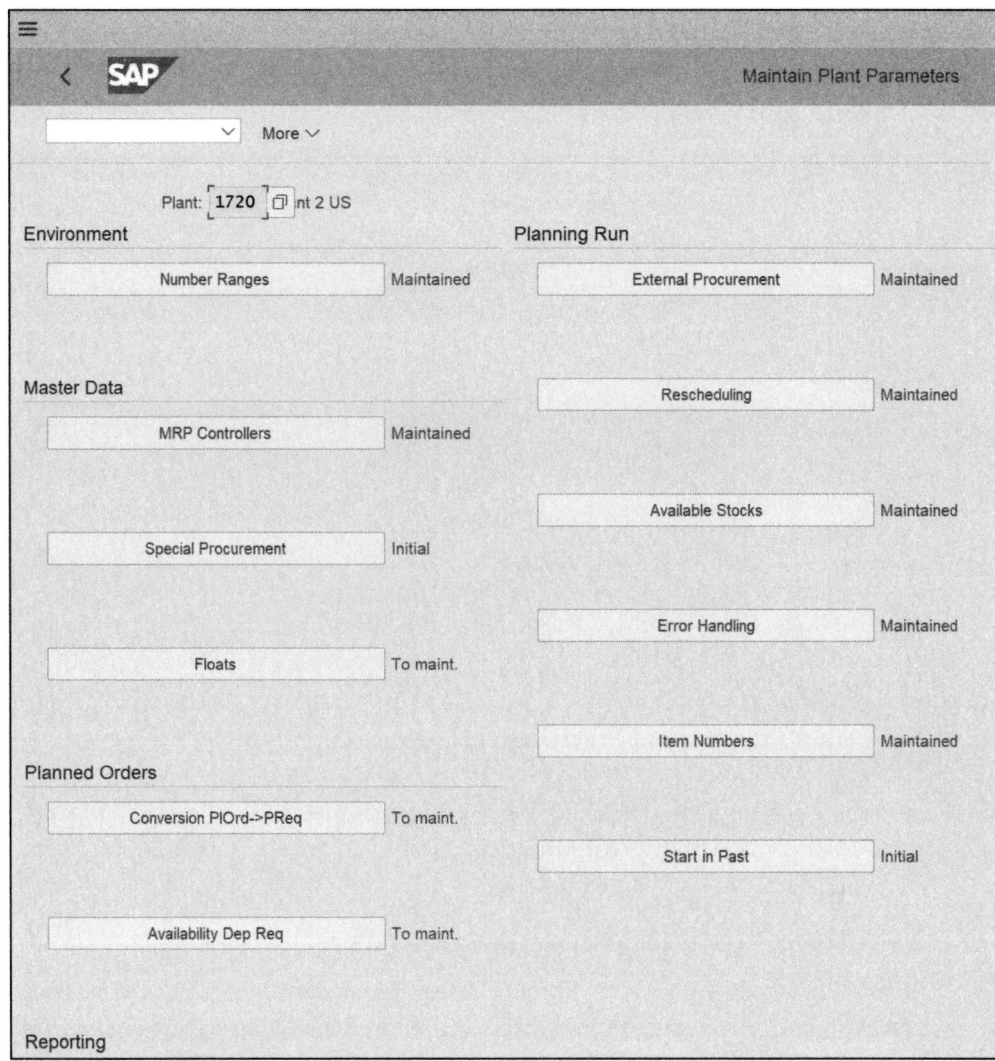

Figure 6.25 Maintain Plant Parameters

Here, you can maintain your MRP controllers and other master data items, planning run parameters, reporting, planned order settings, and the general number ranges for the plant environment.

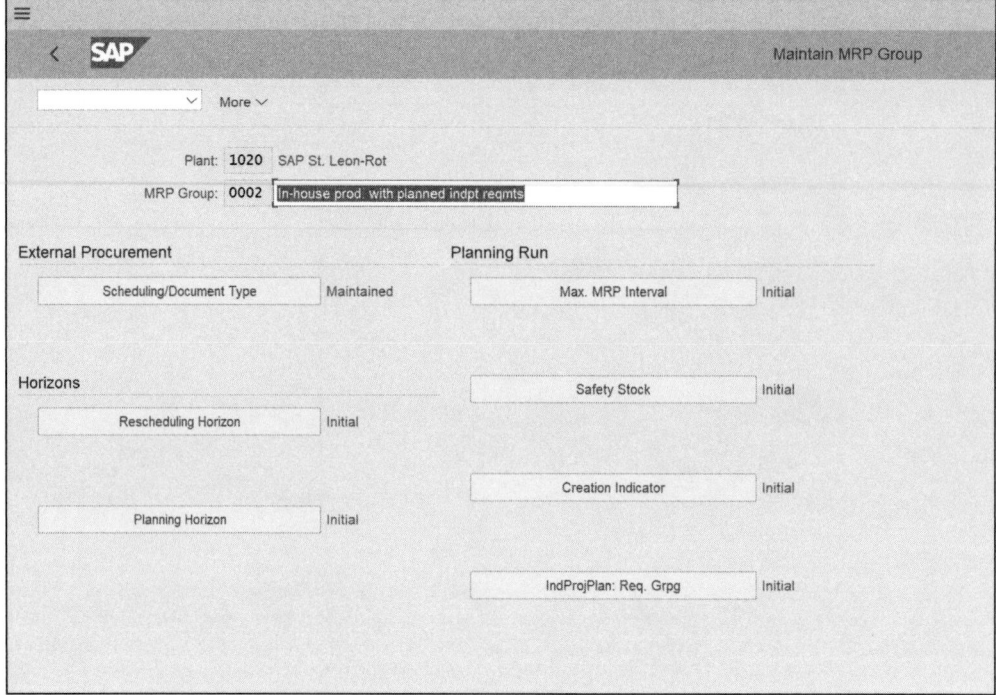

Figure 6.26 Carry Out Overall Maintenance of MRP Groups

If both the plant parameters and the MRP group parameters have been set, the MRP group settings have priority over the plant ones.

6.4.5   Scheduling Agreement Release Collaboration

Scheduling agreement releases, like purchase orders, sometimes require some back-and-forth with the supplier to finalize. With many scheduling releases being triggered automatically via MRP runs, often the only recourse for a supplier looking to finalize or clarify a release line is to pick up the phone. SAP Ariba Supply Chain Collaboration for Buyers provides two-way communication and visibility with suppliers, as well as further automation of the downstream processes on the invoice side of the process.

Under the **Release History** tab in SAP Ariba Supply Chain Collaboration for Buyers, you can review the firm zone-scheduling agreement releases that are confirmed for production, as well as trade-off zone releases—for which you will only be out the material costs if you have to cancel—and planning zone releases (see Figure 6.27).

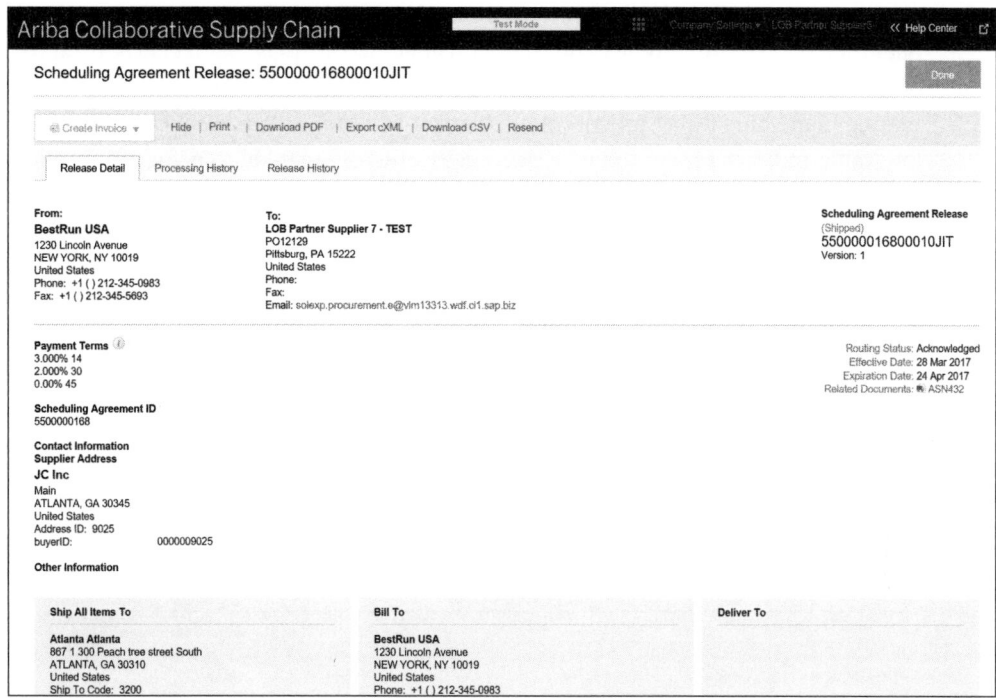

Figure 6.27 Scheduling Agreement Release History in SAP Ariba Supply Chain Collaboration for Buyers

Scheduling agreements are a core direct procurement process and an oft-used alternative to purchase orders in MRP scenarios; scheduling agreements can cut straight to the order if necessary and leverage an existing agreement, versus creating a completely new order. Yet this abridged manner of creating a scheduling agreement release also makes this approach more prone to confusion if the supplier needs to clarify or adjust something. SAP Ariba Supply Chain Collaboration for Buyers supports the end-to-end scheduling agreement process between supplier and buyer, mitigating potential confusion in these areas and helping to fully realize the efficiencies provided by a scheduling agreement ordering approach.

6.4.6   Blanket Purchase Order

Blanket purchase orders are typically used for ordering low-value, high-volume items delivered in an ad hoc manner, sometimes per the customer's request or per an agreement. Rather than create a separate PO for each delivery/order, a blanket PO is established as a kind of bucket with a set amount/quantity and time period. The supplier then delivers and invoices on this blanket PO accordingly. Blanket POs are at the other end of the spectrum from MRP in automating procurement. Rather than automating high-value direct procurement, blanket POs are mostly used for automating low-value indirect procurement. Advantages of using blanket POs for automating procurement include the following:

- Period validity versus one-time order. A blanket PO can cover a period of time during which deliveries can be made and invoices submitted.

- No goods receipt or service entry sheet is required normally for a blanket PO, which cuts down on the process cycles and costs for low-value items.

- Monthly invoices are generally used to further cut down on the processing costs and steps.

Creating a blanket PO or framework order in SAP S/4HANA is much like it was in SAP ERP. In the Create PO app, in advanced mode, select **Framework Order** as the PO type (see Figure 6.28). This is the same as in Transaction ME21N in SAP GUI.

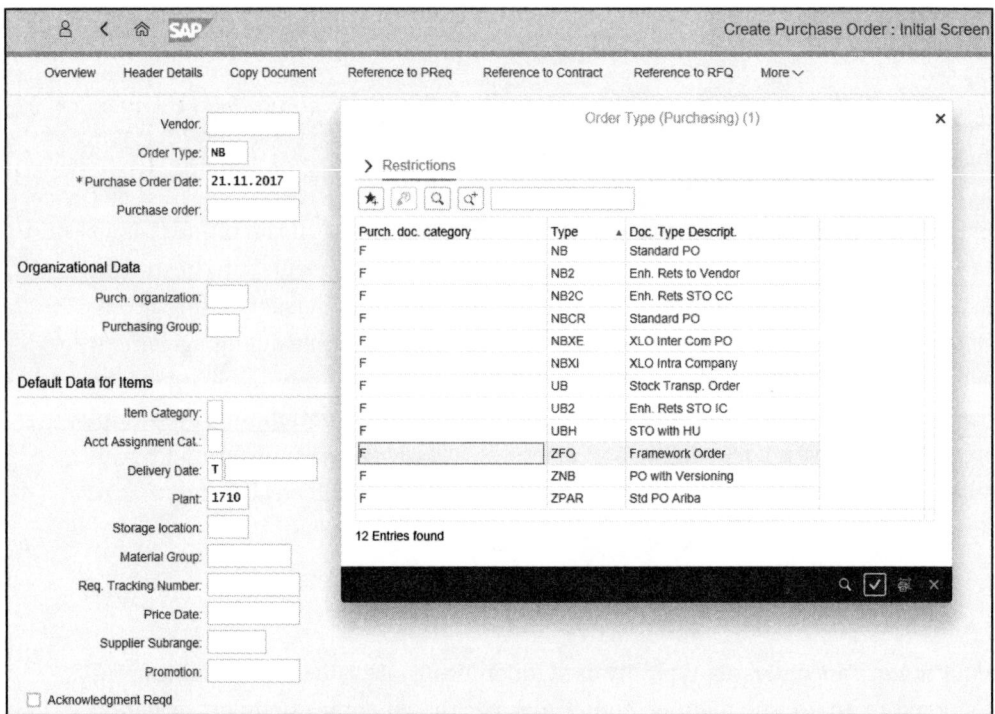

Figure 6.28 Framework PO in SAP S/4HANA

Selecting item type **B** for limit item allows a date range and value to be defined. You don't have to define the account assignment up front as with other orders. It can be set to **Unknown—U** to allow the invoice to perform the correct account assignment at the end of a transaction. In a framework order, you can set multiple delivery dates and a bucket of money from which the supplier invoices as it makes deliveries. The system validates the invoice against the blanket PO's limit and validity period and deducts the amount from the total.

6.4.7   Purchase Orders and Multitier Purchase Orders

SAP Ariba Supply Chain Collaboration for Buyers supports standard purchase orders, as does the Ariba Network in general. However, for direct procurement, there are several variations on the PO process that are the focus of SAP Ariba Supply Chain Collaboration for Buyers. The first is the multitier order. Although rare in indirect procurement, multitier orders can be common in direct procurement. Multitier orders pose challenges to standard purchasing systems. In a multitier order, the order is placed with a contract manufacturer, which then gives the go-ahead to a further supplier.

The multitier order capability allows for both drop-shipping and inbound shipment and receipt visibility, as shown in Figure 6.29.

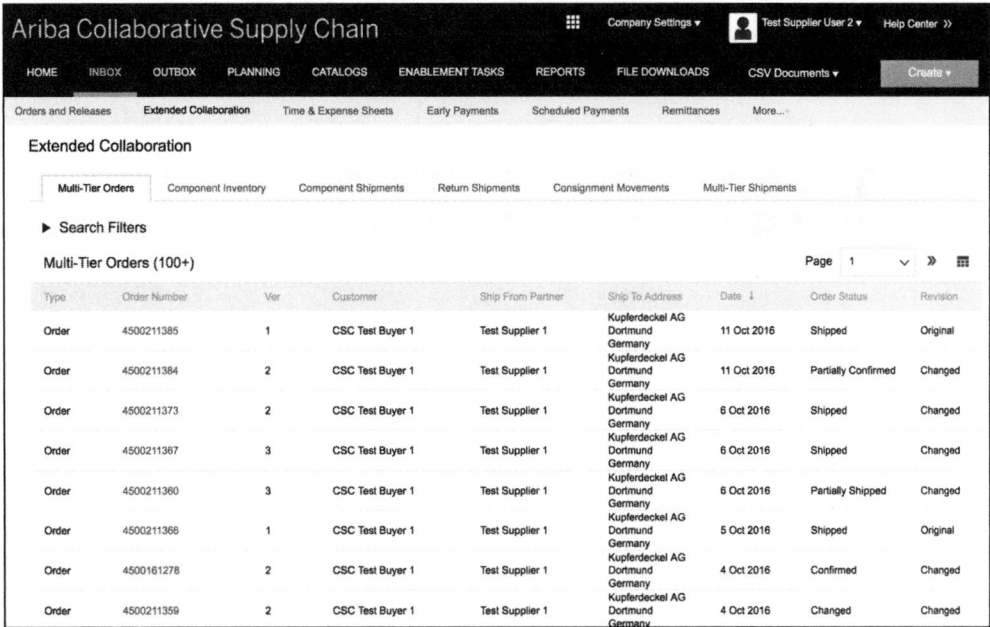

Figure 6.29 Multitier Orders: Drop-Shipping Visibility

This type of collaboration would not be possible directly in SAP S/4HANA because the suppliers need an area to login to and interact within. The Ariba Network effectively creates this space and the functionality to allow both the buyer and suppliers to share data across each other's respective internal systems, even when multiple suppliers are involved in fulfilling the same order.

6.4.8   Subcontracting

Some supplier relationships require you as the purchasing organization to provide the supplier with the components used in their part of the value creation. A typical example in manufacturing would be assembly. Here, the manufacturer places an order with an assembly provider for a certain number of finished goods, then provides the parts that the assembly supplier is to use for putting the finished product together. These components are usually associated with a BOM (see Figure 6.30).

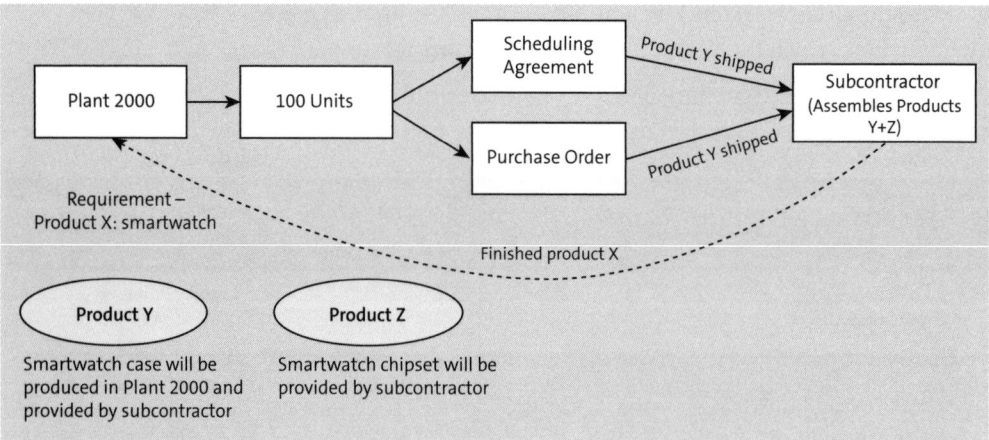

Figure 6.30 Subcontracting Overview

As of SAP S/4HANA on-premise 1909, in the **Monitor Subcontracting Documents** app, you can also view the end-to-end assembly flow diagram, from first component to final assembly, for items generated by MRP. Additional subcontracting app functionality in version 1909 includes the following:

- **Manage Purchase Orders app**
  Subcontracting POs, commitments, and supplier contact information now visible

- **Create Supplier Invoices app**
  Subcontracting invoices supported

Standard Subcontracting Approach

In SAP, there are multiple ways of setting up this transaction, but many approaches add more complexity than they are worth. For example, you can choose to create plants that are technically the supplier's locations and track your inventory as you move it to these locations for finishing. For each transaction requiring subcontracting, you then have to issue a PO and create multiple goods movements and accounting entries internally to support the process. This approach requires more manual effort and accounting acrobatics than is optimal. The most straightforward way to support subcontracting processes is to use the standard subcontracting approach in the system. The process is as follows:

1. Select PO type **L** when creating the purchase order for a subcontracted item. L is the subcontracting PO type and allows you to create subitems manually or via a BOM explosion automatically for the components to be provided to the subcontractor. Although the final product doesn't necessarily require a materials master, the components do require a material master record for this process in SAP.

2. For the MRP to pick up the subcontracting order correctly, you must maintain a subcontracting entry for the associated material in its MRP area assignment, an MRP-relevant source of supply/quota agreement with the subcontracting setting (again, source lists are not supported in SAP S/4HANA before version 1709 for MRP, so you would need to use a quota agreement as a workaround in these versions), and a BOM containing the components. During the MRP run, the system explodes the BOM requirements and classifies dependent subcontracting elements as such.

To flag a material master directly for subcontracting, choose a half finished (**HALB**) or finished (**FERT**) material, and in the **MRP2** tab maintain the **Special Procurement** field with option **30** for the plant, as shown in Figure 6.31.

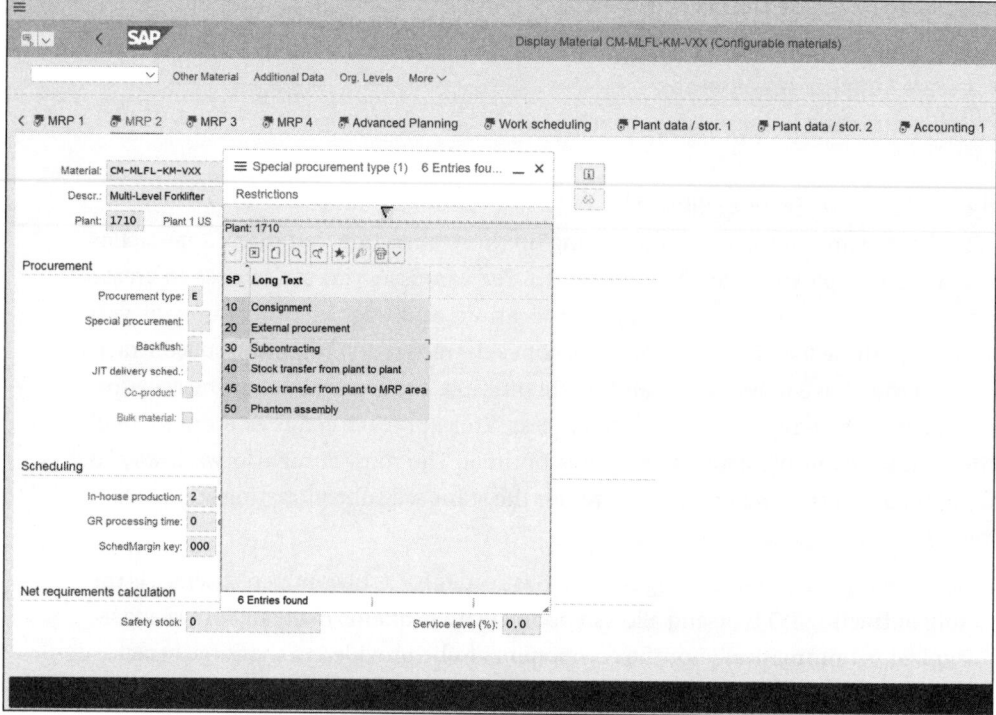

Figure 6.31 Procurement Settings for Subcontracting in Material Master

Subcontracting in SAP S/4HANA

In previous versions of SAP ERP, component materials to be provided to the subcontractor could be planned as a separate stock. However, with SAP S/4HANA, a subcontracting MRP area is the default option for subcontracting planning. Subcontracting will appear under the general plant stock if there is no MRP area maintained for the supplier.

Also in previous versions of SAP ERP, you could check subcontracting stocks by supplier by running reports from a specific IMG menu path. This transaction is now available as an app, Display Subcontracting Stocks by Supplier, in SAP S/4HANA, as shown in Figure 6.32.

In SAP S/4HANA, MRP areas have to be created for every subcontractor; if MRP area–specific material master records don't exist, MRP uses default planning parameters. This differs from classic SAP ERP for subcontracting, in which you could plan either with or without MRP areas.

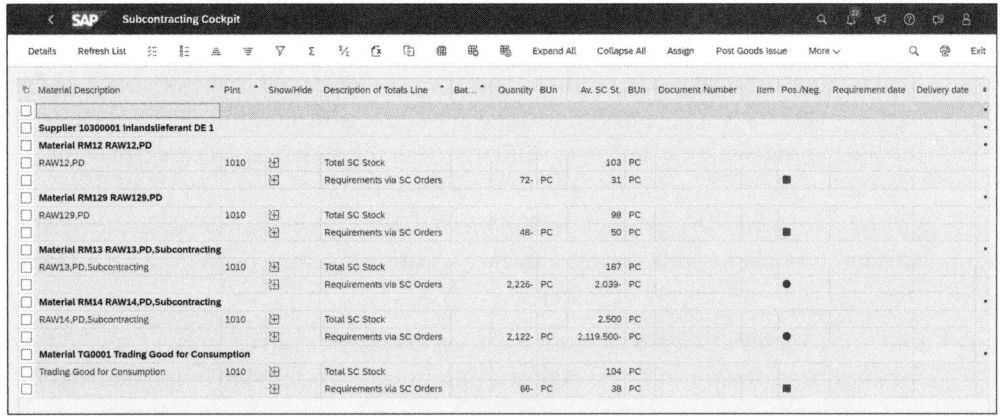

Figure 6.32 Display Subcontracting Stocks by Supplier

If you elected to plan without MRP areas, you weren't able to use the full functionality around lot sizing and were only able to order full lot sizes. If you chose the MRP area route, material data on an MRP area was required for all components. These two options are now combined into one driven by MRP areas, but it doesn't require material data on all components and can support full-lot sizing and sourcing functionality.

Upgrading MRP Subcontracting to SAP S/4HANA

To upgrade MRP subcontracting processes in SAP ERP to SAP S/4HANA, you need to take stock of your existing subcontracting suppliers and processes and identify any gaps, execute a standard upgrade to SAP S/4HANA, and then at postprocessing proceed as follows:

1. Maintain subcontracting MRP areas for all subcontracting suppliers requiring provision stocks to be planned separately from requirements. The customizing entry in the supplier master is sufficient to trigger stock transfers and reservations from the plant to the subcontracting MRP area. You only have to maintain entries in the material masters if special situations exist for lot sizing, purchase requisitions/orders, and/or third-party order processing.

2. Run regenerative MRP and test.

Subcontracting Order Collaboration

As detailed in this chapter, the standard subcontracting process in SAP entails a leap of faith to a degree, which some MRP controllers and their ilk are unwilling to make.

Upon issuing a subcontracting PO and shipping out the components to the supplier, the buyer doesn't technically receive updates on the production of the order until the final product or subassembly with the components is shipped back from the supplier to the buyer. Tracking the materials and valuations, which technically still belong to the buying organization, becomes difficult using the standard process. This often is used as justification by finance and other stakeholders on the buyer side for setting up phantom plants to represent the supplier and then moving and tracking the materials in these plants. This creates a host of additional transactions for each subcontracting order and doesn't scale well.

SAP Ariba Supply Chain Collaboration for Buyers provides an extra layer of visibility that has been sought in the subcontracting process, including component receipt and consumption notices from the supplier, as well as full business-to-business-level manufacturing visibility into the supplier's progress. Using the supplier portal on the Ariba Network, a supplier can login and confirm the consumption of subcontracting components into the assembly, as shown in Figure 6.33.

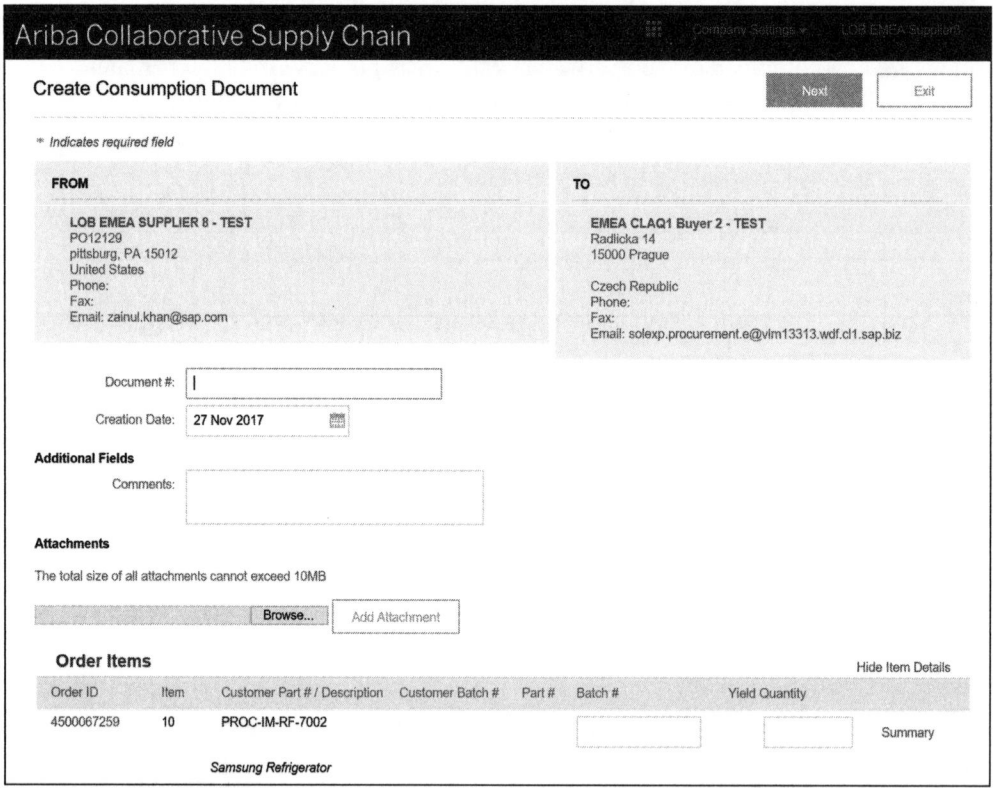

Figure 6.33 Subcontracting Supplier Dashboard: Components Consumed

Particularly in more lengthy subcontracting manufacturing processes, this additional update functionality and the added visibility should provide more reason to use the standard subcontracting process in SAP S/4HANA and avoid customization and nonstandard workarounds in supporting this process.

6.4.9   Consignment Stock

Consignment stock is stored on the buyer's premises but is owned by the supplier until consumed. Typically, consignment stock can be returned to the supplier after an agreed-upon time period if not consumed. The trigger for ownership transfer and consequent payment liability to the supplier is when you transfer a consignment stock item out of your consignment stock. Invoicing is typically conducted on a monthly basis, or potentially at the point of stock transfer if an evaluated receipt settlement (ERS) approach has been defined for vendor invoice payment and/or if the supplier is notified immediately of the transfer.

You can manage multiple consignment stocks from various suppliers and in various currencies. Consignment stock can be allocated to unrestricted, quality-inspection, or blocked-use types as your regular stock materials. You can transfer consignment stock between these three use types, but only the unrestricted use type allows for withdrawals. Using consignment purchasing info records, you can also apply discounts, price quantity scales, and other PIR functionality to consignment stock.

Creating a consignment purchase order is similar to a blanket PO or limit item. In the item category, you select **K** for **Consignment**, as shown in Figure 6.34.

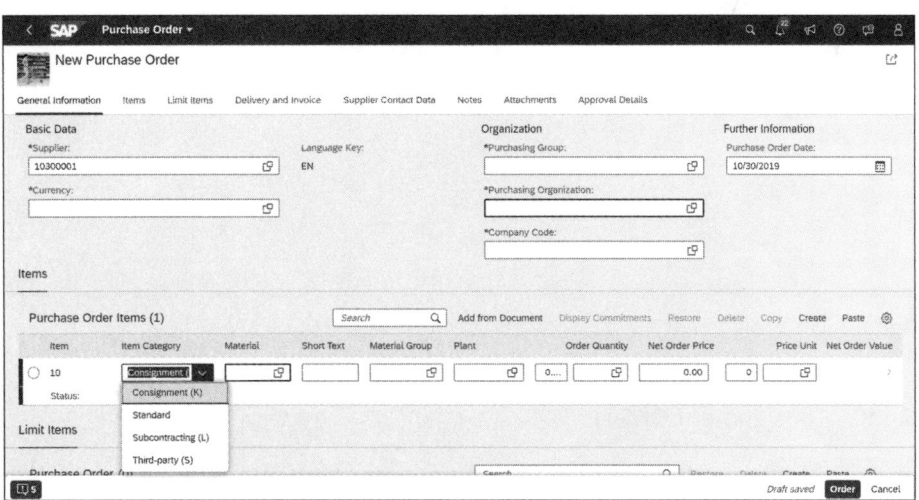

Figure 6.34 Consignment Purchase Order

As far as setup for supporting a consignment order, you must assign the special procurement type key **10** in the material master record under the **MRP 2** tab and maintain the purchasing view, as shown in Figure 6.35. A consignment PIR and any corresponding source list entries must be created to link the material master with the purchasing information.

Many of the orders created in MRP in manufacturing scenarios are for components that are so numerous from a parts and/or volume standpoint that managing these orders and sources of supply can quickly overwhelm buyers with larger procurement scenarios and sourcing activities to worry about. In Section 6.4.12, we'll preview a solution called SAP Supply Base Optimization, which covers this area of spend from price negotiation and sourcing standpoints, using nascent technologies and approaches in artificial intelligence and linear programming.

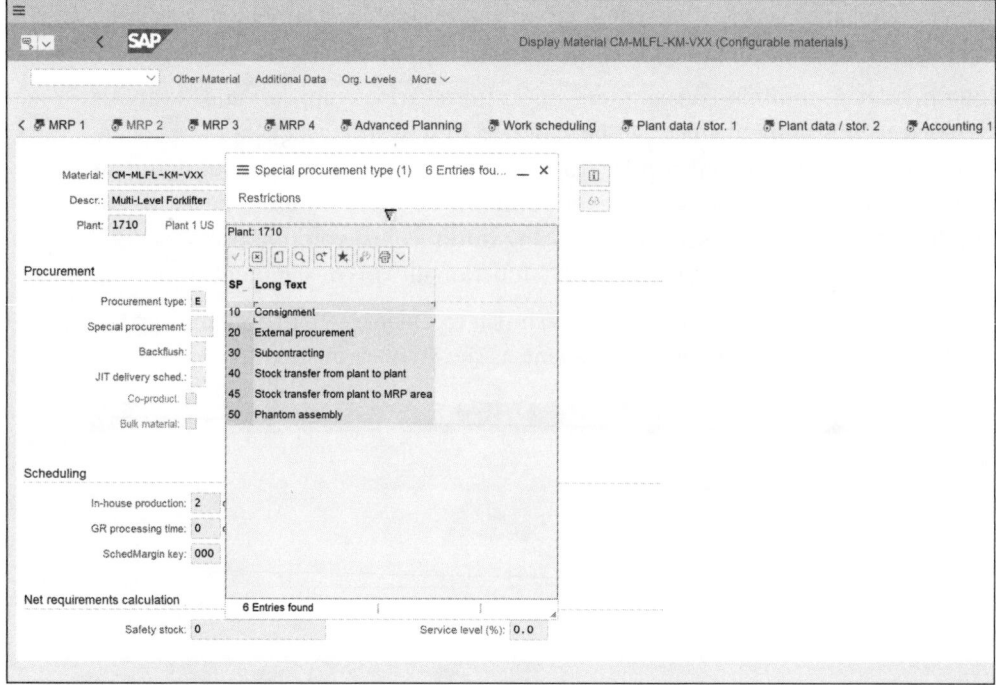

Figure 6.35 Consignment Material Master Setting in MRP 2 Tab

6.4.10   Consignment Orders

In SAP S/4HANA, a consignment stock is provided and owned by the supplier on the buyer's premises; only after consumption does the stock and corresponding payment become the responsibility of the buyer. In this situation, the supplier sometimes has to go onsite to a customer and physically inventory the item prior to submitting an invoice. There may also be incomplete processes for ordering replenishment stock in between inventory cycles in the event the stock is consumed prior to the supplier taking inventory and replenishing automatically. These types of issues run counter to the overarching goal of consignment, which is for the buyer to have real-time access to stock that isn't carried on the buyer's books and for the supplier to have a beachhead at the customer from which the supplier can deepen relationships with and relevance in the customer's supply chain. As with subcontracting, this issue starts with communication, visibility, and management of the consignment stock. Here too, SAP Ariba Supply Chain Collaboration for Buyers provides that last mile of track to bridge these challenges and allow for the consignment process to perform as intended.

The communication focus is from buyer to supplier. Once the consignment stock has been delivered, the buyer needs to provide the supplier with a notification that it has been received and take the items into consignment stock. Upon consumption, another notification is sent to the supplier. In the event that self-billing or ERS is being used for the payment area of the process, a payment is then expedited to the supplier. Alternatively, with the consumption consignment transfer notification, the supplier can now submit a manual invoice for the consignment stock consumed.

This functionality in SAP Ariba Supply Chain Collaboration for Buyers enables you to:

- Replenish and receive consignment inventory and transfer it to your stock as needed
- Obtain and share visibility into material movements with suppliers
- Signal change of ownership of inventory and settle payments to suppliers

SAP Ariba Supply Chain Collaboration for Buyers allows for faster turnaround times in areas that don't technically require another SAP ERP transaction but require further notification to and collaboration with the supplier to close gaps. These are gaps where the customer has technically consumed the inventory and will need billing and possible replenishment from the supplier, but the supplier isn't yet aware of the consumption.

6.4.11   Quality Management Collaboration in SAP Ariba Supply Chain Collaboration for Buyers

Another core topic in direct procurement—which is only tangential in indirect procurement, for the most part—is quality management. For indirect procurement, if an order arrives in subpar quality or with damage, it can be shipped back. If the quality deficiencies aren't caught until the items are consumed, the supplier typically doesn't get further orders from the customer. On the direct side, deficiencies in quality can have catastrophic ramifications, as faulty components are included in finished products, bad batches of pills fill buyer-provided pill packaging and are shipped out, and so on. Inventory management with the quality management functionality allows for some inspection and management of quality for incoming orders, but the in-system communication with and visibility of the supplier is somewhat limited beyond the receipt of the delivery. Often, the supplier may not quite understand why the order was returned. Other times, the supplier is notified too late, after it has already produced and shipped further replications of the defect to the buyer and other customers/partners. SAP Ariba Supply Chain Collaboration for Buyers provides a platform for handling the quality management aspects of the order process, from notification to deviation response/request in real time, allowing suppliers to recognize and correct issues faster, thus lessening the damage to the buyer's and the supplier's production and operations.

In addition to providing the structure for the quality communications, this approach also allows for the entire communication stream to be captured in one area, rather than in several individual emails. This makes the overall transaction flow and issue resolution much clearer from a quality management standpoint, and it allows the buyer and supplier to learn how these issues were resolved previously from older interactions.

6.4.12   SAP Supply Base Optimization

SAP Supply Base Optimization is a cloud-based decision-management tool for buyers that incorporates market benchmark data and applies predictive analytics to optimization and simulation methods to enable intelligent negotiation and business-award decisions with suppliers.

SAP Supply Base Optimization focuses on driving down the price of higher-volume components used in manufacturing products and has a strong value proposition in industries in which component prices continuously fluctuate or decrease, such as tech manufacturing and aerospace. In these industries, the components are numerous and prices trend down as the technology ages and newer versions and general advances are released.

Many buying organizations can't devote full-time employees to drive component price renegotiations, and even quarterly or annual renegotiation cycles are hard to manage. As a result, suppliers can reap a kind of "rent" between the actual, current cost of the component and the price (usually higher) that was initially agreed upon with the customer. The buyer is too busy to be able to focus on renegotiations, which require significant analysis and time investment.

The SAP Supply Base Optimization solution seeks to automate the tedious parts of such analysis and derive actionable insight, target prices, and optimal award splits among suppliers. The high-level business process covered by SAP Supply Base Optimization is as follows:

1. **Scope**
   Propose and refine components for negotiation. Set the target price for negotiation using historic and market benchmark data.

2. **Negotiate**
   Initiate iterative "always-on" negotiations with suppliers. See status of all negotiations at any point in time.

3. **Analyze and award**
   Input business rules and decision logic for optimization. Apply simulation methods to analyze different supplier award scenarios and make final award decision. Auto award for low-priority parts.

4. **Update and report**
   Notify suppliers of updated award decisions. Update master data in the backend ERP system. Provide summary reports by project, supply base manager, commodity group, and so on.

There are two main outputs from SAP Supply Base Optimization for the negotiation and consequent award: target price and award split. The target price is used by the supply base manager to negotiate with suppliers to get the negotiated price as close to the target price as possible. SAP Supply Base Optimization uses predictive analytics libraries to provide a generated target price based on historic and market benchmarking data. The generated target price can be overridden by the supply base manager.

The split calculation provides the supply base manager with a demand quantity share, which can be provided to each supplier based on constraints assigned to the supplier and award process. The split calculation is derived based on linear programming, which in turn leverages machine learning.

As shown in Figure 6.36, SAP Supply Base Optimization provides the supply base manager with a tool to automate analysis and negotiations at the component level, leveraging advances in SAP HANA with real-time availability of both data and analytics, as well as machine learning and linear programming. Expect these types of solutions and approaches to grow in the future as more procurement processes and operations utilize this confluence of technology and applications to automate and refine procurement efficiencies and effectiveness.

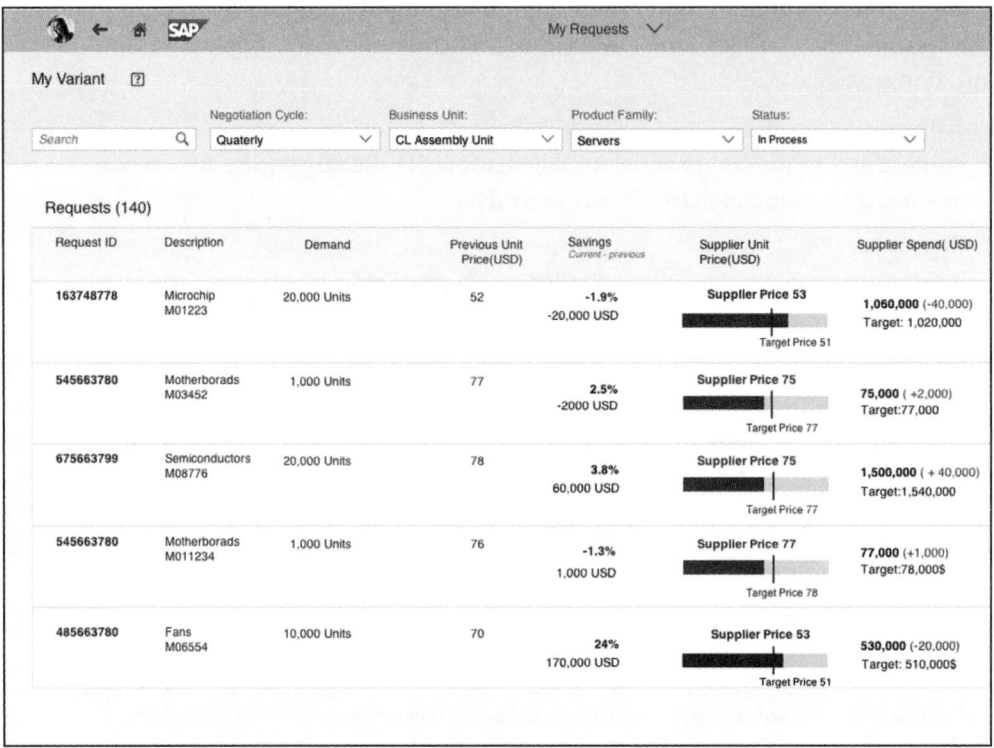

Figure 6.36 SAP Supply Base Optimization: My Requests App

Some of the functionality enhancements available as of SAP Supply Base Optimization release 1908 are as follows:

- Integration with Ariba Network for quote automation. Forwarding of quotes that are initiated in SAP Supply Base Optimization to SAP Ariba Discovery via the Ariba Network to drive supplier responses and collaboration through the Ariba Network.

- Ability for SAP Supply Base Optimization to update contract fields in SAP S/4HANA and SAP ERP with new negotiated prices. Integration content provided as part of delivery.

- Default currency across all projects with local currency support, allowing the supplier to enter a quote response in local currency and the supply base manager to review the quotes in their default currency.

- Tariff data for manufacturer part number (MPN) provided by Paradata, with the supply base manager able to launch Paradata from the SAP Supply Base Optimization workbench to access additional details.

- Supplier quote reset, default end date, and instructions file download now available to support supplier response.

- Item category management in the manage supplier negotiations workbench allows for different handling of items depending on the category assigned—for example, no quote request for a custom part.

6.5   Configuring Automated and Direct Procurement

There are enough parameters in automated and direct procurement that you can configure your setup in an infinite variety of ways to realize your internal business processes and goals. This section covers the main baseline configuration and setup steps required to realize direct material procurement.

6.5.1   Master Data

The prerequisites for direct and automated procurement configuration and execution are as follows:

1. Company code, plant, storage location, purchasing org., and purchasing group have been defined as described in Chapter 3. Without the organization structure, procurement is not possible in the system.

2. Master data objects, including units of measure, material masters, material groups, and suppliers, have been set up appropriately in the system, as described in Chapter 4.

Direct procurement leverages these data elements and the same configuration as defined in Chapter 5. A user can create a PO for either an indirect item or direct material using the Requisitioning app in SAP S/4HANA. The configuration differences and additions for direct procurement are mostly on the automation side in setting up MRP and the usage of different document and item types, such as scheduling agreements and subcontracting. This is the focus of the next section.

Now, we'll cover setting up document types, then setting up the MRP and automation configuration settings.

6.5.2   Document Types

The first step for setting up purchase orders and purchase requisitions is to define the number ranges and document types. For requisitions, you typically just need one range and one document type, as discussed ahead. The requisition then can be used to create different document types at the PO level as required.

Defining Requisition Number Range

First, follow IMG path **Materials Management • Purchasing • Purchase Requisition • Number Range**, then define a number range to be used for your requisitions (see Figure 6.37).

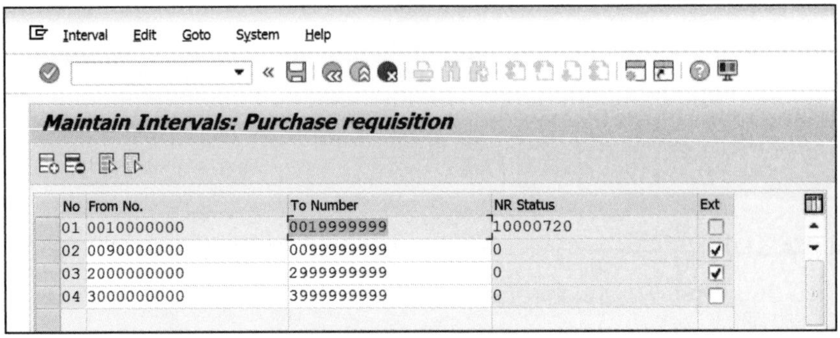

Figure 6.37 Define Number Range for Requisitions

If you have external systems creating requisitions in SAP S/4HANA, this is where you would define these number ranges and flag them as external, as well as the 02- and 03-series number ranges shown in Figure 6.37. Once saved, these number ranges can be assigned to document types.

Defining Document Types for Requisition

Next, you define the document type and use the number range created in the previous step. Follow IMG path **Materials Management • Purchasing • Purchase Requisition •**

Document Type, then set the document type (default is NB), along with the ranges for both internal and external if required (see Figure 6.38).

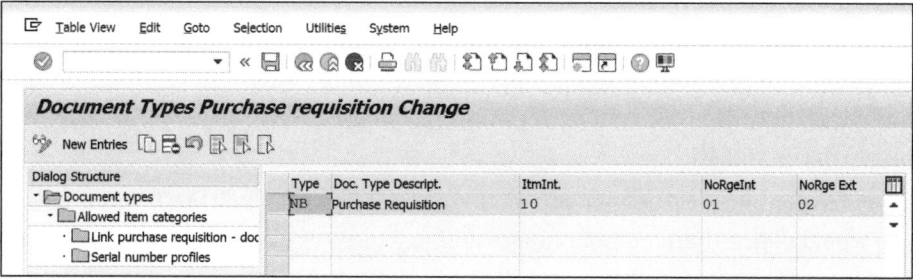

Figure 6.38 Document Type Setting for Requisition

In Figure 6.38, **ItmInt.** refers to the item interval. Setting this to **10** means that each additional item will be spaced 10 digits from the previous item (10, 20, 30…).

Under **Allowed Item Categories**, you can define which item types can be entered on a requisition. This is where standard, service, limit (blanket), and consignment item types can be maintained to support these processes for direct and automated procurement activities (see Figure 6.39). You can also link further document types and define serial number profiles for these item categories in this area by highlighting the targeted item category and then drilling into the applicable folder (e.g., **Link Purchase Requisition—Document**).

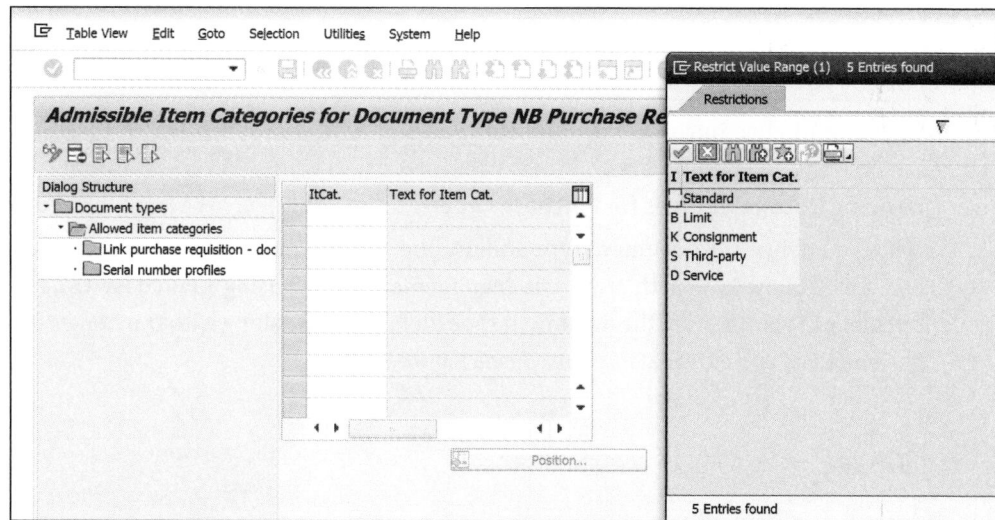

Figure 6.39 Maintaining Item Categories for Requisition Document Type

Now that you've configured the baseline requisition, you can move onto configuring the purchase order.

Defining Purchase Order Number Ranges

Follow IMG path **Materials Management • Purchasing • Purchase Purchase Order • Number Range**, then define number ranges to be used for your purchase orders as shown in Figure 6.40.

If you have external systems creating purchase orders in SAP S/4HANA, this is where you would define these number ranges and flag them as external, as well as the 41-, 44-, 56-, and 61-series number ranges shown in Figure 6.40. Once saved, these number ranges can now be assigned to document types.

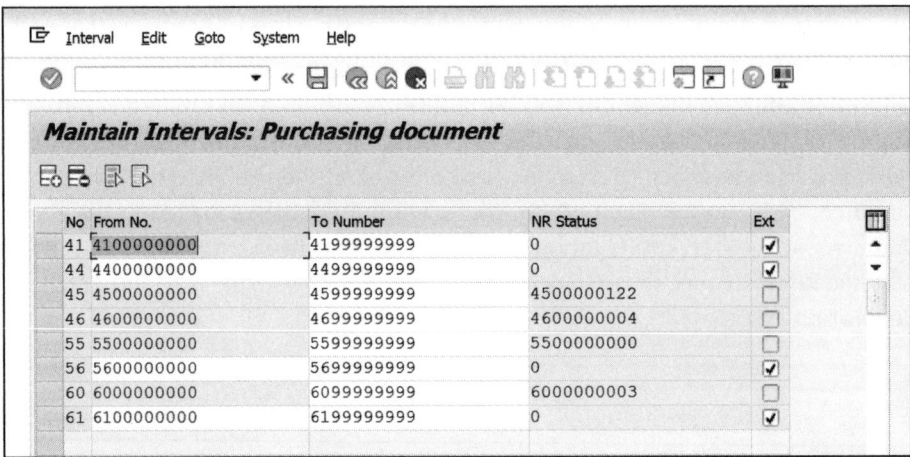

Figure 6.40 Define Purchase Order Number Ranges

Defining Document Types for Purchase Order

Next, you define the document type and use the number range created in the previous step. Follow IMG path **Materials Management • Purchasing • Purchase Order • Document Type**, then set the document type (default is NB), along with the ranges for both internal and external if required (see Figure 6.41).

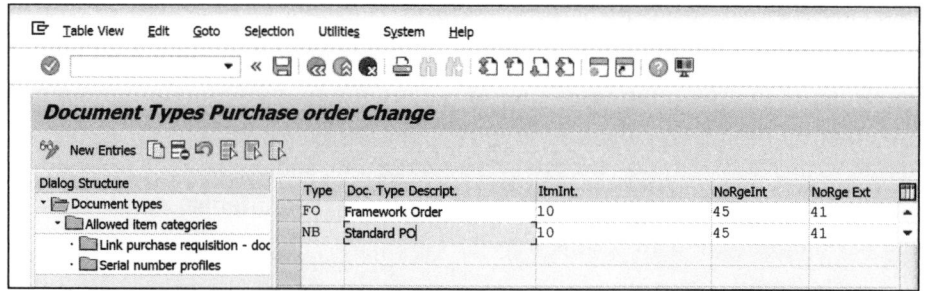

Figure 6.41 Purchase Order Document Type Definition

As with requisitions, under **Allowed Item Categories**, you can define which item types can be entered on a purchase order. This is where standard, service, limit (blanket), and consignment item types can be maintained to support these processes for direct and automated procurement activities. You want to keep these in alignment with the settings you made for requisitions where possible, to avoid scenarios in which a requisition is using an item type unsupported by your purchase order document type settings. You can also link the requisition document types and define serial number profiles for these item categories in this area by highlighting the targeted item category and then drilling into the applicable folder (e.g., **Link Purchase Requisition—Document**; see Figure 6.42).

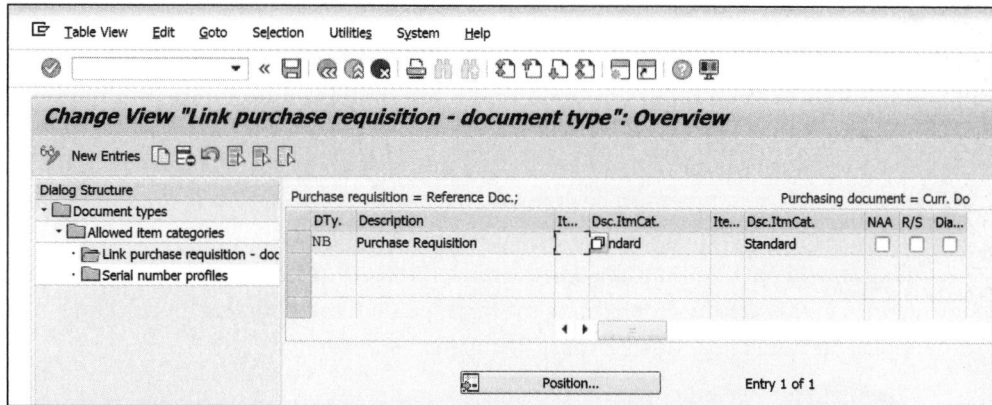

Figure 6.42 Link Purchase Requisition Document Types to PO Doc Type

Now that you've configured the baseline requisition settings and purchase order settings, you're ready to move onto configuring the scheduling agreement document type.

Defining Scheduling Agreement Number Ranges

Follow IMG path **Materials Management • Purchasing • Scheduling Agreement • Number Range**, then define number ranges to be used for your scheduling agreements. Note that number ranges maintained previously to set up purchase orders are reflected in this transaction as well, to avoid overlapping and confusion when setting up further ranges. This also means that you can set up your number ranges for POs and scheduling agreements in one step.

Defining Document Types for Scheduling Agreement

Next, define the document type and use the number range created in the previous step. Follow IMG path **Materials Management • Purchasing • Scheduling Agreement • Document Type**, then set the document type (default is LP), along with the ranges for both internal and external if required (see Figure 6.43).

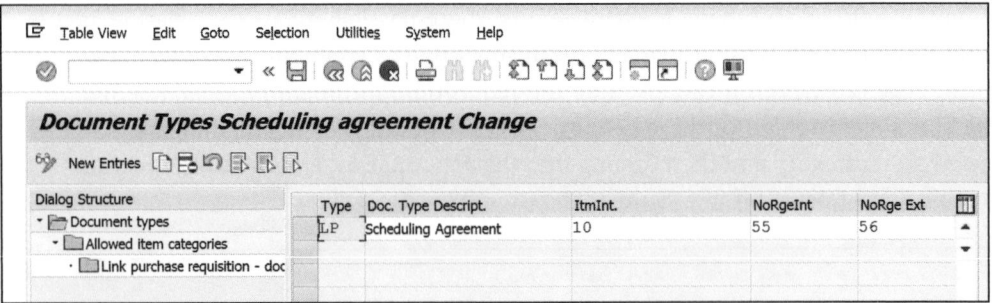

Figure 6.43 Scheduling Agreement Document Type Definition

As with requisitions and purchase orders, under **Allowed Item Categories,** you can define which item types can be entered on a purchase order. This is where standard and consignment item types can be maintained to support these processes for scheduling agreements. You can also link the requisition document types to these item categories in this area by highlighting the targeted item category and then drilling into applicable folder (e.g., **Link Purchase Requisition—Document**).

Now that you've configured the baseline scheduling agreements and the core document types for requisitions and purchase orders, you're ready to configure further areas for MRP.

6.5.3   Forecast Planning

For a forecast to be used for MRP, you must configure the forecast indicator for the corresponding MRP type in IMG menu path **Materials Management • Consumption-Based Planning • Master Data • Check MRP Types**, as shown in Figure 6.44.

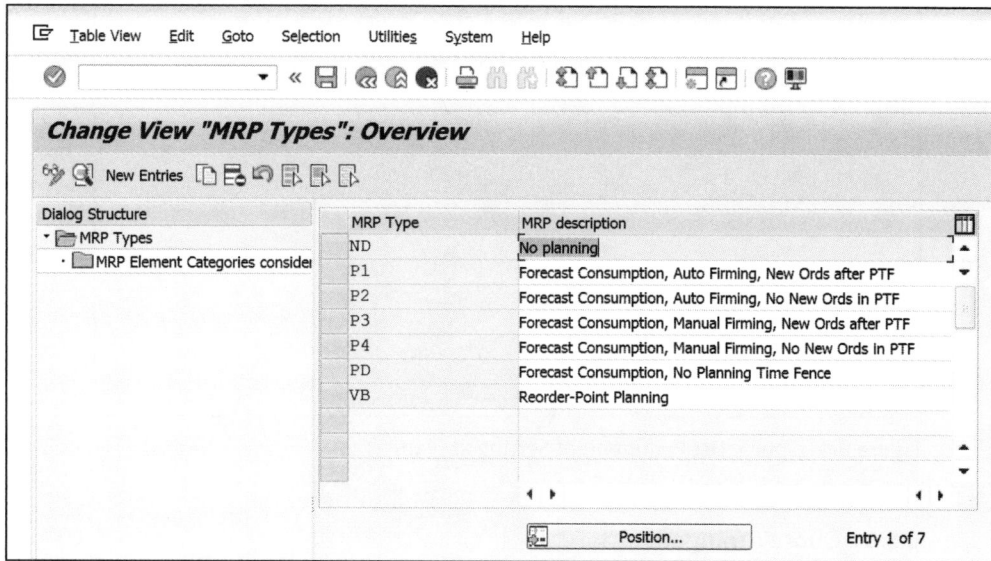

Figure 6.44 Forecast: MRP Types

Option forecast configuration can be set by following IMG menu path **Materials Management • Consumption-Based Planning • Forecast**. Here, you can define weighting groups for moving average, split forecast requirements for MRP, and assign forecast errors to error clauses.

6.5.4   Purchase Info Records

You can maintain a rounding profile in the PIR or in general customizing, in which you define a threshold value for which the system will round the number up to a deliverable unit. For the latter, follow IMG path **Consumption-based Planning • Planning • Lot-Size Calculation • Maintain Rounding Profile**. This allows you to adapt the units of measure in MRP to the delivery and transport units.

6.5.5   Source Lists

Under IMG path **Materials Management • Purchasing • Source List**, you can identify which plants require a source list, as shown in Figure 6.45.

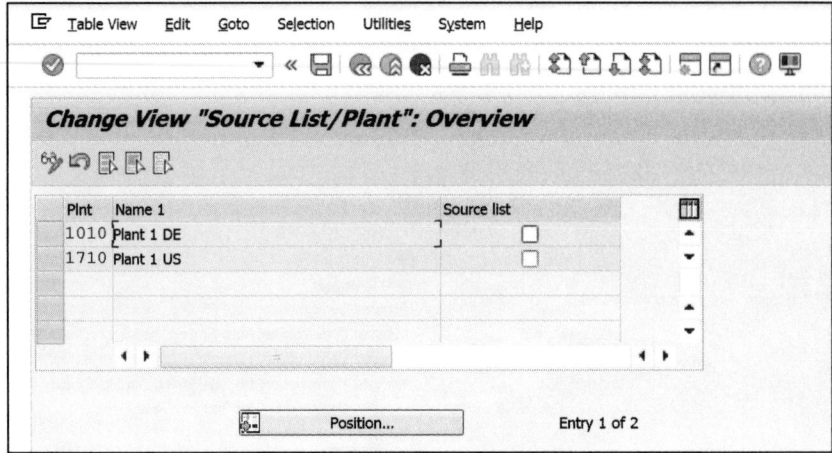

Figure 6.45 Source List Requirement Setting at Plant

6.5.6   Quota Arrangements

The main area of configuration for quota arrangement is the number range. You define this under IMG path **Materials Management • Purchasing • Quota Arrangement • Define Number Ranges** (see Figure 6.46).

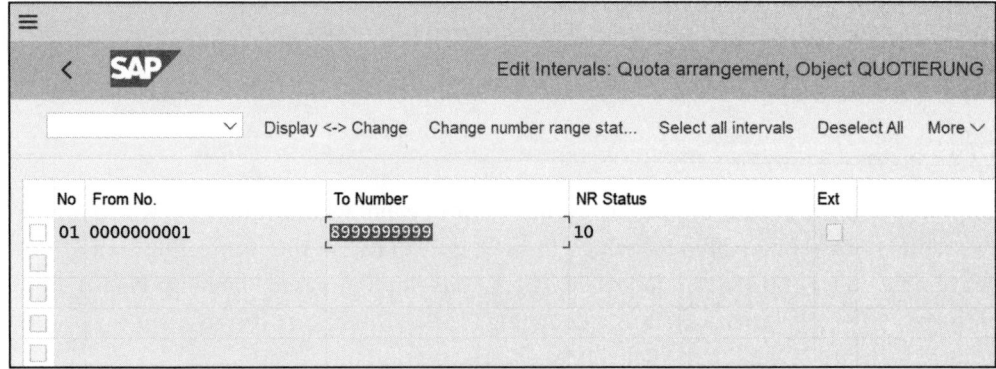

Figure 6.46 Number Range Configuration for Quota Arrangement

This is an overview of baseline configuration in support of direct procurement and automated procurement activities in SAP S/4HANA systems. Direct procurement is embedded in SAP ERP due to the tight linkages with other functionalities that reside in this area, such as production planning, sales and distribution, and finance. These areas and stakeholders will provide further requirements for a project to seamlessly configure a cross-module direct procurement process.

6.6   Integration with SAP Ariba

Let's briefly review two key SAP S/4HANA integration scenarios with SAP Ariba: SAP Ariba Supply Chain Collaboration for Buyers and SAP Ariba Sourcing integration with SAP S/4HANA.

Formerly known as Collaborative Supply Chain, SAP Ariba Supply Chain Collaboration has evolved to support direct procurement processes on the supplier side in the Ariba Network.

The main direct procurement transactions supported now include schedule releases, subcontract orders, consignment inventory checks, and quality notifications/responses on the buyer side. On the supplier side, leveraging the power of the Ariba Network, a supplier can now collaborate on forecasts, confirm POs and component receipts/consumption, provide manufacturing visibility, advise of order deviations, and submit an invoice back to the buyer. With SAP Ariba Supply Chain Collaboration for Buyers and SAP Ariba Strategic Sourcing, there is coverage for all of the following processes in SAP S/4HANA:

- SAP Product Lifecycle Management (SAP PLM), Sourcing, Contracts, and SAP Ariba Strategic Sourcing
- Forecast-to-commit in SAP Integrated Business Planning (SAP IBP): SAP Ariba Strategic Sourcing
- Request, order, make: SAP Ariba Supply Chain Collaboration for Buyers
- Receive, manage, pay: SAP Ariba Supply Chain Collaboration for Buyers

Chapter 10 and Chapter 15 detail the configuration for SAP Ariba Strategic Sourcing and SAP Ariba Supply Chain Collaboration for Buyers, respectively.

6.7   Summary

Automated and direct procurement processes continue to evolve in SAP S/4HANA while leveraging core SAP ERP approaches such as MRP and reorder point planning. Although MRP remains as a unifying automation engine for procurement in SAP S/4HANA, there are simplifications and updates both to the MRP cockpit and to the overall support of different sourcing protocols and forecast methodologies. Scheduling agreements, subcontracting, and consignment procurement processes all continue as viable vehicles for automating purchasing and facilitating direct procurement, in particular in SAP S/4HANA; now these processes have the added option of integrating with the Ariba Network via SAP Ariba Supply Chain Collaboration for Buyers. Long considered a differentiator and an argument for ERP-based procurement, direct procurement integrated with core production and planning modules in SAP S/4HANA continues this tradition while expanding toward a future state of integrated and automated direct procurement processes, enhanced by machine learning and real-time information exchange with suppliers. Much of direct procurement requires management of inventory items once procured. In the next chapter we will dive deeper into this area of inventory management.

Chapter 7
Inventory Management

Proper management and minimization of working capital held in physical stocks is a key need for all enterprises. SAP S/4HANA provides many capabilities in inventory management for recording movements of goods and to report on current and historical stock balances and values.

Inventory management is a core component of SAP S/4HANA Enterprise Management, supporting SAP S/4HANA Sourcing and Procurement with the receipt of goods and services. This component also integrates tightly with other integrated end-to-end logistics business processes, such as order and contract management for sales, service management, product planning, and production orchestration and execution. Inventory management also integrates with internal and external accounting functions, recording the financial impact of goods movements as they happen. Figure 7.1 illustrates how inventory management integrates with other core SAP S/4HANA logistics and financial functions.

Inventory management covers the following core areas of functionality in the SAP S/4HANA system:

- Stock management on both a quantity and value basis
- Planning, entry, and recording of material movements
- Physical inventory processes
- Reporting of goods movements, stock balances, and physical inventory results

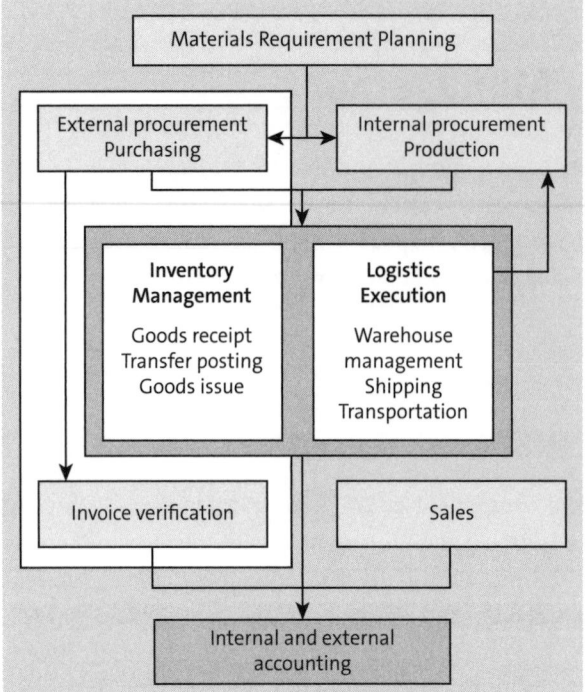

Figure 7.1 Inventory Management Integration

7.1   What Is Inventory Management?

The inventory management area manages and records all movements of goods in the system. It also has capabilities to manage the quantities of physical stocks in all plants in the enterprise. Integration with financial accounting means that financial impacts to general ledgers are posted immediately upon recording the goods movement in the SAP S/4HANA system. Inventory management has extensive reporting capabilities so that stock balances and goods movements can be made visible to the enterprise, facilitating end-to-end process harmonization.

Inventory management in the SAP S/4HANA system has the following solution capabilities:

- Goods receipt
- Goods issue
- Stock transfers

- Transfer postings
- Basic warehouse management
- Basic shipping

For the purposes of this book, we'll focus on the solution capabilities of Inventory Management that impact SAP S/4HANA Sourcing and Procurement business processes, which are goods receipt, goods issue, stock transfers, and transfer postings.

The inventory management data model for stocks in prior versions of SAP ERP was quite complex. Each material document, which is the system record for goods movements, was represented in the system in two tables: a header record containing date, time, and user information, and one or more line items containing information about movement type, material, quantities, units of measure, and so on. Using these tables involved joining the two to obtain a unified dataset for the application or query at hand. Figure 7.2 shows both the SAP Business Suite powered by SAP HANA and the SAP S/4HANA inventory management data models in more detail.

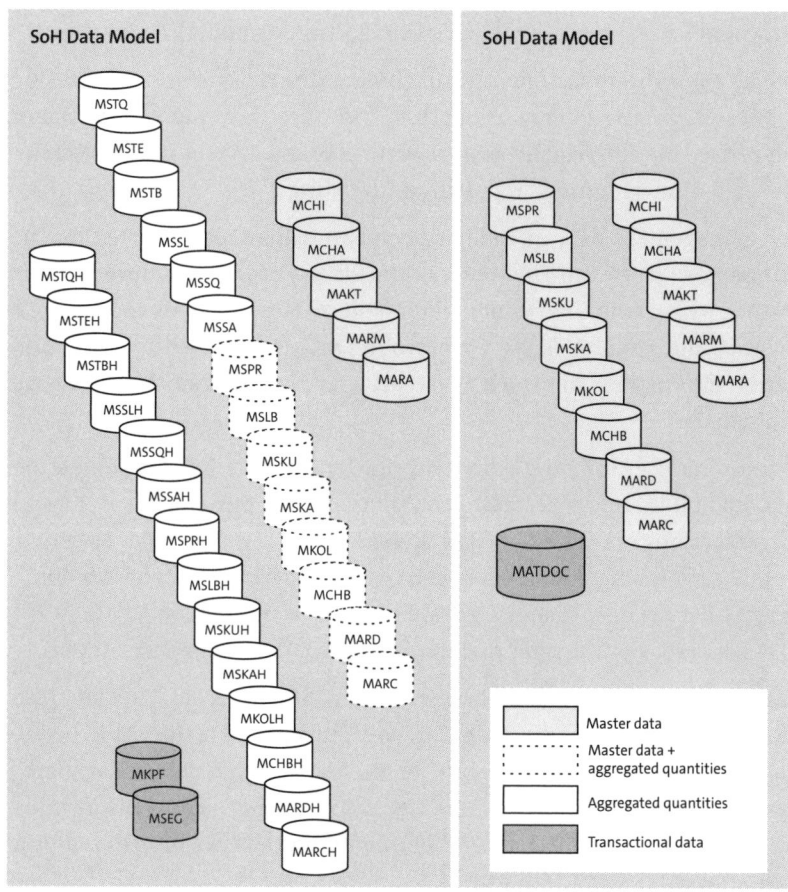

Figure 7.2 Inventory Management Data Model

The material master was involved in inventory management as well. Two tables used for holding material master control attributes—table MARC, for plant-level material attributes, and table MARD, for storage-location-level material attributes—were used to hold stock quantities and values at the plant and storage-location-data levels, respectively. This meant that inserts into the database for goods movements required locking the material master at the respective level being transacted. This was quite problematic for SAP clients with high volumes of goods movements at peak periods because locking issues sometimes prevented these movements from taking place in a timely manner.

In addition, other tables were used to store quantities and values that were specific to the kind of stock being processed. These tables needed to be updated during goods movement postings as well, which further complicated the updates. These included tables MCHB (Stocks at Batch Level), MKOL (Special Stocks from Supplier), and others.

Several aggregate tables were also present in the data model for use in reporting applications. These aggregate tables summarized the stock movement and balance data into time-phased buckets. Finally, historical stock balance tables were also architected into the data model for use in reporting and costing.

The inventory management data model has been completely rearchitected for the SAP HANA in-memory platform. The material document has been reduced to one table, table MATDOC, which contains header and line item data for goods movements. The stock quantity and amount fields, which were previously stored in the hybrid tables, have been eliminated. The stock aggregate and historical stock tables have also been eliminated.

This simplification reduces the total data footprint required to maintain inventory management data and therefore increases the transactional throughput of the system because transactions now don't need to update nearly as many tables as before. It also means that only main tables are needed; redundancy in the database is eliminated. The master data is now clearly separated from the transactional data in the data model. Less data means a smaller memory footprint, increasing throughput.

All stock calculations now harness the power of the SAP S/4HANA database and read table MATDOC directly. This allows stock balances, both current and historical, to be calculated in real time, without use of aggregate tables. Analytics can now be calculated in real time and go to the most granular level. This capability enables inventory managers to react to operational situations and eliminate bottlenecks in material flow through the enterprise.

This architecture also eliminates the need for material master locking during INSERT operations on the database, thus improving transactional throughput by a factor of 10 to 25 times. Analytics now run natively and avoid the overhead involved in JOIN operations on the underlying data tables.

Twenty-one tables were eliminated in the new inventory management data model, and stock aggregate columns in eight additional tables were removed as well.

Material valuation data was previously housed in the accounting tables of the material master. Now the material ledger is required in SAP S/4HANA and is used to house material valuation data. This allows inventory valuation in multiple currencies to be maintained consistently. The valuation tables in the classic SAP ERP data model (table MBEW and others) have been eliminated from the data model. Note that SAP does provide CDS views for those customers who are converting to SAP S/4HANA and who need to preserve their investment in legacy developments to run their business processes. The previous hybrid, aggregate, and historical views of the database are available via CDS views in the system.

7.2   Stock Management in SAP S/4HANA

The identification, tracking, and management of physical stocks is the core purpose of inventory management. The functions of the system allow all goods movements affecting physical stocks to be recorded in real time. This allows stock balances to be instantly obtained, both for the present and for any point in the past. If the material type assigned to the material permits valuation, then the appropriate financial documents are immediately posted in the system when the goods movements are recorded.

It's useful to consider stock management as a collection of multiple data elements that relate to one another. Each data element reflects an individual aspect of the stock—for example, the condition, location, and physical and logistical attributes of the stock itself:

- Material identification
- Location
- Usability
- Ownership
- Batch identification
- Serialization

7.2.1   Material Identification

Each item in stock is identified with a material number. This material number represents a unit of stock that is distinct from another—for instance, different raw materials used in a production process. Each material is represented in the system with a unique material number, which can be up to 40 characters in length. Each material has a *material type* attribute, which defines control features for a grouping of materials.

7.2.2   Location

The location information in inventory management consists of two attributes:

- Plant, the physical location where logistics activities in support of the enterprise are transacted
- Storage location, a subset of a plant used for stock-management purposes

All stock managed in an enterprise must be assigned to a plant. The plant provides the linkage to financial accounting via the company code assigned to that plant.

If the stock is managed in a facility that the enterprise owns or controls, then the stock is assigned to a storage location upon receipt. However, there are other types of stocks in an enterprise that may not have a storage location identified. A good example of this is stock being transferred between two facilities. If goods being transferred have been issued from the supplying plant but haven't yet arrived in the receiving plant, then the stock in SAP S/4HANA is designated as in transit to the receiving plant and doesn't list a storage location. A storage location must be specified on the goods receipt into stock at the physical location.

7.2.3   Usability

Stock type is the term used in SAP to designate the disposition or usability of the stock for materials planning and execution purposes. There are four main stock types supported in SAP S/4HANA:

1. Unrestricted use stock
2. Quality inspection stock
3. Blocked stock
4. Customer returns stock

Unrestricted Use

The *unrestricted use* stock type is used to designate inventory quantities that are free to be considered for materials planning or execution purposes, such as deliveries to customers or consumption for production. Unrestricted use stocks can be freely transferred between plants and storage locations.

Quality Inspection

The *quality inspection* stock type is used for identifying quantities of goods that are undergoing processing by the quality department at the current time. Quality inspection stocks are considered *available* from a materials planning point of view. However, these stocks can't be shipped to a customer or consumed internally until a decision has been made about their usability. They can be transferred between storage locations in a plant but can't be transferred between plants.

Quality inspection stocks may be under the control of the quality management (QM) area. If QM is active for that material in that plant, then its processes control the postings of material into and out of the Quality inspection stock type. If QM isn't active for that material in that plant, then transfer postings are used to post stocks out of Quality inspection stock into other stock types.

Blocked

The *blocked* stock type is used when a material becomes unusable for planning and execution purposes. Blocked stocks generally aren't considered during materials planning. Blocked stocks can't be used for fulfilling customer or production demands. Blocked stocks can be transferred between storage locations within a plant.

Note that unrestricted use, quality inspection, and blocked stocks are considered valuated stocks if the stock type assigned to the material is valuated in the valuation area assigned to the plant.

Customer Returns

The *customer returns* stock type is a less commonly used stock type. It can be used to manage goods that have been delivered back into a storage location from a customer and for which a decision hasn't yet been made as to whether the goods will be accepted back into stock. Customer returns stock is always nonvaluated stock. Once a decision is made to accept the goods, a transfer posting from customer returns to either unrestricted use, quality inspection, or blocked stock is made. This transfer posting posts the quantities into valuated stock and creates an accounting document.

261

7.2.4   Ownership

Most stocks in an SAP S/4HANA system are owned by the enterprise and are reflected in the appropriate stock accounts in financial accounting. However, it's possible to represent stocks that are owned by an external party in the system. Special stock indicators are used to represent these ownership scenarios in inventory management. Each special stock has a unique one-letter identifier in the database.

The following are examples of special stocks that are owned by the enterprise and physically stored at an external location:

- Component stocks provided to supplier for subcontracting (special stock O)
- Finished goods consigned to a customer (special stock W)
- Returnable transport packaging at customer (special stock V)

Note that these special stocks can be in either unrestricted use or quality inspection stock types.

The following are examples of special stocks owned by an external party and physically stored in a plant and storage location:

- Supplier consignment stock (special stock K)
- Supplier-owned returnable transport packaging (special stock M)

7.2.5   Batch Identification

Many industries, such as food or pharmaceuticals, require stock management based on the attributes of a manufacturing lot of a material. SAP S/4HANA provides the batch management area to fill these needs. A *batch* is defined as a subset of a material with a set of attributes that have common values.

If you need a material to be batch-managed in the SAP S/4HANA system, set the batch management indicator on a material master view at the plant level, such as the purchasing view.

A batch can contain one or more characteristics, which are equivalent to the attributes being measured. Each characteristic in a batch can contain one or more values that differentiate one batch from another for that material. Typically, the characteristic values are recorded upon the initial goods receipt of a batch-managed material from production or procurement.

All goods movements for batch-managed materials must identify the unique batch of the material being transacted.

Note that it's very difficult to change the batch management indicator on a material once material movements have been recorded in the system. Therefore, consider carefully before setting the batch management indicator on the material master.

7.2.6 Serialization

Some industries need to identify individual units of a material—for example, consumer electronics or medical devices, for which it's important to track units for customer servicing and warranty purposes. Serial number management is used in SAP S/4HANA to meet these requirements.

Making a material relevant for serialization involves the assignment of a serial number profile in the storage view of the material master. The serial number profile is set up in system configuration and designates the types of business transactions for which serial numbers need to be recorded.

If serialization is active for inventory management for a material in a plant, then serial numbers must be recorded for each unit of material in a goods movement.

7.2.7 Goods Movements

Goods movements are transactions in SAP S/4HANA that result in a change in stock.

There are four main types of goods movements:

1. **Goods receipts**
   These are goods movements that result in an increase in quantities of stock.

2. **Goods issues**
   These are goods movements that result in a decrease in quantities of stock.

3. **Stock transfers**
   These are goods movements that result in quantities of stock moving between two logistics organizational elements. For instance, you can transfer stock between two plants in an enterprise or between two storage locations in a plant.

4. **Transfer postings**
   These are goods movements that result in a change in identity, disposition, or ownership of a material. Transfer postings can be done in conjunction with stock transfers in some cases.

Each goods movement in the SAP S/4HANA system is recorded as a material document. A material document contains information on the type of goods movement, the date and time of posting, the identifier of the user that created the goods movement, the materials transacted, quantities and units of measure, and associated details. The details are recorded in table MATDOC in SAP S/4HANA.

Many goods movements reference other SAP S/4HANA documents. For instance, a goods receipt can reference a purchasing document and line item. This information is recorded in the material document as well.

Each material document line item contains a movement type code. The movement type in the SAP S/4HANA system is represented by a three-character code that identifies the type of goods movement to be recorded (goods receipt, goods issue, transfer posting). Movement types play an important control function in determining what data is required to successfully post the goods movement and to pass information into other system components, such as financial accounting. Special stock indicators are used for some movement types depending on the situation.

Movement types are paired with a reversal movement type. These reversal movement types are used to undo a movement already posted in the system. It is typical to have the reversal movement type be one more than the movement type number. For example, the reversal movement type for a goods receipt for a purchase order (101) is 102.

Examples of movement types important for SAP S/4HANA Sourcing and Procurement include the following:

- 101, Goods Receipt for a Purchasing Document
- 543 O, Goods Issue from Component Stock Provided to Supplier

7.3   Goods Receipts

Goods receipts are goods movements that result in an increase in stock. They are important goods movements for SAP S/4HANA Sourcing and Procurement as they form an important process link between purchasing and financial accounting. Goods receipts usually reference other SAP S/4HANA documents, such as purchase orders or inbound deliveries. This streamlines the entry of the goods receipt data, which can be copied directly from the reference document. However, there are goods receipts that can be entered without any reference, such as when initial stocks are entered into the system at startup.

Goods receipts can be entered into the SAP S/4HANA system in two ways: a material document can be posted directly in the system using the Post Goods Movement app;

or, if the supplier of the goods transmits an advanced shipping notification (ASN) to you, you can then convert this communication into an inbound delivery document in SAP S/4HANA. Inbound delivery documents can be used when available to plan inbound receipts with much more precision because the quantities and dates are much firmer than at the time of purchase order entry or purchase order acknowledgement.

The inbound delivery can be created in the SAP S/4HANA system with reference to one or more purchasing documents. As an alternative, these documents can also be created via the receipt of an advanced shipping notification from the supplier of the goods prior to the actual receipt. EDI or the Ariba Network can be utilized to transmit ASNs to an SAP S/4HANA system. Inbound deliveries allow for more precise planning of the inbound movements and provide up-to-date firm supply data to materials planning.

The confirmation control key entered on the purchasing document line item controls the method by which a goods receipt is posted. If the confirmation control key includes inbound deliveries, then that document must be referenced to receive the goods. Otherwise, the purchase order or scheduling agreement line item can be referenced directly at goods receipt.

- **Movement types for goods receipts with reference to documents:**
  - 101, Goods Receipt with reference to Purchase Order/Production Order
- **Movement types for goods receipts without reference:**
  - 561, Initial Stock Entry for Unrestricted Use Stock
  - 563, Initial Stock Entry for Quality Inspection Stock
  - 565, Initial Stock Entry for Blocked Stock

Goods receipts can be posted using apps that post goods movements directly into inventory management. Some goods receipts also can be posted using integration with shipping documents, such as inbound deliveries. Both types of goods receipts are described in the following sections.

7.3.1   Posting Goods Receipts

There are a variety of SAP Fiori apps for inventory management that can be used to record the arrival of goods at your facility. These apps are described in more detail in the sections ahead.

The following SAP Fiori apps are available in SAP S/4HANA for processing goods receipts:

- Post Goods Receipt for Purchase Order
- Manage Stock
- Material Documents Overview

In addition, the following WebGUI apps are also available for processing goods receipts:

- Post Goods Movement
- Output Material Documents

Post Goods Receipt for Purchase Order

The Post Goods Receipt for Purchase Order app is used to record the physical receipt of goods into a facility. This app requires the receipt of these goods to be made with reference to an existing purchasing document. It is vital that goods receipts reference the correct purchasing documents used to order them for the procure-to-pay business process to work efficiently.

The Post Goods Receipt for Purchase Order app (Figure 7.3) lets you do the following:

- Post the receipt of goods with reference to a purchasing document that contains order items for stock material (procurement for stock)
- Post the receipt of goods with reference to a purchasing document that contains order items with single or multiple account assignments (procurement for direct consumption)
- Post the receipt of goods into supplier consignment stock
- Post the receipt of goods into goods receipt blocked stock, which will be released at a later time
- Post the receipts of shelf-life managed materials into stock
- Assign batches on the item level during goods receipt processing for those materials that require them
- Use predefined output forms in output management for material documents, which can be copied and changed according to your requirements

This app cannot process purchase orders that use non-SAP-delivered purchase order document types.

This app also cannot process purchase order items which fulfill at least one of the following conditions:

- The **Delivery Completed** indicator is set on the line item.
- Account assignment categories that are not supported are included.
- The material is serialized.

If all items of a purchase order fulfill at least one of these three conditions, the purchase order is not able to be processed in this app. Use the Post Goods Movement app as an alternative for processing purchase orders meeting these criteria.

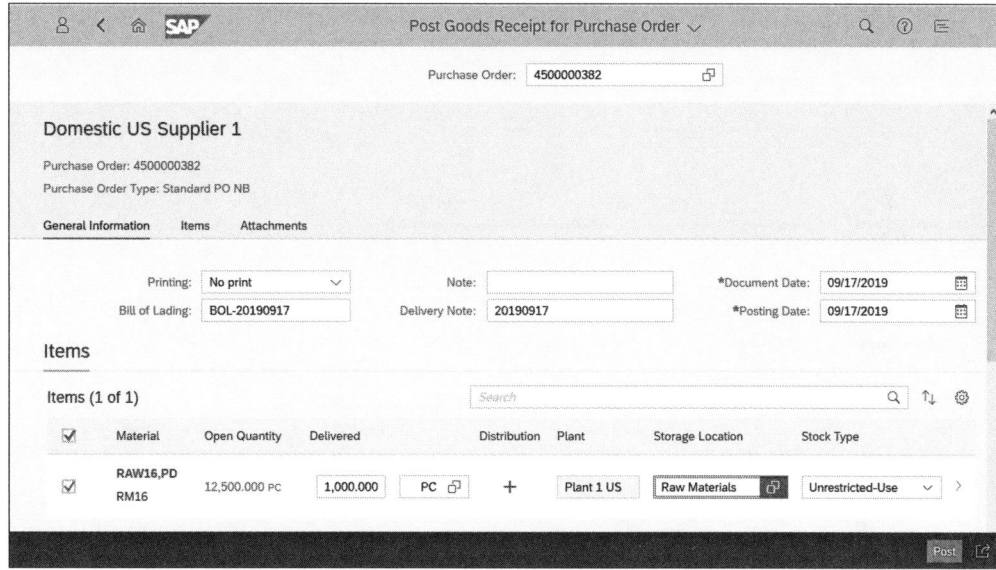

Figure 7.3 Post Goods Receipt for Purchase Order App

The app supports goods receipts for the following account assignments:

- A: Asset
- C: Sales order
- F: (Production) order
- K: Cost center
- P: Project
- S: Third party
- X: All auxiliary account assignments

The following special stocks are also supported:

- Project stock (Q)
- Sales order stock (E)

The Post Goods Receipt for Purchase Order app is assigned to the inventory manager and warehouse clerk standard authorization roles.

Manage Stock

The Manage Stock app (Figure 7.4) lets you perform stock changes in the SAP S/4HANA system.

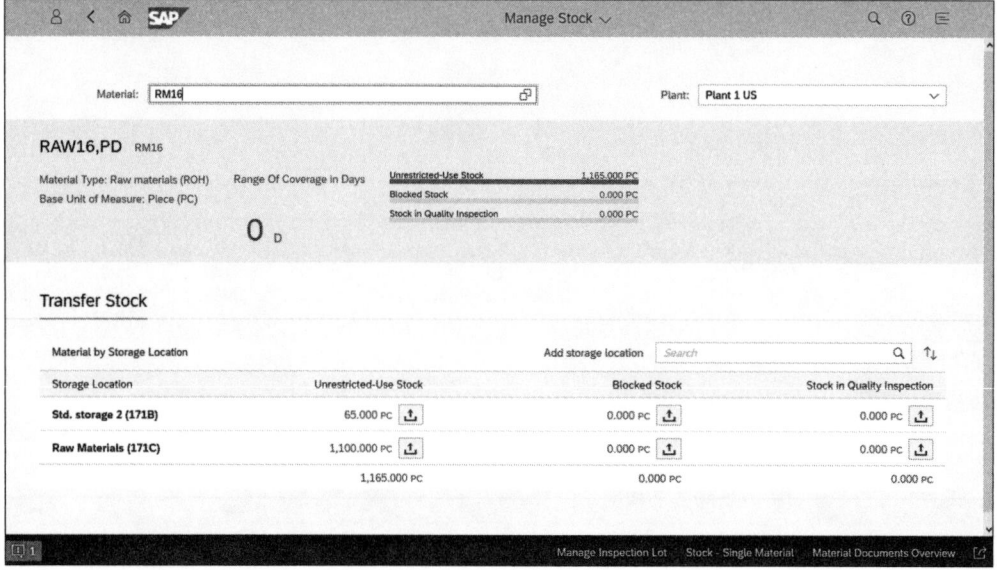

Figure 7.4 Manage Stock App

This app can perform the following types of goods movements:

- Initial entry of stock balances for unrestricted use, quality inspection or blocked stocks
- Scrapping of material

The following special stocks are also supported:

- Project stock (Q)
- Sales order stock (E)

This app supports movement-type-dependent reason codes. Reason codes let you add a short explanation for the underlying purpose of a specific goods movement, such as poor quality. You can also enter free texts for the document header or for an individual line item.

The Manage Stock app lets you check the range of coverage based on the consumption of unrestricted stock in the last 30 days.

If you notice that you've made an error in posting goods movements, you can correct the error by reversing the material document and posting the goods movements again. To reverse the material document, use the Material Documents Overview app.

Note that serialized materials cannot be managed via this app.

The Manage Stock app is assigned to the inventory manager standard authorization role.

Material Documents Overview

The Material Documents Overview app (Figure 7.5) provides the capability to show a list of material document items based on filter criteria and display the details for a selected material document item. You can also reverse a material document.

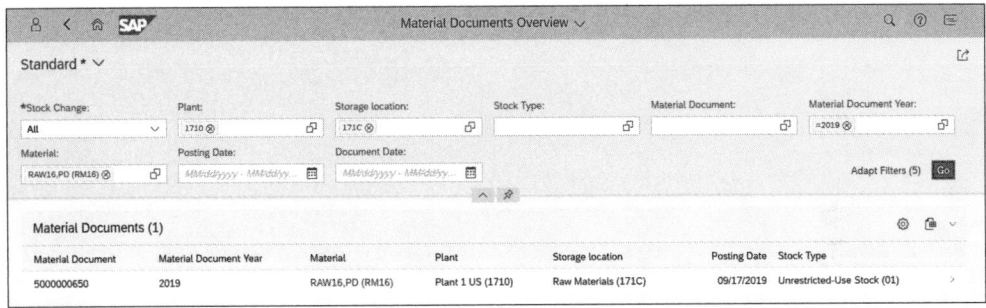

Figure 7.5 Material Documents Overview App

This app can be used to do the following:

- Display a material document item list based on filter criteria
- Display the details for a specific material document item
- Display a graphical process flow for a material document with the relevant preceding and follow-on documents
- Get an overview of material documents, such as goods issue, goods receipt, and material movements with document date, movement type, and document items

- Add attachments to a material document
- Export the result list to a spreadsheet
- Reverse a selected material document

The Material Documents Overview app is assigned to the inventory manager and warehouse clerk standard authorization roles.

Post Goods Movement

The Post Goods Movement app (Figure 7.6) is used to perform goods movements, including goods receipts in the SAP S/4HANA system. It can also be used to review a specific material document and its associated documents.

This app is used when the simplified goods receipt SAP Fiori apps don't support all aspects of the type of goods receipts needed for your enterprise.

The Post Goods Movement app runs directly on the backend SAP S/4HANA system and is functionally equivalent to the classic SAP ERP Transaction MIGO.

The Post Goods Movement app is assigned to the inventory manager and warehouse clerk standard authorization roles.

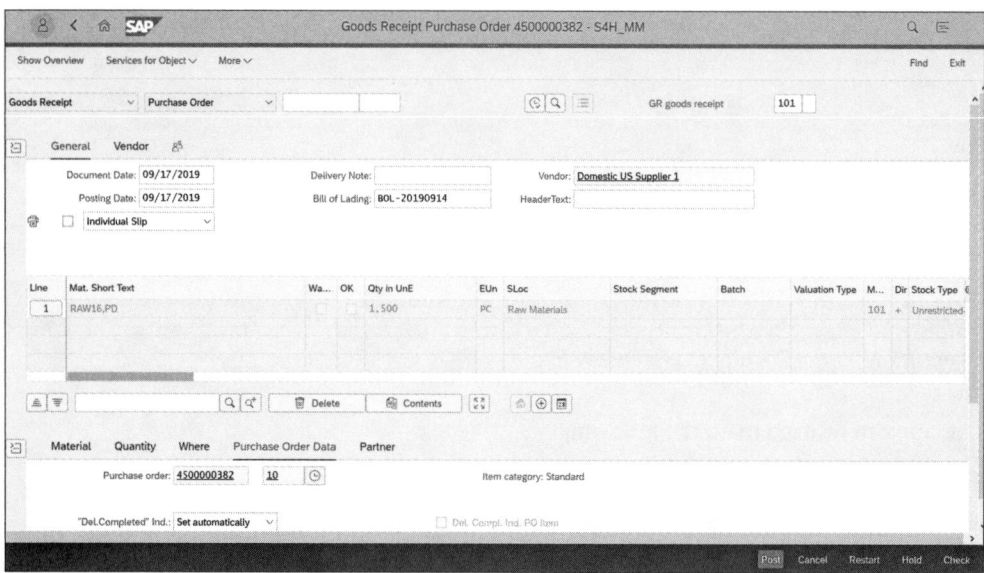

Figure 7.6 Post Goods Movement App

Output Material Documents

The Output Material Documents app (Figure 7.7) is used to create printouts, goods receipt labels, and other types of messages from the inventory management component.

The Output Material Documents app runs directly on the backend SAP S/4HANA system and is functionally equivalent to the classic SAP ERP Transaction MB90.

The Output Material Documents app is assigned to the inventory manager and warehouse clerk standard authorization roles.

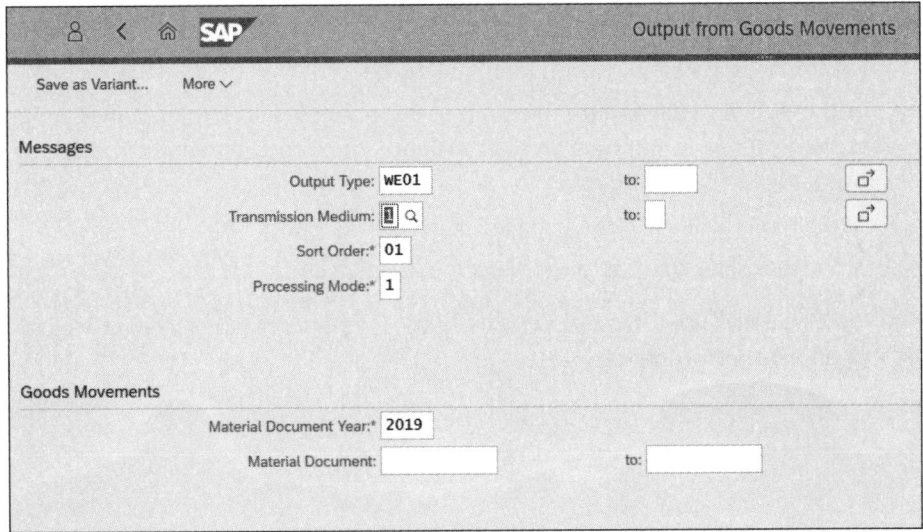

Figure 7.7 Output Material Documents App

7.3.2   Processing Goods Receipts via Inbound Deliveries

There are a variety of SAP Fiori apps that can be used to record the arrival of goods at your facility if your supplier transmits details to you via an advanced shipment notification. These apps are described in more detail in the following sections.

The Post Goods Receipt for Inbound Delivery SAP Fiori app is available in SAP S/4HANA for processing goods receipts via inbound deliveries. In addition, the following Web-GUI apps are also available:

- Inbound Deliveries for Purchase Orders
- Create Inbound Delivery
- Change Inbound Delivery
- Display Inbound Delivery
- My Inbound Delivery Monitor

Post Goods Receipt for Inbound Delivery

The Post Goods Receipt for Inbound Delivery app (Figure 7.8) enables a user to record goods receipts with reference to an inbound delivery document. The app displays a selection of inbound deliveries from the supplier that can be posted.

Note that if an inbound delivery is required for the purchase order, this app must be used to post the receipt of the goods. This requirement is controlled via the confirmation control key on the purchase order line item.

This app can be used to do the following:

- Post the receipt of goods with reference to an inbound delivery containing order items for stock material (procurement for stock)
- Post the receipt of goods with reference to an inbound delivery containing order items with single or multiple account assignments (procurement for direct consumption)
- Post the receipts of shelf-life-managed materials into stock
- Post the receipt of goods into supplier consignment stock

The Post Goods Receipt for Inbound Delivery app is assigned to the receiving specialist standard authorization role.

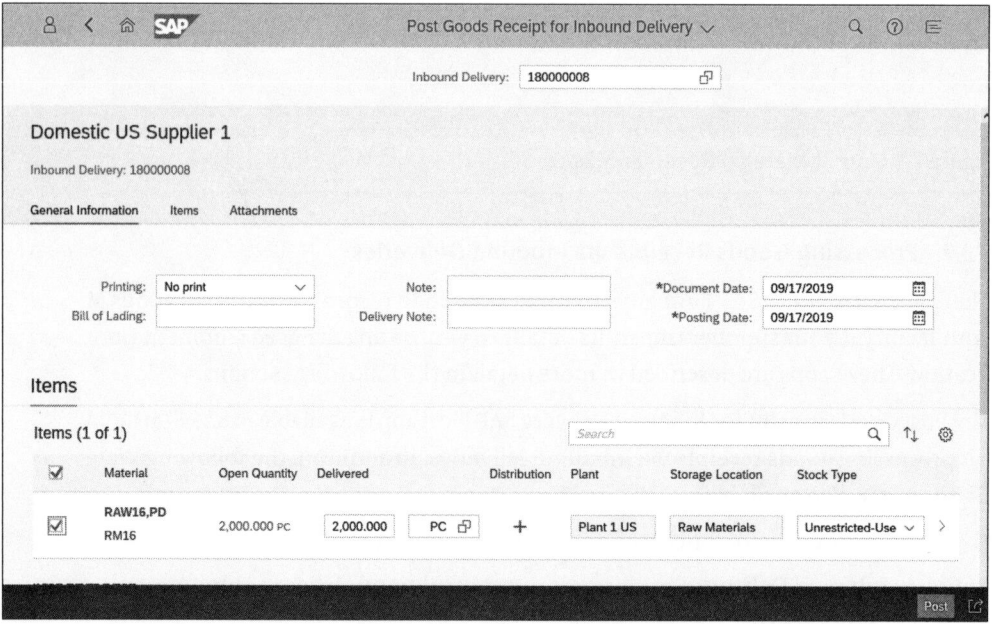

Figure 7.8 Post Goods Receipt for Inbound Delivery App

Inbound Deliveries for Purchase Orders

The Inbound Deliveries for Purchase Orders app (Figure 7.9) is used to list purchase orders that are approved but don't have inbound deliveries created. Users can select the purchase orders for which they wish to create inbound deliveries. A log of the inbound deliveries created is then displayed (Figure 7.10).

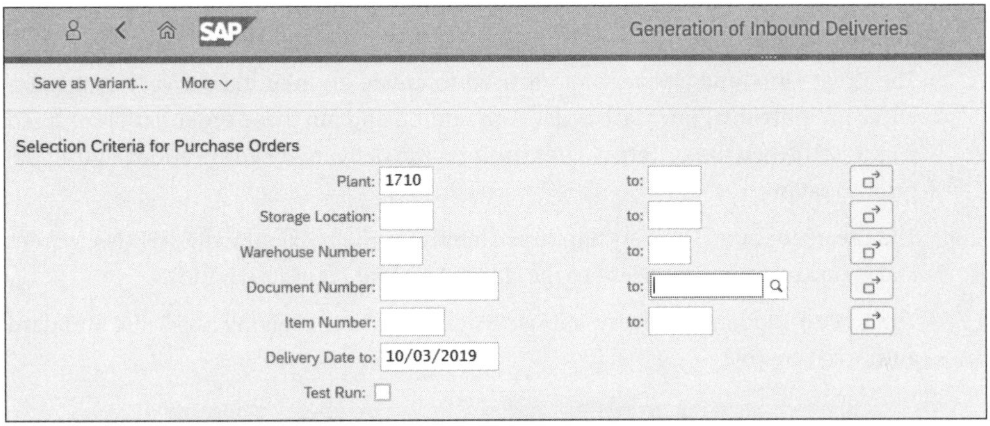

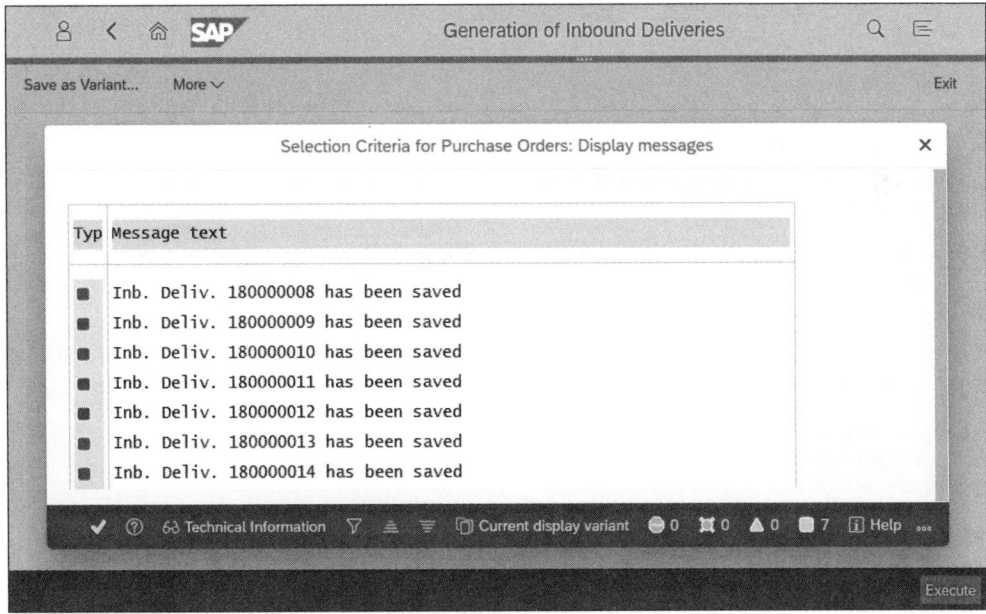

Figure 7.9 Inbound Deliveries for Purchase Orders Selection Screen

Figure 7.10 Inbound Deliveries for Purchase Orders Creation Log

The Inbound Deliveries for Purchase Orders app runs directly on the backend SAP S/4HANA system and is functionally equivalent to the classic SAP ERP Transaction VL34.

The Inbound Deliveries for Purchase Orders app is assigned to the receiving specialist standard authorization role.

Create Inbound Delivery

The Create Inbound Delivery app is used to create an inbound delivery that references an individual purchase order. The referencing purchase order data is entered (Figure 7.11), then the system creates the inbound delivery for verification (Figure 7.12) prior to saving.

The Create Inbound Delivery app runs directly on the backend SAP S/4HANA system and is functionally equivalent to the classic SAP ERP Transaction VL31N.

The Create Inbound Delivery app is assigned to the receiving specialist standard authorization role.

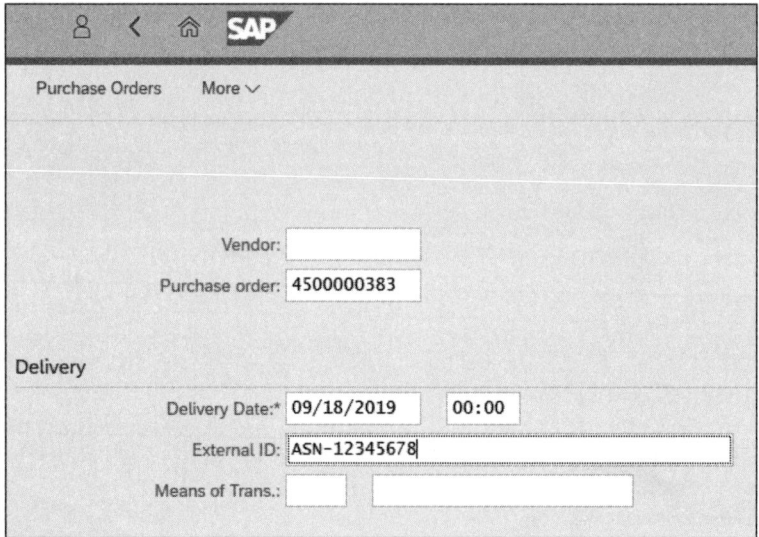

Figure 7.11 Create Inbound Delivery App Selection Screen

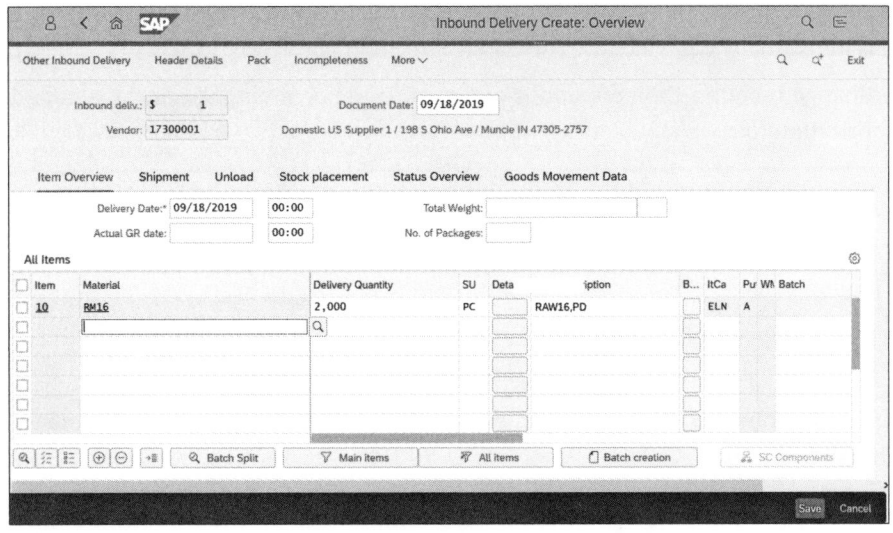

Figure 7.12 Create Inbound Delivery App

Change Inbound Delivery

The Change Inbound Delivery app (Figure 7.13) is used to make changes to an existing inbound delivery. The types of changes that can be made depend on the status of the document.

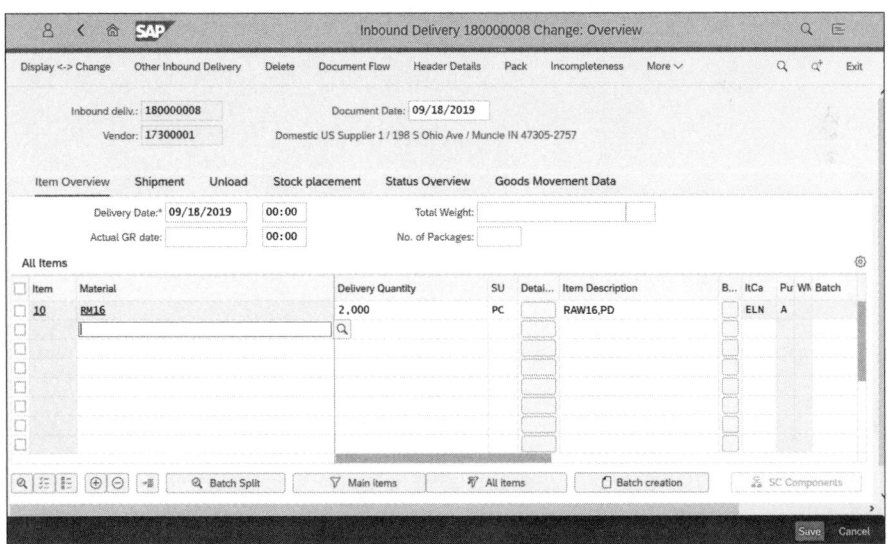

Figure 7.13 Change Inbound Delivery App

The Change Inbound Delivery app runs directly on the backend SAP S/4HANA system and is functionally equivalent to the classic SAP ERP Transaction VL32N.

The Change Inbound Delivery app is assigned to the receiving specialist standard authorization role.

Display Inbound Delivery

The Display Inbound Delivery app (Figure 7.14) is used to show all details for an existing inbound delivery.

The Display Inbound Delivery app runs directly on the backend SAP S/4HANA system and is functionally equivalent to the classic SAP ERP Transaction VL33N.

The Display Inbound Delivery app is assigned to the receiving specialist standard authorization role.

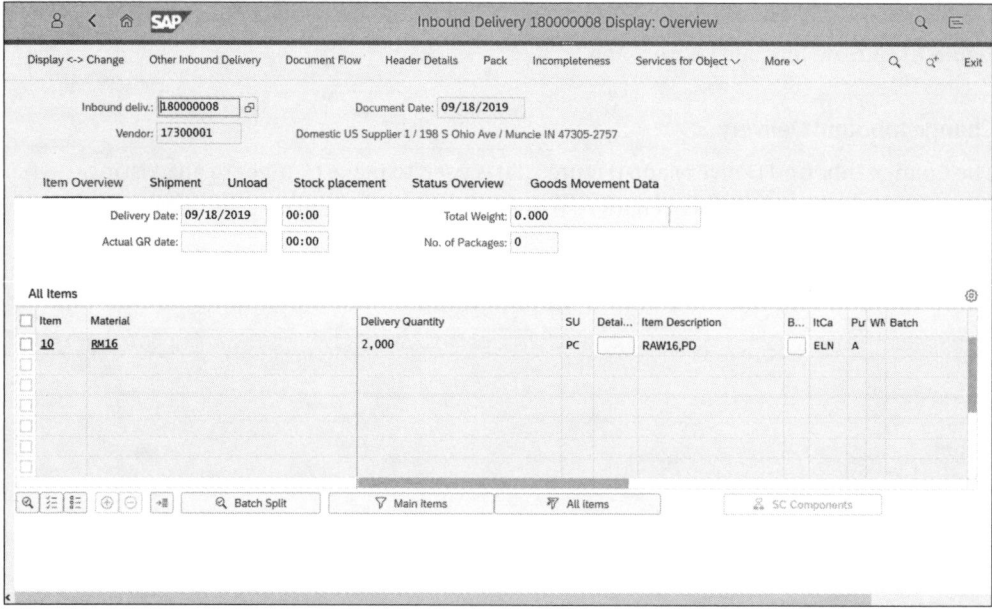

Figure 7.14 Display Inbound Delivery App

My Inbound Delivery Monitor

The My Inbound Delivery Monitor app (Figure 7.15) is used to generate worklists of current inbound deliveries and to take appropriate action on the deliveries displayed. Worklists can be created that allow update of putaway quantities on line items and to post goods receipts against inbound delivery documents. General lists of inbound deliveries that meet entered criteria can also be generated.

The My Inbound Delivery Monitor app runs directly on the backend SAP S/4HANA system and is functionally equivalent to the classic SAP ERP Transaction VL06I.

The My Inbound Delivery Monitor app is assigned to the receiving specialist standard authorization role.

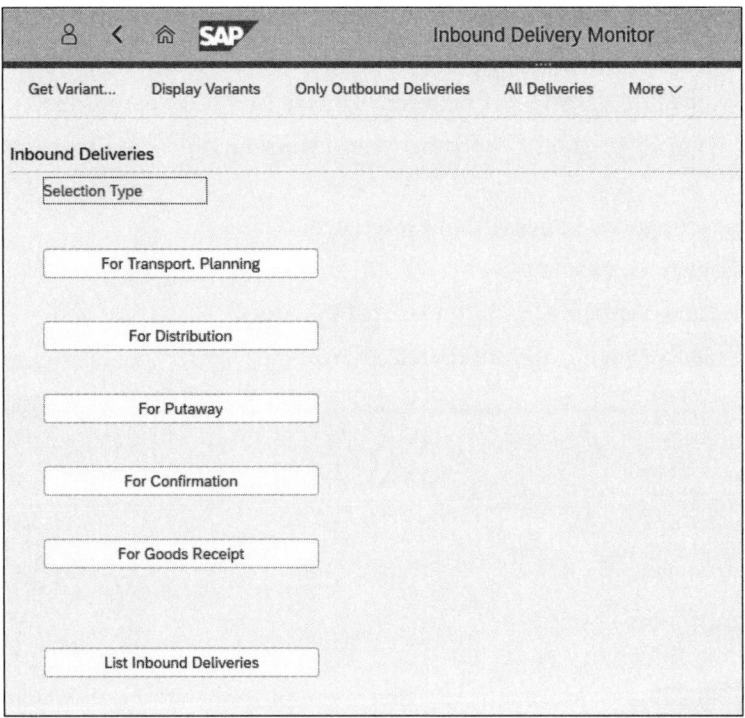

Figure 7.15 My Inbound Delivery Monitor App

7.4 Goods Issues

Goods issues are classified as goods movements that result in a decrease in stock quantities. Goods issues can be planned in the SAP S/4HANA system or can be executed without preplanning.

Planned goods issues are issued with reference to an existing document, such as an outbound delivery to a customer or a reservation. Those customers requiring shipping integration with their goods issue processes will generally reference outbound delivery documents created by the warehouse.

Unplanned goods issues are issued without any reference. Examples include scrapping of defective material or issuing samples from stock.

Here are the movement types for goods issues with and without reference documents:

- **Movement types for goods issues with reference to documents:**
  - 261, Goods Issue to Production Order
  - 601, Goods Issue to Outbound Delivery to Customer
  - 641, Goods Issue to In-Transit Stock between Plants in Same Company Code
  - 643, Goods Issue to In-Transit Stock between Plants in Differing Company Codes
- **Movement types for goods issues without reference:**
  - 201, Goods Issue to Cost Center
  - 333, Goods Issue to Sampling from Unrestricted Use Stock
  - 551, Goods Issue to Scrap from Unrestricted Use Stock

> **Note**
>
> Apps used for goods issues without reference include the following:
>
> - Manage Stock
> - Post Goods Movement
>
> These apps were described in Section 7.3.

If you use outbound delivery documents to manage shipping operations, then you can post goods issues in inventory management via these documents. The following apps can be used to manage outbound deliveries in the SAP S/4HANA system:

- My Purchase Orders—Due for Delivery
- Manage Outbound Deliveries

We'll describe these apps in the following sections.

7.4.1   My Purchase Orders—Due for Delivery

The My Purchase Orders—Due for Delivery app (Figure 7.16) is used to create outbound deliveries for those purchase orders that involve outbound movements of material. These types of purchase orders include returns of material to suppliers or the provisioning of component materials to a subcontractor out of storage location stock. Specific selection criteria are entered, and a list of eligible purchase orders is shown. Outbound deliveries then can be created for the selected orders.

The My Purchase Orders—Due for Delivery app runs directly on the backend SAP S/4HANA system and is functionally equivalent to the classic SAP ERP Transaction VL10B.

The My Purchase Orders—Due for Delivery app is assigned to the shipping specialist standard authorization role.

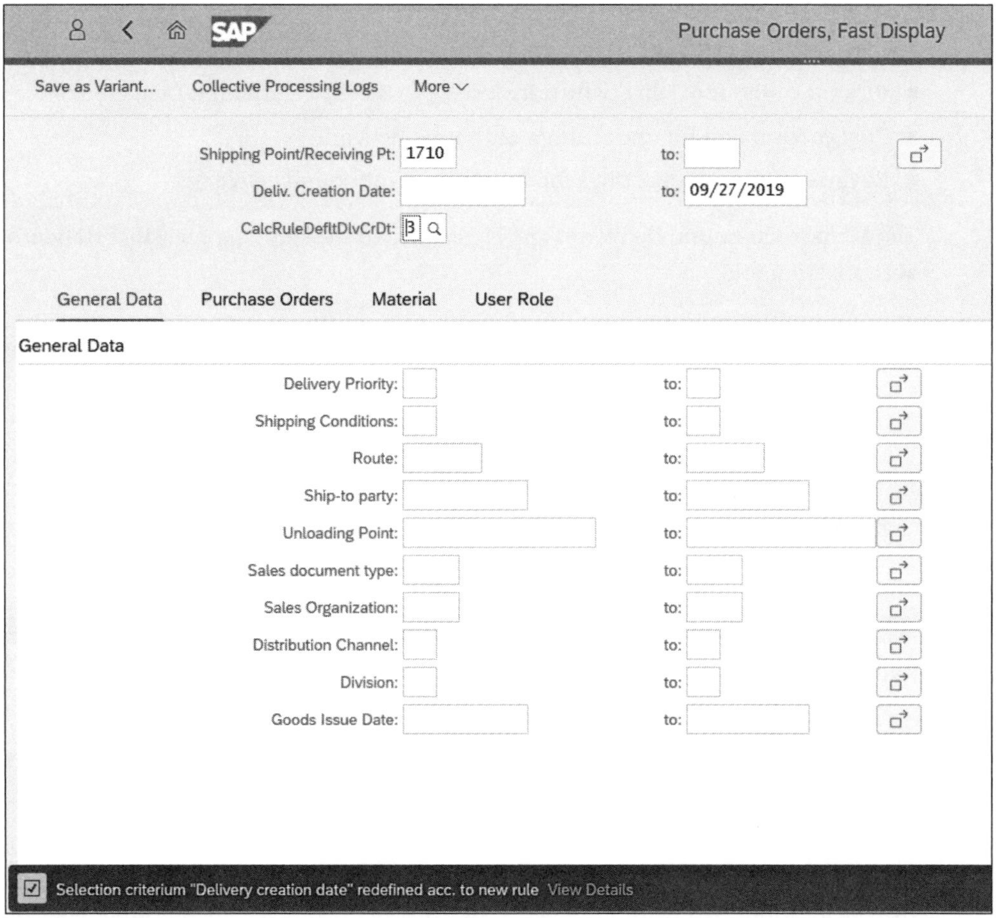

Figure 7.16 My Purchase Orders—Due for Delivery App

7.4.2   Manage Outbound Deliveries

The Manage Outbound Deliveries app (Figure 7.17) produces a list of outbound deliveries to your specifications. You can click a specific outbound delivery to see details about the document, such as the ship-to customer, weights, or volumes. You can then process the documents, depending on the status of the delivery. For instance, you can post a goods issue for a delivery from this app if it has been completely picked. If you subsequently need to change a delivery document, you can use the app to reverse the goods issue posting and then edit the document.

The Manage Outbound Deliveries app is used to do the following:

- Search for outbound deliveries using provided filter criteria
- Sort your table entries in ascending or descending order
- Pick the outbound delivery by transferring to the Pick Outbound Delivery app
- Post goods issues for one or more outbound deliveries
- Reverse goods issue postings for one or more outbound deliveries

The Manage Outbound Deliveries app is assigned to the shipping specialist standard authorization role.

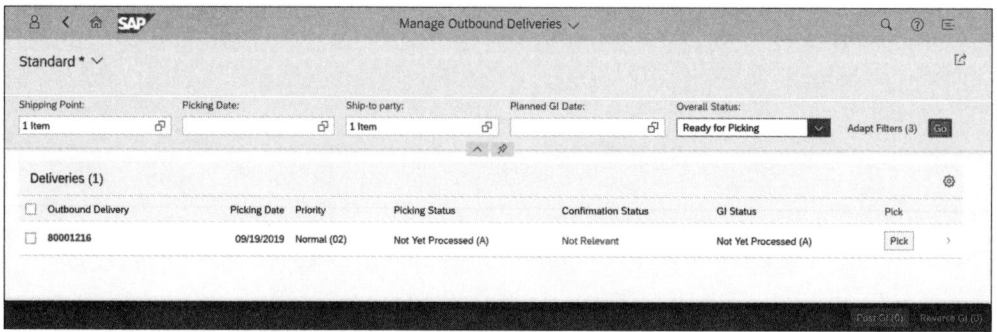

Figure 7.17 Manage Outbound Deliveries App

7.5   Stock Transfers

Stock transfers are goods movements in inventory management that result in a change in location for the goods being transacted. Stock transfers can be between storage locations in a plant or between two distinct plants. There are three types of stock transfers:

- Plant to plant within one company code
- Plant to plant between two company codes
- Storage location to storage location within one plant

Stock transfers can take place using either one-step or two-step processes.

7.5.1   One-Step and Two-Step Stock Transfers

In one-step stock transfers, the material moves from the issuing plant and storage location to the receiving plant and storage location immediately upon posting. One-step stock transfers are typically used when goods movements are performed in the system after the physical transfer takes place or when the transit time between the two storage locations is minimal.

The following movement types are used for one-step stock transfers:

- 301, Plant to Plant
- 311, Storage Location to Storage Location

Two-step transfers are used to record the goods issue from the issuing plant and storage location separately from the goods receipt into the receiving plant and storage location. This two-step process has the benefit of providing visibility into in-transit stock quantities between the two locations.

The following movement types are used for two-step stock transfers:

- 303, Plant to Plant—Goods Issue from Shipping Plant
- 305, Plant to Plant—Goods Receipt in Receiving Plant
- 313, Storage Location to Storage Location—Goods Receipt in Receiving Plant
- 305, Plant to Plant—Goods Receipt in Receiving Plant

Note that these movement types only work with unrestricted use stock.

Simple movements of stock can be recorded in the SAP S/4HANA system with just a material document. The following apps can be used to perform stock transfers using inventory management goods movements:

- Transfer Stock—In-Plant
- Transfer Stock—Cross-Plant
- Manage Stock

We'll describe these apps in the following sections.

> **Note**
>
> The Manage Stock app was described in Section 7.3.1.

Transfer Stock—In-Plant

The Transfer Stock—In Plant app (Figure 7.18) is used to make transfer postings within a plant. Utilize this app to make storage location to storage location stock transfers. You can transfer unrestricted, quality inspection, or blocked stocks. You can move supplier consignment, sales order, or project special stocks between storage locations as well.

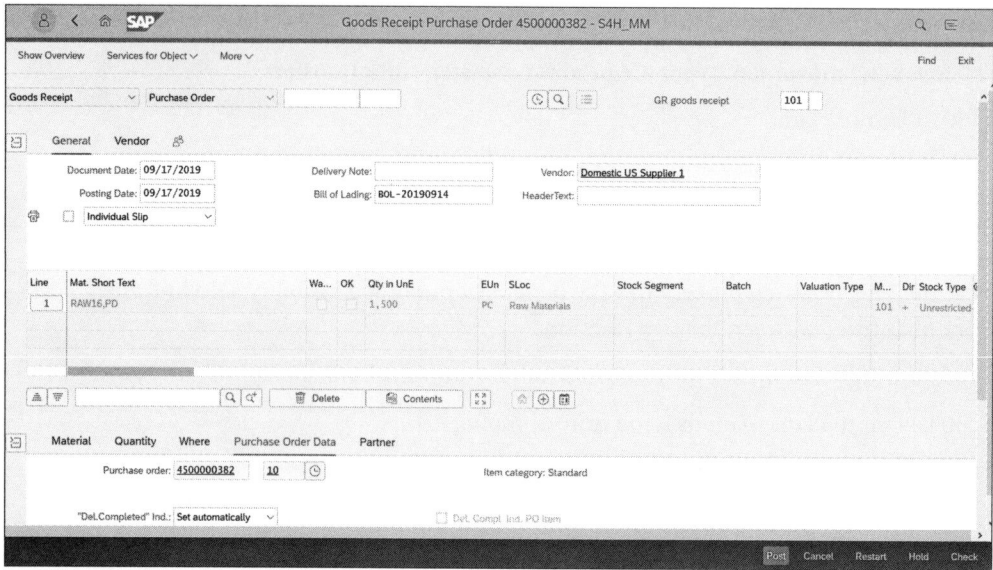

Figure 7.18 Transfer Stock In-Plant App

This app also lets you transfer from one stock type to another. In addition, it allows transfers of ownership from supplier consignment stock to unrestricted use stock. You can also transfer quantities between two sales order stocks or two project stocks, and you can enter free texts for the document header or for an individual line item. You can also check the range of coverage for the existing stocks based on the consumption of unrestricted use stock materials in the last 30 days.

You can branch from this app to other apps, such as Stock—Single Material and Material Documents Overview.

The Transfer Stock—In-Plant app is assigned to the inventory manager and warehouse clerk standard authorization roles.

Transfer Stock—Cross-Plant

Use the Transfer Stock—Cross-Plant app (Figure 7.19) to create transfer postings from one plant to another. You can also transfer stock from one stock type to another using this app.

You can create a stock transport order directly from this app via the **Create Stock Transport Order** button. Note that stock transport order configuration needs to be set in the backend system to support this feature.

You can record free texts for the document header or for an individual line item., and you can use a predictive analytics model to forecast the delivery date for a stock transport order from this app as well.

You can branch from this app to other apps, such as Manage Stock, Transfer Stock—In-Plant, and Material Documents Overview.

The Transfer Stock—Cross-Plant app is assigned to the inventory manager and warehouse clerk standard authorization roles.

Figure 7.19 Transfer Stock—Cross-Plant App

7.5.2   Stock Transfer Execution Using Shipping Integration

It's common to use the shipping component of SAP S/4HANA to transact stock transfers through your facilities. The same apps described earlier for handling goods receipts with inbound deliveries (e.g., Post Goods Receipt for Purchase Order) also can be used for performing receipts for inbound stock transport purchase orders.

7.5.3   Stock Transfer Reporting

It's important to monitor the status of stock transfers in the system, especially those that involve a two-step process. This will ensure that all physical stock transfers are posted in a timely manner and that up-to-date stock information is available for materials planning.

SAP S/4HANA provides the following apps to obtain reports for in-process stock transfers:

- Overdue Materials—Stock in Transit
- Display Stock in Transit

We'll describe these apps in the following sections.

Overdue Materials—Stock in Transit

The Overdue Materials—Stock in Transit app (Figure 7.20) provides information on materials for which a stock transport order has been created and issued, but which have not been received to date. You can identify these materials to complete the stock transfer process or to investigate potential issues with the transfers.

Use the Overdue Materials—Stock in Transit app to do the following:

- Review the stock transport orders for which materials are scheduled to arrive in a plant
- Display a list of stock transport order line items for which the stock transfer process hasn't yet been completed, has been completed, or both
- Follow up on the results by choosing a purchase order or a material from the list, and then choosing one of the following apps: Post Goods Receipt for Purchase Order, Stock—Single Material, or Stock—Multiple Materials
- See the stock value of overdue stocks in transit; stock value calculation is based on stock quantity of the selected reporting date multiplied by the current material price

- Use a predictive analytics model to forecast the delivery date for a stock transport order

The Overdue Materials—Stock in Transit app is assigned to the shipping specialist, receiving specialist, and warehouse clerk standard authorization roles.

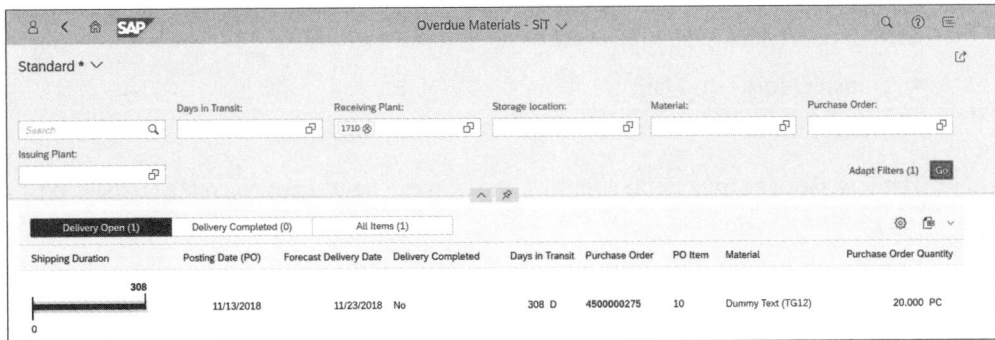

Figure 7.20 Overdue Materials—Stock In Transit App

Display Stock in Transit

The Display Stock in Transit app (Figure 7.21) is used to show all stocks that have been issued from one plant and are currently in transit to another plant. It also shows stock transport purchase order references and the value of the goods transferred.

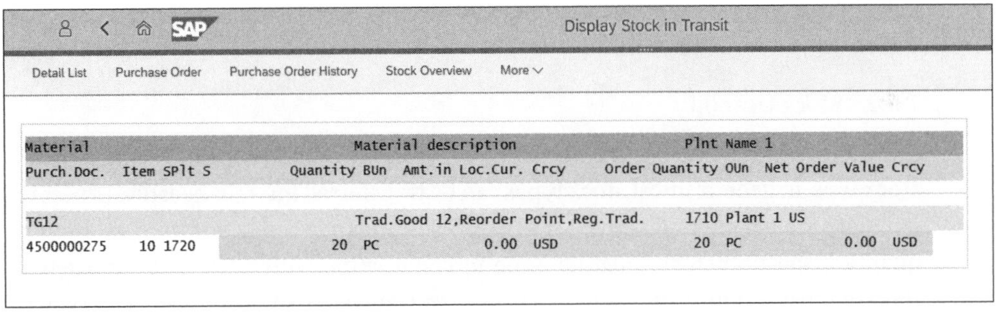

Figure 7.21 Display Stock in Transit App

The Display Stock in Transit app runs directly on the backend SAP S/4HANA system and is functionally equivalent to the classic SAP ERP Transaction MB5T.

The Display Stock in Transit app is assigned to the inventory manager standard authorization role.

7.6   Transfer Postings

Transfer postings are goods movements that result in a change in identity, usability, or ownership for a quantity of stock. Typically, the stock doesn't physically move in the system during a transfer posting. However, it's possible to combine some types of transfer postings with changes in location as well. The following SAP Fiori apps are used to post transfer postings in the SAP S/4HANA system:

- Transfer Stock—In-Plant
- Manage Stock

The Post Goods Movements WebGUI app also can be utilized to create transfer posting goods movements.

Descriptions of these apps can be found in Section 7.5.

7.6.1   Stock Identity

Transfer postings that result in a change in stock identity involve changes in material. Note that a material can only to transferred to the stock of another material if both materials share the same base unit of measure.

If a material is batch-managed in the SAP S/4HANA system, a change in batch identity can also be posted. Both the material and batch can be changed at the same time.

The 309 movement type is used to change material or batch quantities in stock.

7.6.2   Stock Usability

Transfer postings that result in a change in stock usability involve a change in the stock type. In general, most stock types can be transferred interchangeably. However, if quality management is active for a material in a plant, then transfers into or out of quality inspection stock must be done in conjunction with a QM process, such as inbound inspection. Movement types used to transfer stock from one stock type to another are shown in Table 7.1.

From Stock Type	To Stock Type	Movement Type
Quality inspection	Unrestricted use	321
Unrestricted use	Quality inspection	322

Table 7.1 Stock Transfer Movement Types for Usability Changes

From Stock Type	To Stock Type	Movement Type
Blocked	Unrestricted use	343
Unrestricted use	Blocked	344
Blocked	Quality inspection	349
Quality inspection	Blocked	350
Customer returns	Unrestricted use	453
Customer returns	Quality inspection	457
Customer returns	Blocked	459

Table 7.1 Stock Transfer Movement Types for Usability Changes (Cont.)

7.6.3   Stock Ownership

If you have stocks delivered to your facility by a supplier on a consignment basis and you wish to take financial ownership of these stocks, you enter a transfer posting to recognize that fact. Similarly, if you return stock that was delivered on a consignment basis to your customer, you post a transfer posting as well. Movement type 411 K is provided for this purpose.

7.7   Physical Inventory

Good accounting practices require periodic reconciliation of the stock balances found in the SAP S/4HANA system to the physical stocks in the warehouse. These assets need to be reflected accurately on the company's financial statements. Accurate stock balances also optimize the benefits of MRP for assuring availability of material for production and sales processes.

The system provides a variety of physical inventory methods to accomplish this requirement. Regardless of the method used, all physical inventory processes encompass the following three phases (see Figure 7.22):

❶ Creation of the physical inventory documents

❷ Entry of the physical counts into SAP S/4HANA

❸ Posting of physical inventory differences

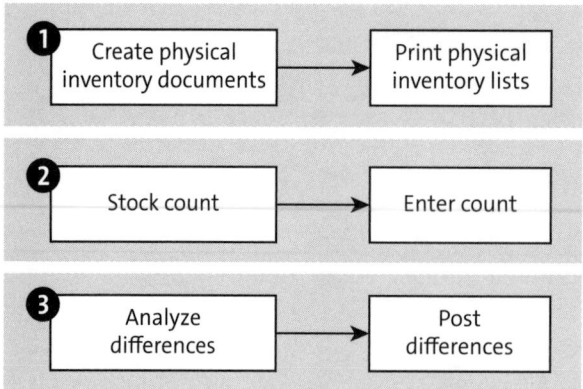

Figure 7.22 Physical Inventory Process Phases

A physical inventory document is needed to begin the process. This document forms the basis for planning and performing a physical inventory, for recording counts, and for posting any differences found between the system and the physical stocks. Physical inventory documents contain a header, which holds information about the count event itself, such as the document number, the person responsible for the count, and the planned count date. Line items on the physical inventory document contain the materials being counted and hold the system and actual count information.

Stocks are counted in inventory management based on the following:

- Material
- Plant
- Storage location
- Stock type
- Valuation type/batch
- Special stock

Each combination of these elements will be counted separately during a physical inventory.

The method of creating physical inventory documents is dependent on the technique used for the count. SAP S/4HANA supports the following techniques:

- Manual physical inventory (spot inventory)
- Annual physical inventory
- Continuous physical inventory

- Cycle counting
- Sample-based physical inventory

For more information on the physical inventory methods available, consult the SAP Help website.

Once the documents are created, it's common to print the physical inventory count sheets. These are then distributed to the counters, who record the physical quantities on the sheet. Count sheets can be transferred to a mobile application for counting as well.

After the physical count is recorded, this information is entered into the SAP S/4HANA system. The system can provide feedback to the entry clerk if the quantity recorded during the count exceeds the system count based on a defined threshold percentage. This helps prevent data entry errors.

Once the counts are entered, they can be analyzed by authorized personnel. This analysis may result in a recount of the material in that storage location.

Once the physical inventory counts are confirmed, any differences detected need to be posted to inventory management so that the physical and system counts are reconciled.

This action results in a goods movement posting either incrementing or decrementing the quantity of goods in stock. Financial postings are also made at the same time.

SAP S/4HANA supplies apps to use in managing the physical inventory processes supported by the system. There are apps to support the execution of a physical inventory and others for monitoring the physical inventory processes and reporting. We'll discuss these apps ahead.

7.7.1 Physical Inventory Execution

SAP supplies the Create Physical Inventory Documents SAP Fiori app to support physical inventory processes.

In addition, the following WebGUI apps are available for execution of physical inventory processes:

- Create Single PI Document
- Change Physical Inventory Document
- Enter Inventory Count
- Change Physical Inventory Count

- Enter PI Count w/o Document
- Enter and Post PI Count w/o Document
- Request Physical Inventory Recount
- Process Physical Inventory Count Results
- Print Physical Inventory Documents
- Create Physical Inventory Documents—Regular Stock
- ABC Analysis for Cycle Counting

These apps are described in more detail in the following sections.

Create Physical Inventory Documents

You use the Create Physical Inventory Documents app (Figure 7.23) to create physical inventory documents for selected materials. You use this app when you want to perform a physical inventory for a specified set of materials of your choosing.

Select the materials that you want using the filter criteria supplied. You can click on a material line to obtain current stock balances, key figures, and material master information. You can then create one or more physical inventory documents based on grouping information you supply to the app.

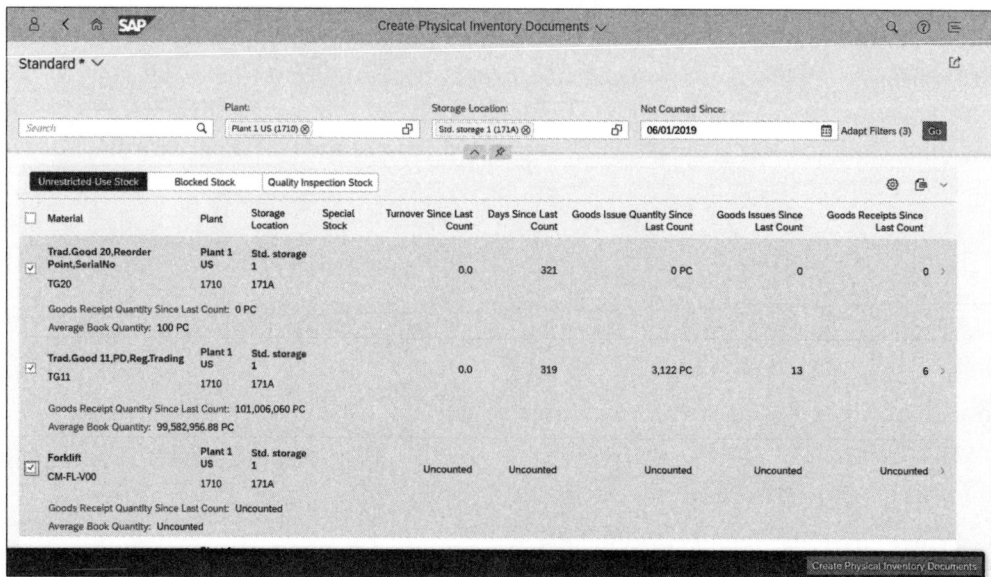

Figure 7.23 Create Physical Inventory Documents App

The Create Physical Inventory Documents app is assigned to the warehouse clerk and inventory manager standard authorization roles.

Create Single PI Document

You use the Create Single PI Document app (Figure 7.24) to manually create a physical inventory document. You use this app when you want to perform a physical inventory for a specific set of materials of your choosing. These are also known as *spot inventories*. You can activate the resulting document at the same time if you wish.

The Create Single PI Document app runs directly on the backend SAP S/4HANA system and is functionally equivalent to the classic SAP ERP Transaction MI01.

The Create Single PI Document app is assigned to the warehouse clerk and inventory manager standard authorization roles.

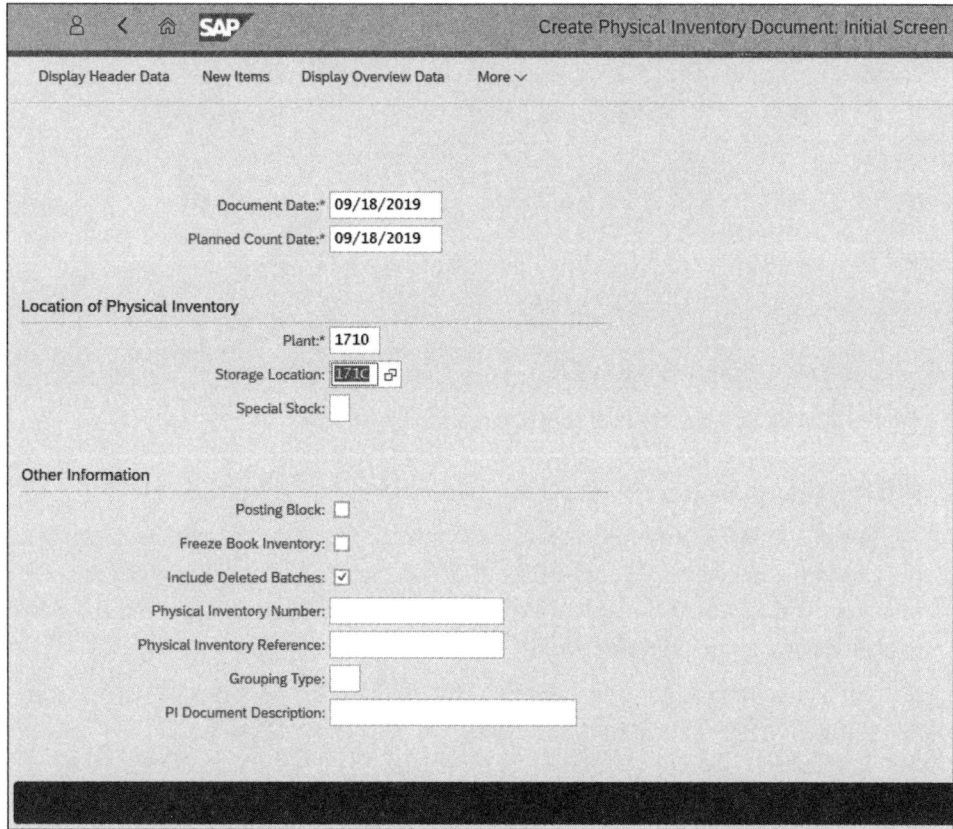

Figure 7.24 Create Single PI Document App

Change Physical Inventory Document

You use the Change Physical Inventory Document app (Figure 7.25) to change an existing physical inventory document. You use this app when you want to add or change materials that need to be counted. You can activate physical inventory documents using this app as well.

The Change Physical Inventory Document app runs directly on the backend SAP S/4HANA system and is functionally equivalent to the classic SAP ERP Transaction MI02.

The Change Physical Inventory Document app is assigned to the warehouse clerk and inventory manager standard authorization roles.

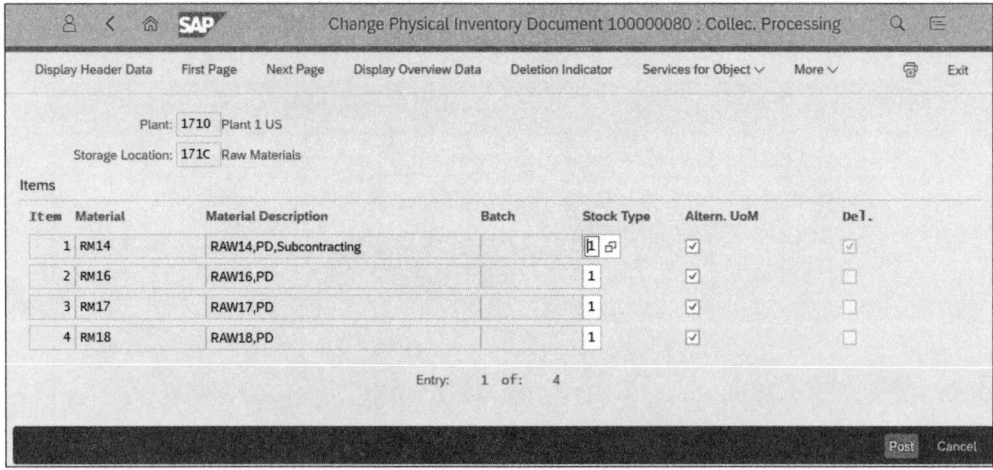

Figure 7.25 Change Physical Inventory Document App

Enter Inventory Count

You use the Enter Inventory Count app (Figure 7.26) to enter the count results that have been recorded by the inventory counter on the physical inventory count sheet. Messages will appear if the entered counted inventory quantities exceed the book quantities by a predefined threshold.

The Enter Inventory Count app runs directly on the backend SAP S/4HANA system and is functionally equivalent to the classic SAP ERP Transaction MI04.

The Enter Inventory Count app is assigned to the warehouse clerk and inventory manager standard authorization roles.

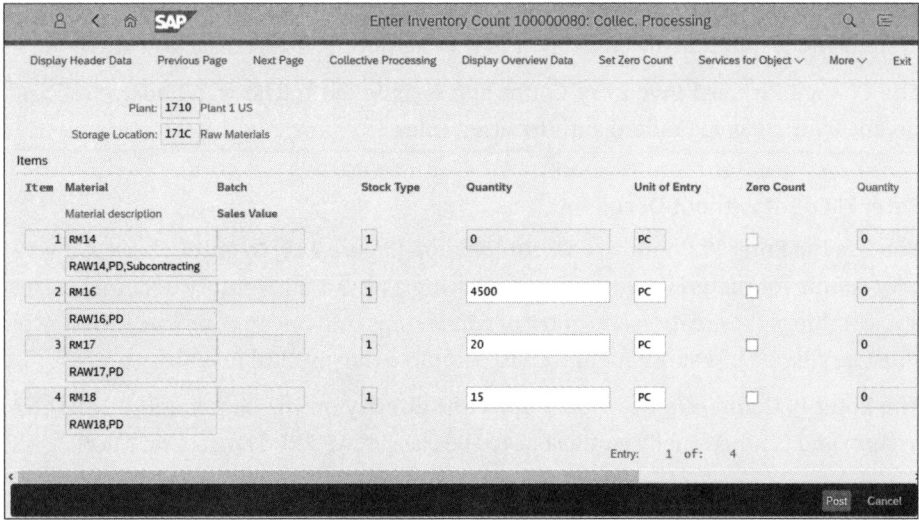

Figure 7.26 Enter Inventory Count App

Change Physical Inventory Count

You use the Change Physical Inventory Count app (Figure 7.27) to modify an entered count for a physical inventory document. You change entered counts until the count differences have been cleared for this document.

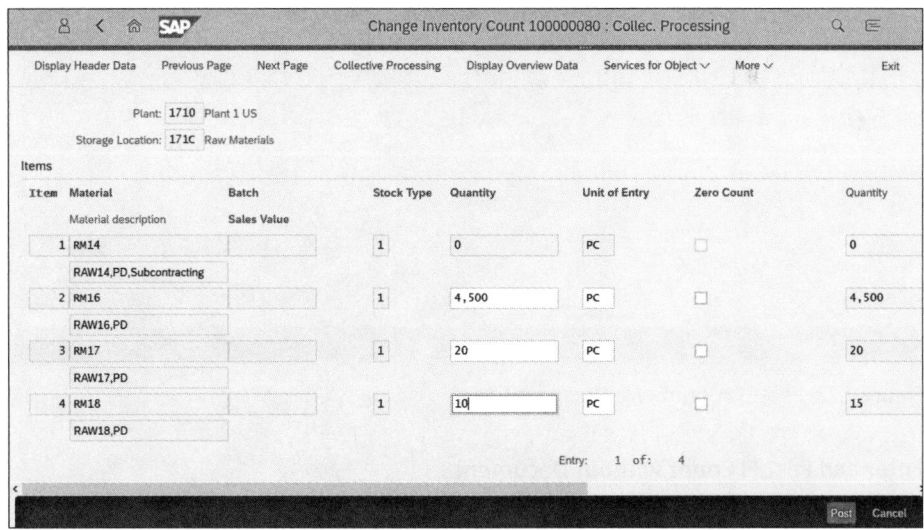

Figure 7.27 Change Physical Inventory Count App

The Change Physical Inventory Count app runs directly on the backend SAP S/4HANA system and is functionally equivalent to the classic SAP ERP Transaction MI05.

The Change Physical Inventory Count app is assigned to the warehouse clerk and inventory manager standard authorization roles.

Enter PI Count without Document

You use the Enter PI Count w/o Document app (Figure 7.28) to enter physical inventory counts for materials without first creating a physical inventory document. This app combines the creation and entry of count steps into one transaction. Differences must be cleared in a subsequent step to complete the physical inventory process.

The Enter PI Count w/o Document app runs directly on the backend SAP S/4HANA system and is functionally equivalent to the classic SAP ERP Transaction MI09.

The Enter PI Count w/o Document app is assigned to the warehouse clerk and inventory manager standard authorization roles.

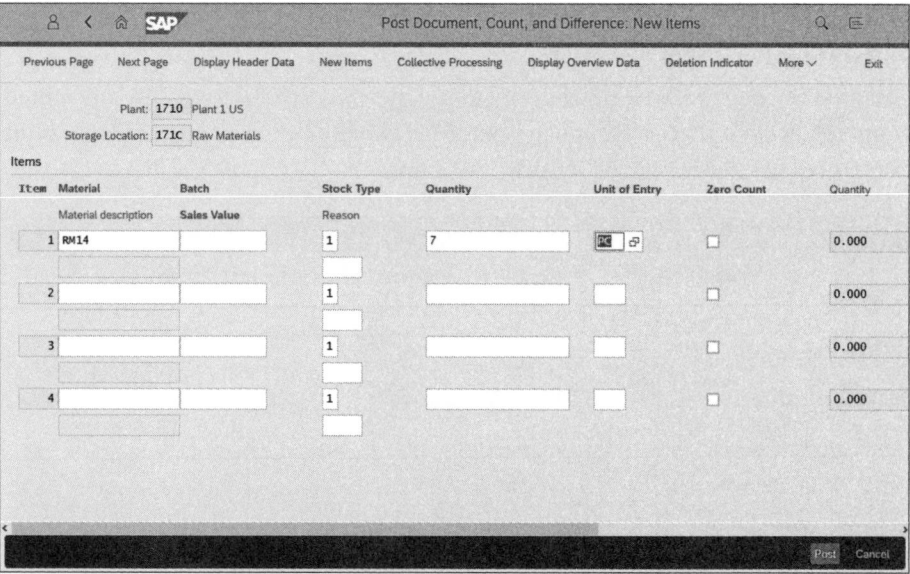

Figure 7.28 Enter PI Count w/o Document App

Enter and Post PI Count without Document

You use the Enter and Post PI Count w/o Document app (Figure 7.29) to enter physical inventory counts and post differences for materials without first creating a physical inventory document. This app combines creation, entering, and clearing of differences steps into one transaction.

The Enter and Post PI Count w/o Document app runs directly on the backend SAP S/4HANA system and is functionally equivalent to the classic SAP ERP Transaction MI10.

The Enter and Post PI Count w/o Document app is assigned to the inventory manager standard authorization role.

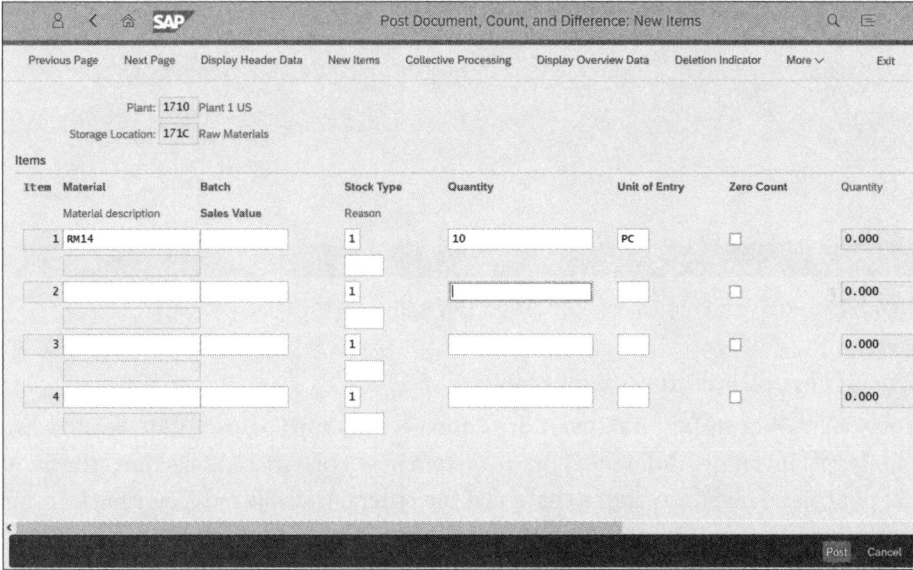

Figure 7.29 Enter and Post P/I Count w/o Document App

Request Physical Inventory Recount

You use the Request Physical Inventory Recount app (Figure 7.30) to recount items from a counted physical inventory document. This creates a new physical inventory document that references the items selected for recount from the original document.

The Request Physical Inventory Recount app runs directly on the backend SAP S/4HANA system and is functionally equivalent to the classic SAP ERP Transaction MI11.

The Request Physical Inventory Recount app is assigned to the inventory manager standard authorization role.

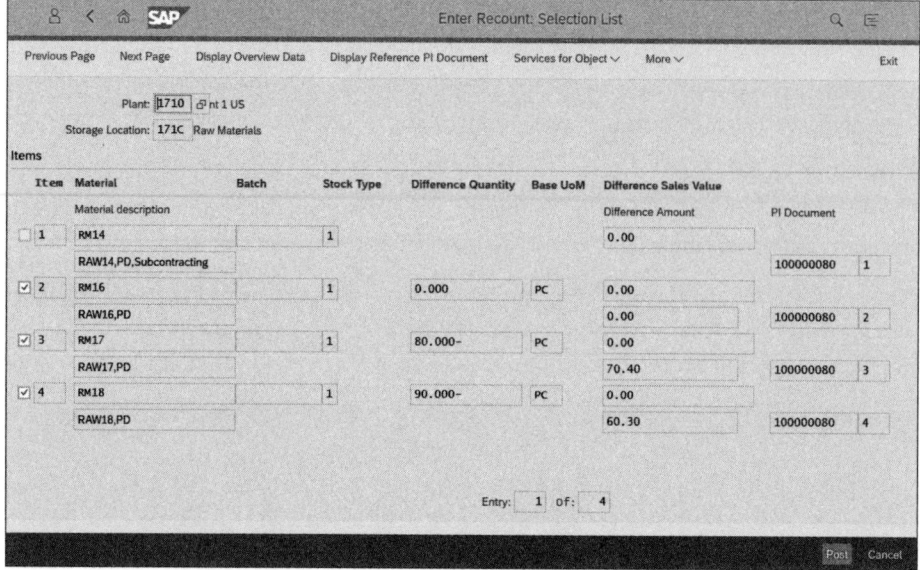

Figure 7.30 Request Physical Inventory Recount App

Process Physical Inventory Count Results

You use the Process Physical Inventory Count Results app (Figure 7.31) to create a list of physical inventory differences in the system based on entered selection criteria. A list of physical inventory items that meet the criteria is displayed. You can clear the differences directly from this list, or you can enter or change count results.

The Process Physical Inventory Count Results app runs directly on the backend SAP S/4HANA system and is functionally equivalent to the classic SAP ERP Transaction MI20.

The Process Physical Inventory Count Results app is assigned to the inventory manager standard authorization role.

PhysInvDoc	Item	Material	Batch	Plant	SLoc	Book Quantity	Qty Counted	Difference Quantity	Unit
100000080	2	RM16		1710	171C	4,500.000	4,500.000	0.000	PC
100000080	3	RM17		1710	171C	100.000	20.000	80.000-	PC
100000080	4	RM18		1710	171C	100.000	10.000	90.000-	PC

Figure 7.31 Process Physical Inventory Count Results App

Print Physical Inventory Documents

You use the Print Physical Inventory Documents app (Figure 7.32) to print activated, uncounted physical inventory documents that can be distributed to the persons performing the count. The system tracks that the physical inventory documents have been printed because these documents are typically controlled documents in an enterprise.

The Print Physical Inventory Documents app runs directly on the backend SAP S/4HANA system and is functionally equivalent to the classic SAP ERP Transaction MI21.

The Print Physical Inventory Documents app is assigned to the warehouse clerk and inventory manager standard authorization roles.

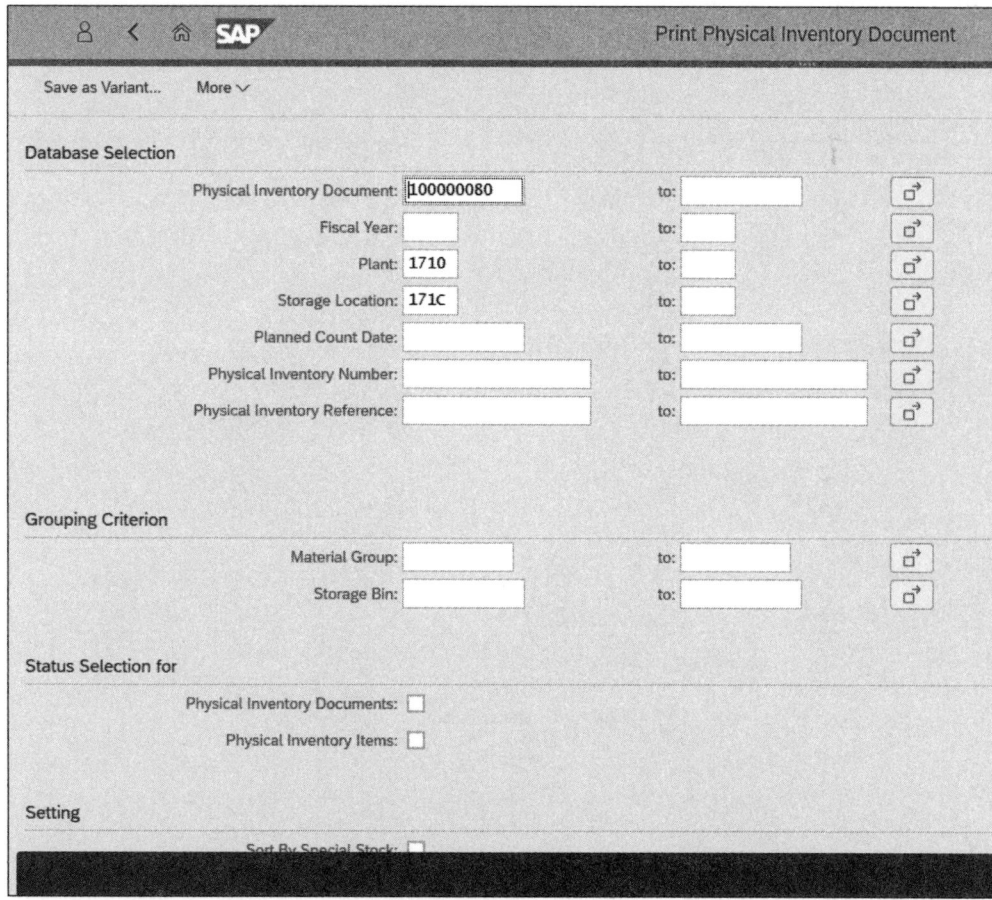

Figure 7.32 Print Physical Inventory Documents App

Create Physical Inventory Documents—Regular Stock

You can use the Create Physical Inventory Documents—Regular Stock app (Figure 7.33) to create several physical inventory documents at one time based on entered selection criteria. The physical inventory documents are then created in a batch run and are available for counting.

Note that this app creates documents for normal storage location stocks only; there are other apps for creating physical inventory counts for special stocks.

The Create Physical Inventory Documents—Regular Stock app runs directly on the backend SAP S/4HANA system and is functionally equivalent to the classic SAP ERP Transaction MI31.

The Create Physical Inventory Documents—Regular Stock app is assigned to the warehouse clerk and inventory manager standard authorization roles.

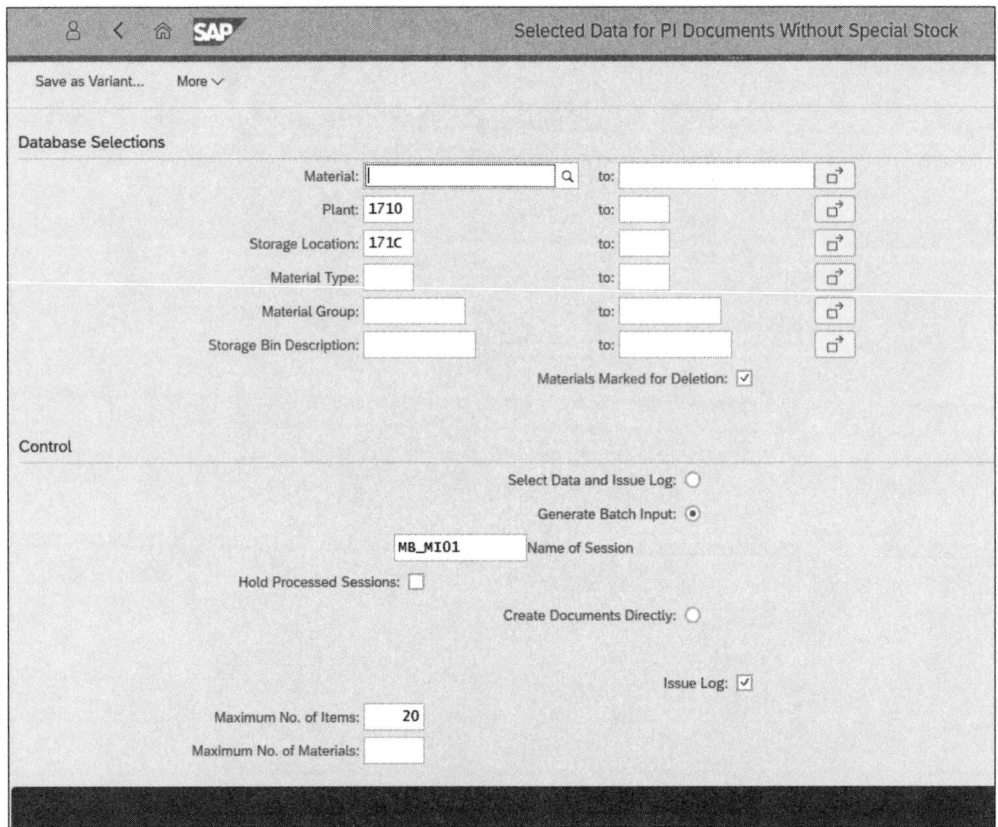

Figure 7.33 Create Physical Inventory Documents—Regular Stock App

ABC Analysis for Cycle Counting

You can use the ABC Analysis for Cycle Counting app (Figure 7.34) to set cycle count indicators on the material master for those materials subject to the cycle counting method of physical inventory. The cycle count indicator determines the frequency per year with which a material needs to be counted per the settings in configuration. The system analyzes consumption or forecast data for that material and plant in the system and sets the cycle count indicator accordingly.

The ABC Analysis for Cycle Counting app runs directly on the backend SAP S/4HANA system and is functionally equivalent to the classic SAP ERP Transaction MIBC.

The ABC Analysis for Cycle Counting app is assigned to the inventory manager standard authorization role.

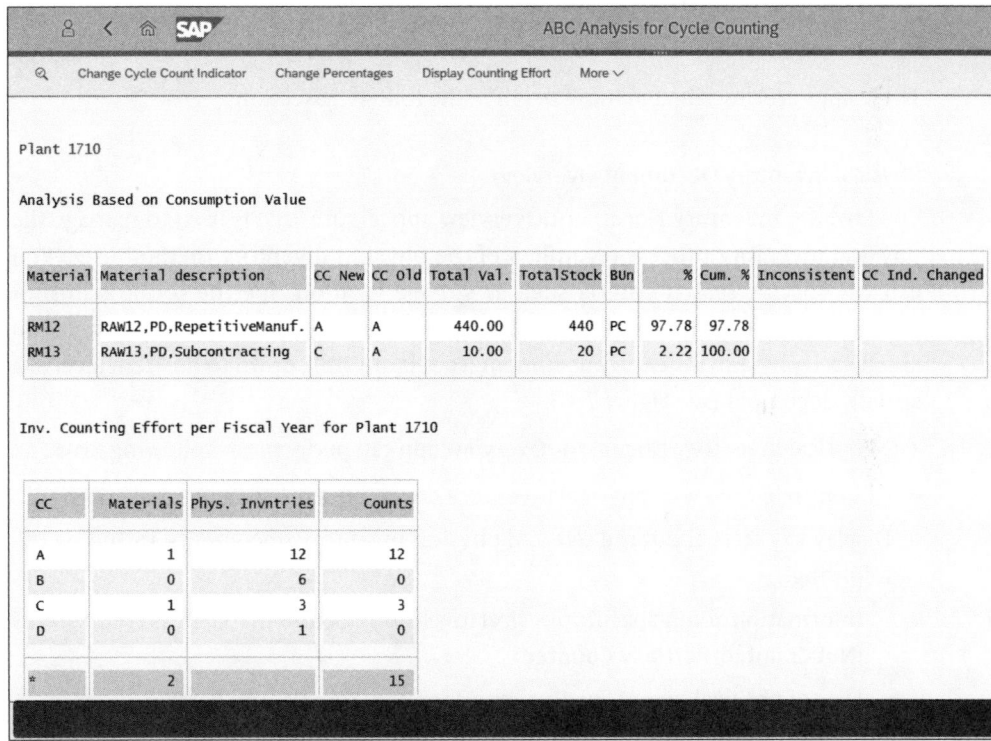

Plant 1710

Analysis Based on Consumption Value

Material	Material description	CC New	CC Old	Total Val.	TotalStock	BUn	%	Cum. %	Inconsistent	CC Ind. Changed
RM12	RAW12,PD,RepetitiveManuf.	A	A	440.00	440	PC	97.78	97.78		
RM13	RAW13,PD,Subcontracting	C	A	10.00	20	PC	2.22	100.00		

Inv. Counting Effort per Fiscal Year for Plant 1710

CC	Materials	Phys. Invntries	Counts
A	1	12	12
B	0	6	0
C	1	3	3
D	0	1	0
*	2		15

Figure 7.34 ABC Analysis for Cycle Counting App

7.7.2 Physical Inventory Monitoring and Reporting

Inventory managers often find it useful to see reports on the progress of physical inventory operations in their facilities. SAP S/4HANA provides reporting capabilities for physical inventory processes to fulfill this need.

The following SAP Fiori apps are available for the inventory manager to monitor the physical inventory processes in their facilities:

- Physical Inventory Document Overview
- Physical Inventory Analysis

In addition, the following WebGUI apps are available for physical inventory process monitoring:

- Display Physical Inventory Progress
- Display PI Document Items for Materials

These apps are described in more detail in the following sections.

Physical Inventory Document Overview

The Physical Inventory Document Overview app (Figure 7.35) is used to manage the physical inventory process regardless of the physical inventory method used. You can use specific search criteria such as storage location, specific count status, or planned count date to filter results. The search result shows detailed information about each physical inventory document (see Figure 7.36), down to the item level of a specific document (see Figure 7.37).

The Physical Inventory Document Overview app can perform the following tasks:

- Obtain an overview of physical inventory documents meeting entered criteria
- Display key facts about the selected physical inventory documents, including the following:
  - Information about specific physical inventory documents, such as count status (**Not Counted, Partially Counted**)
  - Lists of physical inventory document items, materials, and batches
  - Counting progress and posting progress, shown as a bar chart
- Define defaults for the fiscal year, plant, and storage location filters

The Physical Inventory Document Overview app is assigned to the inventory manager standard authorization role.

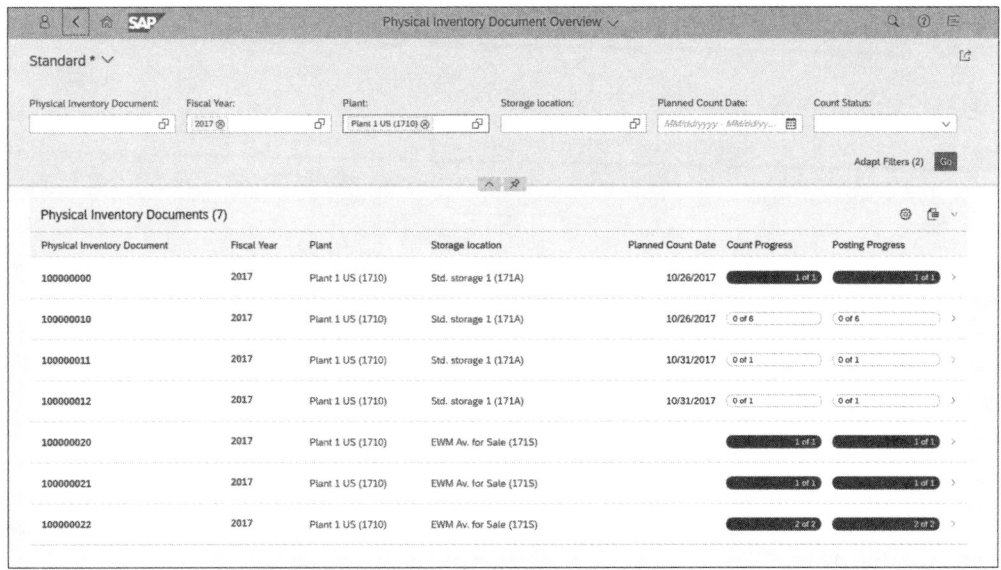

Figure 7.35 Physical Inventory Document Overview App

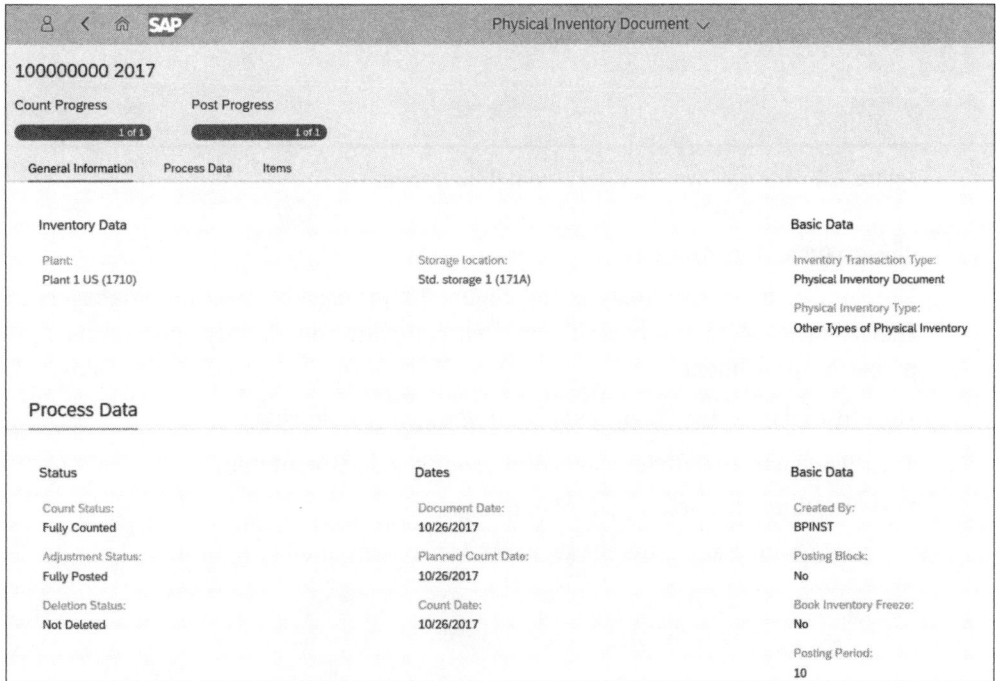

Figure 7.36 Physical Inventory Document Details

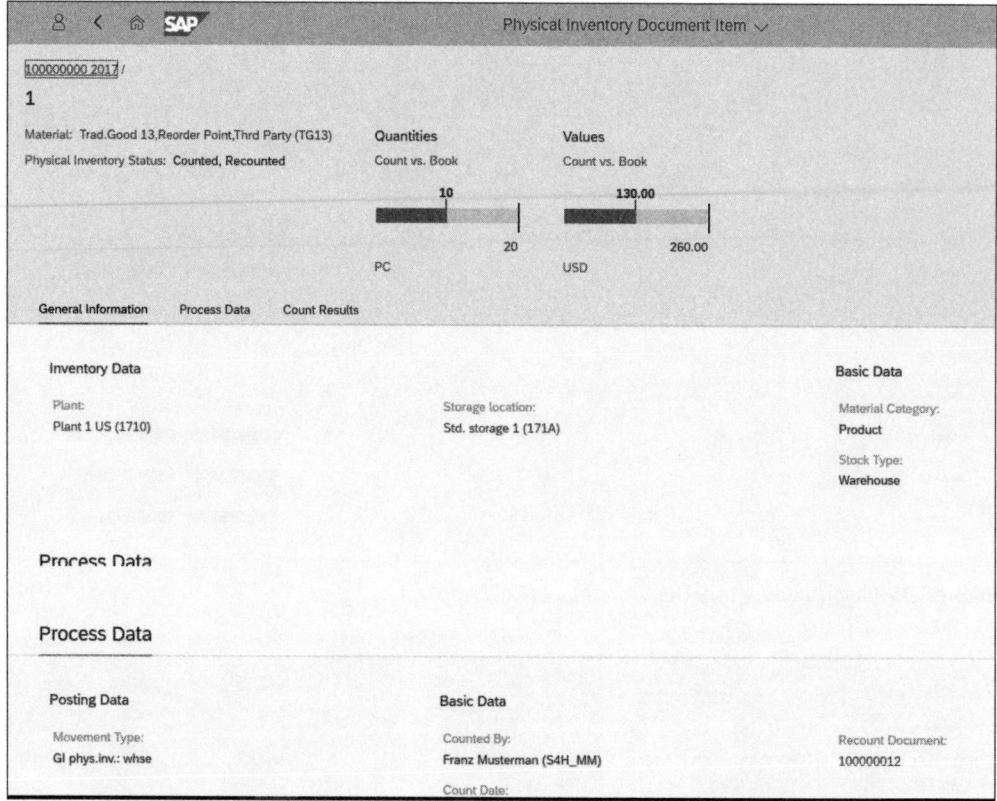

Figure 7.37 Physical Inventory Document Item Details

Physical Inventory Analysis

The Physical Inventory Analysis app (Figure 7.38) is used by inventory managers to analyze physical inventory results in their company and identify opportunities for process improvement.

The Physical Inventory Analysis app lets you do the following:

- Drill down to an individual physical inventory document item
- Define filters to narrow your search scope
- Choose from many different available dimensions and key figures

In addition, this app supports sorting, totaling, and subtotaling, as well as export to Excel. Default filters can be set for fiscal year, plant, storage location, and material.

The Physical Inventory Analysis app is assigned to the inventory manager standard authorization role.

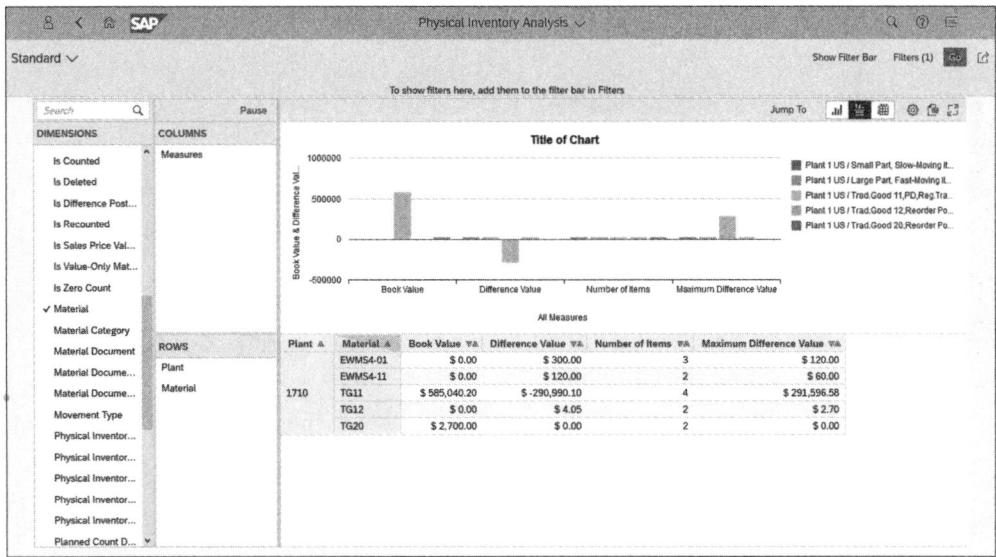

Figure 7.38 Physical Inventory Analysis App

Display Physical Inventory Progress

You can use the Display Physical Inventory Progress app (Figure 7.39) to display a report on the progress of physical inventory activity based on entered selection criteria. You can drill into the resulting list of materials and batches to obtain lists of physical inventory documents created.

The Display Physical Inventory Progress app runs directly on the backend SAP S/4HANA system and is functionally equivalent to the classic SAP ERP Transaction MIDO.

The Display Physical Inventory Progress app is assigned to the inventory manager standard authorization role.

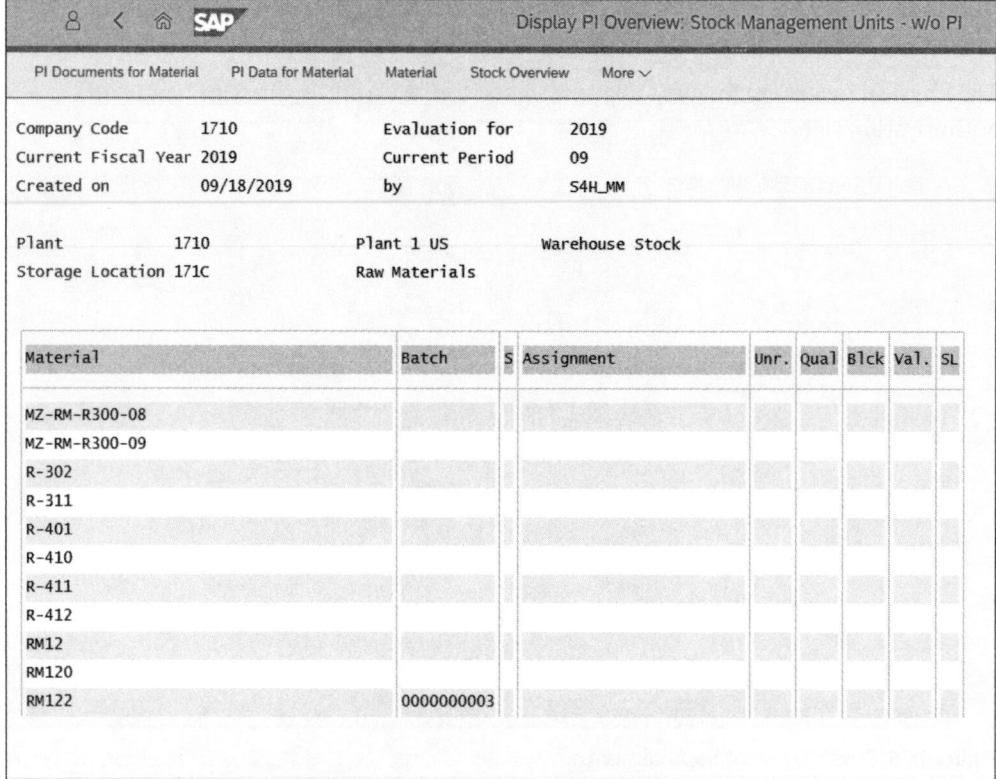

Figure 7.39 Display Physical Inventory Progress App

Display PI Document Items for Materials

You can use the Display PI Document Items for Materials app (Figure 7.40) to list physical inventory items for materials based on entered selection criteria. A list of materials is shown, along with the physical inventory document items for that material.

The Display PI Document Items for Materials app runs directly on the backend SAP S/4HANA system and is functionally equivalent to the classic SAP ERP Transaction MI22.

The Display PI Document Items for Materials app is assigned to the inventory manager standard authorization role.

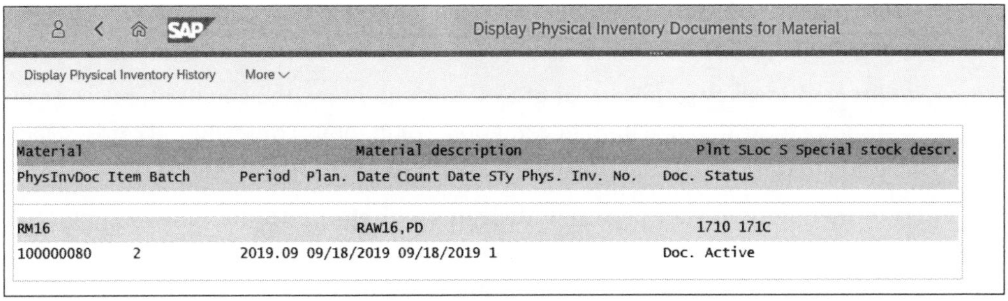

Figure 7.40 Display PI Document Items for Materials App

7.8   Reporting in Inventory Management

Proper control of physical stocks requires a robust set of inventory management reports. SAP S/4HANA builds on SAP ERP's stock balance reporting capabilities by adding new capabilities to visualize the current stock situation, thus enabling fast action in the case of logistics bottlenecks. These capabilities include inventory analytics, which show key performance indicators in real time, and the inventory overview pages, new in SAP S/4HANA, which show multiple key analytics on a single screen.

There are several inventory management reporting apps that come delivered with the SAP S/4HANA system. These can be broadly grouped into four types:

- Inventory overview pages
- Goods movements reporting apps
- Stock balances reporting apps
- Inventory analytics

We'll discuss each type in the sections that follow.

7.8.1   Inventory Overview Pages

Inventory overview pages allow inventory managers, analysts, and warehouse personnel to see all relevant metrics for their operations on one page. These metrics are arranged as actionable cards that can be rearranged or hidden. Filters can be applied to the overview pages, which instantly reflect on the displayed metrics. This allows the user to focus on important items, enabling decision-making and follow-on actions in a timely manner.

For list cards, selecting the header of a card brings you to the app itself; selecting an item shows more detailed item information. For graphical or analytical cards, selecting the card displays detailed analytical information.

There are three overview page apps delivered with the SAP S/4HANA system for use by inventory control personnel:

- Overview Inventory Processing
- Overview Inventory Management
- Inventory Analysis Overview

We'll discuss these apps in the following sections.

Overview Inventory Processing

The Overview Inventory Processing app (Figure 7.41) shows the current and most important information and tasks relevant for a warehousing clerk. The information is displayed on a set of actionable cards. You can therefore focus on the most important tasks, enabling faster decisions and immediate action.

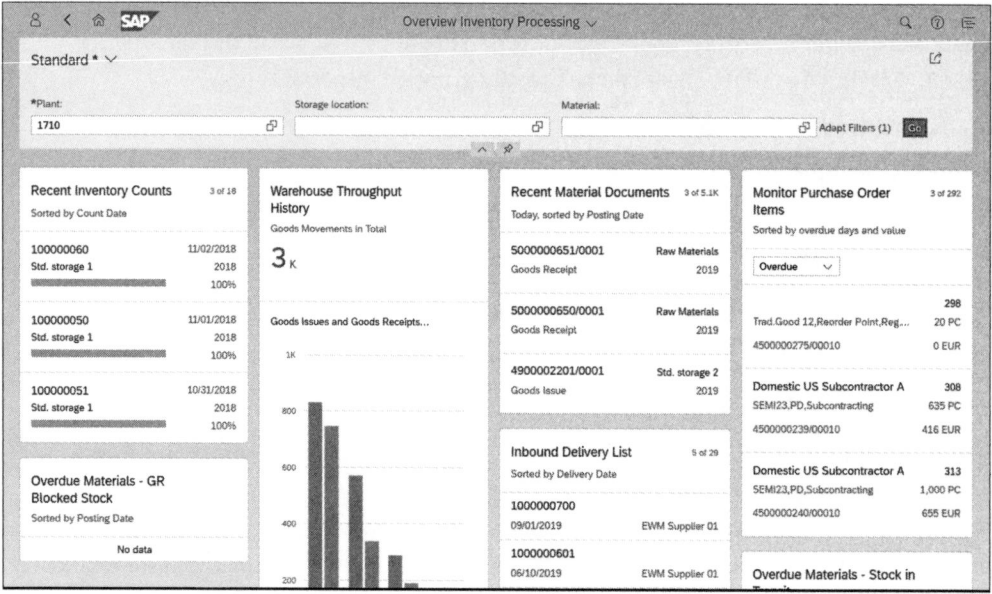

Figure 7.41 Overview Inventory Processing App

The following cards are available in the Overview Inventory Processing app:

- Recent Inventory Counts
- Warehouse Throughput History
- Recent Material Documents
- Monitor Purchase Order Items
- Overdue Materials—GR Blocked Stock
- Outbound Delivery List
- Inbound Delivery List

Additional details on the capabilities of these cards can be found in the app documentation on the SAP Help website.

The Overview Inventory Processing app is assigned to the warehouse clerk standard authorization role.

Overview Inventory Management

The Overview Inventory Management app (Figure 7.42) is used by inventory managers to show the most important information and tasks relevant at the current time. The information is displayed on a set of actionable cards. You can therefore focus on the most important tasks, enabling faster decisions and immediate action.

The following cards are available in the Overview Inventory Management app:

- Recent Material Documents
- Overdue Material—GR Blocked Stock
- Stock Value by Stock Type
- Stock Value by Special Stock Type
- Warehouse Throughput History
- Monitor Purchase Order Items
- Overdue Materials—Stock in Transit

Additional details on the capabilities of these cards can be found in the app documentation on the SAP Help website.

The Overview Inventory Management app is assigned to the inventory manager standard authorization role.

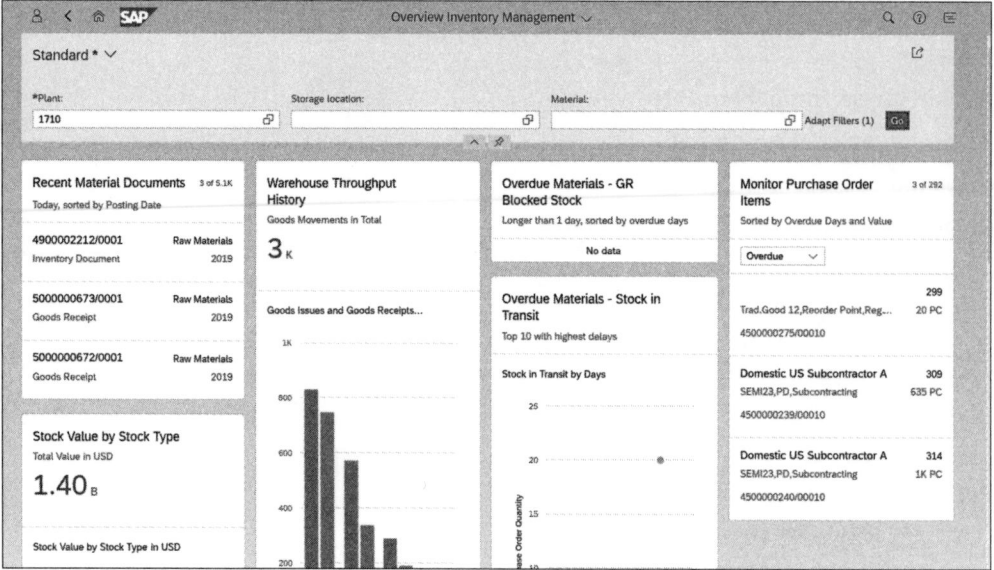

Figure 7.42 Overview Inventory Management App

Inventory Analysis Overview

The Inventory Analysis Overview app is used by inventory analysts to show the most important information and tasks relevant at the current time. The information is displayed on a set of actionable cards. You can therefore focus on the most important tasks, enabling faster decisions and immediate action.

The following cards are available in the Inventory Analysis Overview app:

- Stock Value Increase despite Consumption
- More than 100 Days without Consumption
- Monitor Batches by Longest Time in Storage
- Monitor Batches by Earliest Expiration Date

Additional details on the capabilities of these cards can be found in the app documentation on the SAP Help website.

The Inventory Analysis Overview app is assigned to the inventory analyst standard authorization role.

7.8.2 Goods Movement Reporting

It's often useful to determine how the stock balances in the system were derived. This is especially true when trying to reconcile physical inventory counts with book inventories. Goods movement reports in SAP S/4HANA allow you to list goods movements that meet user-entered selection criteria for analysis and action.

SAP S/4HANA features two apps to report on goods movements recorded in the system:

- **Material Documents Overview**
  The Material Documents Overview app was described in detail in Section 7.3.1.
- **Display Material Documents List**
  The Display Material Documents List app (Figure 7.43) is used to display material documents that meet entered selection criteria.

The Display Material Documents List app runs directly on the backend SAP S/4HANA system and is functionally equivalent to the classic SAP ERP Transaction MB51.

The Display Material Documents List app is assigned to the warehouse clerk and inventory manager standard authorization roles.

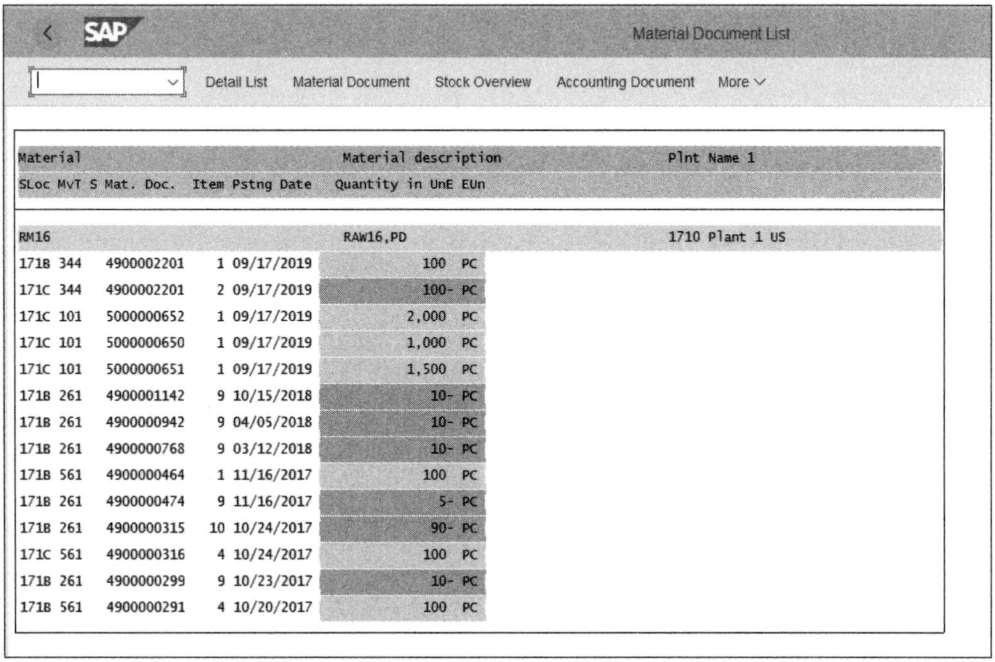

Material						Material description		Plnt Name 1
SLoc	MvT	S	Mat. Doc.	Item	Pstng Date	Quantity in UnE	EUn	
RM16						RAW16,PD		1710 Plant 1 US
171B	344		4900002201	1	09/17/2019	100	PC	
171C	344		4900002201	2	09/17/2019	100-	PC	
171C	101		5000000652	1	09/17/2019	2,000	PC	
171C	101		5000000650	1	09/17/2019	1,000	PC	
171C	101		5000000651	1	09/17/2019	1,500	PC	
171B	261		4900001142	9	10/15/2018	10-	PC	
171B	261		4900000942	9	04/05/2018	10-	PC	
171B	261		4900000768	9	03/12/2018	10-	PC	
171B	561		4900000464	1	11/16/2017	100	PC	
171B	261		4900000474	9	11/16/2017	5-	PC	
171B	261		4900000315	10	10/24/2017	90-	PC	
171C	561		4900000316	4	10/24/2017	100	PC	
171B	261		4900000299	9	10/23/2017	10-	PC	
171B	561		4900000291	4	10/20/2017	100	PC	

Figure 7.43 Display Material Documents List App

7.8.3 Stock Balances Reporting Apps

There are several SAP-supplied SAP Fiori apps to monitor the current quantities of stocks in the SAP S/4HANA system. These include the following:

- Stock—Single Material
- Stock—Multiple Materials
- Manage Batches

In addition, several WebGUI transactions are also supplied by SAP for stock monitoring:

- Batch Information Cockpit
- Display Stock Overview
- Display Warehouse Stock

We'll discuss these apps in the following sections.

Stock—Single Material

The Stock—Single Material app (Figure 7.44) provides an overview of all stocks for one material. You can review your stock by specific plants and storage locations for which you are responsible. The app can display the stock information as a table or a diagram.

The Stock—Single Material app has the following capabilities:

- Display a stock overview for a single material by plant and storage location as a table or a bar graph
- Display the stock history of the material for the last 12 periods as a curve diagram (see Figure 7.45)
- Drill down into the stock history (day-end closing) or to the material documents for each day
- Compare the stock information with the safety stock and minimum safety stock values defined for that material
- Transfer to other apps, such as the following:
  - Manage Stock
  - Transfer Stock—In-Plant
  - Transfer Stock—Cross-Plant
  - Material Documents Overview
  - Stock—Multiple Materials

The Stock—Single Material app is assigned to the shipping specialist, receiving specialist, and inventory manager standard authorization roles.

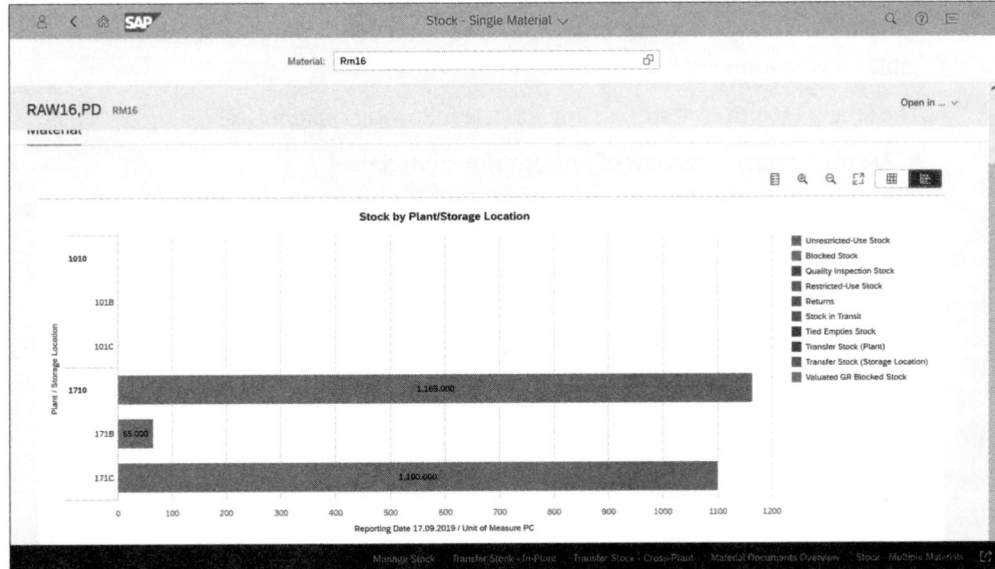

Figure 7.44 Stock—Single Material App

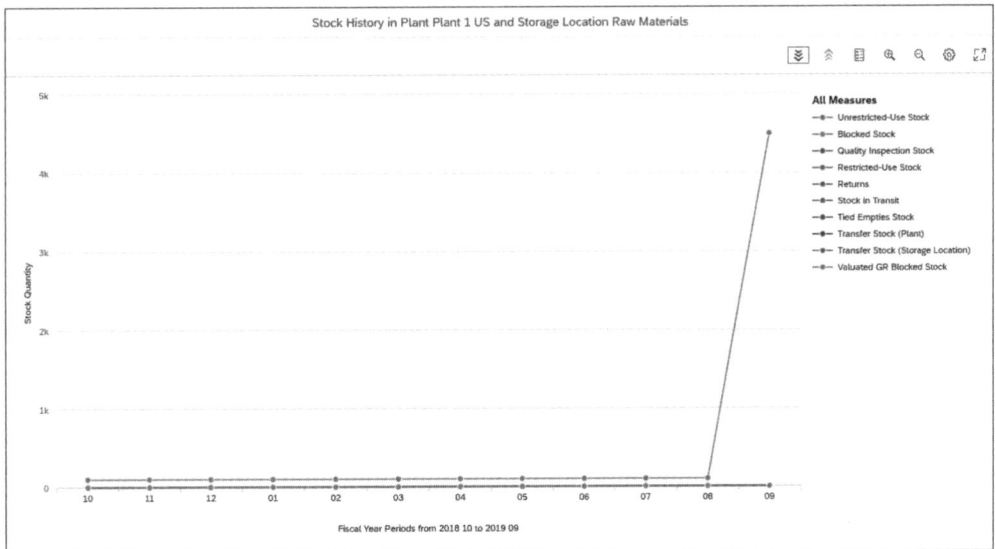

Figure 7.45 Stock History in Plant

Stock—Multiple Materials

The Stock—Multiple Materials app (Figure 7.46) provides an overview of stocks for one or more materials. You can review your stock by specific plants and storage locations for which you are responsible. The app can display the stock information as a table or a diagram.

The Stock—Multiple Materials app has the following capabilities:

- Display a stock overview of one or more materials
- Display the value of your stock; stock value calculation is based on stock quantity of the selected reporting date multiplied by the current material price
- Export the results to a spreadsheet

The Stock—Multiple Materials app is assigned to the shipping specialist, receiving specialist, and inventory manager standard authorization roles.

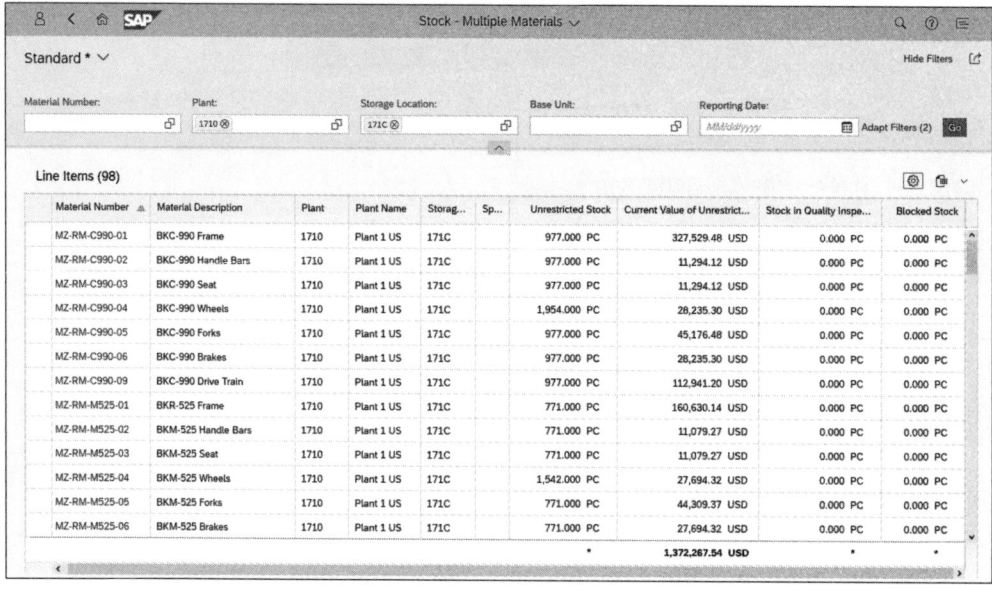

Figure 7.46 Stock—Multiple Materials App

Manage Batches

The Manage Batches app (Figure 7.47) lets you create, edit, and display batches in your SAP S/4HANA system. This app gives you quick and easy access to batch-relevant information.

New or changed batch records can be stored as draft versions. This allows others to locate and review these draft versions using the search or filter options to complete their work.

The Manage Batches app allows you to:

- Search for existing batches or ranges of batches
- Edit existing batch masters
- Create new batch masters
- Obtain information about other business documents related to the batch, such as inspection lots or deliveries
- Save new or changed batches as drafts for others to work on
- Transfer to the Stock—Single Material or Transfer Stock—In-Plant app

The Manage Batches app is assigned to the warehouse clerk and inventory manager standard authorization roles.

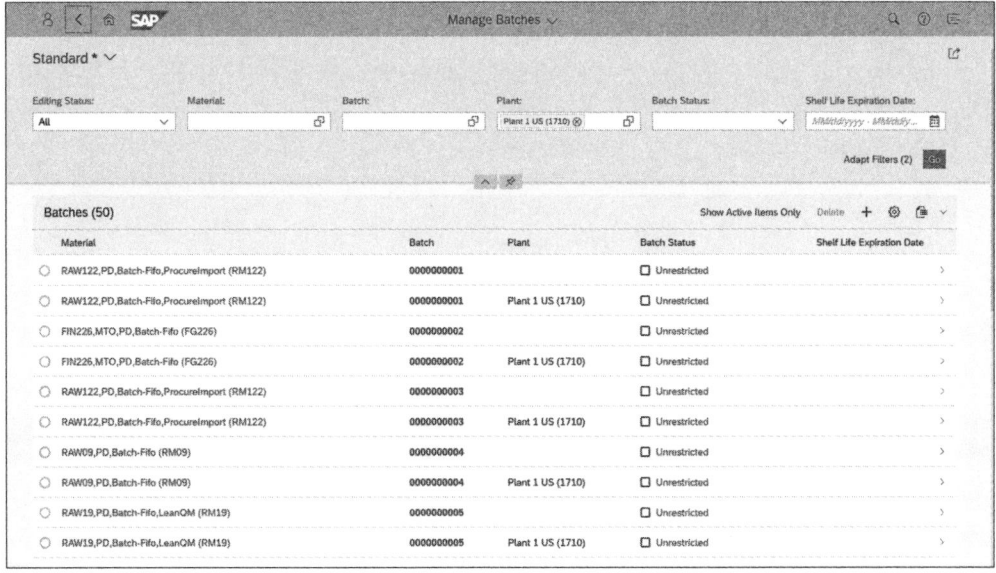

Figure 7.47 Manage Batches App

Batch Information Cockpit

You can use the Batch Information Cockpit app (Figure 7.48) for further analysis and control options, such as calling up the batch master for changing and displaying

master data, classification data, and the batch where-used list, containing information about the lifecycle of a batch.

The Batch Information Cockpit app runs directly on the backend SAP S/4HANA system and is functionally equivalent to the classic SAP ERP Transaction BMBC.

The Batch Information Cockpit app is assigned to the quality technician standard
authorization role.

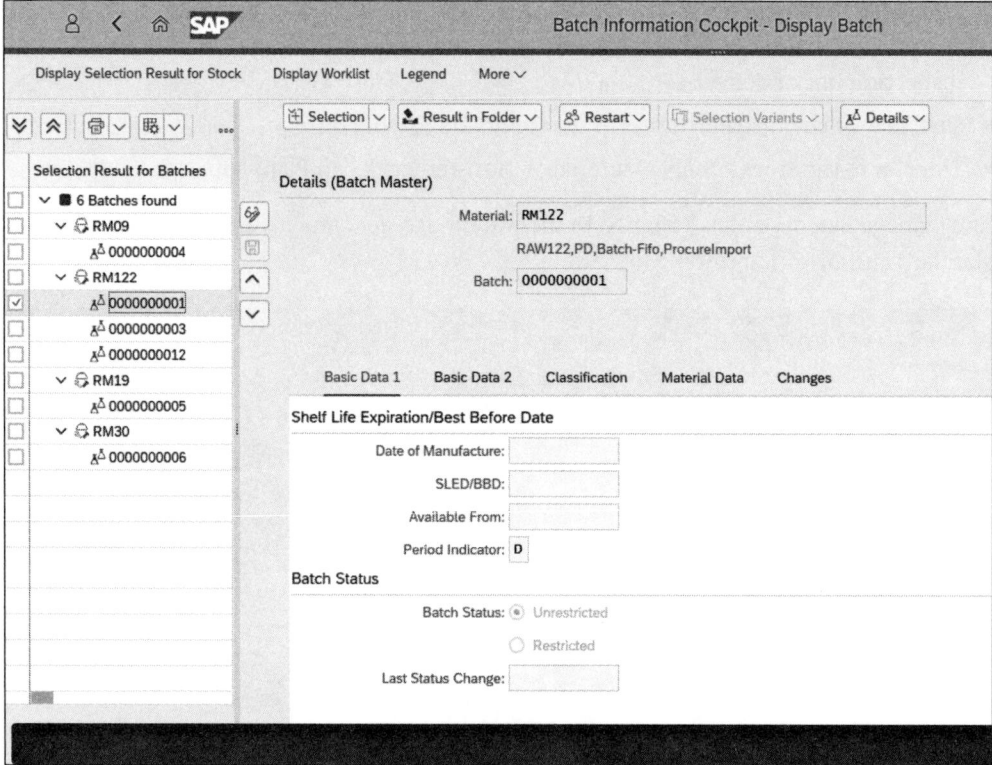

Figure 7.48 Batch Information Cockpit App

Display Stock Overview

The Display Stock Overview app (Figure 7.49) is used to display current stock balances
for a single material in all plants, storage locations, and special stock types across the
enterprise.

The Display Stock Overview app runs directly on the backend SAP S/4HANA system
and is functionally equivalent to the classic SAP ERP Transaction MMBE.

The Display Stock Overview app is assigned to the inventory manager and warehouse clerk standard authorization roles.

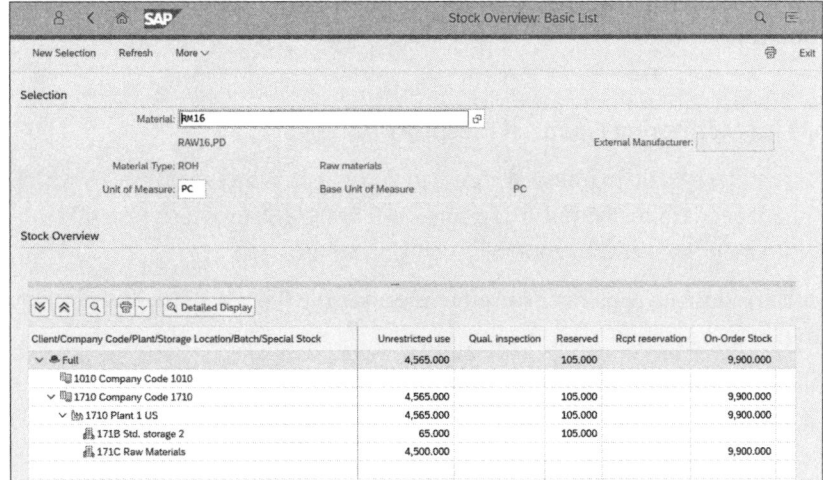

Figure 7.49 Display Stock Overview App

Display Warehouse Stock

The Display Warehouse Stock app (Figure 7.50) is used to display current stock balances for one or more materials in selected plants and storage locations.

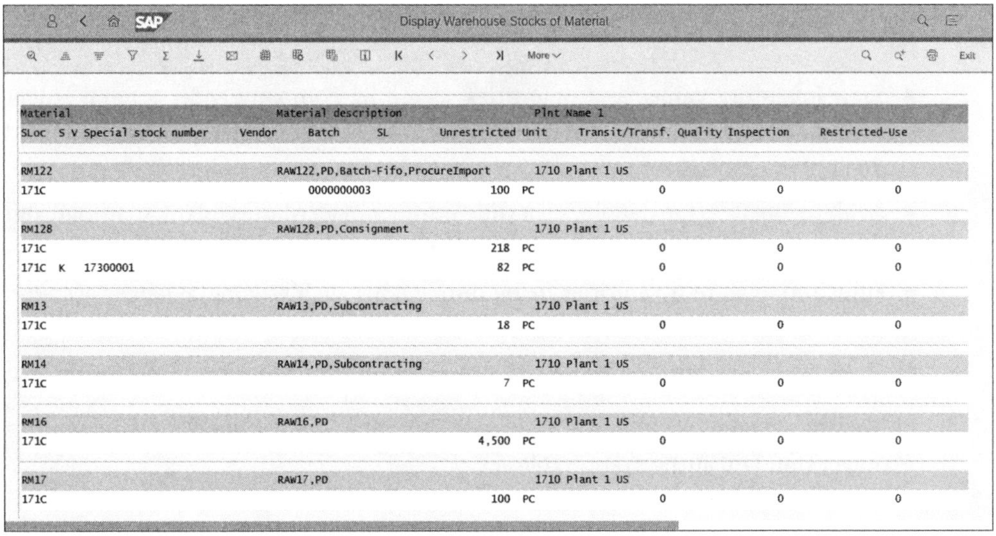

Figure 7.50 Display Warehouse Stock App

The Display Warehouse Stock app runs directly on the backend SAP S/4HANA system and is functionally equivalent to the classic SAP ERP Transaction MB52.

The Display Warehouse Stock app is assigned to the inventory manager standard authorization role.

7.8.4   Apps for Monitoring Financial Inventory Values

The monetary value tied up in physical stocks in your facility is a key metric by which inventory managers are measured. Therefore, SAP S/4HANA provides several standard reports to help manage and control inventory values.

In addition, the following apps can be used to monitor the financial inventory values in the system:

- Material Inventory Values—Balance Summary
- Material Inventory Values—Line Items

We'll discuss these apps in the following sections.

Material Inventory Values—Balance Summary

Use the Material Inventory Values—Balance Summary app (Figure 7.51) to understand the quantities and values of your material inventories on a specific date, which can be current or in the past.

The Material Inventory Values—Balance Summary app allows you to do the following:

- View inventory values and quantities sorted by company code, general ledger account, material group, material, business transaction type, posting date, and document number
- Analyze line items in detail with a wide number of attributes (plant, material) and key figures (inventory quantity, inventory amount in up to three currencies
- Filter and analyze inventories using dimensions such as general ledger account, material, profit center, and fiscal year
- Show the analysis of the line items using graphics, tables, or a combination of both

The Material Inventory Values—Balance Summary app is assigned to the inventory manager standard authorization role.

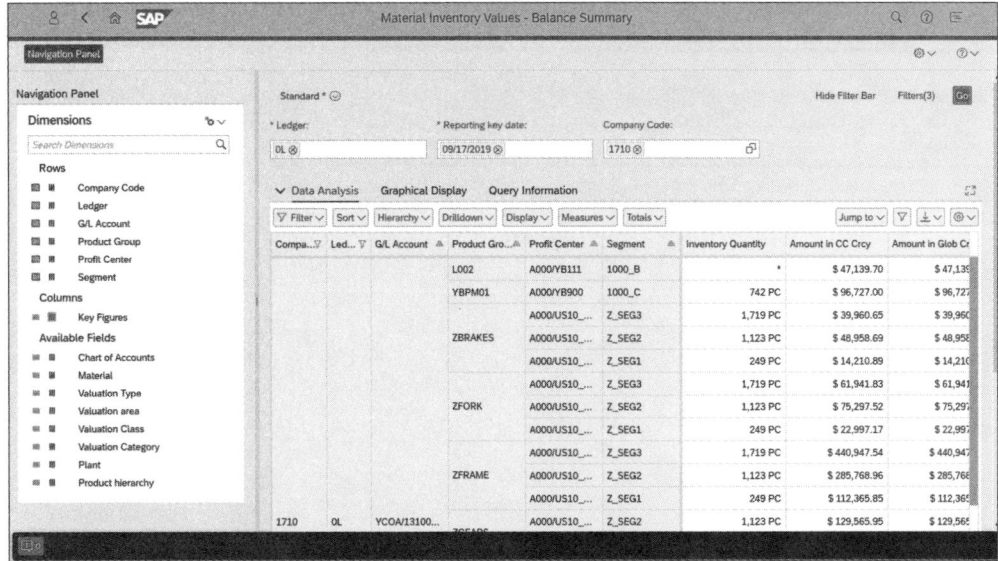

Figure 7.51 Material Inventory Values—Balance Summary App

Material Inventory Values—Line Items

The Material Inventory Values—Line Items app (Figure 7.52) is used to understand quantities and values of your material inventories at the line item level.

This app displays the following information about material inventory values:

- The inventory value and quantity of the journal entries that affect the value of material inventories during a particular period
- The date of the source document, the proposed posting date, and the actual posting date

The Material Inventory Values—Line Items app allows you to do the following:

- View inventory values and quantities sorted by company code, general ledger account, material group, material, business transaction type, posting date, and document number
- Analyze line items in detail with a wide number of attributes (plant, material) and key figures (inventory quantity, inventory amount in up to three currencies)
- Filter and analyze inventories using dimensions such as general ledger account, material, profit center, and fiscal year
- Show the analysis of line items using graphics, tables, or a combination of both

The Material Inventory Values—Line Items app is assigned to the inventory manager standard authorization role.

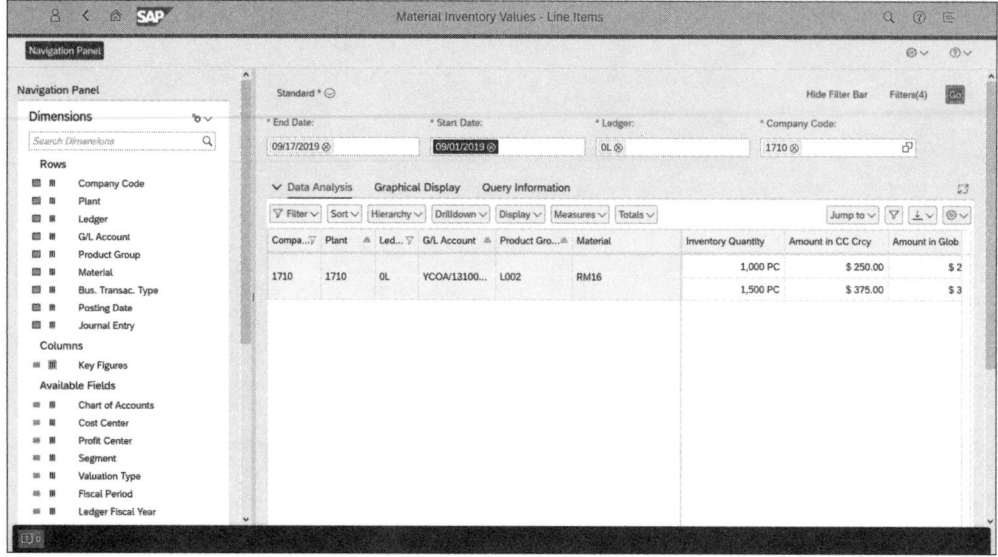

Figure 7.52 Material Inventory Values—Line Items App

7.8.5   Inventory Management Object Pages

There are several object pages available when using inventory management in SAP S/4HANA:

- Material Document
- Material
- Supplier
- Customer
- Inbound Delivery
- Outbound Delivery

We'll discuss these object pages in the following sections.

Material Document Object Page

The Material Document object page (Figure 7.53) displays useful information about the material document posted in the SAP S/4HANA system. Via this object page, you can navigate to related business objects and to transactional apps.

Here, you can do the following:

- Display an overview of material document header and line item data, such as movement type, document date, and materials transacted
- Obtain a graphical process flow of other business documents related to this material document (see Figure 7.54)
- Navigate to additional information relevant to this material document, such as details for related business partners, related master data, or related documents

The Material Document object page is assigned to the inventory manager and warehouse clerk standard authorization roles.

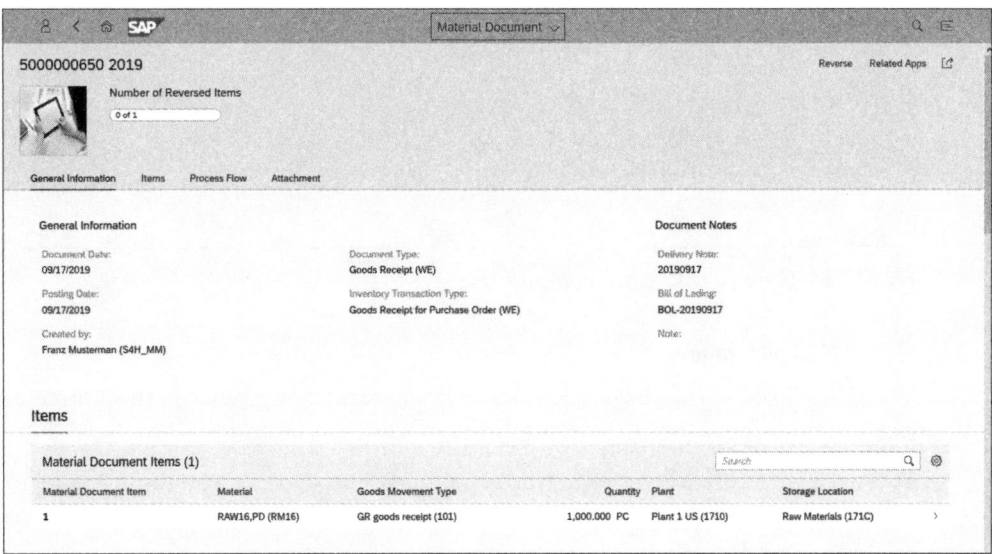

Figure 7.53 Material Document Object Page

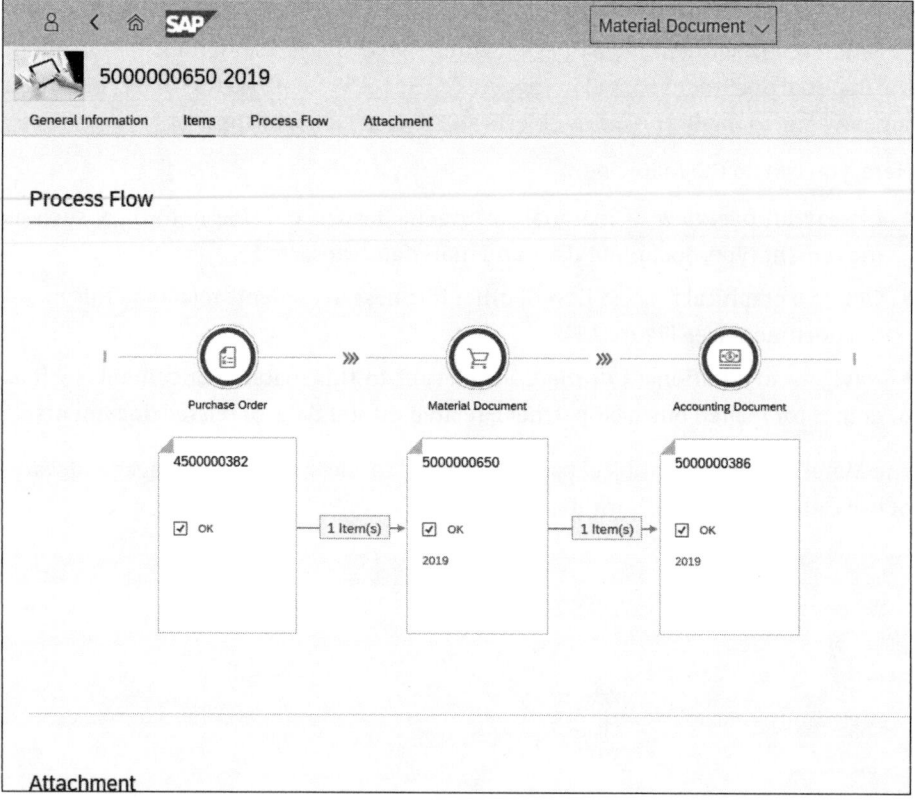

Figure 7.54 Material Document Process Flow

Material Object Page

The Material object page (Figure 7.55) is used to display an overview of a specific material.

You navigate to this object page from other SAP Fiori apps, or you can navigate to additional information related to this material, such as detailed information about related master data or related documents.

The Material object page can also show the following:

- Suppliers of the material, using the purchasing view
- Procurement master data and documents for the material (see Figure 7.56)

The Material object page is assigned to the purchaser, warehouse manager, warehouse clerk, and accounts payable accountant standard authorization roles.

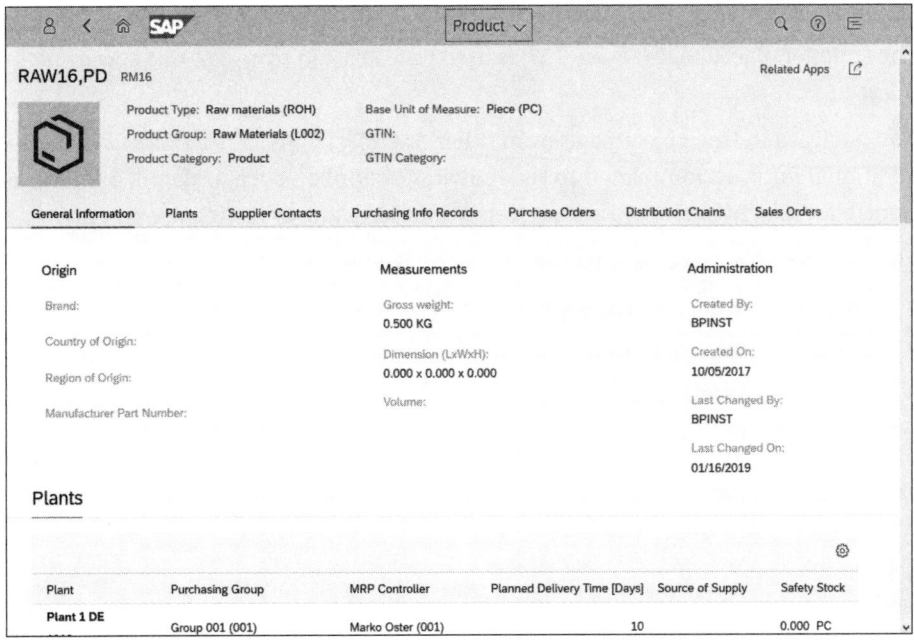

Figure 7.55 Material Object Page

Figure 7.56 Procurement Master Data and Documents for Material

Supplier Object Page

The Supplier object page (Figure 7.57) is used to display an overview of a specific supplier.

You navigate to this object page from other SAP Fiori apps, or you can navigate to additional information related to the individual supplier, such as detailed information about related business partners, related master data, or related documents.

The Supplier object page can also show the following:

- Company code data for the supplier
- Communication and blocking data for the supplier
- Materials provided to your company by the supplier
- Annual spend for the supplier

The Supplier object page is assigned to the strategic buyer standard authorization role.

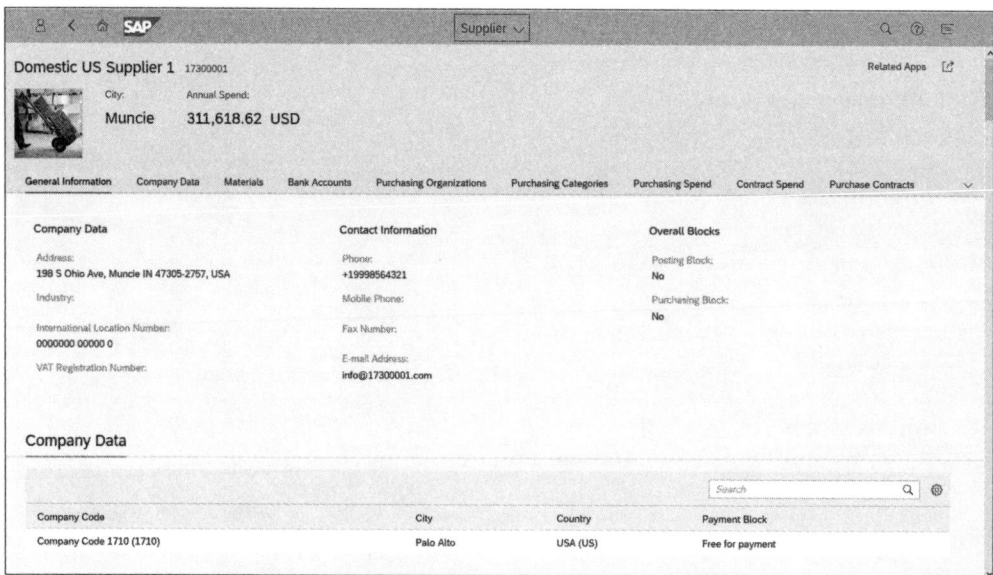

Figure 7.57 Supplier Object Page

Customer Object Page

The Customer object page (Figure 7.58) is used to display an overview of a specific customer.

You navigate to this object page from other SAP Fiori apps, or you can navigate to additional information related to the individual customer, such as detailed information about related business partners, related master data, or related documents.

The Customer object page can also show the following:

- Company code and sales area data for the customer (see Figure 7.59)
- Related sales orders and billing documents for the customer
- Communication data and blocking data for the customer

The Customer object page is assigned to the customer master specialist and accounts receivable accountant standard authorization roles.

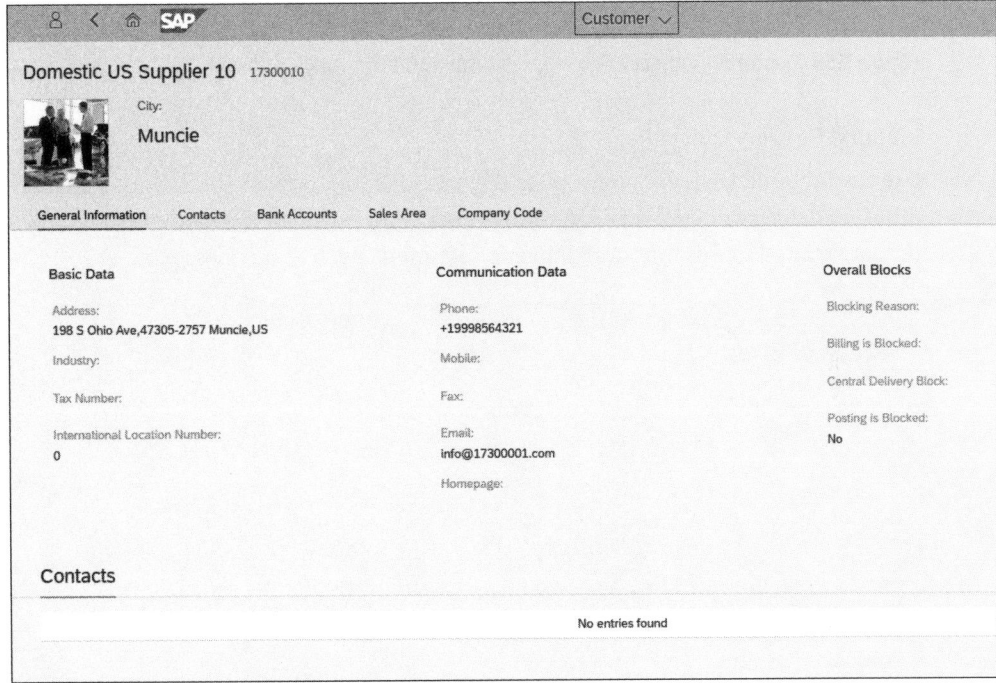

Figure 7.58 Customer Object Page—General Information

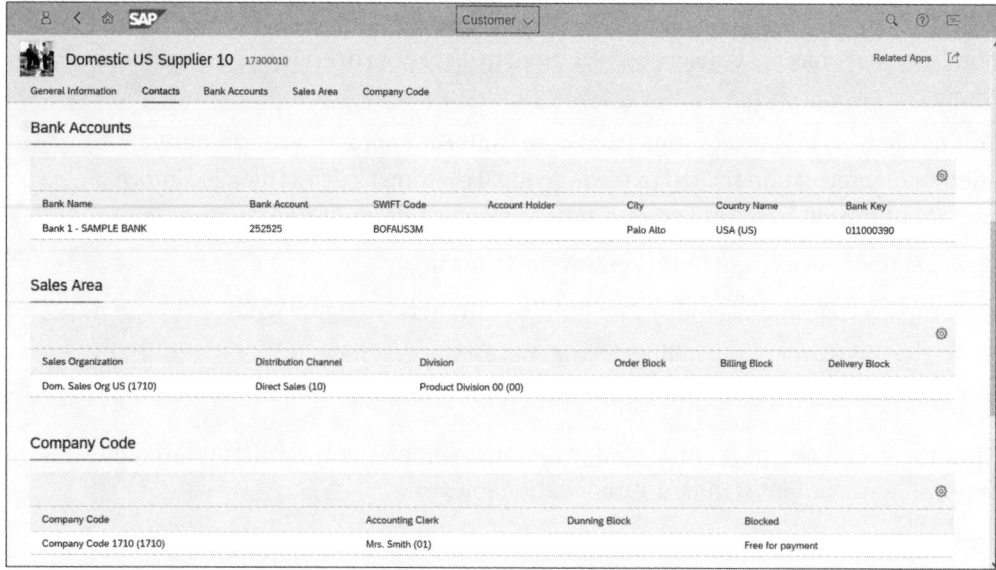

Figure 7.59 Customer Object Page—Sales Area and Company Code Data

Inbound Delivery Object Page

Use the Inbound Delivery object page (Figure 7.60) to display details about a specific inbound delivery document. You can also easily access related documents and master data related to this inbound delivery document, such as business partners.

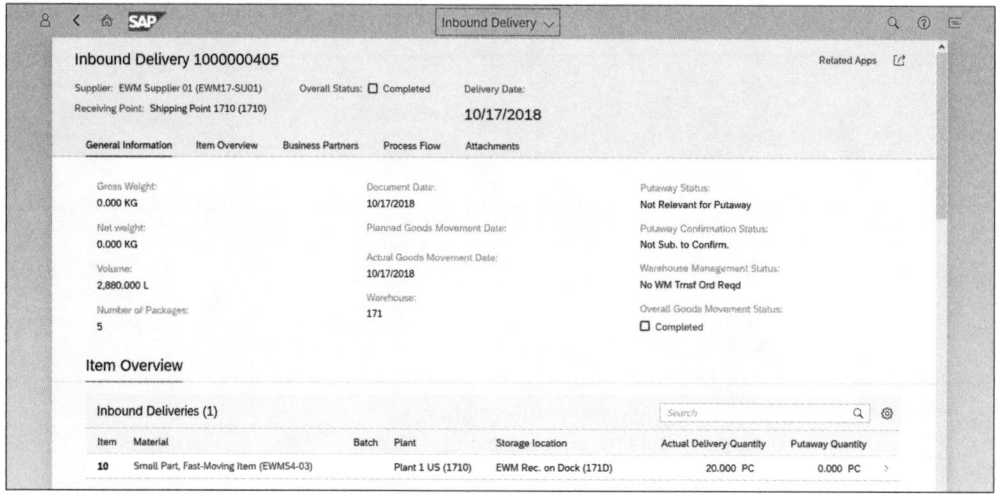

Figure 7.60 Inbound Delivery Object Page—General Information

You can navigate to this app by searching for inbound deliveries from the Enterprise Search area of the SAP Fiori launchpad. You can search for inbound deliveries using key fields such as receiving point, material number, or supplier. The results are shown in a worklist from which you can easily retrieve details for each inbound delivery document listed.

The Inbound Delivery object page can be used to do the following:

- Display attributes of the inbound delivery document, such as receiving point, overall status, and delivery date
- Display the materials to be received, along with quantity and receiving plant and storage location
- Display the contact details of the business partners involved in the outbound delivery
- Display the process flow, a graphical overview of the chain of connected process steps and corresponding business documents (see Figure 7.61)—for example, view the sales order that preceded the outbound delivery or the material document that recorded the goods issue posting for the outbound delivery

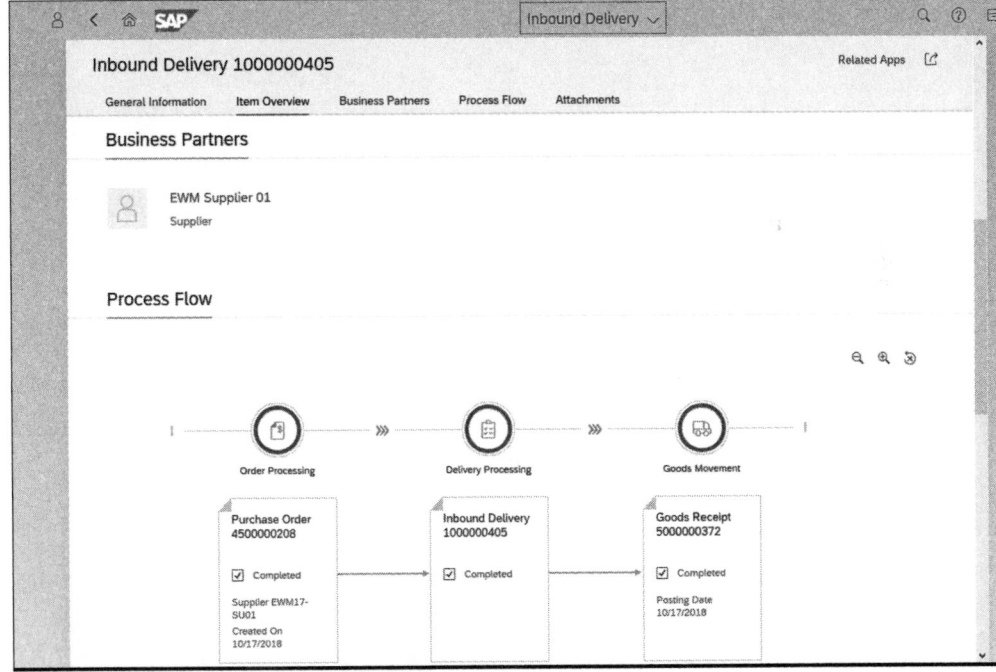

Figure 7.61 Inbound Delivery Object Page—Process Flow

The Inbound Delivery object page is assigned to the receiving specialist, inventory manager, and warehouse clerk standard authorization roles.

Outbound Delivery Object Page

Use the Outbound Delivery object page (Figure 7.62) to display details about a specific outbound delivery document. You can also easily access related documents and master data related to this outbound delivery document, such as business partners.

You can navigate to this app by searching for outbound deliveries from the Enterprise Search area of the SAP Fiori launchpad. You can search for outbound deliveries using key fields such as shipping point, material number, or customer. The results are shown in a worklist from which you can easily retrieve details for each outbound delivery document listed.

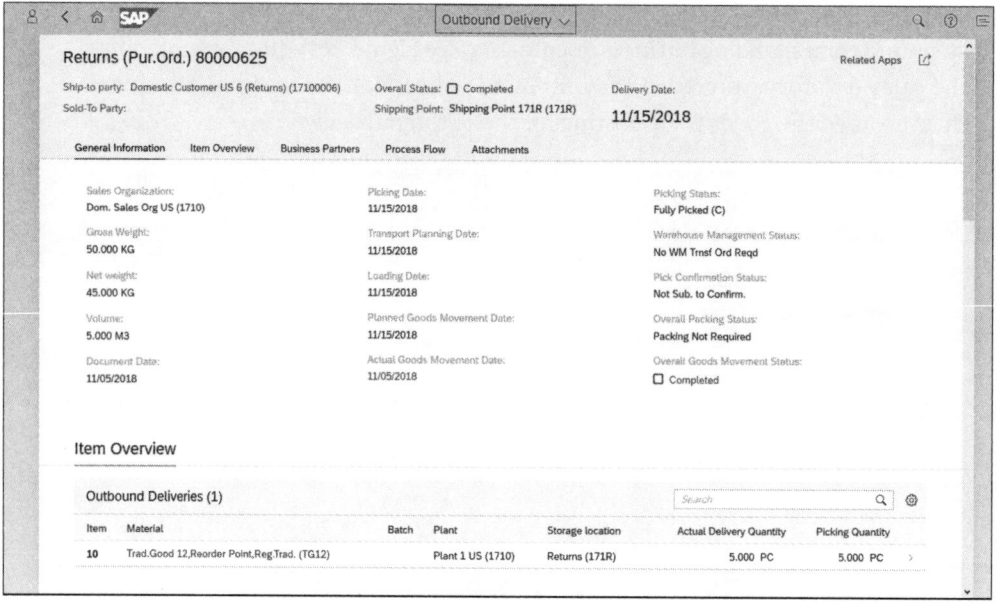

Figure 7.62 Outbound Delivery Object Page—General Information

The Outbound Delivery object page can be used to do the following:

- Display attributes of the outbound delivery document, such as shipping point, overall status, and delivery date
- Display the materials to be shipped, along with quantity and shipping plant and storage location

- Display the contact details of the business partners involved in the outbound delivery
- Display the process flow, a graphical overview of the chain of connected process steps and corresponding business documents (see Figure 7.63)—for example, view the sales order that preceded the outbound delivery or the material document that recorded the goods issue posting for the outbound delivery

The Outbound Delivery object page is assigned to the shipping specialist standard authorization role.

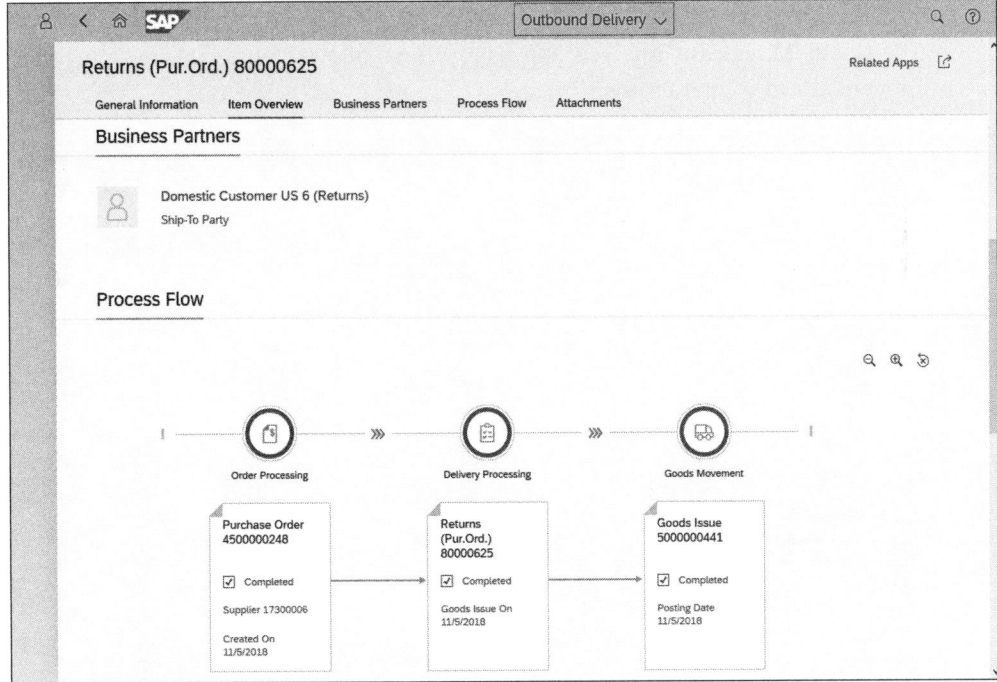

Figure 7.63 Outbound Delivery Object Page—Process Flow

7.8.6   Inventory Management Analytics

Managing the myriad stock items in a typical warehouse can be a daunting task. Warehouse personnel and inventory managers need information to understand how goods are moving in, within, and out of a facility. They also need to understand the velocity of materials so that materials that are moving slowly can be addressed in terms of storage space and placement within the warehouse.

SAP S/4HANA supplies the following analytic apps for use by inventory managers:

- Goods Movement Analysis
- Inventory Turnover Analysis
- Slow or Non-Moving Materials
- Dead Stock Analysis
- Inventory KPI Analysis

We'll discuss each app in the following sections.

Goods Movement Analysis

The Goods Movement Analysis app (Figure 7.64) allows you to investigate goods movements in your enterprise.

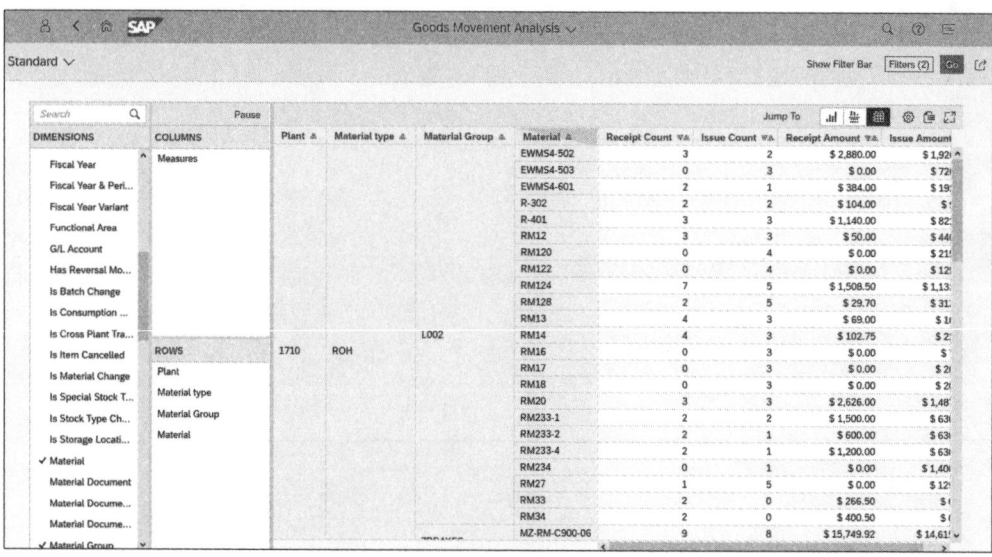

Figure 7.64 Goods Movement Analysis App

The Goods Movement Analysis app has the following features:

- Define filters to narrow your search scope, such as plant, material, and material group
- Choose from a variety dimensions for analysis, such as plant, storage location, material, year/month, calendar week, and day of year
- Choose from a variety of key figures, such as stock change quantity, stock change amount, consumption quantity, consumption amount, movement count, issue count, and receipt count

- Drill down to an individual material document item if required
- Sorting, totaling, and subtotaling
- Export to Excel

The Goods Movement Analysis app is assigned to the inventory manager standard authorization role.

Inventory Turnover Analysis

The Inventory Turnover Analysis app (Figure 7.65) assists you in monitoring the turnover of material in a plant. *Turnover* is defined as the relation between goods issue quantities and stock quantities within a set time period.

This app provides detailed information on materials that have turnover issues based on a specified time horizon.

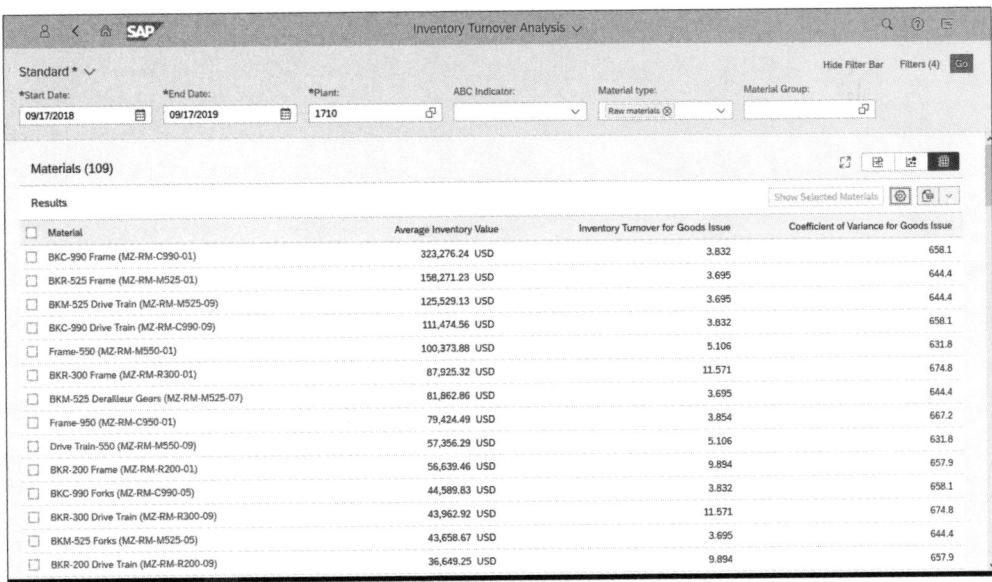

Figure 7.65 Inventory Turnover Analysis App

The Inventory Turnover Analysis app lets you do the following:

- Perform research on turnover-related issues down to individual materials
- Display detailed turnover analysis results using different representations—for example, as a scatter or bubble chart

- See the stock value of materials with turnover issues; stock value calculation is based on stock quantity of the selected reporting date multiplied by the current material price

The Inventory Turnover Analysis app is assigned to the inventory manager standard authorization role.

Slow or Non-Moving Materials

Use the Slow or Non-Moving Materials app (Figure 7.66) to monitor and investigate those materials for which the velocity through the warehouse is slower than normal. Based on this, you can then initiate follow-on actions, such as scrapping.

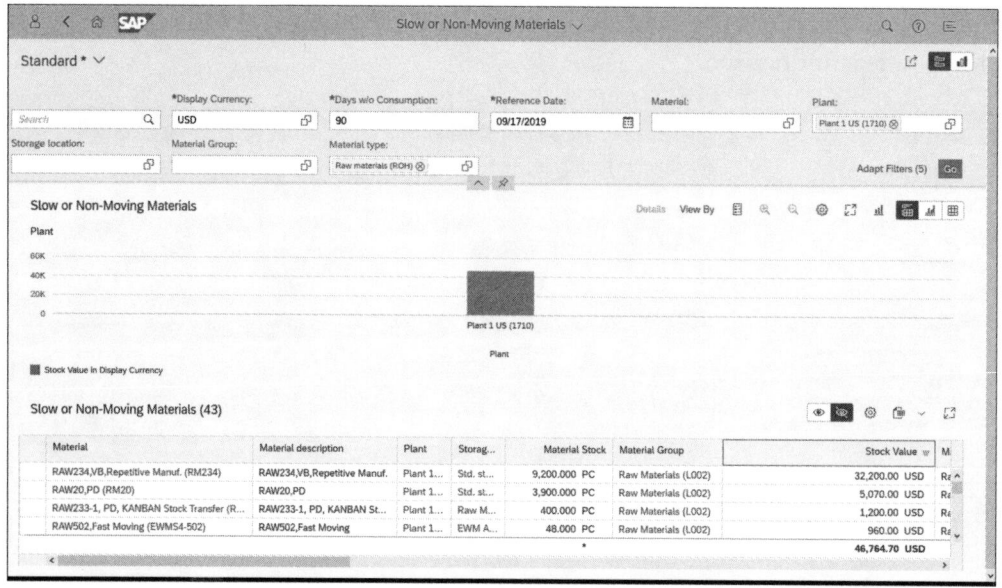

Figure 7.66 Slow or Non-Moving Materials App

The Slow or Non-Moving Materials app has the following features:

- Allows monitoring of slow-moving materials
- Monitors how much working capital is tied up by the slow-moving items
- Execution of follow-up activities based on the analysis results
- Predictive model for the slow-moving indicator for a material in a time period to see if a material may deviate from the previous consumption and stock values

- Additional details on the selected material; see how the slow-moving indicator has changed over the last 12 months
- Inform colleagues about the slow-moving stock situation

The Slow or Non-Moving Materials app is assigned to the inventory manager, receiving specialist, and shipping specialist standard authorization roles.

Dead Stock Analysis

Use the Dead Stock Analysis app (Figure 7.67) to investigate dead stocks in your enterprise. Dead stocks are material and plant combinations for which the stock value has grown larger despite existing consumption postings over a prescribed time period. Dead stocks can impact an enterprise's cash flow and profitability. The Dead Stock Analysis app has the following features:

- Allows monitoring of dead stocks
- Monitor how much working capital is tied up in dead stock
- Monitors dead stock across plants in different countries using a common reporting currency
- Execution of follow-up activities based on the analysis results, such as stock transfers or scrapping
- Inform colleagues about the dead stock situation

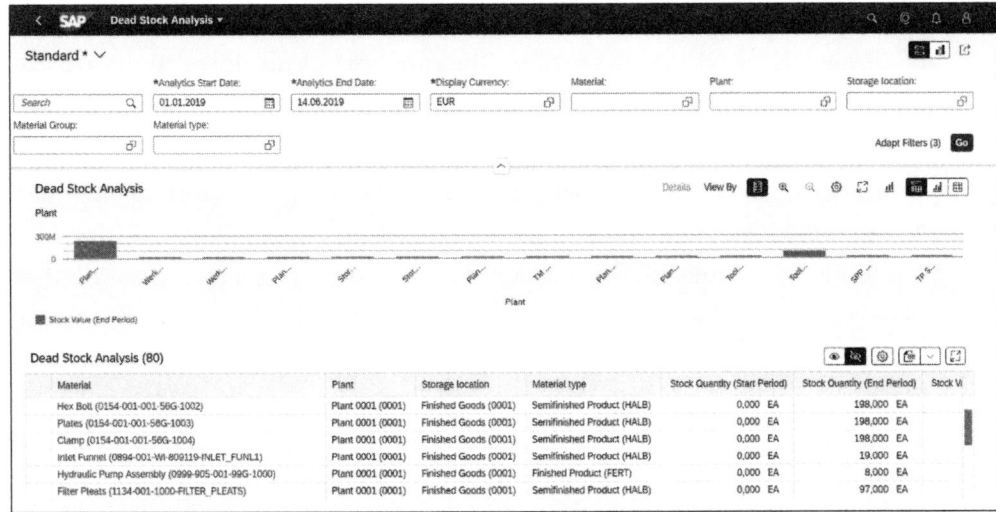

Figure 7.67 Dead Stock Analysis App

The Dead Stock Analysis app is assigned to the inventory manager, receiving specialist, and shipping specialist standard authorization roles.

Inventory KPI Analysis

The Inventory KPI Analysis app allows inventory analysts to monitor KPI changes over time to ensure forecast and inventory accuracy. The app compares the KPI over two defined time periods and visually represents this in a meaningful way.

There are five KPIs that can be monitored using this app:

- **Stock Changes**
  Change in stock values in the company code currency over the specified time period.
- **Consumption Changes**
  Change in consumption values of materials over the time period. Consumption value is the sum of the consumption quantities times the current material price.
- **Inventory Aging Changes**
  Changes in the percentage relationship between the average stock quantity and the consumption quantity over the time period.
- **Inventory Turnover Changes**
  Changes in the relationship between consumption quantities and average stock quantities in the time period.
- **Range of Coverage Changes**
  Changes in the relationship between the current stock quantity and the average consumption (defined as the relationship between consumption and number of days in the time period) in the time period.

Details on the KPI calculation logic can be found in the app documentation on the SAP Help website.

The Inventory KPI Analysis app is assigned to the inventory analyst standard authorization role.

7.9   Configuring Inventory Management

Inventory management is a core supply chain capability of the SAP S/4HANA system. Inventory management is delivered by SAP to work based on standard settings. However, to realize the full features and functionalities of inventory management to support an enterprise's goals, the system does needs to be fine-tuned based on business requirements. This section details the standard SAP-recommended configuration steps for inventory management. These settings are made in the SAP S/4HANA system by following the customizing path provided in the following sections for each step.

With SAP S/4HANA, it's possible to take advantage of the SAP Best Practices activation approach for customizing, as explained in Chapter 2. However, if you use the traditional customizing approach, this section can help. This information also helps validate the SAP standard configuration.

The following management configuration elements are described in the sections ahead:

- **General configuration elements**
  - **Plant Parameters** allows individual inventory management settings to be adjusted for each plant
  - **Number Assignment** assigns customer number ranges to inventory management documents
  - **Define Document Life** assigns archive durations to inventory management documents
- **Configuration elements for goods receipts and goods issues**
  - **Create Storage Location Automatically for Goods Receipts** controls the automated creation of material master views at goods receipt time
  - **Set Expiration Date Check** controls how expiration date checking is done in a plant
  - **Allow Negative Stocks** controls whether negative stock balances are allowed and in which storage locations
- **Configuration elements for movement types**
  - **Record Reasons for Movement Types** assigns specific codes to describe the purpose of a goods movement
  - **Copy, Change Movement Types** allows creation of new movement types
- **Configuration elements for physical inventory**
  - **Default Values for Physical Inventory** sets the values that default into each physical inventory document
  - **Settings for Physical Inventory** sets additional values for the control of the physical inventory process per plant

- **Allow Freezing of Book Inventory** controls the freezing behavior of book inventories during the physical inventory process
- **Cycle Counting** sets specific controls for cycle counting per plant

7.9.1   General Configuration Elements

Here, we'll look at the general configuration elements of inventory management. This includes plant parameters, number assignment, and document life definition. Let's start with plant parameters.

Plant Parameters

There are a number of inventory management settings that can be made for a specific plant. For example, this configuration item allows you to create storage location views automatically for goods movements in one plant, but not in another.

To define plant parameters, navigate to **IMG (SPRO)** • **Materials Management** • **Inventory Management and Physical Inventory** • **Plant Parameters**.

The plant selection screen appears (see Figure 7.68).

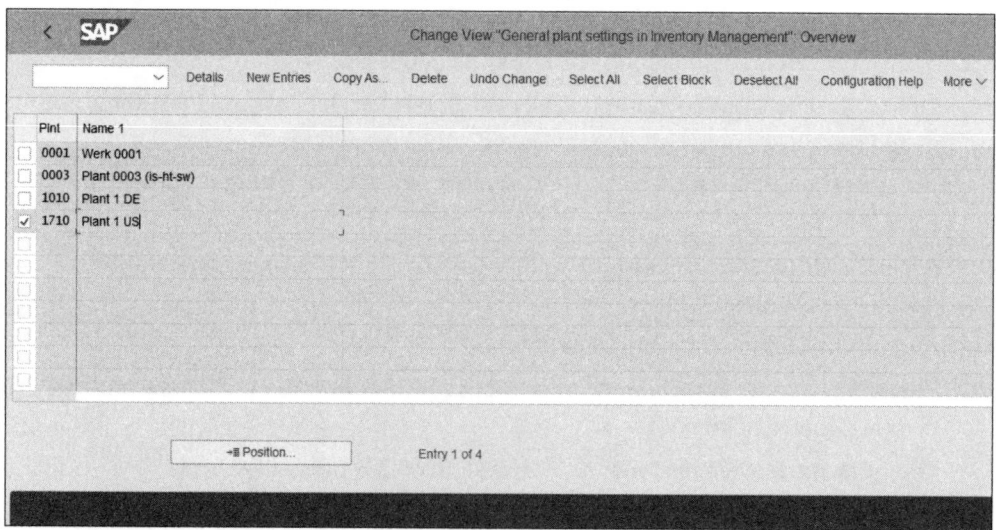

Figure 7.68 Plant Parameters: Plant Selection Screen

Click the check box next to the desired plant, then press **Details**. The detailed screen for plant settings appears (see Figure 7.69).

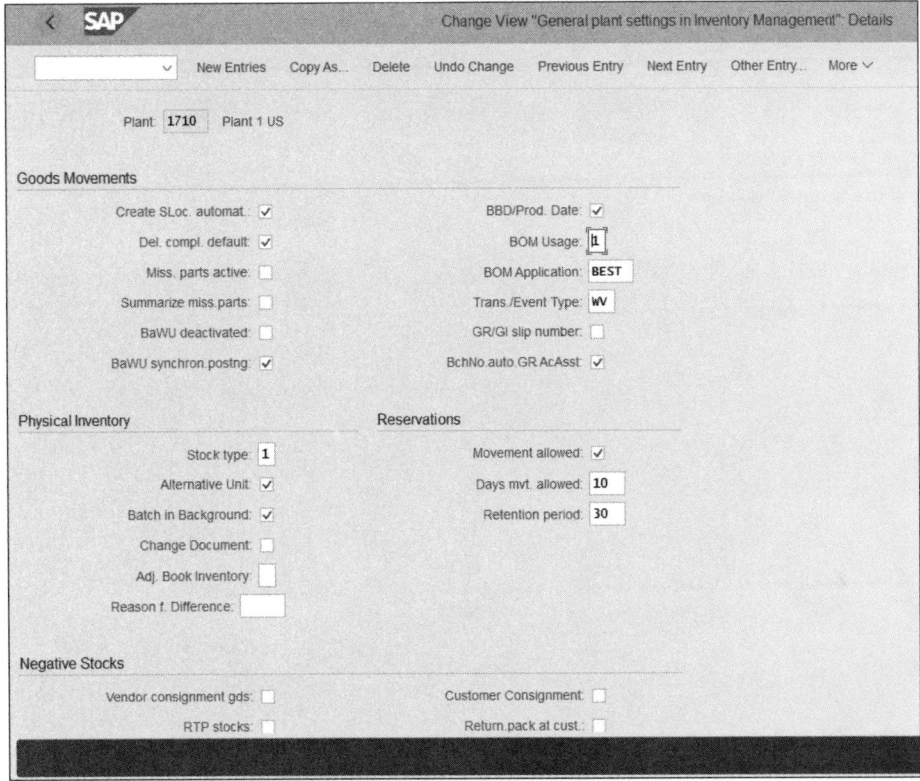

Figure 7.69 Plant Parameters: Details Screen

You can, for example, configure these settings so that storage locations are allowed to be created upon goods receipt for a plant, or set the default stock type on a physical inventory document. Refer to the field documentation in the IMG for detailed explanations for all settings in this configuration element

Make any desired changes to the standard inventory management settings, then press **Save**.

Number Assignment

All goods movements in the SAP S/4HANA system result in material documents. Based on the transaction/event type of the goods movement, a unique number is assigned from a specific number range to the document. Transaction/event types that are relevant for SAP S/4HANA Sourcing and Procurement in the system are listed in Table 7.2.

Transaction/ Event Type Grouping	Number Range	Transaction/ Event Type	Description
Goods receipts	4900000000– 4999999999	WE	Goods receipts for purchase orders
		WO	Subsequent adjustment of subcontract orders
Goods issues/ transfer postings	5000000000– 5999999999	WA	Goods issues, transfer postings, other goods receipts
		WI	Material documents for inventory adjustment postings
Physical inventory	0100000000– 0199999999	IB	Physical inventory documents
		ID	Physical inventory documents for counts and differences without reference
		IN	Physical inventory documents for recounts

Table 7.2 Inventory Management Number Ranges

If you want to use different number ranges than those delivered by SAP, or if you want to reset your number ranges each fiscal year, navigate to **IMG (SPRO) • Materials Management • Inventory Management and Physical Inventory • Number Assignment • Define Number Assignment for Material and Phys. Inv. Docs**.

The **Edit Intervals: Material Document** selection screen appears (see Figure 7.70).

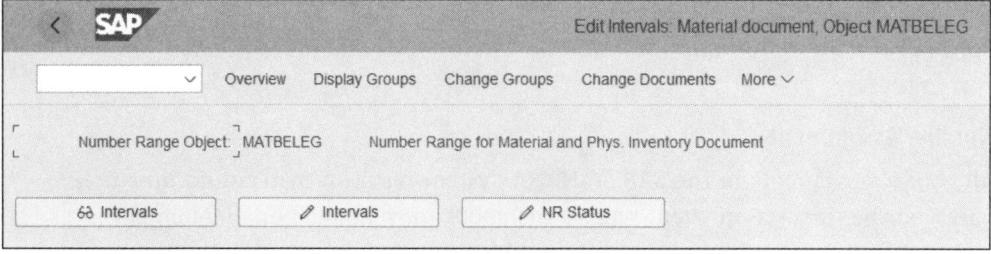

Figure 7.70 Material Document Number Range: Selection Screen

Click the **Change Intervals** button. The **Edit Intervals: Material Document** screen appears (see Figure 7.71).

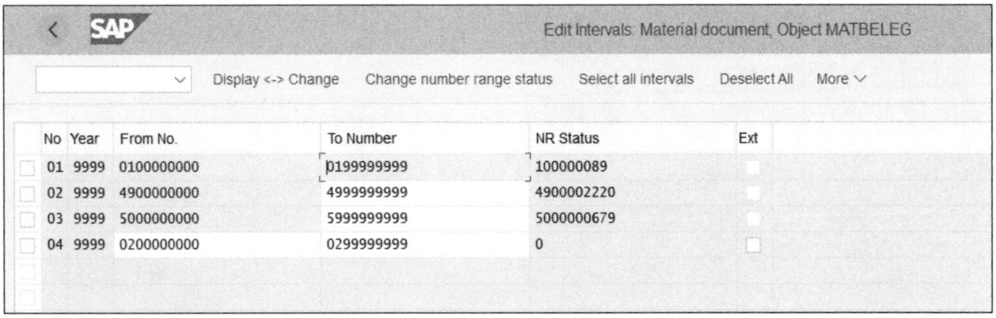
Edit Intervals: Material document, Object MATBELEG
Display <-> Change
Change number range status
Select all intervals
Deselect All
More
No Year From No. To Number NR Status Ext
01 9999 0100000000 0199999999 100000089
02 9999 4900000000 4999999999 4900002220
03 9999 5000000000 5999999999 5000000679
04 9999 0200000000 0299999999 0

Figure 7.71 Material Document Number Range: Interval Maintenance Screen

Make any desired additions or changes to the standard number range intervals or the starting values, then press **Save**.

Note that number range configuration changes have to be transported manually to the source systems. Alternatively, you can maintain number range intervals or statuses directly in the destination system.

Define Document Life

Enterprises often implement an archiving system in their SAP S/4HANA systems for business objects, including material documents. The amount of time that an enterprise requires objects to be available online is typically determined by document retention policies. You can use this configuration item to prevent the accidental archiving of material documents before a certain number of days. This setting is based on plant and transaction/event type.

The menu path to set the document life is **IMG (SPRO) • Materials Management • Inventory Management and Physical Inventory • Define Document Life**.

The **Archiving: Document Lives** screen appears (see Figure 7.72).

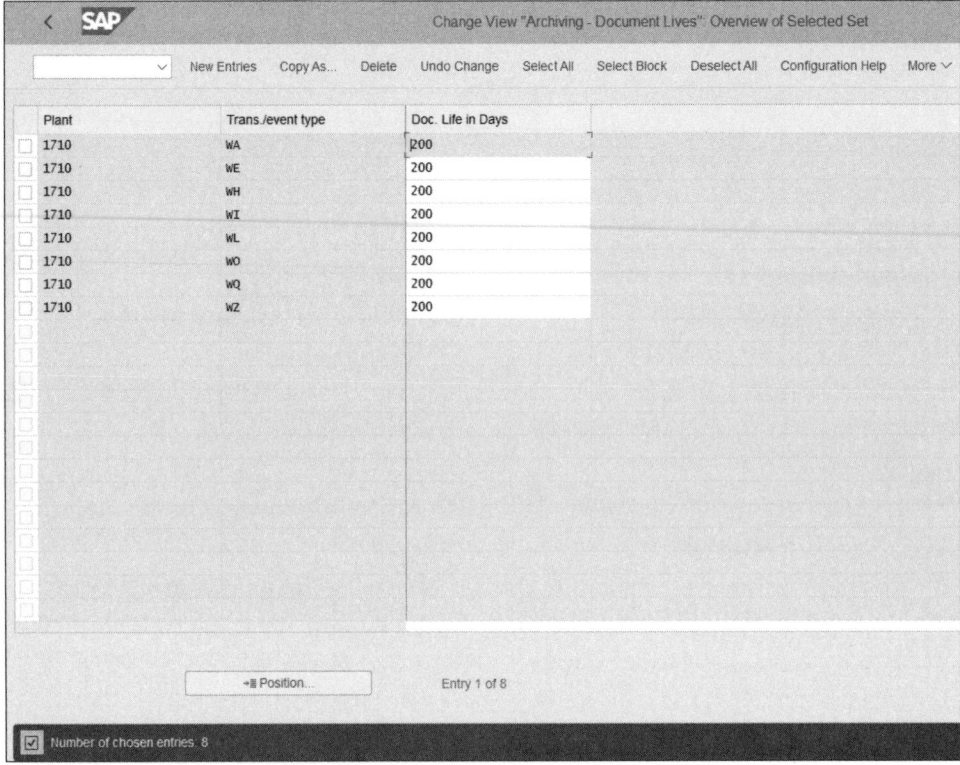

Figure 7.72 Define Document Life

Edit the number of days for the specified plant and transaction/event type, then press **Save**.

7.9.2   Goods Receipts and Goods Issues

Let's take a look at the configuration elements for goods receipts and goods issues. In this section, we'll explore how to create storage locations automatically, how to set expiration date checks, and how to allow negative stocks.

Create Storage Location Automatically for Goods Receipts

This configuration item defines whether storage location data in the material master is created automatically upon the first goods receipt of that item in that storage location. This is a useful feature if you don't want to maintain storage views on the material master ahead of time.

The menu path to create storage location data automatically for goods receipts is **IMG (SPRO) • Materials Management • Inventory Management and Physical Inventory • Goods Receipt • Create Storage Location Automatically**.

The **Create Storage Loc. Automatically** screen appears (see Figure 7.73).

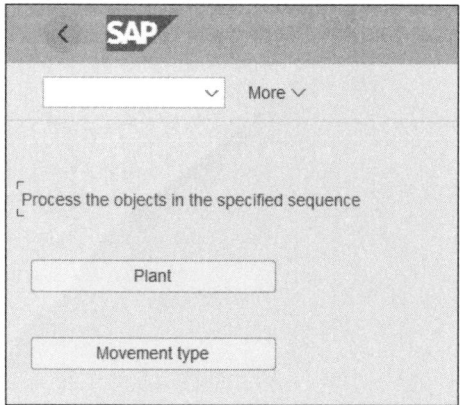

Figure 7.73 Create Storage Location Automatically: Selection Screen

Press the **Plant** button. The **Automatic Creation of Storage Location per Plant** screen appears (see Figure 7.74). Check the **Create Storage Location Automatically** check box for the desired plants, then press **Save**.

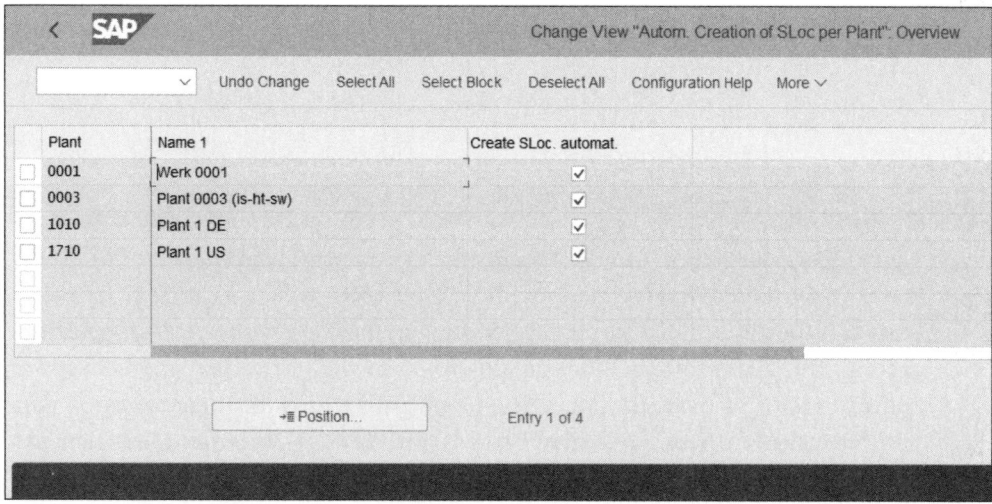

Figure 7.74 Create Storage Location Automatically: Plant Screen

Press the **Movement Type** button. The **Automatic Creation of Storage Location for Movement** screen appears (see Figure 7.75). Check the **Create Storage Location Automatically** check box for the desired movement types, then press **Save**.

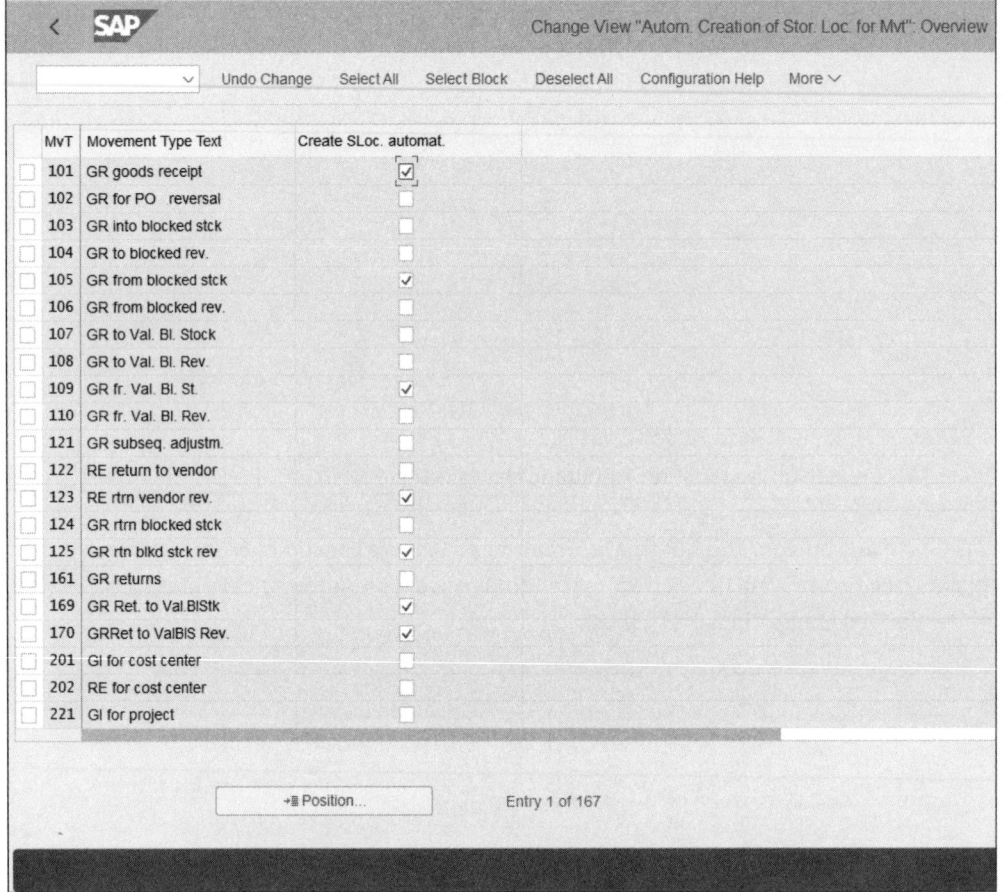

Figure 7.75 Create Storage Location Automatically: Movement Type Screen

Note that there is a similar configuration item in the goods issues/transfer postings section. This allows storage location data to be created for certain goods issues or transfer posting movement types. The menu path to create storage location data automatically for these movement types is **IMG (SPRO)** • **Materials Management** • **Inventory Management and Physical Inventory** • **Goods Issues/Transfer Postings** • **Create Storage Location Automatically**. This configuration item works identically to the one just described.

Set Expiration Date Check

SAP S/4HANA can check that a perishable item has sufficient shelf life remaining at the time of goods receipt. To do this, a minimum remaining shelf life has to be maintained in the material master record. In addition, the ability to check shelf life for each plant and movement type has to be maintained in configuration.

These checks are not enabled in the standard SAP S/4HANA system.

The menu path to enable shelf life expiration date checks is **IMG (SPRO)** • **Materials Management** • **Inventory Management and Physical Inventory** • **Goods Receipt** • **Set Expiration Date Check**.

The **Activate/Deactivate Expiration Date Check** screen appears (see Figure 7.76).

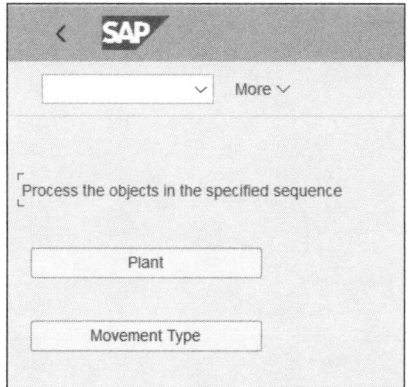

Figure 7.76 Set Expiration Date Check: Selection Screen

Press the **Plant** button. The **Activate Expiration Date View per Plant** screen appears (see Figure 7.77). Check the **Best By Date/Production Date** check box for the desired plants, then press **Save**.

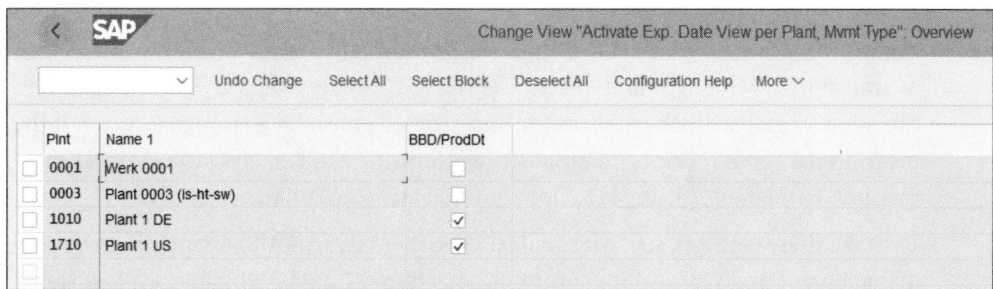

Figure 7.77 Set Expiration Date Check: Plant Screen

Press the **Movement Type** button. The **Expiration Date per Movement** screen appears (see Figure 7.78). Check the **Check Shelf Life Expiration Date** for the desired movement types, then press **Save**.

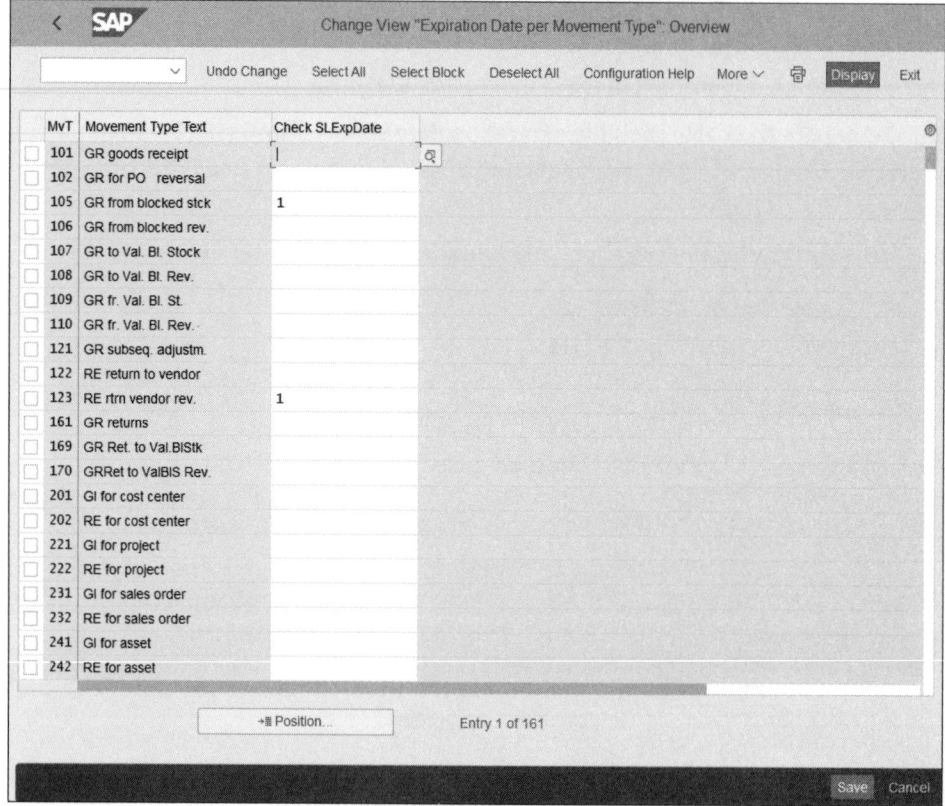

Figure 7.78 Set Expiration Date Check: Movement Type

Allow Negative Stocks

Normally there needs to be sufficient stock in a storage location prior to a goods issue or transfer movement that depletes the stock. However, the SAP S/4HANA system can allow negative stock balances for unrestricted stocks in a storage location if the recording of goods receipts into that storage location can't always be done in a timely manner. The default setting is to not allow negative stock balances.

To make these settings, navigate to **IMG (SPRO) • Materials Management • Inventory Management and Physical Inventory • Goods Issue/Transfer Postings • Allow Negative Stocks**.

The **Allow Negative Stocks for Valuation Area** selection screen appears (see Figure 7.79).

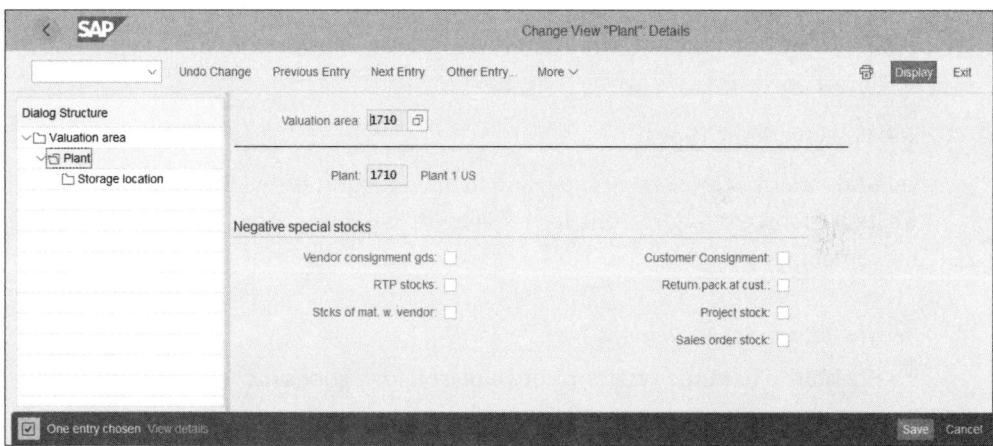

Figure 7.79 Allow Negative Stocks: Valuation Area Screen

Click the **Negative Stocks** checkbox for each valuation area in which negative stocks should be allowed. Then click the check box to the left of the valuation area, then click on the **Plant** level in the hierarchy tree.

The **Allow Negative Stocks for Plant** screen appears (see Figure 7.80).

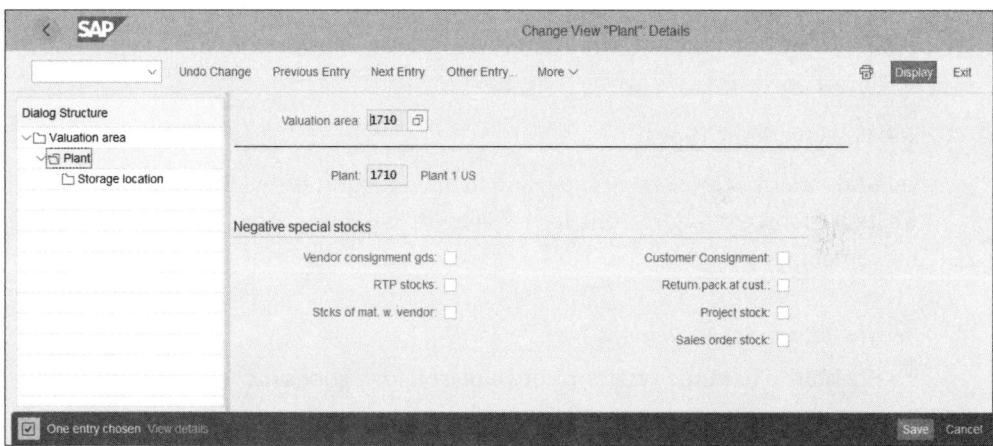

Figure 7.80 Allow Negative Stocks: Plant Screen

Click the checkboxes for any special stock categories for which negative stocks in that plant are allowed. Then click the **Storage Location** level in the hierarchy tree.

The **Allow Negative Stocks for Storage Location** screen appears (see Figure 7.81).

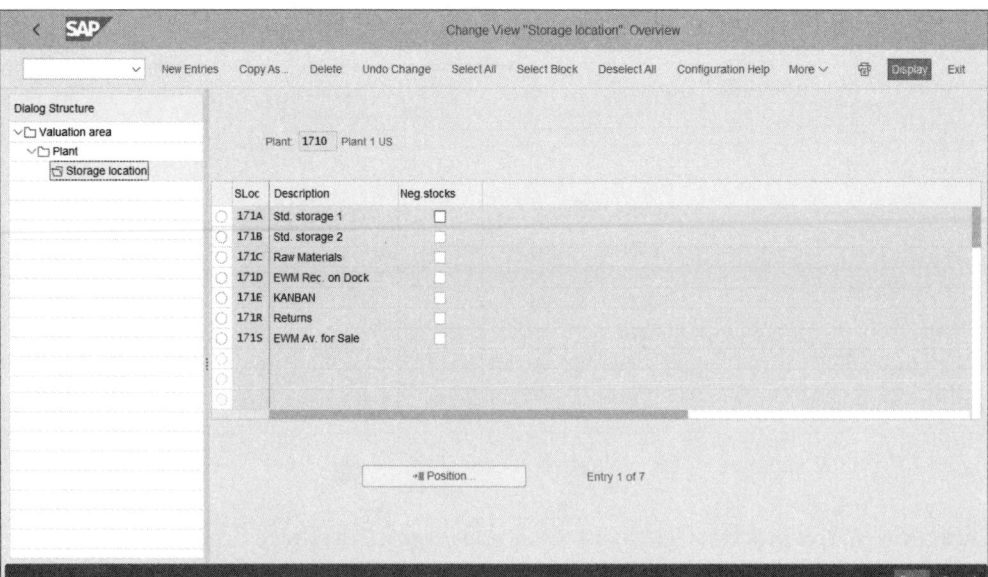

Figure 7.81 Allow Negative Stocks: Storage Location Screen

Click the **Negative Stocks** checkbox for any storage locations for which negative stocks in that plant are allowed. Then click the **Save** button.

7.9.3   Movement Types

Let's take a look at movement types and their configuration elements. In this section, we'll discuss recording reasons for movement types, and how to copy and change movement types.

Record Reason for Movement Types

It's possible to have the system record a reason for a goods movement at the time of posting. For example, you can require a reason to be entered when a goods issue to scrapping is performed. With this configuration item, you can require the entry of a reason for a specific movement type and also maintain the valid reasons that can be selected.

To make these settings, navigate to **IMG (SPRO)** • **Materials Management** • **Inventory Management and Physical Inventory** • **Movement Types** • **Record Reasons for Movement Types**. The **Reason for Movement** screen appears (see Figure 7.82).

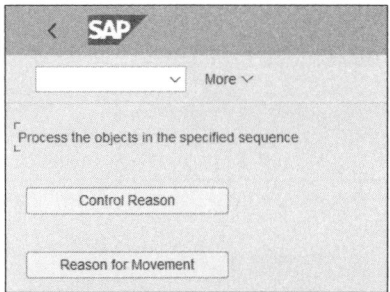

Figure 7.82 Record Reason for Movement Types: Selection Screen

Press the **Control Reason** button. The **Control Reason for Movement** screen appears (see Figure 7.83). For each movement type, enter a valid control reason code (required, suppressed, or optional). Press the **Save** button to record your changes.

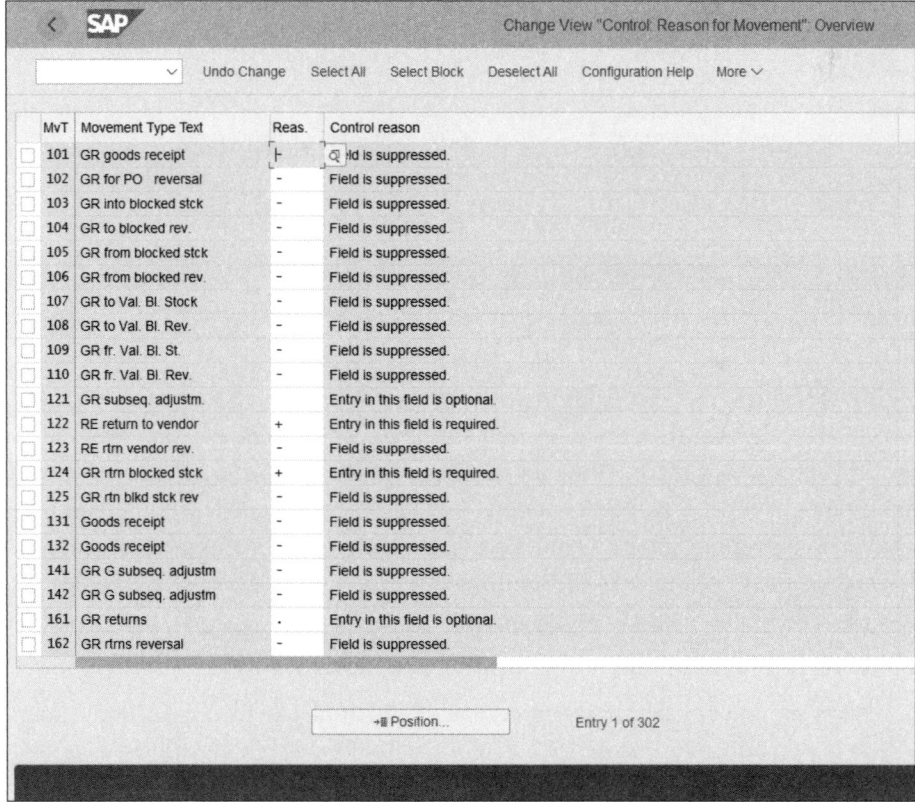

MvT	Movement Type Text	Reas.	Control reason
101	GR goods receipt	⊦	Field is suppressed.
102	GR for PO reversal	-	Field is suppressed.
103	GR into blocked stck	-	Field is suppressed.
104	GR to blocked rev.	-	Field is suppressed.
105	GR from blocked stck	-	Field is suppressed.
106	GR from blocked rev.	-	Field is suppressed.
107	GR to Val. Bl. Stock	-	Field is suppressed.
108	GR to Val. Bl. Rev.	-	Field is suppressed.
109	GR fr. Val. Bl. St.	-	Field is suppressed.
110	GR fr. Val. Bl. Rev.	-	Field is suppressed.
121	GR subseq. adjustm.		Entry in this field is optional.
122	RE return to vendor	+	Entry in this field is required.
123	RE rtrn vendor rev.	-	Field is suppressed.
124	GR rtrn blocked stck	+	Entry in this field is required.
125	GR rtn blkd stck rev	-	Field is suppressed.
131	Goods receipt	-	Field is suppressed.
132	Goods receipt	-	Field is suppressed.
141	GR G subseq. adjustm	-	Field is suppressed.
142	GR G subseq. adjustm	-	Field is suppressed.
161	GR returns	.	Entry in this field is optional.
162	GR rtrns reversal	-	Field is suppressed.

Entry 1 of 302

Figure 7.83 Record Reason for Movement Type: Control Reason Screen

Press the **Movement Type** button. The **Reason for Movement** screen appears (see Figure 7.84). Maintain entries for any movement types for which reason codes are required or optional, then press **Save**.

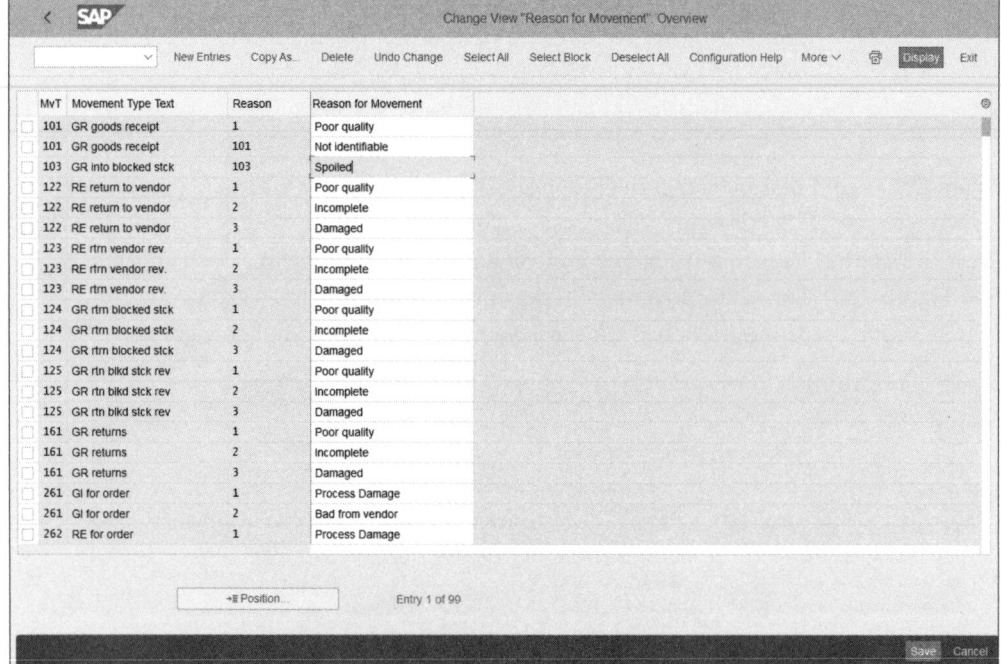

Figure 7.84 Record Reason for Movement Type: Reason Codes Screen

Copy and Change Movement Types

SAP S/4HANA comes with many movement types, which handle nearly every business inventory transaction. However, it's sometimes desirable to set up new movement types to handle specific situations in your enterprise. For instance, you may want new movement types to handle a goods issue for consumption to support research and development. SAP S/4HANA allows you to create new movement types to support your enterprise's requirements.

There are three rules to follow when creating new movement types:

1. Always copy an existing movement type that is similar to the type of movement you are creating. For example, if you're creating a new goods issue movement type, copy an existing goods issue movement type. Copy all dependent entries, as there is a large amount of integration of inventory management with other areas

of SAP S/4HANA, such as finance and quality management. Don't attempt to create a movement type from scratch!

2. Always copy the copied movement type's reversal movement type as well. All movement types require a reversal movement.

3. There are ranges of codes that SAP sets aside for customer-created movement types. Most SAP S/4HANA customers create new movement types that start with Y, Z, or 9.

To copy movement types, navigate to **IMG (SPRO) • Materials Management • Inventory Management and Physical Inventory • Movement Types • Copy, Change Movement Types**.

The **Field Selection** dialog box is shown (see Figure 7.85). Click the **Movement Type** checkbox, then press the green checkmark at the bottom of the dialog.

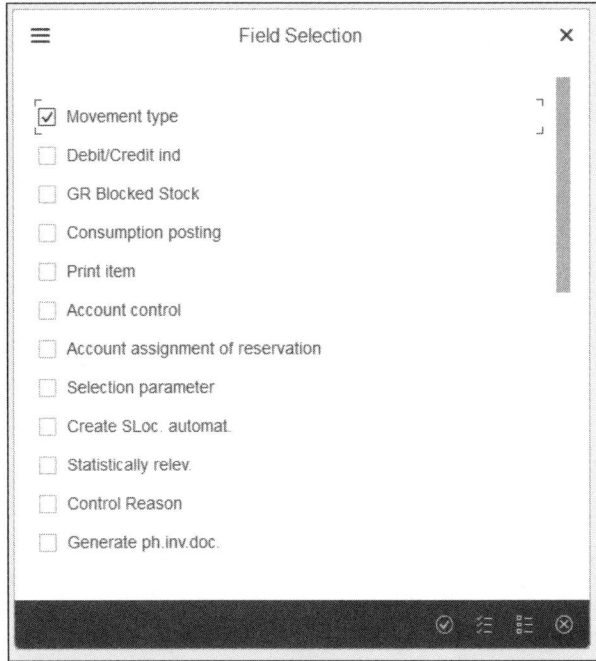

Figure 7.85 Change, Copy Movement Types: Field Selection Screen

The **Copy Movement Type** screen is shown (see Figure 7.86). Check the movement types you wish to copy in the fields provided, then press the green checkmark at the bottom of the dialog.

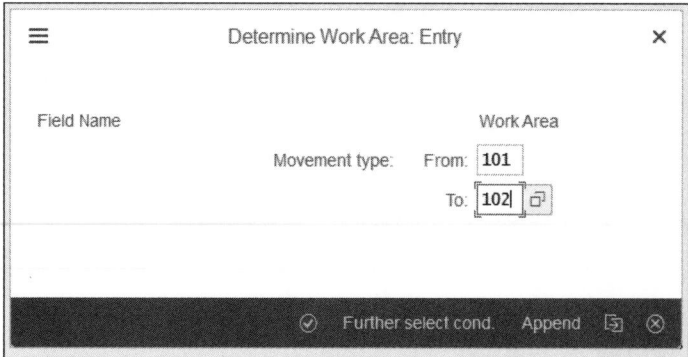

Figure 7.86 Copy, Change Movement Types: Copy Movement Type

The **Field Selection** dialog box is shown (see Figure 7.87). Click the checkbox next to the movement type you want to change. In the dialog box, enter the new movement type and description, then press ⌜Enter⌟.

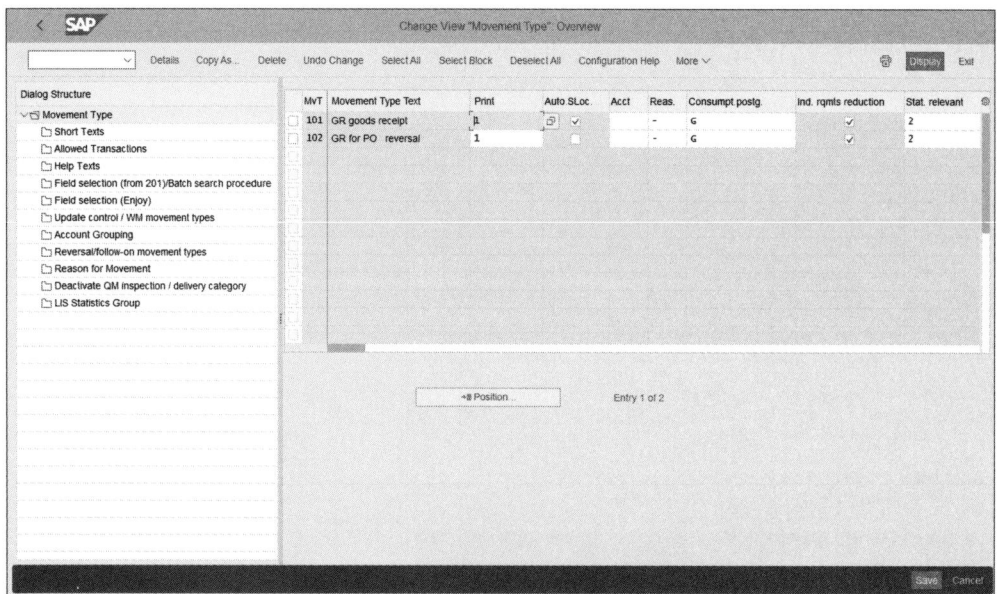

Figure 7.87 Copy, Change Movement Types: Movement Type Selection

Double-click the **Short Texts** folder in the hierarchy tree in the left frame. The **Short Texts** maintenance screen is shown (see Figure 7.88). Maintain the short and long texts for the new movement type in the fields provided.

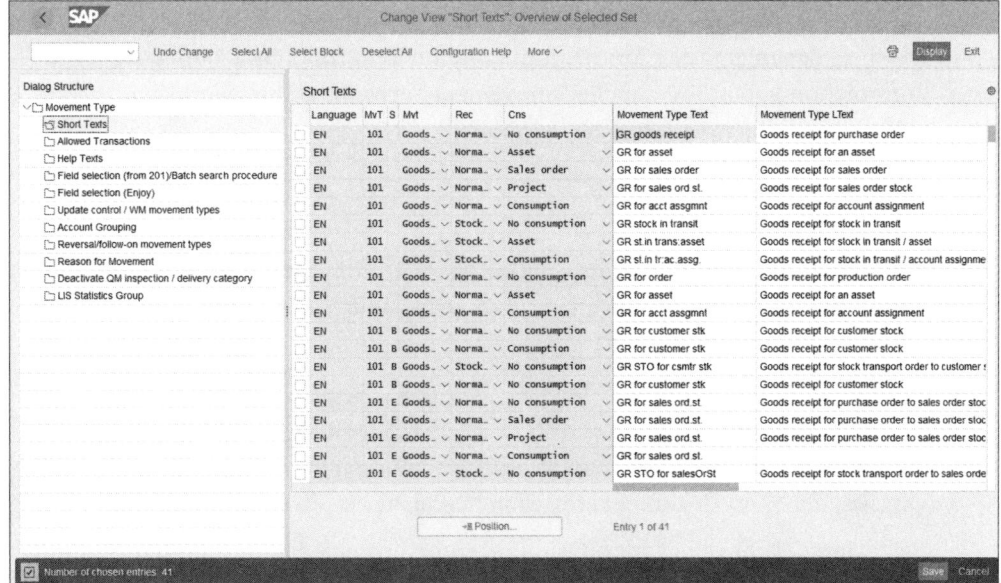

Figure 7.88 Copy, Change Movement Types: Short Texts Maintenance Screen

Double-click the **Reversal/Follow-On Movement Types** folder in the hierarchy tree in the left frame. The **Reversal Movement Type** maintenance screen is shown (see Figure 7.89). Maintain the reversal movement types for your new movement type. Press the **Save** button to save your entries.

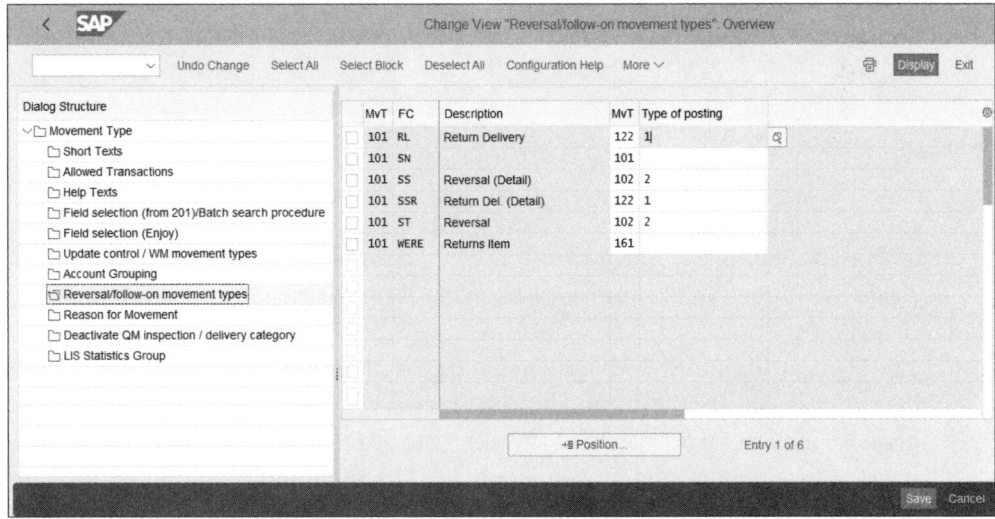

Figure 7.89 Copy, Change Movement Types: Reversal Movement Type Screen

Repeat the preceding steps for the reversal movement type to be created.

The help documentation for this configuration item contains a lot of good, detailed information about SAP-supplied movement types, how they work, and the stock types and special stocks that they support.

7.9.4   Physical Inventory

Now let's take a look at the configuration elements for physical inventory. Here we'll see how to configure default values, settings, freezing balances, and cycle counting.

Default Values for Physical Inventory

This configuration item allows you to set the default values used in the physical inventory processes for each plant. Settings are established that default into each physical inventory document created in that plant.

To review default values for physical inventory, navigate to **IMG (SPRO)** • **Materials Management** • **Inventory Management and Physical Inventory** • **Physical Inventory** • **Default Values for Physical Inventory**.

The **Physical Inventory Settings** screen appears (see Figure 7.90). Click the checkbox next to the plant for which you want to maintain default values, then click the **Details** button.

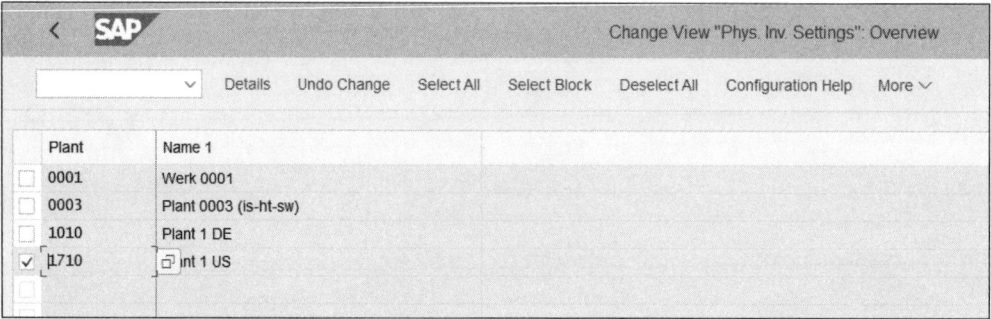

Figure 7.90 Default Values for Physical Inventory: Plant Selection Screen

The **Physical Inventory Settings** screen appears (see Figure 7.91). Determine the default stock type for the documents (1 is unrestricted stock). Click the **Batch in Background** checkbox for the batches in inventory to be predetermined and copied to the physical inventory document being created. Click the **Alternative Unit of Measure** checkbox if you want to be able to record counts in alternative units of measure. You can also maintain a default reason for inventory differences if desired. Press the **Save** button.

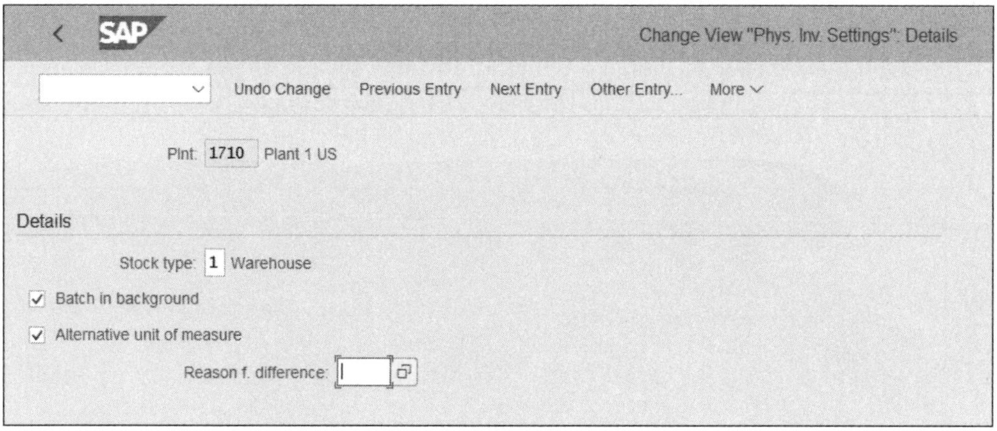

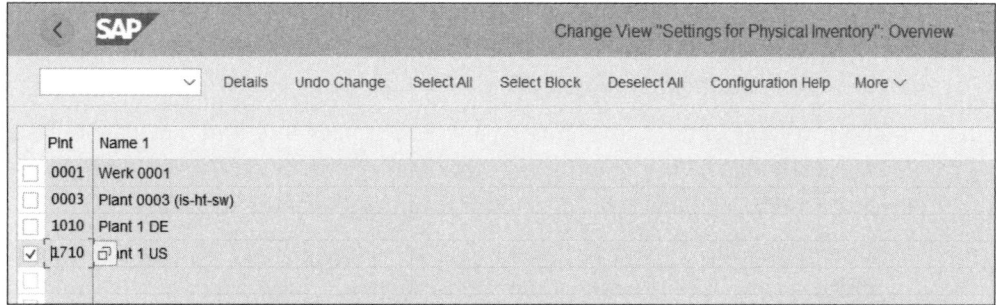

Figure 7.91 Default Values for Physical Inventory: Plant Details Screen

Settings for Physical Inventory

This configuration item allows you to make additional detailed settings for physical inventory processing for each plant. Default settings are set by SAP and can be adjusted as necessary.

To review default values for physical inventory, navigate to **IMG (SPRO) • Materials Management • Inventory Management and Physical Inventory • Physical Inventory • Settings for Physical Inventory**.

The **Settings for Physical Inventory** screen appears (see Figure 7.92). Click the checkbox next to the plant for which you want to maintain settings, then click the **Details** button.

Figure 7.92 Settings for Physical Inventory: Plant Selection Screen

The **Settings for Physical Inventory** screen appears (see Figure 7.93). You can set the system so that it creates change documents when physical inventory documents are maintained or counts are changed. You can control how the system reacts when book inventories are frozen but goods movements are posted. You can specify if and how serial numbers are displayed on physical inventory count sheets as well. Details of these settings can be found in the field documentation in the IMG. Press the **Save** button.

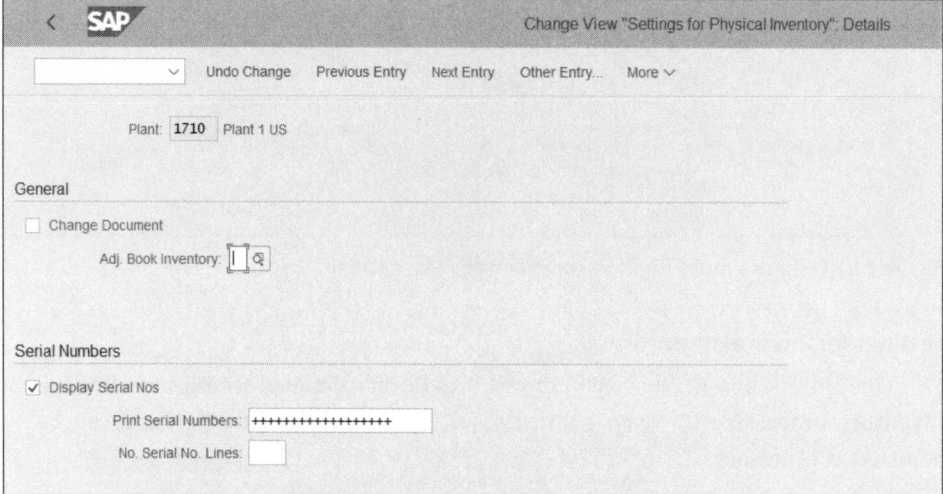

Figure 7.93 Settings for Physical Inventory: Plant Details Screen

Allow Freezing of Book Inventory Balances in Storage Locations

This configuration item allows you to determine if freezing of book inventories will be done when physical inventory documents are activated. If book inventories are frozen, inventory differences found during the count will be calculated from the frozen stock balance. If book inventories are not frozen, then inventory differences will be calculated from the stock balance at the time the count is recorded. This indicator can be set at the storage location level.

To allow freezing of book inventory valances in storage locations, navigate to **IMG (SPRO)** • **Materials Management** • **Inventory Management and Physical Inventory** • **Physical Inventory** • **Allow Freezing of Book Inventory Balances in Storage Locations**.

The **Determine Work Entry** dialog box is displayed (see Figure 7.94). Enter the plant for which settings will be made, then press the green checkmark at the bottom of the dialog.

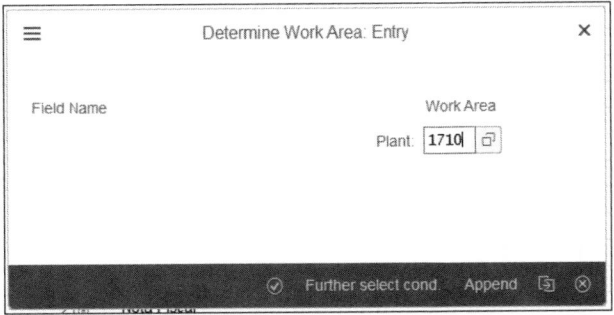

Figure 7.94 Allow Freezing of Book Inventories: Plant Selection

The **Storage Location** screen appears (see Figure 7.95). Click the checkbox next to each storage location in the specified plant for which you want to allow freezing of book inventories at the time of physical inventory document activation. Press the **Save** button.

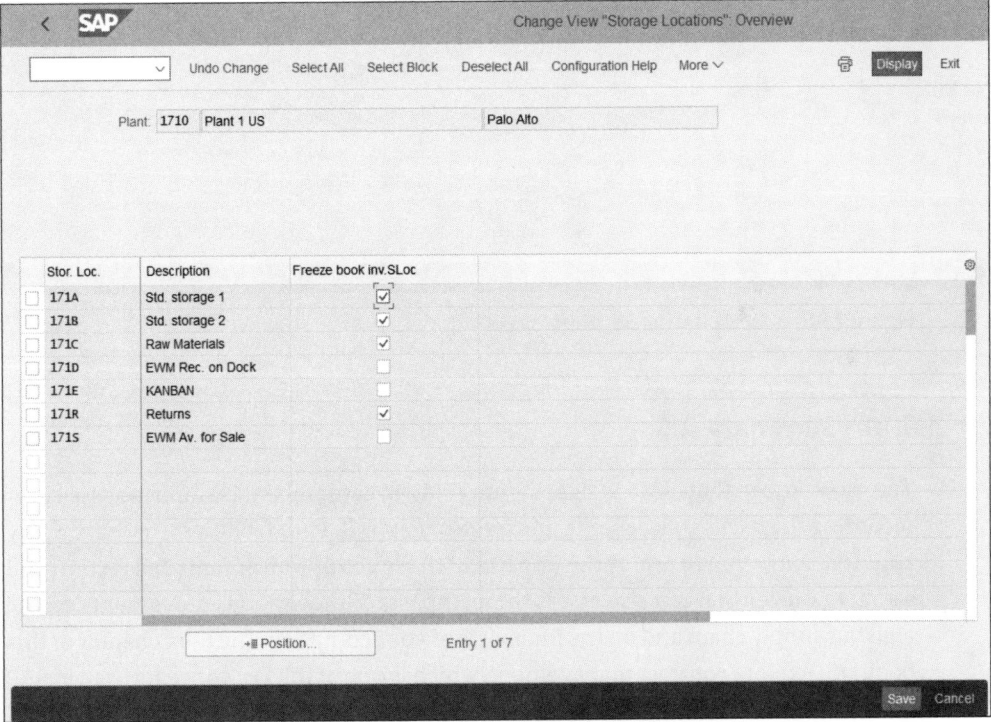

Figure 7.95 Allow Freezing of Book Inventories: Storage Location Details

Cycle Counting

This configuration item allows you to make necessary settings for using the cycle counting method of physical inventory. For each plant, the cycle counting indicators are defined along with settings to determine the frequency of count and float time. These cycle count indicators are set on the material master to determine which materials are subject to cycle counting and their relative count frequency.

To make cycle counting settings for your plants, navigate to **IMG (SPRO) • Materials Management • Inventory Management and Physical Inventory • Physical Inventory • Cycle Counting**.

The **Settings for Cycle Counting** screen is displayed as shown in Figure 7.96. Enter the plant, associated cycle counting indicators, and associated settings. Refer to the field documentation in the IMG documentation for detailed explanations of the available settings.

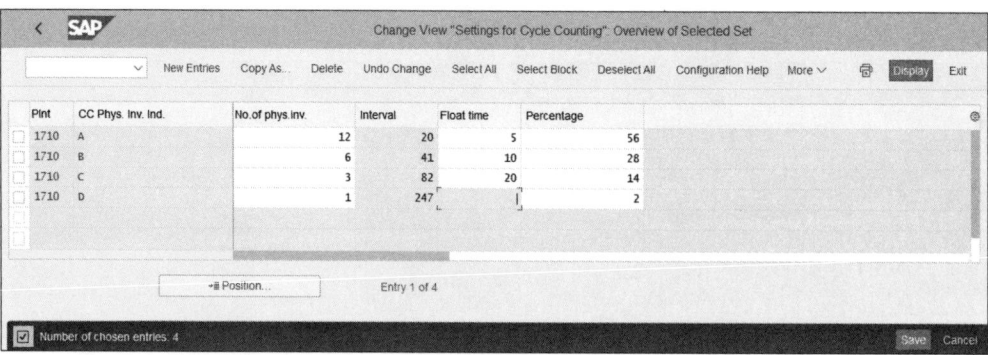

Figure 7.96 Cycle Counting Settings

7.10   Summary

You now know that SAP S/4HANA provides a comprehensive app portfolio for recording the receipt, placement, and issue of goods in your facilities. There are many apps that allow you to report the impacts of those goods movements at a tactical and a strategic level. You can also assess these impacts of those goods movements on the logistics supply chain and on the financials of your company. The next chapter of this book will explore contract management, which is one of the key concepts used in SAP S/4HANA Sourcing and Procurement for securing and administering long-term supply arrangements for your company.

Chapter 8
Contracts Management

Purchasing contracts are agreements made by a buying organization with a supplier for supply of materials and services. Contract management in purchasing is the process of managing such contracts, which includes creation, execution, monitoring, analysis, and renewal of contracts in SAP S/4HANA.

This chapter explains the contract management process and the SAP Fiori apps relevant to contract management and related analytics. We've also provided the detailed configuration steps required in SAP S/4HANA to run contract management.

Businesses are becoming increasingly competitive and success-driven in today's digital economy. To be a successful organization, it's essential that the procurement process, which is one of the core lines of business for any industry, is run with high efficiency and low costs. Most companies use the concept of longer-term purchasing agreements with suppliers to achieve procurement process optimization and improved financial performance. Such agreements are defined as *outline purchase agreements*, which may be referred to as *blanket* or *umbrella agreements* outside SAP systems. Outline purchase agreements within SAP S/4HANA comprise contracts, centrally agreed upon contracts, distributed contracts, scheduling agreements, and scheduling agreements referencing a centrally agreed upon contract. The solution addressing these agreements is referred to as *purchase contract management* under the sourcing and contract management stream in SAP S/4HANA, as shown in Figure 8.1.

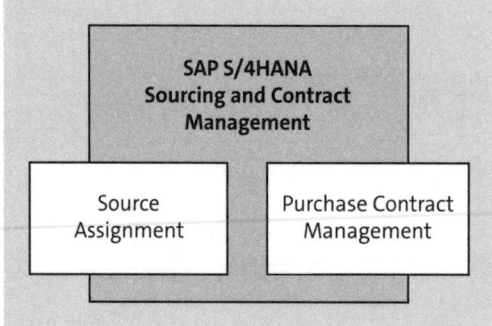

Figure 8.1 Sourcing and Contract Management

8.1   What Is Contract Management?

Contract management within SAP S/4HANA Sourcing and Procurement refers to the management of long-term purchasing arrangements with suppliers for supply of materials or performance of services. Purchases made with reference to these purchasing agreements help streamline the procurement process. Well-designed contract management can help reduce prices and guarantee on-time supply, which helps plan and optimize the business processes of both the purchasing organization and the supplying organization. The analytics capabilities and innovations offered by SAP S/4HANA enables contract management processes that are in real time and efficient.

8.1.1   Contract Creation

A contract is a document created and maintained in the SAP S/4HANA system. This document holds all the information relevant to the purchasing agreement between the organization and the supplier. Once the quantities, prices, terms, and conditions are finalized, the contract is created in the system. The different types of contracts and how they're created in the system are explained in this section.

8.1.2   Types of Contracts

A contract is a type of outline agreement with suppliers in SAP S/4HANA that allows for the issue of release orders (a.k.a., call-off orders) for the agreed-upon materials or services of the contract. These purchase contracts in SAP S/4HANA consist of *items*, which are materials, material groups, or services. It's possible to create the following contracts, depending on the business requirements:

- **Quantity contract**

  This type of contract stipulates the quantity, negotiated price, and conditions for purchase of materials or services from the supplier with whom the contract is established. This allows the purchaser to issue multiple release orders to the supplier with reference to the contract until the total quantity reaches the value defined in the contract.

- **Value contract**

  These contracts are generally used for purchasing materials or services that belong to certain material groups defined in materials management. These contracts stipulate the total value of the contract—which is also known as the *target value*—and of the material groups and the supplier. Specific materials or services are not listed as line items in the contract, but the contract allows purchase of materials or services that belong to the material groups that are listed as line items in the contract. Purchasers can create release orders for materials or services that belong to the material groups identified in the contract.

- **Contract release order**

  It's possible to create a release order, which is simply a PO referencing a contract, using SAP GUI Transaction ME21N. In this transaction, if you enter the contract number in the **Outline Agreement** field under the **Items** pane, the system will populate all the information from the contract and expect you to input the quantity and delivery date. After creating the release order, it's possible to edit and display the document using Transactions ME22N and ME23N, respectively. With the introduction of SAP Fiori apps in SAP S/4HANA, the UI has moved away from the old SAP GUI-based transactions to the new SAP Fiori UX, which is explained in the next section.

8.1.3   Manage Purchase Contracts

Contracts can be created either directly by entering all the data manually or by referencing purchase requisitions, RFQs/quotations, or existing contracts. The SAP GUI Transaction ME31K is used for creating a contract, and this transaction is also available from the SAP Fiori launchpad. With the introduction of SAP Fiori apps for

SAP S/4HANA, the Manage Purchase Contracts SAP Fiori app is used for creating or editing contracts, as follows:

1. Logon to the SAP Fiori launchpad and click the **Manage Purchase Contracts** tile to open the app.

2. Click the **Create** button to create a contract. The header screen, shown in Figure 8.2, is presented for entering header information.

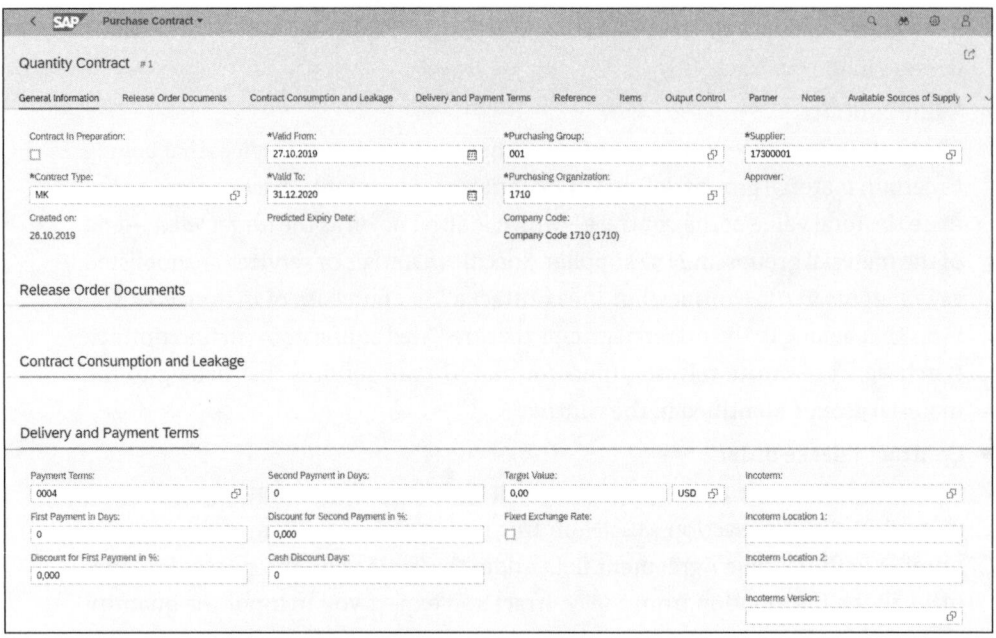

Figure 8.2 Create Contract: Header

3. After entering the **Contract Type**, **Purchasing Organization**, **Purchasing Group**, **Supplier**, and **Valid From** and **To** dates in the **General Information** tab, navigate to the **Delivery and Payment Terms** tab and enter **Payment Terms**, **Incoterms**, and **Target Value** if applicable.

4. In the **Reference** tab, you can enter **Reference, Quotation, AND SALESPERSON** if available. In this tab, you can also enter the **Invoicing Party** and **Goods Supplier** if different from the **Supplier** entered in the **General Information** tab (as in Figure 8.3).

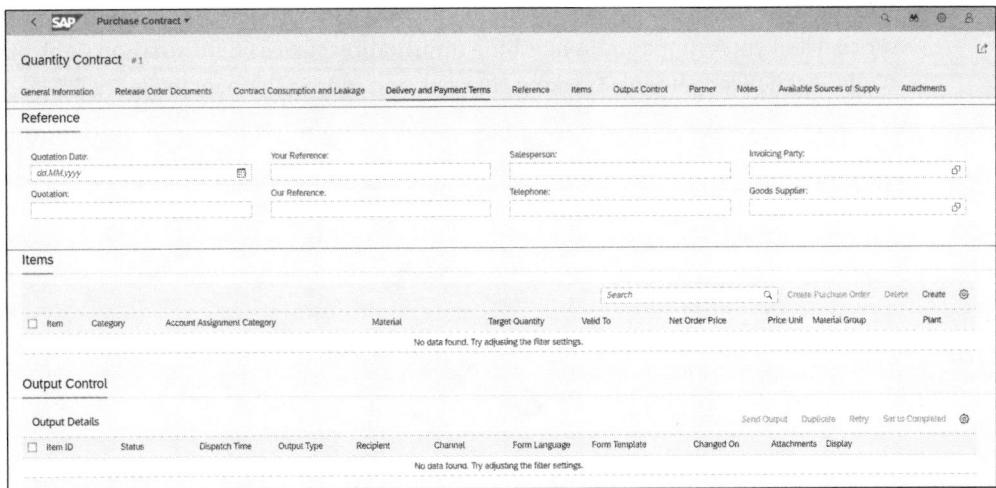

Figure 8.3 Create Contract — Reference

5. Then you can enter notes for the supplier if any in the **Notes** tab. It's also possible to add attachments.

6. Once you've entered all the header information, choose the **Item** tab and click the **Create** button to add item details for the contract. Input the **Material** number, **Plant**, **Item Category**, and **Storage Location** in the **General Information** tab, as shown in Figure 8.4.

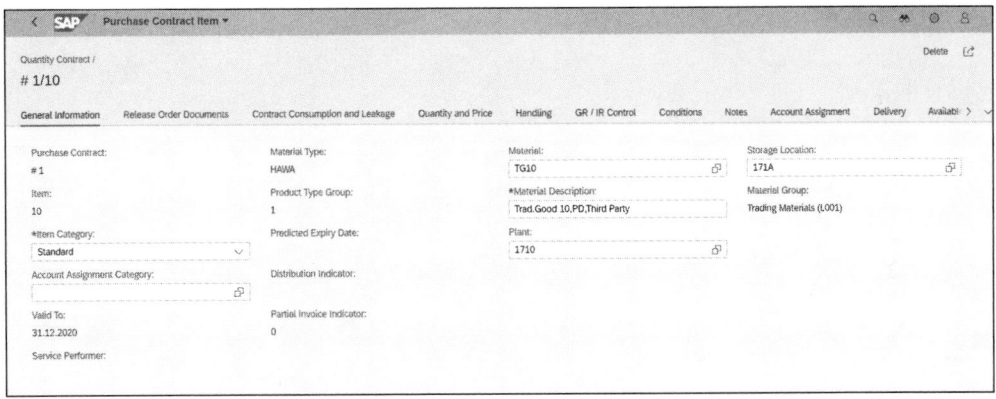

Figure 8.4 Create Contract Item: General Information

7. On the **Item Detail** screen, enter **Target Quantity** and **Release Order Quantity** and **Price**. Then you can maintain handling information such as **Confirmation Control**, **Order Acknowledgement**, **Tracking Number**, and more, as shown in Figure 8.5.

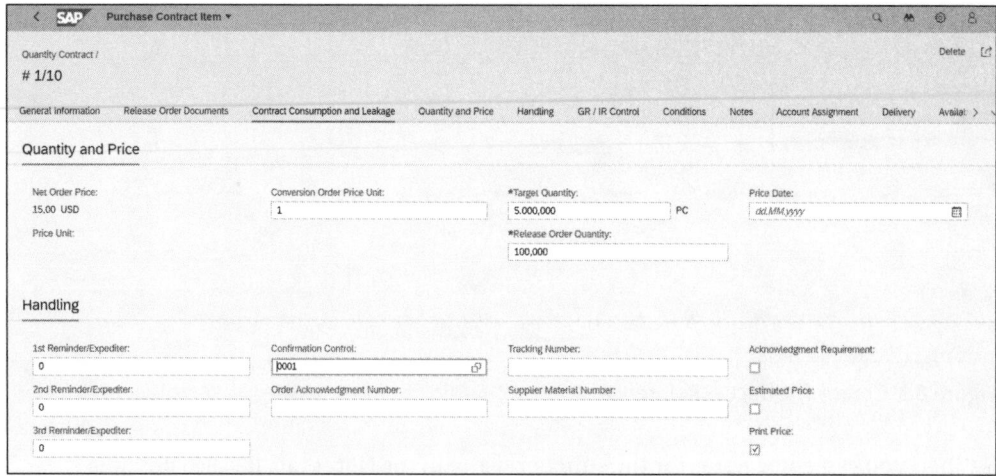

Figure 8.5 Create Contract Item: Quantity and Price

8. Go to the **GR/IR Control** tab and enter tolerance limits and stock type as applicable. Flags to indicate the requirement of GR, IR, GR-based invoice verification, and more can be added, as shown in Figure 8.6.

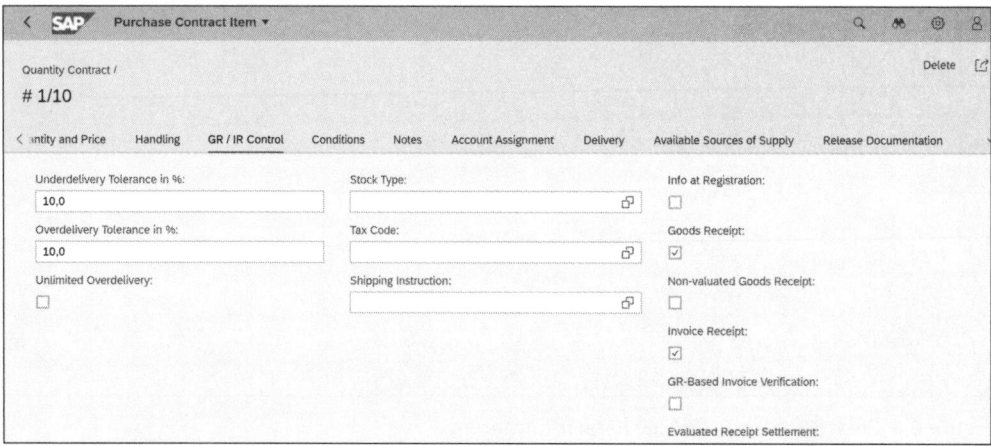

Figure 8.6 Create Contract Item: GR/IR Control

9. Go to the **Conditions** tab and add (**+**) conditions, as shown in Figure 8.7.

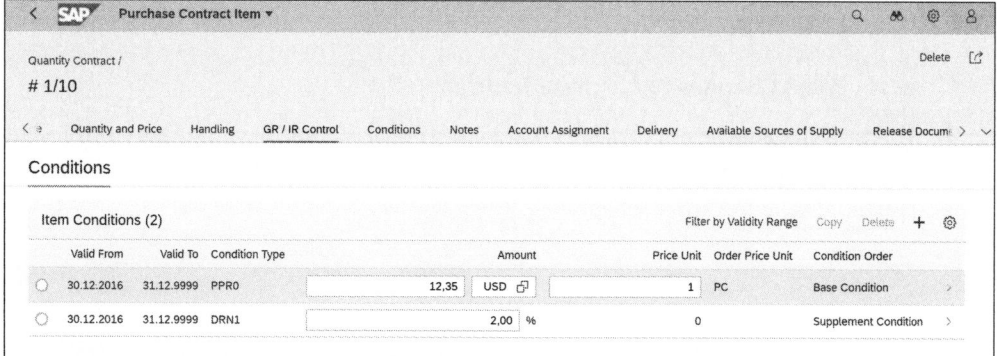

Figure 8.7 Create Contract Item: Conditions

10. Check all the entries and click the **Apply** button to apply the conditions; then save the contract. This completes the process of creating a contract.

This app also provides the capability to search for contracts based on a wide range of criteria, including supplier, purchasing organization, purchasing group, rating, creation date, validity status, and so on. As shown in Figure 8.8, it's also possible to navigate to the contract in display mode and edit it from there ❶.

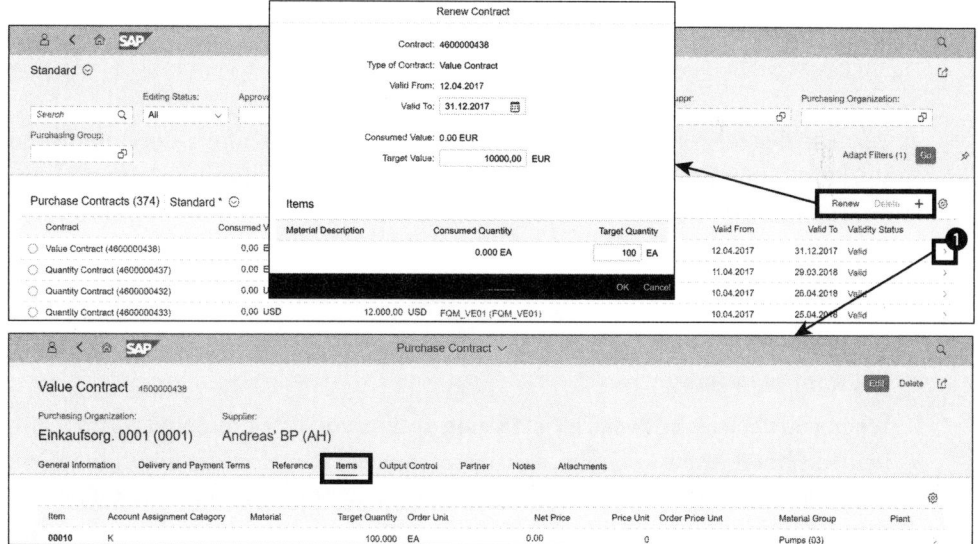

Figure 8.8 Manage Purchase Contract

Selecting a contract from the list and clicking the **Renew** button allows the user to extend the validity period, target quantity, or target value of the contract.

8.1.4   Mass Changes to Purchase Contract

This app enables the purchaser to change the fields of multiple purchase contracts at the same time (see Figure 8.9). It's possible to export the list of contracts from this app externally to a spreadsheet.

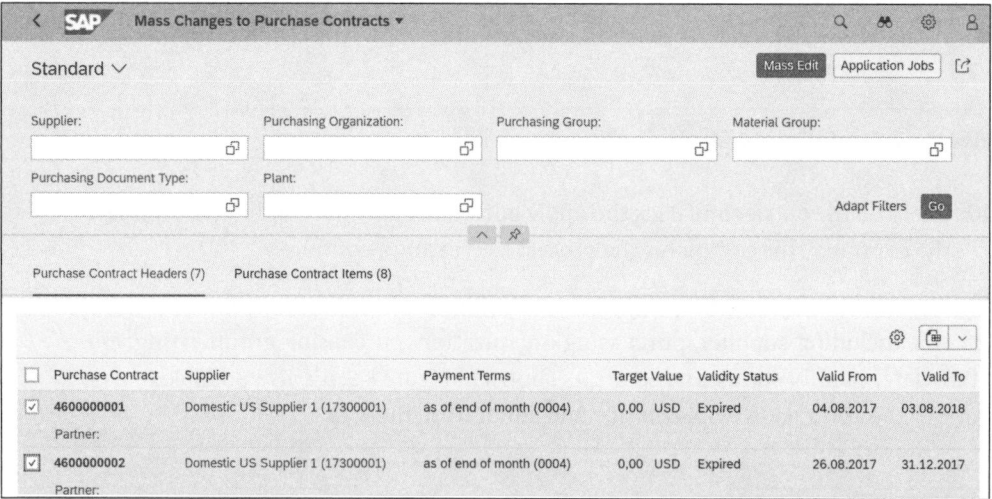

Figure 8.9 Mass Changes to Purchase Contracts

1. The initial screen displays all the contracts based on the filters selected on the screen To make changes to multiple contacts at the same time, select all the contracts you want to change and press the **Mass Edit** button. On the pop-up screen, you'll see three options for each header value:
   - **Keep Existing Value**
   - **Replace Field Value**
   - **Clear Field Value**

2. When you choose the **Replace Field Value** option, you'll be presented with a blank field to enter the new value. Once you've completed the selections and entered the new values as needed, you can press the **Apply Mass Changes** button, as shown in Figure 8.10. The fields available for changes include **Terms of Payment, Purchasing**

Group, Exchange Rate, Fixed Exchange Rate, Target Value, and **Purchasing Document Name**. Similar actions can be performed for contract items as well by selecting the purchase contract items in the app.

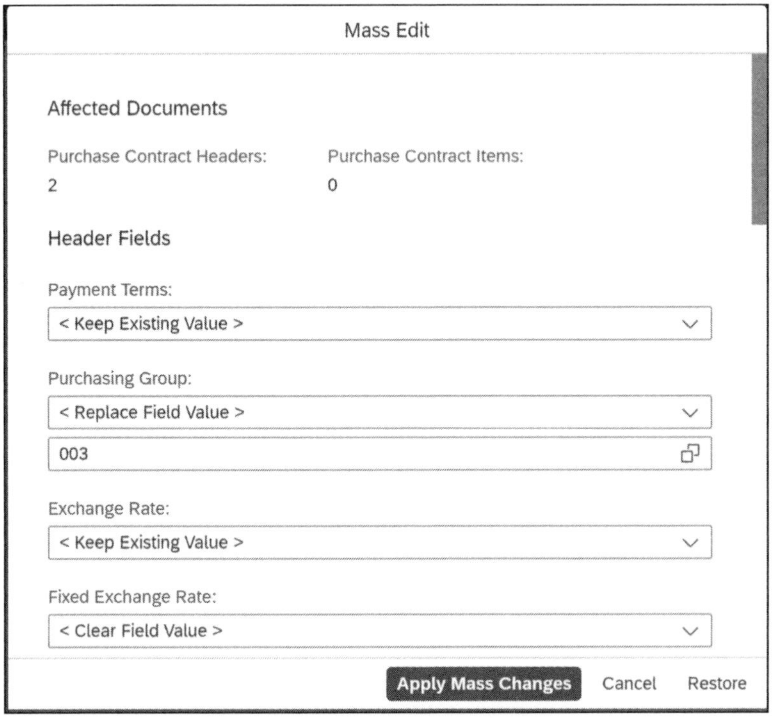

Figure 8.10 Purchase Contracts: Apply Mass Changes

The app allows the user to view the status of the changes made to the contract by pressing the **Application Jobs** button. From the list of contracts displayed, it's possible to navigate to the object pages for the purchase contract and supplier by clicking an object link to view the contextual information related to those objects.

8.2   Contract Consumption

Purchase managers and buyers want to monitor existing contracts in the system and analyze consumption patterns. They also want to obtain advance information about both planned and predicted expiry dates of contracts. This information helps the purchasing organization regulate consumption and initiate contract renewal or the renegotiation process. This section describes the SAP Fiori apps available in SAP S/4HANA to both analyze and predict contract data.

8.2.1   Value Contract Consumption

Login to the SAP Fiori launchpad and navigate to the Value Contract Consumption SAP Fiori app, then click the tile to execute the app. This SAP Fiori app analyses the value contracts in the system and displays target and released amounts and the consumption percentage over the last 365 days. It's possible to display the KPIs by supplier, purchasing group, purchasing organization, document, and trend, as shown in Figure 8.11. The output can be filtered by **Purchase Contract, Document Type, Supplier, Calendar Week/Month/Quarter/Year, Purchasing Group/Organization, Supplier, Currency, Company Code,** and **Created By**, as shown in Figure 8.11 ❶.

Note that the table is coded by **Released Amount, Target Amount,** and **Consumption %** ❷.

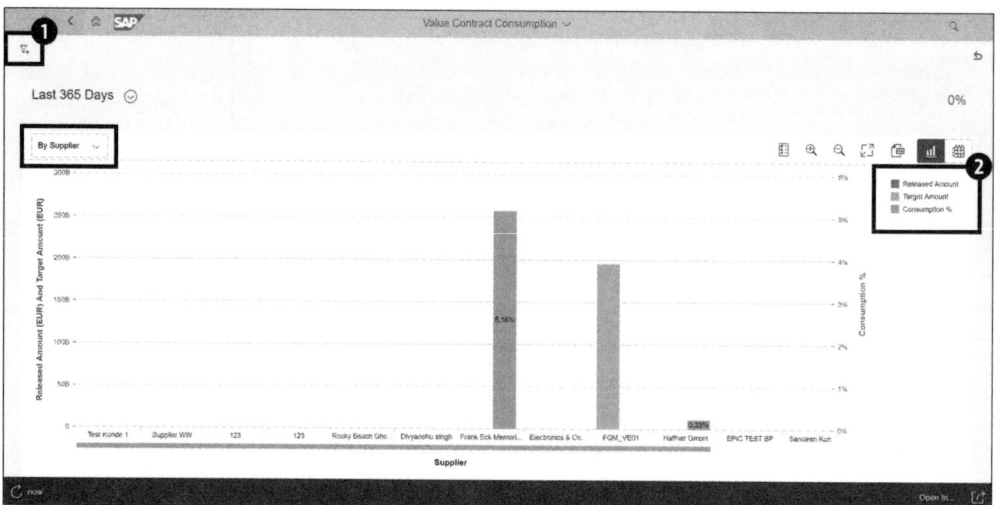

Figure 8.11 Value Contract Consumption

From the initial display—for example, **By Supplier**—it's possible to drill down by clicking on any bar (representing one supplier's data) and selecting one of the options, as shown in Figure 8.12, to go to the next level. Once you choose, for example, **Purchasing Group** from the options, you'll see the values for the selected supplier per purchasing group.

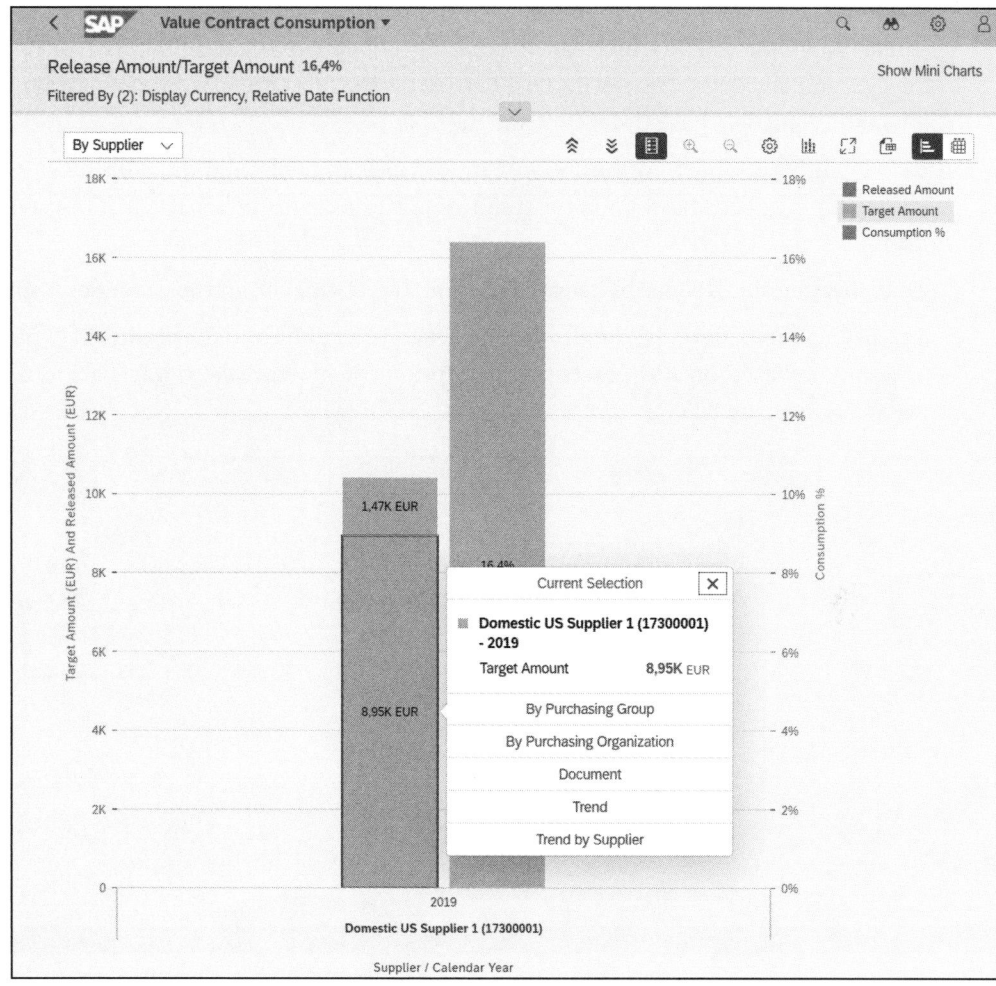

Figure 8.12 Value Contract Consumption: Drilldown

8.2.2   Quantity Contract Consumption

Login to the SAP Fiori launchpad and navigate to the Quantity Contract Consumption SAP Fiori app; click its tile to execute the app. This SAP Fiori app determines the percentage of consumption of quantity type contracts. It also displays the target and released quantities of contracts. The results can be viewed by supplier, purchasing group, purchasing organization, purchasing category, material group, cost center, document, and trend. It's also possible to filter each view by **Purchase Contract**, **Calendar Week/Month/Quarter/Year**, **Purchasing Group/Organization**, **Supplier**, **Currency**, **Company Code**, **Created By**, **Cost Center**, **Purchasing Category**, **Material Group**, **Material**, **Plant**, **Purchase Order Unit** and more ❶.

The Quantity Contract Consumption app provides an additional measure for predicted contract consumption in the trend view, based on historical data from closed contracts.

Note that the table is coded by **Released Amount**, **Target Amount**, and **Consumption %** ❷.

In the document view, the predicted contract consumption and the predicted expiration date based on 100 percent consumption for individual contracts are provided (as in Figure 8.13).

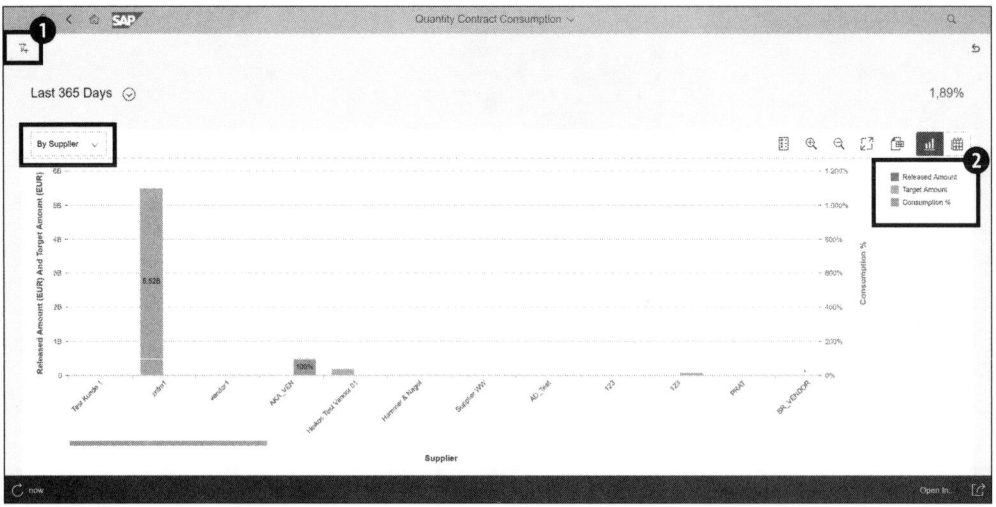

Figure 8.13 Quantity Contract Consumption

From the initial display—for example, **By Supplier**—it's possible to drill down by clicking on any bar (representing one supplier's data) and selecting one of the options, as shown in Figure 8.14, to go to the next level. Once you choose, for example, **Purchasing Group** from the options, you'll see the values for the selected supplier per purchasing group.

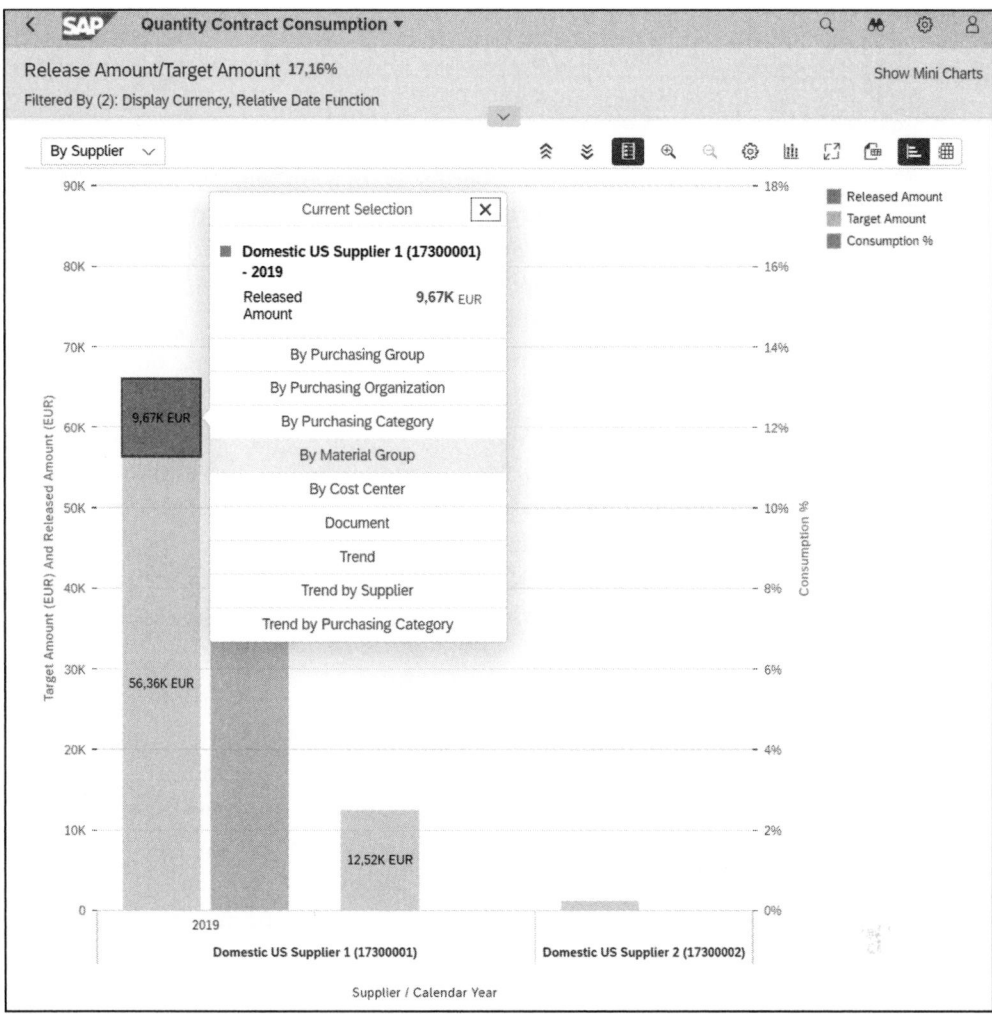

Figure 8.14 Quantity Contract Consumption: Drilldown

8.3   Contract Dashboard Reporting and Expiration Notification Setting

Reporting in contract management has undergone major changes in SAP S/4HANA. The capability that comes with the in-memory technology of SAP S/4HANA and the SAP Fiori UI has made it possible to offer a number of innovations in the areas of reporting and analytics. This section provides a detailed explanation of all the SAP Fiori apps that come with SAP S/4HANA. It's also important to note that SAP has embarked on a new journey to introduce more innovative apps as part of every new release.

SAP Fiori provides its role-based, consumer-grade UX across all lines of business. SAP Fiori 3.0 is the latest evolution of the UX for SAP S/4HANA and provides consistency, intelligence, and integration. It provides a harmonized look and feel across products, enables embedded machine learning and automation of mundane tasks, and makes integration of content from different products simpler. SAP Fiori 3.0 enriches the UX with intuitive, easy-to-use apps that run on both mobile devices and computers. SAP Fiori apps help zero in on key functions, tasks, and activities for the user. SAP Fiori overview pages allow users to get live KPIs and action items, including lists of contracts that will expire in the near future. SAP Fiori apps are categorized as transactional, analytical, and object page types. Transactional apps run business transactions, and object page apps display master data and documents. Analytical apps, as the name suggests, are used to analyze live data for instant business insights. These apps also provide capability to act based on insights. Detailed information on all the apps is available at *http://s-prs.co/500303*.

SAP Fiori 3.0 design provides a harmonized user experience across all SAP applications including cloud solutions. The SAP Fiori visual theme known as Quartz comes in light and dark flavors. SAP Fiori apps are not developed yet for some SAP GUI transactions. However, these classic SAP GUI transactions are made available in the SAP Fiori theme to support a seamless user experience across the SAP Fiori launchpad. These apps run in the backend as SAP GUI applications but are presented via a harmonized user experience. This helps users access the system from a central SAP Fiori launchpad, enjoy the new UX, and avoid the need to log on to SAP GUI. It's worth mentioning that SAP is replacing additional SAP GUI transactions with SAP Fiori apps in each SAP S/4HANA release. The SAP Fiori apps discussed in the following sections are available within the contract management solution in SAP S/4HANA.

8.3.1   Unused Contracts

This app identifies all the contracts that haven't been t used within the last 365 days from the current date and displays the target and released amounts (Figure 8.15). The output can be displayed by supplier, purchasing group, purchasing organization, purchasing document category, or document in tabular format or as a chart. You can drill down to view the related documents by clicking any of the bars in the bar chart view and selecting the **Documents** navigation option.

Log in to SAP Fiori launchpad, navigate to the Unused Contracts SAP Fiori app, and click its tile to execute the app. This app provides insight into unused contracts and enables the buyer to analyze and take necessary action to better utilize the contract.

In Figure 8.15 ❶, you can filter by purchase contract, calendar year, purchasing group/organization, supplier, currency, company code, and who it was created by. You may select **By Supplier** to search by supplier, by purchasing group or organization, or document ❷. Note that the table is coded by **Target Amount**, **Released Amount**, and **Unused Contracts** ❸.

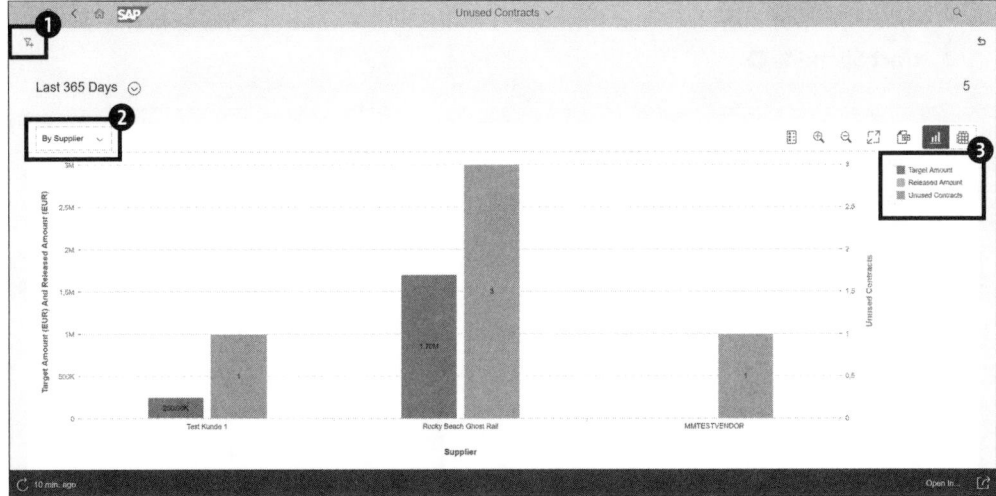

Figure 8.15 Unused Contracts

8.3.2   Off-Contract Spend

Often, purchases are made without a negotiated price for materials or services. Procurement managers always want to know how much or what percentage of materials are procured outside of negotiated contracts. Analyzing this information helps buyers determine the types of products and areas in need of further contracts and negotiated prices. The Off-Contract Spend app (Figure 8.16) enables the buyer to analyze and control such purchases, resulting in improved procurement processes and reduced costs.

Log in to the SAP Fiori launchpad, navigate to the Off-Contract Spend SAP Fiori app, and click its tile to execute the app. In this app, the total amount of purchase order items without any contract reference is expressed as a percentage of the total amount of all the purchase order items over a period of one year from the previous year to date. The app shows both the off-contract spend amount and the spend percentage.

In Figure 8.16 ❶, you can filter by calendar week/month/quarter/year, company code, supplier, supplier country, material, plant, purchasing group/organization, material group, purchasing category, purchasing order, currency, and who it was created by. You may select **By Supplier** to search by supplier, by purchasing category or material group, by purchasing group or organization, plant, cost center or WBS element, document, or trend ❷. Note that the table is coded by **Off Contr. Spend Amt** and **Off Contract Spend %** ❸.

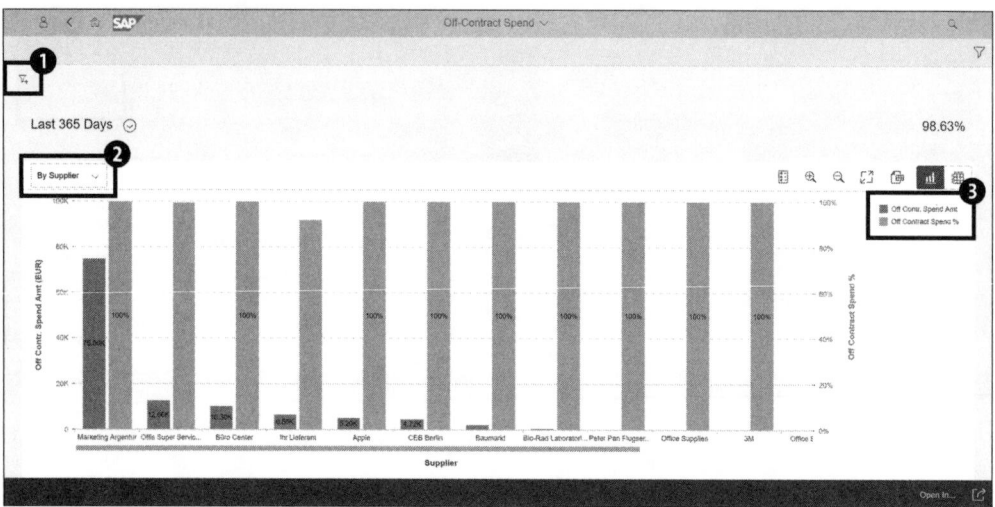

Figure 8.16 Off-Contract Spend

The values can be displayed by supplier, purchasing group, purchasing organization, purchasing category, or material group, plant, WBS element, cost center, and trend in tabular format or as a chart. The app can display all documents that contribute to the spend. It's also possible to analyze the trend of the spend by purchasing category or by supplier.

8.3.3 Contract Leakage

The Contract Leakage app (Figure 8.17) is used to identify purchase order spend on items procured without referencing an existing contract that could have been used. Such a buying pattern is likely to increase costs and decrease efficiency. The Contract Leakage app helps monitor such spending that happens outside contracts even though a contract is in place. For each view, the list of documents that contribute to the spend amount can be displayed as well. This app enables the buyer to analyze whether the leakage is increasing or decreasing and which supplier or purchasing category contributes to the leakage. You can drill down by supplier, purchasing group, purchasing organization, purchasing category, material group, and document in this app by clicking any of the bars in the bar chart view and selecting the appropriate navigation option.

Log in to the SAP Fiori Launchpad, navigate to the Contract Leakage SAP Fiori app, and click its tile to execute the app.

In Figure 8.17 ❶, you can filter by calendar week/month/quarter/year, material, plant, material group, purchasing category, purchasing order, supplier, supplier country, company code, currency, and accounting objects. You may select **By Supplier** to search by supplier, by purchasing category or material group, by purchasing group or organization, plant, cost center or WBS element, document, or trend ❷. Note that the table is coded by **Leakage Amount**, **Non-Leakage Amount**, and **Leakage %** ❸.

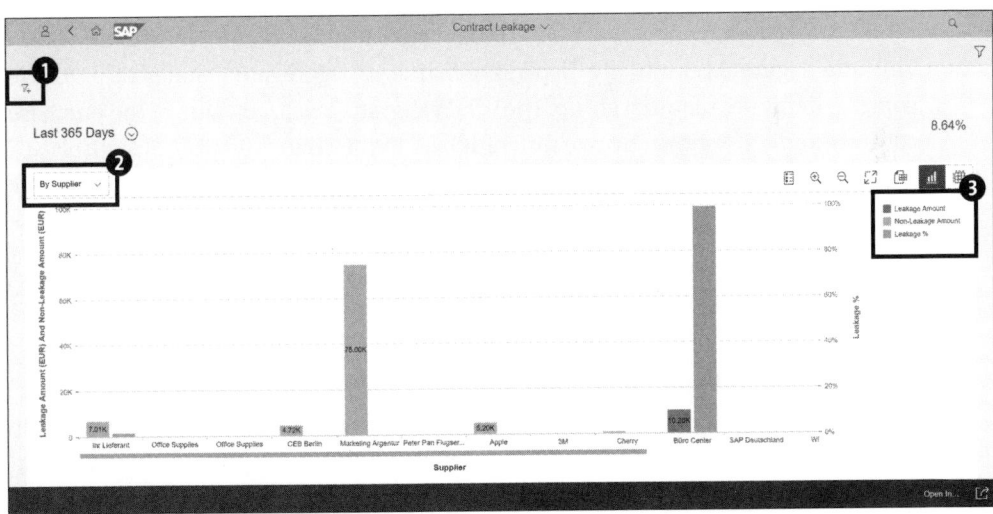

Figure 8.17 Contract Leakage

8.3.4   Purchase Contract Items by Account Assignment

This app displays purchase contract items grouped by their cost centers, using filter criteria such as **Purchase Contract, Cost Center, Order, WBS Element, Asset,** and so on. Clicking any cost center of the result output lets you view details such as material, supplier, account assignment category description, net value, and account assignment quantity for each purchase contract item assigned to that cost center. The app allows you to drill down further to view the corresponding purchase orders and general information. It also allows navigation to object pages for material and supplier.

Log in to the SAP Fiori launchpad, navigate to the Purchase Contract Items by Account Assignment SAP Fiori app, and click its tile to execute the app (seen in Figure 8.18).

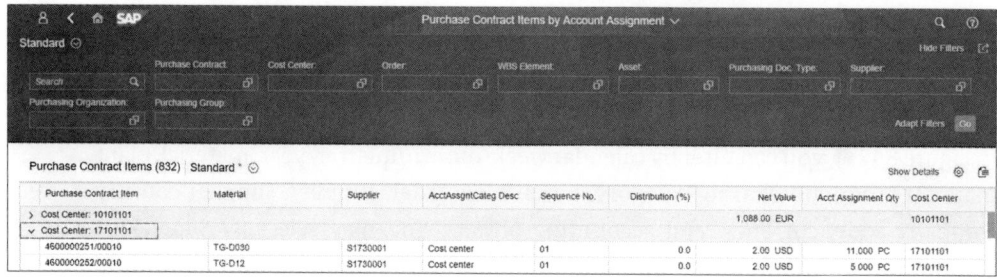

Figure 8.18 Purchase Contract Items by Account Assignment

8.3.5   Monitor Purchase Contract Items

This app (Figure 8.19) initially displays a chart with aggregated values of purchase contract items per material group. The total value and released value of the purchase contract items are shown by two different bars in the chart. The page also displays a list of purchase contract items below the chart. When you click any of the bars in the chart, the list below shows only purchase contract items that are relevant to the selected bar.

Log in to the SAP Fiori launchpad, navigate to the Monitor Purchase Contract Items SAP Fiori app, and click its tile to execute the app.

Purchase contract items can be displayed based on filter criteria such as **Display Currency, Purchase Contract, Material Group, Material, Supplier, Cost Center,** and so on. It's possible to drill down further to view detailed information for any dimension. In the chart, the Y-axis represents the measure and the X-axis represents the dimension.

It's possible to click any purchase contract item and view the item details. This app allows you to navigate to contextual information related to a purchase contract and material from the items list.

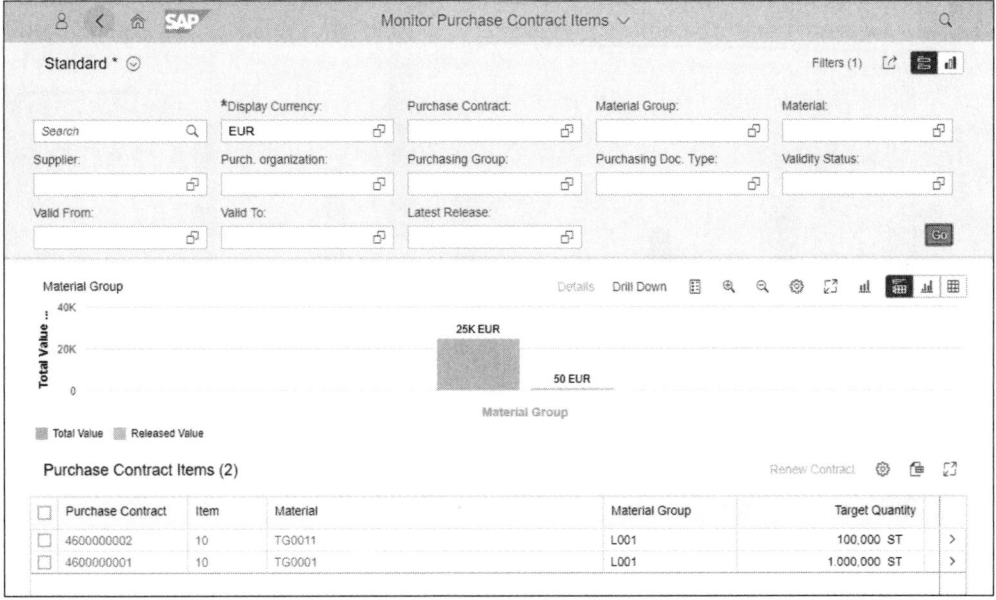

Figure 8.19 Monitor Purchase Contract Items

8.3.6   Contract Expiry

This app identifies contracts that are expiring within a certain time period and can display the number of expiring contracts, target amount, and released amount. The output can be displayed by supplier, purchasing group, purchasing organization, purchasing category, or material group, in tabular format or as a chart. As shown in Figure 8.20 ❶, it's also possible to filter the data by purchase contract, validity start/end, created by, currency, purchasing group/organization, supplier, and company code. You may select **By Supplier** to search by supplier, by purchasing group or organization, or by document ❷. Note that the table is coded by **Expiring Contracts**, **Released Amount**, and **Target Amount** ❸.

Log in to the SAP Fiori launchpad, navigate to the Contract Expiry SAP Fiori app, and click its tile to execute the app.

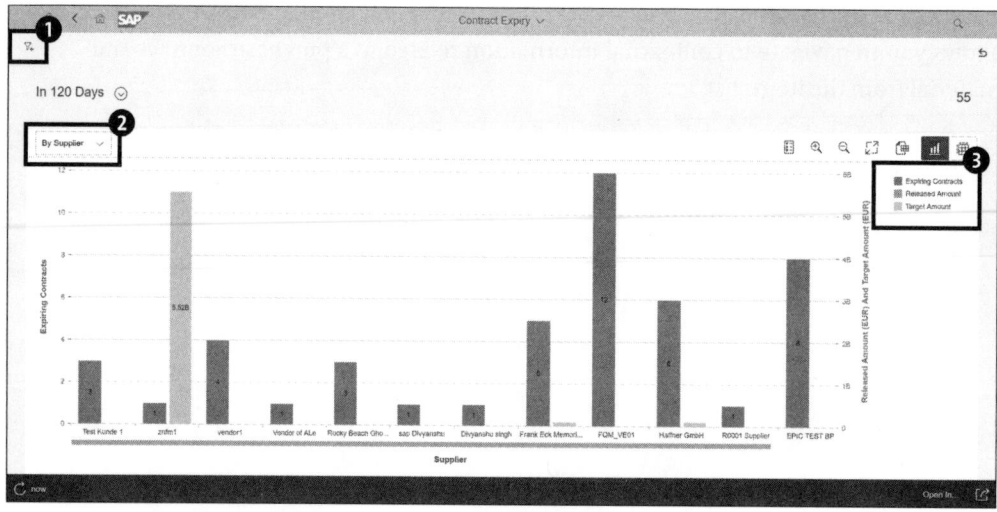

Figure 8.20 Contract Expiry

8.4   Configuration

To realize the features and functionalities of contract management, the system needs to be configured based on business requirements. This section provides the details of standard SAP-recommended configuration steps for contract management. These settings are made in the SAP S/4HANA system by following the customizing paths provided in the following sections for each step.

8.4.1   Configuring Contracts

With SAP S/4HANA, it's possible to take advantage of the SAP Best Practices activation approach for customizing, as explained in Chapter 2. However, if you use the traditional customizing approach, this section can help. This information also helps validate the SAP standard configuration.

Define Document Types

Contracts are managed in the system as documents. Document types, which act as a key to group contracts, are defined in configuration. To define document types, navigate to **IMG (SPRO)** • **Materials Management** • **Purchasing** • **Contract** • **Define Document Types**. Table 8.1 provides the SAP-standard settings; it's possible to define additional contract document types depending on business requirements. Number ranges are assigned to each document type defined in the system. New number ranges may also be defined and used as required. The menu path to set number ranges is **IMG (SPRO) • Materials Management • Purchasing • Contract • Define Number Ranges** (see Figure 8.21).

Field Name	Value (First Entry)	Value (Second Entry)
Type	MK	WK
Doc. Type Description	Quantity Contract	Value Contract
Item Number Interval	10	10
Number Range—Internal	46	46
Number Range—External	44	44
Update Group Statistics	SAP	SAP
Field Selection Key	MKK	WKK

Table 8.1 Define Document Types

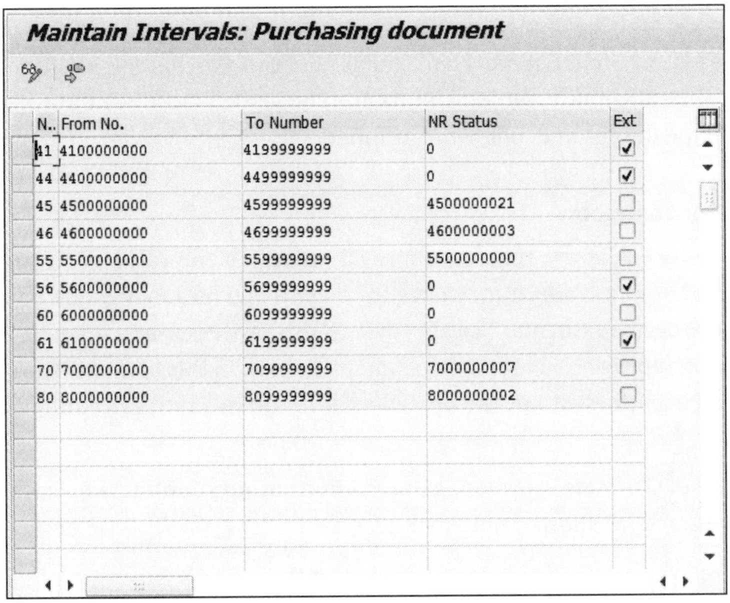

Maintain Intervals: Purchasing document

N..	From No.	To Number	NR Status	Ext	
41	4100000000	4199999999	0	✔	
44	4400000000	4499999999	0	✔	
45	4500000000	4599999999	4500000021	☐	
46	4600000000	4699999999	4600000003	☐	
55	5500000000	5599999999	5500000000	☐	
56	5600000000	5699999999	0	✔	
60	6000000000	6099999999	0	☐	
61	6100000000	6199999999	0	✔	
70	7000000000	7099999999	7000000007	☐	
80	8000000000	8099999999	8000000002	☐	

Figure 8.21 Define Number Ranges: Contract

Allowed Item Categories

After defining the document types, select the line for the **Doc Type** defined in the previous step and double-click **Allowed Item Categories**. On the admissible item categories for the document type, the item categories listed in Table 8.2 can be configured depending on business requirements.

Item Category	Description	Use Case
Blank	Standard	N/A
M	Material unknown	Used when similar materials are negotiated for same price but with different material number
W	Material group	Only for value contract with material groups but without item price or quantity
D	Service	When contract is created for performance of services
K	Consignment	When contract is created for consignment materials
L	Subcontracting	When contract is created for subcontracting activities

Table 8.2 Item Categories in Contracts

Then, select the line for each **Item Category** and double-click **Link Purchase Requisition Document Type**. On the **Change View "Link Purchase Requisition-Document Type": Overview** screen, define the allowed follow-on documents.

Release Procedure for Contracts

A *release procedure* is used for the contract approval process. If the value of a contract exceeds $10,000, for example, it may have to be approved by a manger before the contract can be processed further. The approver in this process uses a predetermined release code to approve (release) the document. *Release* in this context refers to approving contracts in the system. The procedure is set up in a series of configuration steps:

1. Navigate to **IMG (SPRO)** • **Materials Management** • **Purchasing** • **Contract** • **Release Procedure for Contracts**, as shown in Figure 8.22.

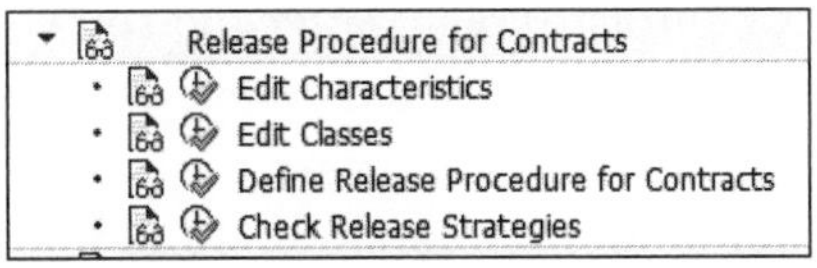

Figure 8.22 Release Procedure for Contracts

2. Create characteristics.

3. Create classes.

4. Set up the release procedure for contracts.

5. Create release group.

6. Create release code.

7. Create release indicator.

8. Create release strategy.

9. Check release strategies.

Texts for Contracts

Text types are used while creating contracts, and text maintained under each text type is generally used to provide additional information either at the header level or item level within the contract. For this functionality to work, text types must be defined. In this customizing step, it's possible to check the SAP defined standard text types and create new text types if needed. In addition, you can define copying rules for adopting texts from other objects, such as RFQ, quotation, contract, and so on:

1. To begin the configuration, navigate to **IMG (SPRO)** • **Materials Management** • **Purchasing** • **Contract** • **Texts for Contracts**, as shown in Figure 8.23.

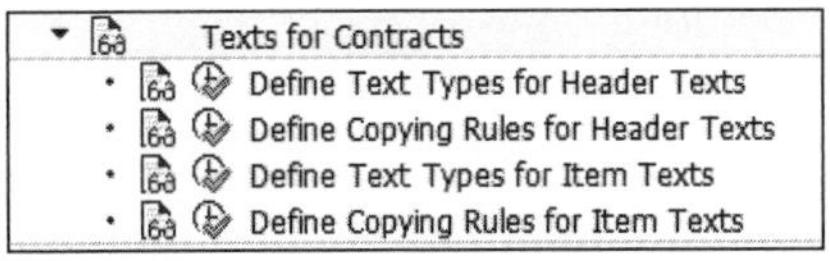

Figure 8.23 Texts for Contracts

Then, you can check the available text types and define your own text types for header texts if needed.

2. After the text types are defined, open the **Define Copying Rules for Header Texts** node, select the text type for which copying rules need to be defined, and choose **Text Linkages**.

3. On the **Maintain Text Linkages: Header Text Contract** screen, enter the source object and source text type from which the text can be copied to the contract text type (target text). For example, you can configure an RFQ as the source object and the header text of the RFQ as source text and configure the target as the header text of the contract. If this setting is done in the system, the system will copy the header text of the RFQ into the header text of the contract while creating a contract. It's possible to set the copying rule to any one of the following options:

   – Text automatically adopted in target object
   – User can have text adopted in target object
   – Text can't be adopted in target object

This customizing activity is repeated for item text types.

Set Up Authorization Check for General Ledger Accounts

In this step, you set the general ledger account authorization check to **Active** in contracts. Navigate to **IMG (SPRO) • Materials Management • Purchasing • Contract • Set Up Authorization Check for G/L Accounts** (as in Figure 8.24). This indicator is set at the company code level. Whenever a contract is created with an item requiring account assignment, the system checks whether the creator of the contract has the necessary authorization for the general ledger account entered. This setting is used as a control mechanism based on the business requirements per company code.

Figure 8.24 Authorization Check for General Ledger Accounts

8.4.2   Manage Workflows for Purchase Contracts

This SAP Fiori app is based on the flexible workflow, which is a general function available for purchasing documents. The Manage Workflow for Purchase Contracts app allows users to define one-step or multistep approval processes for purchase contracts according to the business requirements of the organization. Setting up a workflow using this app for purchase contract is simple and doesn't require any development skills:

1. Login to the SAP Fiori launchpad, navigate to the Manage Workflows for Purchase Contracts app, and click its tile to execute the app.

2. Click the **Add** button to create a new workflow. Enter a name and description if desired and the validity period for the workflow, as shown in Figure 8.25.

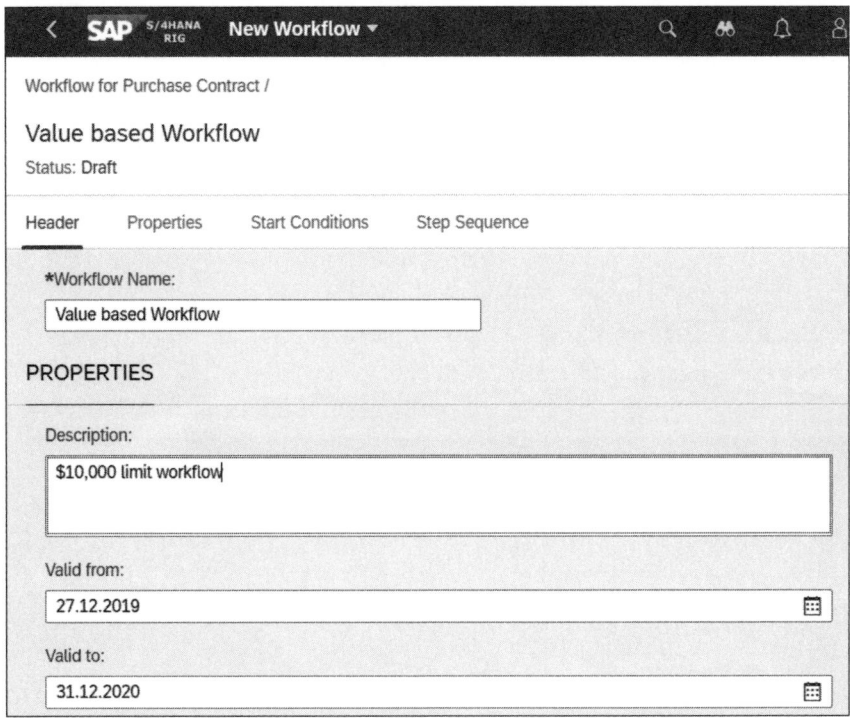

Figure 8.25 Value-Based Workflow Header

3. Scroll down and add a start condition, as shown in Figure 8.26. The standard start conditions center on account assignment, company code, material group, purchasing group, target value, and others.

4. Scroll down to the **Step Sequence** tab and click the **Add** button to add steps as shown in Figure 8.27. One or more steps can be defined here; for each step, enter recipients (approvers) and step conditions, if any.

5. Save the workflow and activate for the workflow to take effect.

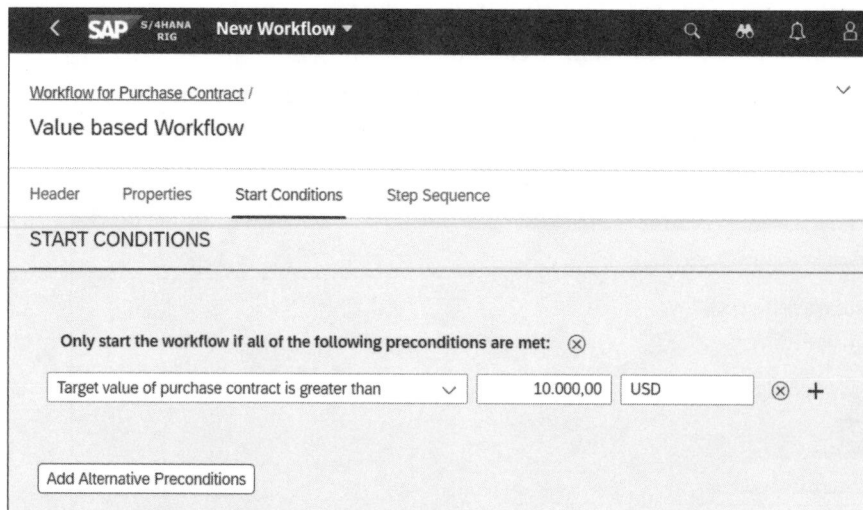

Figure 8.26 Value-Based Workflow Start Conditions

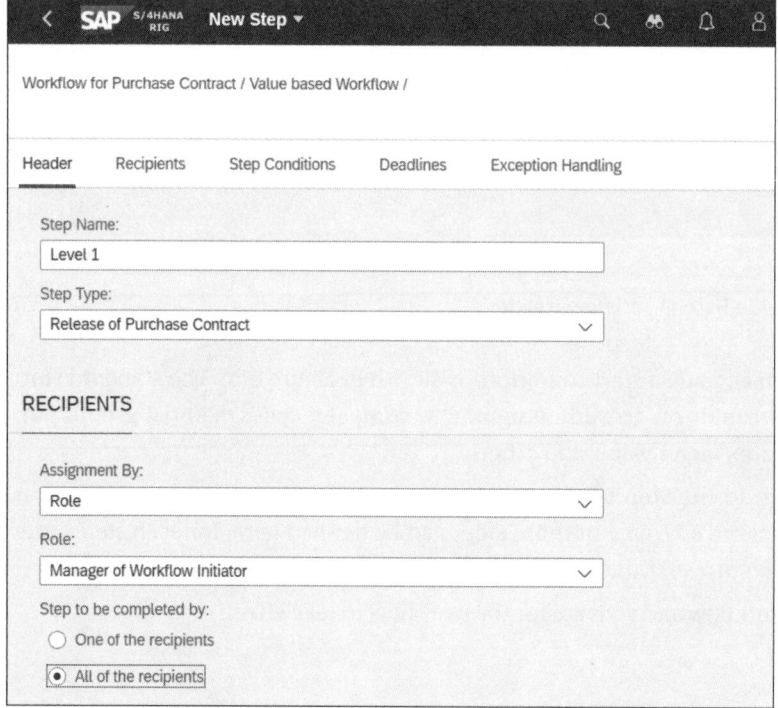

Figure 8.27 Step Sequence

8.5   Scheduling Agreement

Scheduling agreements are another form of outline purchase agreement in SAP S/4HANA. These agreements are used to procure materials over a specified period of time following a set schedule of delivery. The predetermined delivery schedules in the agreement indicate quantities of items and dates of delivery. Conditions can be maintained at the header level, which applies to all the items, or at the item level, which applies only to a specific item. These agreements have the account assignment function, which allows the buyer to allocate costs by maintaining details of controlling objects at the item level within the document at the time of creation.

The benefits of using scheduling agreements include the following:

- Shorten processing times and reduce the amount of paperwork required otherwise
- Delivery schedule can replace a large number of discrete purchase orders or contract release orders
- Reduced inventory
- Possible to run manufacturing operations on the just-in-time principle
- Suppliers require shorter lead times with smaller deliveries spread over a long period, resulting in better planning and efficient resource allocation for suppliers
- Scheduling agreement can work in conjunction with MRP, especially in repetitive manufacturing involving large quantities

8.5.1   Scheduling Agreement Types

Scheduling agreements types are determined by document types defined in customizing. The three document types that are predefined in the standard system are explained in the following sections. In addition to these three, it's possible to define your own custom document types depending on your business requirements. More details are provided in Section 8.6.

Scheduling Agreement with Release Document

This type of agreement is created by choosing scheduling agreement document type LPA. In this case, the schedule lines entered within the agreement aren't transmitted to the supplier at the time of creation of the agreement and are internal to the system. The schedule lines maintained in this agreement can be changed at any time during the life of the agreement, which allows some level of flexibility in scheduling procurement. Whenever a scheduling agreement release is created, the information stored in the schedule lines is used to create and transmit the releases to the supplier. Two types of releases available with this type of scheduling agreement (LPA) are the forecast delivery schedule (FRC) and the just-in-time delivery schedule. The release documentation generated in this process provides information about the releases transmitted to the supplier over a set period.

Scheduling Agreement without Release Document

This type of agreement is created by choosing scheduling agreement document type LP. The scheduling lines created in this type of agreement are external and official. This means that the scheduling lines are transmitted to the supplier as soon as they're created. Also, there is no release documentation associated with this agreement.

Stock Transport Scheduling Agreement

If a company is procuring materials internally from another plant on a regular basis, it's possible to set up a stock transport scheduling agreement by choosing document type LU at the time of creation. SAP standard uses item category U (Stock Transfer) for this type of agreement.

8.5.2   Creating Scheduling Agreements

Scheduling agreements can be created manually or by referencing purchasing documents such as purchase requisitions, RFQs/quotations, other scheduling agreements, or centrally agreed-upon contracts. It's possible to create a scheduling agreement by copying any one of the purchasing documents and then making changes before saving the agreement.

8.5.3   Manage Scheduling Agreement

The Manage Scheduling Agreement SAP Fiori app provides the capability to search and filter scheduling agreements by purchasing organization, agreement type, supplier, material, status, validity period, and more. It allows the user to display, copy, edit, create, and delete scheduling agreements. It's possible to maintain schedule lines within scheduling agreements. The app also highlights those scheduling agreements that are expiring soon and allows the user to renew them by clicking the **Renew Agreement** button, as shown in Figure 8.28.

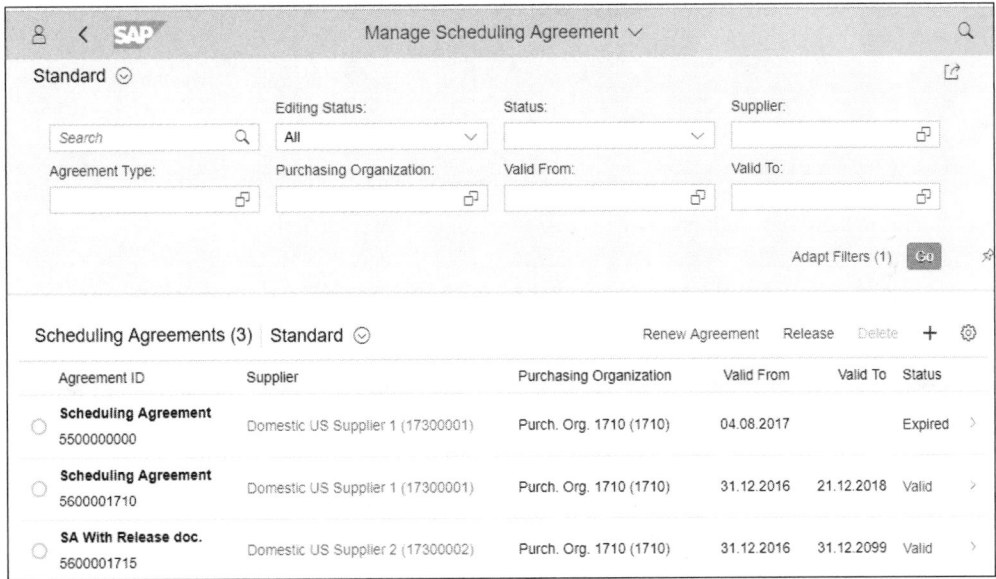

Figure 8.28 Manage Scheduling Agreement

To create a new scheduling agreement, proceed as follows:

1. Log on to the SAP Fiori launchpad and click the tile for the Manage Scheduling Agreement app.

2. Click the **Create** button to bring up the input screen for creating a new scheduling agreement.

3. Enter an agreement type, validity dates, a purchasing organization, and a supplier under the **General Information** tab, as shown in Figure 8.29.

Figure 8.29 Scheduling Agreement Header General Information

4. Scroll down and enter payment terms, a target value, and incoterms under the **Delivery and Payment** tab, as shown in Figure 8.30.

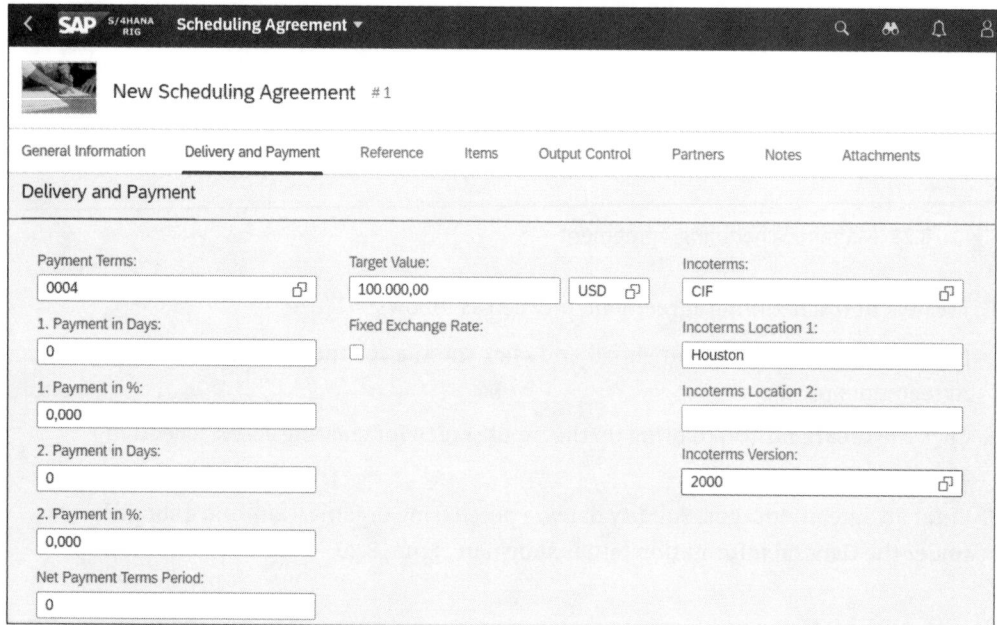

Figure 8.30 Delivery and Payment

5. Enter reference information such as quotation info and salesperson, if applicable, under the **Reference** tab.

6. Scroll down to the **Items** tab and click the **Create** button to bring up the **Item Details** page. On this page, enter the material number, plant, and storage location under the **General Information** tab and the target quantity and price under the **Quantity And Price** tab, as shown in Figure 8.31.

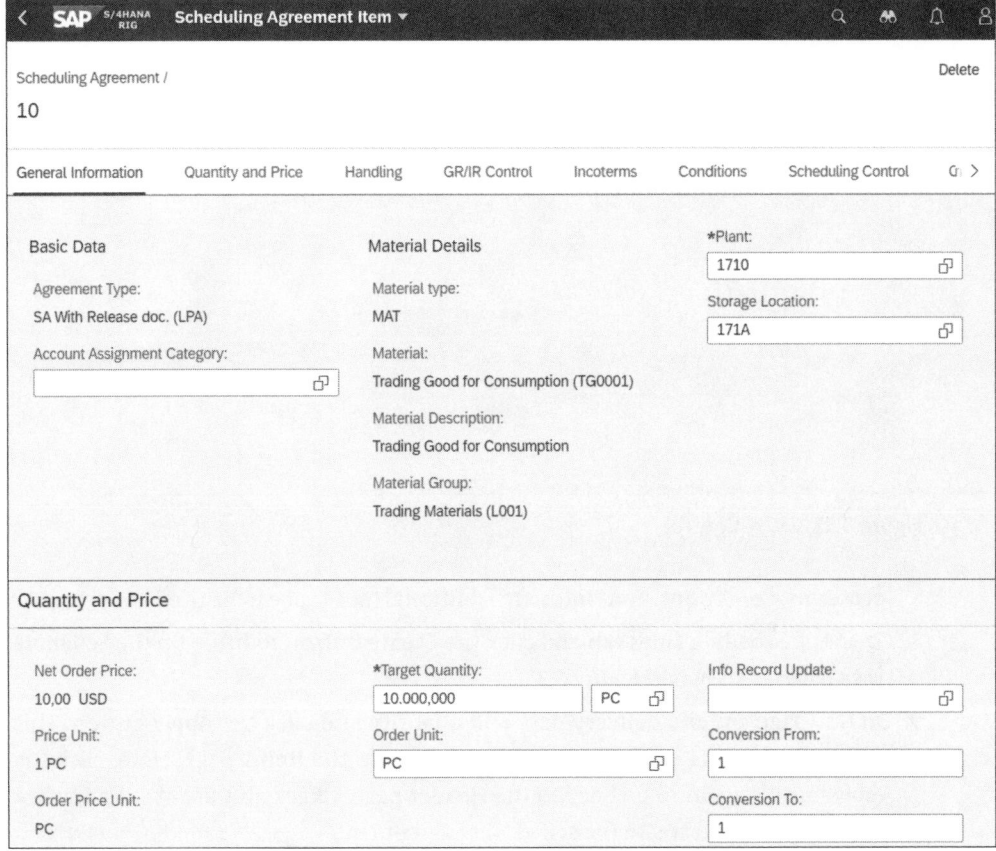

Figure 8.31 Scheduling Agreement Item

7. Scroll down and enter the tolerance and GR/IR requirements under the **GR/IR Control** tab, as shown in Figure 8.32.

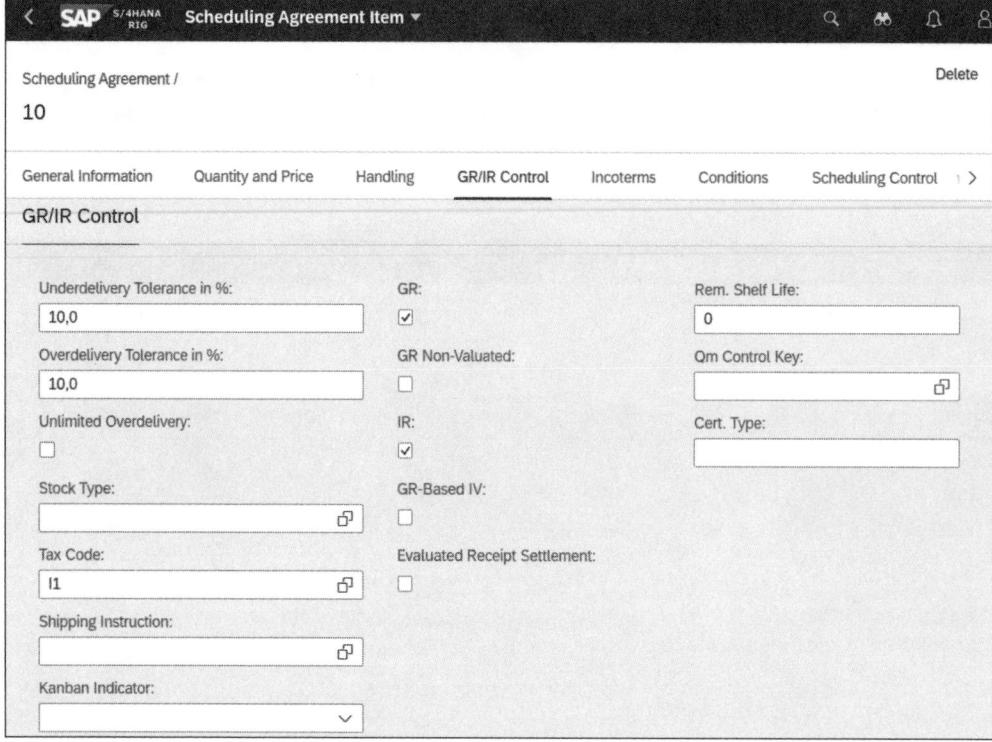

Figure 8.32 GR/IR Control

Incoterms, Conditions, and Notes are additional tabs that can be used as necessary.

8. Go to the **Schedule Lines** tab and click the **Create** button to bring up the **Schedule Lines** page, as shown in Figure 8.33.

9. On this page, enter a delivery date and quantity and click the **Apply** button. This will apply the data entered and take you back to the **Items** page. Here, click the **Apply** button again to go back to the **Header** page. Check all the entries and click the **Save** button to create the scheduling agreement.

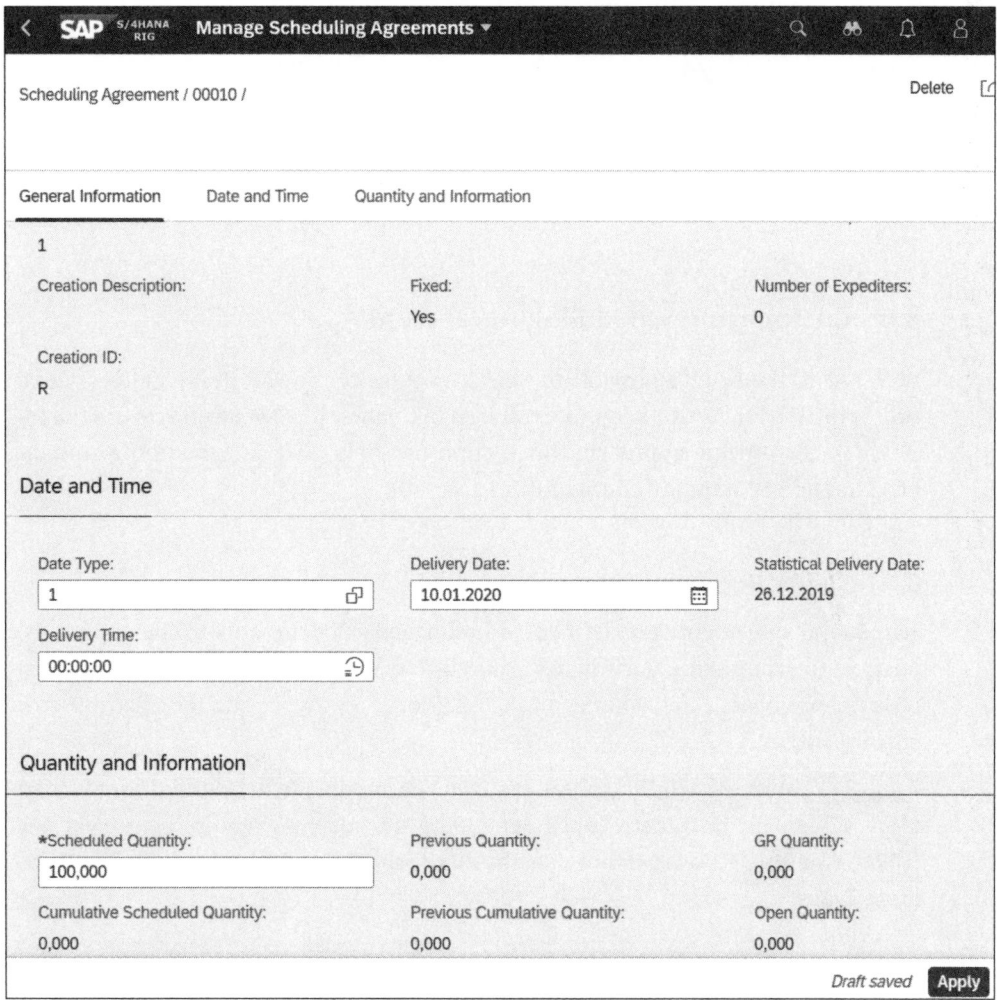

Figure 8.33 Schedule Lines

Note

The following is a list of GUI transactions for which apps are available in SAP Fiori:

- Display Scheduling Agreement (Transaction ME33L)
- Create Scheduling Agreement (Transaction ME31L)
- Display Scheduling Agreement Schedule (Transaction ME39)
- Change Scheduling Agreement (Transaction ME32L)

- Print Scheduling Agreement (Transaction ME9L)
- Print Scheduling Agreement Releases (Transaction ME9E)
- Create Scheduling Agreement Releases (Transaction ME84)
- Create Transport Scheduling Agreement (Transaction ME37)
- Release Scheduling Agreement (Transaction ME35L)

8.6   Customizing Scheduling Agreements

With SAP S/4HANA, it's possible to take advantage of the SAP Best Practices activation approach for customizing, as explained in Chapter 2. However, if you use the traditional customizing approach, this section can help. This information also helps validate the SAP standard configuration.

8.6.1   Define Document Types

Scheduling agreements are defined and managed as documents in the system. It's possible to group these documents under different document types based on business requirements. First, you need to define document types and their attributes in customizing.

Table 8.3 provides the SAP-standard settings; it's possible to define additional scheduling agreement document types depending on business requirements, via **IMG (SPRO)** • **Materials Management** • **Purchasing** • **Scheduling Agreement** • **Define Document Types**.

Field Name	Value (First Entry)	Value (Second Entry)	Value (Third Entry)
Type	LPA	LP	LU
Doc. Type Description	SA With Release Doc.	Scheduling Agreement	Stock Trans. Sch. Agreement
Item Number Interval	10	10	10
Number Range—Internal	55	55	55

Table 8.3 Define Document Types

Field Name	Value (First Entry)	Value (Second Entry)	Value (Third Entry)
Number Range—External	56	56	56
Update Group Statistics	SAP	Blank	SAP
Field Selection Key	LPL	Blank	LUL
Control	Blank	Blank	T
Time-Dependent Conditions	Checked	Unchecked	Checked
Release Document	Checked	Unchecked	Unchecked

Table 8.3 Define Document Types (Cont.)

New number ranges may also be defined and used as required. This step generally is required if new document types are defined in the previous step. The menu path for creating number ranges is **IMG (SPRO)** • **Materials Management** • **Purchasing** • **Scheduling Agreement** • **Define Number Ranges**.

8.6.2   Allowed Item Categories

After defining the document types for scheduling agreements, select the line for the **Doc Type** and double-click **Allowed Item Categories**. On the **Admissible Item Categories for Document Type** screen, maintain the item categories as needed from the list in Table 8.4. These item categories can be configured depending on business requirements. This configuration determines what item categories can be selected for a given document type by the business user while creating the scheduling agreement.

Item Category	Description	Use Case
Blank	Standard	Default
K	Consignment	When scheduling agreement is created for consignment materials
L	Subcontracting	When scheduling agreement is created for subcontracting activities

Table 8.4 Item Categories in Scheduling Agreements

Item Category	Description	Use Case
U	Stock transfer	Can be used only with document type LU (Stock Transfer Scheduling Agreement)

Table 8.4 Item Categories in Scheduling Agreements (Cont.)

Now, select the line for each **Item Category** and double-click **Link Purchase Requisition-Document Type**. On the **Change View "Link Purchase Requisition-Document Type": Overview** screen, define the allowed follow on documents.

8.6.3   Maintain Release Creation Profile

A *release creation profile* is used to determine the period in which releases (types of delivery schedule) are generated against a scheduling agreement and transmitted to the vendor. This also controls the creation periodicity of the releases; the aggregation of scheduled quantities, starting from the day after release creation; and the implementation of a tolerance check. In this step, a release creation profile is maintained for scheduling agreements with a release document. This profile determines the release creation strategy and how backlog and immediate requirements are considered in the release creation. To maintain the release creation profile, navigate to **IMG (SPRO)** • **Materials Management** • **Purchasing** • **Scheduling Agreement** • **Maintain Release Creation Profile for SA with Release Document**.

The following criteria also can be set up in the profile:

- **Aggregation and release horizon**
  If and how delivery schedules are to be aggregated with the release creation
- **Release creation periodicity**
  The frequency with which scheduling agreement releases are generated
- **Tolerance profile**
  For releases that need to be generated because of changed delivery schedules, a tolerance check is carried out
- **Last goods receipts**
  If and how last inbound deliveries and goods receipts are determined and outputted during the release creation

- **Internet release**
  If, during the release creation, internet releases are to be generated

- **Printing with Smart Forms**
  Which additional information in scheduling agreement releases is outputted if you use the ISAUTO_ESCR_FRC_JIT print form, based on Smart Forms

- **Criteria for dynamic stopping**
  On the basis of which criteria scheduling agreement releases are subject to dynamic stopping

> **Note**
>
> For more customizing steps, such as the following, Section 8.4. The explanation provided for contracts apply to scheduling agreements as well:
>
> - Release procedure for scheduling agreements
> - Define screen layout at document level
> - Texts for scheduling agreements
> - Set up authorization check for general ledger accounts

8.7   Summary

Contract management is a core area for procurement organizations. Without an existing agreement in place, it's difficult to drive disciplined pricing and terms. Contracts can be tied to catalog items to underpin a clear ordering process and UX, representing a model way to conduct corporate purchasing. SAP S/4HANA updates many older transaction codes and screens with SAP Fiori apps, but much of the setup and configuration remains the same. However, there are now shortcuts in the form of SAP Best Practices activation, which automatically sets up standard functionality in the system.

Having the functionality to craft agreements with suppliers is half of the equation. The other half is finding the right supplier for each these agreements. The next chapter will focus on enterprise contract management and assembly.

Chapter 9

Enterprise Contract Management and Assembly

SAP S/4HANA Cloud for enterprise contract management and assembly is a suite of applications designed and developed for the creation and governance of legal content in enterprises. It can be integrated into all core business processes, such as procurement processes, sales and distribution and internal policies, and intercompany agreements.

SAP S/4HANA Cloud for enterprise contract management and assembly provides a central repository for all legal documents, such as contracts, policies, and nondisclosure agreements. This solution provides the capability to trace both internal and external tasks, signatures, and responsibilities. In this chapter, we'll cover the features and functionalities provided by this solution and the SAP Fiori apps for process executions. We've provided the customizing steps required in SAP S/4HANA for implementation of this solution.

SAP offers this solution to create and manage legal content in an organization. This offering comprises two innovative solutions to manage enterprise contracts and other legal content across the enterprise: SAP S/4HANA cloud for enterprise contract management and SAP S/4HANA Cloud for enterprise contract assembly are seamlessly integrated here.

9.1 What Is Enterprise Contract Management and Assembly?

Legal content in SAP S/4HANA includes contracts, agreements, security policies, and other documents with legal significance in an organization. Such content is generated throughout an enterprise as part of different business processes, including procurement and sales and distribution. Legal content could include company policies and intercompany agreements as well. The SAP S/4HANA Cloud for enterprise contract management and assembly intelligent solution is designed and developed for the creation and management of legal content in enterprises This solution allows such legal content to be integrated into the core business processes of SAP S/4HANA and also provides the ability to store the content in a single repository. This means that an organization has complete control over all the legal content relevant to the company. Some of the challenges faced by businesses today in enterprise contract management include distributed repositories for storage of legal content, lack of comprehensive search capabilities, unstructured content in multiple formats, no consistent risk and compliance management, inefficient or unclear workflow in document processing, and content management in silos within the organization.

The new approach with enterprise contract management in SAP is to provide a central layer for legal content within SAP S/4HANA. The concept is to use legal content as master data and allow all information to follow the same data structure and be categorized semantically. This makes it possible to create and reuse text blocks and adapt to changing regulations and business needs.

The new features offered within enterprise contract management are as follows:

- Single repository for all legal documents
- Search for legal content (e.g., contracts)
- Request a new contract
- Manage different versions of legal documents
- Upload of a signed contract into a contract repository
- Monitor contracts (e.g., expiration, open issues)
- Link legal content to an operational real estate contract
- Link legal content to an operational purchase contract
- Link legal content to an RFQ
- Trigger/create workflows for reviewing, informing, approving and process legal content
- Collaborate internally
- Send reminders about action items for managed contracts
- Manage contract relationship hierarchies
- Save all contract related documentation and communication together with the contracts
- Standardize contract management scenarios

Enterprise contract management provides the following SAP Fiori applications designed for creation and management of legal content in enterprises that can be integrated into all core business processes:

- Enterprise Contract Management Overview (Legal Content Overview)
- Manage Contexts
- Request Legal Content
- Manage Legal Transactions
- Categories
- Manage Legal Documents
- Manage Legal Tasks

We'll discuss these apps in the following sections.

9.2   Enterprise Contract Management Overview App

This page provides an overview of the most critical tasks in just one screen based on the data from the underlying apps. It allows you to analyze and identify upcoming important dates, reminders, and transactions and take necessary action directly from the cards. It also includes actionable cards, which show critical information such as expiration, risk, or status. For example, the Legal Transactions with Open Issues card shows the transactions that are at risk and allows you to take the necessary action from the card.

Login to SAP Fiori Launchpad, navigate to the Enterprise Contract Management Overview app, and click its tile to execute the app. Click the header of any card to open it. You can click any item shown within the card to go directly to the item details. Different cards may have varying significance to different users. By dragging and dropping, you can rearrange the cards within the initial page of the app and customize the overview page according to your needs and responsibilities.

All the cards provided by default on the overview page may not be required for all the users. Depending on their needs, users can hide or show a card by following these steps:

1. In the shell bar (uppermost section of the SAP Fiori launchpad), select the **User** icon and select **Manage Cards** (Figure 9.1).

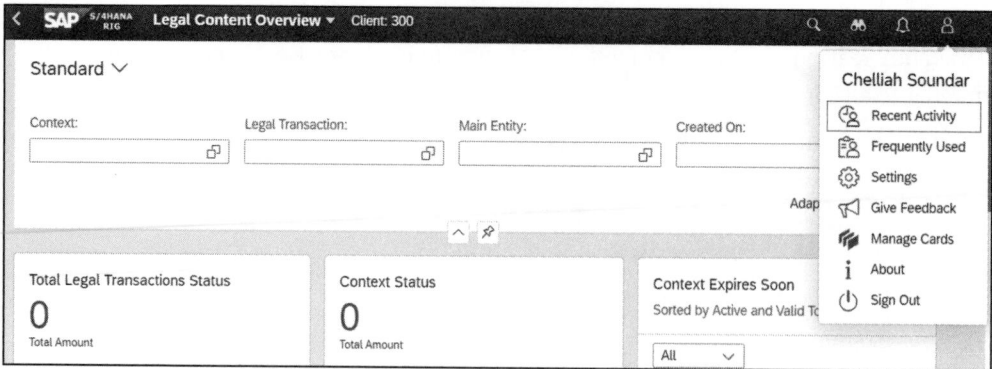

Figure 9.1 Manage Cards

2. This will bring up the Manage Cards screen (Figure 9.2). Use the switch control to hide or show the relevant card. Select **OK**.

3. To reset the view to the default settings, select **Restore** in the **Manage Cards** window (Figure 9.2).

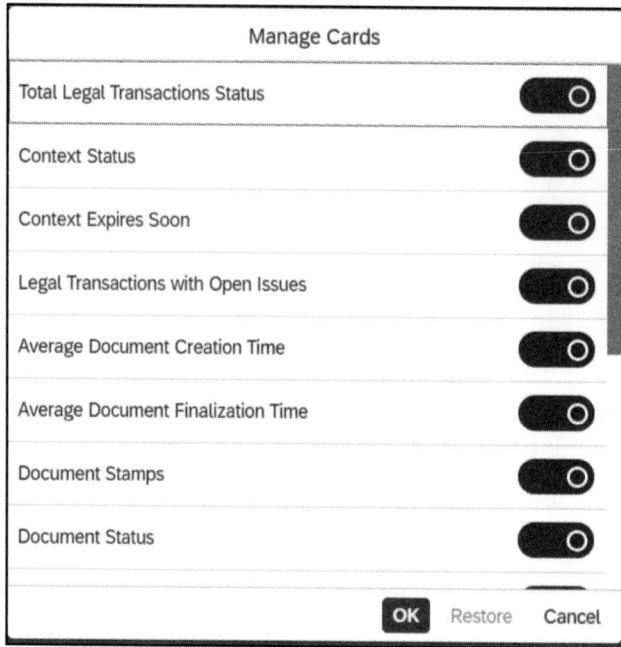

Figure 9.2 Show or Hide Card

The displayed information can be filtered by applying the available filters, such as **Contexts, Legal Transaction**, and **Main Entity**. These filters will apply to all relevant cards. For example, you can filter the content of all cards according to a specific legal context or main entity by choosing the respective filters.

The following cards are available in this app:

- **Context Expires Soon**
  Displays expiring contexts sorted by earliest **Valid To** date.

- **Legal Transactions with Open Issues**
  Displays legal transactions that are at risk sorted by the creation date of the legal transaction.

- **Legal Transaction Status**
  Displays the total number of legal transactions and a pie chart showing the status of legal transactions for the current quarter. By clicking each of the status segments in the pie chart, you can display the list of those specific transactions within the Manage Legal Transactions app.

- **Context Status**
  Displays the total number of contexts and a pie chart showing the status of the contexts for the current quarter. By clicking each of the status segments in the pie chart, you can display the list of those specific contexts within the Manage Contexts app.

- **Document Stamps**
  Displays the total number of legal documents that have been stamped and a pie chart showing the total stamp names of such documents for the current quarter. By clicking each of the statuses in the pie chart, you can display the list of those specific documents within the Manage Legal Documents app.

- **Document Status**
  Displays the total number of legal documents and a pie chart showing the status of the documents for the current quarter. By clicking each of the statuses in the pie chart, you can display the list of those specific documents within the Manage Legal Documents app.

- **Open Documents**
  Displays the total number of open documents out of the overall documents sorted by the **Created** or **In Process** status. By clicking the **View All** link, you can display the list report of Manage Legal Documents, with all documents filtered based on the status **In Process** or **Created**. If you click the object stream of this stack of cards,

9

you can display the open documents. From here, you can edit or download these documents.

- **Signed and Accepted Documents**
  Displays the total number of documents with status **Accepted** and total number of documents that have the stamp **Signed**, sorted by date and time

- **Upcoming Dates**
  Displays the upcoming dates of the legal transactions, sorted by earliest transaction first.

- **Upcoming Reminders**
  Displays legal transactions for which reminders have been set and their reminder types and dates, sorted by earliest reminder date first.

- **Average Document Creation Time**
  Displays average time taken to create legal documents per quarter.

- **Average Document Finalization Time**
  Displays average time taken to finalize a legal document per quarter.

- **Pending Tasks of My Legal Transaction**
  Displays legal workflow tasks that are pending. The display list is grouped by legal transaction. This card also displays the total number of pending tasks and the tasks completed in the current year, last six months, or last 30 days.

- **Average Task Processing Time**
  Displays average time taken to process each workflow task per quarter, based on task types. This card also displays the total number of tasks processed in a year and the number of tasks processed in a day.

- **Task Completion**
  Displays the number of tasks completed per quarter, based on task types and the total number of tasks completed in a year.

9.2.1   Manage Contexts

This app helps create and manage context used as a template when creating a legal transaction. Context covers a particular business scenario, such as procurement or sales and distribution processes, and provides a foundation for how a legal transaction is processed and what kind of information needs to be provided. Login to the SAP Fiori launchpad, navigate to the Manage Contexts app, and click its tile to execute the app.

This app displays existing contexts and allows for filtering/search by **Context** ID, **Owner**, **Status**, **Editing Status**, and validity dates, as shown in Figure 9.3.

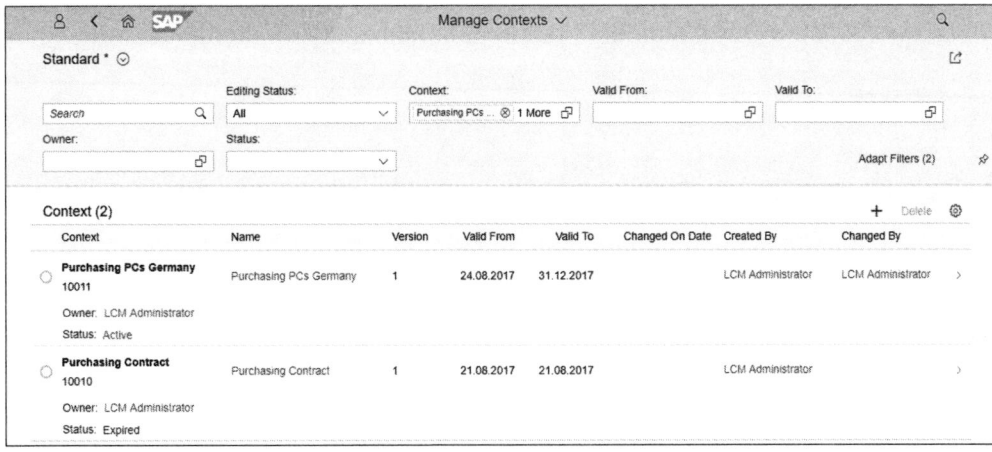

Figure 9.3 Manage Contexts

The following functions are provided in the app:

- **Live update function**
  The list of contexts in the content area is updated immediately when a user changes the filter criteria.

- **Deleting contexts**
  Select a context and delete it directly from the list. Deleting a context is possible only if it isn't yet assigned to a legal transaction.

- **Personalization of the table settings**
  Display additional columns and rearrange the order of the displayed columns.

- **Creating contexts**
  From this app, create a new context by clicking the **+** sign (**Create Object**). As shown in Figure 9.4, first the header and general information are filled in, and then the required information is provided in all the tabs:

  - Under the **Categories** tab, enter the categories that describe the business scenario covered by the context.

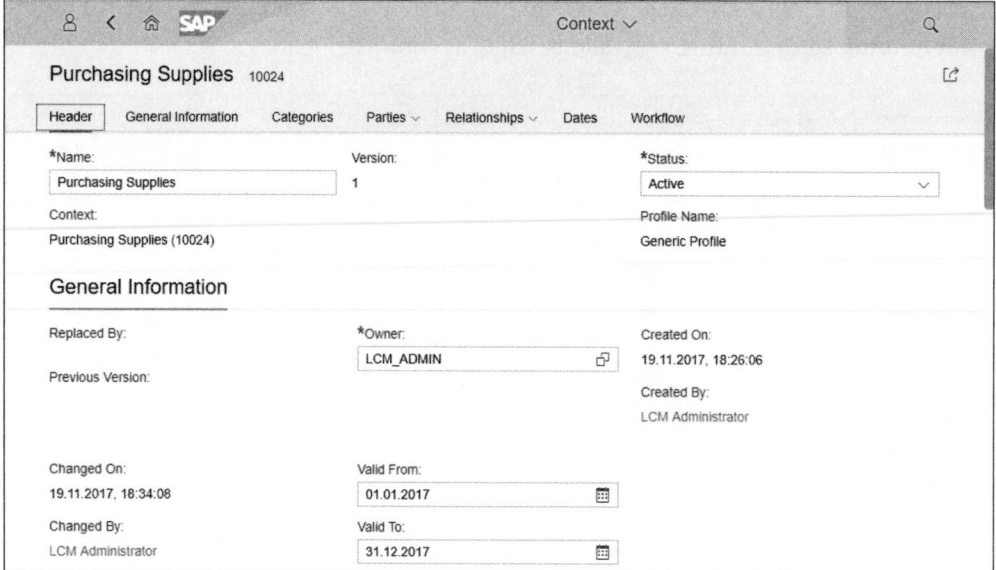

Figure 9.4 Create Context

- In the **Parties** section, define the parties involved in the business scenario represented by this context. Parties can be entities such as suppliers or purchase organizations, internal contacts, and external contacts. Entities marked as **Main Entity** in the context are mandatory and can't be deleted in the legal transaction process.

- In the **Relationships** section, define the legal transactions used in the business scenario covered by this context. For example, in a context for a supplier contract, a legal transaction for the purchase order may be considered a relationship.

- In the **Dates** tab, enter timelines and milestones for the business scenario covered by this context.

- It's possible to define a simple release or even a complex workflow process under the **Workflow** tab.

- **Editing contexts**

  From the list of contexts displayed in the Manage Contexts app, you can navigate to the item details and review or edit the context. Here, you can add, display, edit, or remove categories, parties, relationships, workflow steps, and dates. Depending on the type of change, a new version of the context can be created.

9.2.2   Categories for Legal Content

This app displays existing categories and allows for filtering/search by **Category** ID, **Type**, **Status**, and so on, as shown in Figure 9.5. This SAP Fiori app can be accessed from the SAP Fiori launchpad by clicking its tile.

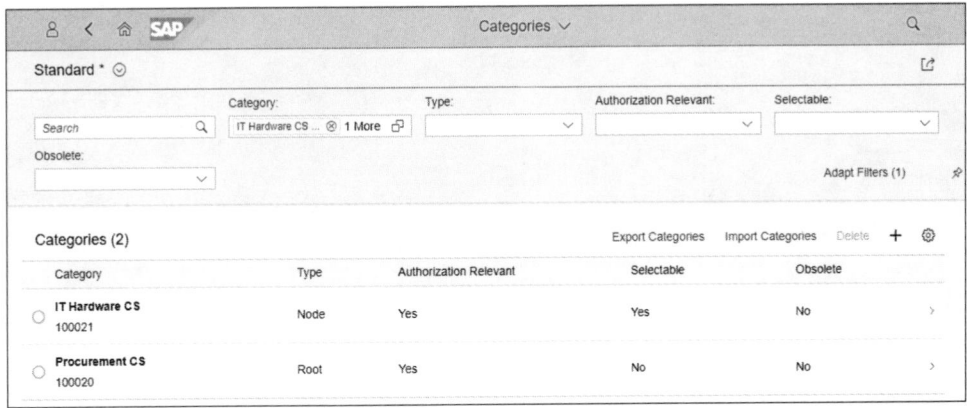

Figure 9.5 Categories for Legal Content

By clicking the **Create** button, you can create new categories. By clicking any of the categories listed, you can go to the details of the category and make changes as needed and also add or edit children categories. The delete function is also available on the initial page of the app. From the initial page on which all the categories are listed, you can export the categories to an Excel file. The app allows import of categories as well.

The categories created in this app can be used in the Manage Context, Request Legal Content, and Manage Legal Transactions apps.

9.2.3   Request Legal Content

This app allows a user to submit a request for a legal content. The app comes with an intuitive wizard to take you through a multistep process of providing necessary information and submitting a request for legal content. Based on the information provided through this app, a legal transaction is created and sent to the responsible person or team for further processing. This app allows you to add or remove documents and mark a document as mandatory or nonmandatory. It's also possible to upload an attachment through this app. This SAP Fiori app can be started from the SAP Fiori launchpad by clicking the **Request Legal Content** tile.

The steps involved in submitting a request for legal content are as follows:

1. **Basic Data**

   Enter a **Name** and choose a **Context ID** (as shown in Figure 9.6). This should have already been created in the Manage Contexts app. The context selected here provides information for the following steps based on the template of the context.

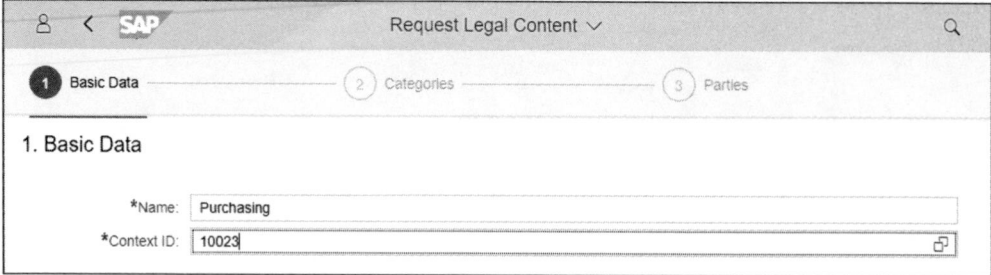

Figure 9.6 Request Legal Content: Step 1

2. **Categories**

   The **Group**, **Path**, and **Category** are filled in based on the context (see Figure 9.7). If the category is marked as **Required**, it can't be removed or changed. However, the user can add additional categories if needed.

Figure 9.7 Request Legal Content: Step 2

3. **Parties**

   Parties are entities such as customers or vendors, internal contacts such as purchase managers or legal counsels, or external contacts such as contact persons or signing authorities (see Figure 9.8). If the context selected in step 1 has predefined parties, the system adds those parties automatically. It isn't possible to remove main or required entities, but it's possible to add additional parties.

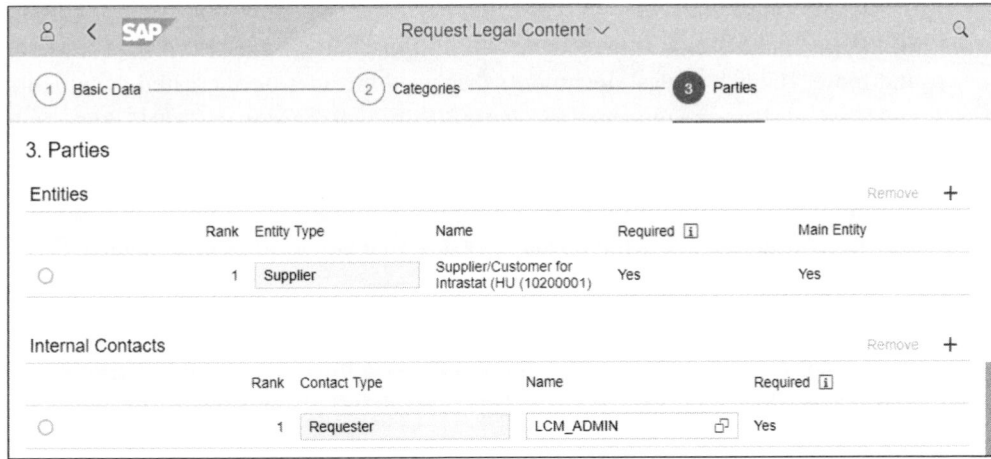

Figure 9.8 Request Legal Content: Step 3

4. **Relationship**
   Add relationships in this step. Based on the type of the legal request—for example, a nondisclosure agreement—enter the legal transaction that deals with the master agreement.

5. **Dates**
   Enter dates, such as the start date, end date, or renewal date, in this step.

6. **Review**
   Once all the information needed for the legal content request has been entered, the user can review all the entries in this step and correct or update as needed.

Depending on the context selected in step 1, the overall number of steps can vary. If, for example, no relationships are predefined in the context, step 4 won't be shown in the wizard. It's possible to add relationships if needed at a later stage after the legal transaction is created from this legal request.

Now the legal content request is submitted. At this point, the system creates a legal transaction based on the request. This legal transaction will be available in the work-list of the Manage Legal Transactions app.

9.2.4   Manage Legal Documents

Log in to SAP Fiori launchpad, navigate to the Manage Legal Documents app, and click its tile to execute the app. When this app is started, a list of available legal documents is displayed, together with the filter bar, which includes filters such as **Editing Status**, **Document**, **Legal Transaction**, **Content Type**, **Access Level**, **Main Organization**, and more. The list of legal documents displayed includes both created documents and the ones that were uploaded as a static file through the Manage Legal Transaction app.

This app provides the following capabilities and features:

- Select any document from the list displayed that you want to download and click the **Download** button to download the document.

- Select a document and click the **Send for e-Sign** button to send the document for e-signature. Enterprise contract management is integrated with the e-signature provider DocuSign, which allows legal documents to be sent to the DocuSign account.

- This app shows the e-signature status of a legal document in the header section of the document.

- From inside a legal document, the user can edit the document and cancel the e-sign process if the signature isn't needed.

- The app allows users to delete legal documents.

9.2.5   Manage Legal Tasks

This app helps manage the legal workflow tasks that are in the user's inbox. The workflow tasks are grouped per legal transaction from where these tasks were triggered. You can launch this app from the SAP Fiori Launchpad, the steps are as follows:

1. When you open the app, it displays the workflow tasks and allows you to filter by **Task Type**, **Processor**, **Agent Role**, **Status**, **Processed On**, and **Last Notified On**.

2. From the initial page of the app, you can open any of the legal tasks that are listed by clicking it. Once the legal task details are displayed, you can forward the task to another agent if the current agent is unavailable. Notes can be added for the receiving agent while forwarding the task.

3. From the initial list page, key users can notify the responsible agent about tasks that are pending or those tasks that are about to expire. This action can be performed from within the task as well.

4. By clicking a task, the user can view its details in the object page. The object page provides the details under different tabs, such as **General Information, Related Task, Agents** (details of the agents who have processed this task), **Notified On**, and **Comments**.

9.2.6   Manage Legal Transactions

This app is used to manage a legal transaction through its lifecycle. It's possible to define the renewal and termination dates for legal transactions using this feature. In addition, the app offers a situation handling feature to define situations to notify the legal counsel when the status synchronization of a legal transaction has failed and should be processed to ensure successful synchronization. The app displays existing legal transactions and allows filtering/search by **Legal Transaction Number, Context, Editing Status, Created By, Changed By, Health** (status), and so on, as shown in Figure 9.9.

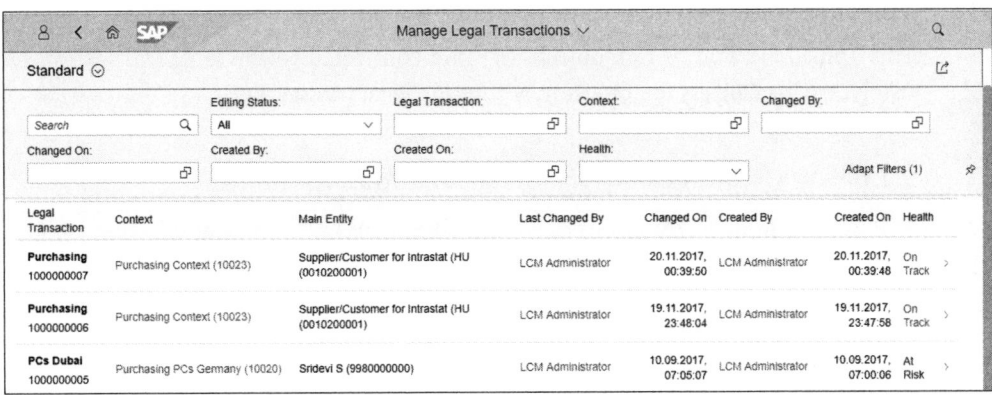

Figure 9.9 Manage Legal Transactions

The display columns of the results can be personalized by rearranging columns or showing additional columns. From the list displayed, it's possible to navigate to individual legal transactions and edit them as well. From within the legal transaction, it's possible to create a task and start the workflow. A **History** function to display the change log for the legal transaction is also provided in this app. Figure 9.10 shows the **Edit** view of an existing legal transaction; it allows the user to navigate to tabs for **Categories, Parties, Relationships, Dates, Reminders**, and **Tasks** and to edit data. From the **Documents** tab, it's possible to add documents to the legal transaction.

Figure 9.10 Edit Legal Transaction

From the initial page of the app, you can select an existing transaction and create a reference transaction by clicking the **Create with Reference** button. This defines a relationship and ensures traceability between the source and reference transactions.

From the initial page of the app, you can select an existing legal transaction and use the **Copy** button to create a new legal transaction.

This app allows you to link objects that are connected to the legal transaction by using the **Link Objects** feature from within the legal transaction.

9.2.7   SAP S/4HANA Cloud for Enterprise Contract Assembly

SAP S/4HANA Cloud for enterprise contract assembly is a new application on SAP Cloud Platform. This cloud solution lets you create and manage the complete lifecycle of templates and text blocks that can be used for generating virtual legal documents that are used in enterprise contract management. This solution offers the legal experts of the enterprise a way to create and manage clauses and templates for the creation of legal content. It integrates seamlessly into SAP S/4HANA Cloud for enterprise contract management and enables the automatic assembly of legal contracts and other legal documents based on clauses and templates developed by legal experts. The integration of SAP S/4HANA Cloud for enterprise contract management with SAP S/4HANA Cloud for enterprise contract assembly enables the business to integrate with all core business processes.

Manage Templates

This SAP Fiori app is available within the SAP S/4HANA Cloud for enterprise contract assembly solution. To access this app, log in to the SAP Fiori launchpad, navigate to the Manage Templates app, and click its tile. The Manage Templates app enables the user to create and manage both templates and text blocks.

After opening the app, you see the list view, which displays the templates that exist in the system. From this page, you can search or filter templates by **Template Name**, **Content Type**, **Governing Law**, **Language**, **Validity Dates**, and **Owner of the Template**.

Create Template

From the initial list page of the app, choose **+** (create) to create a new template. On the create page, enter a name for the template and enter the values for **Content Type** such as nondisclosure agreement, master procurement contract, and so on; **Governing Law**, such as US law, German law, and so on; **Language**; and a validity period, and click the **Create** button.

Insert Text Block

Open the template created in the previous section and click **Edit** to modify it. Click **+** (add) either from the actions bar or at the bottom of the template to open the text block library. From the dropdown menu, choose **Insert Existing Clause from Library** to open the **Text Block Library** pane on the right side of the screen. Search for and find the required text block from the available list and select it by clicking the checkbox next to the text block title. You will see a preview of the text block within the template at your cursor position. Check the preview and choose **Insert**. This action will insert the selected text block into the template at the cursor position. Then choose **Save** to save the template.

Create Text Block

A text block is a passage of text with a specific meaning that can be used in a template or a document. From the initial page of the Manage Templates app, open a template and choose **Show Library**. Then click **+** (create text block) which opens a pop-up screen for **New Clause**. Enter a title and enter required values, then click the **Create** button. That will create a new text block that will be added to the text block library. This text block will be available from the library in the future to insert into a template.

9.3   Customizing Enterprise Contract Management

Enterprise contract management requires some basic customizing to be done in the SAP S/4HANA system. The functionalities explained in the previous section work based on the values maintained in this section. We've provided the details of the standard settings and values, but it's possible to customize the system according to varying business requirements. For example, the business object types defined here are for the purpose of classifying object types to meet business requirements and context.

9.3.1   Number Ranges

At the time of creation of legal transactions, contexts, categories, and documents, the system assigns IDs. These IDs are assigned base on the range maintained in this customizing step. SAP-standard number ranges are shown in Table 9.1. These values are maintained via the following menu path: **IMG (SPRO) • Legal Content Management • General Settings • Number Ranges • Maintain Number Ranges for Legal Transactions/ Maintain Number Ranges for Contexts/Maintain Number Ranges for Categories/ Maintain Number Ranges for Documents**.

Object	Number Range Number	From Number	To Number
Legal transactions	01	1000000000	9999999999
Contexts	01	10000	99999
Categories	01	100000	999999
Documents	01	1000000000	9999999999

Table 9.1 Maintain Number Ranges for Legal Content Management

9.3.2   Reminder Types

Reminder emails are used to manage legal transactions. In this customizing step, reminder types are defined (see Figure 9.11), and it's possible to assign email templates for each reminder type. A few basic reminder types are provided in Table 9.2. The customizing values are maintained in the system via the following menu path: **IMG (SPRO) • Legal Content Management • General Settings • Define Reminder Types**.

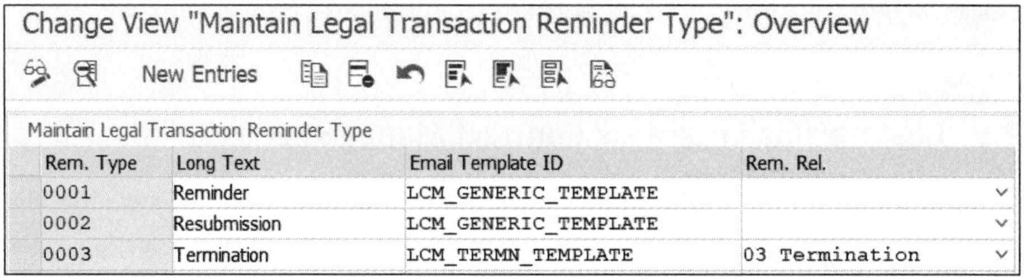

Change View "Maintain Legal Transaction Reminder Type": Overview

New Entries

Maintain Legal Transaction Reminder Type

Rem. Type	Long Text	Email Template ID	Rem. Rel.	
0001	Reminder	LCM_GENERIC_TEMPLATE		⌄
0002	Resubmission	LCM_GENERIC_TEMPLATE		⌄
0003	Termination	LCM_TERMN_TEMPLATE	03 Termination	⌄

Figure 9.11 Define Reminder Types

Field Name	Entry 1	Entry 2	Entry 3
Reminder Type	0001	0002	0003
Long Text	Reminder	Resubmission	Termination Notification
Email Template ID	LCM_GENERIC_ TEMPLATE	LCM_GENERIC_ TEMPLATE	LCM_GENERIC_ TEMPLATE

Table 9.2 Define Reminder Types

9.3.3   Date Types

Different date types are used in legal transactions, and those date types are defined in this customizing activity. It's possible to define the date as a single date or a period by marking the **True** checkbox, as shown in Figure 9.12. Set the values provided in Table 9.3 at the following menu path; the values shown in the table are only representative: **IMG (SPRO) • Legal Content Management • General Settings • Define Date Types**.

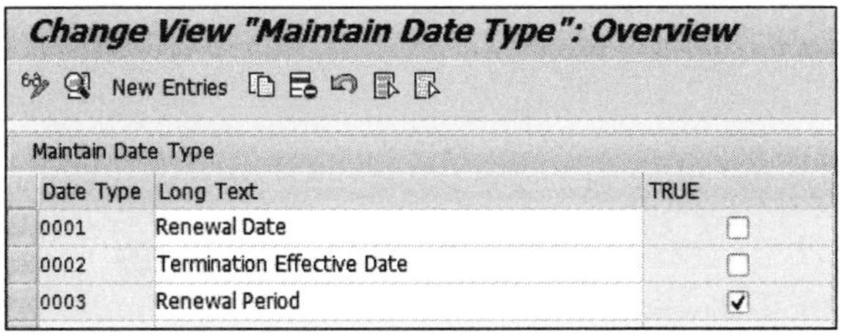

Figure 9.12 Define Date Types

Field Name	Value 1	Value 2	Value 3
Date Type	0001	0002	0003
Long Text	Renewal Date	Termination Effective Date	Renewal Period
True	Unchecked	Unchecked	Checked

Table 9.3 Define Date Types

9.3.4   Internal Contacts

In this step, the internal contact types are defined, which are assigned to the internal contacts in legal transactions (see Figure 9.13). These types determine the role of internal contacts in legal transactions. Make the necessary entries shown in Table 9.4

at the following menu path: **IMG (SPRO) • Legal Content Management • General Settings • Define Internal Contacts**.

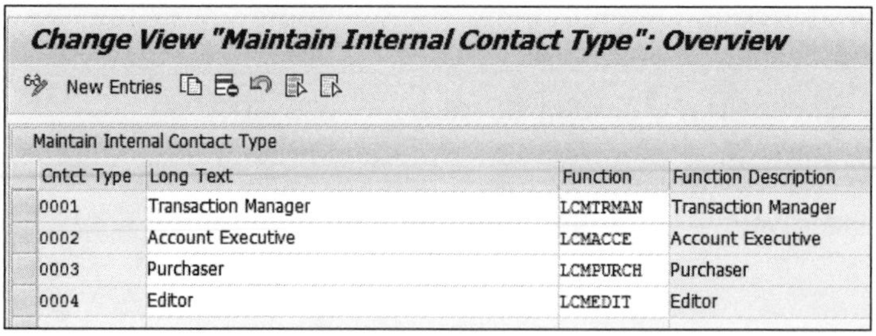

Figure 9.13 Define Internal Contact Types

Field Name	Value 1	Value 2	Value 3	Value 4
Contact Type	0001	0002	0003	0004
Long Text	Transaction Manager	Account Executive	Purchaser	Editor
Function	LCMTRMAN	LCMACCE	LCMPURCH	LCMEDIT

Table 9.4 Define Internal Contacts

9.3.5   Entity Types

An organization involved in a legal transaction in enterprise contract management is identified as an *entity* in the system. In this customizing activity, the entity types are defined, and these types are assigned to entities in a legal transaction (see Figure 9.14). The types defined here determine the role of an entity within a legal transaction. Make the necessary settings shown in Table 9.5 at the following menu path: **IMG (SPRO) • Legal Content Management • General Settings • Define Entity Types**.

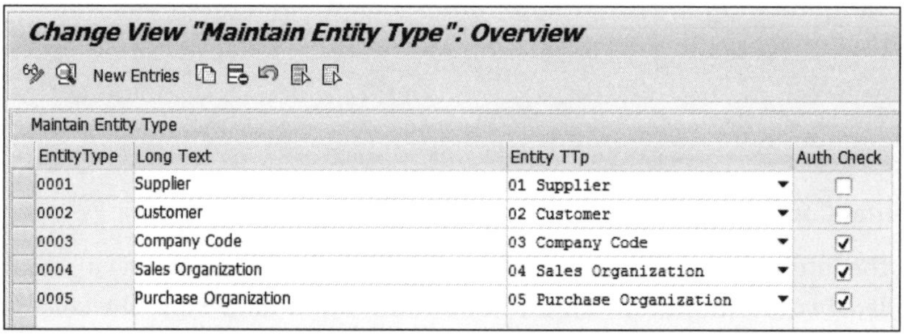

Figure 9.14 Define Entity Types

Field Name	Entity Type	Long Text	Entity Technical Type	Authorization Check
Value 1	0001	Supplier	Supplier	Unchecked
Value 2	0002	Customer	Customer	Unchecked
Value 3	0003	Company Code	Company Code	Checked
Value 4	0004	Sales Organization	Sales Organization	Checked
Value 5	0005	Purchase Organization	Purchase Organization	Checked

Table 9.5 Define Entity Types

9.3.6   External Contacts

External contact types are defined in this activity, and these types are assigned to external contacts in legal transactions. The type defined here determines the role of external contacts in legal transactions. Standard and basic values are provided in Table 9.6. Follow this menu path to complete this customizing activity: **IMG (SPRO)** • **Legal Content Management** • **General Settings** • **Define External Contacts** (see Figure 9.15).

Field Name	Value 1	Value 2	Value 3	Value 4
Contact Type	0001	0002	0003	0004
Long Text	Main Contact	Signer	Legal Contact	Account Manager

Table 9.6 Define External Contacts

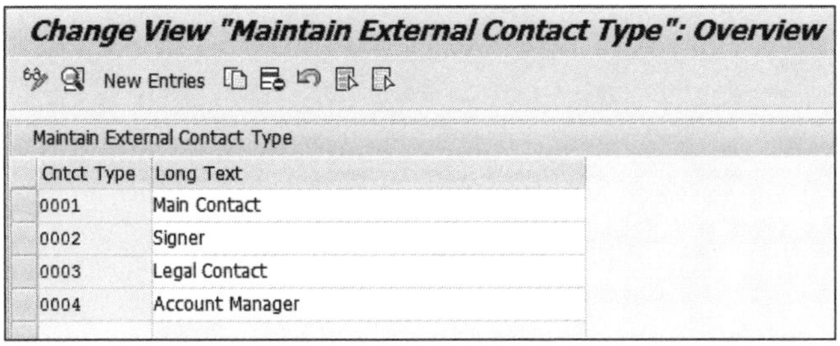

Figure 9.15 Define External Contact Types

9.3.7   Technical Types for Linked Object Types

Linked object types are defined as described in Section 9.3.8 ahead. In this section, the technical types are defined for the linked object types. Linked objects are business objects linked through a legal transaction. Table 9.7 shows the standard technical object types. To complete this step, go to **IMG (SPRO)** • **Legal Content Management** • **General Settings** • **Define Technical Types for Linked Object Types** (see Figure 9.16).

Field Name	Value 1	Value 2	Value 3	Value 4	Value 5
Lnk.Obj. Tech. Type	PC	PO	SO	SQ	RFQ
Lnk.Obj. Tech. Cat.	Internal SAP	Internal SAP	Internal SAP	Internal SAP	Internal SAP
Business Entity	I_PURCHASE-CONTRACT	I_PURCHASE-ORDER	I_SALES-ORDER	I_SALES-QUOTATION	I_REQUEST-FORQUOTA-TION
Semantic Object	Purchase-Contract	Purchase-Order	SalesOrder	Sales-Quotation	Request-ForQuota-tion
Semantic Object Attr.	PURCHASE-CONTRACT	PURCHASE-ORDER	SALES-ORDER	SALES-QUOTATION	REQUEST-FORQUOTA-TION

Table 9.7 Technical Types for Linked Object Types

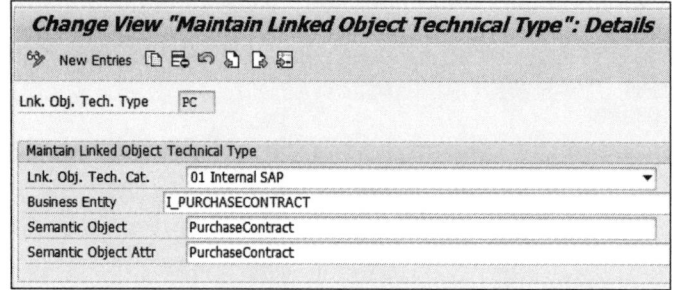

Figure 9.16 Define Technical Types for Linked Object Types

9.3.8 Linked Object Types

A linked object is a business object in the system that is linked to a legal transaction. For example, purchase orders or sales orders may be considered linked business objects for a given legal transaction. The linked object types defined here determine the purpose of the linked object within the legal transaction. The values provided in Table 9.8 are generally used for linked objects. To make the necessary settings in customizing, go to **IMG (SPRO)** • **Legal Content Management** • **General Settings** • **Define Linked Object Types** (see Figure 9.17).

Field Name	Linked Object Type	Long Text	Lnk.Obj.Tech. Type	Integration Link
Value 1	0001	Purchase Order	PO	BLANK
Value 2	0002	Purchase Contract	PC	Purchase Contract
Value 3	0003	Request for Quotation (RFQ)	RFQ	Reference for Quotation
Value 4	0004	Sales Order	SO	BLANK
Value 5	0005	Sales Quotation	SQ	BLANK

Table 9.8 Define Linked Object Types

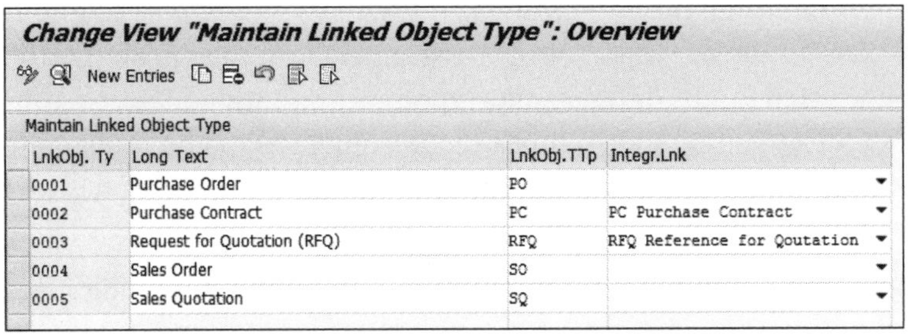

Figure 9.17 Define Linked Object Types

9.3.9 Content Types

The *content type* describes the purpose of documents such as an amendment or master agreement used in legal transactions. The content types defined in this customizing step are assigned to documents from within the Manage Documents app. Enter the values provided in Table 9.9 at the following menu path: **IMG (SPRO)** • **Legal Content Management** • **Documents** • **Define Content Types**.

Field Name	Value 1	Value 2	Value 3
Content Type	AMD	MC	NDA
Long Text	Amendment	Master Contract	Nondisclosure Agreement

Table 9.9 Define Content Types

9.3.10 Document Stamps

Document stamps indicate the status of documents in enterprise contract management. Stamps defined in this customizing step can be assigned to documents in the application. Maintain the values provided in Table 9.10 via menu path **IMG (SPRO)** • **Legal Content Management** • **Documents** • **Define Document Stamps**.

Field Name	Value 1	Value 2
Stamp Name	0001	0002
Long Text	Published	Reviewed Externally

Table 9.10 Define Document Stamps

9.3.11 Profiles

The profiles defined in this step can be assigned to contexts and legal transactions in the Manage Contexts and Manage Legal Transactions apps. The profiles predefine the values that can be selected for the different data types, such as entities, internal contacts, dates, and so on, for a legal transaction. Customizing profiles and profile sets helps reduce the number of values presented for selection in the UI to the ones that are relevant for a specific business scenario.

This customizing activity has three steps to complete. In the first step, a profile set is maintained for the entity type, internal contact type, external contact type, and so on by maintaining the values provided in Table 9.11 at the following menu path: **IMG (SPRO)** • **Legal Content Management** • **Profiles** • **Define Profiles** (see Figure 9.18).

Field Name	Profile Set	Set Type	Long Text
Value 1	G1	1 Entity	Generic Entities
Value 2	G2	2 Internal Contact	Generic Internal Contacts

Table 9.11 Define Profile Set

Field Name	Profile Set	Set Type	Long Text
Value 3	G3	3 External Contact	Generic External Contacts
Value 4	G4	4 Date	Generic Dates
Value 5	G5	5 Linked Object	Generic Linked Objects
Value 6	G6	6 Reminder	Generic Reminders
Value 7	G7	7 Document Content	Generic Document Contents

Table 9.11 Define Profile Set (Cont.)

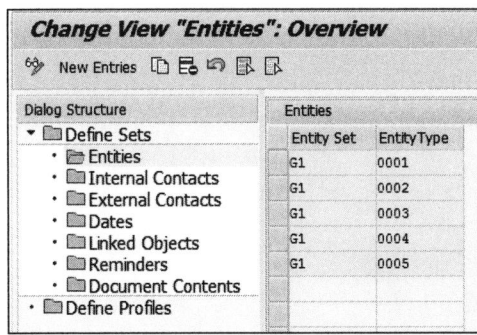

Change View "Define Sets": Overview

New Entries

Dialog Structure	Define Sets		
▼ Define Sets	Prf. Set	Set Type	Long Text
• Entities	G1	1 Entity	Generic Entities
• Internal Contacts	G2	2 Internal Contact	Generic Internal Contacts
• External Contacts	G3	3 External Contact	Generic External Contacts
• Dates	G4	4 Date	Generic Dates
• Linked Objects	G5	5 Linked Object	Generic Linked Objects
• Reminders	G6	6 Reminder	Generic Reminders
• Document Contents	G7	7 Document Content	Generic Document Contents
• Define Profiles			

Figure 9.18 Define Profile Sets

In the second step, for each profile set created—for example, G1 Entity—a list of entity types is maintained. This is achieved by selecting **Profile Set G1** and double-clicking the **Entities** node under **Define Sets** in the dialog structure (see Figure 9.19) and then maintaining the values provided in Table 9.12.

Change View "Entities": Overview

New Entries

Dialog Structure	Entities	
▼ Define Sets	Entity Set	EntityType
• Entities	G1	0001
• Internal Contacts	G1	0002
• External Contacts	G1	0003
• Dates	G1	0004
• Linked Objects	G1	0005
• Reminders		
• Document Contents		
• Define Profiles		

Figure 9.19 Define Entity Set

Field Name	Entity Set	Entity Type	Long Text
Value 1	G1	0001	Supplier
Value 2	G1	0002	Customer
Value 3	G1	0003	Company Code
Value 4	G1	0004	Sales Organization
Value 5	G1	0005	Purchase Organization

Table 9.12 Define Entity Set

This step is repeated for **Internal Contact Set** (Table 9.13), **External Contact Set** (Table 9.14), **Date Set** (Table 9.15), **Linked Objects Set** (Table 9.16), **Reminders Set** (Table 9.17), and **Document Contents Set** (Table 9.18).

Field Name	Internal Contact Set	Internal Contact Type	Long Text
Value 1	G2	0001	Transaction Manager
Value 2	G2	0002	Account Executive
Value 3	G2	0003	Purchaser
Value 4	G2	0004	Editor

Table 9.13 Define Internal Contact Set

Field Name	External Contact Set	Contact Type	Long Text
Value 1	G3	0001	Main Contact
Value 2	G3	0002	Signer
Value 3	G3	0003	Legal Contact
Value 4	G3	0004	Account Manager

Table 9.14 Define External Contact Set

Field Name	Date Set	Date Type	Long Text
Value 1	G4	0001	Renewal Date

Table 9.15 Define Date Set

Field Name	Date Set	Date Type	Long Text
Value 2	G4	0002	Termination Effective Date
Value 3	G4	0003	Renewal Period

Table 9.15 Define Date Set (Cont.)

Field Name	Linked Obj. Set	Linked Obj. Type	Long Text
Value 1	G5	0001	Purchase Order
Value 2	G5	0002	Purchase Contract
Value 3	G5	0003	Request for Quotation (RFQ)
Value 4	G5	0004	Sales Order
Value 5	G5	0005	Sales Quotation

Table 9.16 Define Linked Object Set

Field Name	Reminder Set	Reminder Type	Long Text
Value 1	G6	0001	Reminder
Value 2	G6	0002	Obligation Check

Table 9.17 Define Reminder Set

Field Name	Document Content Set	Content Type	Long Text
Value 1	G7	AMD	Amendment
Value 2	G7	MC	Master Contract
Value 3	G7	NDA	Nondisclosure Agreement

Table 9.18 Define Document Content Set

The third step in this customizing activity is to define profiles, which consist of the profile sets defined in the first step. The profiles defined here can be assigned to contexts and legal transactions. This third step is completed by double-clicking **Define**

Profiles in the dialog structure, as shown in Figure 9.18. Then, maintain the values provided in Table 9.19.

Field Name	Value
Profile	GENERIC
Long Text	Generic Profile
Entity Set	G1
Internal Contact Set	G2
External Contact Set	G3
Date Set	G4
Linked Object Set	G5
Reminder Set	G6
Document Content Set	G7

Table 9.19 Define Profiles

9.3.12   Document Types

A *document* is defined as an instance of legal content tailored to a specific transaction or activity in a certain business context. In this customizing step, a new document type, LCM, is defined for legal content management. To define a document type for legal content management, first navigate to **IMG (SPRO)** • **Cross-Application Components** • **Document Management** • **Control Data** • **Define Document Types**, then enter the values provided in Table 9.20, as shown in Figure 9.20.

Field Name	Value
Document Type	LCM
Document Type description	Legal Content Mgmt
Use KPro	X
Version Assignment	Unchecked
Archiving Authorization	Unchecked

Table 9.20 Define Document Type

Field Name	Value
Internal Number Range	02
External number range	01
Number exit	MCDOKZNR
Vers. No. Incr.	2
Document Status	+
Document Desc.	+

Table 9.20 Define Document Type (Cont.)

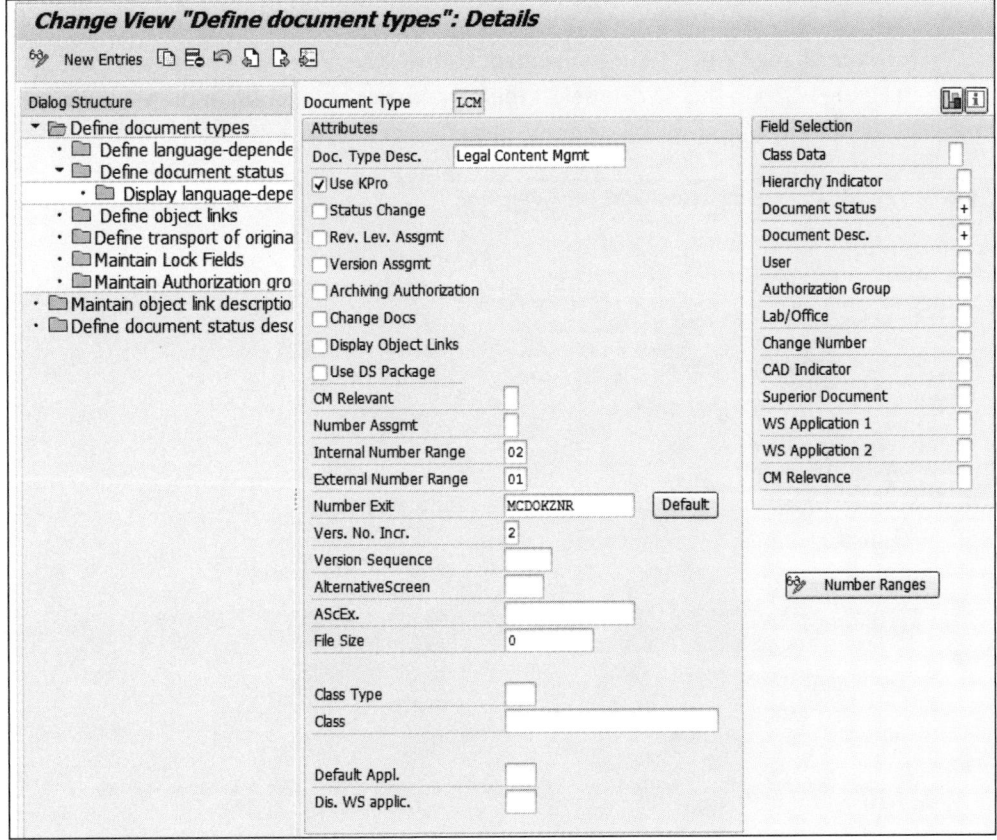

Figure 9.20 Define Document Type LCM

Click the green arrow to go back, then select document type **LCM**. Double-click **Define Document Status** in the **Dialog Structure** area (see Figure 9.21).

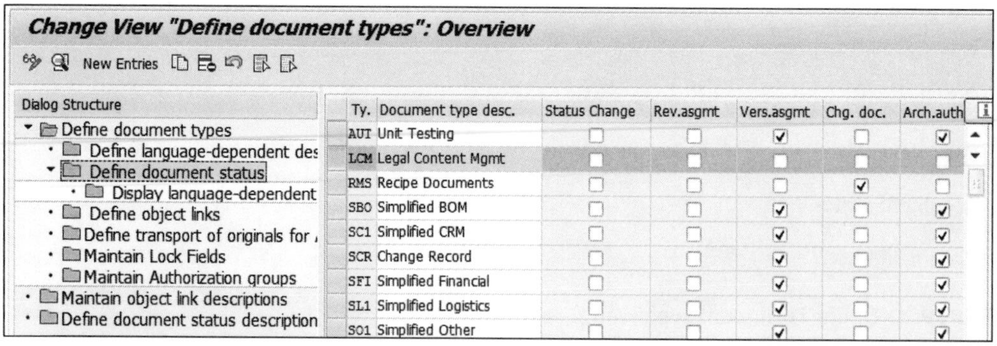

Figure 9.21 Define Document Status

Now the **Change View "Define document status": Overview** screen appears, as shown in Figure 9.22. On this screen, select the new entries and maintain the values shown in Table 9.21.

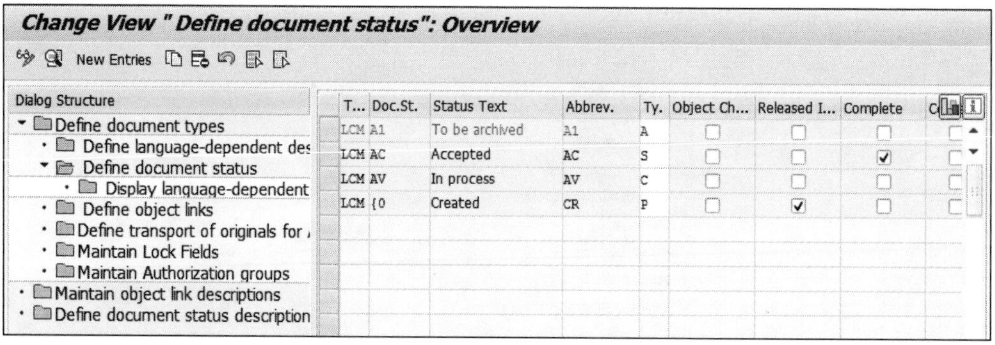

Figure 9.22 Define Document Status Overview

Field Name	Value 1	Value 2	Value 3	Value 4	Value 5
Document Status	{0	AV	AC	A1	{2
Status	CR	AV	AC	A1	IW
Status Text	Created	In Process	Accepted	To Be Archived	In Work

Table 9.21 Define Document Status

Field Name	Value 1	Value 2	Value 3	Value 4	Value 5
Status Type	P	C	S	A	O
Status Type Description	Primary Status	Check-In Status	Locked Status	Archive Status	Original Processing Status
Prev. 1		{0	AV	AC	AV
Prev. 2		AC		AV	{0
Prev. 3		A1			
Prev. 4		{2			
Complete for Enterprise Contract Management			Checked		

Table 9.21 Define Document Status (Cont.)

Now, go back to the overview screen, open the **Maintain Object Links** folder, and maintain the following values, as shown in Figure 9.23:

- Language (**Lang.**): **EN**
- **Object**: **LCMDOC**
- **Object Description**: **Lgl Content Mgmt Doc**

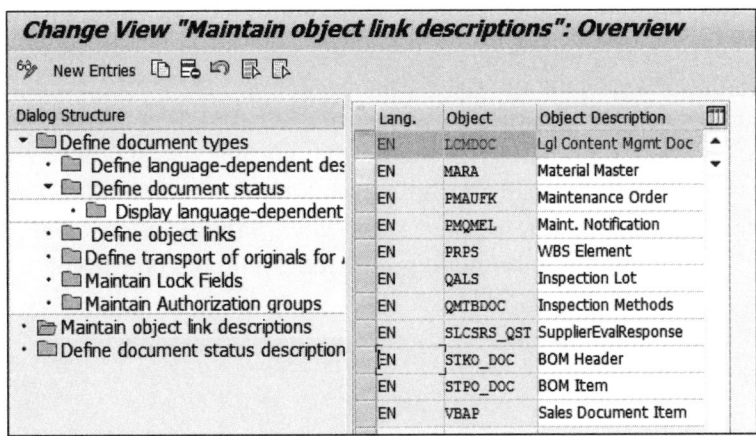

Figure 9.23 Maintain Object Link Descriptions

Return again to the overview screen, select document type **LCM**, open the **Define Object Links** folder, and maintain the following values, as shown in Figure 9.24:

- **Document Type**: LCM
- **Object**: LCMDOC
- **Dynpro No.**: 500

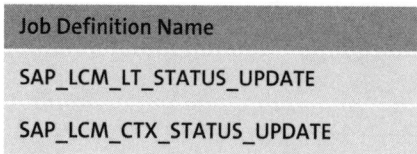

Figure 9.24 Define Object Links

9.3.13   Background Job Definitions

SAP S/4HANA comes with a job repository for scheduling technical background jobs (see Table 9.22). Scope-dependent jobs need to be defined in this repository before they can be activated. The application components to which these jobs belong need to be active in the system before maintaining the related table, table STJR_JOBD_SCOPE. For this activity, go to **IMG (SPRO)** • **SAP NetWeaver** • **Application Server** • **System Administration** • **Activation of Scope-Dependent Background Job Definitions (S/4HANA)**.

Job Definition Name
SAP_LCM_LT_STATUS_UPDATE
SAP_LCM_CTX_STATUS_UPDATE

Table 9.22 Scope-Dependent Background Job Definitions

Job Definition Name
SAP_LCM_LT_SEND_EMAIL_REMINDERS
SAP_LCM_SYNCHRONIZE_CATEGORIES
SAP_LCM_CTX_REMOVE_OBS_CATEG

Table 9.22 Scope-Dependent Background Job Definitions (Cont.)

9.4   Summary

SAP S/4HANA Cloud for enterprise contract management and assembly makes it easy to request contracts online, automate contract creation, use workflows, manage document versions, and standardize reviews, approvals, and processing, which makes enterprise-wide access to all legal content easy and fast. This solution ensures legal compliance and increases contracting performance. It also helps corporations to conduct business more effectively, keep customers and suppliers happy, and outperform competitors. The next chapter will focus on the external sourcing functionality in both SAP S/4HANA and SAP Ariba, which is used to drive the correct source of supply for each contract.

Chapter 10

External Sourcing

Procurement of materials and services is one of the main functions of most business organizations. Identifying the best sources for those materials and services in terms of price, timeliness, quality, and so on is one of the important tasks of a purchasing organization.

Whether fulfilling a one-time requirement of high-value items or a continuous requirement of any item, a buyer engages in a strategic process of finding one or more sources to fulfill the requirement from a pool of competing suppliers. This process is generally known as *strategic sourcing* and sometimes known as *external sourcing*.

Sourcing within a procurement function by definition is the process of finding suppliers of goods and services for an organization. Sourcing in SAP S/4HANA uses the *request for quotation* process, which begins with a purchase requisition and ends with creation and award of a purchase order or a contract. This process involves communication between the purchasing organization and suppliers who are external to the SAP S/4HANA system. SAP traditionally offered SAP Supplier Relationship Management (SAP SRM) along with supplier self-service for sourcing solutions using the RFx process. This approach required an organization to implement SAP SRM and supplier self-service applications, including a dedicated supplier portal. With the introduction of SAP S/4HANA, this sourcing solution is offered as an extended solution linked to SAP Ariba's cloud applications, which enables external communication and interaction with the suppliers. SAP provides standard integration between SAP S/4HANA and the SAP Ariba solutions required for this sourcing process. Because SAP Ariba solutions are used by both buyers and suppliers, this approach eliminates the need for every purchasing organization to create a dedicated portal for the suppliers to interact.

In this chapter, we'll cover the complete end-to-end external sourcing business process, including variations available within sourcing in SAP S/4HANA. All the SAP Fiori apps offered in this solution are explained and illustrated with screenshots. We've also provided the configuration steps and illustrative screenshots to help you implement the entire solution.

10.1   Sourcing Strategies

A sourcing solution was offered in SAP ERP along with SAP SRM, but now in SAP S/4HANA the solution is offered along with SAP Ariba. The new strategy is more efficient and simpler because SAP S/4HANA is tightly integrated with SAP Ariba Sourcing and the Ariba Network. The Ariba Network helps establish easy and quick connections to millions of suppliers worldwide who are already in the network. In this new approach, the sourcing process is initiated in SAP S/4HANA, from which you reach out to suppliers in the Ariba Network, identify the sources through SAP Ariba Sourcing, award the suppliers in SAP Ariba Sourcing, and bring the data back to SAP S/4HANA to create a purchase contract or purchase order to complete the process.

10.1.1   Sourcing Process Flow

The process flow is shown in Figure 10.1. Within SAP Best Practices, this scope item is known as Sourcing with SAP Ariba Sourcing.

10.1.2   Sourcing Optimization

Sourcing optimization is achieved in SAP S/4HANA with the help of the new SAP Fiori apps described in the next section, as well as the features and functionalities available within SAP Ariba solutions. The sourcing solution helps achieve the following:

- Provide visibility and identify savings opportunities
- Standardize source-to-contract processes across business units
- Drive materials cost savings and optimization across all spend categories
- Increase speed and efficiency across different teams
- Reduce risk by finding better suppliers and innovation partners

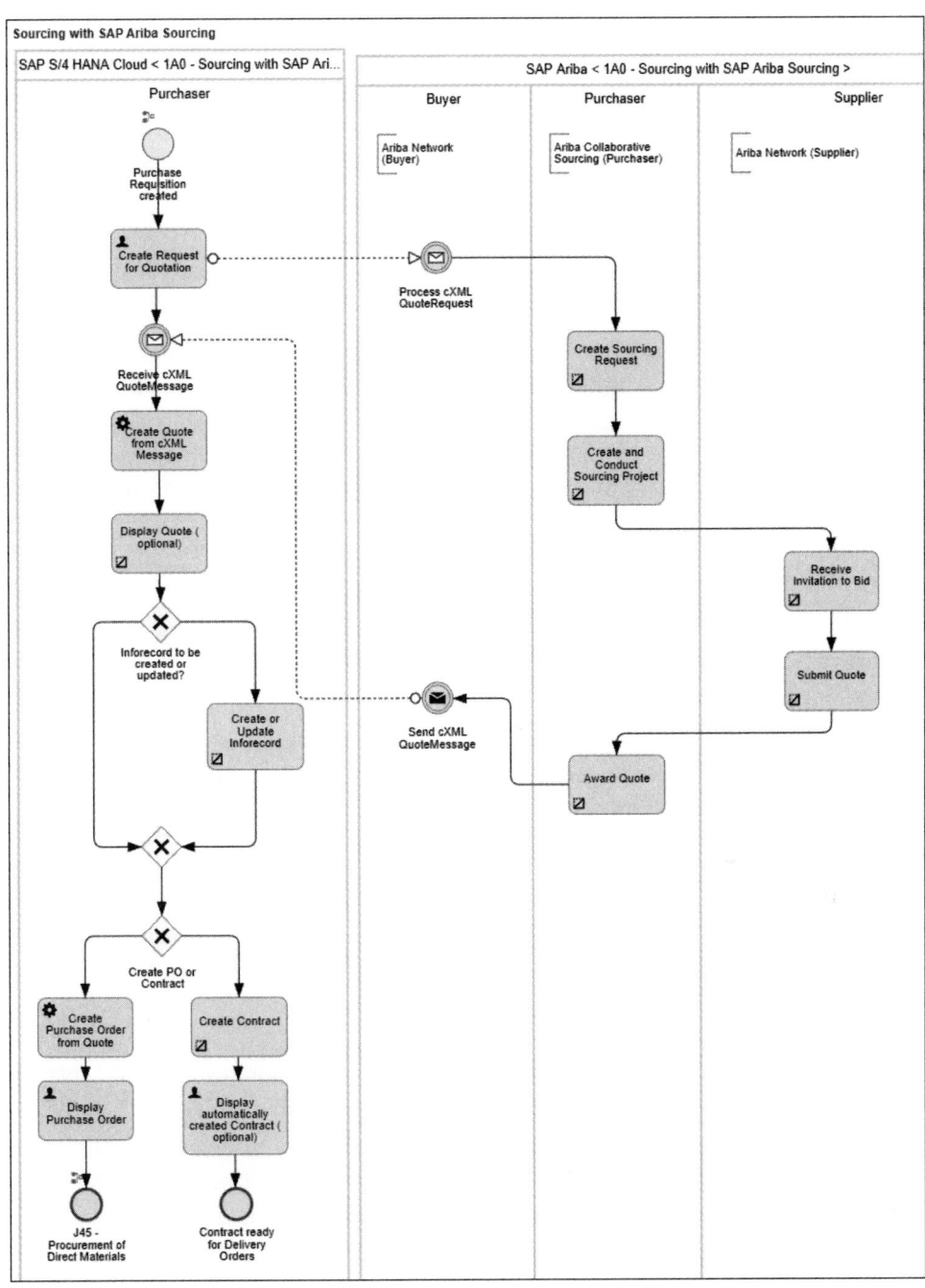

Figure 10.1 Process Flow

10.2   Request for Quotation

A *request for quotation* is a request from a purchasing organization of a company that's sent to suppliers, soliciting them to submit a quotation for the supply of materials or services. The request for quotation document (RFQ) is a purchasing document created in the SAP S/4HANA system either from a purchase requisition or by copying an existing RFQ. RFQs also can be created manually without referencing any other document. RFQs for lean services can be created by selecting **Services** as the **Product Type Group** at the item level.

It's possible to create a single RFQ that contains both material and service items. It's important to note that the RFQs created in the new SAP Fiori app can't be viewed or processed in the SAP GUI environment and vice versa. The RFQ and quotation solution offered using SAP GUI processes and transactions in SAP ERP (MM-PUR-RFQ) isn't a strategic choice in SAP S/4HANA. Support for this solution is likely to end at some point in the future.

10.2.1   Sourcing with SAP Ariba Sourcing

Sourcing is the ability of the purchasing organization to work in collaboration with the millions of suppliers available in the Ariba Network. The buyers together with the suppliers can improve efficiency and meet compliance requirements across the entire sourcing process. This approach incorporates seamless processes, transparent communications between the buyers and suppliers, and trust between the parties involved in the sourcing process. Sourcing capability is achieved through SAP Ariba Sourcing. This section explains the process steps on the SAP S/4HANA side. In this process, once the RFQ is created and published in SAP S/4HANA, it's sent to SAP Ariba Sourcing, where a sourcing request is created based on the RFQ received from SAP S/4HANA. The RFQ type used for this process in SAP S/4HANA is an *external sourcing request*.

The buyer then creates a sourcing project in SAP Ariba Sourcing with reference to the sourcing request and publishes the project. This sourcing project results in RFQs in the SAP Ariba Sourcing application for the suppliers to respond to. The suppliers can access these RFQs and submit their responses or quotations through their SAP Ariba accounts in SAP Ariba Sourcing. After the RFQ closing time, the buyer can review all the responses from different suppliers, compare them, and award one or more suppliers in SAP Ariba Sourcing. The awarded quotations are automatically sent to SAP S/4HANA, in which purchase orders or contracts are created, depending on the document type selected in SAP Ariba Sourcing while awarding.

10.2.2   Quote Automation for Procurement

If a purchasing organization is interested in requesting only price and quantity information or shipping costs, it's possible to use the external price request RFQ type. This RFQ type, once saved and published in SAP S/4HANA, is sent to the Ariba Network, where the suppliers can create their responses. These bids submitted by suppliers through their SAP Ariba accounts are sent back to SAP S/4HANA, where they can be processed. The buyer can compare the bids (quotations) received, award one of those in the SAP S/4HANA system, and create a purchase order or contract. Within SAP Best Practices, this scope item is known as Ariba—Quote Automation Integration for Procurement.

10.2.3   Request for Price

This RFQ process helps the buyer to create price requests in SAP S/4HANA and send them directly to suppliers by email or send a printed version by mail. The internal sourcing request RFQ type is used for this process. Suppliers respond to the RFQ by providing their quotations via email or mail. The buyer manually creates quotations in the SAP S/4HANA system using the Manage Supplier Quotations app based on the quotations received from the suppliers. The quotations created in the SAP S/4HANA system are compared, and the best one is awarded. It's possible to award the best quotation in one of the following ways: directly within the quotation by clicking **Award**, from the list in the Manage Supplier Quotations app, or from the list in the Compare Supplier Quotations app. After awarding the quotation, the follow-on document, either a purchase order or a contract, is created in SAP S/4HANA. Quotations that do not meet the requirements should be set to **Rejected** or **Completed** manually. After completion of this process, the RFQ may be set to **Completed** as well. The process flow is shown in Figure 10.2. Within SAP Best Practices, this scope item is known as Request for Price.

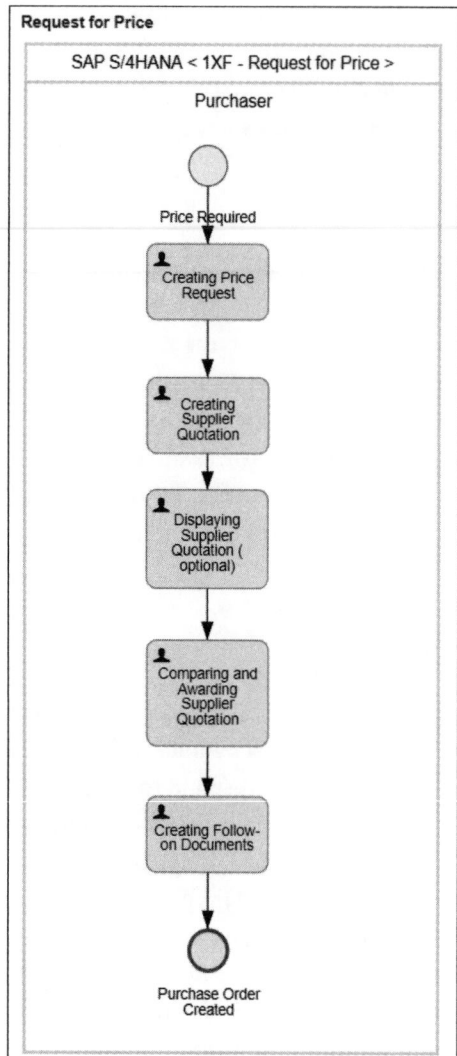

Figure 10.2 Request for Price

10.2.4   Manage Request for Quotation

This SAP Fiori app is used to create RFQs in the SAP S/4HANA system. The RFQ created is sent to SAP Ariba Sourcing based on the configuration explained later in this chapter. Then the sourcing process is carried out in Ariba and the awarded quotation is sent back to SAP S/4HANA to create a purchase order or purchase contract.

This SAP Fiori app provides the capability to display the list of all existing RFQs and to search for RFQs by **RFQ Number**, **RFQ Type**, **Status**, **Company Code**, **Purchasing Org.**, **Purchasing Group**, **Quotation Deadline**, and so on. This app also helps copy an existing RFQ, create a new RFQ from scratch, and delete an RFQ. It's possible to customize the filters and display columns, as shown in Figure 10.3.

Here you can see:

❶ Customize and save own filter settings

❷ Customize filter bar individually

❸ **Copy**, **Delete**, or **Add** (Create new) request for quotation

❹ Customize and save own table layout

From this app, you also can display an existing RFQ by clicking any of the listed RFQs. This allows the user to review all the information within the RFQ, including output details/status, legal transactions associated with the RFQ, and process flow. You may select **Standard** to customize and save filter settings and **Adapt Filters (1)** to customize the filter bar individually. You may also **Copy**, **Delete**, or **+** (create new) requests for quotations. By selecting the gear icon, you can customize and save your own table layout.

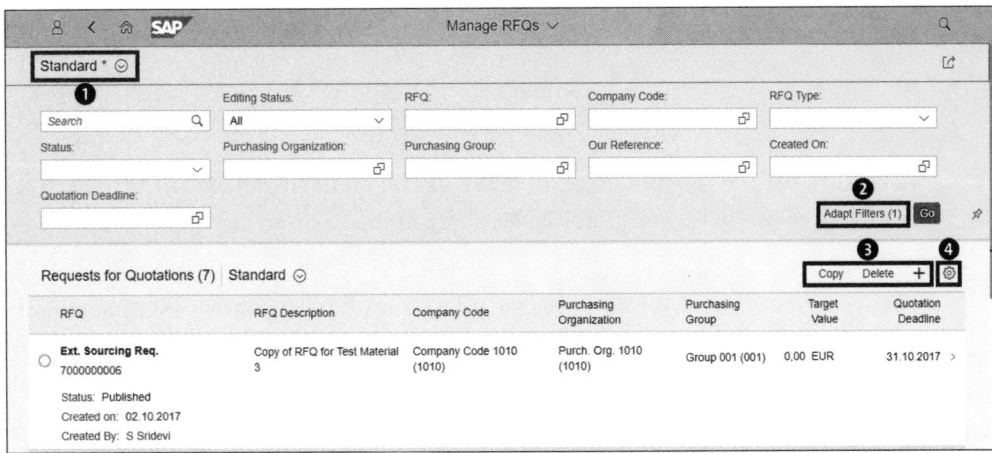

Figure 10.3 Manage RFQs

10.2.5   Create Request for Quotation

To create an RFQ from an existing purchase requisition, access the Manage Purchase Requisitions SAP Fiori app, select the purchase requisition, and click the **Create RFQ** button, as shown in Figure 10.4.

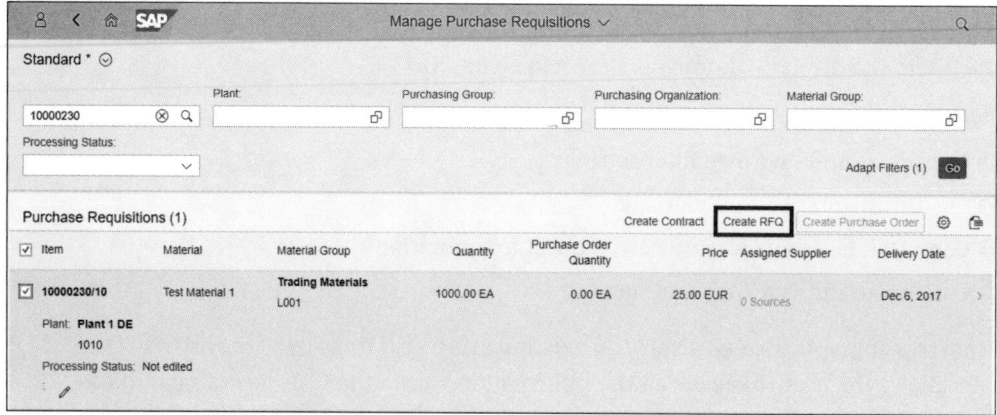

Figure 10.4 Manage Purchase Requisition

This action will take you to the **Request for Quotation** creation screen (Figure 10.5), where the RFQ type, quotation deadline, and organizational information such as company code and purchasing organization are entered.

Here you can see how to:

❶ Publish RFQ to Ariba Sourcing once all data is complete

❷ Edit details of existing request for quotation

To create a request for quotation, fill in the header and item details, select bidders to send RFQ requests to, and publish RFQs to SAP Ariba Sourcing for follow-on processes.

The system adds all the information, including item details, from the purchase requisition. It's also possible to specify the follow-on document, either a purchase order or contract, for the RFQ on this screen. This app allows you to maintain delivery and payment terms, add bidders if desired, and add attachments. Once all values are entered, the RFQ is published. At this point, the RFQ is sent from SAP S/4HANA to SAP Ariba Sourcing.

Then the sourcing process is carried out in SAP Ariba and the awarded quotation is sent back to SAP S/4HANA to create a purchase order or purchase contract.

Figure 10.5 Create/Edit Request for Quotation

10.2.6 Monitor Request for Quotation Items

This app, shown in Figure 10.6, enables the strategic purchaser to monitor RFQ items. It allows the user to display the list of all the RFQ items in a table view, along with a chart for awarded quotation value and submitted quotation value. By default, the chart is displayed per suppliers; you can change the settings to display the chart per company code, plant, purchasing organization, and many more options. The app provides options to choose the chart type from a variety of types, such as bar chart, line chart, pie chart, and more. The output results can be filtered by RFQ number, RFQ type, quotation deadline, purchasing category, material group, company code, plant, purchasing org., and so on. The user can select any RFQ item to view the corresponding quotes and general information and navigate to view contextual information related to a supplier or material.

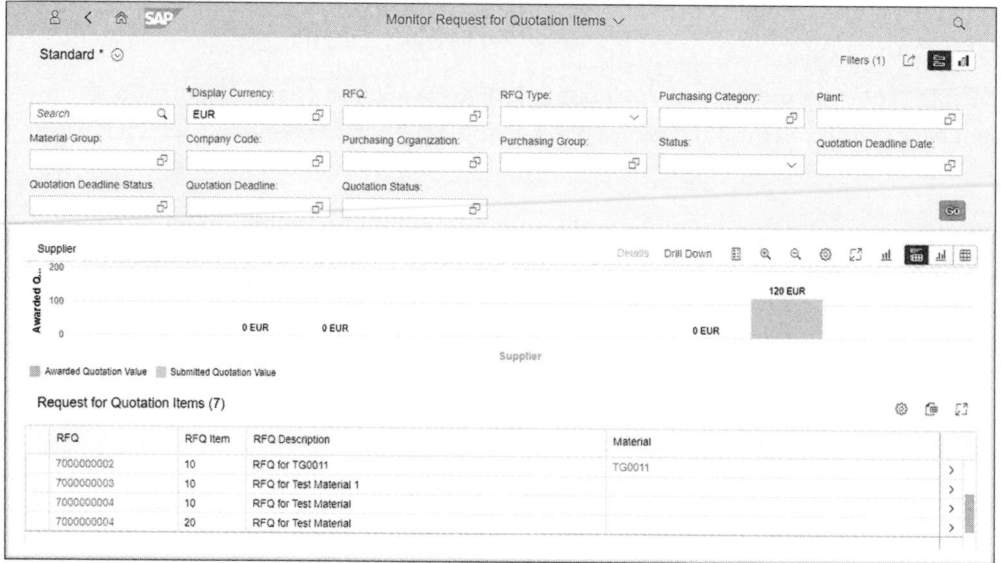

Figure 10.6 Monitor RFQ Items

10.2.7   Compare Supplier Quotations

This app (Figure 10.7) enables the purchaser to compare supplier quotations received against an RFQ and to find the best offer. It allows you to search for a specific RFQ and display all quotations received for it; it also allows you to check whether all the invited suppliers have submitted their quotations. To select the best quotation, press **8000000001.** Selecting **Award** creates a purchase order or contract, and the **Document** icon exports the list of quotations to a spreadsheet.

In this app, you can see how to:

❶ Select the best quotation

❷ Creates a purchase order or contract

❸ Export the list of quotations to a spreadsheet

It displays an overview of all quotations for a selected RFQ, providing information such as basic supplier data, total net value (which reflects the complete net costs for the goods or services, including transportation costs), and fully quoted items (fully quoted items are items that the supplier can deliver in the requested quantity).

This app identifies the lowest-priced item as the best-priced item. Other factors, such as supplier evaluation score, are not included in the calculation. The purchaser can award the best quotation directly from this app and create a PO or contract.

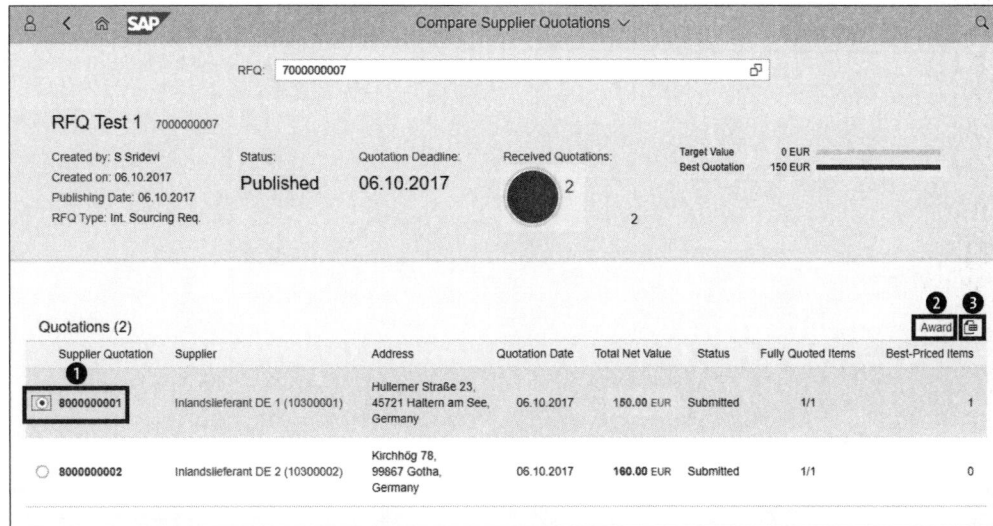

Figure 10.7 Compare Supplier Quotations

10.2.8   Manage Supplier Quotation

This app (Figure 10.8) enables the user to display all supplier quotations that have been received for different RFQs. It also allows the user to select any quotation and view its detailed information. The app features include the following:

- Search for a quotation by quotation number, type, status, submission date, supplier, RFQ number, RFQ type, and more
- Display detailed information for a quotation by selecting the quotation from the search result list
- Display item details, such as the actual item, quantity, and pricing details
- Submit quotations that are in the **In Preparation** status
- Edit quotations that are in the **In Preparation** or **Submitted** status
- Delete quotations that are in the **In Preparation** status
- Award quotations

- Set quotations to **Completed**
- Navigate to detailed information about suppliers and RFQs

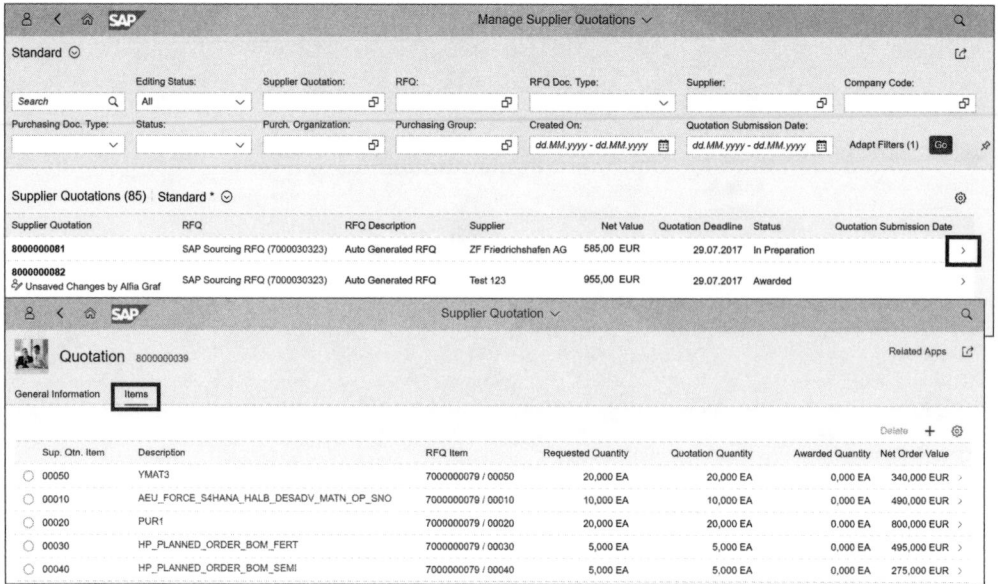

Figure 10.8 Manage Supplier Quotations

10.2.9   Manage Workflows for RFQs

This app enables the business process specialist to configure workflows for RFQs in the SAP S/4HANA system. Both one-level approval by the manager of the workflow initiator and multilevel approval by the manager of the workflow initiator and by higher-level managers are possible.

This app allows the user to perform the following activities:

- Display the list of existing workflow definitions.
- Display the detailed information for a workflow definition.
- Create new workflows and define the step sequence. You can define the start conditions and the order in which the start conditions are checked. You can also define the order of the steps. If you have more than one workflow defined, the workflow is selected depending on the fulfilment of the start condition.
- Copy an existing workflow and modify it according to your business needs.
- Set validity periods for workflows and activate or deactivate workflows.

10.2.10   Manage Workflows for Supplier Quotation

This app lets you define an approval process for supplier quotations, which allows the approver to check the awarded quotations before a follow-on document is created. The awarded quotation can be approved or rejected.

For external quotation (RE) types, the workflow process isn't relevant because these quotations are approved and awarded in SAP Ariba Sourcing. The default setting for quotations of the price quotation (RSI) and internal quotation (RQ) types is automatic approval. This app helps the user define a workflow process based on the business requirements for these quotation types. Both one-level approval by the manager of the workflow initiator and multilevel approval by the manager of the workflow initiator and by higher-level managers are possible.

This app comes with the following standard features:

- Display the list of existing workflow definitions
- Display the details of an existing workflow definition
- Create new workflows by defining preconditions and step sequence
- Copy an existing workflow to create a new one
- Activate or deactivate workflows

Setting up a workflow for quotations using this app doesn't require any development skills. This app helps the business user to set up a workflow by following the steps described ahead. Figure 10.9 shows the steps involved. Start the Manage Workflows for Supplier Quotation app and click the **Add** button to create a workflow. Enter a name for the workflow and provide a description if necessary. You can set up a validity period for this workflow. Choose one or more preconditions for the workflow to start. In this example, preconditions are set to **10,000.00** ❶. The workflow will start only if the selected preconditions are met. Standard preconditions available are as follows:

- **Quotation Follow-On Document Category**
- **Quotation Follow-On Document Type**
- **Initiator of Workflow**
- **Quotation Document Currency**
- **Quotation Document Type**
- **Supplier Quotation Creator**
- **Quotation Total Net Amount Is Greater Than**
- **Quotation Total Net Amount Is Less than or Equal To**

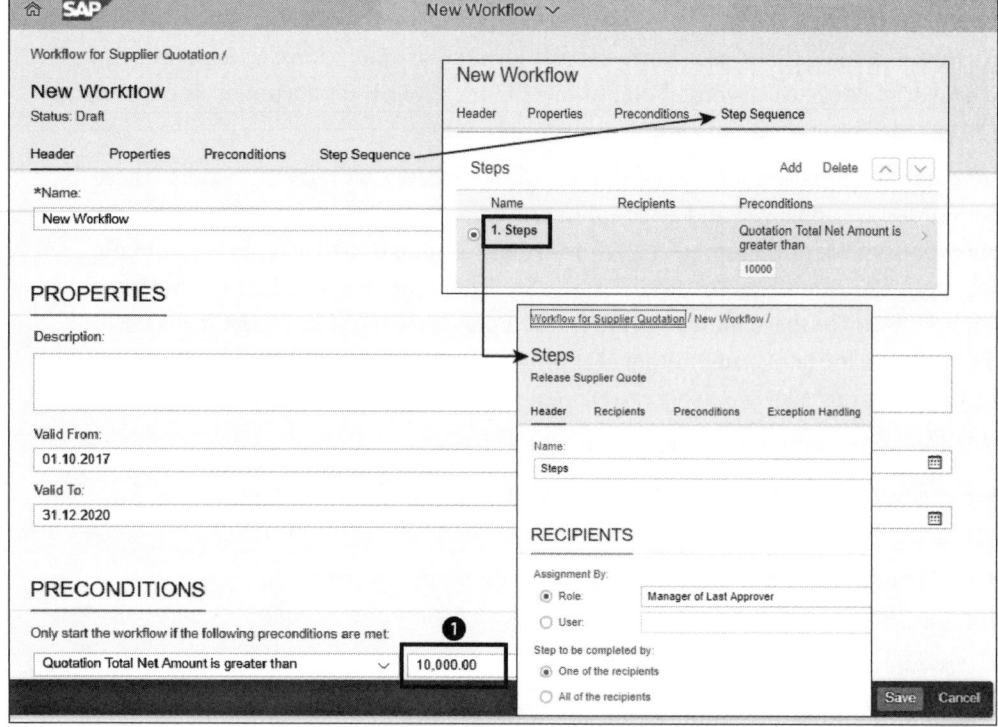

Figure 10.9 Create Workflow for Quotations

The next step in setting up the workflow is to add a step sequence, as listed in Table 10.1.

Step Sequence Type	Precondition	Recipient	Exception Handling
Automatic Release of Supplier Quote	Allowed/ Selectable	N/A	Allowed/ Selectable
Release Supplier Quote	Allowed/ Selectable	Allowed/ Selectable	Allowed/ Selectable

Table 10.1 Workflow Step Sequence

10.2.11   My Inbox

This app displays the list of all quotations that have been sent for approval. The user can perform the following actions through this app:

- Approve quotations
- Reject quotations
- Claim a quotation so that only he/she can approve or reject it
- Forward a quotation to another user for approval
- Suspend a quotation for a certain period of time
- Display the workflow or task log

10.3   Configuring Request for Quotation

With SAP S/4HANA, you can take advantage of the SAP Best Practices activation approach for customizing, as explained in Chapter 2. However, if you choose the traditional customizing approach, this section can help. This information also helps validate the customer settings against SAP-standard configuration. For the sourcing process (RFQ) to work in SAP S/4HANA along with SAP Ariba, the configuration described in the following sections needs to be done in the SAP S/4HANA system.

10.3.1   Number Ranges

Request for quotation and *supplier quotation* are the two types of documents that need to be configured for the sourcing solution in SAP S/4HANA. These documents are assigned a unique number at the time of creation for identification. The system will use a number from within the number range defined in this step. Number ranges, which include starting and ending numbers and assignment type (external or internal), are defined using the values shown in Table 10.2 via menu path **IMG (SPRO) • Materials Management • Purchasing • Supplier Quotation Process • Define Number Ranges**.

No	From No	To Number	NR Status	External Assignment
70	7000000000	7099999999	0	Unchecked
80	8000000000	8099999999	0	Unchecked

Table 10.2 Define Number Ranges

10.3.2   Document Types for RFQ

The SAP system manages RFQs as documents, and this customizing step allows for creation of document types necessary for the business. The standard customizing

settings can be made by following menu path **IMG (SPRO) • Materials Management •
Purchasing • Supplier Quotation Process • Define Document Types for RFQ**.

This menu path will bring up the **Document Types RFQ Change** screen; here, you can
create new entries. The values required for creating the three standard document
types are shown in Table 10.3.

Type	Doc. Type Description	No. Range Int.	External Processing	Awarding
RE	Ext. Sourcing Req.	70	Ariba Sourcing Request	External
RQ	Int. Sourcing Req.	70	Blank	Internal
RSI	Ext. Price Request	70	Ariba Quote Automation	Internal

Table 10.3 Document Types for RFQ

Then, select each document type and double-click **Allowed Item Categories** in the dialog structure area, as shown in Figure 10.10. This brings up the **Admissible Item Categories for Document Type** screen; on this screen, create entries as shown in Table 10.4.

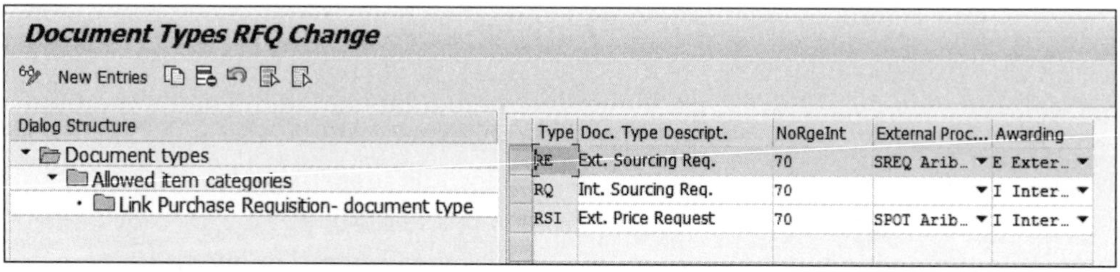

Figure 10.10 Define Document Types for RFQ

Entry	Item Cat.	Text for Item Cat.
Admissible Item Categories for Document Type RE Ext. Sourcing Req.	Blank	Standard
Admissible Item Categories for Document Type RQ Int. Sourcing Req.	Blank	Standard
Admissible Item Categories for Document Type RSI Ext. Price Request	Blank	Standard

Table 10.4 Admissible Item Categories for RFQ Document Type

Return to the **Document Types RFQ Change** screen. Select each document type and double-click the **Link Purchase Requisition document type** in the **Dialog Structure** area. This brings up the **Change View "Link Purchase Requisition—Document Type": Overview** screen. On this screen, create new entries as shown in Table 10.5.

Entry	DTy.	Description	Item Cat	Dsc. Item Cat.	Item Cat.	Dsc. Item Cat
For Doc. Type RE	NB	Purchase Requisition	Blank	Standard	Blank	Standard
For Doc. Type RQ	NB	Purchase Requisition	Blank	Standard	Blank	Standard
For Doc. Type RQ	NBS	Purchase Req. NBS	Blank	Standard	Blank	Standard
For Doc. Type RSI	NB	Purchase Requisition	Blank	Standard	Blank	Standard

Table 10.5 Link Purchase Requisition Document Type

10.3.3 Document Types for Supplier Quotation

The SAP system manages supplier quotations as documents, and this customizing step allows for creation of document types as necessary for the business. The standard customizing settings can be made by following **IMG (SPRO) • Materials Management • Purchasing • Supplier Quotation Process • Define Document Types for Supplier Quotation**.

This menu path will bring up the **Document Types Quote Change** screen; here, create new entries, as shown in Table 10.6.

Type	Doc. Type Description	No. Range Int.
RE	External Quotation	80
RQ	Internal Quotation	80
RSI	Price Quotation	80

Table 10.6 Define Document Types for Supplier Quotation

Now select each document type and double-click **Follow-On Document Categories** in the **Dialog Structure** area, as shown in Figure 10.11. This will open the **Change View "Follow-on Document Categories": Overview** screen, on which you can create new entries, as shown in Table 10.7.

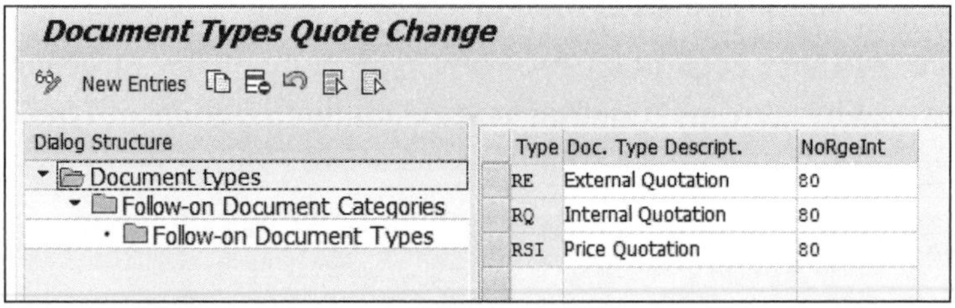

Document Types Quote Change

New Entries

Dialog Structure	Type	Doc. Type Descript.	NoRgeInt
▾ ☐ Document types	RE	External Quotation	80
▾ ☐ Follow-on Document Categories	RQ	Internal Quotation	80
• ☐ Follow-on Document Types	RSI	Price Quotation	80

Figure 10.11 Define Document Type for Quote

	Target Document Category	Description
For Doc. Type RE	F	Purchase Order
For Doc. Type RE	K	Contract
For Doc. Type RQ	F	Purchase Order
For Doc. Type RQ	K	Contract
For Doc. Type RSI	F	Purchase Order

Table 10.7 Follow-On Document Categories

Select **F** for **Target Document Category** and double-click **Follow-On Document Types** in the **Dialog Structure** area. This will bring up the **Change View "Follow-on Document Types": Overview** screen and on this screen, create the new entries shown in Table 10.8.

Target Doc. Type	Target Doc. Type Description
NB	Standard PO

Table 10.8 Follow-On Document Type for Category F

Now, select **K** for **Target Document Category** and double-click the **Follow-On Document Types** in the **Dialog Structure** area. This will bring up the **Change View "Follow-on Document Types": Overview** screen. Here, create new entries as shown in Table 10.9.

Target Doc. Type	Target Doc. Type Description
MK	Quantity Contract
WK	Value Contract

Table 10.9 Follow-On Document Type for Category K

10.3.4   External Processing for Supplier Quotation Process

In this activity, you define the external processing for a request for quotation. The standard customizing settings can be made by following **IMG (SPRO)** • **Materials Management** • **Purchasing** • **Supplier Quotation Process** • **Define External Processing for Supplier Quotation Process**. The external processing types defined here, as shown in Table 10.10, are used in the customizing activity Define Document Types for RFQ.

External Processing	External Processing in External System	External Processing Text
SPOT	QuoteAutomation	Ariba Quote Automation
SREQ	sourcingRequest	Ariba Sourcing Request

Table 10.10 External Processing for Supplier Quotation Process

10.3.5   Activate cXML Message Types

In this customizing activity, you determine the cXML message types that you want to exchange with the Ariba Network.

Start by navigating to **IMG (SPRO)** • **Integration with Other SAP Components** • **Business Network Integration** • **Integration with the Ariba Network** • **Framework Settings** • **Define Basic Message Settings**. Then, maintain the recommended settings as shown in Table 10.11.

Application Component ID	Object Type	Object Type Description	cXML Message Type	Direction	Active
BNS-ARI-SE-ERP	RFQS4H	Request for Quotation	QTEQ	Outbound	Active
BNS-ARI-SE-ERP	QUOTES4H	Quote	QTEM	Inbound	Active

Table 10.11 cXML Message Types

10.3.6   Credentials and Endpoints

In this customizing activity, the credentials that identify your company on the Ariba Network is identified and the endpoints are enabled. The values to be used for this configuration are explained ahead. The values shown in Figure 10.12 are only examples; the values in real projects are unique to each customer.

Start by navigating to **IMG (SPRO)** • **Integration with Other SAP Components** • **Business Network Integration** • **Integration with the Ariba Network** • **Framework Settings** •

Define Credentials and End Points for Ariba Network. Choose **New Entries** and enter the following values:

- **Ariba Network ID**: The ID of your buyer account
- **Shared Secret**: Your Ariba Network buyer account shared secret
- **Test Account**: Check this box if it's a test account
- **Enable System ID**: Used if multiple buyer systems use the same Ariba Network buyer account
- **System ID**: Enter system ID here if system ID is enabled
- **Enable End Points**: Select for authentication and polling

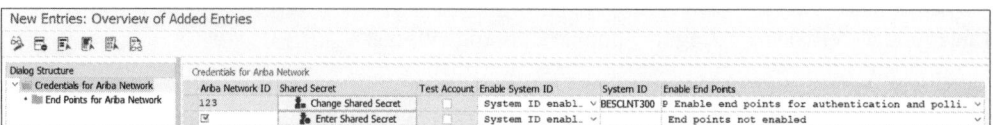

Figure 10.12 Credentials for Ariba Network

After completing these settings, select the newly created entry, double-click **End Points for Ariba Network**, and enter values as shown in Figure 10.13. The values shown in Figure 10.13 are only examples; the values in real projects are unique to each customer. Enter the following:

- **SAP-Internal Key**: System ID, entered in the previous step
- **Ariba End Point ID**: Endpoint ID "<S/4 HANA>", created in the Ariba Network buyer account (usually the same as the system ID)
- **Shared Secret**: Ariba Network buyer account shared secret

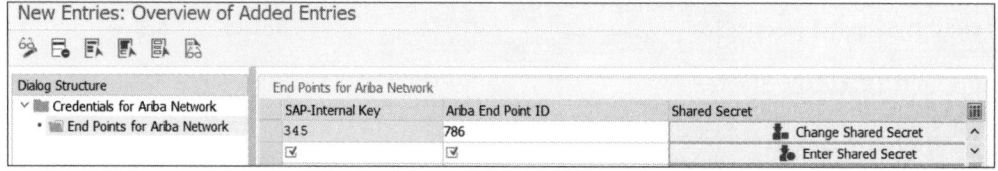

Figure 10.13 Endpoints for Ariba Network

10.3.7   Assign Network ID to Company Code

In this activity, the Ariba Network ID is assigned to company codes in the SAP S/4HANA on-premise system. The Ariba Network ID assigned here will be sent with each document sent to the Ariba Network and is used to identify the sender. You need to assign this ID to each company code that communicates with SAP Ariba.

Start by navigating to **IMG (SPRO)** • **Integration with Other SAP Components** • **Business Network Integration** • **Integration with the Ariba Network** • **Application Specific Settings** • **Assign Ariba Network ID to Company Code**. Choose **New Entries** and enter the **Ariba Network ID** and **Company Code** as needed and save the entries.

10.3.8   Schedule Job

Messages, which are quotes received in the Ariba Network buyer account, will have to be picked by the SAP S/4HANA system periodically. To achieve this, the following background job is scheduled:

- **Program Name**: ARBFND_FETCH_CXML_MESSAGES_NEW
- Variant attributes:
  - **Ariba Network ID**: <ID of the buyer account>○
  - **CXML Message Type**: QTEM5

The batch job may be set up in the system to run every two minutes using Transaction SE36.

10.3.9   Output Parameter Determination and Use

In this customizing activity, settings needed for output determination for requests for quotation are made.

Follow menu path **IMG (SPRO)** • **Integration with Other SAP Components** • **Business Network Integration** • **Integration with the Ariba Network** • **Application-specific Settings** • **Define Message Output Control** • **Method 2: Use SAP S/4HANA-Based Output Management** • **Define Business Rules for Output Determination**.

The **Output Parameter Determination** screen is displayed, as shown in Figure 10.14. Under **Select Business Rules**, choose the following:

- **Show Rules for**: Request for Quotation
- **Determination Step**: Channel

Next, make the following entry in the table:

- **Output Type**: EXTERNAL_REQUEST
- **Channel**: XML
- **Exclusive Indicator**: -(false)

After entering theses values, activate and save.

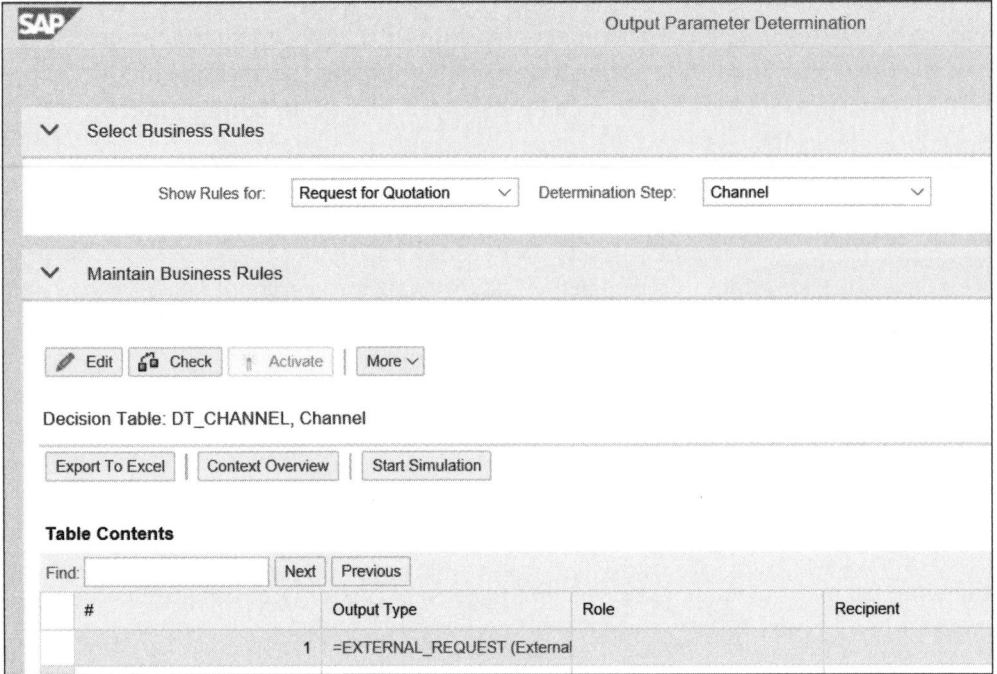

Figure 10.14 Output Parameter Determination

10.4   Configuring Flexible Workflow

In SAP S/4HANA, the process owners—for example, the person responsible for the sourcing process—are provided with the tools necessary to configure the approval workflow relevant to the business processes they own. They can configure the workflow needed for the business processes themselves without needing to go to the IT department. This strategy empowers the process owner and eliminates costs associated with development. The Manage Workflows SAP Fiori app allows process owners to use this new flexible workflow procedure in SAP S/4HANA. This approach also provides the flexibility to change the workflow as and when required to meet changing requirements.

This section describes the configuration steps required for the Manage Workflows for Supplier Quotation app to work.

10.4.1 Scenario Activation

Workflow IDs are provided in the system for each scenario, such as release purchase order, release supplier quotation, and so on. To activate the scenario relevant to the business process in question, follow menu path **IMG (SPRO) • SAP NetWeaver • Application Server • Business Management • SAP Business Workflow • Flexible Workflow • Scenario Activation** (see Figure 10.15).

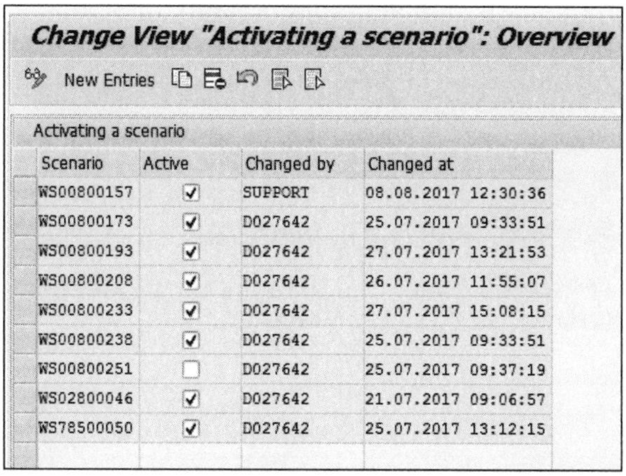
Change View "Activating a scenario": Overview

New Entries

Activating a scenario

Scenario	Active	Changed by	Changed at
WS00800157	☑	SUPPORT	08.08.2017 12:30:36
WS00800173	☑	D027642	25.07.2017 09:33:51
WS00800193	☑	D027642	27.07.2017 13:21:53
WS00800208	☑	D027642	26.07.2017 11:55:07
WS00800233	☑	D027642	27.07.2017 15:08:15
WS00800238	☑	D027642	25.07.2017 09:33:51
WS00800251	☐	D027642	25.07.2017 09:37:19
WS02800046	☑	D027642	21.07.2017 09:06:57
WS78500050	☑	D027642	25.07.2017 13:12:15

Figure 10.15 Scenario Activation

The supplier quotation workflow scenario is activated by creating an entry as shown in Table 10.12. This setting makes the scenario visible in the Manage Workflows for Supplier Quotation app.

Scenario	Active
WS00800193	Select

Table 10.12 Scenario Activation

10.4.2 Register Event for Subsequent Workflow

For triggering a subsequent workflow, further triggering events need to be determined in addition to the event Assigned. To do this, a check function module is implemented. To start, follow menu path **IMG (SPRO) • SAP NetWeaver • Application Server • Basis Services • Archive Link • Customizing Incoming Documents • Workflow Scenarios • Register Event for Subsequent Workflow.**

This will open the **Change View "Event Type Linkages": Overview** screen; on this screen, create the entries shown in Table 10.13. Then configure the receiver call as shown in Table 10.14.

Customizing settings made in this step are shown in Figure 10.16.

Object Category	Object Type	Event	Receiver Type
ABAP Class	CL_MM_PUR_WF_OBJECT_QTN	SUBMITTED_FOR_APPROVAL	WS00800193

Table 10.13 Register Event for Subsequent Workflow

Receiver Call	Receiver Function Module	Event Delivery	Linkage Activated	Behavior Upon Error Feedback	Receiver Status
Function Module	SWW_WI_CREATE_VIA_EVENT_IBF	Using tRFC (Default)	select	System defaults	No errors

Table 10.14 Receiver Configuration

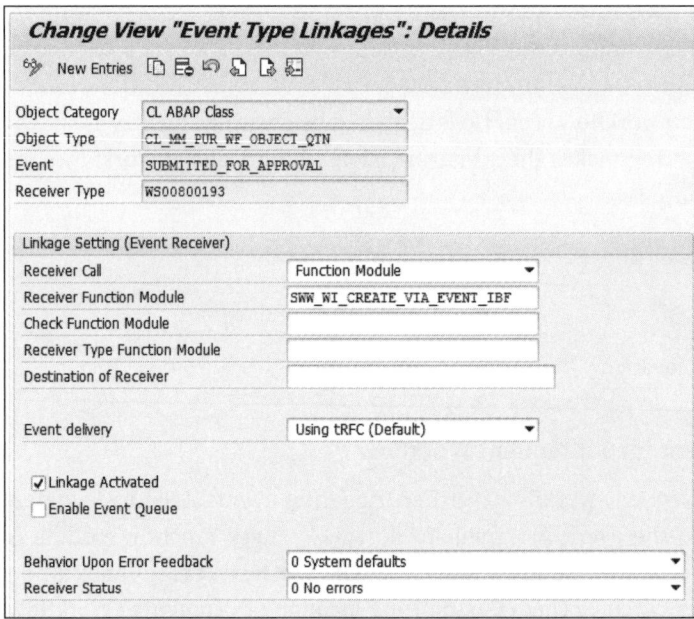

Figure 10.16 Event Type Linkages

10.4.3   Maintain Task Names and Decision Options

Each workflow ID is assigned a step ID, and possible decision keys such as approve and reject need to be maintained. The step ID determines the task, and the decision keys determine the possible decisions within the workflow.

Begin by navigating to **IMG (SPRO)** • **SAP NetWeaver** • **SAP Gateway Service Enablement** • **Content** • **Workflow Settings** • **Maintain Task Names and Decision Options**.

This opens the screen shown in Figure 10.17.

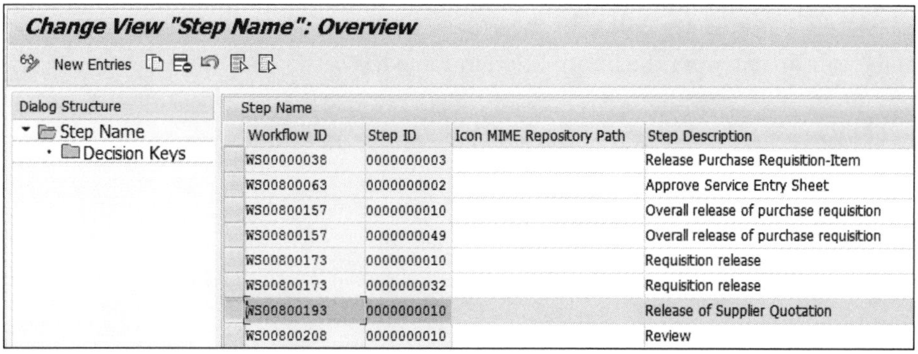

Change View "Step Name": Overview				
New Entries				
Dialog Structure	**Step Name**			
▼ 🗁 Step Name	Workflow ID	Step ID	Icon MIME Repository Path	Step Description
• 🗁 Decision Keys	WS00000038	0000000003		Release Purchase Requisition-Item
	WS00800063	0000000002		Approve Service Entry Sheet
	WS00800157	0000000010		Overall release of purchase requisition
	WS00800157	0000000049		Overall release of purchase requisition
	WS00800173	0000000010		Requisition release
	WS00800173	0000000032		Requisition release
	WS00800193	0000000010		Release of Supplier Quotation
	WS00800208	0000000010		Review

Figure 10.17 Maintain Task Names and Decision Options

In this customizing activity, the workflow step ID and description are maintained for the workflow ID as shown in Table 10.15.

Workflow ID	Step ID	Step Description
WS00800193	10	Release of Supplier Quotation

Table 10.15 Workflow Step

On the **Change View "Step Name": Overview** screen, select the entry with **Workflow ID WS00800193**, double-click **Decision Keys** in the **Dialog Structure**, and maintain entries as shown in Table 10.16.

Key	Decision Text	Nature
1	Approve	Positive
2	Reject	Negative

Table 10.16 Decision Keys

10.4.4   Visualization of SAP Business Workflow

The metadata required for visualization of SAP Business Workflow is defined in this step. The metadata for each task type relevant to the workflow scenario is defined here.

Begin by navigating to **IMG (SPRO)** • **SAP NetWeaver** • **Application Server** • **Business Management** • **SAP Business Workflow** • **Visualization of SAP Business Workflow Metadata** • **Client-Dependent Configuration**.

On the **Change Visualization Metadata for Work Items and Objects** screen (see Figure 10.18), select **SAPUI5 My Inbox** for the **Worklist Client** field. Then, select the **Task** tab and create an entry per the information in Table 10.17.

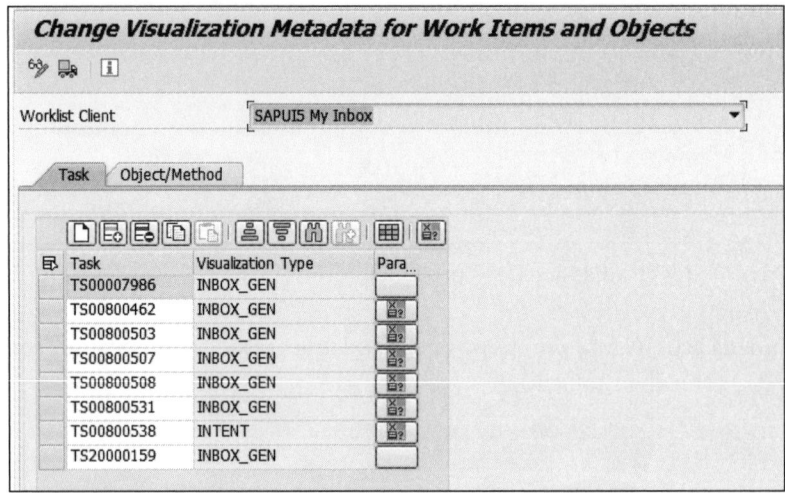

Figure 10.18 Visualization of SAP Business Workflow

Task	Visualization Type
TS00800462	INBOX_GEN

Table 10.17 Visualization Type

Then, select the **Parameters Available** button for task **TS00800462**; on the **Parameter for TS00800462** screen, maintain the values as parameter values (as given in Table 10.18).

Parameter Name	Visualization Parameter Value
APPLICATION_PATH	N/A
COMPONENT_NAME	cross.fnd.fiori.inbox.annotationBasedTaskUI
QUERY_PARAM00	service=/sap/opu/odata/sap/MM_PUR_QTN_MAINTAIN_SRV
QUERY_PARAM01	entity=/C_SuplrQuotationEnhWD(SupplierQuotation='{&_WI_Object_ID.MS_SUPPLIER_QUOTATION.SUPPLIERQUOTATION&}', DraftUUID=guid'00000000-0000-0000-0000-000000000000', IsActiveEntity=true)
QUERY_PARAM02	annotations=/sap/opu/odata/IWFND/CATALOGSERVICE;v=2/Annotations(TechnicalName='MM_PUR_QTN_MAINTAIN_ANNO_MDL',Version='0001')/$value/
SCHEME	SAPUI5

Table 10.18 Parameter Values

10.4.5   Scenario Definition

Scenarios (e.g., Workflow for Supplier Quotation) that are to be consumed by the task gateway service need to be defined. Each scenario needs to be assigned to at least one consumer type (e.g., mobile, desktop, tablet).

Begin by navigating to **IMG (SPRO)** • **SAP NetWeaver** • **SAP Gateway Service Enablement** • **Content** • **Task Gateway** • **Task Gateway Service** • **Scenario Definition**. This will open the screen shown in Figure 10.19.

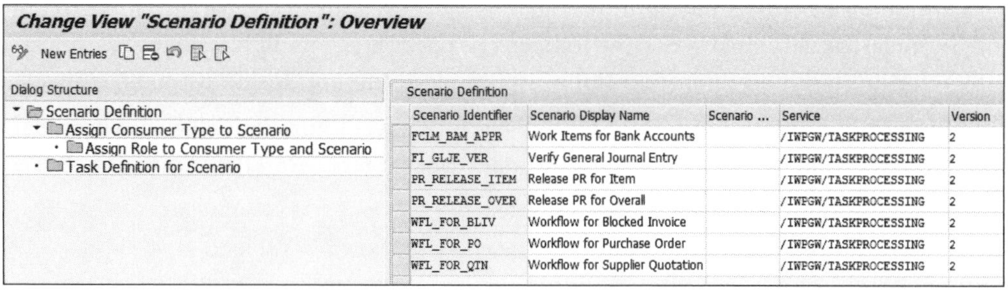

Change View "Scenario Definition": Overview

Scenario Identifier	Scenario Display Name	Scenario ...	Service	Version
FCLM_BAM_APPR	Work Items for Bank Accounts		/IWPGW/TASKPROCESSING	2
FI_GLJE_VER	Verify General Journal Entry		/IWPGW/TASKPROCESSING	2
PR_RELEASE_ITEM	Release PR for Item		/IWPGW/TASKPROCESSING	2
PR_RELEASE_OVER	Release PR for Overall		/IWPGW/TASKPROCESSING	2
WFL_FOR_BLIV	Workflow for Blocked Invoice		/IWPGW/TASKPROCESSING	2
WFL_FOR_PO	Workflow for Purchase Order		/IWPGW/TASKPROCESSING	2
WFL_FOR_QTN	Workflow for Supplier Quotation		/IWPGW/TASKPROCESSING	2

Dialog Structure:
- Scenario Definition
  - Assign Consumer Type to Scenario
    - Assign Role to Consumer Type and Scenario
  - Task Definition for Scenario

Figure 10.19 Scenario Definition

On the **Change View "Scenario Definition": Overview** screen, create a new entries per the information in Table 10.19.

Scenario Identifier	Scenario Display Name	Technical Service Name	Version	EntitySet External Name	Property External Name
WFL_FOR_QTN	Workflow for Supplier Quotation	/IWPGW/TASKPROCESSING	2	Task	TaskDefinitionID

Table 10.19 Scenario Definition Values

On the **View "Scenario Definition": Overview** screen, select the entry for **Scenario Identifier: WFL_FOR_QTN**, double-click **Assign Consumer Type to Scenario** in the **Dialog Structure** area, and create the following entry: "tablet".

Return to the overview screen, select **WFL_FOR_QTN**, choose **Task Definition for Scenario** in the **Dialog Structure** area, and create the entry shown in Table 10.20.

SAP System Alias	Task Type
LOCAL_TGW	TS00800462

Table 10.20 SAP System Alias

10.4.6   Maintain Attribute for Workflow Task

There are two levels of agent assignment in SAP Business Workflow: determining possible agents and determining responsible agents. The work item is only sent to the responsible agents, but the responsible agents must also be possible agents. We recommend that all employees in the company be possible agents. By classifying the task as a general task, we guarantee that the responsible agents are also always possible agents.

Begin by navigating to **IMG (SPRO)** • **SAP NetWeaver** • **Application Server** • **Basis Services** • **ArchiveLink** • **Customizing Incoming Documents** • **Workflow Scenarios** • **Determine Possible Agents for a Task**.

On the **Task: Maintain** screen, fill in the entry as shown in Table 10.21.

Task Type	Task
Standard Task	00800462

Table 10.21 Task Maintain Values

Choose **Display** to see the screen shown in Figure 10.20.

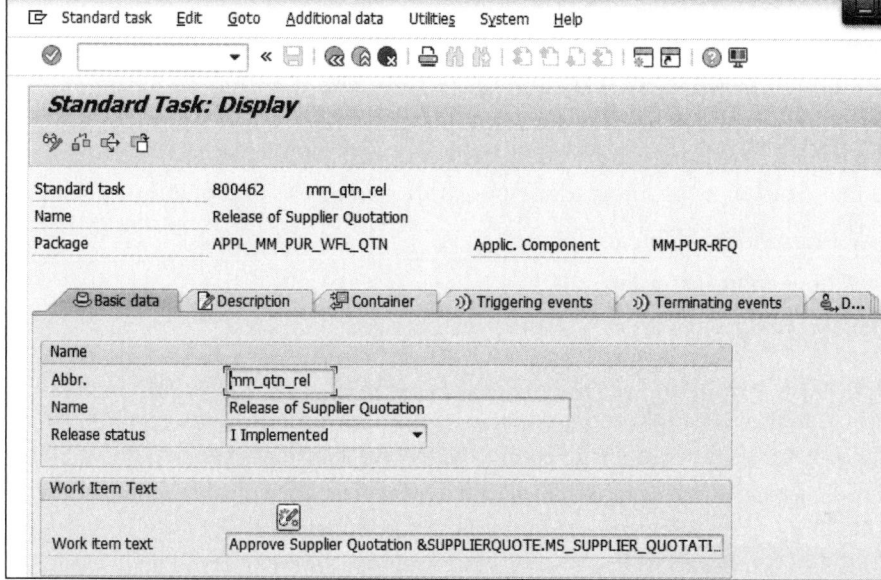

Figure 10.20 Maintain Attribute for Workflow Task

On the **Standard Task: Display** screen, go to **Additional Data** • **Agent Assignment** • **Maintain**.

On the **Standard task: Maintain Agent Assignment** screen (see Figure 10.21), select the row shown in Table 10.22.

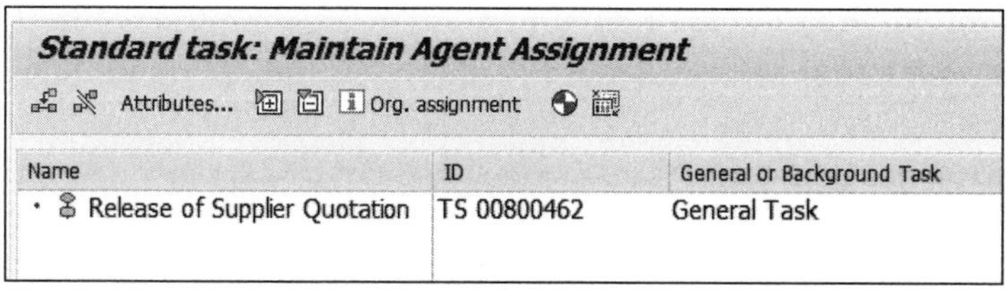

Figure 10.21 Maintain Agent Assignment

Name	ID
Release of Supplier Quotation	TS 00800462

Table 10.22 Agent Assignment

Click **Attributes**, then, on the **Task** screen, choose **General Task** and click **Transfer**. Then, go back twice and complete the activity.

10.5   Integration with SAP Ariba

SAP provides three integration options between SAP S/4HANA and SAP Ariba's cloud solutions. The following integration options are available as of the time of writing:

- SAP Cloud Platform Integration
- SAP Process Orchestration
- Direct connectivity via SAP S/4HANA webservices

However, SAP's strategic approach for SAP Ariba integration is SAP Ariba Cloud Integration Gateway. This solution is enabled by SAP Cloud Platform Integration, which provides a fast and simple way to connect SAP Ariba solutions with backend systems and trading partners. This approach eliminates the need for multiple adapters for different solutions and scenarios. SAP Ariba Cloud Integration Gateway comes with intuitive self-service tools that enable quick and easy configuration and testing. The self-service wizard provides the following features:

- Automated testing and scenarios
- Real-time monitoring and alerts
- Automatic upgrades
- Alignment with SAP
- Security safeguards

10.6   Summary

Sourcing—more specifically, external sourcing—involves collaboration with suppliers outside the organization. SAP has strategically used SAP Ariba solutions as the way to achieve this external communication and collaboration. Tight integration optimizes the overall solution capability. In this chapter, we focused on the SAP S/4HANA side of the solution. The next chapter will explore the final step in a source-to-pay process, in which an invoice is submitted and it comes time for the procuring organization to pay their receivers.

Chapter 11
Invoice and Payables Management

Entry of a supplier invoice, matching this information with data from purchasing and receiving, and the subsequent processing of invoice data to facilitate payment completes the procure-to-pay process cycle enabled by SAP S/4HANA.

Invoice management and payables management are essential end-to-end processes delivered with SAP S/4HANA Sourcing and Procurement. The entry and validation of a supplier's invoice into the system records the billing details and enables the matching and approval processes. Once the invoice is entered, matched, and optionally approved, the process to pay a supplier for the goods and services rendered is performed. These two processes complete the procure-to-pay end-to-end business process.

This chapter will describe the applications supplied by SAP S/4HANA to enable the invoice processing and accounts payable business processes. We'll first delve into supplier invoice processing, describing how to manage the entry and validation of invoices in the SAP S/4HANA system. Then we'll explore the transactional and analytic apps that enable accounts payable, which results in optimal payments being rendered to suppliers.

11.1 What Are Invoice and Payables Management?

In invoice management, all pertinent details of a supplier invoice are entered into the system, which are then verified against both the purchasing documents to which they reference and the quantities of goods or services that have been received to date. If the document details, such as the prices and quantities in the entered invoice, match the information contained in the SAP S/4HANA system, then the supplier invoice document is accepted and posted to the system. If discrepancies are found, then the documents can be held or parked and the discrepancies addressed with the supplier and with the purchasing and receiving departments. Once the discrepancies are reconciled, then the supplier invoice document can be successfully posted in the system, with appropriate accounting documents created to reflect the general ledger impact of the invoice entry.

In payables management, the accepted invoice becomes eligible for payment. A payment proposal is generated by the system. Once the proposal is reviewed and approved, it's included in a subsequent payment run. Funds are then transferred from the enterprise to the supplier's banking accounts via a variety of payment methods.

The SAP S/4HANA system contains integrated capabilities to handle the complete invoice verification and payables processes. There are three main solution capabilities available in SAP S/4HANA:

- **Invoice processing**
  Entry and validation of supplier invoices into the system
- **Accounts payable**
  Processing of payments due to suppliers
- **Invoice collaboration**
  Working with suppliers to integrate invoices and payables via the Ariba Network

We'll describe each solution's capabilities in detail in the following sections.

11.2   Invoice Processing

The invoice processing capability of SAP S/4HANA Sourcing and Procurement is focused on the entry, validation, and posting of supplier invoice details in the SAP S/4HANA system. The information contained in the invoice presented by the supplier is checked for accuracy against the customer's referenced purchasing documents and the goods receipts that have been logged into the system. Price, quantity, tax, and accounting information are all checked.

If the total invoice amount is in balance with the reference documents, then the invoice document can be posted successfully in the system. The appropriate financial postings are also posted at the same time due to the integration of invoice processing with financial accounting.

If the total invoice amount isn't found to be in balance or additional information or expertise is needed to process the invoice document, then the invoice entry can be held or parked by the invoice entry processor for later processing by knowledgeable personnel.

Entry of supplier invoices that reference purchasing documents is supported, as are financial invoices (finance only) without a specific purchase document reference.

SAP S/4HANA brings many innovations to invoice processing. Managing supplier invoices in classic SAP ERP involved a good deal of transferring back and forth between multiple screens. First, selection criteria had to be entered on an invoice listing screen. The resulting report listed all invoice documents that satisfied the entered selection criteria. Detecting issues and resolving them involved moving back and forth between the invoice list screen and the invoice details screen. If you needed to change the selection criteria of the invoice list, you needed to fully regenerate the invoice list first.

With SAP S/4HANA, the dynamic search capabilities in the Supplier Invoices List app provide a streamlined way of selecting and managing invoices of concern.

The many apps available to support invoice processing make the job of entering supplier invoices streamlined and simple. The following native SAP Fiori apps for invoice processing are available:

- Create Supplier Invoice
- Supplier Invoices List
- Display Supplier Balances

Note

The following WebGUI transactional apps for invoice processing are also available from SAP:

- Create Supplier Invoice (Advanced)
- Display Supplier Invoice (Advanced)
- Release Blocked Invoices
- Clear GR/IR Clearing Account
- Display/Cancel Account Maintenance
- Create Consignment and Pipeline Settlement
- Create Evaluated Receipt Settlement

11.2.1   Supplier Invoice Documents

The supplier invoice document in SAP S/4HANA is a representation of the presentation and acceptance of a bill from a supplier to a customer. It also passes information needed to complete the procure-to-pay cycle to financial accounting. Entry of a supplier invoice document is a necessary step in most procure-to-pay processes; it ensures that a supplier will be paid for the goods or services provided.

There are four types of supplier invoice documents supported by the SAP S/4HANA system:

- Supplier invoice
- Credit memo
- Subsequent credit
- Subsequent debit

Supplier Invoice

A *supplier invoice* is a document presented by a supplier for reimbursement of goods or services rendered. It contains details about the supplier, bank information, identification of items and quantities purchased, supplier pricing, unplanned delivery costs, and tax and account determination information.

Credit Memo

A *credit memo* is a document used to record the entry of an invoice for a credit claimed from the supplier. This document arises from a return of defective goods, a reduction of an invoice, or for other reasons.

These documents can be considered debits for the vendor. The accounting postings for credit memos typically are the reverse of a normal supplier invoice posting.

Credit memos can be entered directly into the system or can be generated automatically via evaluated receipt settlement (ERS).

Subsequent Credit

A *subsequent credit* invoice document is posted when you've entered and settled an invoice for which the supplier has billed you at too high a price. The subsequent credit memo entered is a value-only document and doesn't affect the quantities originally invoiced. It's valuable to enter subsequent credits when needed in the system to preserve the invoice history.

Subsequent Debit

A *subsequent debit* invoice document is posted when you've entered and settled an invoice for which the supplier has billed you at too low a price. The subsequent

debit memo entered is value-only as well and doesn't affect the quantities originally invoiced.

Automatic Settlements

Invoice documents can be created automatically in the system, based on regularly
scheduled settlements of procurement processes. These include ERS, consignment or
pipeline settlement, or billing based on invoicing plans. These processes produce
invoice documents based on data in your SAP S/4HANA system, rather than relying
on a bill submitted by the supplier directly.

11.2.2   Results of Invoice Processing

The following actions take place on successful posting of an invoice document in SAP
S/4HANA:

- A logistics invoice document is created to reflect the supplier billing details.
- One or more financial documents are created based on the data entered. These
  finance documents reference and are traceable to the logistics invoice document.
  These documents post the amounts entered for the invoice line items to the
  appropriate general ledger accounts.
- The purchase order history in the referenced purchasing document line items is
  updated, which provides a complete audit trail of activities linked to line items.
- If required, the prices on the material master are adjusted.

11.2.3   Types of Supplier Invoice Verification

There are two types of supplier invoice verification supported by the SAP S/4HANA
system. They differ in the data that is proposed during the entry of the invoice document. These two types are purchase order-based invoice verification and goods
receipt-based invoice verification.

Purchase Order–Based Invoice Verification

In this technique, illustrated in Figure 11.1, the system generates one invoice line for
each referenced purchase order item. The quantities proposed during invoice entry
are determined by the difference between the total delivered quantity and the total
invoiced quantity. If the quantities and amounts on the supplier invoice differ from
those proposed, as in the case of a partial goods receipt, these items will need to be
adjusted by the invoice processor.

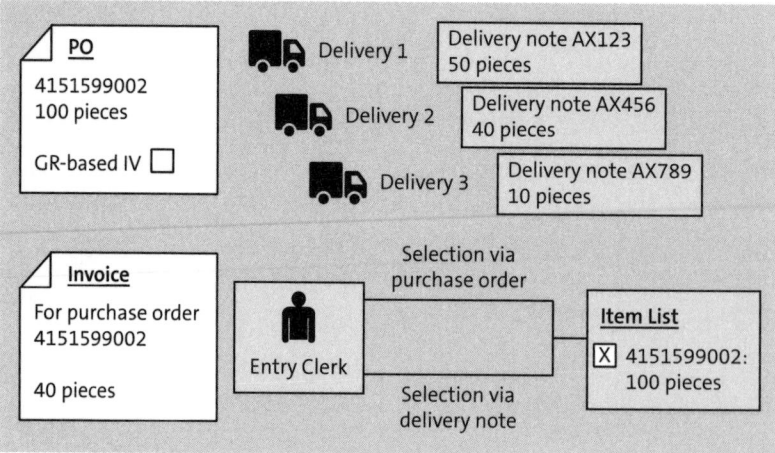

Figure 11.1 Purchase Order–Based Invoice Verification

Goods Receipt–Based Invoice Verification

In this technique, illustrated in Figure 11.2, the quantities and amounts proposed on the invoice entry must match one or more goods receipts recorded in the SAP S/4HANA system. With goods receipt-based invoice verification, the invoice can't be entered without a goods receipt reference. This procedure is useful if you want to assure that goods have been received prior to posting a supplier's invoice.

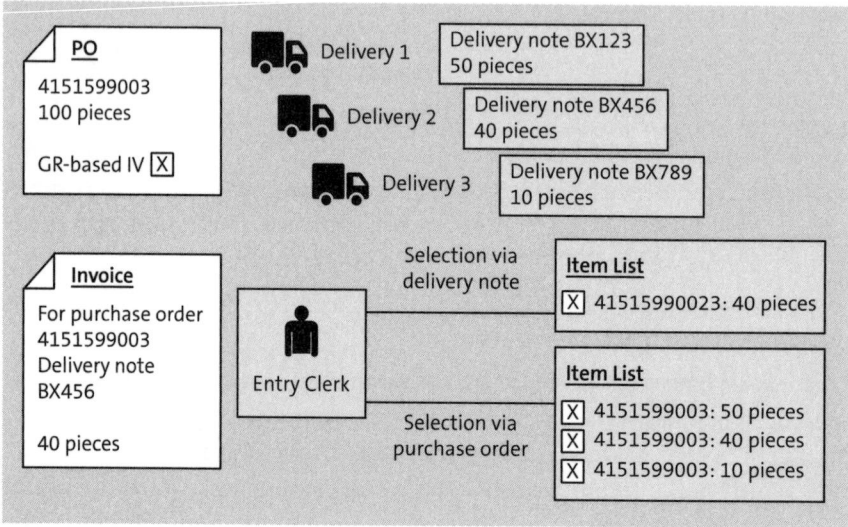

Figure 11.2 Goods Receipt–Based Invoice Verification

The invoice lines created are proposed from each partial delivery connected to the referenced purchasing documents or delivery notes. This allows goods receipts and invoice receipts to be aligned in the purchase order history.

This function is controlled by setting the GR-based **Invoice Verification** indicator on the purchasing organization views for the supplier business partner role. The value here is adopted into the purchasing document. If desired, this same setting can be made at the purchasing organization and plant levels as well by maintaining alternate purchasing data for the business partner. The setting at the plant level supersedes the value from the purchasing organization view.

The GR-based **Invoice Verification** indicator can be set or unset on a PIR as well. This setting for a PIR is adopted into the purchasing document preferentially over the settings maintained in the supplier master.

11.2.4   Entry of Invoice Documents

A supplier's invoice can be entered via a variety of techniques into the SAP S/4HANA system. It's possible to utilize all types of invoice entry techniques, depending on the supplier and your business requirements:

- Invoice entry online, using SAP Fiori apps
- Invoice entry via EDI
- Invoice entry via the Ariba Network

Online Invoice Entry Using SAP Fiori Apps

Use the available online SAP Fiori apps to enter a supplier invoice when the document is presented to you via normal delivery methods, such as the postal service or email. The SAP S/4HANA system automatically adopts referenced documents to minimize data entry, and it verifies that the prices and quantities presented by the supplier match the information in your system.

Basic header data about the invoice is entered into the system, such as the invoice date, invoice reference from the supplier, and total invoice amount. A tax code can be entered here if needed.

References to purchasing documents such as purchase orders, scheduling agreements, or service entry sheets are then entered. The system will adopt key information from these documents such as quantities, prices, and tax information, thereby speeding up invoice data entry and reducing errors.

The system checks that the invoice data from the supplier matches the information in the reference documents. If the total amount doesn't balance or is outside of configured tolerances, then the system will flag the invoice and won't allow posting until corrections are made.

Sometimes freight charges passed onto you from the supplier are present on an invoice. If these weren't planned for in the purchase order itself, this amount can be added to the invoice in the form of unplanned delivery costs.

The invoice can be held, parked, saved as complete, or posted by the invoice processor as needed. Figure 11.3 shows these invoice statuses.

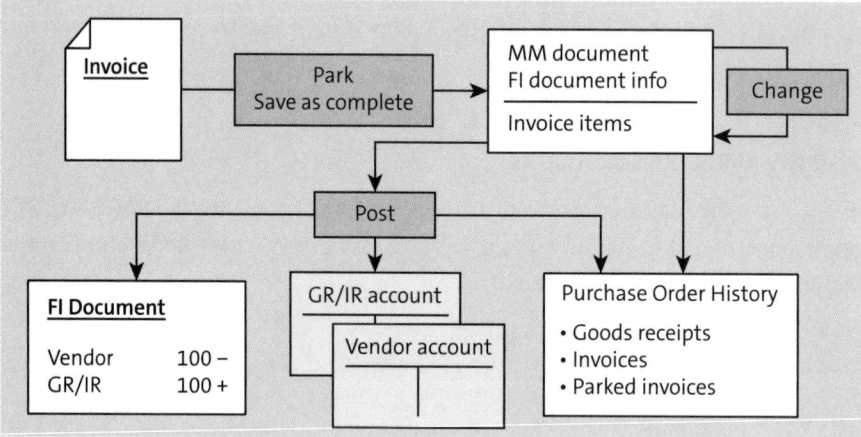

Figure 11.3 Supplier Invoice Statuses

Holding a document lets you save the invoice document in its current state, with only the minimum amount of validation. The system only checks for the existence of the company code and supplier. A logistics invoice document is created during hold, but no financial documents are posted and no updates to purchase order history are performed. Held invoices need to be monitored and subsequently processed for the procure-to-pay process to continue.

Parking an invoice document is useful if you're missing data needed for posting and you don't want to have to reenter the data. The invoice document doesn't have to be in balance to be parked. A logistics invoice document is created, and the purchase order history is updated as well. An open, parked supplier line item is also generated and finance document numbers assigned. A duplicate invoice check also occurs at this time. Parking a document can trigger a workflow to commence further processing on the invoice document.

Save as complete is another option that you can use if you have a complete, balanced document but don't want to post the document at that point. Like parked documents, a logistics invoice document is created, and the purchase order history is updated as well. An open, saved as complete supplier line item also is generated and finance document numbers assigned. A duplicate invoice check also occurs at this time.

The SAP Fiori apps used to enter an invoice into the SAP S/4HANA system are described in more detail in the following sections.

If required, entered invoices can go through an approval process. There are standard workflows available in the SAP S/4HANA system to route a supplier invoice document to approvers based on your company's requirements.

Posting a supplier invoice in SAP S/4HANA will typically result in the following postings:

- Debit to the supplier subaccount of the invoicing supplier partner on the invoice
- Credit to the GR/IR account

Invoice Entry Using Electronic Data Interchange

EDI can be used between two trading partners to facilitate the exchange of documents. Transmitting a supplier invoice and the subsequent posting of that document in the system is a key process often enabled via this technique. The system validates the data sent by the supplier and, if acceptable, posts the invoice into the system without the need for human intervention. SAP S/4HANA supports multiple EDI protocols for the transmission and acceptance of supplier invoice documents.

Invoice Entry via the Ariba Network

The Ariba Network is a cloud-based business-to-business marketplace in which buyers and suppliers can connect and do business on a single, networked platform. Exchange of supplier invoices is just one of the standard integrations built into SAP Ariba that can be integrated into the SAP S/4HANA system.

Invoice Reduction

If you dispute the values or quantities on the supplier invoice presented, you can reduce the invoice entered to match what you think is correct. This is known as *invoice reduction* in SAP S/4HANA (see Figure 11.4). To reduce an invoice, take the following steps:

- Mark the line item as **Vendor Error: Reduce Invoice**.
- Enter the reduced value or quantity (or both) into the reduction fields provided.
- Verify the values and quantities given on the supplier invoice and enter them in the fields provided.

The system posts two documents when invoice reduction is used. First, an invoice document for the invoiced quantities and values is created. Second, a credit memo is generated for the difference quantities and values. Optionally, you can also generate a complaint document that can be transmitted back to the supplier in this situation.

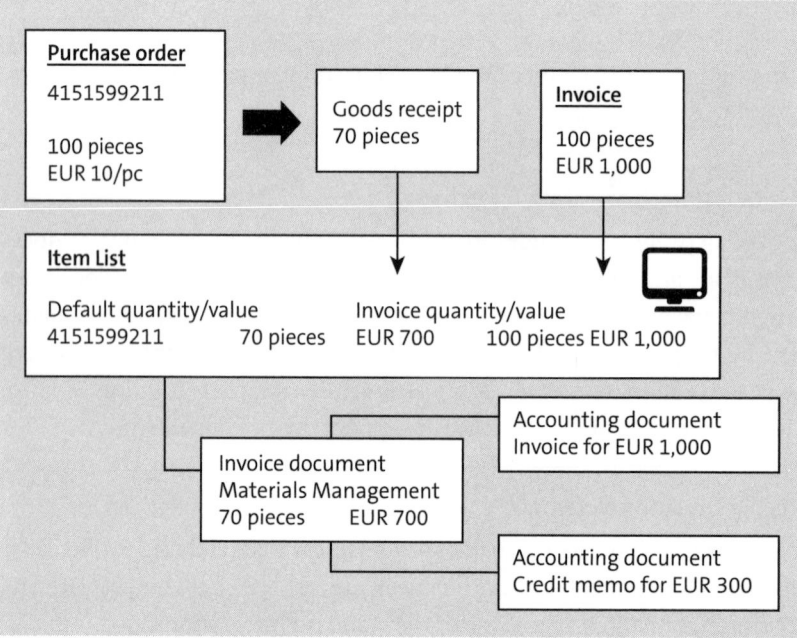

Figure 11.4 Invoice Reduction

Simulation of Invoice Postings

SAP S/4HANA can simulate the accounting postings for an invoice prior to the actual posting of the invoice document. This capability allows the invoice processor to observe the general ledger account postings based on the entered data.

Click the **Simulate** button to see the resulting simulated postings. You can also post the invoice directly from the simulation if you wish.

11.2.5 Invoice Processing

There are a variety of SAP Fiori transactional apps available to enter and process supplier invoice documents and monitor the GR/IR accounts in SAP S/4HANA:

- Create Supplier Invoice
- Create Supplier Invoice—Advanced
- Import Supplier Invoices

Create Supplier Invoice

This native SAP Fiori app allows you to create and display a supplier invoice based on information received from your supplier. You can note one or more purchase order items to which this invoice refers. Once entered, SAP S/4HANA compares the quantity and amount data for each supplier invoice item with the data of the related purchase order item. If goods receipt–based invoice verification has been defined for a purchase order item, the system compares the supplier invoice data with the related goods receipt data as well. If the quantities or amounts lie outside defined tolerances, the invoice is posted as automatically blocked for payment. An approval process also can be triggered by the system. When looking at the details, you can reverse a posted supplier invoice or release a blocked invoice. These features are available in the Create Supplier Invoice app (as shown in Figure 11.5 and Figure 11.6):

- Create a new supplier invoice document; you can create credit memos, subsequent credits, and subsequent debits as well.
- Edit fields on the invoice document, which the system then transfers to financial accounting.
- Change the currency exchange rate displayed, if allowed by customization.
- Relate all entered invoice items for one or multiple purchase order references for which the invoice was received. You can deselect items that are not relevant.

- It's possible to create a supplier invoice without a purchase order reference. In this case, additional data will need to be entered manually in the invoice document, such as currency, baseline date, terms of payment, and invoicing party.
- Create additional general ledger account items as required.
- Enter and check tax data for the invoice.
- Edit payment terms if the payment terms pulled from the purchase order need to be altered.
- Enter unplanned delivery costs presented on the supplier's invoice.
- Add one or more attachments to the invoice document.
- Simulate, hold, or post the supplier invoice.
- Reduce the invoice, which generates a credit memo alongside the invoice document.
- Output specific business documents, such as letters of complaint to the invoicing party arising due to invoice reduction.

The Create Supplier Invoice app is assigned to the accounts payable accountant—procurement standard authorization role.

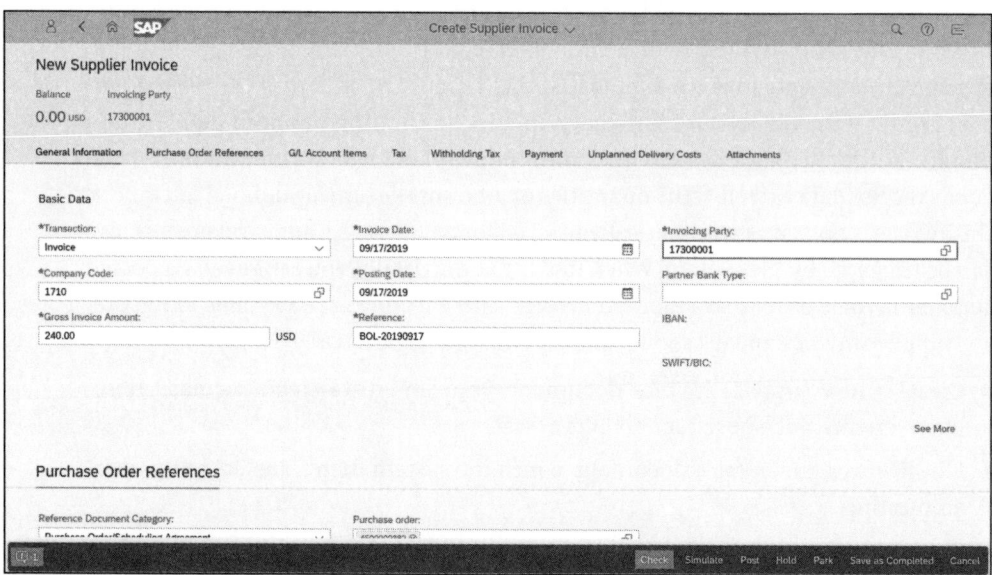

Figure 11.5 Create Supplier Invoice App: General Information

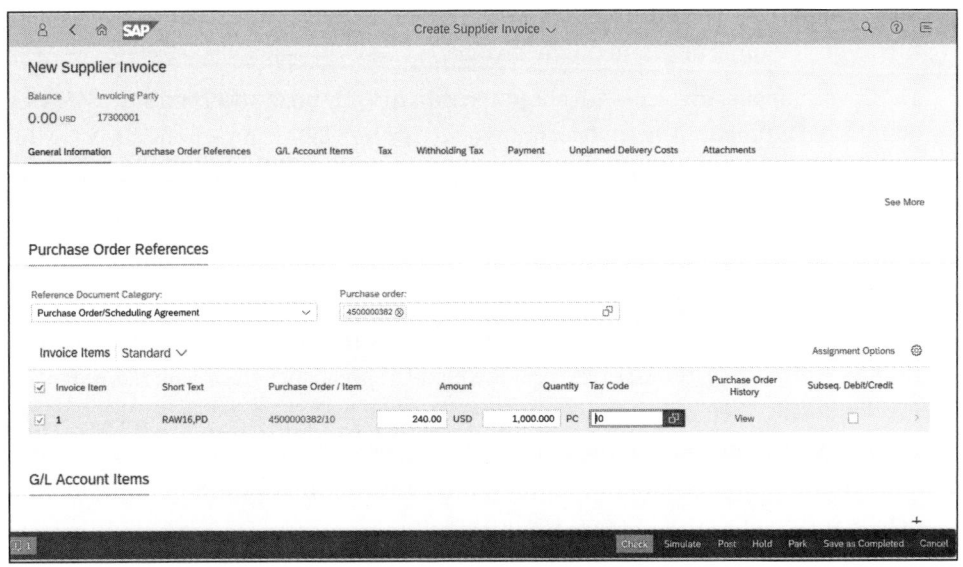

Figure 11.6 Create Supplier Invoice App: Purchase Order Reference

Create Supplier Invoice—Advanced App

The Create Supplier Invoice—Advanced app (Figure 11.7) is used when the supplier invoice is too complex to enter using the Create Supplier Invoice native SAP Fiori app.

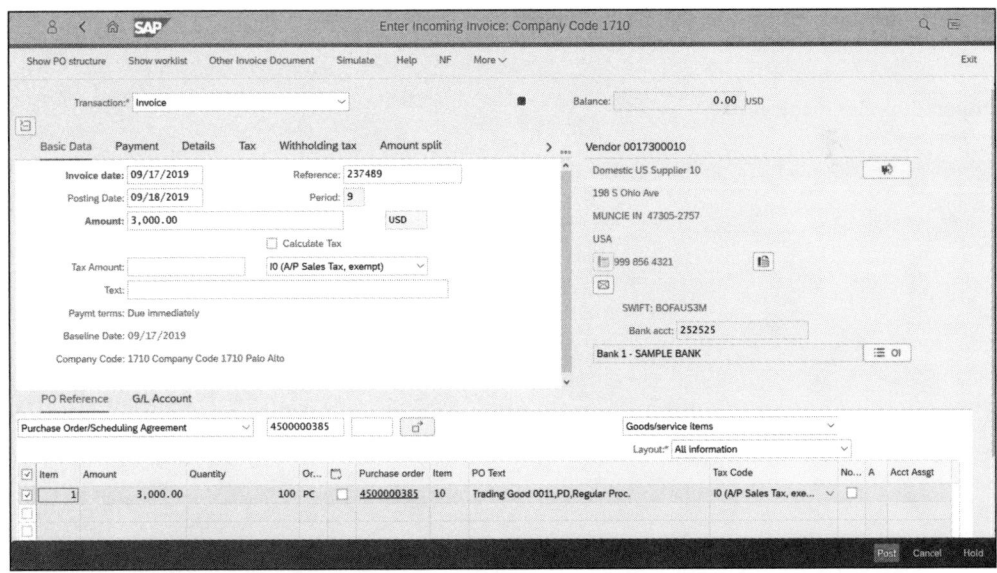

Figure 11.7 Create Supplier Invoice—Advanced App

This situation can occur, for example, if you need to register multiple account assignments for the same line item on the invoice.

The Create Supplier Invoice—Advanced app runs directly on the backend SAP S/4HANA system and is functionally equivalent to the classic SAP ERP Transaction MIRO.

The Create Supplier Invoice—Advanced app is assigned to the accounts payable accountant—procurement standard authorization role.

Import Supplier Invoices

The Import Supplier Invoices app allows you to import multiple supplier invoices into the SAP S/4HANA system at once. You download a spreadsheet template file, enter the invoice details, then upload the completed file back into the app (see Figure 11.8 and Figure 11.9). The entered information is verified. You may then post the invoices from the app. You can also navigate to the Create Supplier Invoice app to view invoice details, correct any errors, or post the invoice.

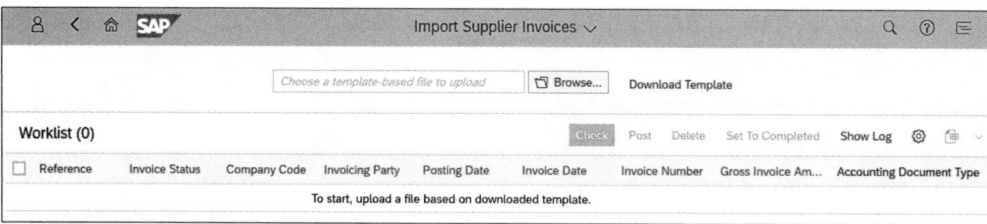

Figure 11.8 Import Supplier Invoices App

Import Supplier Invoices

Last Updated 09/18/2019

	Header Data						
	COMPANYCODE	SUPPLIERINVOICETRANSACTIONTYPE	INVOICINGPARTY	SUPPLIERINVOICEIDBYINVCGPART	DOCUMENTDATE	POSTINGDATE	ACCOUNTINGDOCUI
*Invoice ID	*Company Code (4)	*Transaction (1) 1=Invoice; 2=Credit Memo	*Invoicing Party (10)	Reference (16)	*Document Date	*Posting Date	*Document Type (2)
1	1710	1	17300001	DL-6664	10/2/2019	10/2/2019	RE
2	1710	1	17300001	DL-6665	10/2/2019	10/2/2019	RE
3	1710	1	17300004	54345355345	10/2/2019	10/2/2019	RE
4	1710	1	17300004	54345355346	10/2/2019	10/2/2019	RE
5	1710	1	17300004	54345355350	10/2/2019	10/2/2019	RE
6	1710	1	17300004	54345355450	10/2/2019	10/2/2019	RE
7	1710	1	17300004	54345356001	10/2/2019	10/2/2019	RE
8	1710	1	17300010	INV-20191001-015	10/2/2019	10/2/2019	RE
9	1710	1	17300010	INV-20191001-016	10/2/2019	10/2/2019	RE
10	1710	1	17300010	INV-20191001-017	10/2/2019	10/2/2019	RE
11	1710	1	17300010	INV-20191001-018	10/2/2019	10/2/2019	RE
12	1710	1	17300010	INV-20191001-019	10/2/2019	10/2/2019	RE
13	1710	1	17300010	INV-20191001-020	10/2/2019	10/2/2019	RE
14	1710	1	17300010	INV-20191001-021	10/2/2019	10/2/2019	RE
15	1710	1	17300010	INV-20191001-022	10/2/2019	10/2/2019	RE

Figure 11.9 Import Supplier Invoices Template

Extensive documentation on the invoice entry template can be found in the app documentation available at the SAP Help site. Up to 500 invoice line items may be imported in one execution of the app.

The Import Supplier Invoices app is assigned to the accounts payable accountant—procurement standard authorization role.

Several other invoice processing apps are available within the SAP S/4HANA system:

- Release Blocked Invoices
- Print Supplier Invoices
- Clear GR/IR Clearing Account
- Display/Cancel Account Maintenance
- Create Consignment and Pipeline Settlement
- Create Evaluated Receipt Settlement

We'll discuss these in the following sections.

Release Blocked Invoices

Invoices may be blocked in SAP S/4HANA for a variety of reasons, such as exceeding invoice tolerances or a stochastic (random) block.

The Release Blocked Invoices app allows you to obtain a list of all blocked invoice documents and selectively release any documents that were blocked and for which the root cause of blocking (e.g., a missing goods receipt) has been addressed. Invoices that were manually blocked during invoice entry can be released using this app as well (as shown in Figure 11.10 and Figure 11.11).

This app runs on the backend SAP S/4HANA system and is functionally equivalent to the classic SAP ERP Transaction MRBR.

The Release Blocked Invoices app is assigned to the accounts payable accountant—procurement standard authorization role.

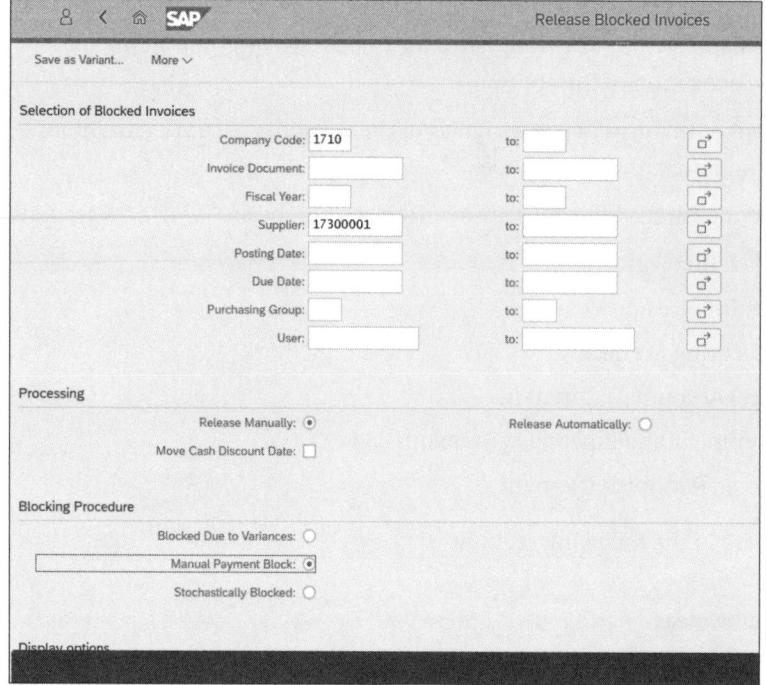

Figure 11.10 Release Blocked Invoices App: Selection Screen

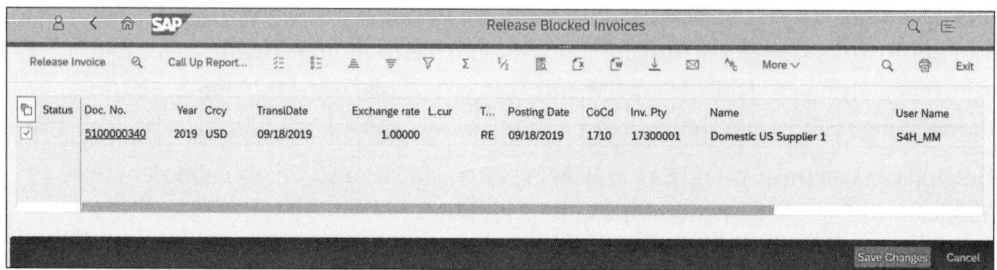

Figure 11.11 Release Blocked Invoices App: Worklist

Print Supplier Invoices

This app allows you to print outputs from invoice processing in real time (see Figure 11.12 and Figure 11.13). These outputs include complaint communications from invoice reduction and ERS documents.

This app runs on the backend SAP S/4HANA system and is functionally equivalent to the classic SAP ERP Transaction MR90.

The Print Supplier Invoices app is assigned to the accounts payable accountant—procurement standard authorization role.

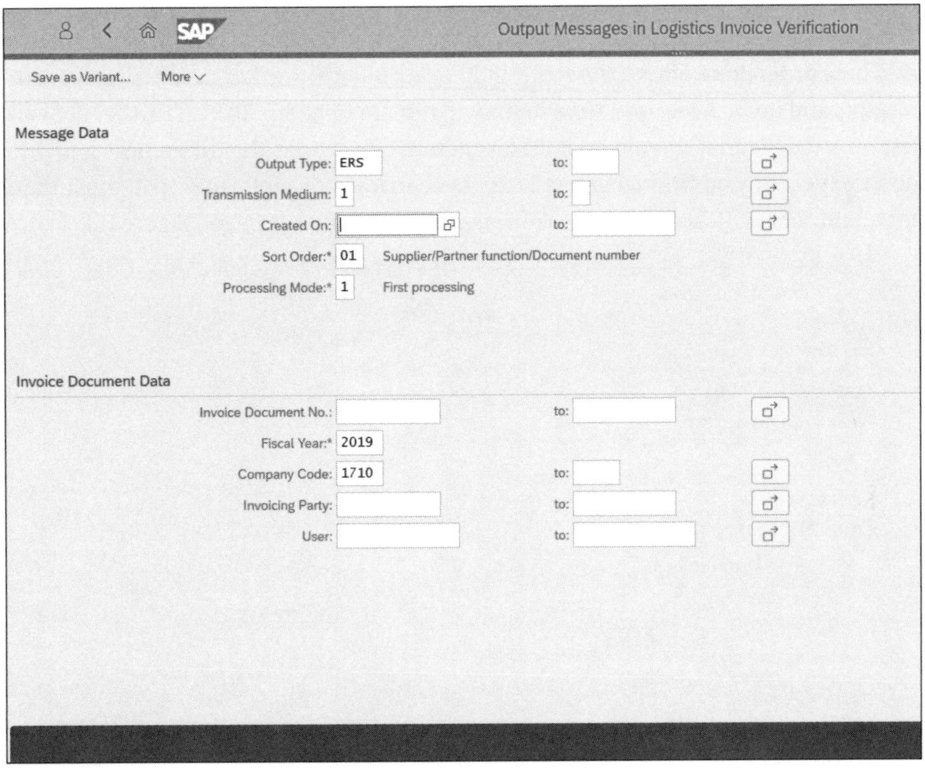

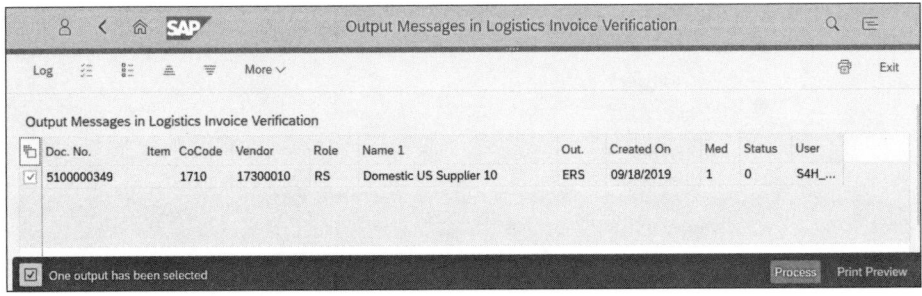

Figure 11.12 Print Supplier Invoices App: Selection Screen

Figure 11.13 Print Supplier Invoices App: Worklist Screen

Clear GR/IR Clearing Account App

The goods receipt/invoice receipt (GR/IR) clearing account is a general ledger account used for clearing quantities and amounts from goods receipts and supplier invoices. The GR/IR account is cleared if the delivered quantity and the invoiced quantity for a purchase order line item are the same. If there are quantity differences between goods receipts and invoice receipts, then items will remain open in GR/IR. If further deliveries, return deliveries, invoices, or credit memos don't clear the differences and you don't expect any additional goods receipts or invoice receipts, then you must then maintain the GR/IR account manually (as shown in Figure 11.14 and Figure 11.15).

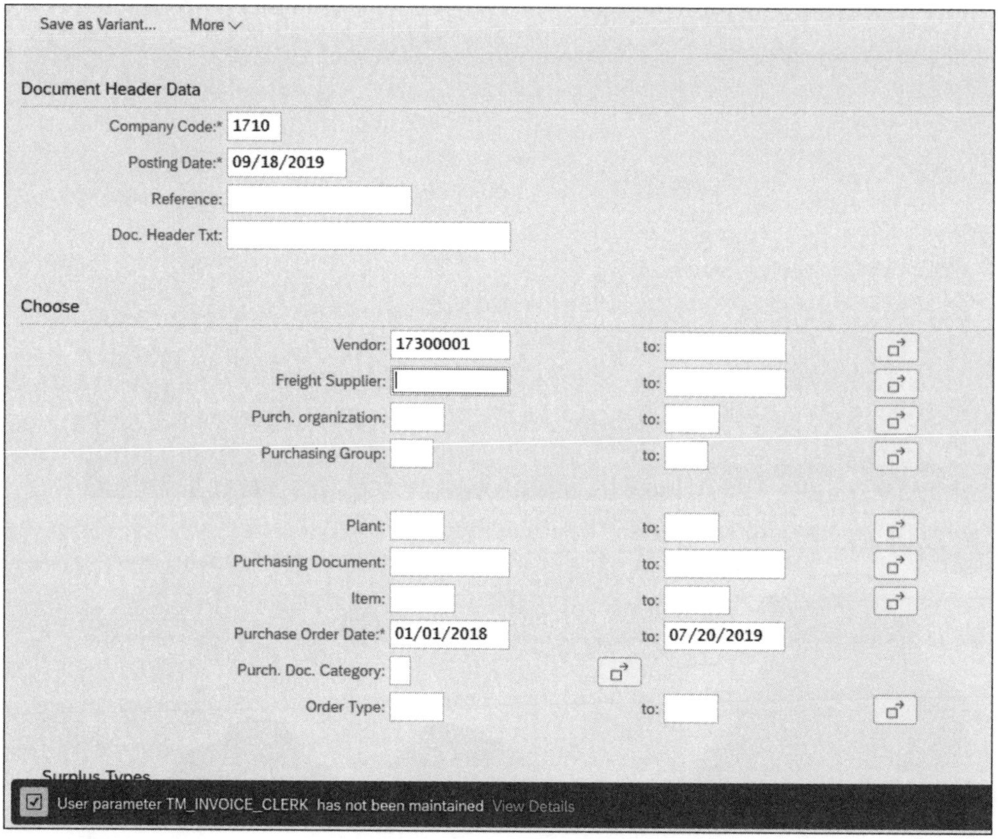

Figure 11.14 Clear GR/IR Clearing Account App: Selection Screen

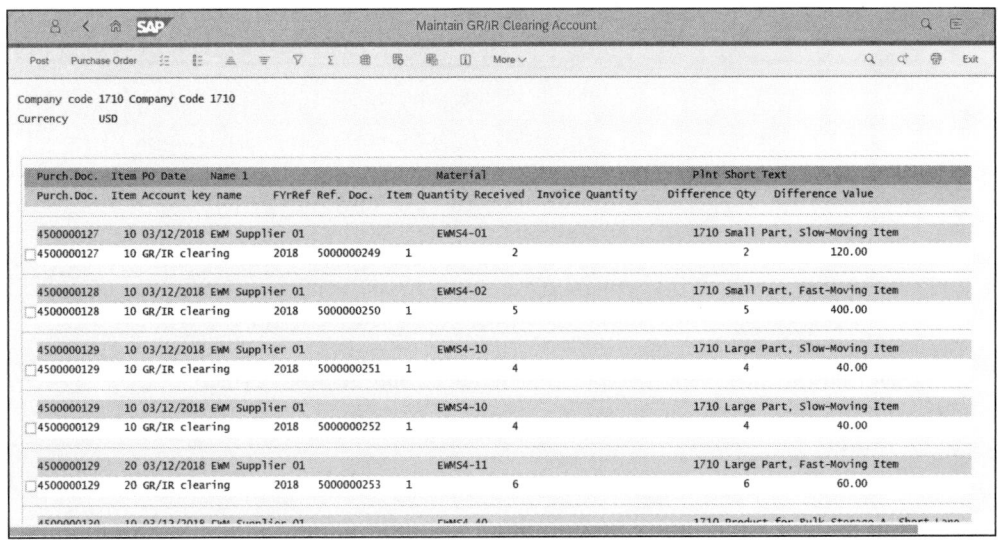

Figure 11.15 Clear GR/IR Clearing Account: Worklist Screen

The Clear GR/IR Clearing Account app allows you to clear leftover quantities from the GR/IR general ledger account as needed. The system creates an account maintenance document to record this transaction.

This app runs on the backend SAP S/4HANA system and is functionally equivalent to the classic SAP ERP Transaction MR11.

The Clear GR/IR Clearing Account app is assigned to the accounts payable accountant—procurement standard authorization role.

Display/Cancel Account Maintenance

The Display/Cancel Account Maintenance app allows you to show or cancel a GR/IR account maintenance document that was previously posted to the database. You may need to cancel these documents if, for example, the documents were posted in error. This app is shown in Figure 11.16 and Figure 11.17.

This app runs on the backend SAP S/4HANA system and is functionally equivalent to the classic SAP ERP Transaction MR11SHOW.

The Display/Cancel Account Maintenance app is assigned to the accounts payable accountant—procurement standard authorization role.

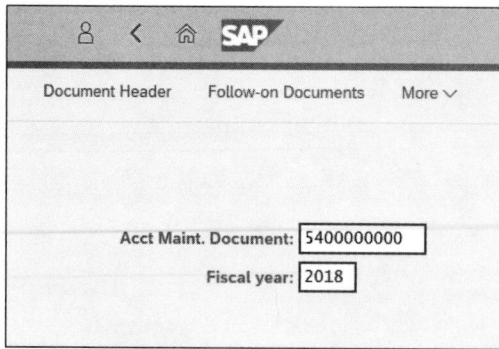

Figure 11.16 Display/Cancel Account Maintenance App: Selection Screen

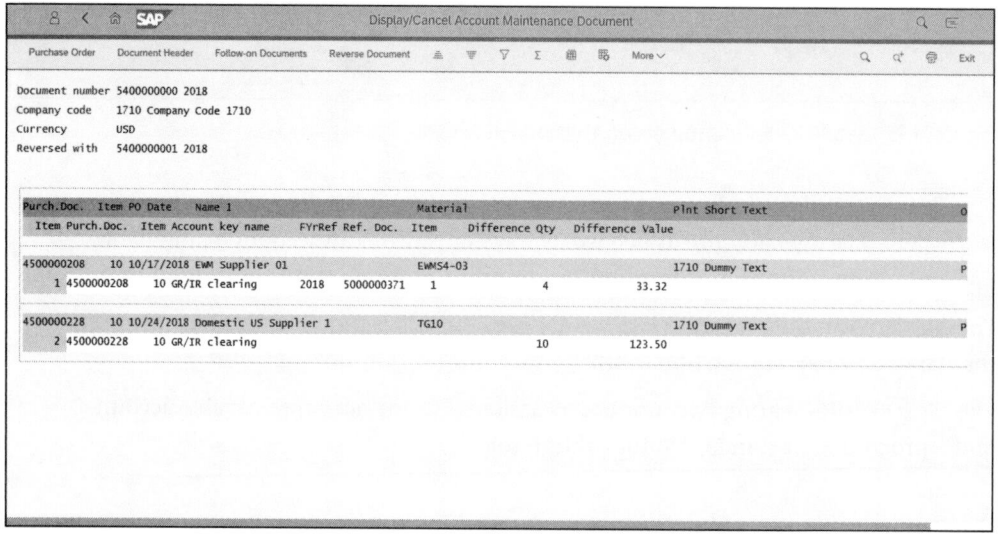

Figure 11.17 Display/Cancel Account Maintenance App: Worklist Screen

Create Consignment and Pipeline Settlement

The Create Consignment and Pipeline Settlement app allows you to periodically settle consignment and pipeline liabilities that occur during normal business. This app is shown in Figure 11.18 and Figure 11.19.

Because consignment and pipeline withdrawals are made in the system in inventory management, a supplier liability record is recorded in the system with a price that's valid at the date of withdrawal. This price isn't on record in the referenced purchase order; it's obtained from the consignment or pipeline PIR.

474

This settlement function will post an invoice document in the system automatically for any supplier consignment or pipeline liabilities that it finds based on the selection criteria entered into the SAP S/4HANA system.

This app runs on the backend SAP S/4HANA system and is functionally equivalent to the classic SAP ERP Transaction MRKO.

The Create Consignment and Pipeline Settlement app is assigned to the accounts payable accountant—procurement standard authorization role.

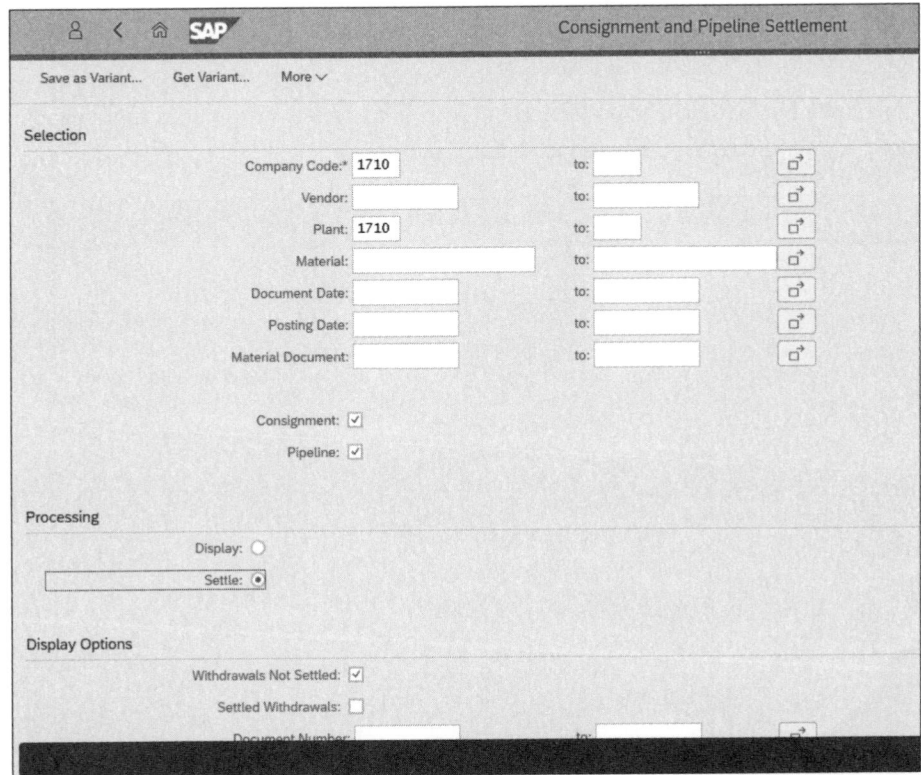

Figure 11.18 Create Consignment and Pipeline Settlement App: Selection

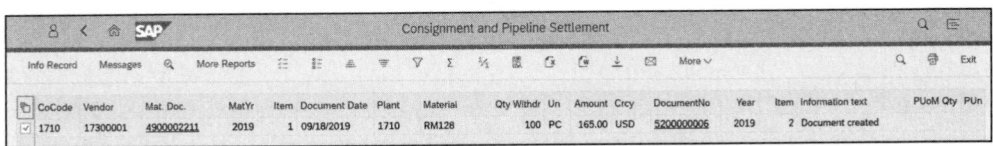

Figure 11.19 Create Consignment and Pipeline Settlement App: Worklist

Create Evaluated Receipt Settlement

The Create Evaluated Receipt Settlement app allows you to automatically create invoice documents for purchase order items that have been received from specified suppliers. The supplier doesn't send an invoice for its shipments; rather, you create invoices based on the goods receipt quantities and the purchase price found on the purchase order line items. You can generate a message to the supplier informing it of the invoices generated via this procedure. This app is shown in Figure 11.20 and Figure 11.21.

This app runs on the backend SAP S/4HANA system and is functionally equivalent to the classic SAP ERP Transaction MRRL.

The Create Evaluated Receipt Settlement app is assigned to the accounts payable accountant—procurement standard authorization role.

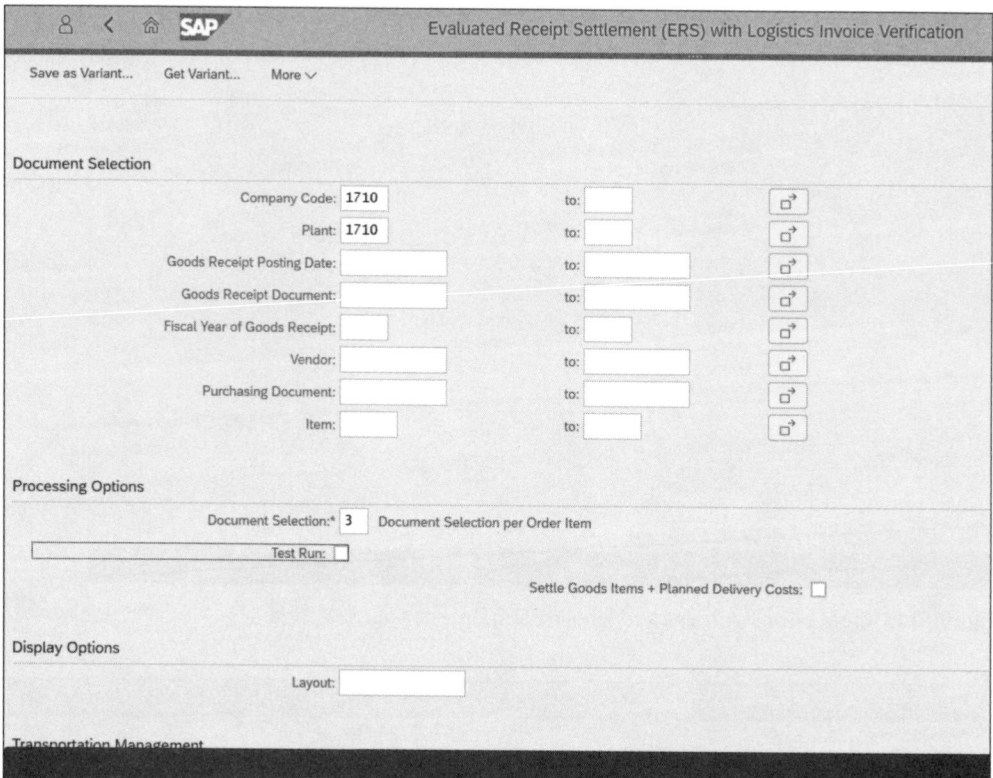

Figure 11.20 Create Evaluated Receipt Settlement App: Selection Screen

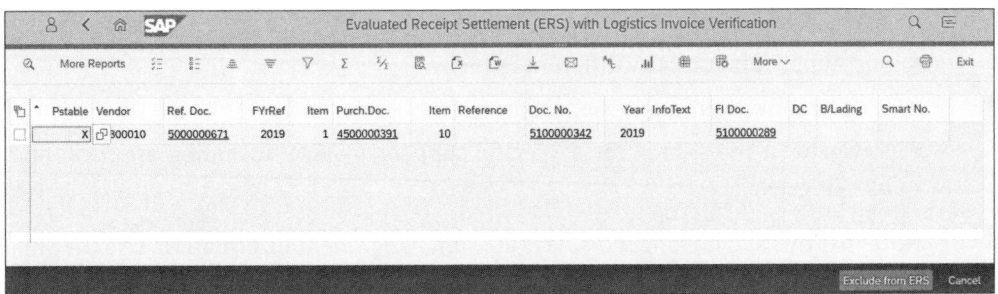

Figure 11.21 Create Evaluated Receipt Settlement App: Worklist Screen

11.2.6 Reporting in Invoice Processing

There are three tactical reporting apps delivered with SAP S/4HANA for use in invoice processing:

- Supplier Invoices List
- Supplier Invoice Items by Account Assignment
- Display Supplier Invoice—Advanced

We'll discuss each app in the following sections.

Supplier Invoices List

The Supplier Invoices List app (Figure 11.22) allows you to search for supplier invoices and use the resulting search result as a worklist to display and process details for these invoices. This is very useful for day-to-day invoice management because you can, for example, display a list of blocked supplier invoices and release or reverse these documents easily.

Once you've selected a document, you can drill into it to see all the details for that transaction. The system automatically knows if the invoice can be displayed via the native SAP Fiori app or if the Display Invoice Document—Advanced app is required. Certain complex invoices can't be rendered in the native SAP Fiori app. SAP S/4HANA automatically detects these documents and displays them in the appropriate app.

In the header section of the worklist, you can filter invoices in the list by entering filter values in the selection fields. You can also create your own variants or hide the filter bar if you wish.

477

You can also do the following:

- Sort supplier invoices by different criteria
- Hide or show columns in the worklist
- Navigate to the details for a specific supplier invoice, including approval and blocking details

Note that this app no longer displays account assignment information. Use the Supplier Invoice Items by Account Assignment app to see this information.

The Supplier Invoices List app is assigned to the accounts payable accountant—procurement standard authorization role.

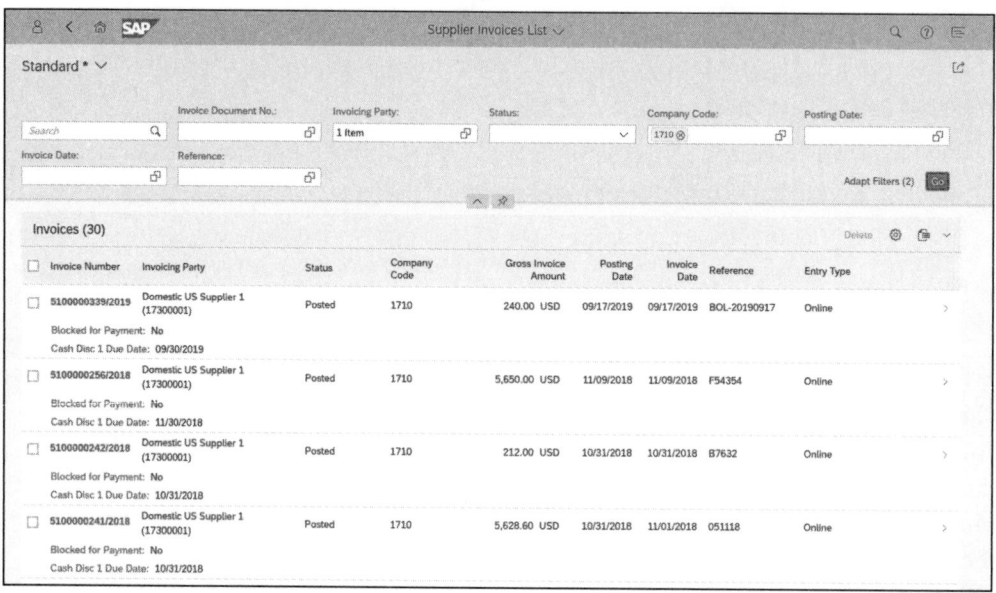

Figure 11.22 Supplier Invoices List App

Supplier Invoice Items by Account Assignment

The Supplier Invoice Items by Account Assignment app (Figure 11.23) is used to display supplier invoice item details based on their account assignments, such as cost centers.

For each supplier invoice item, details such as the account assignment type, company code, posting date, amount, and quantity are shown. You can navigate to the Supplier Invoices List app if you need additional details.

The Supplier Invoice Items by Account Assignment app is assigned to the accounts payable accountant—procurement standard authorization role.

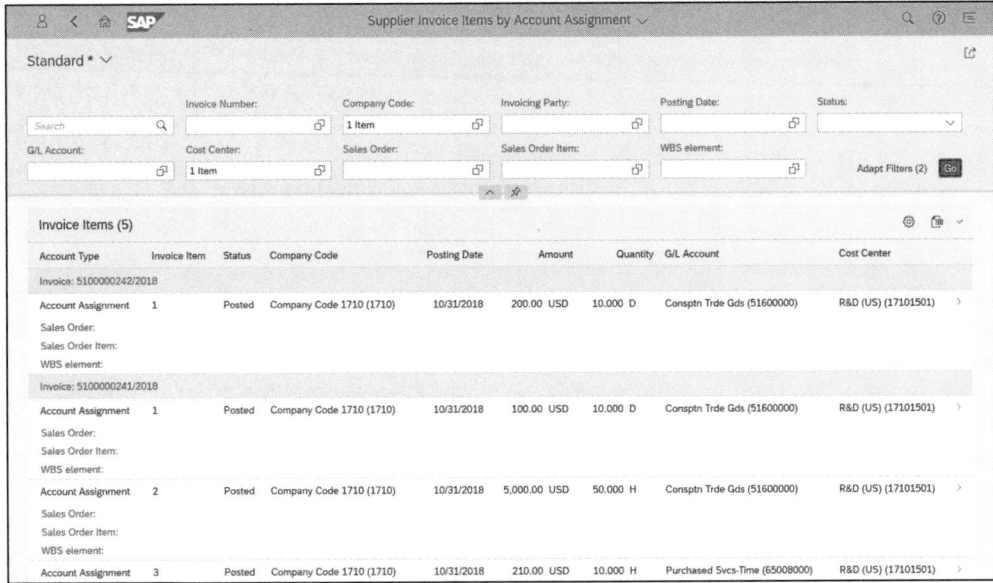

Figure 11.23 Supplier Invoice Items by Account Assignment App

Display Supplier Invoice—Advanced

The Display Supplier Invoice—Advanced app shows all details available for a supplier invoice document in the system. This app is useful for viewing invoices that were created in both the Create Supplier Invoice and Create Supplier Invoice—Advanced apps, or through SAP Ariba Supply Chain Collaboration via the Ariba Network (as shown in Figure 11.24 and Figure 11.25).

The Display Supplier Invoice—Advanced app runs directly on the backend SAP S/4HANA system and is functionally equivalent to the classic SAP ERP Transaction MIR4.

The Display Supplier Invoice—Advanced app is assigned to the accounts payable accountant—procurement standard authorization role.

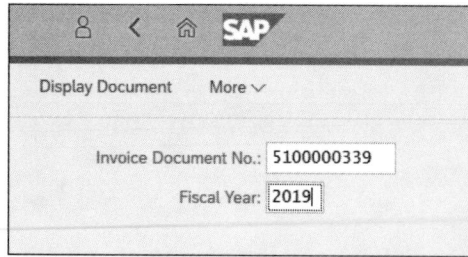

Figure 11.24 Display Supplier Invoice—Advanced App: Selection Screen

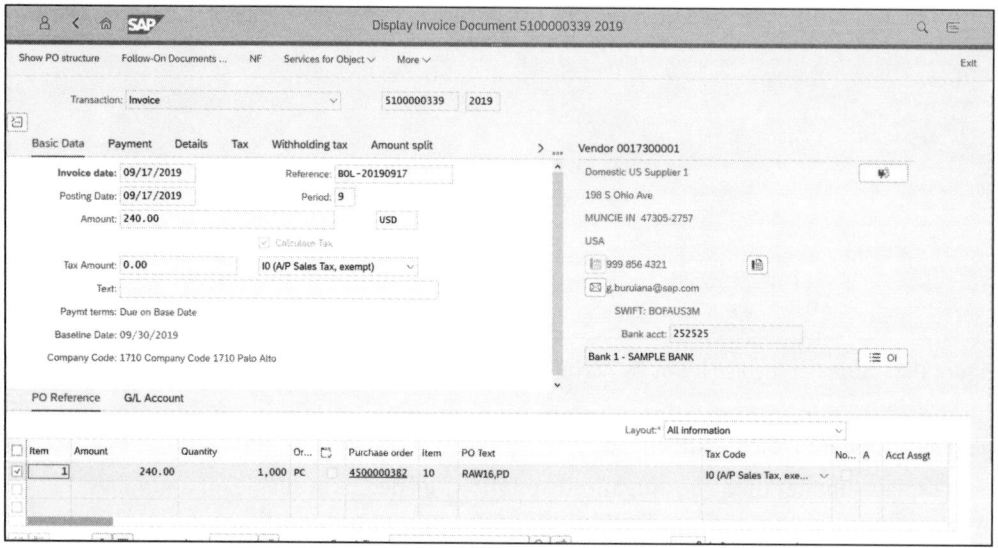

Figure 11.25 Display Supplier Invoice—Advanced App: Details Screen

11.2.7   Object Pages

There are two object pages available in the invoice processing capability of the invoice and payables management area:

- Supplier Invoice
- Supplier Accounting Document

Many of the transactional SAP Fiori apps allow you to click a supplier invoice document or a supplier accounting document to obtain details for these items.

Supplier Invoice Object Page

The Supplier Invoice object page displays detailed information about an individual supplier invoice document stored in the SAP S/4HANA system. This object page is called in a variety of ways in the SAP Fiori system: from context-sensitive links in the List Supplier Invoices app, for example, or from global search.

Use the Supplier Invoice object page to obtain details for an invoice document of interest. You can also link to the Purchase Order object page from this app.

You can display an overview of the supplier invoice header data, such as the supplier and bank details, referenced purchasing documents, and key facts, such as gross invoice amount, fiscal year, and payment status. You can also obtain details about related business partners, master data, and related purchasing documents (see Figure 11.26, Figure 11.27, and Figure 11.28).

The Supplier Invoice object page is assigned to the accounts payable accountant—procurement standard authorization role.

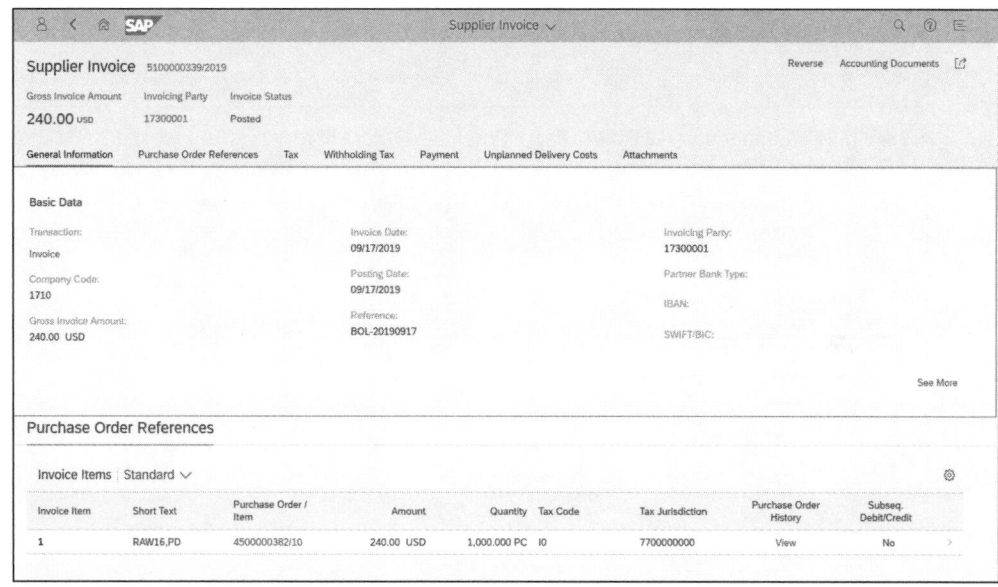

Figure 11.26 Supplier Invoice Object Page: General Information

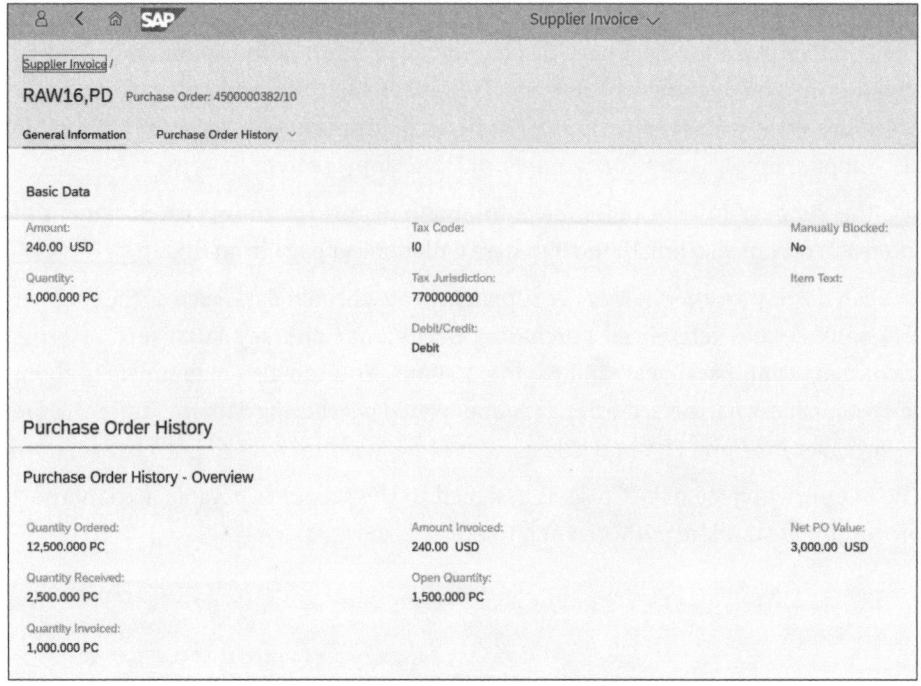

Figure 11.27 Supplier Invoice Object Page: Purchase Order History

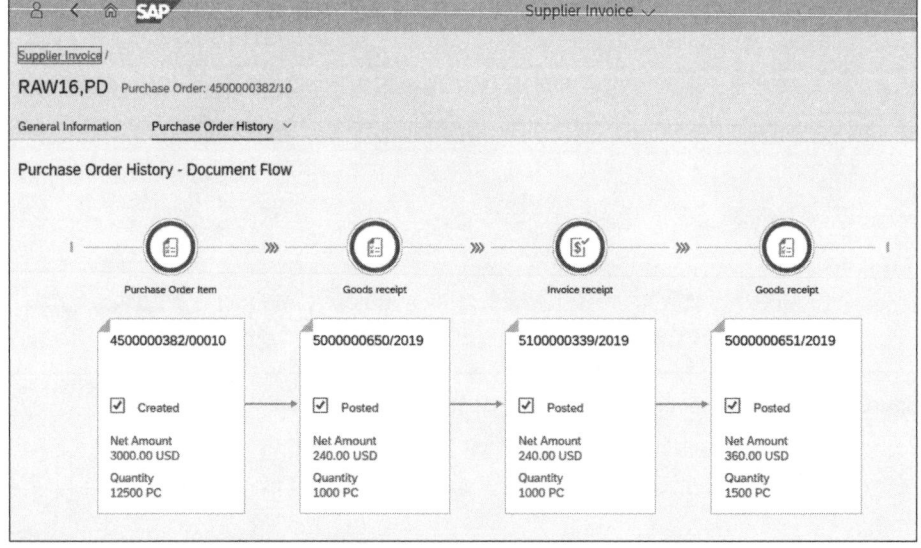

Figure 11.28 Supplier Invoice Object Page: Document Flow

Supplier Accounting Document Object Page

The Supplier Accounting Document object page (Figure 11.29) displays information about supplier accounting documents. These documents are produced when accounting postings are made during supplier invoice document processing in SAP S/4HANA.

You can display an overview of the accounting document data, including the supplier, amount, document status, and document posting date. You also can navigate to its related business objects, such as purchase order, supplier, or journal entry.

The Supplier Accounting Document object page is assigned to the accounts payable accountant, accounts payable manager, warehouse clerk, and inventory manager standard authorization roles.

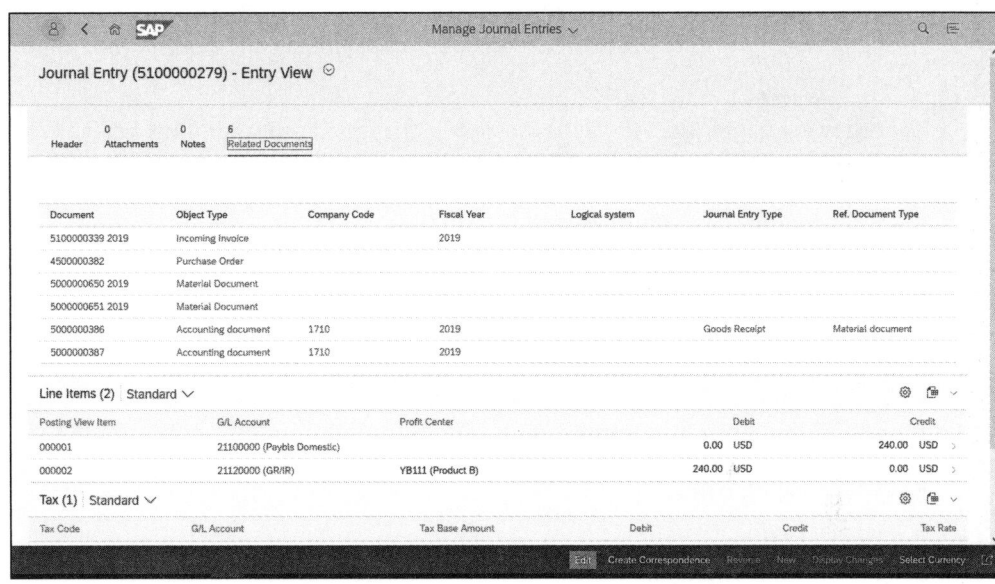

Figure 11.29 Supplier Accounting Document Object Page

11.3   Accounts Payable

Accounts payable is the second capability provided by the invoicing and payables functionality in SAP S/4HANA Sourcing and Procurement.

Accounts payable departments handle invoice entry and payment processes so that an enterprise's suppliers are paid while optimizing cash flow. There is tight integration between the invoice processing and payables processing components of SAP S/4HANA Sourcing and Procurement: one feeds the other.

There are three major areas of accounts payable that the SAP S/4HANA system supports:

- Supplier payment processing
- Supplier account management
- Correspondence

11.3.1   Supplier Payment Processing

Supplier payment processing apps assist the accounts payable accountant in running the operational payables function and assure that payments are made to the suppliers at the optimal time.

The following native SAP Fiori apps for supplier payment processing are available:

- Post Outgoing Payments
- Clear Outgoing Payments (Manual Clearing)
- Manage Payment Blocks
- Manage Automatic Payments
- Revise Payment Proposals
- Manage Supplier Down Payment Requests
- Monitor Purchase Order Down Payments
- Create Single Payment
- Manage Payment Media
- Approve Bank Payments
- Monitor Batches and Payments

Note

The following WebGUI transactional apps for supplier payment processing are also available:

- Create Supplier Down Payment Requests (Transaction F-47)
- Post Supplier Down Payments (Transaction F-48)

- Schedule Automatic Payments (Transaction F110)
- Post Supplier Outgoing Payments (Transaction F-58)

We'll discuss these apps in the following sections.

Post Outgoing Payments

The Post Outgoing Payments app (Figure 11.30) allows you to post and clear a single outgoing payment in one step. Normally, enterprises process outgoing payments automatically based on payment proposals. However, if you want to perform a payment to a supplier immediately, you need to enter the payment data manually. You can clear these outgoing payments with open supplier line items. You can also post an outgoing payment to a general ledger account or on account.

The following features are available in the Post Outgoing Payments app:

- List open items that can be cleared with the outgoing payment.
- Add or change the discount to be applied to each invoice.
- Create residual items by entering a residual amount and assigning one or more reason codes and reference information about the business partner. You can define in configuration if a new item is to be posted to the business partner account or if the difference is to be cleared.
- Post an outgoing payment to a general ledger account, if required with account assignment.
- Post an outgoing payment *on account*, which means to a customer or supplier account without reference to a specific item if clearing isn't possible.
- Search for open items of selected suppliers or of all suppliers via fuzzy logic.
- Create notes and affix attachments while posting the clearing document.
- Enter characteristics for profitability-related postings to assign profitability segments in profitability analysis.
- Arrange open items using an invoice reference.
- Simulate the resulting journal entry.
- Clear the payment with the selected open items.

The Post Outgoing Payments app is assigned to the accounts payable accountant standard authorization role.

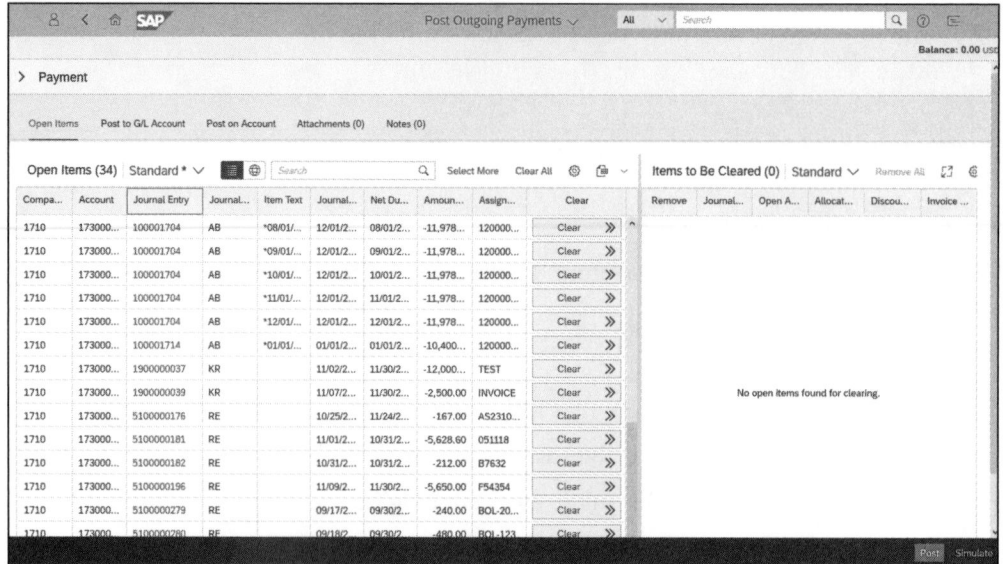

Figure 11.30 Post Outgoing Payments App

Clear Outgoing Payments (Manual Clearing)

Normally, the system will clear outgoing payments automatically. However, if you've paid your supplier manually without reference to an open item, you can use this app to find the matching items and clear the payment manually.

The Clear Outgoing Payments (Manual Clearing) app (Figure 11.31) can provide the following functions:

- View open outgoing payments in your area of responsibility in My Worklist.
- List open items to clear the open payments.
- Apply or change the discount to be applied to each invoice.
- Create residual items by entering a residual amount and assigning one or more reason codes and reference information about the business partner.
- Post an outgoing payment to a general ledger account, if required with account assignment.
- Post an outgoing payment on account—that is, to a customer or supplier account without reference to a specific item—if clearing isn't possible.
- Search for open items of selected suppliers or of all suppliers via fuzzy logic.

- Enter characteristics for profitability-related postings to assign profitability segments in profitability analysis.
- View the withholding tax posted for each open item.
- Create notes and attachments while posting the clearing document.
- Simulate the resulting journal entry.
- Clear the open payment with the selected open items that match the payment.
- Clear open items for a supplier account instead for a payment.
- Clear open items for down payments.

The Clear Outgoing Payments (Manual Clearing) app is assigned to the accounts payable accountant standard authorization role.

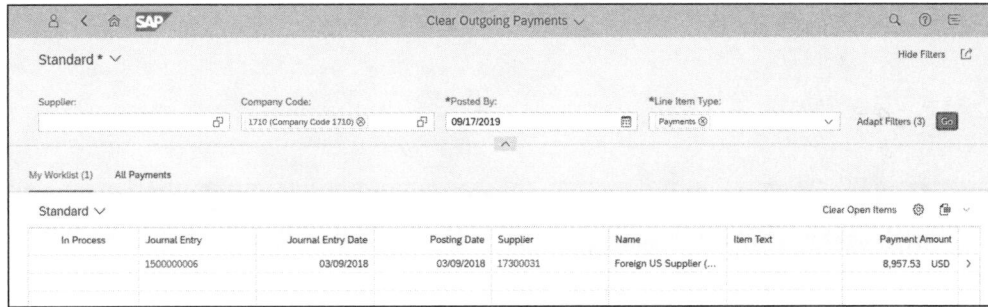

Figure 11.31 Clear Outgoing Payments (Manual Clearing) App

Manage Payment Blocks

Payment blocks on invoices or supplier accounts can be set or removed using the Manage Payment Blocks app (Figure 11.32). You can use the search and sort functions to select and display invoice documents that are blocked.

The Manage Payment Blocks app provides the following functions:

- Search for open invoices by supplier, purchase order, invoice number, or journal entry.
- Display supplier accounts and open invoices and view their blocking status.
- Display open invoices with payment details and related documents.
- View the status of invoices and supplier accounts.
- Select supplier accounts and invoices to block them for payment or unblock them.
- Enter payment block reasons and comments.

The Manage Payment Blocks app is assigned to the accounts payable accountant standard authorization role.

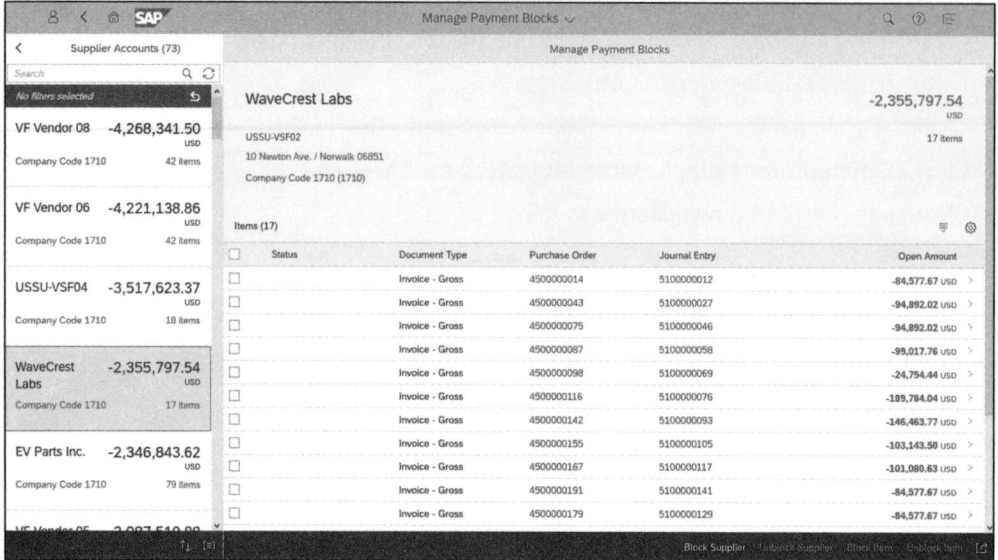

Figure 11.32 Manage Payment Blocks App

Manage Automatic Payments

The Manage Automatic Payments app (Figure 11.33) allows you to schedule payment proposals or payments. You then can obtain an overview of the status of the proposals or payments.

The Manage Automatic Payments app has the following features:

- Schedule payment proposals or payments directly.
- Automatically create payment media after scheduling payment runs. You can find the created payment media in the Manage Payment Media app.
- Create payment advices.
- Search proposals and payments by identifier, run date, user ID, and company code.
- Check for completeness via the log.

The Manage Automatic Payments app is assigned to the accounts payable accountant standard authorization role.

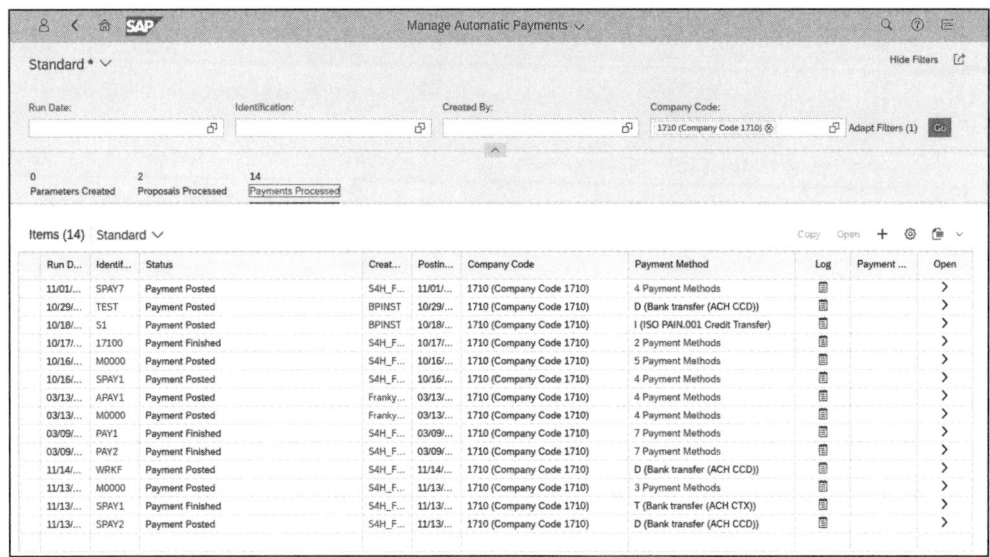

Figure 11.33 Manage Automatic Payments App

Revise Payment Proposals

The Revise Payment Proposals app (Figure 11.34) allows you to check and revise payment proposals and the details of open items. This assures that all supplier payments are made in a timely and accurate manner and that these payments remain compliant with company policies.

You can perform the following using the Revise Payment Proposals app:

- Display open payment proposals.
- Edit payment proposals to change payment methods, partner bank account, or other payment-related information if needed.
- Block and unblock items in payments and reallocate items among payments.
- Mass block items in payments.
- Calculate the total payment amount by payee, currency, and other criteria.
- Check the exceptions log.
- Navigate to the Manage Payment Proposals app.

The Revise Payment Proposals app is assigned to the accounts payable accountant standard authorization role.

> **Note**
>
> The key performance indicator shown on the **Revise Payment Proposals** tile displays only the number of outgoing payments; it doesn't include incoming payments that could be part of a payment proposal.

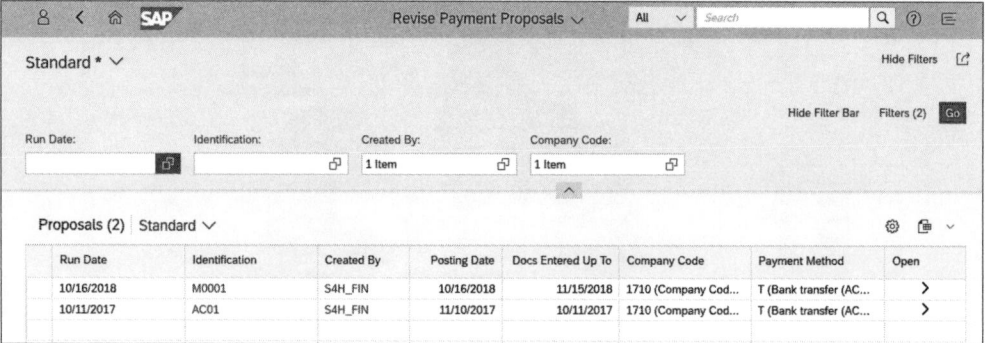

Figure 11.34 Revise Payment Proposals App

Monitor Purchase Order Down Payments

The Monitor Purchase Order Down Payments app (Figure 11.35) is used to keep tabs on supplier down payment information maintained in purchase orders.

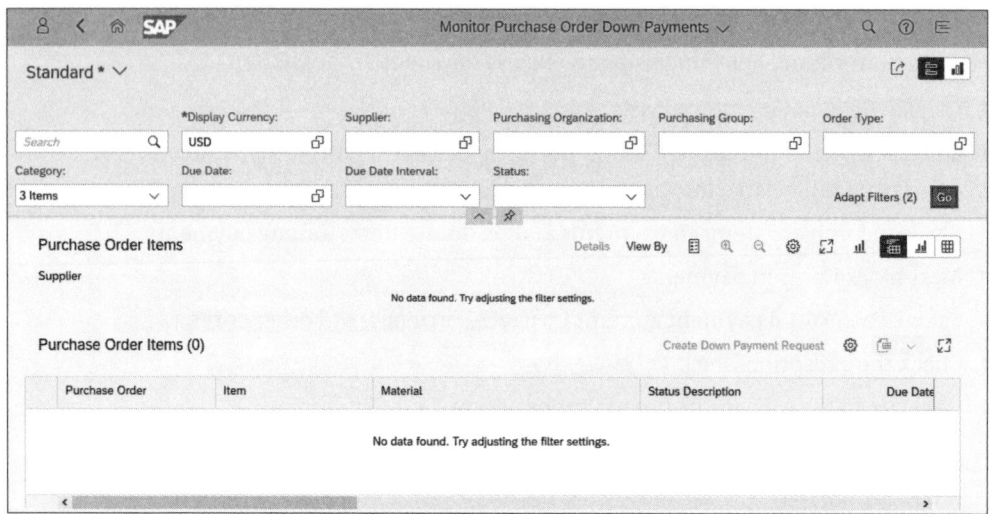

Figure 11.35 Monitor Purchase Order Down Payments App

This app can be used for the following tasks:

- View purchase order items using filter criteria such as down payment due date.
- Create a new down payment request.
- Monitor item counts by category, due date interval, and status.
- See purchase order item details.
- Drill down to see additional down payment details.

The Monitor Purchase Order Down Payments app is assigned to the accounts payable accountant standard authorization role.

Manage Supplier Down Payment Requests

Ordinarily, down payment requests are generated in the SAP S/4HANA system based on information entered in the purchase order document. However, there are times when you may need to create a down payment request manually. Use the Manage Supplier Down Payment Requests app (Figure 11.36) in these cases to create down payment requests as needed. Once the payment run has made the down payment, the payment run also automatically clears the corresponding down payment request. In some cases, you may need to clear the down payment request manually. The Manage Supplier Down Payment Requests app allows you to perform the following tasks:

- View existing down payment requests from suppliers.
- Change existing down payment requests.
- Create new down payment requests.
- Add notes and attachments to down payment requests.
- Export the table of existing down payment requests to a spreadsheet.

The Manage Automatic Payments app is assigned to the accounts payable accountant standard authorization role.

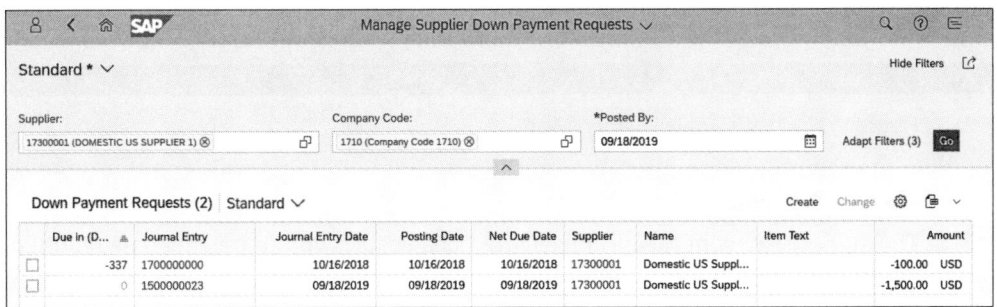

Figure 11.36 Manage Supplier Down Payment Requests App

Create Single Payment

The Create Single Payment app (Figure 11.37) lets you make direct payments to suppliers that have open supplier line items and haven't presented an invoice. Supplier and bank information and amounts to be paid are entered, and a payment is created. This payment posts as a down payment request. This document is used to trigger a payment run. The open items selected are cleared when the payment run completes.

This app allows you to perform the following tasks:

- Execute one-off payments in one step without an invoice.
- Trigger the payment process for specified open supplier line items.
- Add attachments to the payment.
- Get a log of the results when payment is made.

The Create Single Payment app is assigned to the accounts payable accountant standard authorization role.

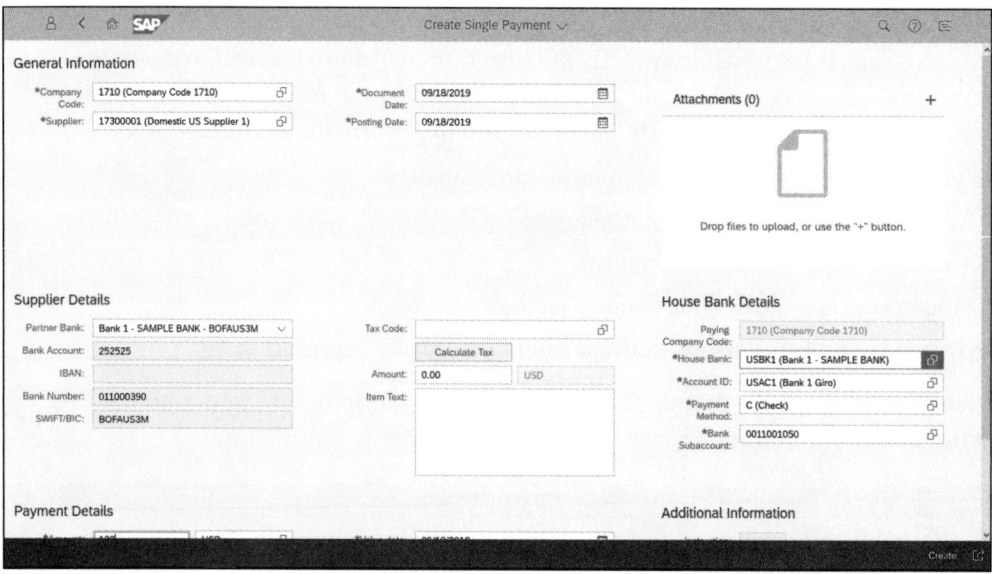

Figure 11.37 Create Single Payment App

Manage Payment Media

The Manage Payment Media app (Figure 11.38) enables you to transfer data required for electronic payment transactions to banks via a data medium. A payment medium is created with each successful payment run.

The Manage Payment Media app allows you to perform the following tasks:

- View existing payment media along with their processing statuses.
- Download payment media.
- Delete payment media.
- Display and analyze payment summary information.

The Manage Payment Media app is assigned to the accounts payable accountant standard authorization role.

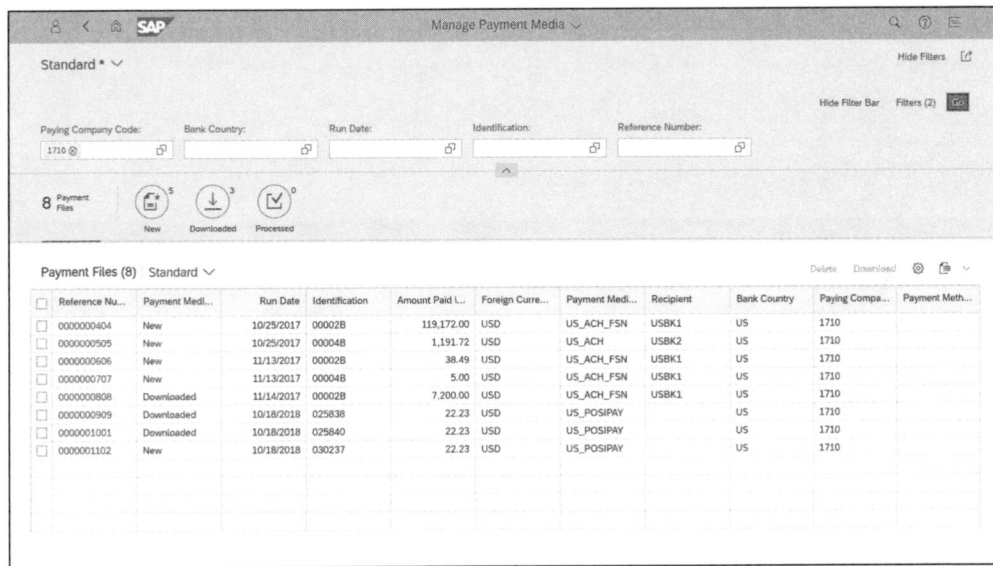

Figure 11.38 Manage Payment Media App

Approve Bank Payments

The Approve Bank Payments app (Figure 11.39) lets an accounts payable manager review and process payment batches. You can check the payments contained in the batch and approve, reject, or defer individual payments or entire batches if you wish.

This app lets you perform the following tasks:

- Search for payment batches by batch number, company code, and house bank.
- Edit payment batch due dates and instruction keys for payments.
- Defer payments to a future date.

The Approve Bank Payments app is assigned to the accounts payable manager standard authorization role.

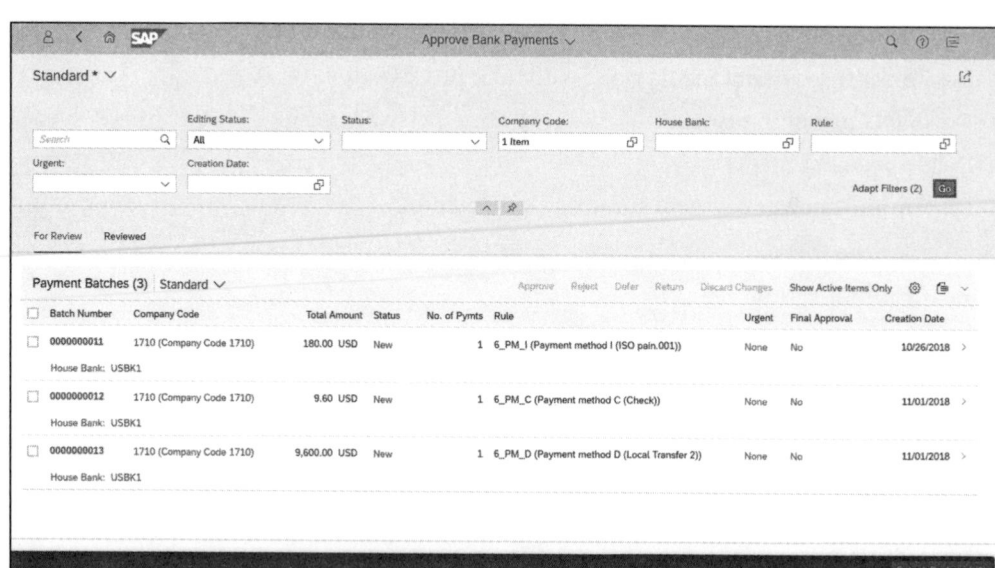

Figure 11.39 Approve Bank Payments App

Monitor Batches and Payments

The Monitor Batches and Payments app (see Figure 11.40 and Figure 11.41) is used to review details of batches and the payments they contain. You can observe the statues of each batch and payment in a batch at all stages of the payment process.

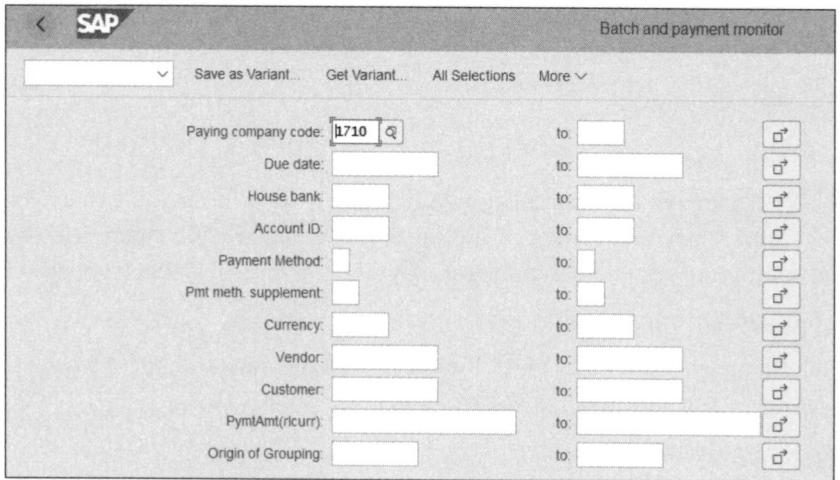

Figure 11.40 Manage Batches and Payments App: Selection Screen

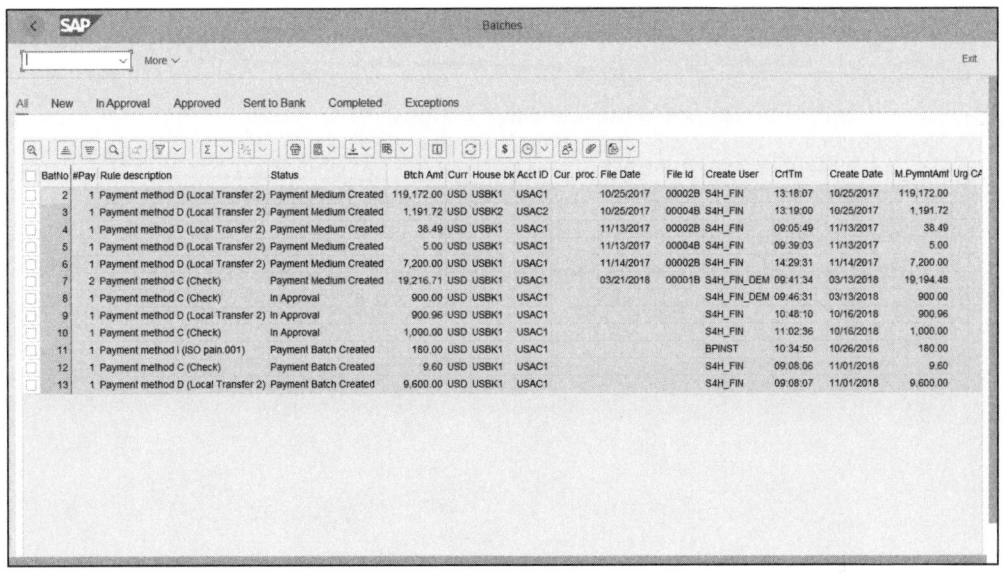

Figure 11.41 Monitor Batches and Payments App: Report Screen

This monitoring app is useful for performing the following tasks:

- View the history of a payment batch.
- Edit payment batch due dates and instruction keys for payments.
- Review all payment batch approvers and their contact information.
- View the payment medium file details associated with the batch.

The Monitor Batches and Payments app is assigned to the accounts payable accountant standard authorization role.

This app runs on the backend SAP S/4HANA system and is functionally equivalent to the classic SAP ERP Transaction BNK_MONI.

11.3.2   Supplier Account Management

The accounts payable department periodically needs to review supplier account data to assure that all transactions for those suppliers are correctly represented in the system and that payments are being made at the optimum time.

The following transactional apps support the accounts payable accountant in managing supplier accounts:

- Manage Supplier Line Items
- Display Supplier Balances

We'll discuss these apps in the following sections.

Manage Supplier Line Items

The Manage Supplier Line Items app (Figure 11.42) is used to find supplier line items using a wide range of search criteria. For example, you can see all line items of a supplier account or all open supplier invoices for a company code that are overdue at a key date.

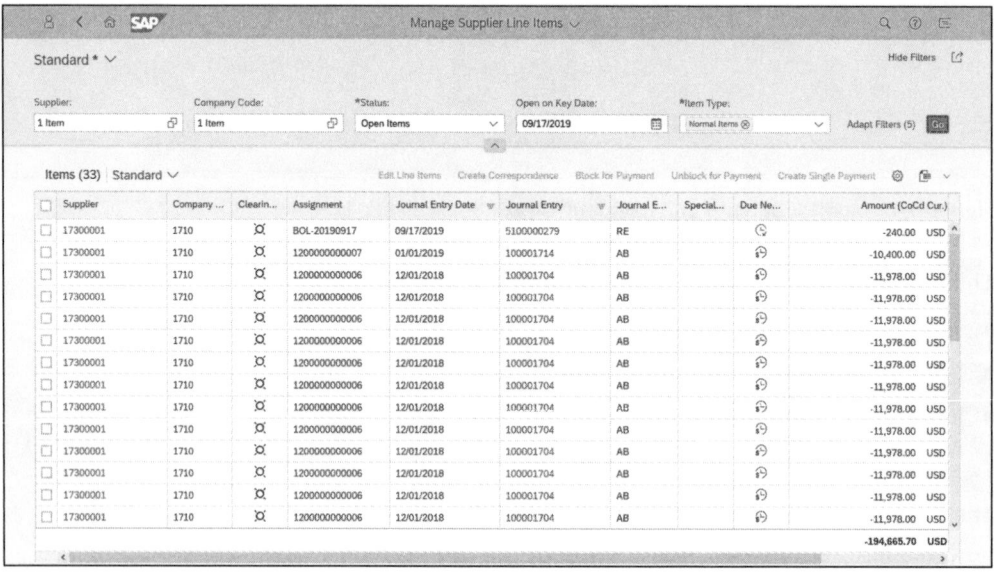

Figure 11.42 Manage Supplier Line Items App

In addition to displaying data, you can also take actions such as setting a payment block or creating a manual payment. The app is also accessed from other apps, allowing users to drill down to supplier line items.

The Manage Supplier Line Items app lets you perform the following actions:

- Find supplier line items using a wide range of search criteria.
- Set or remove payment blocks.

- Change line item attributes such as payment data, assignment, or line item text.
- Create manual payments.

The Manage Supplier Line Items app is assigned to the accounts payable accountant standard authorization role.

Display Supplier Balances

The Display Supplier Balances app (Figure 11.43) can be used to view debits, credits, and balances on supplier accounts by company code, fiscal year, and supplier. The app allows you to further analyze amounts by drilling down to related line items. Furthermore, you can compare purchases between two fiscal years.

The Display Supplier Balances app is useful for the following:

- Displaying balances, debits, credits and imputed interest on supplier accounts.
- Searching for supplier balances by company code, fiscal year, and supplier.
- Comparing purchases from the current and the previous year.

The Display Supplier Balances app is assigned to the accounts payable accountant standard authorization role.

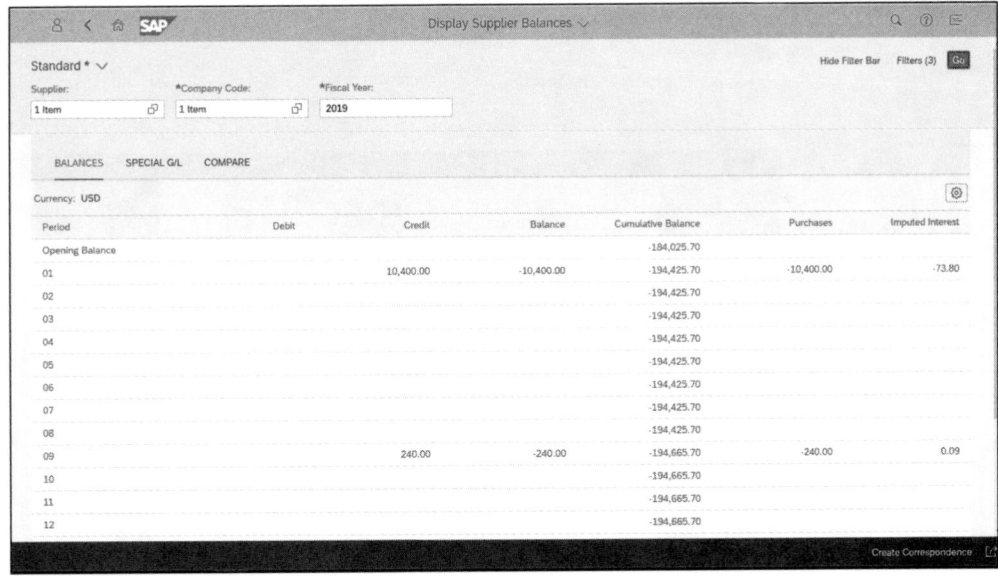

Figure 11.43 Display Supplier Balances App

Create Correspondence

Sometimes, you'll need the SAP S/4HANA system to issue a formal communication to a supplier. The Create Correspondence app (Figure 11.44) facilitates these types of requests. Correspondence can include issuing a supplier statement or a dunning notice for late delivery.

> **Note**
>
> In addition, there are multiple WebGUI apps available in SAP S/4HANA to produce correspondence as well. These apps include the following:
>
> - Create Balance Confirmations (for Suppliers): Transaction F.18/F18P
> - Create Periodic Account Statements: Transaction F.27
> - Create Dunning Notices: Transaction F150
> - Create Standard Letters (for Suppliers): Transaction F.66
> - Create Correspondence (for Internal Documents): Transaction F.62
> - Print Correspondence Requests: Transaction F.61
> - Delete Correspondence Requests: Transaction F.63

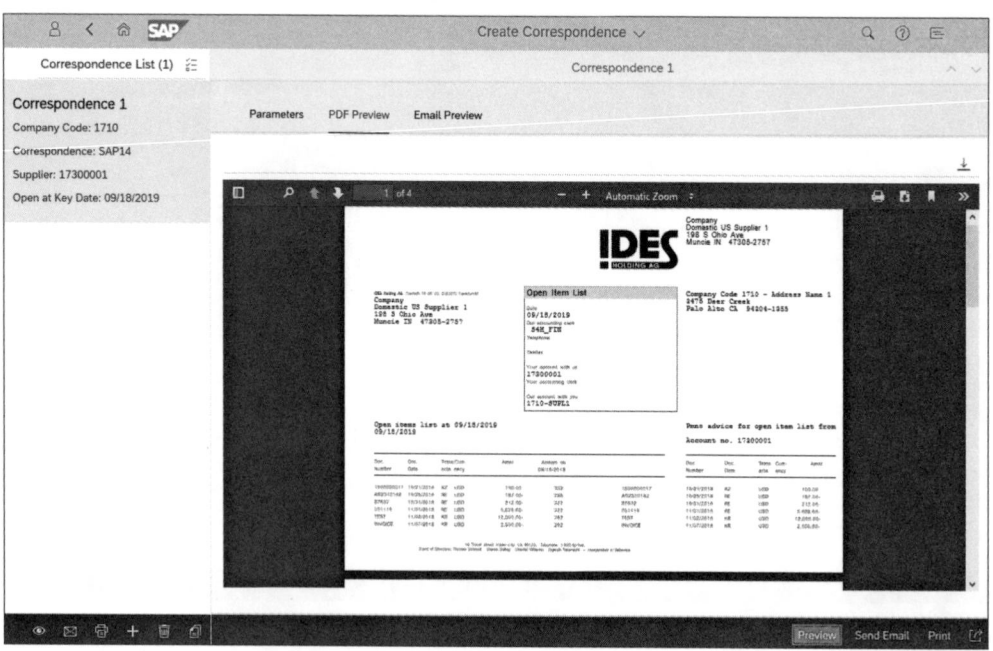

Figure 11.44 Create Correspondence App

The Create Correspondence app lets you manage many types of correspondence with your suppliers. You can review, email, print, fax, or download individual items. This is a standalone app, but it's also called from a number of other accounts payable apps, such as Display Supplier Balances.

The app lets you do the following:

- Create correspondence for a supplier.
- Preview the correspondence prior to transmission.
- Email, fax, print, or download correspondence in PDF format.

> **Note**
>
> This app is also used by accounts receivable personnel to create correspondence to customers.
>
> The data required for generating documents depends on whether they're intended for a customer or a supplier and on the type of correspondence being transmitted.

The Create Correspondence app is assigned to the accounts payable accountant standard authorization role.

11.4   Invoice and Payables Management Analytics and Reporting

The UI platform for analytics and reporting in SAP S/4HANA is app-centric. The core dashboard apps of a typical accounts payable manager are shown in Figure 11.45.

Figure 11.45 Accounts Payable Analytic Apps

These apps show actionable values on their respective tiles, whether for overdue payables, future payables, days payable outstanding, or invoice processing statistics. You can set KPIs, and the apps will refresh their data automatically. These analytics apps also can be refreshed manually without going into the app itself by clicking the **Now** icon in the lower-left-hand corner. Note that some metrics can appear in green and red. The red measures indicate that the KPI threshold set has been exceeded. A user thus is notified instantly in a simplified manner if something is going off target, without needing to enter the report itself.

SAP S/4HANA analytics and reporting apps extend the entire process flow for procure-to-pay. On the payment side, there are a comparable number of analytic options and reports, to provide accounts payable and invoice users with up-to-the-second insight into payables and cash flow position.

There is a variety of analytic apps for use by accounts payable roles in the SAP S/4HANA system. These apps include the following:

- Accounts Payable Overview
- Aging Analysis
- Overdue Payables
- Future Payables
- Cash Discount Forecast
- Cash Discount Utilization
- Days Payable Outstanding
- Days Payable Outstanding—Indirect Method
- Invoice Processing Analysis
- Supplier Payment Analysis (Manual and Automatic Payments)
- Supplier Payment Analysis (Open Payments)

Let's take a closer look at each of these apps.

11.4.1   Accounts Payable Overview

The Accounts Payable Overview app (Figure 11.46) allows you to easily monitor key accounts payable indicators. You can then access the relevant accounts payable apps to quickly react to the information presented to you. The information is displayed in a series of actionable cards in a common display currency.

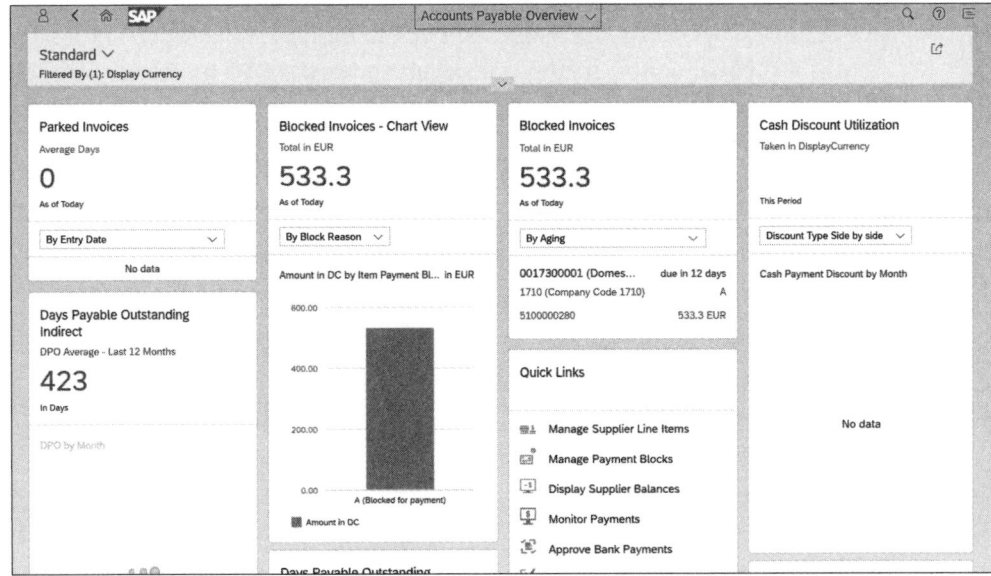

Figure 11.46 Accounts Payable Overview App

This overview app allows you to monitor the following key process indicators:

- **Parked Invoices**
  This card displays the KPI for the average days parked of your parked invoices. You can sort the displayed parked invoices list. You can navigate to the Manage Supplier Line Items app from this card.

- **Blocked Invoices Chart**
  This card shows the total amount of all blocked invoices. You can sort the displayed blocked invoices list. You can navigate to the Manage Supplier Line Items app from this card.

- **Blocked Invoices**
  This card shows the total amount of all blocked invoices. You can sort the displayed blocked invoices list. You can navigate to the Manage Supplier Line Items app from this card.

- **Cash Discount Utilization**
  This card shows the KPI total amount of cash discounts taken during the specified period. The chart shows the lost cash discounts and cash discounts taken in the

current and prior months. You can navigate to the Cash Discount Utilization app from this card.

- **Days Payable Outstanding Indirect**
This card displays the KPI average days payable outstanding over the last 12 months using the indirect method. The chart shows the DPO by month over the last 12 months. You can navigate to the Days Payable Outstanding—Indirect Method app from this card.

- **Days Payable Outstanding Direct**
This card displays the KPI average days payable outstanding over the last 12 months calculated at the document level. The chart shows the DPO by month over the last 12 months. You can navigate to the Days Payable Outstanding app from this card.

- **Payable Aging**
This card shows the KPI for the total overdue invoice amount. The chart shows open invoices separate into age intervals. You can navigate to the Aging Analysis app from this card.

- **Suppliers with Debit Balances**
This card shows the KPI for the debit balance as of today. The chart displays a list of supplier accounts with debit balances, sorted by amount. You can navigate to the Manage Supplier Line Items app from this card.

- **Invoices Blocked in Supplier Master Data**
This card shows the KPI for the sum of all blocked invoices based on blocks set in the supplier master data. You can navigate to the Manage Supplier Line Items app from this card.

- **Posted Invoices in Current Period**
This card shows the sum of all invoices posted in the current period. Cumulative statistics by entry date are also shown.

- **My Inbox**
This card shows your open work items, such as invoice approvals for your attention.

- **Due Invoices Free for Payment**
This card shows the KPI for the total amount of due invoices that are free for payment as of today's date. The chart displays due invoices that are free to be paid

grouped by days in arrears. You can navigate to the Manage Supplier Line Items app from this card.

- **Invoice Processing Statistics**
  This card shows the average time in days it took to process invoices for the processing step and period selected. Other statistics are available from this card as well.

- **Posted Invoices**
  This card shows the KPI for the amount or count of posted invoices in the last six fiscal periods. The chart shows a breakdown of amount or count per fiscal period.

- **Quick Links**
  Shows links to useful accounts payable apps.

The Accounts Payable Overview app is assigned to the accounts payable manager standard authorization role.

11.4.2   Aging Analysis

The Aging Analysis app is useful for viewing aging payables across the organization. This will allow you to identify negative trends in total payables, net due, and overdue amounts. You can then react to these negative trends and take appropriate actions to counter them.

The **Aging Analysis** tile displays the **Payable Amount** KPI, which is calculated as the sum of total open payables. Open payables are defined as the sum of past-due payables and future payables.

The Aging Analysis app, as shown in Figure 11.47, allows you to do the following:

- Display the payables amount, including the overdue amount and the net due amount, by company, aging, business area, reconciliation accounts, currency, payment method, and supplier group.
- Use the company code, aging interval, business area, reconciliation account, and payment method filters to focus your aging payables analysis.

The Aging Analysis app is assigned to the accounts payable manager standard authorization role.

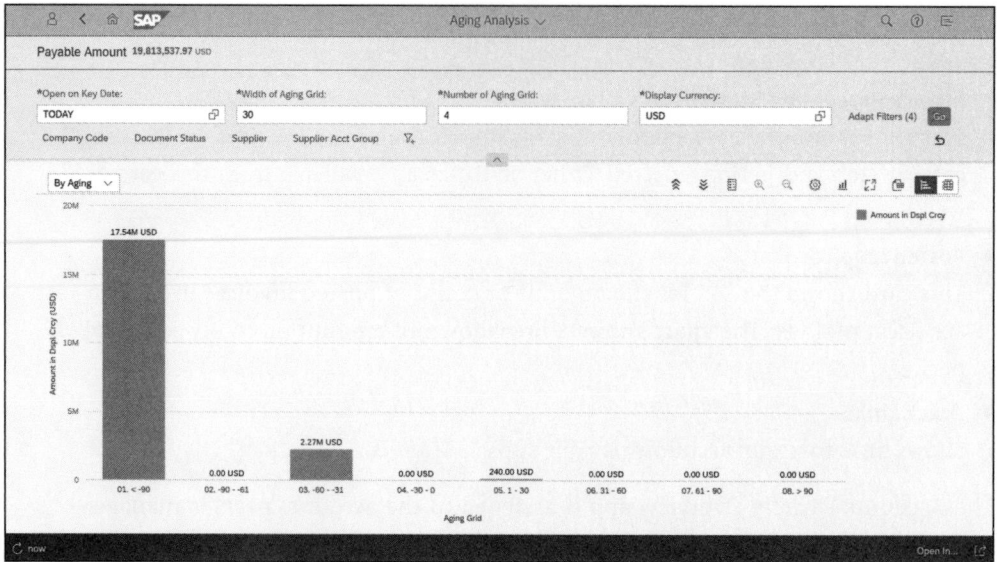

Figure 11.47 Aging Analysis Report

11.4.3   Overdue Payables

The Overdue Payables app is used to check payable amounts overdue to your suppliers by company code, supplier group, supplier, and reason for payment block. You can monitor the status of the overdue payments for critical suppliers. Use this app to take action on payables due to your key suppliers.

The **Overdue Payables** tile shows three metrics:

- **Uncritical Overdue**
  The sum of all uncritically overdue payables amounts

- **Critical Overdue**
  The sum of all critically overdue payables amounts

- **Overdue Payables**
  The sum of uncritically overdue payables and critically overdue payables

In configuration, you can define the threshold for critically overdue in days for your company. Note that payables due on today's date are included in the calculation.

The Overdue Payables app, as shown in Figure 11.48, allows you to do the following:

- Display the overdue payable amount and the payable amount that isn't yet overdue.

- Distinguish between critically overdue amounts and uncritically overdue amounts.
- Analyze the payable amount by different views, including company code, supplier group, reason for payment block, and supplier.
- Break the overdue payable amount into four intervals before today when you analyze the amount by supplier.

The Overdue Payables app is assigned to the accounts payable manager standard authorization role.

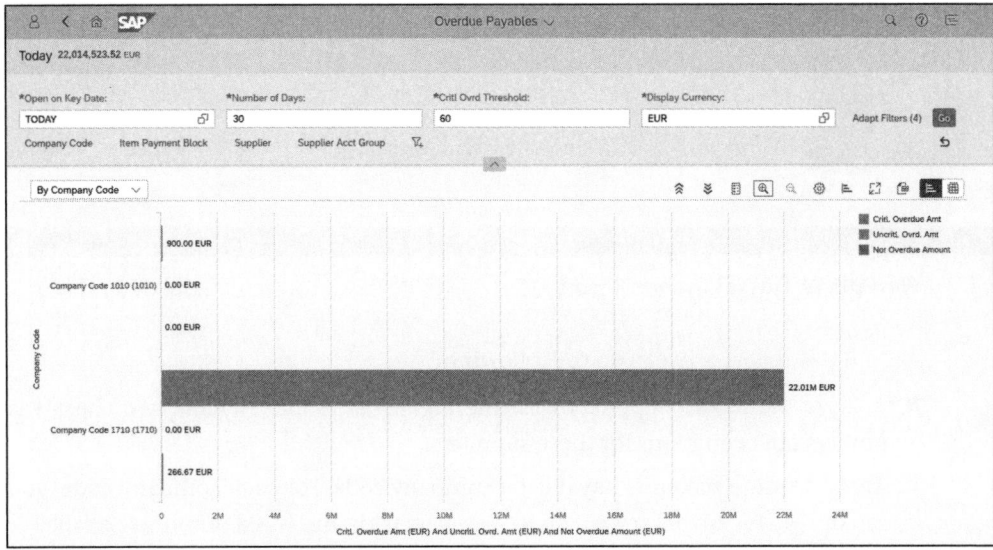

Figure 11.48 Overdue Payables Report

11.4.4   Future Payables

The Future Payables app allows you to analyze your future payables in a variety of ways.

The **Future Payables** tile displays the **Future Payables** KPI, which is calculated as the total amount of all invoices due in the future.

You can analyze your payables for predefined due periods by drilling into the Future Payables app. For each due period, you can drill down further to the 10 suppliers with the largest amounts payable, as shown in Figure 11.49. These due periods are customizable.

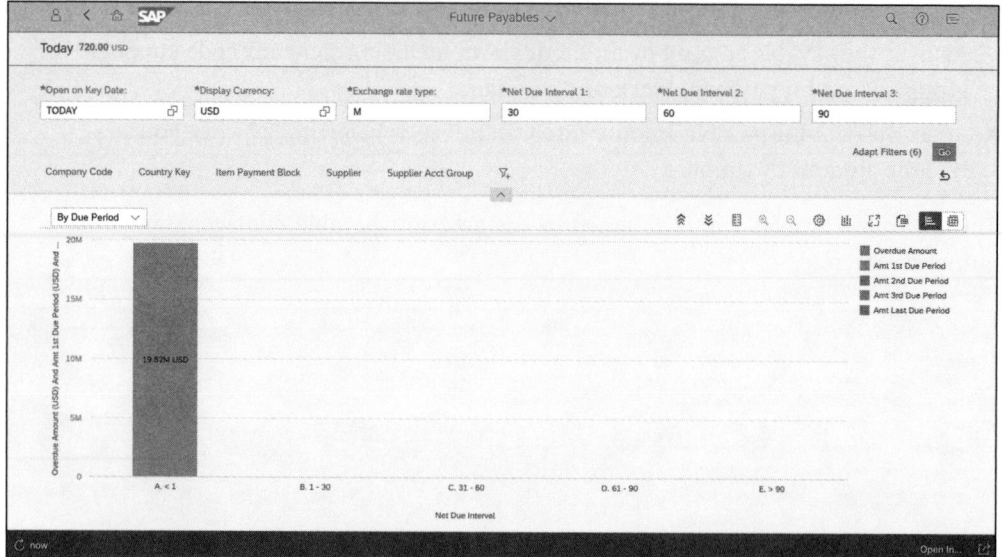

Figure 11.49 Future Payables Report

Within this report, you can do the following:

- Analyze the top 10 suppliers with the highest amounts payable and check the numbers of open items for these suppliers.
- Analyze future accounts payable by company code. For each company code, you can drill down further to the top 10 suppliers with the largest amounts payable.
- Filter accounts payable based on payment blocking reasons. For example, you can choose a certain reason that a supplier is blocked and search for suppliers blocked for that reason. You can also navigate to the **Supplier** object page as well.

The Future Payables app is assigned to the accounts payable manager standard authorization role.

11.4.5   Cash Discount Forecast

The Cash Discount Forecast app lets you predict all available cash discounts in the short-term future period.

The **Cash Discount Forecast** tile displays the **Available Amount** metric, which is defined as the total amount of cash discounts available on open invoices.

Drilling into the Cash Discount Forecast app (Figure 11.50), you can do the following:

- Display the cash discounts expiring in the future. Cash discounts are available on the key date but will expire by the end of the period you define.
- Analyze the expiring cash discounts by company or by payment terms by displaying the expiring cash discounts, the available cash discounts on the key date, and the expired cash discounts before the key date. The available cash discounts on the key date refer to the cash discounts available from the key date to the future.
- Analyze expiring cash discounts by payment day by displaying the cash discounts that are expiring between that payment day and the next. You also can display the cash discounts for blocked within the set period. You then can take action to pay these invoices before the discounts expire.

The Cash Discount Forecast app is assigned to the accounts payable manager standard authorization role.

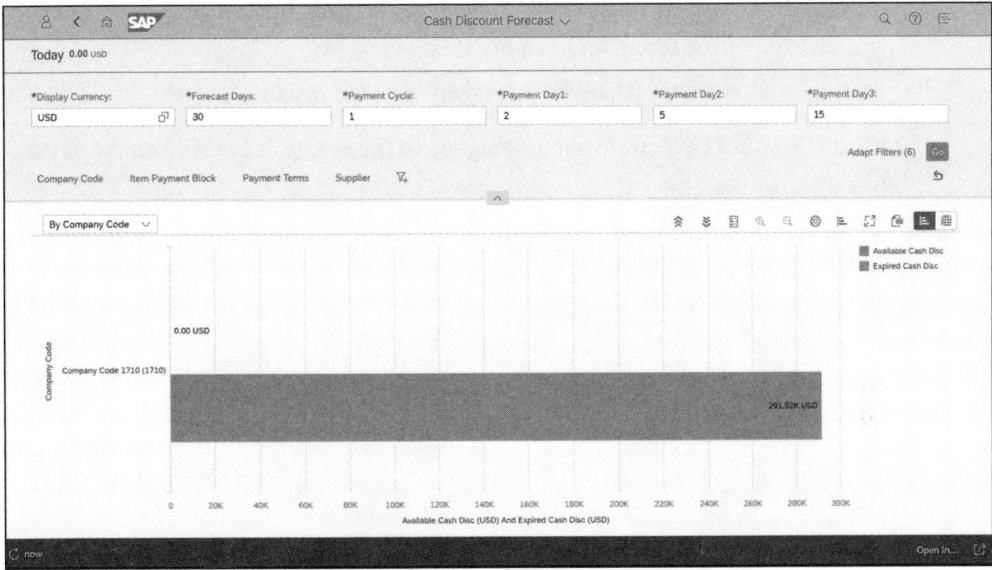

Figure 11.50 Cash Discount Forecast Report

11.4.6   Cash Discount Utilization

The Cash Discount Utilization app allows for monitoring of cash discount utilization in real time. You can find out which company codes or locations could make better use of the cash discounts available to them. You can also determine the reasons for cash discount loss so that it can be avoided in the future.

The **Cash Discount Utilization** tile displays the **Cash Discount Utilization Ratio**. This is defined as the sum of cash discounts taken divided by the sum of cash discounts offered over a defined time period in the past through today.

The app allows you to perform the following tasks:

- Display the utilization rate of cash discounts in a defined period in the past. This is defined as the cash discounts taken divided by the sum of the cash discounts taken and cash discounts lost.
- Compare the current versus the targeted utilization rate and measure compliance.
- Check whether the current utilization rate is acceptable, needs attention, or is critically low. This utilization-rate level is configurable in the SAP S/4HANA system.
- Analyze cash discount utilization by company, country, supplier group, payment terms, and cause of cash discount loss.
- Distinguish between discounts expired and discounts missed and display their corresponding amounts when you analyze cash discount utilization by cause of cash discount loss, as shown in Figure 11.51.
- Distinguish between cash discounts taken and cash discounts lost.

The Cash Discount Utilization app is assigned to the accounts payable manager standard authorization role.

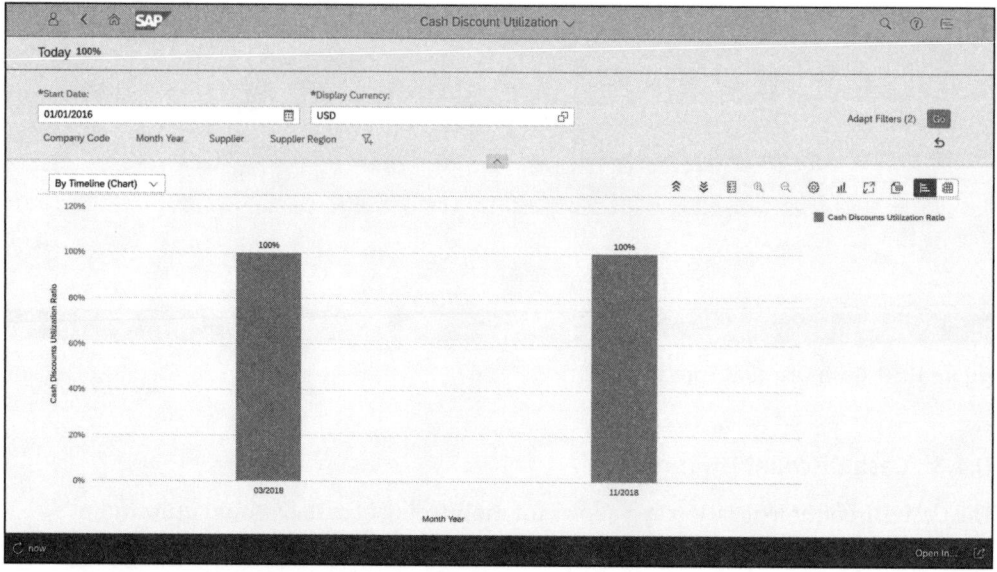

Figure 11.51 Cash Discount Utilization Report

11.4.7   Days Payable Outstanding

The Days Payable Outstanding app gives you information to analyze and understand the key accounts payable performance indicator: days payable outstanding (DPO). DPO measures the number of payables a company has at the current moment. It lets you drill down to find suppliers with low or high days outstanding. You can view the data by company code, supplier, supplier's country, and timeframe, in either a chart or a table view.

The **Days Payable Outstanding** tile shows a monthly breakdown of DPO for the last year.

The Days Payables Outstanding app allows you to analyze DPO in a variety of ways:

- View days payable outstanding in the last rolling calendar year. For each month, as in Figure 11.52, you can drill down to the 10 suppliers with the highest/lowest days payable outstanding.
- View the top 10 DPOs by supplier.
- View DPO by company code. For each company code, you can drill down further to the top 10 suppliers with the highest/lowest DPO value.
- Filter DPO by supplier.

The Days Payable Outstanding app is assigned to the accounts payable manager standard authorization role.

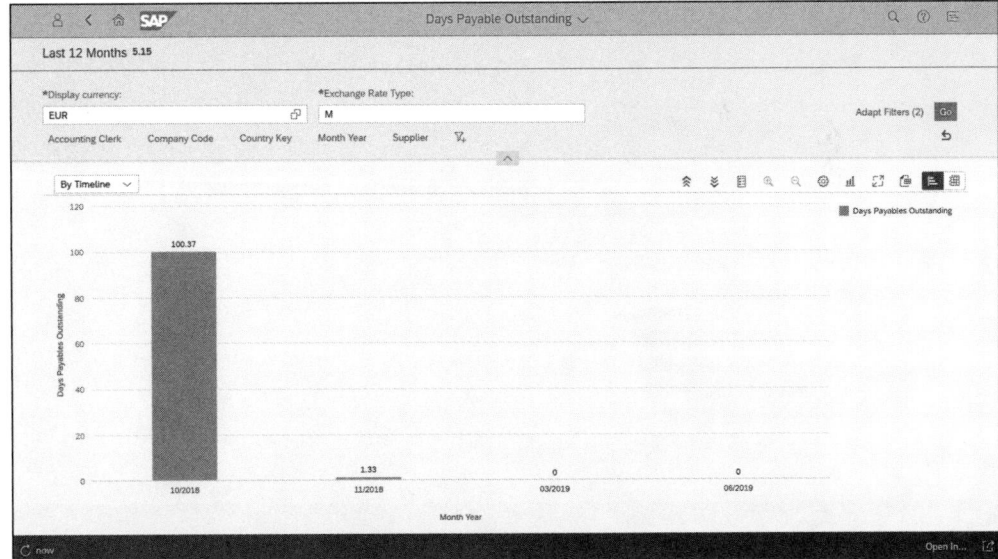

Figure 11.52 Days Payable Outstanding Report

11.4.8   Days Payable Outstanding—Indirect Method

The Days Payable Outstanding—Indirect Method app gives you similar information as the previous app. However, it calculates DPO on an aggregate level, rather than on the level of individual documents. It calculates DPO for the last 12 months using rolling monthly averages for the accounts payable balances and purchases. You can customize the parameters and the number of months to analyze.

The **Days Payable Outstanding—Indirect Method** tile shows a monthly breakdown of DPO for the last year.

The Days Payables Outstanding—Indirect Method app allows you to analyze DPO in a variety of ways:

- View days payable outstanding in the last rolling calendar year. For each month, as in Figure 11.53, you can drill down to the 10 suppliers with the highest/lowest days payable outstanding.
- View the top 10 DPOs by supplier.
- View DPO by company code. For each company code, you can drill down further to the top 10 suppliers with the highest/lowest DPO value.
- Filter DPO by supplier.

The Days Payable Outstanding—Indirect Method app is assigned to the accounts payable manager standard authorization role.

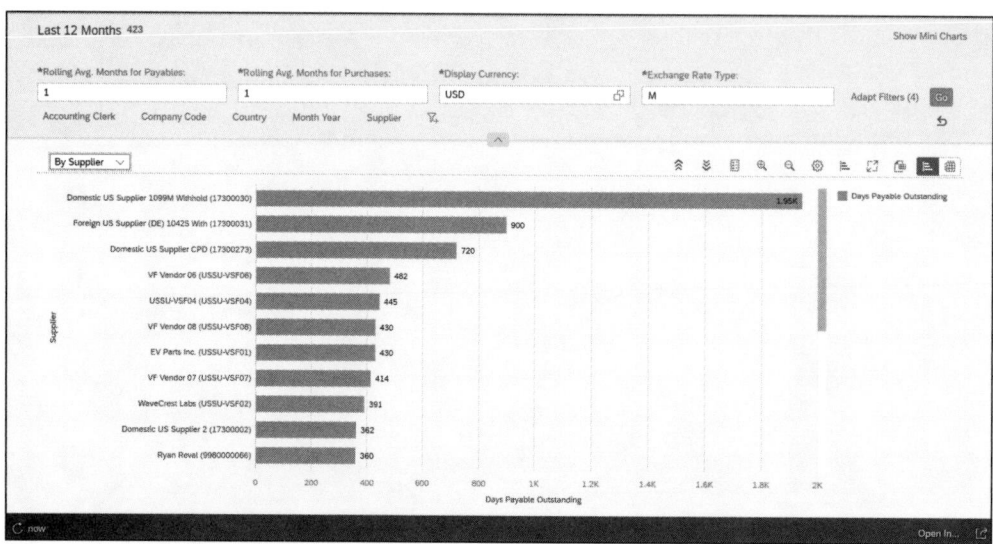

Figure 11.53 Days Payable Outstanding—Indirect Method Report

11.4.9 Invoice Processing Analysis

The Invoice Processing Analysis app lets you see information about the invoices processed in a period, such as the total number of posted invoices and posted line items.

The **Invoice Processing Analysis** tile displays the **Total Amount** metric, which is defined as the sum of the amounts of invoices posted in the designated period.

The Invoice Processing Analysis app can be used to perform the following tasks:

- See the total amount of invoices and line items posted in a certain month, as shown in Figure 11.54.

- See the total amount of invoices and line items posted for a certain supplier or by a specified user.

- See the total amount of invoices and line items posted in each of the following four processing statuses:
  - **Free for Payment**
  - **Cleared**
  - **Blocked**
  - **Parked**

The Invoice Processing Analysis app is assigned to the accounts payable manager standard authorization role.

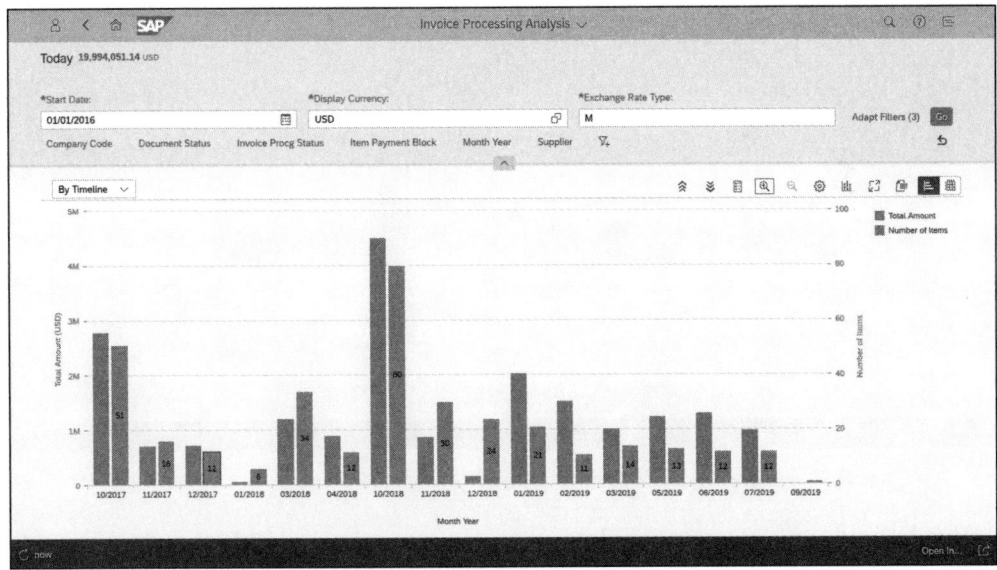

Figure 11.54 Invoice Processing Analysis Report

11.4.10   Supplier Payment Analysis (Manual and Automatic Payments)

The Supplier Payment Analysis (Manual and Automatic Payments) app is used to get insight into payments made in the last 365 days. Automatic payments are all payments posted directly by Transaction F110. Manual payments include all other payments made in the SAP S/4HANA system.

The **Automatic and Manual Payments** tile shows the **Payments for the Last Year** metric, which is defined as the sum of the amount of payments that were made today through 365 days in the past.

The Supplier Payment Analysis (Automatic and Manual Payments) app lets you perform the following tasks:

- Display aggregate data for all payment documents posted in the last year, as shown in Figure 11.55

- Display payment data by company code, supplier, user, or currency

The Supplier Payment Analysis (Manual and Automatic Payments) app is assigned to the accounts payable manager standard authorization role.

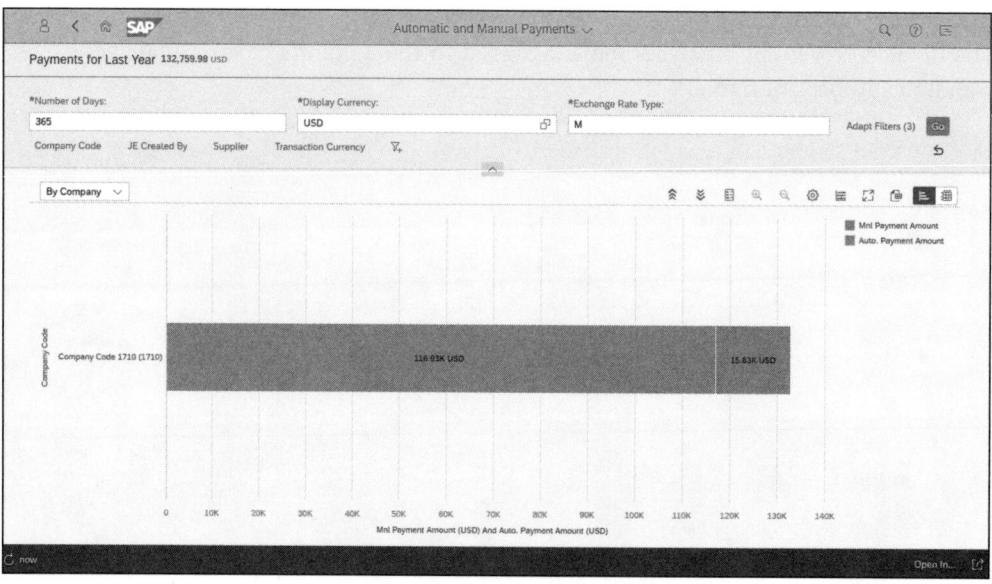

Figure 11.55 Supplier Manual and Automatic Payments Report

11.4.11   Supplier Payment Analysis (Open Payments)

The Supplier Payment Analysis (Open Payments) app is used to get insight into open payments. You can look at open payments by company code, supplier, user, or currency, for example.

The **Supplier Payment Analysis (Open Payments)** tile shows the **Open Payments** metric, which is defined as the sum of the amount of payments not cleared with invoices. Down payments are excluded from this analysis.

This app can be used to perform the following tasks:

- Display data for all payment documents not reconciled with invoices
- Display open payment data by company code, supplier, user, or currency, as shown in Figure 11.56

The Supplier Payment Analysis (Open Payments) app is assigned to the accounts payable manager standard authorization role.

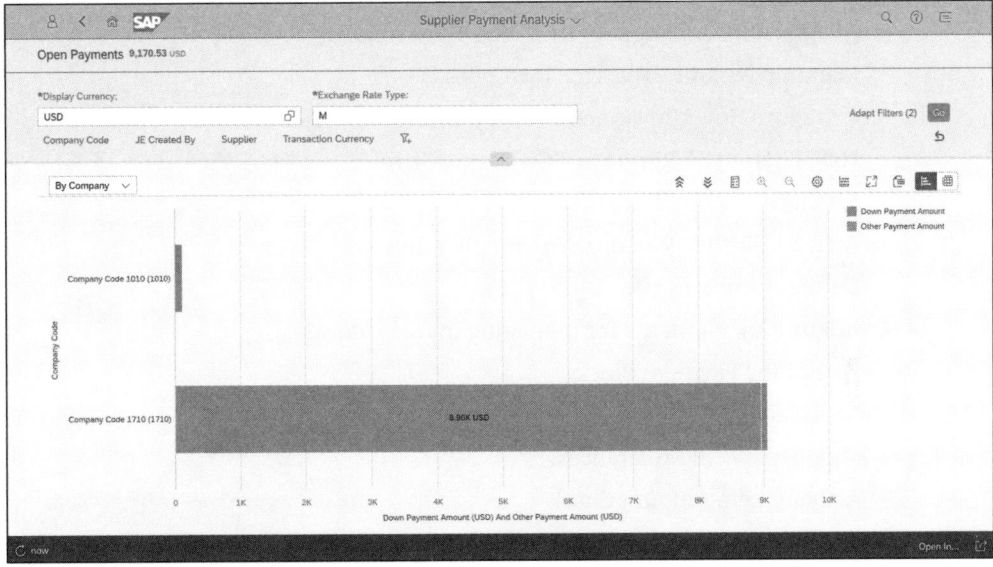

Figure 11.56 Supplier Open Payments Report

11.5   Configuring Invoice and Payables Management

Invoicing and payables management in SAP S/4HANA is delivered by SAP to work based on standard settings. However, to realize the full features and functionalities of these capabilities management to support the enterprise's goals, the system can be fine-tuned based on business requirements. This section provides the details of standard SAP-recommended configuration steps for invoice and payables management. These settings are made in the SAP S/4HANA system by following the customizing paths provided in the following sections for each step.

With SAP S/4HANA, it's possible to take advantage of the SAP Best Practices activation approach for customizing, as explained in Chapter 2. However, if you use the traditional customizing approach, this section can help. This information also helps validate the SAP standard configuration.

This configuration section is divided into two areas: a set of configuration elements for control of the entry of inbound invoices from suppliers, and a set of configuration elements controlling the circumstances by which entered invoices are blocked for subsequent processing. Here's a list of available apps for each:

- **Configuration elements for managing incoming invoices**
  - Maintain Number Range Interval for Invoice Documents
  - Assign Number Ranges to Invoicing Transactions
  - Maintain Default Values for Tax Codes
  - Configure How Unplanned Delivery Costs are Posted
  - For GR-Based IV, Reversal of GR Despite Invoice
  - Set Check for Duplicate Invoices
  - Activate Flexible Workflow for Supplier Invoices
  - Define Document Life

- **Configuration elements for managing invoice blocks**
  - Determine Payment Blocks
  - Set Tolerance Limits
  - Supplier-Specific Tolerances
  - Activate Item Amount Check
  - Set Item Amount Check
  - Activate Stochastic Block
  - Set Stochastic Block

11.5.1   Configuration Elements for Managing Incoming Invoices

Let's take a look at the configuration elements for managing incoming invoices. Here we'll cover number range intervals for invoice documents, number range assignment for invoicing transactions, default values for tax codes. Unplanned delivery cost configuration, and more.

Maintain Number Range Interval for Invoice Documents

When an invoice document is created by SAP S/4HANA, it's assigned a unique number. If you wish to assign a different number range to invoice documents, you need to establish a number range interval.

Navigate to **IMG (SPRO) • Materials Management • Logistics Invoice Verification • Incoming Invoice • Number Assignment • Maintain Number Assignment for Logistics Documents • Maintain Number Range for Invoice Documents**. The **Edit Intervals: Invoice Document** selection screen appears (see Figure 11.57).

Edit Intervals: Update document, Object RE_BELEG
Overview
Change Documents
More
Number Range Object: RE_BELEG
Decentral invoice verification document
Intervals
Intervals
NR Status

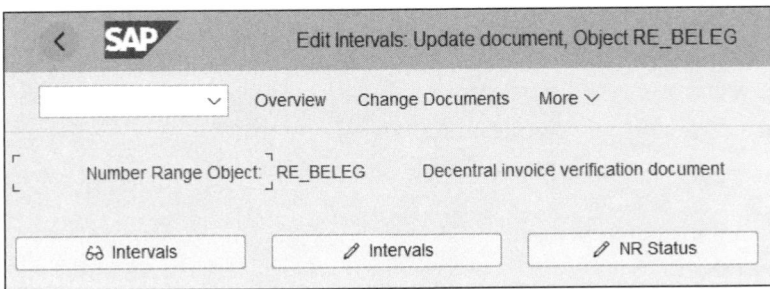

Figure 11.57 Maintain Number Range for Invoice Documents: Selection

Click the **Change Intervals** button. The **Edit Intervals: Invoice Document** screen appears (see Figure 11.58).

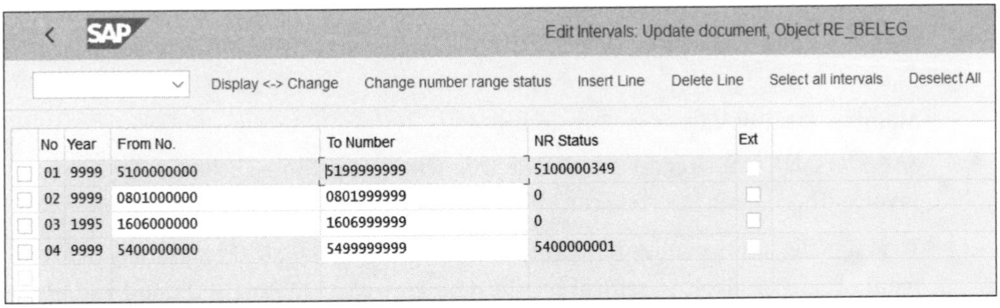

Edit Intervals: Update document, Object RE_BELEG
Display <-> Change
Change number range status
Insert Line
Delete Line
Select all intervals
Deselect All
No Year From No. To Number NR Status Ext
01 9999 5100000000 5199999999 5100000349
02 9999 0801000000 0801999999 0
03 1995 1606000000 1606999999 0
04 9999 5400000000 5499999999 5400000001

Figure 11.58 Maintain Number Range for Invoice Documents: Maintenance

Make any desired additions or changes to the standard number range intervals, then press **Save**.

Note that number range configuration changes have to be transported manually to the source systems. Alternatively, you can maintain number range intervals or statuses directly in the source system.

Assign Number Range to Invoicing Transactions

The number range then needs to be assigned to invoicing transactions. There are two invoicing transactions in the SAP S/4HANA system: Transaction RD (Invoice Posting), and Transaction RS (Invoice Cancellation, ERS, Invoicing Plan).

To assign number ranges to invoicing transactions, navigate to **IMG (SPRO) • Materials Management • Logistics Invoice Verification • Incoming Invoice • Number Assignment • Maintain Number Assignment for Logistics Documents • Transaction - Assign Number Range**.

The **Number Ranges: Logistics Invoice Verification** screen appears (see Figure 11.59).

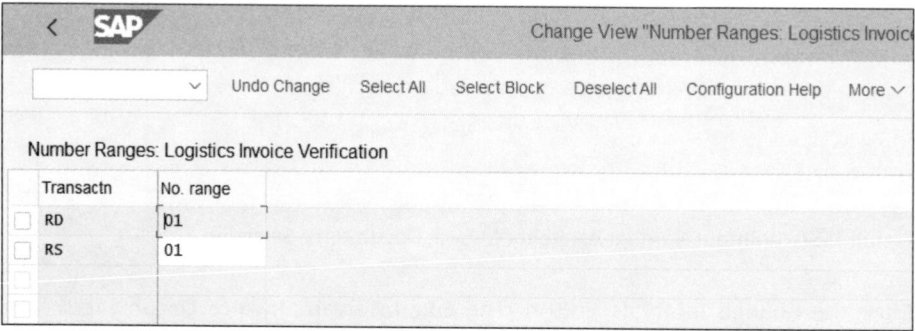

Figure 11.59 Transaction: Assign Number Range

Assign the desired number range to the invoicing transactions, then press **Save**.

Maintain Default Values for Tax Codes

SAP S/4HANA can suggest a tax code that will default into an incoming domestic invoice. This default tax code can be set by company code.

To assign default tax codes for invoices, navigate to **IMG (SPRO) • Materials Management • Logistics Invoice Verification • Incoming Invoice • Maintain Default values for Tax Codes**.

The **Tax Defaults in Invoice Verification** screen appears (see Figure 11.60).

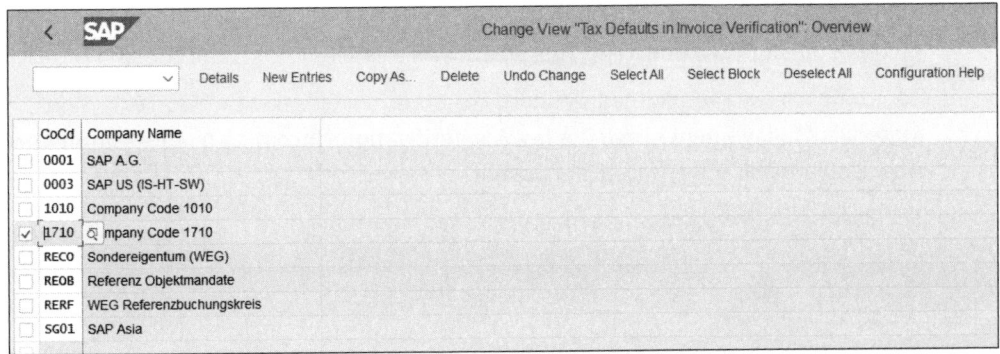

Figure 11.60 Maintain Default Values for Tax Codes: Company Code

Click the checkbox next to the company code, then press the **Details** button. The **Tax Defaults in Invoice Verification—Company Code** screen appears (see Figure 11.61).

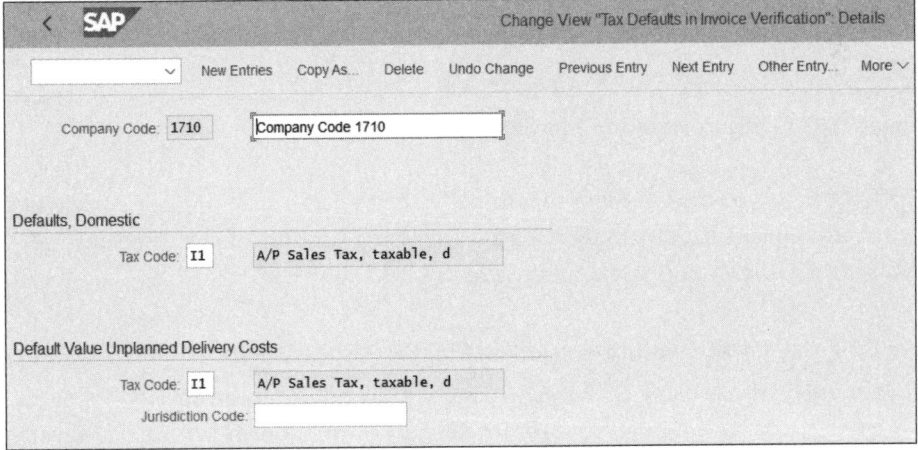

Figure 11.61 Maintain Default Values for Tax Codes: Maintenance

Use the dropdown list for the **Tax Code** field to select a valid tax code for the selected company code. You can maintain default values for unplanned delivery costs as well. When you're done, press **Save**.

Configure How Unplanned Delivery Costs Are Posted

You can control how unplanned delivery costs that come in on a supplier invoice are posted. You can either have the unplanned delivery costs distributed proportionally over the invoice line items, or you can have them posted in a separate general ledger account, one for each line item. This posting logic is set by company code.

To configure how unplanned delivery costs are posted, navigate to **IMG (SPRO)** • **Materials Management** • **Logistics Invoice Verification** • **Incoming Invoice** • **Configure How Unplanned Delivery costs are posted**.

The **Posting Delivery Costs** screen appears (see Figure 11.62).

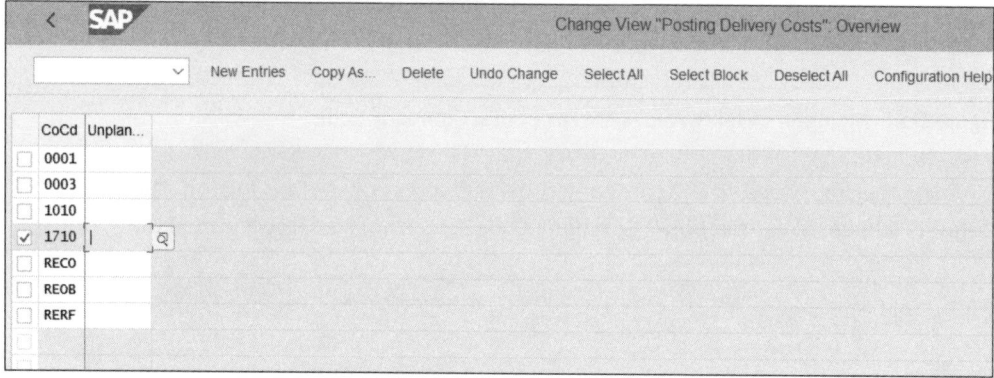

Figure 11.62 Configure How Unplanned Delivery Costs are Posted

Click the checkbox next to the company code, then select a valid unplanned delivery cost option (blank for distribution across line items, **1** for posting to a separate general ledger). When you're done, press **Save**.

For GR-Based Invoice Verification, Reversal of GR Despite Invoice

If your enterprise is using GR-based invoice verification, you can specify if you can reverse a goods receipt or create a return delivery if the supplier invoice has already been posted. If you don't allow this option, the supplier invoice will need to be cancelled prior to entering the reversal or supplier return.

This setting is made by reversal or return movement type. It can't be set by company code.

To configure whether reversals or returns can be made after invoice posting, navigate to **IMG (SPRO)** • **Materials Management** • **Inventory Management and Physical Inventory** • **Goods Receipt** • **For GR-Based IV, Reversal of GR Despite Invoice**.

The **For GR-Based IV, Reversal of GR Despite Invoice** screen appears (see Figure 11.63).

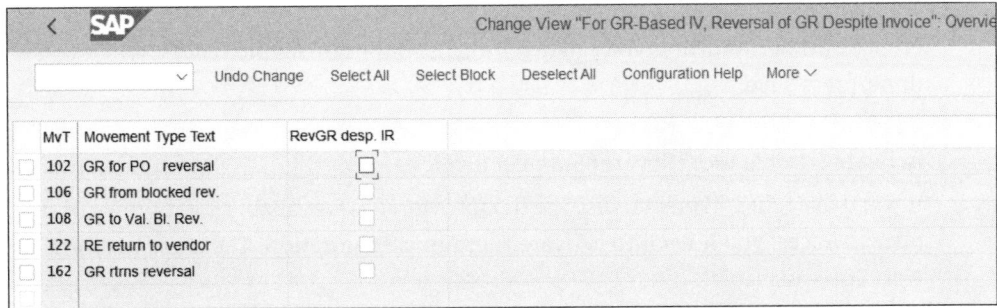

Figure 11.63 For GR-Based IV, Reversal of GR Despite Invoice

Click the checkbox next to the movement types for which reversals or returns are allowed without cancellation of the supplier invoice. When you're done, press **Save**.

Set Check for Duplicate Invoices

With this configuration item, you can check that the same invoice is not inadvertently entered into the SAP S/4HANA system more than once, so that duplicate payments are not made. The system can check that the supplier, currency code, company code, gross invoice amount, reference document number, and invoice date are unique. These settings apply to a company code.

To configure whether the system should check for duplicate invoices, navigate to **IMG (SPRO)** • **Materials Management** • **Logistics Invoice Verification** • **Incoming Invoice** • **Set Check for Duplicate Invoices**.

The **Duplicate Invoice Check** screen appears (see Figure 11.64).

CoC...	Name	Check co. code	Check reference	Check inv. date
0001	SAP A.G.	✓	✓	✓
0003	SAP US (IS-HT-SW)	☐	☐	☐
1010	Company Code 1010	✓	✓	✓
1710	Company Code 1710	✓	✓	✓
RECO	Sondereigentum (WEG)	✓	✓	✓
REOB	Referenz Objektmandate	✓	✓	✓
RERF	WEG Referenzbuchungskreis	✓	✓	✓

Figure 11.64 Set Check for Duplicate Invoices

For each company code, you can select if the system will check the company code, reference number, and/or invoice date during the duplicate invoice check. When you're done, press **Save**.

Activate Flexible Workflow for Supplier Invoices

If you'd like SAP S/4HANA to use the flexible workflows available for approval of supplier invoices, you'll need to activate them in configuration. There are two flexible workflows available:

- Workflow for Approval of Invoices on Payment Block
- Workflow to Release Completed Invoices for Payment

To configure whether the system uses the flexible workflow for supplier invoices, navigate to **IMG (SPRO) • Materials Management • Logistics Invoice Verification • Incoming Invoice • Activate Flexible Workflow for Supplier Invoices**.

The **Activate Flexible Workflow for Supplier Invoices** screen appears (see Figure 11.65).

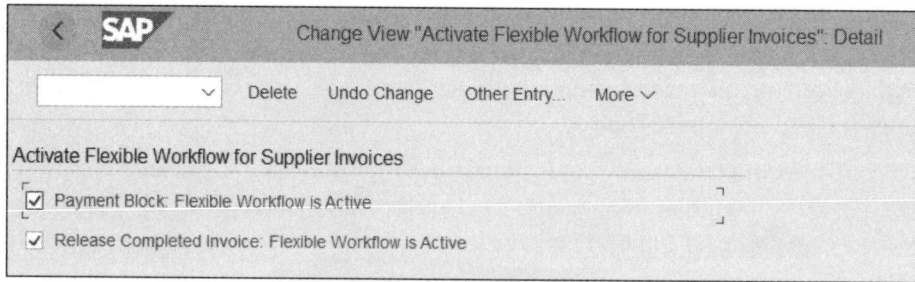

Figure 11.65 Activate Flexible Workflow for Supplier Invoices

Click the checkbox for each flexible workflow you wish to use. When you're done, press **Save**.

Define Document Life

Enterprises often implement an archiving system in their SAP S/4HANA systems for business objects, including supplier invoices. The amount of time that an enterprise requires objects to be available online is typically determined by document retention policies. You can use this configuration item to prevent the accidental archiving of supplier invoices before a certain number of days. This setting is based on company code.

The menu path to set the document life is **IMG (SPRO) • Materials Management • Logistics Invoice Verification • Define Document Life**.

The **MR Document Archiving: Document Life** screen appears (see Figure 11.66).

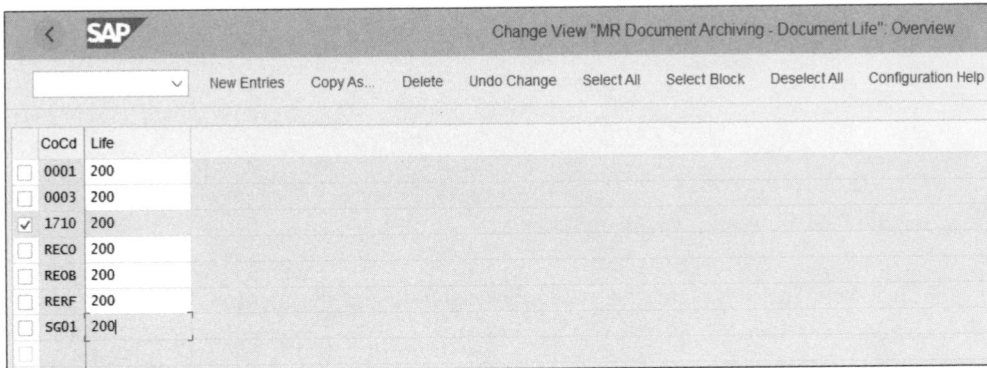

Figure 11.66 Define Document Life

Edit the number of days for the specified company code, then press **Save**.

11.5.2   Configuration Elements for Managing Invoice Blocks

Let's take a look at the configuration elements for managing invoice blocks. We'll begin with determining payment blocks, setting tolerance limits, and a supplier-specific tolerances. Then we'll activate item amount checks, set item amount checks, and do the same for stochastic blocks.

Determine Payment Blocks

You can create payment block reasons to suit your enterprise's requirements. These can be manually applied to the invoice at the time of entry.

The menu path to create payment block codes is **IMG (SPRO) • Materials Management • Logistics Invoice Verification • Invoice Block • Determine Payment Block**.

The **Reasons for Blocking Payment** screen appears (see Figure 11.67).

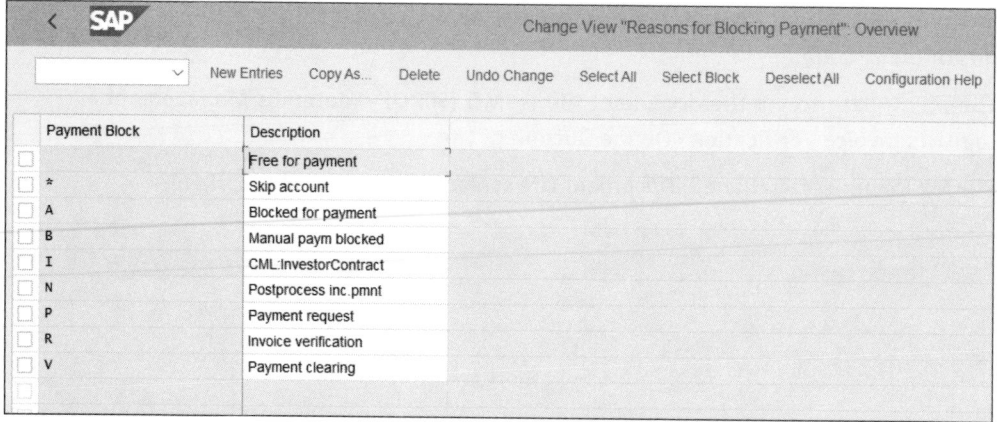

Figure 11.67 Determine Payment Blocks

Click **New Entries** to create a new blocking code and description. When you're finished, press **Save**.

Set Tolerance Limits

The SAP S/4HANA system checks each invoice item for variances between the invoice and the purchase order and goods receipt. Each variance is defined as a tolerance key. Each company code has its own set of tolerance keys that can be configured. The system uses the following tolerance keys and settings during invoice processing:

- AN: Amount of Item without Order Reference
- AP: Amount for Item with Order Reference
- BD: Form Small Differences Automatically
- BR: Percentage Order Price Unit Variance (IR before GR)
- BW: Percentage Order Price Unit Variance (GR before IR)
- DQ: Exceed Amount: Quantity Variance
- DW: Quantity Variance when GR Quantity = Zero
- KW: Variance from Condition Value
- PP: Price Variance
- PS: Price Variance: Estimated Price

- ST: Date Variance (Value x Days)
- VP: Moving Average Price Variance

If a variance exceeds a tolerance limit, the user receives a message. If an upper limit is exceeded, then the invoice will be blocked for payment. Please refer to the configuration help documentation for detailed explanations of each tolerance key and how they work.

The menu path to set tolerance limits is **IMG (SPRO)** • **Materials Management** • **Logistics Invoice Verification** • **Invoice Block** • **Set Tolerance Limits**.

The **Tolerance Limits** screen appears (see Figure 11.68).

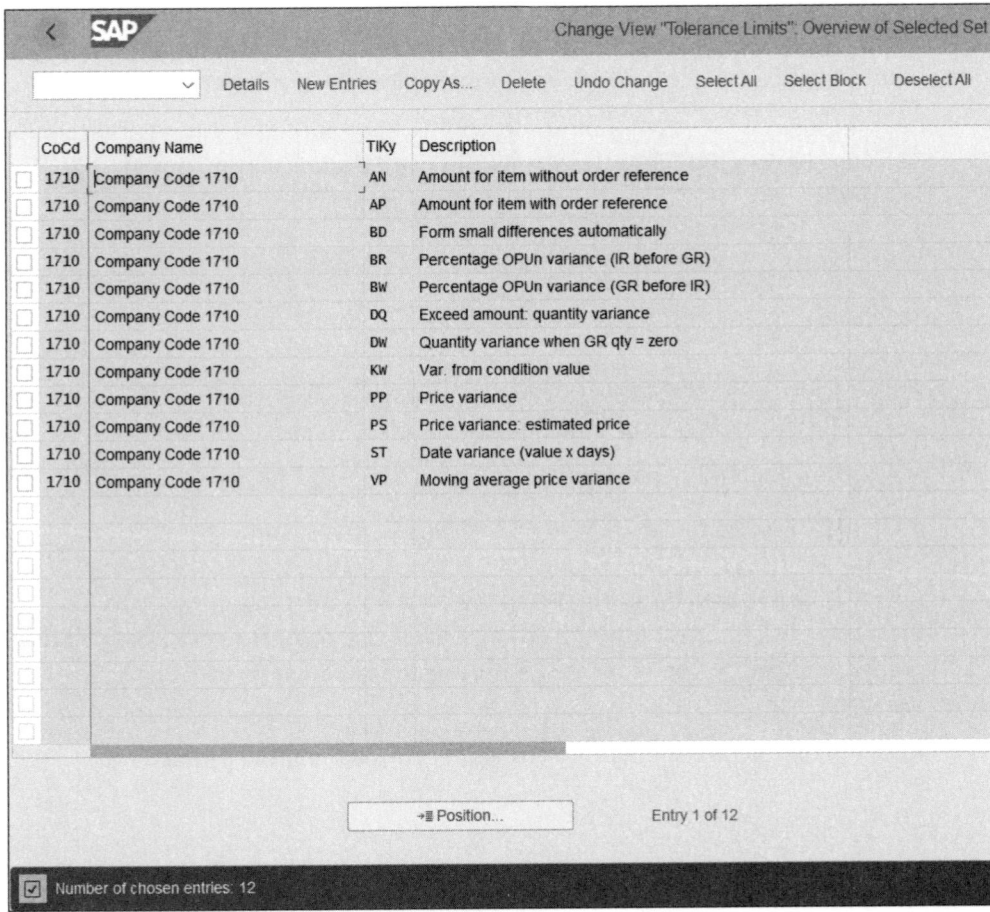

Figure 11.68 Set Tolerance Limits

Click the checkbox next to the company code and tolerance key combination you wish to maintain, then press the **Details** button. The screens will depend on the tolerance key being maintained. When you're finished, press **Save**.

Supplier-Specific Tolerances

There are some tolerances that can be applied to specific suppliers in a company code if you wish. This is done using a tolerance group. You define tolerance groups per company code, then assign them to suppliers via the business partner vendor maintenance screens. You can configure how the system reacts to certain variances that occur, both positive and negative. Refer to the configuration help documentation for detailed explanations of each tolerance setting and how they work.

The menu path to set supplier-specific tolerances is **IMG (SPRO)** • **Materials Management** • **Logistics Invoice Verification** • **Incoming Invoice** • **Configure Supplier-Specific Tolerances**.

The **Supplier-Specific Tolerances Company Code Selection** screen appears (see Figure 11.69).

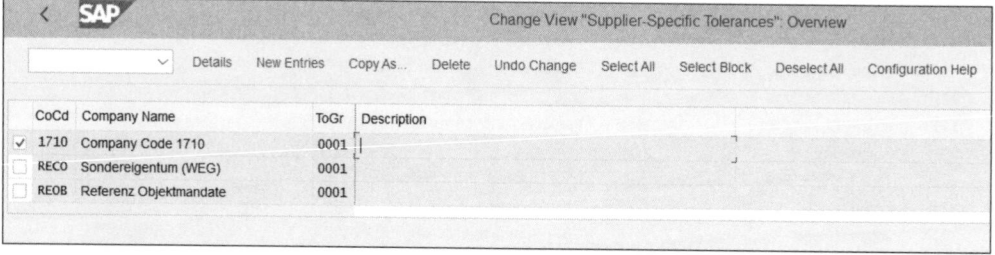

Figure 11.69 Supplier-Specific Tolerances: Company Code Selection

Click the checkbox next to the company code and tolerance group you wish to maintain. Click the **New Entries** field to create a new company code and tolerance group combination. The **Supplier-Specific Tolerances Details** screen appears (see Figure 11.70).

Maintain the tolerance limits and settings. When you're finished, press **Save**.

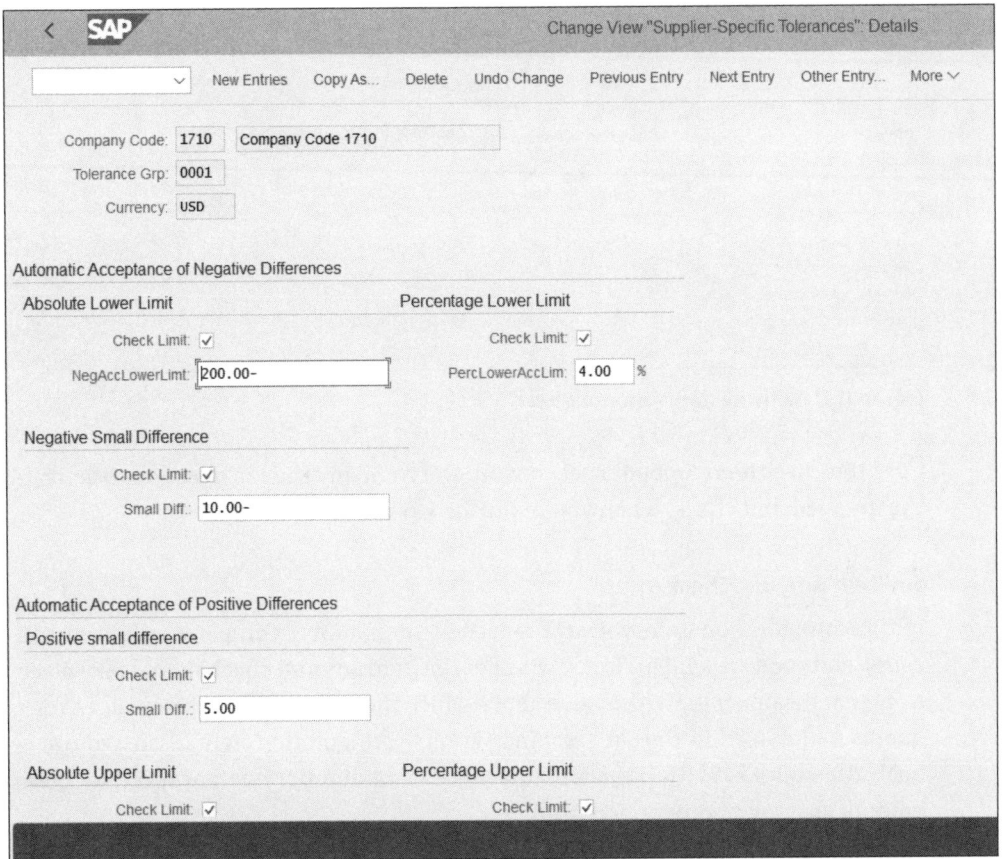

Figure 11.70 Supplier-Specific Tolerances: Maintenance

Activate Item Amount Check

You can instruct the SAP S/4HANA system to block an invoice line item that exceeds a specified amount. You activate this check using this configuration item. The check is set by company code.

The menu path to activate the item amount check is **IMG (SPRO) • Materials Management • Logistics Invoice Verification • Invoice Block • Item Amount Check • Activate Item Amount Check**.

The **Activate Block Due to Item Amount** screen appears (see Figure 11.71).

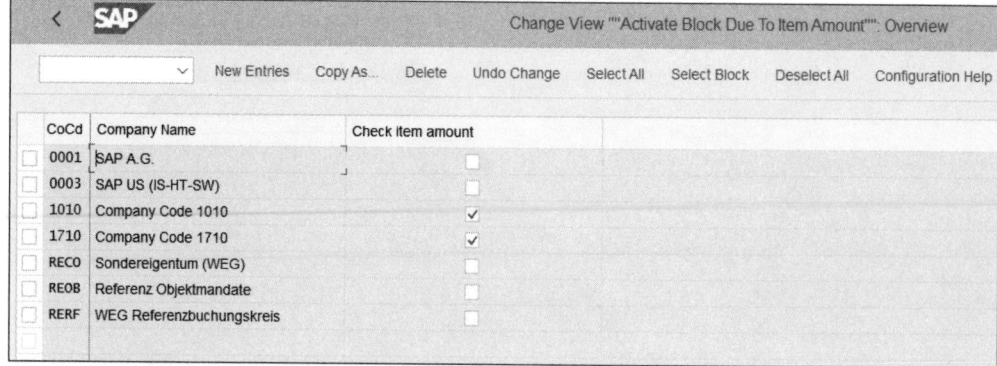

Figure 11.71 Activate Item Amount Check

Click the **Check Item Amount** checkbox for the company code in question to activate the item amount check. When you're finished, press **Save**.

Set Item Amount Check

In this configuration item, you set for each combination of company code, item category, and goods receipt indicator whether the item amount check should take place. Note that the upper limit (the value above which the system should block the invoice line) is maintained in the Set Tolerance Limits configuration item discussed previously (tolerance keys AN [item amount check without order reference] and AP [item amount check with order reference]).

The menu path to activate the item amount check is **IMG (SPRO) • Materials Management • Logistics Invoice Verification • Invoice Block • Item Amount Check • Set Item Amount Check**.

The **Invoice Verification Amount Check** screen appears (see Figure 11.72).

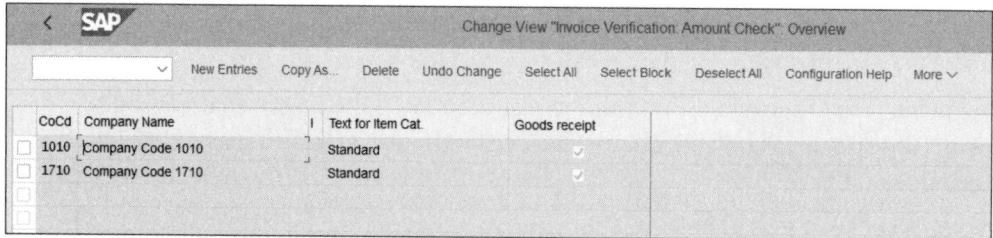

Figure 11.72 Set Item Amount Check

Maintain all combinations of company code, item category, and goods receipt indicator for which the item amount check should be active. When you're finished, press **Save**.

Activate Stochastic Block

The system provides the capability for randomly blocking invoices for further review and approval. This capability is known as *stochastic blocking*. You enable stochastic blocking by company code.

The menu path to activate the stochastic block is **IMG (SPRO) • Materials Management • Logistics Invoice Verification • Invoice Block • Stochastic Block • Activate Stochastic Block**.

The **Stochastic Block Activation** screen appears (see Figure 11.73).

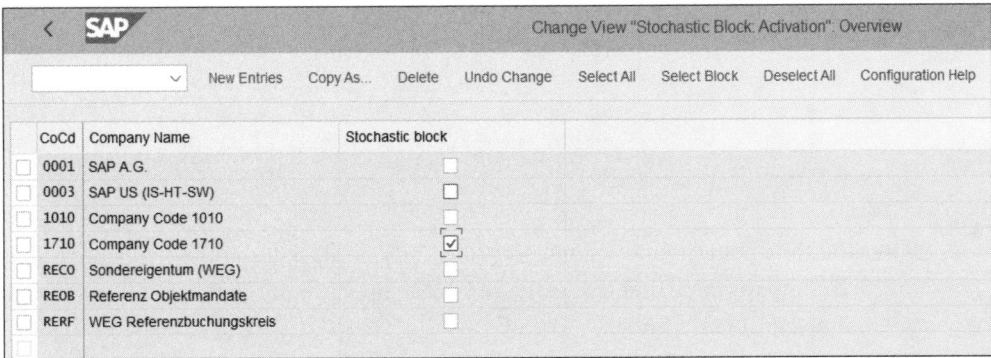

Figure 11.73 Activate Stochastic Block

Click the **Stochastic Block** checkbox for the correct company code to activate the stochastic block capability. When you're finished, press **Save**.

Set Stochastic Block

In this configuration item, you set the threshold and percentage values that determine how likely it is that the stochastic blocking will happen. If the total invoice value is greater than or equal to the threshold value, the probability that the invoice will be blocked is the same as the percentage. However, if the total invoice value is less than the threshold value, the probability that the invoice will be blocked is proportional to the given percentage. This guarantees that invoices less than the threshold are blocked less often than ones that warrant further review. Stochastic checks are performed after all other invoice block checks are complete. You set stochastic blocking thresholds and percentages by company code.

The menu path to activate the stochastic block is **IMG (SPRO) • Materials Management • Logistics Invoice Verification • Invoice Block • Stochastic Block • Set Stochastic Block**.

The **Stochastic Block Values** screen appears (see Figure 11.74).

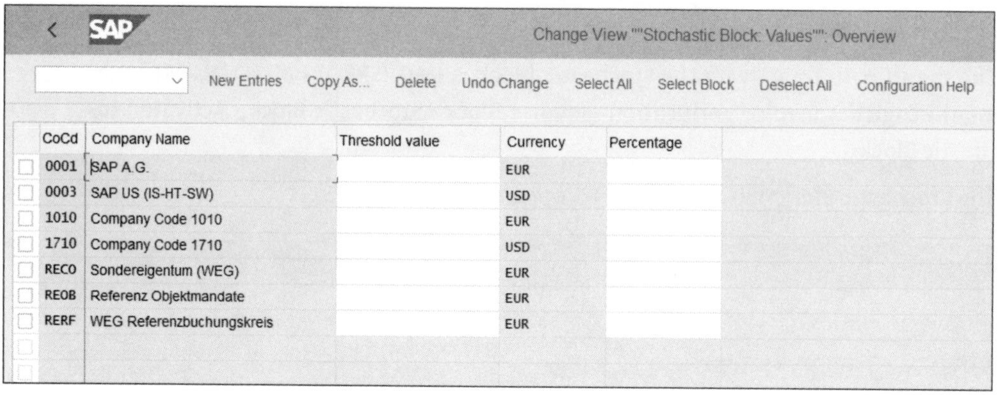

	CoCd	Company Name	Threshold value	Currency	Percentage	
☐	0001	SAP A.G.		EUR		
☐	0003	SAP US (IS-HT-SW)		USD		
☐	1010	Company Code 1010		EUR		
☐	1710	Company Code 1710		USD		
☐	RECO	Sondereigentum (WEG)		EUR		
☐	REOB	Referenz Objektmandate		EUR		
☐	RERF	WEG Referenzbuchungskreis		EUR		

Figure 11.74 Set Stochastic Block

Enter the threshold invoice value and probability of blocking in the fields provided for each company code that was activated in the previous configuration item. When you're finished, press **Save**.

11.6   Summary

You've now learned that SAP S/4HANA provides a complete solution for managing the entry of supplier invoices into the SAP S/4HANA system. Once the invoice data is entered and verified in the system, control then passes to accounts payable for supplier payment. There are many reporting and analytic apps that allow accounts payable personnel to monitor and optimize the invoicing and payment process from end to end. Now, let's take a look at supplier management.

Chapter 12
Supplier Management

Managing suppliers and the relationships between suppliers and the buying organization is at the heart of procurement. SAP S/4HANA Sourcing and Procurement functionality focuses on supplier evaluation, classification, and segmentation. This chapter will provide an overview of these capabilities, as well as configuration steps.

Supplier Management in SAP S/4HANA centers on three core topics: classification, segmentation, and evaluation. This is also how the chapter unfolds, providing an overview of supplier management and then going deeper into these three areas, finishing with configuration steps for each area.

12.1 What Is Supplier Management?

Supplier management is an interchangeable term with *procurement* in general. All procurement involves a counterparty, even if the procurement is internal and the counterparty merely another part of the overall organization. Supplier management ensures your organization receives value from the selected supplier and transactions by identifying, onboarding, and tracking suppliers during their lifecycle with your organization.

Some organizations strive to have tight relationships with their strategic suppliers, co-innovating and building new products and markets in tandem with their core supply base. This type of strategy is deployed in a variety of scenarios, even in counterintuitive ones like fast food. McDonalds is widely cited as having deep relationships with its suppliers and working on products jointly with these suppliers to obtain a signature flavor or product. This approach enables McDonalds to ensure quality standards are met uniformly across the world by their suppliers and fosters loyalty on the part of its suppliers, who may not be able to replace a customer the size of McDonalds if the supplier were to damage this relationship.

Other organizations look at purchasing as a commodity acquisition activity and seek to obtain the lowest prices; they choose the supplier who currently can provide this, switching whenever necessary to the lowest price. This type of approach works well in procurement situations with low switching costs and commodity-type materials and services.

Whatever the approach, supplier management is a must for a procurement organization if it's to contribute to the success of a company in the long term. Buying from the wrong supplier can have disastrous consequences for the buyer. Managing the supply base to obtain competitive pricing based on your volumes and negotiating can mean success or failure in a competitive marketplace.

Supplier management and evaluation functionality in SAP S/4HANA has been augmented with additional, subjective criteria and survey capabilities that were previously the domain of SAP Supplier Relationship Management (SAP SRM). This chapter will detail supplier management from qualification to classification/segmentation to onboarding to evaluation, highlighting new functionality and nuances in SAP S/4HANA.

12.1.1   Supplier Discovery, Qualification, and Onboarding

Supplier discovery, qualification, and onboarding are not in scope for SAP S/4HANA Sourcing and Procurement and SAP S/4HANA in general. These areas are best handled using the SAP Ariba Discovery and SAP Ariba Supplier Lifecycle and Performance cloud solutions. Alternatively, you can also implement SAP Supplier Lifecycle Management if you require an on-premise version of this capability. The following is a high-level overview of each solution's capabilities.

SAP Ariba Discovery and SAP Ariba Supplier Lifecycle and Performance

SAP Ariba Discovery allows you to create a posting for your desired item or service, post it to the Ariba Network, have suppliers submit proposals, review the proposals, and select the best one. You can also post more generic requests to identify category suppliers or search from 1.5 million suppliers in 233 countries covering over 20,000 commodity codes (material groups) on the Ariba Network worldwide. Once you've selected a supplier, you can enter it into SAP S/4HANA directly and begin transacting, or further qualify it and have the supplier maintain its own record using SAP Ariba Supplier Lifecycle and Performance.

SAP Ariba Supplier Lifecycle and Performance provides the following capabilities:

- Vendor data model with two-way sync between the solution and SAP S/4HANA
- Registration and onboarding with supplier portal
- Supplier-managed information
- Supplier 360-degree view
- Reports and analysis
- Supplier performance management (scorecards, questionnaires, KPIs)
- Reports and analysis (based on category, location, and business unit)
- Supplier segmentation, qualification, and development
- Supplier lifecycle and performance management
- Risk assessments and due diligence intelligence
- Risk-exposure monitoring (reputational, compliance, financial, sustainability, and operational risks)
- Engagement-level inherent risk and residual risk calculation to drive actions for sourcing and contracts
- Risk mitigation (flexible workflows for procurement and risk management teams)

In a standard SAP Ariba Supplier Lifecycle and Performance integration with SAP S/4HANA, the main part to be integrated with the SAP ERP backend is the supplier master record. This exchange can leverage the existing MDG-S integration with SAP Ariba, which enables SAP Master Data Governance, Supplier to integrate directly and exchange supplier master data with SAP Ariba solutions. If your requirements are more extensive, you can build a custom integration leveraging the SAP Ariba Cloud Integration Gateway. Add-ons and documentation to support your integration requirements are available at *service.sap.com*. SAP Ariba Supplier Lifecycle and Performance uses the new SAP S/4HANA business partner model. To integrate to older versions of SAP ERP, such as ECC, a CVI conversion of the vendor/customer records is a prerequisite. For more information on this topic, see Chapter 4.

SAP S/4HANA Sourcing and Procurement separates supplier management into two distinct areas: classification and segmentation, and supplier evaluation, as shown in Figure 12.1. First, a user can leverage capabilities to classify suppliers and create segments or groups of similar suppliers. Once the suppliers have been organized in this manner from an analysis standpoint, the user can begin conducting objective and subjective exercises to determine the optimal suppliers and supplier mixes to support the organizational procurement objectives.

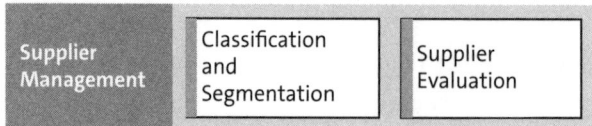

Figure 12.1 SAP S/4HANA Sourcing and Procurement: Supplier Management

The most comprehensive solution for supplier management should include a network approach to facilitate supplier self-services and collaboration. For this, the go-to solution at SAP remains the Ariba Network, the largest network of its kind, as well as SAP Ariba Supplier Lifecycle and Performance. SAP S/4HANA doesn't have functionality or plans to replace the supplier-side approaches supported in the Ariba Network and SAP Ariba Supplier Lifecycle and Performance's supplier management and onboarding solutions. It makes sense to onboard a supplier via a network, as the suppliers don't need to register repeatedly at their customers' individual supplier portals and maintain their commercial details for conducting business. Having a network at the size and feature depth of the Ariba Network, via which over a trillion dollars in transactions take place annually between millions of suppliers and customers, means that a supplier can register on the Ariba Network, maintain its information in a centralized location, and have this information curated and up-to-date for a majority of its customers in one area. This includes customers running SAP S/4HANA as their digital core, as SAP S/4HANA comes with prebuilt linkages and a roadmap for further deepening of these integration points in future releases.

In short, SAP S/4HANA Sourcing and Procurement doesn't plan to encompass self-registration or self-service data maintenance by suppliers directly but focuses only on supplier classification and supplier evaluation. These supplier onboarding activities are instead conducted directly by the buyer in SAP S/4HANA, who registers the supplier internally and updates the data on the supplier record or via an integration with SAP Ariba Supplier Lifecycle and Performance to allow for supplier self-service.

Although sell-side processes for supplier self-registration and supplier self-maintenance are not currently available in SAP S/4HANA and not planned, on the buyer side, SAP S/4HANA supports the following:

- Supplier data creation and maintenance
- Supplier hierarchies
- Supplier classification
- Supplier evaluation
- Supplier risk with Dun & Bradstreet

- Supplier qualification via activity management
- Certificate management via attachments
- Activity management
- Category management and purchasing categories

On the buyer side, therefore, SAP S/4HANA supports qualification, portfolio management, visibility, and performance management for the customer's supply base. The basic steps in the supplier lifecycle are registration and onboarding, classification and segmentation, analysis, and supplier-performance management. The next section reviews the SAP on-premise solution for conducting these processes in SAP Supplier Lifecycle Management.

SAP Supplier Lifecycle Management

Customers occasionally can't leverage a cloud solution due to control sensitivities in their supply base or a need to customize the system beyond a multitenant, public cloud solution's abilities to accommodate. SAP Supplier Lifecycle Management is an on-premise solution that integrates with SAP S/4HANA and provides the following capabilities:

- **Onboarding and registration**
  Provides automated workflows and supplier self-services for registration and maintenance of supplier records
- **Qualification**
  Including questionnaires, reusable libraries, and weighted scoring
- **Classification and segmentation**
  Creates a searchable, collaborative classification system for suppliers
- **Portfolio management of suppliers**
  Provides industry reports and promotion processes
- **Performance management**
  KPI-driven analysis capabilities

If your organization requires qualification capabilities, onboarding, and/or supplier-driven maintenance of supplier records, it may be preferable to leverage the aforementioned functionalities in SAP Ariba Supplier Lifecycle and Performance, foregoing the duplication of these in SAP S/4HANA. This means having SAP Ariba Supplier Lifecycle and Performance drive the supplier qualification, onboarding, and evaluation processes, with SAP S/4HANA receiving the updated supplier record outputs from this process. Similarly, if you elect to implement SAP Supplier Lifecycle Management as part of your SAP S/4HANA landscape, you can focus the supplier registration, qualification, evaluation, and classification in this system rather than mixing supplier management processes in SAP Supplier Lifecycle Management and SAP S/4HANA.

12.1.2   Classification and Segmentation

SAP S/4HANA Sourcing and Procurement has new functionality and a new focus for classification and segmentation. With classification and segmentation, the procurement organization groups similar expenditure items into purchasing categories of spend. Apply further analysis and reporting, and an organization can begin to see which categories of spend are strategic to the organization, where the most money is being spent by category, and possible areas for expansion and consolidation of spend. Once this insight is gleaned from classification and segmentation, suppliers can be evaluated based on their performance and the types of materials and services they provide.

Suppliers are managed in SAP S/4HANA using attributes in their master data, as well as continuous activity and task management based on their objective and subjective performance metrics. Activity and task management are new concepts and features in SAP S/4HANA Sourcing and Procurement, as is the integration with Dun & Bradstreet for data. Unlike previous versions of SAP ERP, SAP S/4HANA supports additional functionality for supplier management, including the ability to classify suppliers and conduct analysis in the system using Dun & Bradstreet data overlays. These additional features provide an integrated overview that's leveraged directly in procurement transactions in real-time, enabling a user to move from insight to action seamlessly in SAP S/4HANA.

12.1.3   Evaluation

Evaluating a supplier's performance is critical to make the supplier lifecycle management process smarter and more collaborative with your stakeholders and the supplier. A supplier may not know they have performance issues with a customer unless the feedback is there. An organization may not realize the extent of the value or impacts of a supplier without conducting such analysis. Once you compile the classification and segmentation metrics and collect objective (on-time delivery, price variance to PO, quality and other measures) and subjective (from surveys and user feedback) performance data, you can report on this using the supplier evaluation tools available in SAP S/4HANA, explained further in Section 12.3.

12.2   Classification and Segmentation

The main apps in SAP S/4HANA Sourcing and Procurement for the segmentation and classification area include the following (these apps can be found in the SAP Fiori app library at *http://s-prs.co/500304*):

- **Manage Purchasing Category**
  Create/maintain/view purchasing categories

- **Translate Purchasing Category**
  Maintain a translation for a purchasing category in another language

- **Manage Activities**
  Review purchasing activities touching suppliers in the system

- **Monitor Tasks**
  Monitor purchasing activities and tasks assigned in the system

- **Process Tasks**
  View worklist of tasks assigned to you and display or edit the tasks

Previous versions of SAP ERP and the segmentation and classification area for supplier evaluation focused on classifications existing in the systems. Material groups were used to create categories for classification of the type of supplier. Using this classification, you could then use objective criteria available in the system from transactions and subjective criteria from creating surveys system riding sidecar to the SAP ERP instance, such as SAP SRM. This has changed in SAP S/4HANA; now, both survey and objective data converge in the core ERP system, as do the analytics and reporting themselves. The next section focuses on a new concept in SAP S/4HANA: purchasing categories.

12.2.1   Purchasing Categories

SAP S/4HANA leverages a purchasing category approach for segmentation and classification that extends beyond a single material group to capture all of the spend and suppliers in a particular area of the business for procurement-centric analysis. Accessed via the aforementioned Manage Purchasing Category app, a *purchasing category* can be used group to several material groups into one purchasing category, essentially providing a metalayer capability to allow purchasing departments to connect otherwise unrelated and related material groups into a larger set for the classification and segmentation of suppliers. This is also a key feature for purchasing departments to classify and segment materials as you can use an aggregate, business-centric view without having to rely on UNSPSC roll-ups or other approaches.

Once the suppliers have been logically grouped into purchasing categories, buying departments can organize work around these categories and drive efficiencies in key areas of the organization's activities and business. With the addition of certification data in attachments, as shown in Figure 12.2, qualified suppliers can be grouped by their certifications, purchasing category, and evaluations/feedback on performance.

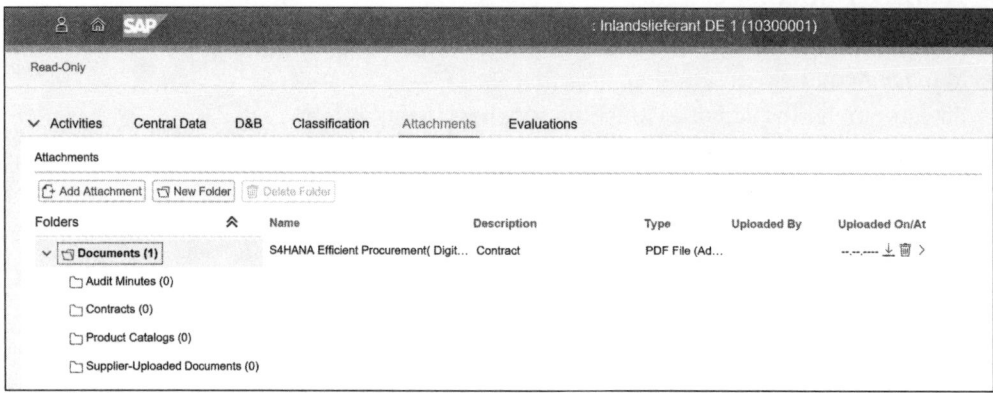

Figure 12.2 Attachments Tab in SAP S/4HANA Supplier Record

Both the buying departments and supplier groups are flexible in the system, allowing for dynamic adjustments. SAP S/4HANA Sourcing and Procurement isn't a pure transactional system from this standpoint, but a system capable of providing in-system overviews and analytics to aid in the purchasing process. To create, manage, and translate purchasing categories in SAP S/4HANA, you simply click the corresponding app's tile (see Figure 12.3). Once created, a purchasing category can be further managed and translated.

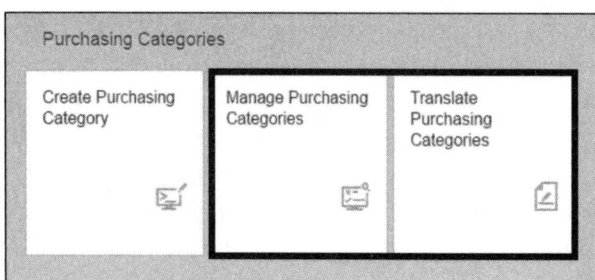

Figure 12.3 Purchasing Category Apps

To create a purchasing category, open the Purchasing Category SAP Fiori app, as shown in Figure 12.4, and enter both the applicable material groups and suppliers, as well as applicable activities.

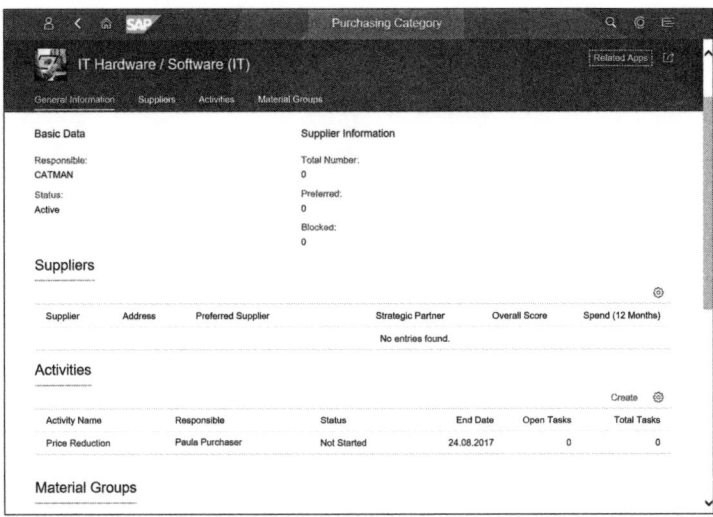

Figure 12.4 Creating Purchasing Category

One-to-many suppliers, activities, and material groups can be assigned to one purchasing category, further enabling aggregated purchasing spend analytics and efficient commodity management.

> **Note**
>
> Although many material groups can be assigned to one purchasing group, a material group can only be assigned to one purchasing group.

The data entered in the purchasing category updates at the supplier record level, facilitating analysis as in Figure 12.5. Here, users can review classification data, scorecards, spend and revenue information, and risk, further informing their transaction decisions and strategies. In the **Central Data** tab of a supplier record, the buyer can review the assigned purchasing categories for this supplier, as in Figure 12.6.

Access to supplier records typically is limited to maintain the quality of the master data in the SAP S/4HANA environment. The app for accessing the supplier record is the Manage Supplier Data app, and this app is typically assigned to the supplier master data manager/owner, rather than to the extended buyer population.

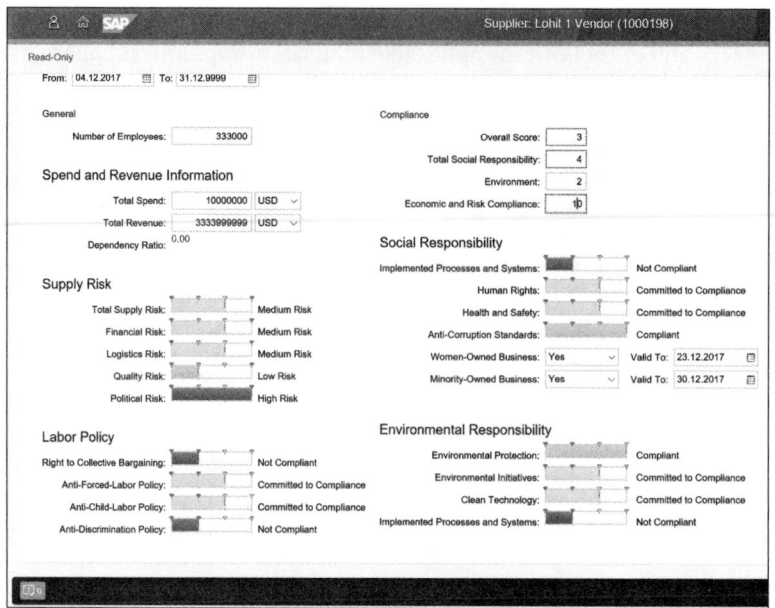

Figure 12.5 Supplier Record with Analysis and Classification Data

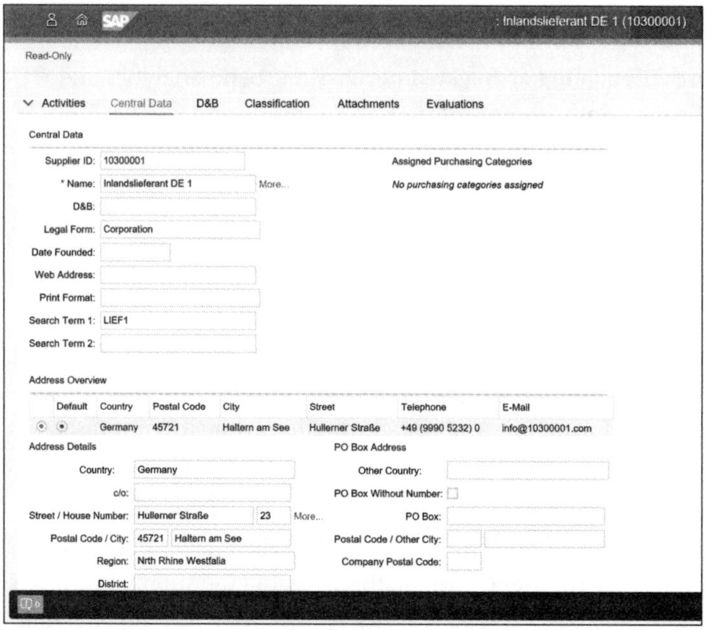

Figure 12.6 Central Data Tab: Supplier

Managing a Purchasing Category

To manage purchase categories at an overview level, a user can navigate to the Manage Purchase Categories app and search or filter on specific purchasing categories, as in Figure 12.7.

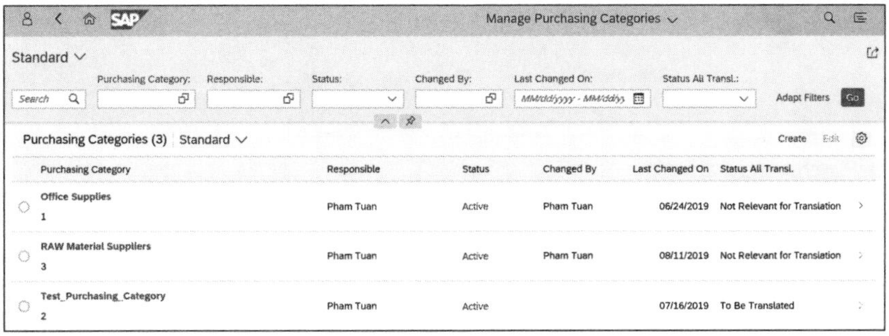

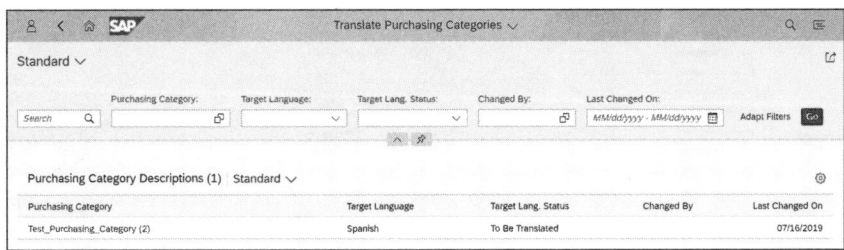

Figure 12.7 Manage Purchasing Categories

Translating a Purchasing Category

If you're running a global system with global procurement operations, you may also be managing the purchasing categories at an international level, requiring translations for the various supported system languages and regions. In the Translate Purchasing Categories app, a user can review purchasing categories that have been translated into other languages, as well as the status of in-process translations, as shown in Figure 12.8.

Figure 12.8 Translate Purchasing Categories App

12.2.2 Supplier Activities and Tasks

Suppliers can be assigned activities and tasks assigned to these activities in SAP S/4HANA Sourcing and Procurement. To make an assignment, open the Manage Activities app from the **Purchasing Activities** section in SAP S/4HANA (see Figure 12.9).

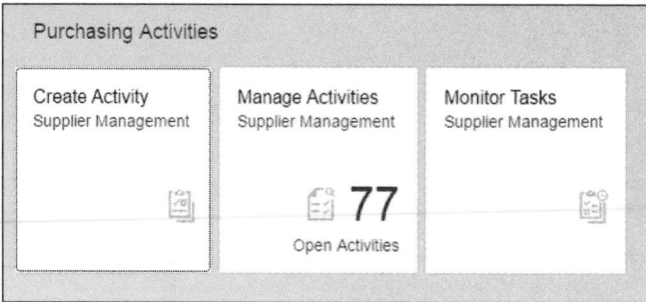

Figure 12.9 Purchasing Activities

You create purchasing activities in this app by selecting **Create** and filling out the fields for **Description**, **Status**, and who is **Responsible** for this activity. Purchasing activities and tasks are created using Web Dynpro transactions in SAP S/4HANA. Once an activity's been created, you can search for and manage activities in the SAP Fiori-based Manage Activities app (see Figure 12.10).

Activity	Activity Type	Status	Purchasing Category	Responsible	Priority	Start Date	End Date
Quantity Contract (11)	Supplier Development	Not Started		Buyer Buyer	Low		06.07.2017
domestic (12)	Supplier Development	Not Started		Buyer Buyer	Low		10.07.2017
Activity (13)	Supplier Development	Not Started		Buyer Buyer	Low		10.07.2017
Activity (14)	Supplier Development	Not Started		Paula Purchaser	Low		10.07.2017
14 (15)	Supplier Development	Not Started		Paula Purchaser	Low		11.07.2017
14 (16)	Supplier Development	Not Started		Paula Purchaser	Low		11.07.2017
14 (17)	Supplier Development	Not Started		Paula Purchaser	Low		11.07.2017
17 (18)	Supplier Development	Not Started		Paula Purchaser	Low		18.07.2017
15 (19)	Supplier Development	Not Started		Paula Purchaser	Low		13.07.2017
Price Reduction (21)	Supplier Development	Not Started	IT Hardware / Software (1)	Paula Purchaser	Low	03.08.2017	24.08.2017
Quantity Contract (31)	Supplier Development	Not Started		Paula Purchaser	Low		31.08.2017
Collaborate on price variance (41)	Supplier Development	Not Started		Paula Purchaser	Low		20.09.2017
Supplier Contact (42)	Supplier Development	Not Started		Paula Purchaser	Low		28.09.2017
Lieferantenbewertung (51)	Supplier Development	Not Started		Paula Purchaser	Low		20.10.2017
Quantity Contract (61)	Supplier Development	Not Started		Paula Purchaser	Low		30.11.2017
Check the Questionnaire (1)	Supplier Development	Not Started		Buyer Buyer	Low	31.03.2017	31.03.2017

Figure 12.10 Manage Activities App

Once a task has been created, it too can be monitored in the Monitor Tasks app (see Figure 12.11). You can assign an internal employee to a task, for example, and then navigate to the task in the monitor and drill into it by clicking it, which then sends you to the Web Dynpro transaction.

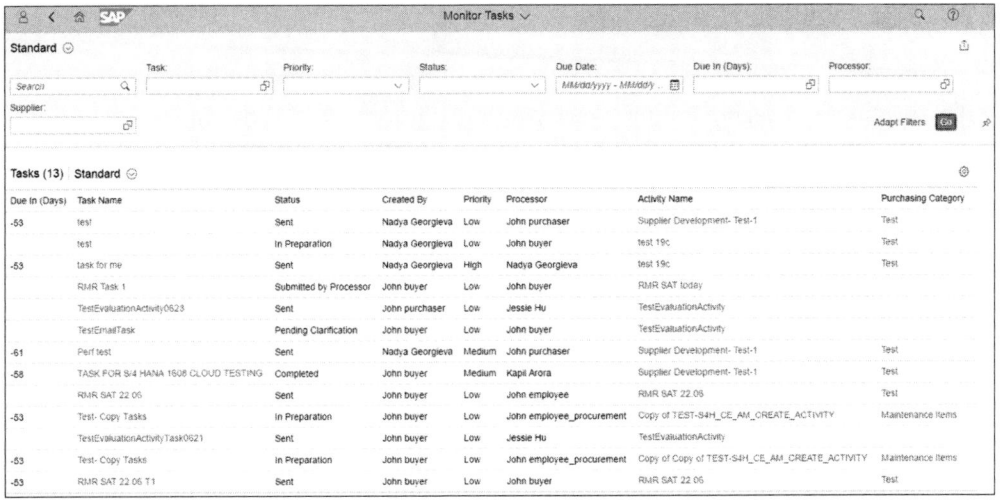

Figure 12.11 Monitor Tasks App

If you're assigned a task in a purchasing activity, you can process the task by going to the Process Tasks app and selecting the task you wish to process, as shown in Figure 12.12.

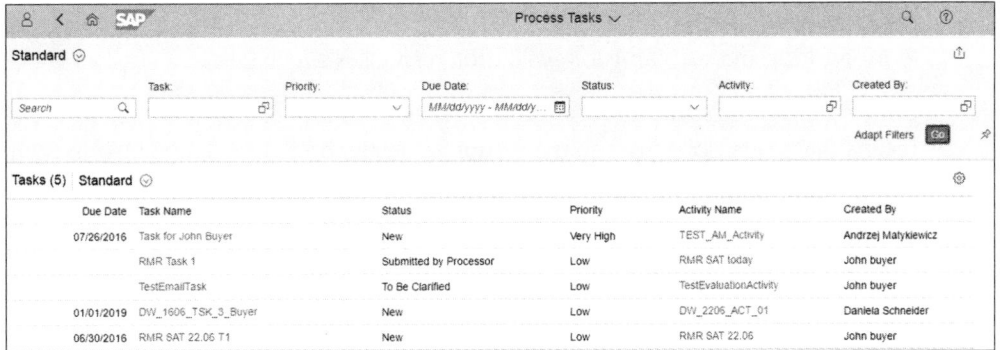

Figure 12.12 Process Tasks App

This section covered the first step in the supplier management process in SAP S/4HANA, which is to segment and classify your suppliers in system. In the following section, we'll review the second area of supplier management: supplier evaluation.

12.3   Supplier Evaluation

Supplier evaluation in SAP S/4HANA Sourcing and Procurement leverages the classification and segmentation overlay an organization establishes in the system, the
objective transaction and performance metrics generated during the transactions of
the supplier with the organization in the system, and the subjective user feedback
from evaluation surveys and questionnaires to establish a comprehensive view of
the supplier. All of these activities and feedback data points roll into a unified score
for the supplier. Based on these scores, it's possible to further group and segment
your suppliers into performance categories and identify low performers in need of
improvement or high performers deserving of further business and spend volumes.

In classic SAP ERP, users had to use SAP SRM, SAP Supplier Lifecycle Management, or
another platform to create supplier evaluations and questionnaires. Alternatively, a
user could manually score a supplier in SAP ERP. Supplier evaluation for soft facts
using questionnaires wasn't available in SAP ERP directly.

SAP S/4HANA Sourcing and Procurement has the codeset from SAP Supplier Lifecycle
Management embedded, which means the following capabilities are now native:

- Questionnaire definition directly in SAP S/4HANA
- Evaluation requests and distribution to appraisers
- Consolidated evaluation results review in evaluation scorecards
- Monitoring and searching for evaluation responses and details

Bringing increased speed and real-time capabilities to bear on supplier management
means that users can consume these supplier evaluation views embedded in their
transactions and processes. New innovations in supplier evaluation functionality in
SAP S/4HANA include the following:

- Functionality to define questionnaires in SAP S/4HANA directly
- Creating evaluation requests and distributing to appraisers
- Consolidated evaluation results in evaluation scorecards
- Monitor and search flexibility for evaluation responses and navigation to
  response details

There are numerous supplier evaluation apps, which center on two main areas (see
Figure 12.13). First, there are questionnaire-focused apps like Manage Questions,
Translate Questions, Manage Templates, Monitor Responses, and Manage Question-
naires. The second area includes the scorecard apps, such as Supplier Evaluation by
Quantity, Time, and Price, as well as Overall Supplier Evaluation Score. In many of
these evaluation apps, you can set KPIs, which are displayed in green, yellow, or red

on the tiles for an individual supplier or metric, allowing a user to understand up front how the supplier or area is tracking to targets.

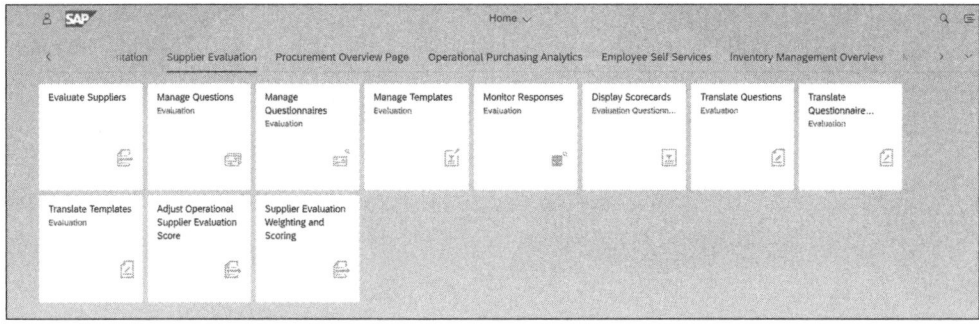

Figure 12.13 Supplier Evaluation Apps

These apps can be obtained from the SAP Fiori app library by searching for "supplier evaluation" as shown in Figure 12.14. Note that the app library also flags new apps available, as in this case with **Schedule Migration of Purchasing Data for Analytics** and **Supplier Evaluation Score History**.

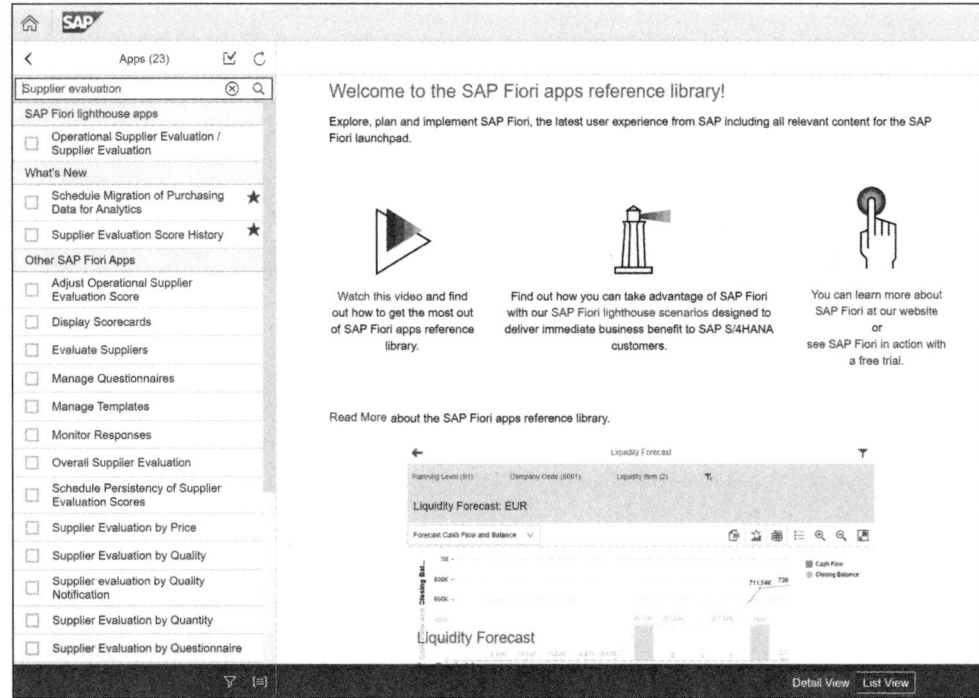

Figure 12.14 Supplier Evaluation App Search in Library

12.3.1   Supplier Evaluation Scorecard

Another app from the SAP Fiori app library search is the Manage Scorecards app. In SAP S/4HANA, the performance of suppliers is updated continuously, comparing purchase order data with goods receipt and invoice data. Employees and purchasers also rate performance by filling out questionnaires periodically. The KPI shows the scores across both hard and soft ratings and data points. As you can see in Figure 12.15, the scorecard itself provides an overall score, but it also provides details about both the objective and subjective ratings, as well as survey responses and survey response rates.

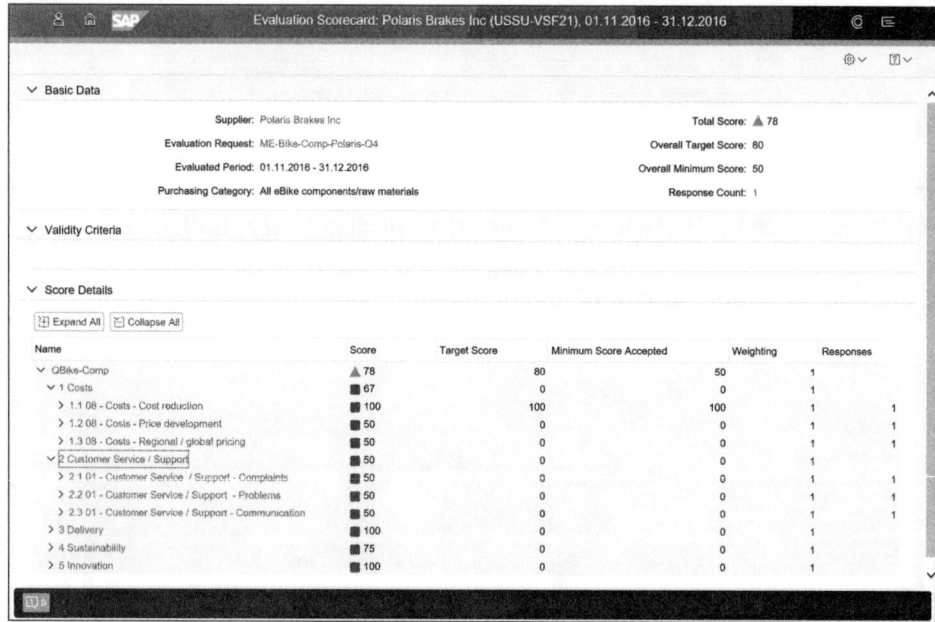

Figure 12.15 Supplier Evaluation Scorecard

The scorecard also lists a target score for the supplier, essentially a KPI setting, so that a user can understand what the organization feels is a reasonable rating to have in this purchasing category. You also have the option of maintaining validity criteria to timebox the scorecard and assign guidance for applicability.

12.3.2   Individual Supplier Evaluation

Individual supplier evaluation apps provide specific views into performance, such as the Supplier Evaluation by Quantity app shown in Figure 12.16. Here, variances in quantities ordered versus quantities delivered can be viewed by a supplier, allowing a user to understand the accuracy of each supplier in terms of order fulfillment.

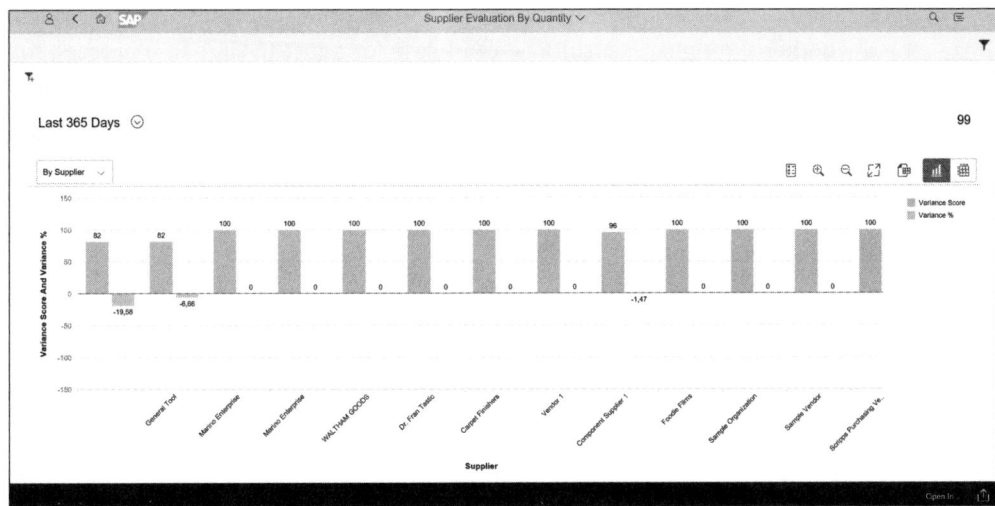

Figure 12.16 Supplier Evaluation by Quantity

12.3.3   Supplier Evaluation by Time

If timeliness is of the essence for the transaction being evaluated, the user can view the supplier's delivery punctuality, as shown in the Supplier Evaluation by Time app in Figure 12.17.

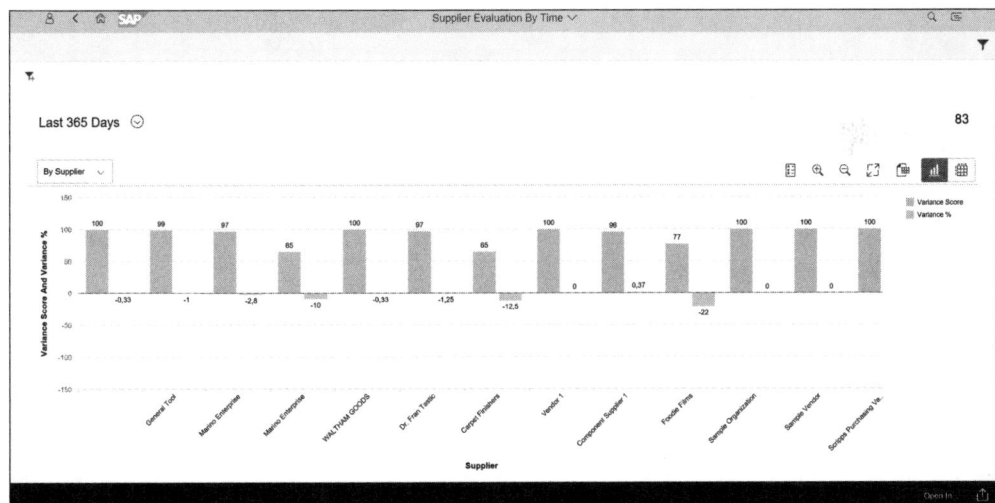

Figure 12.17 Supplier Evaluation by Time

Here, adherence to the delivery date is shown graphically, allowing a user to understand whether a supplier is a suitable candidate for a just-in-time (JIT) process, for example. If a supplier routinely misses its delivery dates based on this report, a user would want to think twice about including them in a mission-critical manufacturing process running in a JIT fashion.

12.3.4   Supplier Evaluation by Price

Perhaps most importantly in some commodity procurement situations, how faithfully a supplier adheres to the quoted price in the PO can be assessed by selecting the Supplier Evaluation by Price app. As shown in Figure 12.18, if a supplier has wide variance in its quoted price, this may warrant further investigation to determine if there are transportation/logistics costs not being quoted up front or even a more nefarious bait-and-switch problem with the supplier.

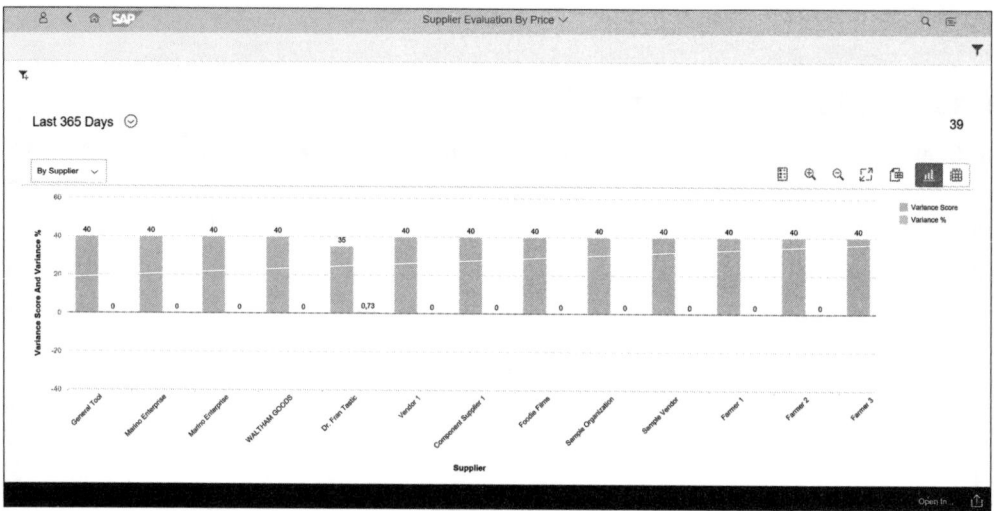

Figure 12.18 Supplier Evaluation by Price

12.3.5   Supplier Evaluation by Questionnaire

Statistics is a slippery slope if the data isn't there in sufficient volumes to underpin a correlation, much less causation. One survey or sample does not a statistical analysis make, and it would be premature to pass judgement too quickly or harshly based on sparse data, no matter how tempting. Ideally, you should have over 35 samples to begin analysis. The Supplier Evaluation by Questionnaire app, shown in Figure 12.19, shows which suppliers have reached such a level in the survey response area and which ones require more follow-up.

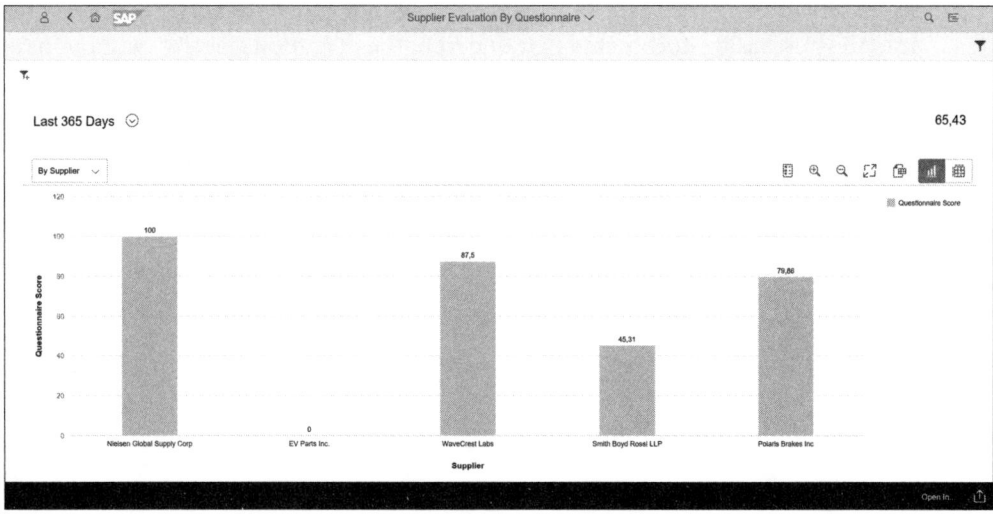

Figure 12.19 Supplier Evaluation by Questionnaire

To create a questionnaire, go to the Create Questionnaire app in SAP S/4HANA and fill out the information in the **Add Evaluation** screen, as shown in Figure 12.20.

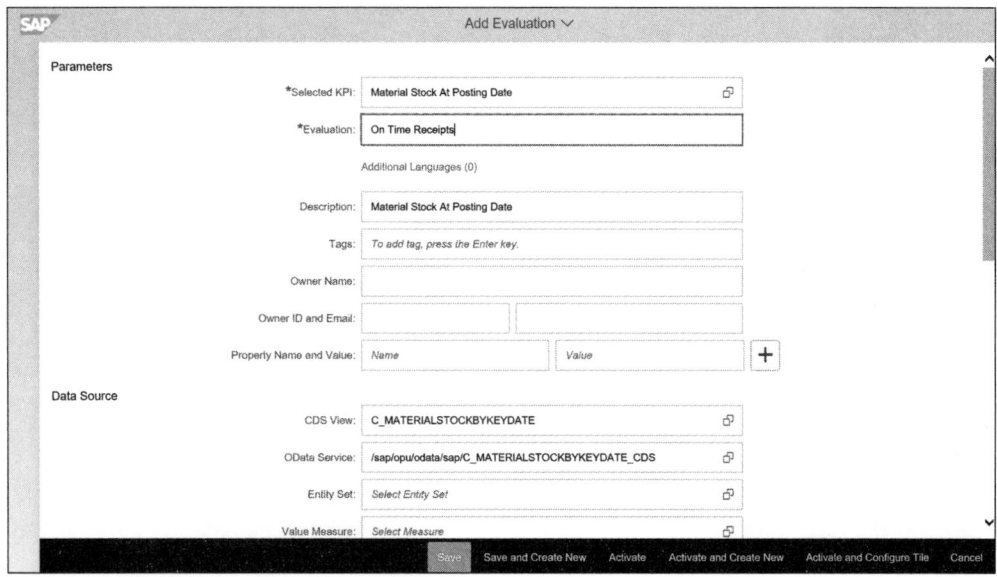

Figure 12.20 Add Supplier Questionnaire

12.3.6   Combined Scorecard

Combined operational and questionnaire scores can be viewed in a graphical format by drilling into the scorecard as shown in Figure 12.21. Similarly, you can drill further into the purchasing documents that underpin the operational score—without having to change systems, as in days of yore.

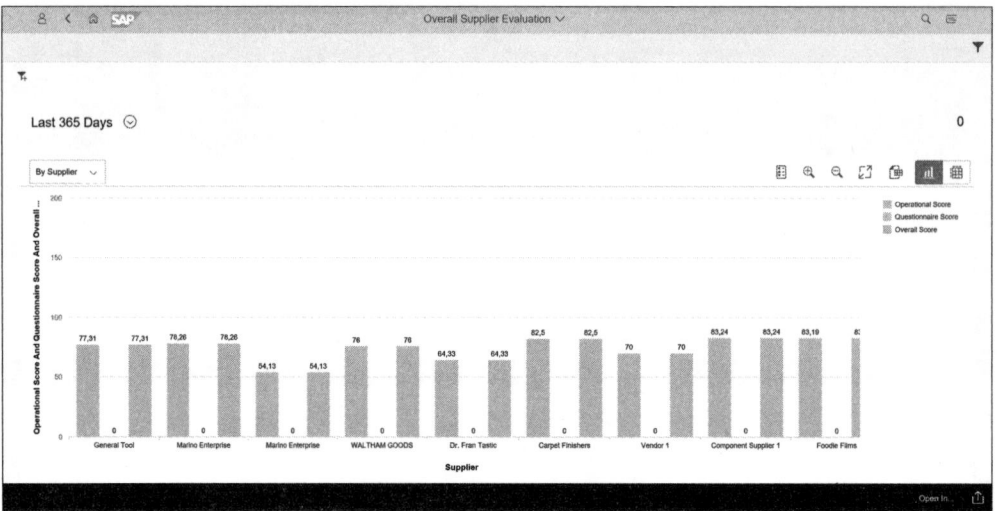

Figure 12.21 Combined Scorecard: Operational and Questionnaire Scores

12.3.7   Operational Supplier Evaluation

Supplier scores can also be reviewed in a graphical fashion side by side in the Supplier Evaluation/Operational Supplier Evaluation app, shown in Figure 12.22. Here, the operational scores and weighted averages for time, price, and quantity are displayed, along with an overall operational score.

As noted in the library apps and as of SAP S/4HANA OP 1909, there is a further reporting app now available for supplier evaluation in the form of the Supplier Evaluation Score History app, shown in Figure 12.23. As the name implies, this app allows users to view the historical evaluations by suppliers, which are updated via a job.

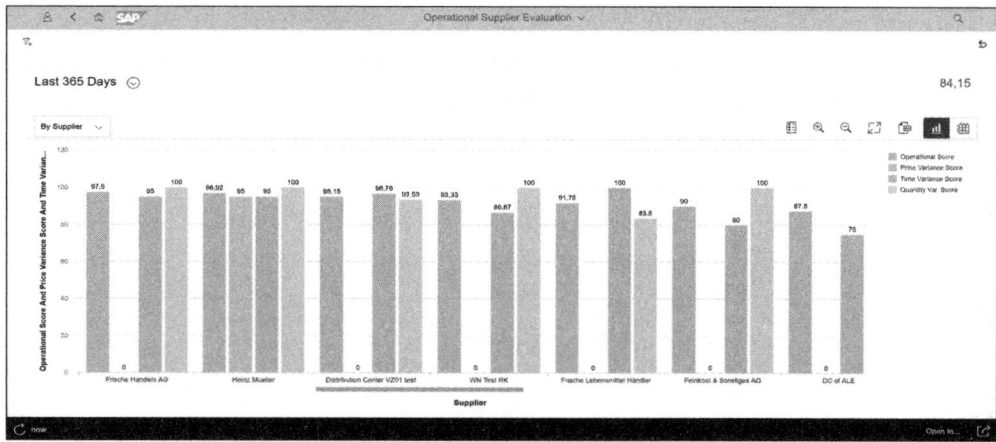

Figure 12.22 Operational Supplier Evaluation

Job ID	Supplier	Calendar Year	Calendar Month	Overall Score	Questionnaire Score
00001	1000108	2019	8	9.9	0
00001	1000129	2019	9	9.9	0
00001	1005500	2019	10	9.9	0
00001	1005549	2019	8	0	0
00001	1005549	2019	9	9.9	0
00001	1005852	2019	9	9.9	0
00001	1006153	2019	9	9.9	0
00001	1006211	2019	9	9.9	0
00001	1006212	2019	9	9.9	0
00001	1006213	2019	9	9.9	0
00001	10100088	2019	8	9.9	0
00001	10200001	2019	8	9.9	0
00001	10200001	2019	9	9.9	0

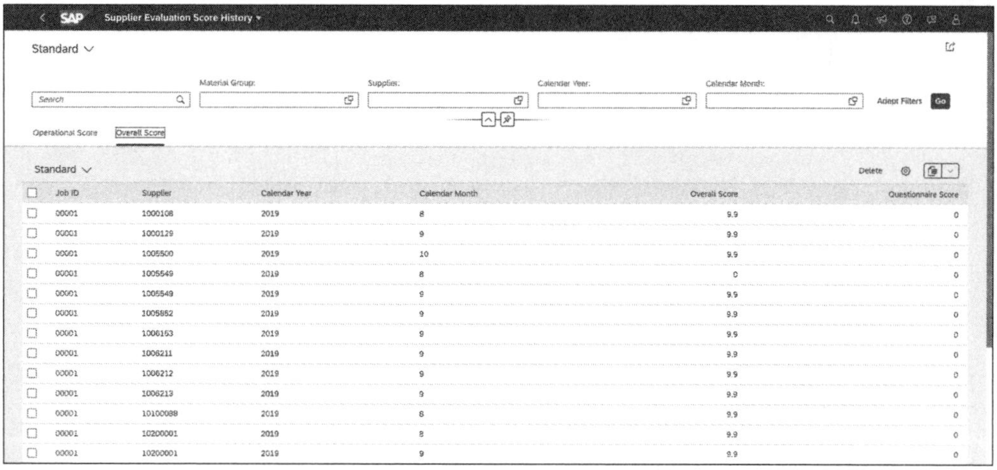

Figure 12.23 Supplier Evaluation Score History

12.4 Configuration

In addition to installing the supplier evaluation apps outlined in Figure 12.14, you need to complete some basic configuration to enable both supplier and category management in the SAP S/4HANA system.

12.4.1 Supplier and Category Management Configuration

First, follow IMG menu path **Materials Management • Purchasing • Supplier and Category Management • Purchasing Categories**, as shown in Figure 12.24.

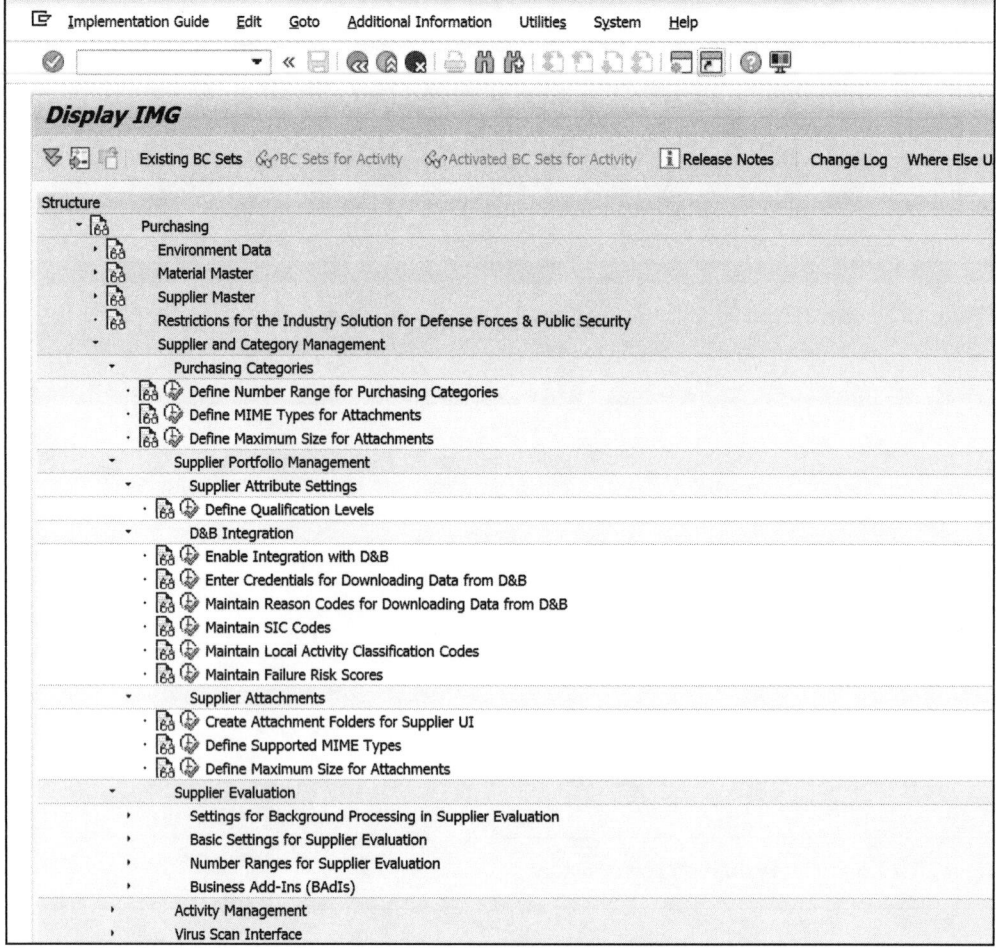

Figure 12.24 Supplier and Category Management

Next, select **Define Number Ranges** as shown in Figure 12.25.

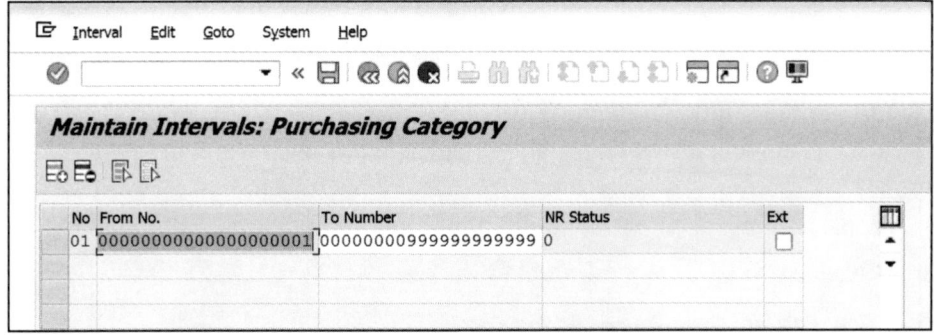

Figure 12.25 Define Number Ranges for Purchasing Categories

Once you've defined your number ranges, save and move to IMG menu path **Materials Management • Purchasing • Supplier and Category Management • Purchasing Categories • Define MIME Types for Attachments and Define Maximum Size for Attachments**. *MIME* here stands for Multipurpose Internet Mail Extensions, which allows you to further define which types of attachments are allowed, as well as their maximum size.

Next, proceed to **Materials Management • Purchasing • Supplier and Category Management • Supplier Portfolio Management • Supplier Attribute Settings • Define Qualification Levels**. Here, you can define qualification levels required by your organization by selecting **New Entries** and entering both a key and a description, as shown in Figure 12.26.

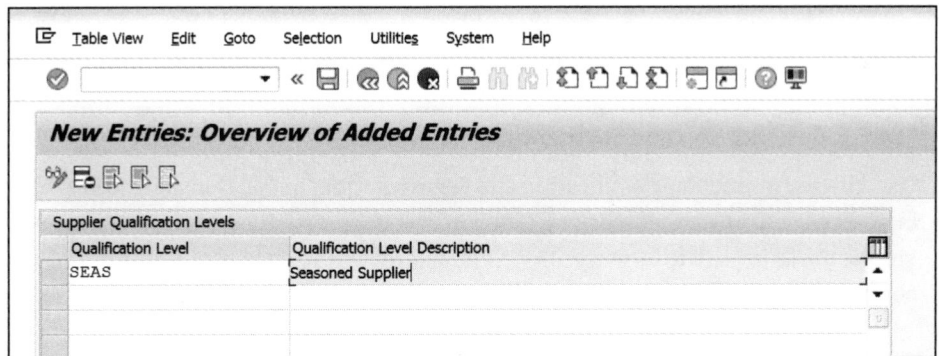

Figure 12.26 Supplier Qualification Levels

Next, if required, you can activate integration with Dun & Bradstreet via **Materials Management • Purchasing • Supplier and Category Management • Supplier Portfolio Management • D&B Integration • Enable Integration with D&B**. Note that a Dun & Bradstreet subscription is required prior to setting up this configuration. Select the switch for Dun & Bradstreet integration, mark it **Active**, and save, as in Figure 12.27.

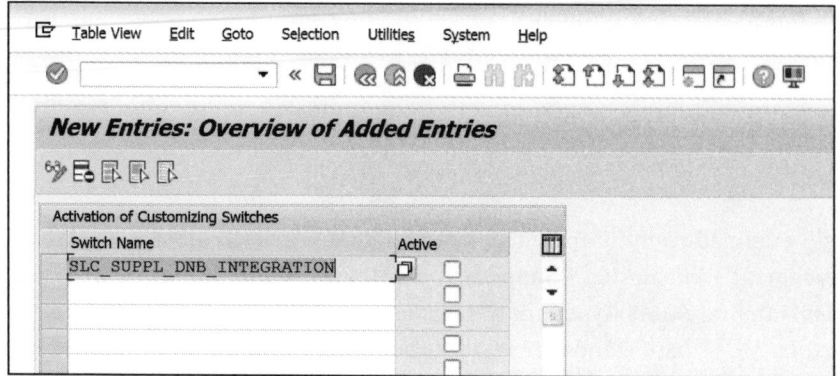

Figure 12.27 Dun & Bradstreet Activation

In the remaining activation steps, you must maintain your credentials for logging in at Dun & Bradstreet in **Materials Management • Purchasing • Supplier and Category Management • Supplier Portfolio Management • D&B Integration • Enter Credentials for Downloading Data from D&B**. If you have reason codes for downloading, or other settings for failure risk scores and codes, you maintain them in the general section **Materials Management • Purchasing • Supplier and Category Management • Supplier Portfolio Management • D&B Integration** under the applicable configuration areas.

12.4.2 Classification and Segmentation

To configure and set up classification and segmentation, install the Manage Purchasing Category, Translate Purchasing Category, Manage Activities, Monitor Tasks, and Process Tasks apps. The functionality, KPIs, and reporting is then available out of the box.

12.4.3 Supplier Evaluation Configuration

For supplier evaluation configuration, you must configure the number ranges in **Materials Management • Purchasing • Supplier and Category Management • Supplier**

Evaluation • Number Ranges for Supplier Evaluation (see Figure 12.28). Any objects you plan to use will require a number range. If using, define number ranges for the following:

- Questions
- Sections
- Question and section groups
- Evaluation questionnaire
- Supplier evaluation templates
- Supplier evaluation requests
- Evaluation responses
- Evaluation scorecards

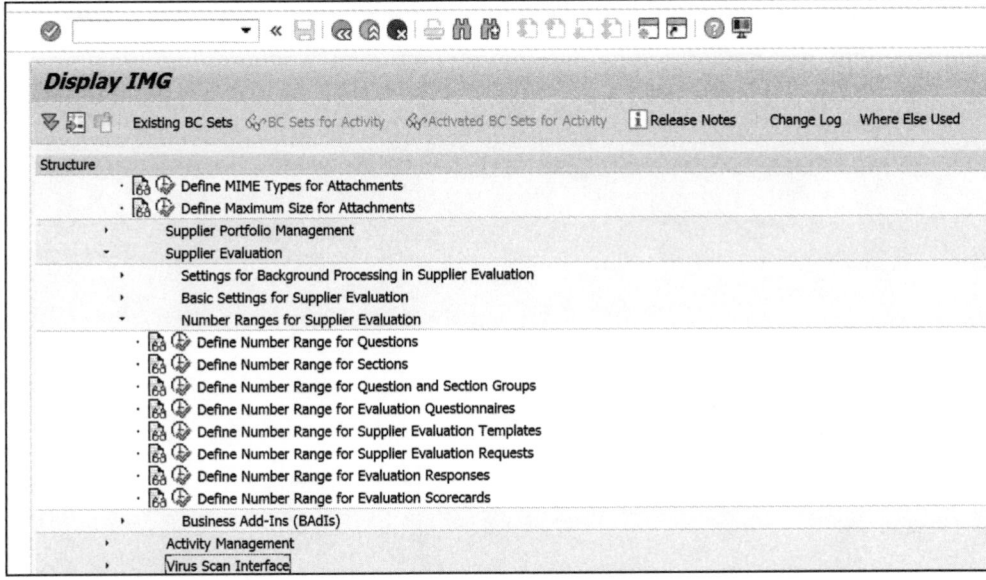

Figure 12.28 Define Number Ranges for Supplier Evaluation

Next, define a language for the question library for questionnaires via IMG menu path **Materials Management • Purchasing • Supplier and Category Management • Supplier Evaluation • Create Question Library for Supplier Evaluation**. You'll need the /SRMSMC/REPORT_EXEC_ADMIN role assigned to you to run this transaction. Select a language on the first screen, as shown in Figure 12.29.

Then, execute the transaction. Your question library has now been created. If you want to use another language other than the one you've defined here, you'll need to create a translation of the question. Once the library is activated, you can further define and assign MIME types and attachment sizes as for the previous area in **Materials Management • Purchasing • Supplier and Category Management • Supplier Evaluation • Maintain Settings for Mails and Other Texts in Evaluation** or **Define MIME Types for Attachments** or **Define Maximum Size for Attachments**.

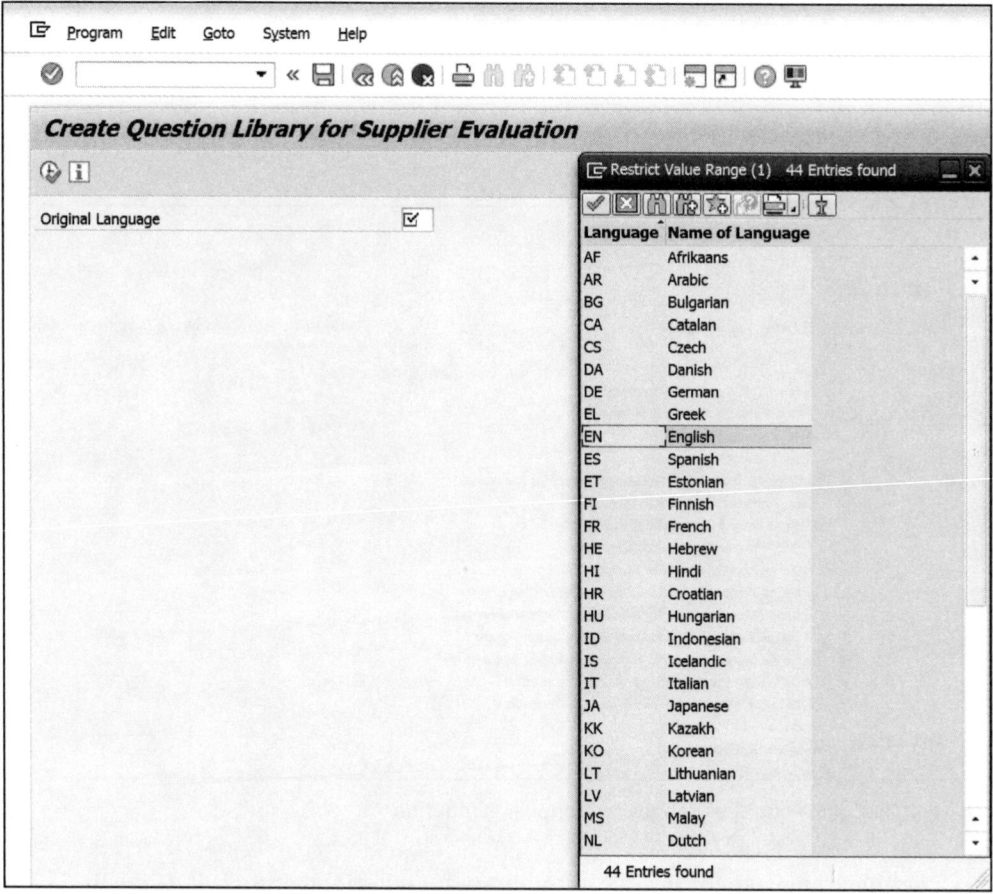

Figure 12.29 Define Language for Question

12.5 Summary

A procurement operation run without any kind of reflection or analysis of its supply base is unable to make improvements over time, much less realize the true potential in SAP S/4HANA or its marketplace. Never before have supplier evaluation, classification, segmentation, and analysis been as deeply embedded and dynamic as in the SAP S/4HANA environment today. Organizations can segment and classify their suppliers, assign KPIs, and perform analysis while executing transactions simultaneously in a fluid manner, knowing that the data they're viewing is current and that the comparisons they're making between suppliers is underpinned by sound classification and segmentation of their major spend areas. What happens when the suppliers are spread across multiple ERP systems? In the next chapter, we will review central procurement in SAP S/4HANA, a solution that can orchestrate procurement activities in multiple ERPs and can integrate with SAP Ariba.

12

Chapter 13

Centralized Procurement

This chapter provides an overview of the SAP S/4HANA for central procurement functionality and scenarios, the migration path from a distributed SAP Supplier Relationship Management environment with multiple backends to SAP S/4HANA for central procurement, and the integration approach for central procurement with SAP Ariba guided buying.

Large enterprises often manage multiple ERP environments. SAP S/4HANA for central procurement allows an organization to manage procurement across multiple SAP ERP systems. This chapter outlines the capabilities, areas, and configuration of SAP S/4HANA for central procurement, beginning with an overview, moving into the distinct process areas, and finishing with sections on configuration.

13.1 What Is Centralized Procurement?

SAP S/4HANA for central procurement is a product within SAP S/4HANA Sourcing and Procurement. SAP S/4HANA for central procurement represents a solution for SAP ERP customers with multiple ERP systems to manage their procurement activities in a centralized manner, similar to SAP Supplier Relationship Management (SAP SRM), while realizing the advantages of SAP's procurement solutions in the cloud, such as SAP Ariba solutions. SAP S/4HANA for central procurement represents both a transformation path from SAP SRM and a future-ready, intelligent ERP platform for connecting to and consuming SAP Cloud solutions to seamlessly augment the process agility, capabilities, and user experience in the overall landscape. Not only is SAP S/4HANA the ERP platform, but it can also be deployed as a central procurement system integrated with multiple backend SAP ERP systems, including older versions of SAP ERP, down to SAP ERP 6.0 EHP 6.

With SAP's introduction of SAP S/4HANA as the digital core and the discontinuation of SAP SRM, for which maintenance expires in 2025, customers are searching for ways, solutions, and software to augment and transform their procurement processes and ensure an orderly migration from SAP SRM. One of the most obvious challenges for a migration from SAP SRM was ensuring like-for-like capabilities in the eventual replacement system. One important value proposition of SAP SRM was its capability to act as the central procurement instance in front of multiple (ERP) backends, providing the procurement department with the capability to organize, govern, and control their tasks from within a central environment. Procurement departments especially valued SRM's capability to manage workload, documents, and approvals centrally, in a procurement-focused manner, above the fray and complexities of ERP environments. When the sunsetting of SAP SRM was announced, a natural question from the SAP SRM customer base was, What is SAP proposing to replace its multi-ERP-management functionality?

In an ideal world, every organization would only have a single ERP instance, but this is often not the case. Many companies and organizations running SAP ERP accumulate more than one system instance. Whether through the acquisition of another company in which the SAP ERP environment wasn't consolidated or a division that created its own SAP ERP instance due to specific requirements, ERP systems in large, multinational organizations sometimes proliferate. Distributed procurement landscapes with numerous backend systems are quite common across larger companies. For example, nearly two-thirds of large enterprises in Europe, the Middle East, and Africa with an SAP SRM system are using it as a procurement hub in front of their diverse, multibackend landscapes.

Merely removing SAP SRM and upgrading the ERP backends to SAP S/4HANA creates challenges in multiple areas, but procurement is particularly impacted by this lack of centralization in an ERP landscape. As a business function, procurement benefits from scale and volumes. The more volume you put through a supplier or into purchasing an item, the bigger the cost savings and efficiencies. Not only can you conduct fewer transactions, saving time and effort, you also realize the volume discount most suppliers offer for saving piecemeal efforts of fulfilling individual orders. Managing procurement in a centralized manner also provides a platform from which to understand your procurement activities holistically, creating a virtuous cycle, whereby each procurement iteration becomes more efficient than the last in obtaining the goods and services your organization needs from the best supplier mix possible for operations and to orchestrate your organization's value creation for the marketplace.

When faced with a distributed environment, the first impulse of problem-solving IT executives of yore was to attempt to consolidate ERP systems into one. This proved time-consuming and very complex in some cases. Master data from an acquired company's SAP ERP environment and overall structure may not have matched the receiving environment. Processes may have been different. The expense of consolidation may have outweighed the upside or, from a budgeting standpoint, lacked a sufficient business case to prioritize the consolidation.

SAP's strategic direction is now focused upon cloud solutions such as SAP Ariba, leveraging SAP S/4HANA for the digital core. SAP SRM will be supported until 2025, and much of its procurement capabilities are being rolled into SAP S/4HANA and SAP Ariba. The capability to tie together multiple SAP ERP backends for procurement is now available in SAP S/4HANA for central procurement. In addition, SAP S/4HANA for central procurement allows for the coupling of more SAP Ariba Solutions on top, to further leverage cloud solutions and advanced capabilities. The diagram on the left in Figure 13.1 shows the current scenario, which is SAP SRM managing a distributed landscape.

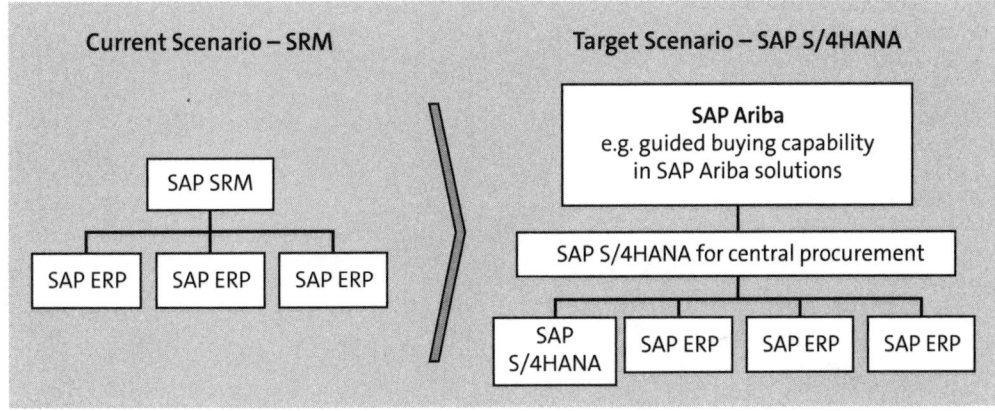

Figure 13.1 From SAP SRM to SAP S/4HANA for Central Procurement

On the right in Figure 13.1, you see the target environment for customers migrating from SAP SRM managing procurement for multiple backend ERPs. Here, SAP Ariba guided buying acts as the gateway for all procurement, providing users with a consumer-grade shopping experience married with a wide spectrum of organization-specific controls, functionality, and content. Connected to SAP Ariba guided buying is SAP S/4HANA for central procurement, which in turn coordinates central requisitioning, central purchasing, central contracts, and central analytics with various versions of SAP ERP, including SAP S/4HANA and SAP ERP versions.

With this migration path from SAP SRM and set of capabilities, SAP S/4HANA and SAP Ariba provide customers with the tools and platform to not only cope and keep up with the ever-faster pace of change in procurement, but also to drive innovation and disruption by leveraging new technologies such as machine learning and blockchain or enabling the Internet of Things.

SAP S/4HANA for central procurement pushes purchase orders out to the respective ERP systems connected in the landscape as per Figure 13.2. It still allows leveraging of ERP-specific data and processes to continue. For example, a PO created in the SAP S/4HANA for central procurement hub could use country-specific localization in ERP1, customer-specific process optimization in ERP2, or company-specific legal nuances in ERP3.

SAP S/4HANA is the digital core in SAP's present and future landscapes. From this platform, SAP customers can leverage a diverse array of SAP Cloud solutions, as well as centralize the management of procurement activities in further SAP S/4HANA and SAP ERP instances.

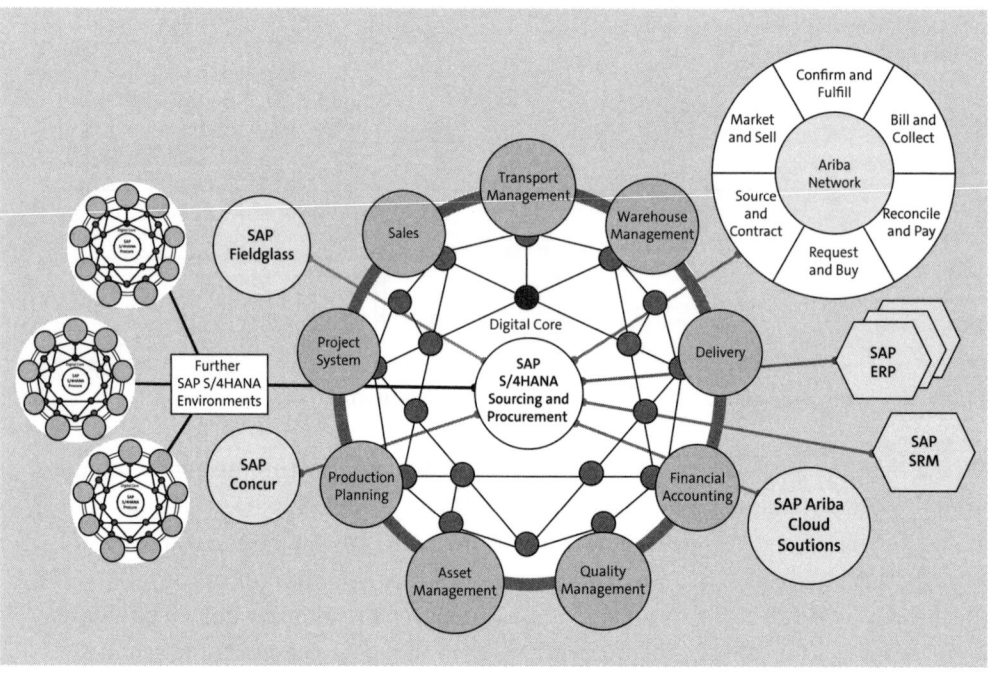

Figure 13.2 SAP S/4HANA as Integrated Platform

Figure 13.2 includes connections to SAP Fieldglass for contingent labor management, SAP Concur for travel and expense management, SAP Ariba (both the Ariba Network and other cloud solutions), and additional SAP S/4HANA, SAP SRM, and SAP ERP environments. SAP customers may only use a portion of these options for their procurement landscape, but the options are there in the event you need to deploy further functionality. Figure 13.3 details the numerous solution options available in this regard.

The processes supported by SAP S/4HANA for central procurement center around the "hub" SAP S/4HANA system where central procurement resides, pushing documents to the respective systems for further processing, as well as pulling updates from various ERP environments for central analysis. The main scenarios supported are central requisitioning, central contract management, and central purchasing, as in Figure 13.3.

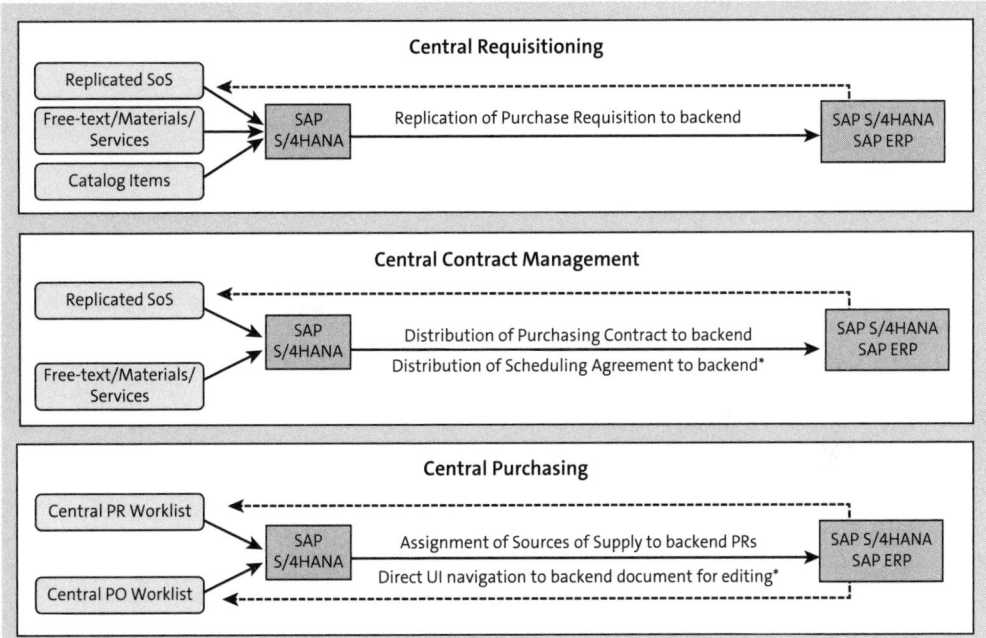

Figure 13.3 Central Procurement Scenarios

For central contract management, the contracts are centrally approved, distributed at the header level, line-item level, or both to the respective ERP system, with central views available in SAP S/4HANA for central procurement for monitoring contract consumption across the landscape and BAdI user exits provided for data mapping. In central purchasing, you can leverage integrated responsibility management, central approvals, and output management, as well as follow-on documents and direct editing of these documents in the hub. In the next sections, we'll dive deeper into the various scenarios for central procurement, beginning with central requisitioning.

13.2   Central Requisitioning

In central requisitioning, sourced requisitions from catalogs, material or service masters, or free text items are created and approved via central procurement for a backend ERP system. Central requisitioning leverages online backend F4 helps, central approval of self-service procurement for requisitions, and pushing approved requisitions to backend ERP systems, where they can be converted automatically to a PO. In Figure 13.4, the demand originates in the central procurement instance of SAP S/4HANA in the form of a requisition.

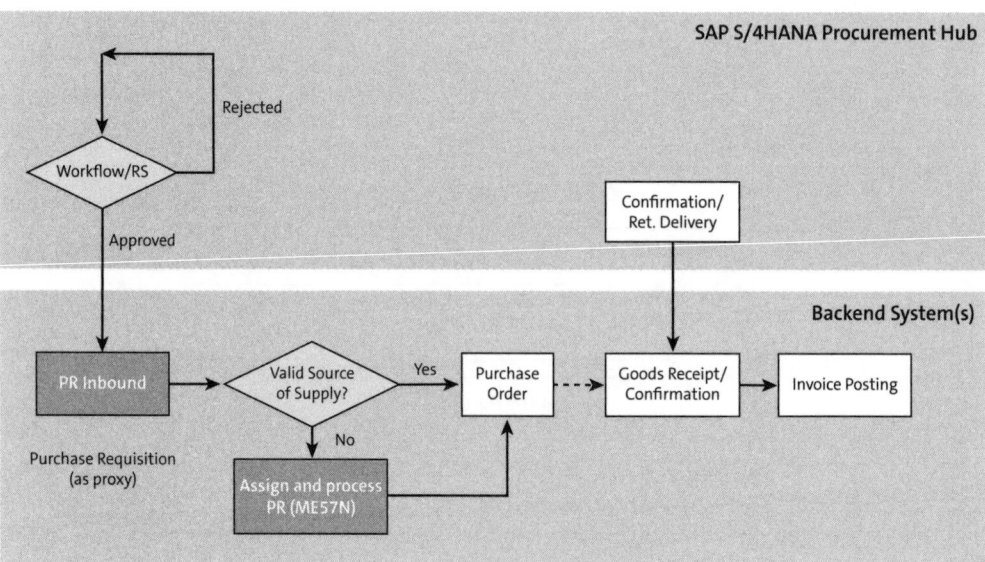

Figure 13.4 Central Procurement Process Flow: Requisitioning

This can be a requisition created directly in central procurement or in an SAP Ariba solution such as SAP Ariba guided buying, which then pushes this requisition back to central procurement for the appropriate routing to the ERP destination. In Figure 13.5, Steps ❶ and ❷ take place in SAP Ariba guided buying, and the follow-on steps then occur in SAP S/4HANA for central procurement and the respective backend ERP systems.

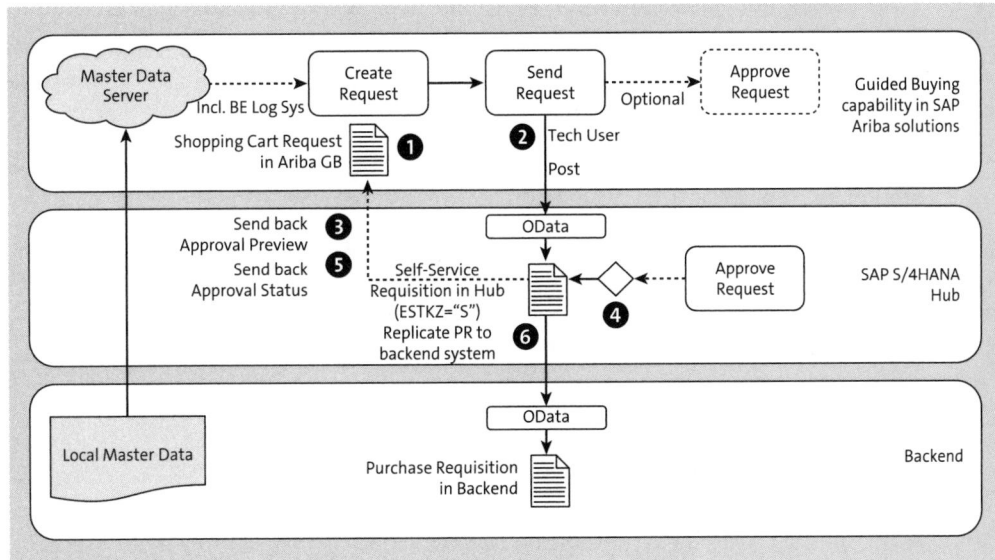

Figure 13.5 Central Requisitioning with SAP Ariba Guided Buying

As of SAP S/4HANA for central procurement release 1909, the requisitioning scenario includes the following:

- Using the Manage Purchase Requisitions Centrally app to manage purchasing and initiate a central sourcing process across distributed ERP systems

- Closing and deferring purchase requisitions in the Manage Purchase Requisitions Centrally app

- Synchronizing with the connected system the critical changes in delivery date, material, quantity, price and deletion of purchase requisitions in the central purchase requisition

- Adding a purchase requisition to an existing purchase order

- Ability for casual user to change a scenario themselves, as well as edit the plant and company code in the User Defaults app

- Search help integrated with purchasing organization and accounting value in connected ERP sytems

- Availability of new class-based workflow in the Manage Workflow for Purchase Requisitions app to support simulation and adding deadlines to drive resolution of pending overdue approvals

If the **Central Purchase Requisition ID** field is maintained in the SAP S/4HANA requisition, this indicates that the purchase requisition has been created within the central requisitioning scenario, transferred to the backend, and is now available for processing in SAP S/4HANA for central procurement.

If the **Blocked for Central Processing** switch is on, as in Figure 13.6, the purchase requisition item is blocked from automatic purchase order conversion in the backend.

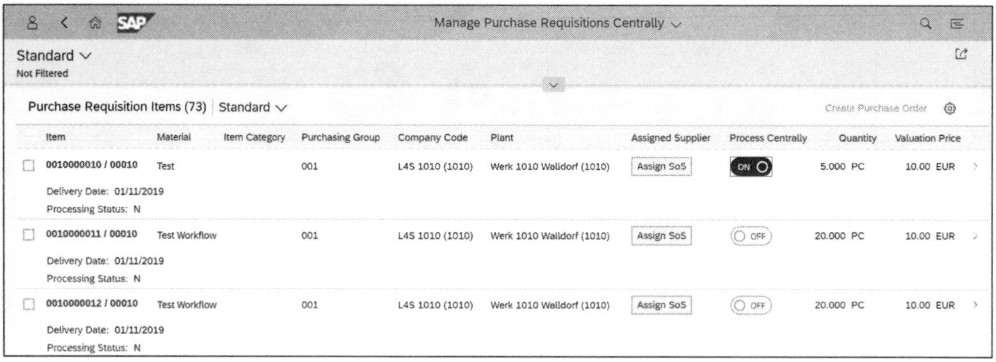

Figure 13.6 Process Centrally Switch in Manage Purchase Requisitions Centrally App

The block ensures that after a source of supply is assigned to the requisition, it can continue to be processed manually by the purchaser and not be immediately picked up by conversion jobs running in the backend and converted into a purchase order.

13.3   Central Purchasing

The central purchasing scenario of SAP S/4HANA for central procurement provides a workplace for the purchaser to create and manage all of the purchase documents for connected backend systems. The purchaser can monitor, display, access, and change the purchasing documents irrespective of whether they are created centrally by an employee using central requisitioning or in any of the connected systems. Central purchasing allows the purchaser to manage and organize the daily tasks and workload to ensure that demands are met, sourced, and converted into purchase orders. Once the purchase orders are released and sent to the supplier, they can then be monitored for follow-on processes such as goods receipts and invoicing processes.

For managing, monitoring, and sourcing in the central purchasing scenario, the Manage Purchase Requisitions Centrally app is available. Purchase orders can be managed, created, or changed via this app. Similar to Manage Purchase Requisitions Centrally, Manage Purchase Orders Centrally follows the same SAP Fiori-based UX design, as shown in Figure 13.7.

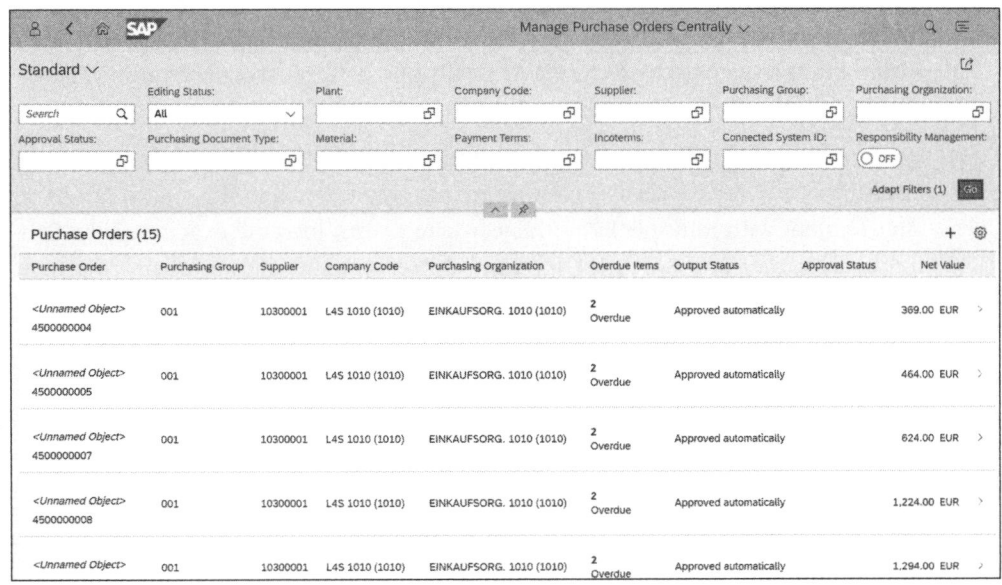

Figure 13.7 Manage Purchase Orders Centrally App

The Manage Purchase Orders Centrally app provides the following main features:

- Search and filter purchase orders from different backend systems—for example, by approval status or overdue items
- Display purchase order details
- Create purchase order manually from scratch directly in the backend system
- Open and change the purchase order directly in the backend system

Central procurement apps such as Manage POs and Manage Requisitions Centrally leverage a data cache, so-called proxy tables, for fast searches and to make use of the capabilities of the SAP HANA in-memory database. The original documents still reside in the backend, and data validation, checks, and enrichment happen directly in the backend system.

Due to this architecture, the business document IDs remain the original IDs of the backend document. Unlike in other integrated systems, such as SAP SRM and SAP ERP, in which there are sometimes external and internal numbers required for the same PO document, no separate IDs are created for external purchase requisitions or purchase orders in central procurement and there is no need to sync number ranges or define extensive ID mappings. Each procurement document keeps its number assigned by the number ranges in the connected system, making them clearly identifiable to all parties, regardless of whether they are accessing the document from within the Manage Purchase Orders Centrally app or a transaction such as Transaction ME23n directly in the backend.

Even in a single ERP instance, analyzing procurement activities often requires data from disparate areas, such as materials management and accounts payables. In an environment with multiple ERPs, this complexity can increase exponentially. Central analytics for SAP S/4HANA for central procurement allows for procurement activities to be analyzed throughout the SAP S/4HANA and SAP ERP connected systems. As of SAP S/4HANA Cloud version 1808 and on-premise SAP S/4HANA, on premise edition 1809, the core analytics supported are with regard to central contracts functionality. Central analytics also has more analytics functionality planned and coming with each release beyond SAP S/4HANA 1809. Section 13.5 explains the basic concepts and introduces the available analytics within SAP S/4HANA and SAP Analytics Cloud.

13.4   Central Purchasing Contracts

With the SAP S/4HANA for central procurement central contracts scenario, a single, central contract can be distributed and managed in various ERP environments in a coordinated manner. This enables a centralized approach for creating and distributing a contract from an SAP S/4HANA for central procurement instance for the multiple connected ERP systems to then consume, monitor, and update simultaneously. Central procurement supports both contracts and scheduling agreements. As with contracts, scheduling agreements are used primarily in direct procurement activities, maintaining a delivery schedule to coordinate the supplier delivery of items or services when they are required in the production process. Scheduling agreements permit an organization to better manage inventories and minimize additional purchase orders and contract release orders while enabling suppliers to understand their actual demand and delivery requirements up front. Many types of scheduling agreements also allow for an additions of line items or quantity changes on the fly. Scheduling agreements still need to be configured in your central procurement system and the connected systems, including document types LP (Scheduling Agreement) and LPA (Scheduling Agreement with Release Document). For information on the general configuration of scheduling agreements by release, visit the site for SAP Best Practices for SAP S/4HANA at *http://s-prs.co/500305*.

The configuration steps for central contracts are delineated further in Section 13.7.3. Once these configuration steps have been completed, you can perform the following processes in central contracts:

1. Create central contracts in the central hub system via the Manage Purchase Contracts app, including partial distribution of the central contract to the connected ERP systems by company code, quantity, and/or percentage levels. At the central contract item level, you can create items from imported material masters, free text materials, and lean service items. Using lean service items is only possible for a free text service and results in the creation of a line item with the item category D in the central contract. However, central contracts limit their creation to item category Standard at the header level.

2. Approve contracts via the My Inbox app.

3. Distribute the contracts to connected ERP systems.

4. Create release orders in an individual ERP system against the distributed contract directly.

5. Import these release orders into the central procurement system via the Schedule Import of Release Orders app. You can start the job immediately or at a specified time, as well as set up the job to be reoccurring or one-time only. You can set the job to do a full, delta, or ad hoc import of the release orders.

With release orders imported into central contracts, purchasers have an overview of all of the release orders released against the central contract in the Manage Central Contracts app.

13.5   Central Analytics

Central analytics for SAP S/4HANA for central procurement looks to provide the user with centralized analysis and capabilities for understanding procurement areas holistically, as well at the individual, granular, connected system level with KPIs as in Figure 13.8.

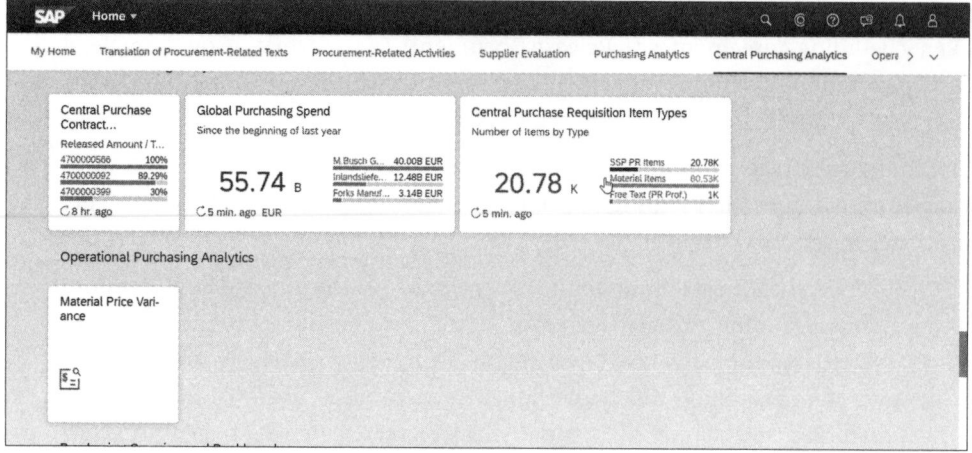

Figure 13.8 Central Procurement Analytics Tiles

With SAP S/4HANA Cloud version 1808 and up and SAP S/4HANA Enterprise version 1809 and up, you have central purchase contract analytics apps available. This allows for transparency of purchase contract consumption across an entire organization and enables you to identify where global contracts are not being utilized or being underutilized in areas of the organization. As of SAP S/4HANA, on-premise edition 1809 and SAP S/4HANA Cloud 1808, there are two main apps for central analytics: Central Purchase Contract Consumption (Figure 13.9) and Monitor Central Purchase Contract Items (Figure 13.10).

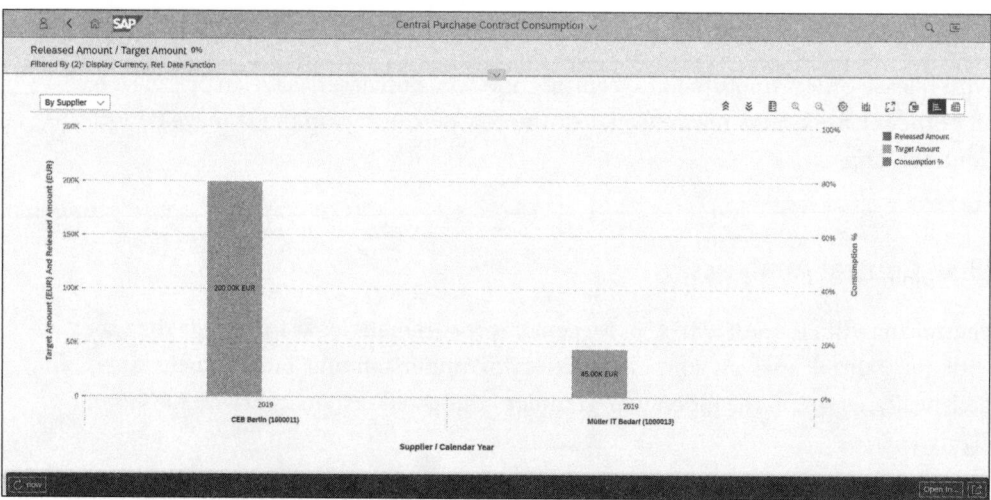

Figure 13.9 Central Purchase Contract Consumption

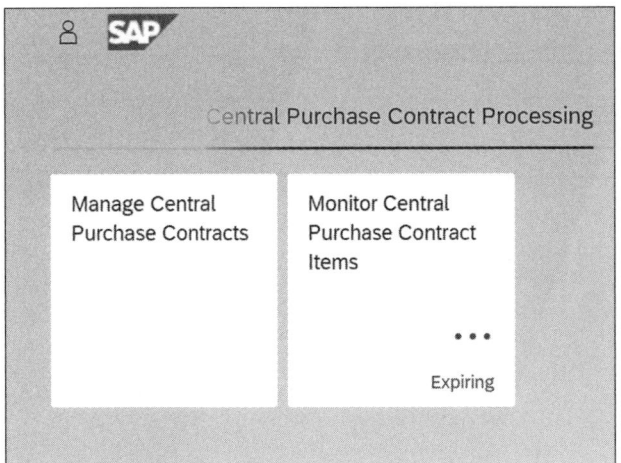

Figure 13.10 Monitor Central Purchase Contract Items

The Central Purchase Contract Consumption key performance indicator shows the values for central contract target versus released amount that are available for the persona buyer and analyzes the release versus target spend amounts on contracts by various dimensions:

- Supplier
- Backend purchasing group
- Backend purchasing organization
- Backend plant
- Purchasing category
- Material group
- Document
- Trend
- Trend by supplier
- Trend by purchasing category

13

The user can click a supplier to use it as a filter for analyzing other dimensions for that specific supplier, such as material group, as per Figure 13.11.

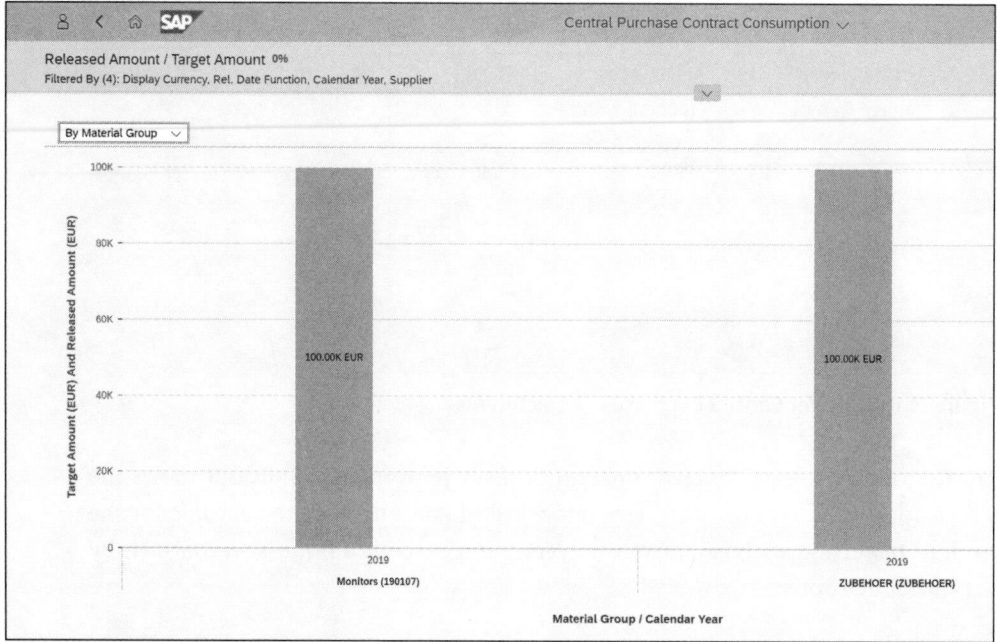

Figure 13.11 Central Purchase Contract Consumption by Material Group

The end user can display the data in Central Purchase Contract Consumption using predelivered visualizations, dimensions, and measures, as well as by individual settings and visualizations, by using the configuration options listed in the dropdown menu shown in Figure 13.12.

The document view in Figure 13.13 provides the buyer with the complete release history of all central purchase contracts. By sorting the release percentage, the user can view the most consumed contracts on top. If the buyer wants to see the details of a specific contract, drilldown capability is provided.

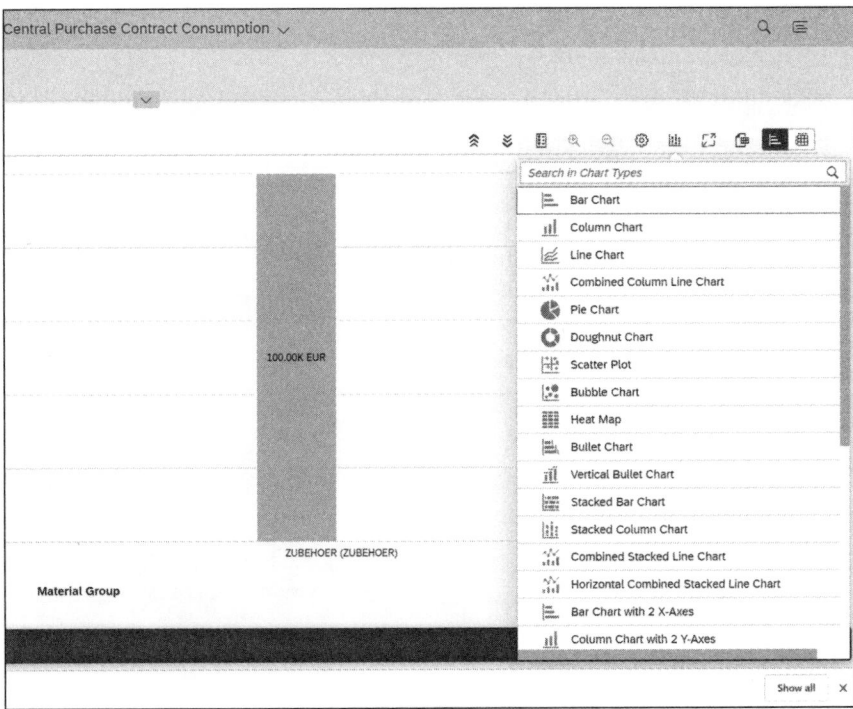

Figure 13.12 Contract Consumption Data Visualization Options

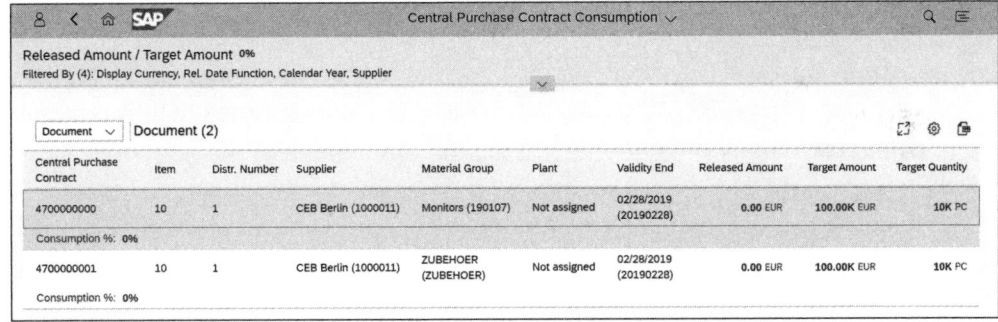

Figure 13.13 Contract Data by Document

13.6   SAP S/4HANA for Central Procurement with SAP Ariba

As per Figure 13.14, SAP S/4HANA for central procurement serves as a nexus layer for accessing numerous SAP Ariba solutions:

- SAP Ariba Supplier Lifecycle Performance and SAP Ariba Supplier Risk Management for supplier management
- SAP Ariba Sourcing and SAP Ariba Contract Management for identifying and transacting with the optimal suppliers for the various spend categories
- Ariba Network for PO/IV collaboration and automation, financing, and payment facilitation with SAP Ariba Payables
- Content management with SAP Ariba Catalog
- Direct procurement with SAP Ariba Supply Chain Collaboration
- Analytics with SAP Analytics Cloud

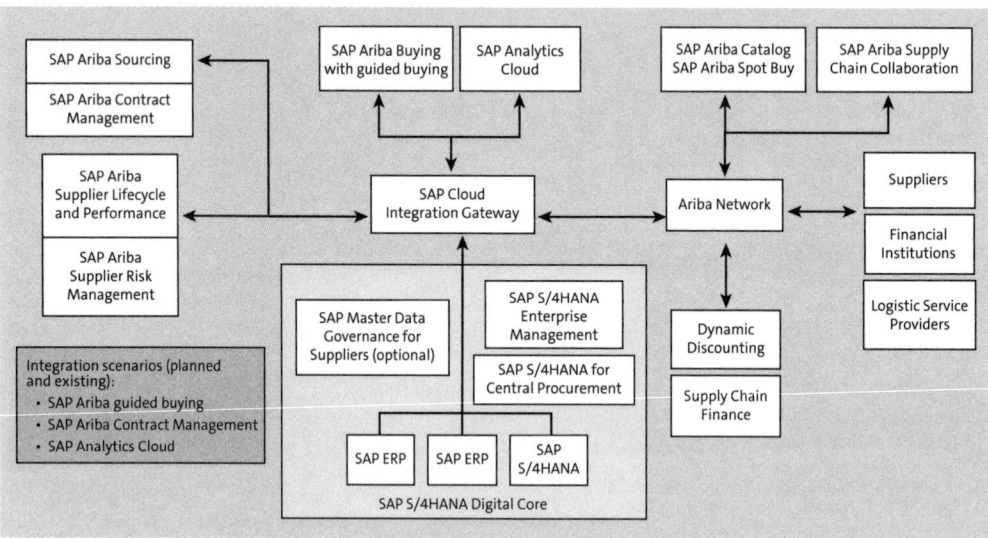

Figure 13.14 Procurement Reference IT Landscape for SAP S/4HANA and SAP Ariba

The main focus area for SAP S/4HANA for central procurement is SAP Ariba guided buying, which provides a consumer-grade buying experience on top of SAP S/4HANA for central procurement. SAP S/4HANA supports this integration from a relative position of strength. SAP S/4HANA has an expanding prebuilt portfolio of native integrations that can take advantage of solutions in SAP Ariba. However, many of these native integrations that exist today for SAP S/4HANA and SAP Ariba are not automatically applicable for central procurement. For example, SAP Ariba Sourcing is not directly integrated with SAP S/4HANA for central procurement as it is with SAP S/4HANA.

In addition, the existing integration with SAP Ariba guided buying and central procurement has restrictions for the document flow. You cannot create a requisition in SAP Guided Buying and convert it to a PO in SAP Ariba. In central procurement's standard integration with SAP Ariba guided buying, the latter has to send a requisition to the former and have the remainder of the process for converting the requisition to a purchase order occur in central procurement and/or the respective backend systems. The requisition created in SAP Ariba guided buying is updated with the purchase order document created in central procurement. This is along the lines of what's called a classic scenario in SAP SRM connected to a backend ERP system. SAP SRM creates a requisition/shopping cart and then sends a requisition down to SAP ERP for PO conversion once the SAP SRM shopping cart has been approved. The follow-on processes for PO creation and invoice reconciliation/accounts payable occur in the backend ERP system, with SAP SRM reflecting the follow-on documents. The leading documents after the SAP SRM shopping cart are effectively in SAP ERP. SAP SRM also has an *extended classic* scenario, whereby the requisition *and* the purchase order are created in SAP SRM and managed there. No such scenario exists for the SAP Ariba guided buying to SAP S/4HANA for central procurement integration. Change PO processes requiring a workflow and registering contract consumption in SAP Ariba Contracts are limited in a classic scenario.

The other challenge is the data model. Central procurement is flexible in terms of managing multiple backend systems and some duplication in the data. If the same supplier record appears in two different forms in two different backend systems, central procurement running without SAP Ariba can still route documents to the correct ERP environment because central procurement creates the document directly in the ERP environment.

When adding SAP Ariba guided buying and the Ariba Network for purchase order and invoice processing, a one-to-one relationship is needed for supplier data. SAP Ariba guided buying cannot maintain this duplication of supplier records easily. A supplier logging in to the Ariba Network expects one login and not multiple ones, based on the backend origin of the supplier record. Maintaining a single catalog for the organization quickly breaks down with the complexities of presenting a single catalog item tied to multiple versions of a supplier, depending upon which company code and backend SAP ERP system will ultimately receive this order. Add in partner functionality/supplier hierarchies for multiple invoice locations of a supplier from an SAP ERP environment, and a seemingly simple integration can quickly encounter challenges. In these situations, a further data harmonization step is often required via SAP Master Data Governance (SAP MDG), which is a project (and license) of its own.

13.7   Configuring SAP S/4HANA for Central Procurement

From an architectural standpoint, SAP S/4HANA for central procurement is an integrated part of the SAP S/4HANA system and code and can be activated and implemented on any SAP S/4HANA instance in parallel with the existing processes, subject to the purchase of the additional license. This means that any existing SAP S/4HANA instance can be converted into the procurement hub system and that there is no need to purchase additional hardware. Existing processes in this central instance remain untouched and can be run simultaneously without interfering. Within this system you could run the existing SAP S/4HANA procurement processes, often also referred to as *local procurement*, and connect them to the central processes of SAP S/4HANA for central procurement. These local processes are mostly treated like any other backend.

With its cloud-first strategy, SAP introduced a concept for SAP S/4HANA in which new developments are designed, developed, and deployed based on cloud principals but then are also made available on premise. Similarly, central procurement as an integrated part of SAP S/4HANA can be deployed in the cloud or on premise. Although there are huge differences between these deployment models, especially with regards to ease of consumption, upgrade speed, and software lifecycle, both options provide the same set of functionalities. Differences exist, due to the nature and requirements of the cloud, in how the connection to the backend landscape is realized. The following systems are supported as backends, as shown in Figure 13.15:

- SAP ERP EHP 6 or greater
- SAP Business Suite on SAP HANA
- SAP S/4HANA 1709 or later
- SAP S/4HANA Cloud

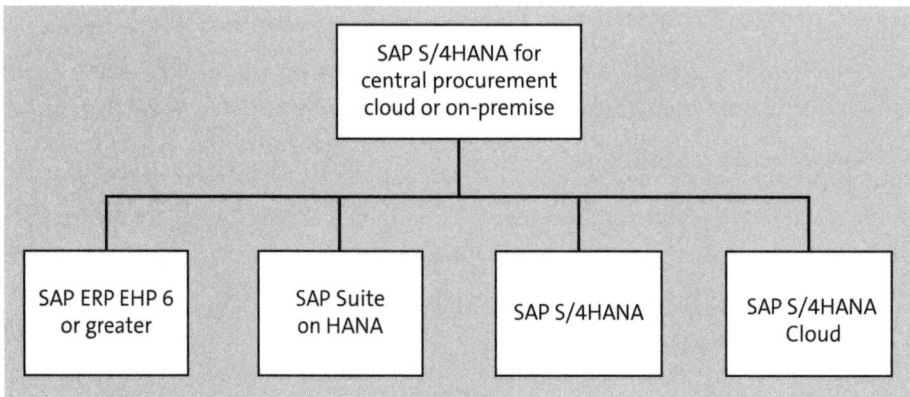

Figure 13.15 Versions of Backend Systems Connected to SAP S/4HANA for Central Procurement

For communication with the backends, OData or SOA services are used. Transactional data, such as data in purchase requisitions, is usually transferred via asynchronous SOA services, whereas data validation, lookups, or actions are usually performed with synchronous OData service calls to the backends.

The needed interfaces are provided for the on-premise backends as part of an *integration add-on*—an additional software component that needs to be installed in the backend systems. This component can be installed easily in the backend and decouples the lifecycle of the interfaces from the complex and costly lifecycle of underlying SAP ERP or SAP S/4HANA systems.

For any business process that is spread across multiple systems, the biggest challenge is master data. In case of procurement, this data includes materials, suppliers, and accounting information, but also organizational information like material groups or the purchasing organization. In the case of a central system architecture, as with any central procurement hub system, two options can be distinguished: either all master data, business logic and all business objects can be consolidated into the central system, or the workplace and business object access and workload organization can be centralized.

Consolidation can be a tedious and arduous task. It requires a companywide understanding of which processes and process-specific data needs to be incorporated into the central process flow, master data harmonization across many systems, or the creation of a mapping and data governance infrastructure. It comes with high TCO, and consolidated processes are usually error-prone and require constant maintenance effort, especially if the backend processes are very heterogenous. In addition, it can slow down innovation cycles in the backends, as well as in the hub, and new features need to be introduced synchronously in the central system and the backend.

As shown in Figure 13.16, centralization keeps the business logic and all business documents in the backends, which reduces the need to harmonize or map master data significantly. Only very few master data elements need to be harmonized or mapped. Mainly these are material groups and purchasing organizations. For central contract management alone, harmonized material master data is required across the backend landscape at this point in time.

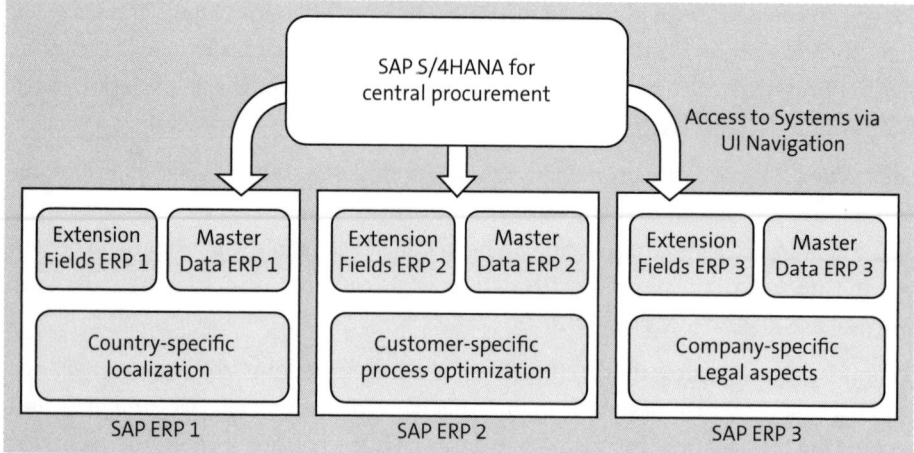

Figure 13.16 Centralizing of Procurement Workplace and Workload

SAP S/4HANA for central procurement is not merely a consolidated purchase order creation app, but a purchasing control center, which allows customers to (remotely) control a global, distributed, and diverse operational procurement ecosystem, while maintaining analytical and operational transparency and compliance.

Before embarking on an SAP S/4HANA for central procurement implementation or any other implementation, it's important to review the online documentation for the latest information, as well as the version release notes. For SAP S/4HANA for central procurement 1909, the release note is SAP Note 2817365.

13.7.1   Establishing Connectivity to ERP Systems

The first step is setting up connectivity to the ERP systems to be managed by SAP S/4HANA for central procurement. This is a cross-scenario-configuration activity for SAP S/4HANA for central procurement. With the SAP_BR_BPC_EXPERT and SAP_BR_ADMINISTRATOR roles or their equivalents assigned to your user, you first need SAP Basis to create RFC connections to each ERP environment using Transaction SM59. SAP Basis should create ABAP and HTTPS connection RFCs, along with an SAP Gateway system alias in table /IWFND/V_DFSYAL. SAP Basis then needs to create the logical system references in your SAP S/4HANA for central procurement environment for each connected ERP system using Transaction BD54. Finally, SAP Basis ties the RFCs to the logical systems' BAPI calls in in Transaction BD97 by entering the RFC connection in the field shown in Figure 13.17.

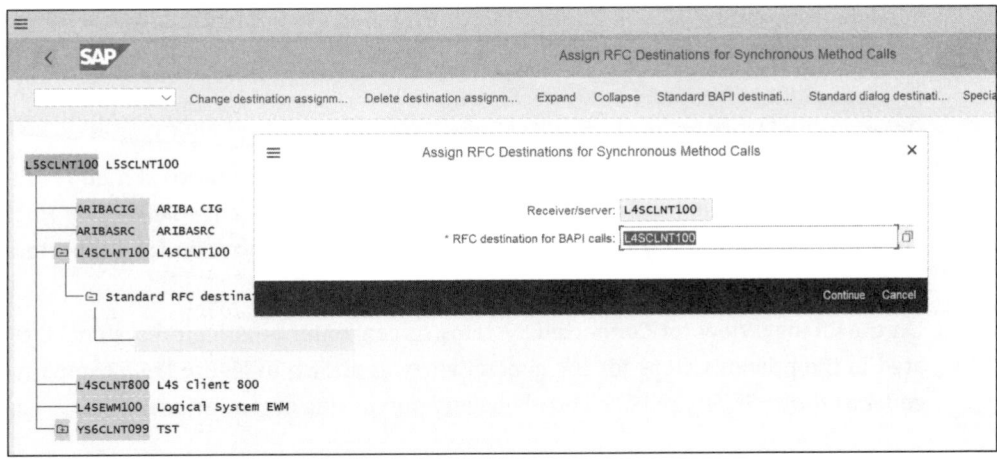

Figure 13.17 Assign RFC Destination for BAPI Calls

The following services/namespaces in Table 13.1 need to be configured to integrate an on-premise SAP S/4HANA for central procurement system via SAP PI or point-to-point connections. The SAP S/4HANA hub system namespaces can be found at *http://s-prs.co/500306*, and in a connected system at *http://s-prs.co/500307*.

SAP S/4HANA Hub system:	In connected system:
PurchaseRequisitionReplicationRequest_Out	PurchaseRequisitionReplicationRequest_In
PurchaseRequisitionReplicationConfirmationB_In	PurchaseRequisitionReplicationConfirmation_Out
PurchaseRequisitionSourcingNotification_In	PurchaseRequisitionSourcingNotification_Out

Table 13.1 Services Namespaces for SAP S/4HANA for Central Procurement

> **Note**
>
> If you set up communication from the SAP S/4HANA for central procurement system to the connected system via P2P, you will need to configure user-defined search for SOA services. If you set up communication via SAP PI, you need to configure user-defined search for the integration engine. User-defined search is required for central purchasing contracts when using the Central Procurement Operations Monitor app.

For detailed webservice configuration steps, please refer to Configuring Web Services in SOA Manager, available at *http://s-prs.co/500308*.

Defining Org Structure and Logical Systems

Next, define the company codes and plants to be used in the scenarios at menu path **SPRO • Materials Management • Purchasing • Central Procurement—Settings in Hub System • Define Company Code, Plant, and Purchasing Organization for Connected System**.

On the **Change View for Connected Systems** screen, enter your logical systems created in the previous steps for the general entry as shown in Figure 13.18, company codes as shown in Figure 13.19, and plants and purchasing organizations.

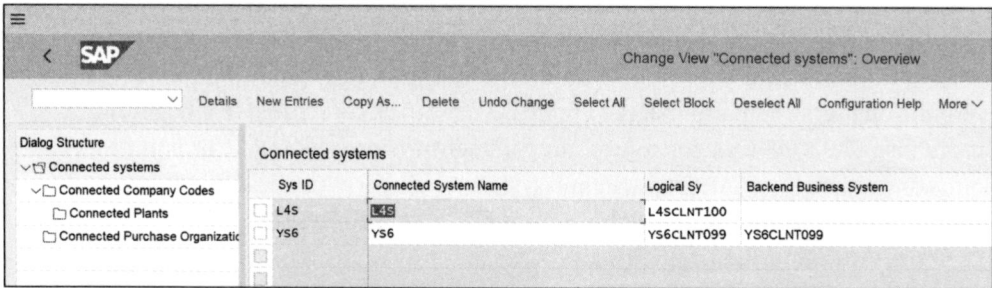

Figure 13.18 Connected Systems Central Procurement

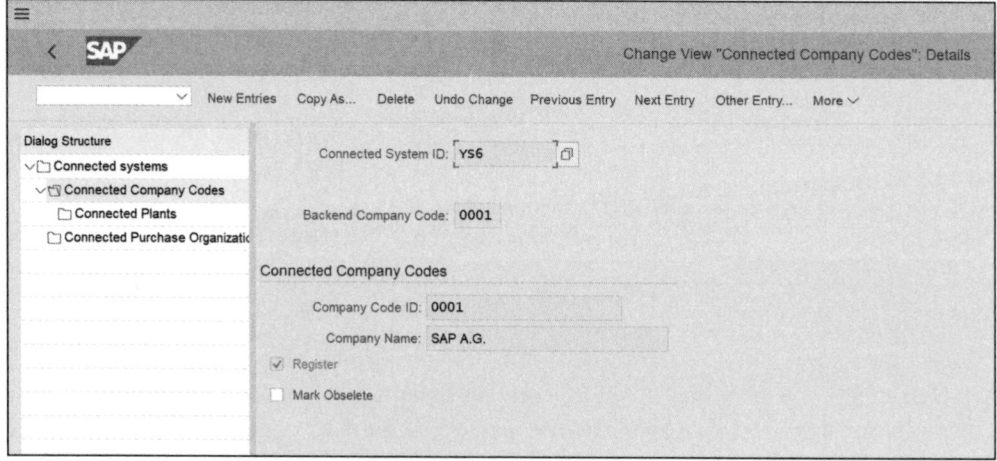

Figure 13.19 Connected Company Codes

Once completed, update table /UI2/VC_SYSALIAS using Transaction SM30 for the con-nected system ID (the backend systems defined in the company code, plant, and pur-chasing organization step).

Next update the mapping of the system alias in the same Transaction SM30, in table /UI2/V_ALIASMAP, as in Figure 13.20.

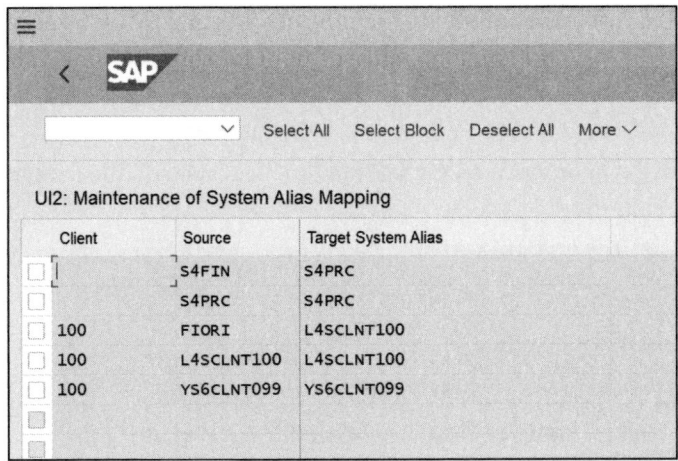

Figure 13.20 Table /UI2/V_ALIASMAP

As of version 1909, you can also maintain the control plane for the APIs of central procurement by following **SPRO • Materials Management • Purchasing • Central Pro-curement—Settings in Hub System • Configure Control Plane for APIs of Central Pro-curement**. For more information on this topic, review the SAP Best Practices Central Requisitioning documentation at *http://s-prs.co/500309*.

For central purchasing, you can find the setup documentation at *http://s-prs.co/500310*.

Job Scheduling

Next schedule a job to extract data for catalog items from the backend systems based on your filter settings, as follows:

1. Login into the SAP Fiori launchpad with a user that has the SAP_BR_BPC_EXPERT role.

2. In the **Purchasing Configuration** section, go to the Schedule Import of Catalog Data application.

3. On the **Application Jobs** screen, select **New**.

4. In the **General Information** area, **Job Template** and **Job Name** can be named **Import Catalog Data**. The job name can be changed if required.

5. To change the scheduling options, click **Define Recurrence Pattern**. Otherwise, the job will start immediately.

6. On the **Scheduling Information** screen, choose the required option and maintain the fields accordingly and confirm with **OK**.

7. In the **Catalog Data** area, under **Customizing Parameters**, the import parameters are automatically picked based on the customizing done in the previous steps.

8. In the **Catalog Data** area, under **Web Service**, select **Multi_Backend** and then enter the following import parameters:
   - **Connected System**: Connected system
   - **Company Code**: Company code in the connected system
   - **Plant**: Plant in the connected system
   - **Choose Import Type**: Full import or delta import
   - **Full Import**: Choose either **Material Group** or **Material**
   - **Material Group From**: If you want to, specify the material group range
   - **Material Group To**: If you want to, specify the material group range
   - **Material From**: If you want to, specify the material range
   - **Material To**: If you want to, specify the material

9. Choose **Schedule** and verify completion under **Application Jobs** and **Scheduled Jobs**.

To monitor system messages and perform troubleshooting activities, you will need to access the Central Procurement Operations Monitor app with the following catalog roles assigned to your user:

- SAP_MM_BC_CPRC_MONITOR_PC (Materials Management—Central Procurement Operations Monitoring)

- SAP_CA_BC_COM_ERR_PC (Communication Management—Message Monitoring and Error Handling)

- SAP_MM_BC_APPLJOB_CONFIG_PC (Materials Management—Job Scheduling)

Establishing OData Connections

SAP Basis now needs to establish OData connections between the backend connected systems and the SAP S/4HANA for central procurement environment. The OData services in Table 13.2 need to be established for each connected backend system.

OData Service Name	Technical Name	Description
Catalog Data Extraction Services	MMPUR_CAT_EXTRACT_SRV	Used to extract materials based on source of supply
OData Service for Purchase Requisition Check	MM_PUR_REQ_CHECK_SRV	Used to check consistency of purchase requisition (PR) in backend
Purchase Requisition History	MM_PUR_REQ_BE_HISTORY_SRV	Used to get history for purchase requisition
SSP Requisition Goods Receipt Hub Backend Services	MMPUR_REQ_SSP_GR_BE_SRV	Checks whether purchase requisition is ready for goods receipt (GR) and also responsible for posting GR in connected system
Service for Return Delivery	MMPUR_SSP_RDEL_BACKEND_SRV	Manages return delivery functionality in Return Delivery app
Search Help	MMPUR_REQ_SRV_BE_SRCH_HLP_SRV	Manages search help in Default Settings for Users, Create PR, and My PRs apps
Hub Service for Delivery Address and General Ledger Account	MMPUR_BE_DETERMINE_DEFAULTS_SRV	For general ledger account determination and assignment and plant address determination and assignment to PR delivery address
Material Value Help Service	MMPUR_BE_VALUE_HELP_SRV	Used for material search and assignment in Create PR app
Sync Business Processes Completed and Deleted PR from Connected System	MMPUR_REQ_BE_EOP_DELETE_SYNC_SRV	Used for synchronizing PRs

Table 13.2 OData Services for Central Procurement

OData Service Name	Technical Name	Description
Backend Accounting Value Helps in Procurement	MMPUR_ACC_BE_ VALUE_HELP_SRV	Accounting value search helps in procurement for Create PR app
Central Procurement Admin Monitor Backend Status for SSP	MM_PUR_ CPROC_OPS_ MNTR_SSP_ BE_SRV	Monitor backed status for Central Procurement Interface Monitor app

Table 13.2 OData Services for Central Procurement (Cont.)

For information about how to activate and maintain the OData services, please refer to SAP Gateway Foundation (SAP_GWFND), at *http://s-prs.co/500311*. Here you should also have SAP Basis set up an SAP Gateway cache management approach (determining how often the cache will be checked and cleared, as well as whether parallelization for batch queries is required).

Activating Change Pointers

Next, activate change pointers by following menu path **SPRO • SAP Netweaver • Application Server • IDoc Interfaces/ALE • Modeling and Implementing Business Processes • Master Data Distribution • Replication of Modified Data • Activate Change Pointers** or using Transaction BD61.

For central requisitioning, you next need to enter and maintain two message types, HUBSOS and HUBPR, by following menu path **SPRO • Integration with Other Components • Advanced Planning and Optimization • Basic Settings for the Data Transfer • Change Transfer • Change Transfer for Master Data • Activate ALE and Change Pointers for Message Types**. You'll need to update these message types via menu path **SPRO • Logistics • General • Material Master • Global Data Synchronization • Set Change Document Items for Message Type**.

For the latest guidance and document items to add to these two message type checks, as well as the differences between maintaining message types for SAP ERP and SAP S/4HANA on-premise and/or SAP S/4HANA Cloud, visit *http://s-prs.co/500312* and go to the **Set Change Document Items for Message Type** section.

13.7.2   Validating Data and Identifying Gaps

With SAP S/4HANA for central procurement utilizing centralization as its key principal, the need to synchronize data, including master data, is greatly reduced.

To provide fast access, easy search capabilities, and analytical functions, SAP S/4HANA for central purchasing uses the underlying SAP HANA in-memory database technology. Information about the business documents from the different backends is updated continuously into SAP S/4HANA for central procurement, and all read access to any document happens via this cached data within the SAP S/4HANA for central procurement solution. Via OData interfaces in the backends, changed or newly created business objects are updated as per Figure 13.21.

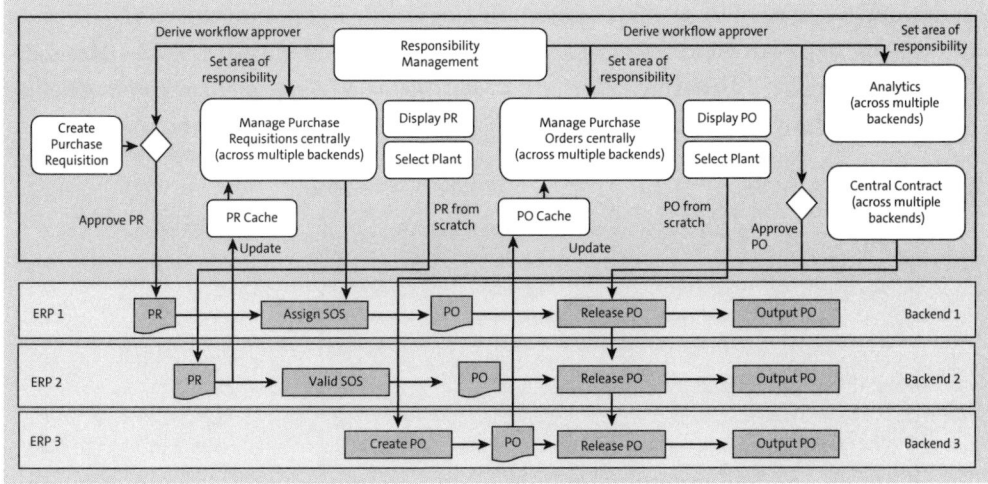

Figure 13.21 Overview of SAP S/4HANA for Central Procurement Architecture and Data Flow

The update cycles can be customized, and programs for initially filling the cache tables in the hub are available. The option to restrict the business objects to be transferred to the central system also is available. The data import is consistently tracked and monitored by appropriate logging functionality so that errors can be identified and resolved. With the ad hoc import functionality, it's also possible to manually import only specific documents at any given point in time.

If you want to filter data extracted to SAP S/4HANA for central procurement, follow menu path **SPRO • Materials Management • Purchasing • Central Procurement • Settings in Hub System • Define additional Filter Options for Source of Supply Extraction**.

Here you maintain the backend logical system and the types of records to be extracted, as shown in Figure 13.22.

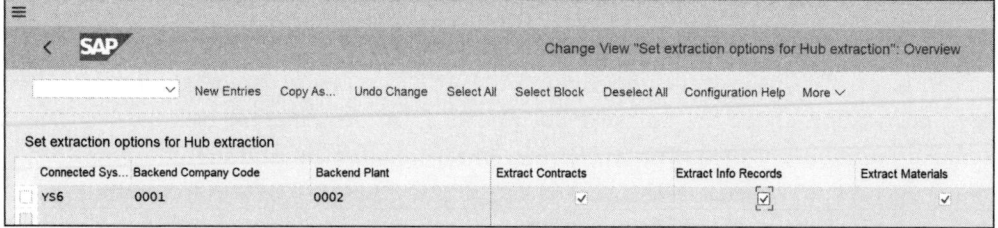

Figure 13.22 Setting Central Procurement Extraction Options

Next, if you want to be able to search catalogs using a common currency, you must enable the search bar for cross-catalog search. Go to menu path **SPRO • Materials Management • Purchasing • Purchase Requisition • Self-Service Procurement • Define Settings for Cross-Catalog Search**. Clear the **Hide Search Bar** checkbox and save, as shown in Figure 13.23.

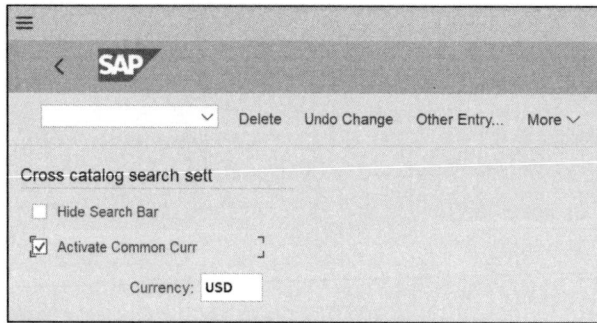

Figure 13.23 Cross-Catalog Search Settings

Next, if you need to harmonize material groups across systems—that is, if your backend ERP systems have differing material groups from the other systems and/or the SAP S/4HANA environment—you can access Transaction OMSF in your SAP S/4HANA for central procurement system or follow menu path **SPRO • Logistics • General • Material Master • Settings for Key Fields • Define Material Groups** and enter these additional material groups as shown in Figure 13.24.

Similarly, if you have purchasing groups in your ERP systems, you can create them in the SAP S/4HANA environment by following menu path **SPRO • Materials Management • Purchasing • Create Purchasing Groups** and selecting **Create Purchasing Groups**.

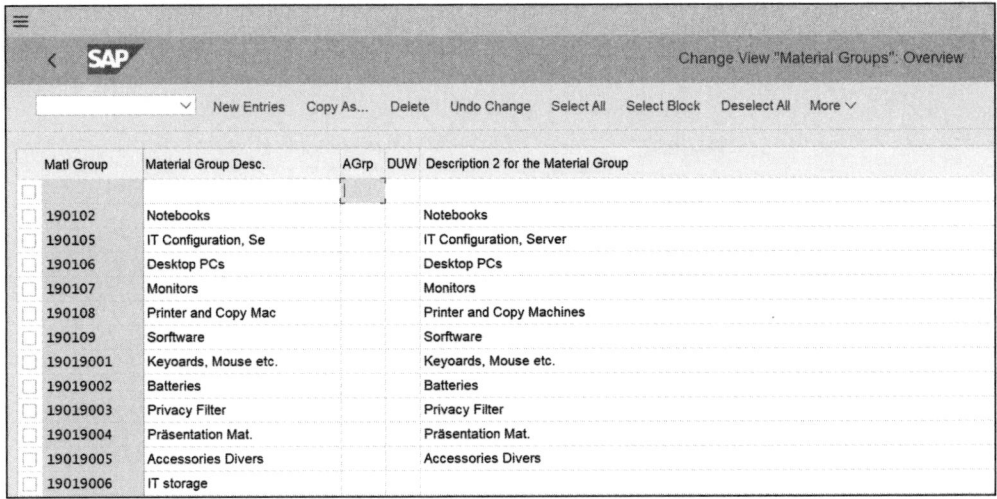

Figure 13.24 Define Material Groups

You can also align your account assignment types and purchasing documents with the backend ERP systems by following **SPRO • Materials Management • Purchasing • Account Assignment • Maintain Account Assignment Categories** and **SPRO • Materials Management • Purchase Requisition • Define Document Types**.

Note that job SAP_MM_PUR_HUB_SYNC_EOP_DEL is scheduled by default to run every 12 hours and update the archiving/deletion/end of purpose (EOP) status of requisitions to the corresponding backend system. You can change the frequency as you would any other job in Transaction SE38.

13.7.3   Configuring SAP S/4HANA for Central Procurement Scenarios

SAP S/4HANA for central procurement covers a wide array of functionalities that can be used to manage procurement activities in a distributed ERP environment. Customers can choose to deploy all the available central procurement scenarios or only select ones. The central procurement scenarios available include requisitioning, purchasing, contracts, and analytics. The following sections detail further steps required for configuring individual scenarios, beginning with requisitioning, for SAP S/4HANA for central procurement 1909 on-premise. For the most current setup documentation for all available versions, including cloud versions, visit *http://s-prs.co/500313*.

Central Requisitioning

The steps for activating requisitioning after completing the general connectivity steps are as follows:

1. Login into the SAP S/4HANA hub system and execute Transaction SPRO.

2. Navigate to the configuration activity via menu path **SPRO • Materials Management • Purchasing • Central Procurement • Settings in Hub System • Activate SAP S/4HANA Procurement Hub and Scenarios**.

3. In the **Change View "Hub Activation" Overview** screen, shown in Figure 13.25, choose **New Entries** and then enter the following entries: **Activate HUB: Check**.

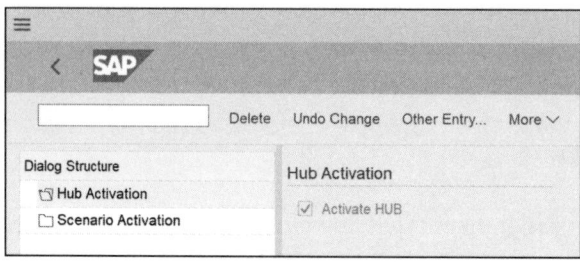

Figure 13.25 Hub Activation

4. Choose **Save**. Note that once saved, the SAP S/4HANA environment becomes a hub for central procurement. This step is a permanent step, so be sure that you have confirmed the environment prior to saving.

5. In the dialog structure area, choose **Scenario Activation**.

6. In the **Change View "Scenario Activation": Overview** screen, choose **New Entries** and then enter **Activate Scenarios for Procurement Hub: Central Requisitioning** as shown in Figure 13.26.

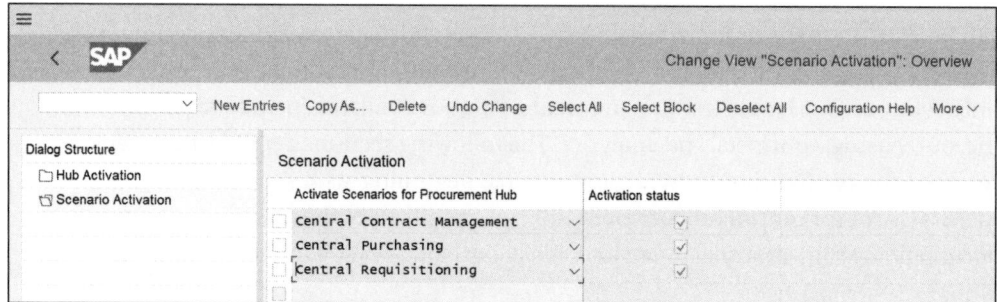

Figure 13.26 Activate Central Requisitioning

7. Choose **Save**.

If you want to modify the requisitions using an enhancement, BAdI MM_PUR_S4_ SSP_HUB_PR_MODIFY (Manage Purchase Requisitions During Replication) allows for checking and changing custom fields, account assignment information, and other data.

If you want to have purchase requisitions automatically convert into POs in the backend systems, an option is available for later releases of SAP ERP via menu path **SPRO • Materials Management • Purchasing • Purchase Order • Enable Automatic Creation of PO from Replicated Central PR** as shown in Figure 13.27.

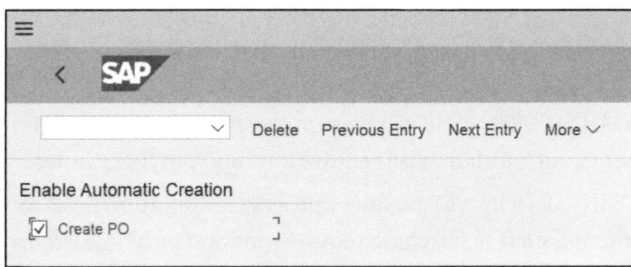

Figure 13.27 Enable Automatic Creation of PO

In older versions of SAP ERP, you can enable the automatic creation of the PO by following these steps:

1. Log in into the connected system (SAP ERP) and execute Transaction SM30.

2. Enter "VMMPUR_POCREATE" for the **View Name**, and then choose **Edit**.

3. Choose the **Create PO** check box.

4. Choose **Save**.

Central Purchasing

As with central requisitioning and central purchasing contracts, ensure that the general steps for establishing connectivity and validating data outlined in this configuration section have been reviewed first. If you want to centrally manage, approve, and release requisitions—that is, release all items of a purchase requisition simultaneously—follow menu path **SPRO • Materials Management • Purchasing • Central Procurement—Settings in Hub System • Central Purchasing • Activate Release of Centrally Managed Purchase Requisitions**. In the change view for the customizing table for **Central PR Approval**, select **New Entries** and enter the **Connected System ID, Order Type** (your PR type), **Description**, and **Overall Release** (whether you want to release the items together), then **Save**.

You can leverage the following BAdIs in Central Purchasing to extend the functionality:

- MM_PUR_S4_MODIFY_EXTRACTED_PR for modifying purchase requisition data during extraction
- MM_PUR_S4_MODIFY_EXTRACTED_PO for managing purchase order data during extraction
- MMPUR_PR_RPL_WORKFLOW_AGENTS for determining agents centrally for approving replicated PRs
- MMPUR_PROXY_PO_SEARCH_FLDS_DEF for assigning default values to search fields for proxy POs
- MMPUR_BUSPROC_AUTMN_ACTION_CHK business process automation BAdI for checking various documents, such as purchase requisitions and purchase orders
- MMPUR_BUSPROC_AUTMN_ACTION_SET business process automation BAdI for modifying various documents, such as purchase requisitions and purchase orders
- MMPUR_PREQ_CENTRAL_APPR change text ID for storing approval/rejection text for central approval of purchase requisition

You can now schedule an import job for purchasing orders and purchasing texts via the following steps:

1. Log on to the SAP Fiori launchpad with the user that has the SAP_BR_BPC_EXPERT role template.
2. In the **Job Scheduling for Purchasing** section, go to the Schedule Import of Purchasing Documents application.
3. On the **Application Jobs** screen, choose **New**.
4. On the **New Job** screen, enter the following values under **General Information**:
   - **Job Template**: **Import Purchase Orders from Connected Systems**
   - **Job Name**: For example, "Import Purchase Orders from Connected Systems"
   Note that **Scheduling Options** is set to start immediately by default, as in Figure 13.28.
5. To change the scheduling options, choose **Define Recurrence Pattern** as in Figure 13.29.

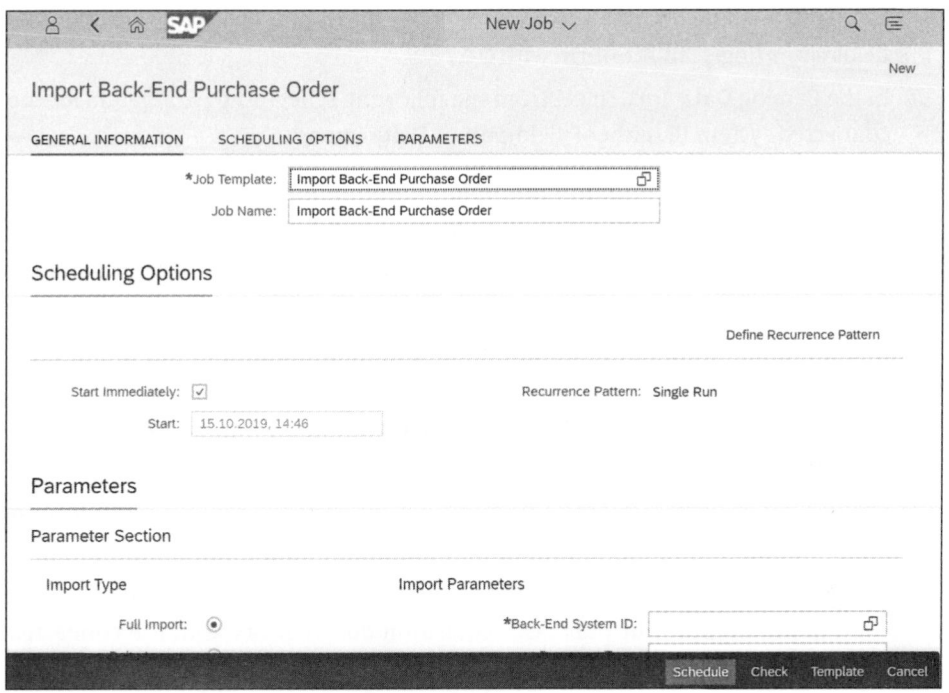

Figure 13.28 Schedule Job to Import POs

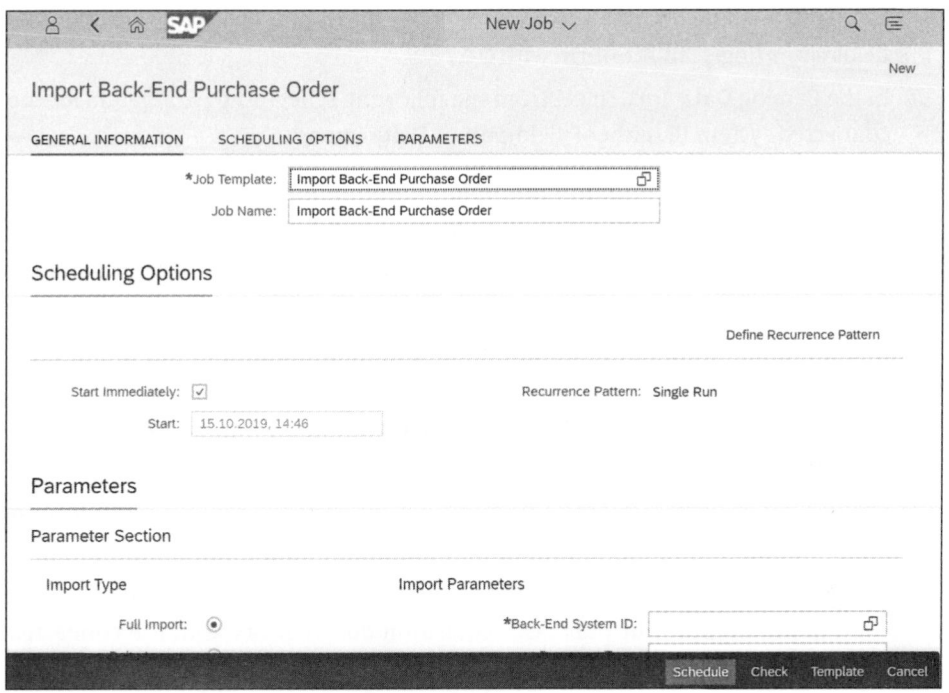

Figure 13.29 Define Recurrence Pattern

6. On the **Scheduling Information** screen, choose the option you want, maintain the fields accordingly, and confirm with **OK**.

7. In the **Catalog Data** area, select from the following scheduling parameters for the connected system ID: either **Full Import** or **Delta Import**.

8. Repeat these steps for purchasing texts.

Next, configure the central settings for purchase requisitions and purchase orders that need to be approved centrally. To configure active central settings for purchase orders in the connected system, perform the following steps:

1. Log on to the connected system and enter Transaction SPRO.

2. Navigate to the configuration activity via **SPRO • Materials Management • Purchasing • Central Procurement • Settings in Connected Systems—Central Purchase Requisition • Manage Central Settings for Purchase Requisitions**.

3. On the **Change View Activate Central Settings for Purchase Requisitions Overview** screen, choose **New Entries** and then make the following entries:

   – **Document Category**: Purchase Requisition

   – **Document Type**: Your purchase requisition document type in the connected system

   – **Purchasing Org**: Your purchasing organization in the connected system

   – **Purch. Group**: Your purchasing group in the connected system

   – **Plant**: Your company code in the connected system

   – **Creation Ind.**: Creation indicator of purchase requisition is set to **Active**

   – **Central Approval**: Check **4**

4. **Save**.

Next, perform the following steps for purchase orders:

1. Log on to the connected system and enter Transaction SPRO.

2. Navigate to the configuration activity via **SPRO • Materials Management • Purchasing • Central Procurement—Settings in Connected Systems • Central Purchase Order • Activate Central Settings for Purchase Orders**.

3. On the **Change View Activate Central Settings for Purchase Orders Overview** screen, choose **New Entries** and then make the following entries:

   – **Document Category**: Purchase Order

   – **Document Type**: Your purchase order document type in the connected system

   – **Purchasing Org**: Your purchasing organization in the connected system

- **Purch. Group**: Your purchasing group in the connected system
- **Plant**: Your company code in the connected system

4. **Save**.

Next, determine the text types to save release information for the purchase orders:

1. Log on to the connected system and enter Transaction SPRO.
2. Navigate to the configuration activity via **SPRO • Materials Management • Purchasing • Central Procurement—Settings in Connected Systems • Central Purchase Order • Determine Text Types to Save Release Information of Purchase Orders**.
3. On the **Change View Maintain Central Settings for Release text of Purchase Order: Overview** screen, choose **New Entries** and then make the following entries:
   - **Text ID**: Your purchase order text ID in the connected system
   - **Default Text**: Check this checkbox
4. **Save**.

Now, after completing the general activation of change pointers, for central purchasing, maintain two message types, MMPUR_PURCHASEORDER_ARCHIVE and EBAN_ARCH. To do so, follow menu path **SPRO • Integration with Other Components • Advanced Planning and Optimization • Basic Settings for the Data Transfer • Change Transfer • Change Transfer for Master Data • Activate ALE and Change Pointers for Message Types**. You can also use Transaction BD50.

Now set the system to log changes for purchase order archiving data by entering Transaction BD52 in the connected system, then entering message type MMPUR_PURCHASEORDER_ARCHIVE. Add the new entries listed in Table 13.3 on the **Change Document Items for Message Type** screen.

Object	Table Name	Field Name
EINKBELEG	EKKO	BSART
EINKBELEG	EKKO	EBELN
EINKBELEG	EKKO	LOEKZ

Table 13.3 Items for MMPUR_PURCHASEORDER_ARCHIVE

You can review the up-to-date setup documentation for both SAP S/4HANA on-premise and SAP S/4HANA Cloud for central purchasing at *http://s-prs.co/500314*.

Central Purchasing Contracts

In SAP S/4HANA for central procurement, central purchasing contracts requires many of the configuration steps covered in Sections 13.7.1 and 13.7.2.

To set up your systems for central contracts, complete the following steps:

1. Define the SAP S/4HANA hub system.
2. Configure/connect the receiving ERP systems.
3. Maintain the organizational data in the SAP S/4HANA for central procurement system.
4. Harmonize the data between hub and connected systems (data in the hub system must be similar to that in the spoke systems).
5. Use the Schedule Import of Catalog Data app to import catalog items and sources of supply information from the different connected systems.
6. The Manage Workflows for Central Contracts app is used to configure the workflow processes for approving central contracts. Using this app, you can
   - set triggers for workflow and the order in which these conditions are to be checked;
   - activate or deactivate a workflow and display the details of each workflow; and
   - define workflow properties, such as validity period and description, as well as preconditions, such as company code, purchasing group, and other variables.

Note that if you do not configure workflows, the contract will automatically go through the Automatic Approval workflow, which is set as the initial default. This workflow should be placed at the end of your ordered workflows to ensure that final approval ensues once your defined workflow steps have been completed.

Now let's look at the contracts-specific configuration steps for SAP S/4HANA 1909 on-premise. Upon completing the connectivity set up, if not already done for another central procurement scenario, configure control plane for the APIs of central procurement. To do so, follow menu path **SPRO • SAP Reference IMG • Materials Management • Purchasing • Central Procurement—Settings in Hub System • Configure Control Plane for the APIs of Central Procurement**.

Select the **Change View API Control Plane for Bounded Content Overview** screen, then select **New Entries**. Using your connected system ID, with bounded context set to CCM, API version 1, and **Activate Driver** checked for each row, enter the values in Table 13.4.

Operation	Message Protocol	API Name	API Driver
2AH Archive Local Contracts	ODATA	MM_PUR_CCTR_ARCHIVE_SRV	CL_MMPUR_CENTRL_CTR_D RIVER
2CD Central Contract Check Distribution	ODATA	MM_PUR_CCTR_CHECK_SRV_1	CL_MMPUR_CENTRL_CTR_D RIVER
2DI Central Contract Distribute	SOAP	PURCHASECONTRACT-DISTRIBUTIONREPLICATION-REQUEST_IN	CL_MMPUR_CENTRL_CTR_D RIVER
2OM Central Procurement Operations Monitor for CCM	ODATA	MM_PUR_CPROC_OPS_MNTR_CC TR_BE_SRV	CL_MMPUR_CENTRL_CTR_D RIVER
2RD Central Contract Read Release Info	ODTA	MM_PUR_CCTR_CALLOFF_SRV	CL_MMPUR_CENTRL_CTR_D RIVER
2RM Central Contract Read Material	ODATA	MMPUR_BE_VALUE_HELP_SRV	CL_MMPUR_CENTRL_CTR_D RIVER
2RR Central Contract Read Related Information		MMPUR_CCTR_BE_SRV	CL_MMPUR_CENTRL_CTR_D RIVER

Table 13.4 Control Plane APIs for Central Procurement

Next, maintain condition type mapping for purchasing documents, as follows:

1. Log in into the SAP S/4HANA hub system and execute Transaction SPRO.

2. Navigate to configuration activity via menu path **SAP Reference IMG Materials Management • Purchasing Central Procurement • Settings in Hub System • Maintain Condition Type Mapping for Purchasing Documents**.

3. On the **Change View "Maintain Condition Type Mapping for Purchasing Documents": Overview** screen, choose **New Entries** and then enter the following:

   – **Sys ID**: Your system ID

   – **Con. Typ. in HUB Sys.**: Your condition type in the SAP S/4HANA for central procurement system

   – **Con. Type in Backend**: Your condition type in the backend ERP system

4. Save.

Next, extract/activate AIF content. First, log on to SAP S/4HANA for central procurement and enter Transaction SE38. Enter "/AIF/CONTENT_EXTRACT_NEW" and "SAP_COM_0090" as the deployment scenario as shown in Figure 13.30. Execute.

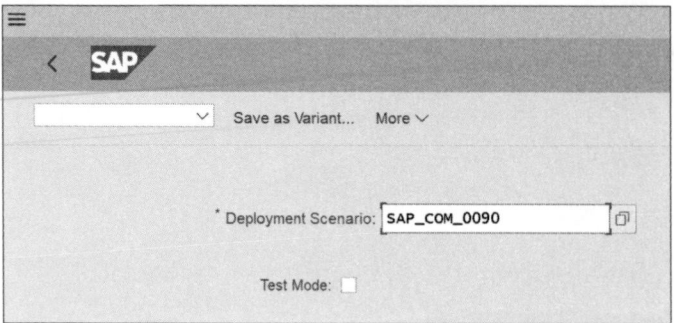

Figure 13.30 Activating AIF Content

For contract master data, validate that the following master data exists in both systems (the hub and the backend):

- Supplier
- Pricing schema
- Inco terms
- Payment terms
- Unit of measures
- Currency
- Tax code

You can leverage the following BAdIs in central purchasing contracts to extend the functionality:

- MM_PUR_S4_CCTR_CHECK for check of central purchase contract; also can be set up to raise messages to help guide the user
- MM_PUR_S4_CCTR_MODIFY_HEADER for change of central purchase contract before saving at header level
- MM_PUR_S4_CCTR_MODIFY_ITEM for change of central purchase contract item before saving at the item level

- MM_PUR_S4_CCTR_FLDCTRL_SIMPLE to manage field controls for central contracts, to make fields hidden, read-only, mandatory, or optional

As mentioned in Section 13.7.1, user-defined search is required for central purchasing contracts for using the Central Procurement Operations Monitor app. The setup steps depend upon whether you are using SOA webservices or SAP PI for your integration.

For both setup steps and the latest setup information, visit *http://s-prs.co/500315*.

Central Analytics

As of version 1908, analytics for central procurement have been enhanced in SAP S/4HANA in the following apps:

- The Central Purchase Requisition Item Types app now can run analyses based on item types.
- The Monitor Purchase Requisition Centrally analytical list page app now has an analytics page for reviewing purchase requisitions, as shown in Figure 13.31.

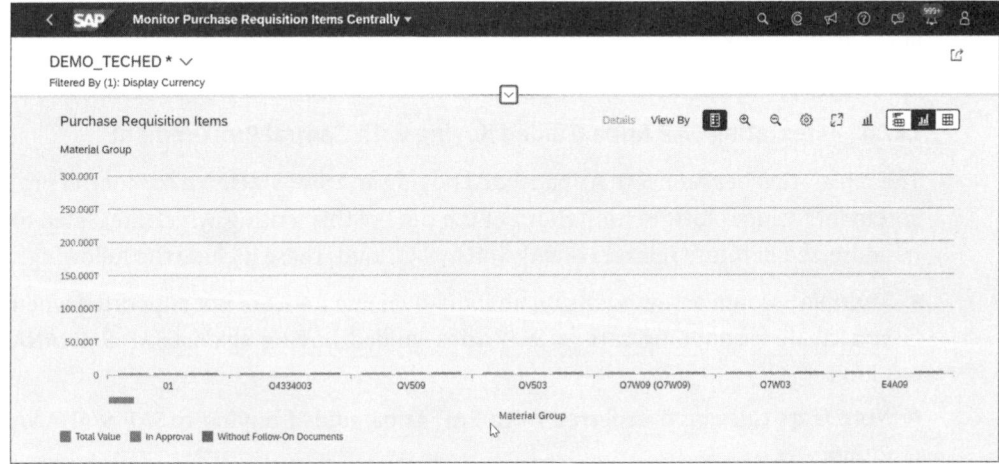

Figure 13.31 Monitor Purchase Requisition Items Centrally

You also have access to an analytical list page app for purchase orders now, as shown in Figure 13.32.

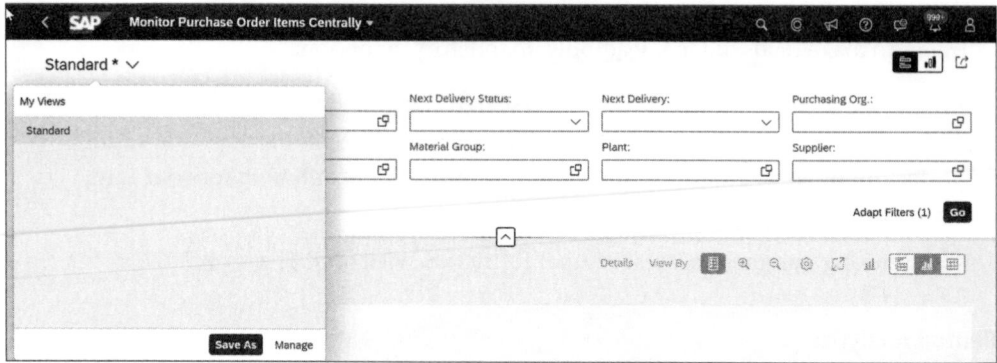

Figure 13.32 Monitor Purchase Order Items Centrally

- The Global Purchasing Spend report in the Central Purchasing Analytics app allows you to analyze all your purchase orders, including central purchase orders and local orders, across the landscape.

To configure and set up central analytics, install these apps and allow the proxy tables to fill with data from the connected systems. The KPIs and reporting are then available out of the box.

13.7.4   Integrating SAP Ariba Guided Buying with Central Procurement

The integration between SAP Ariba guided buying and SAP S/4HANA for central procurement includes further limitations at the time of this writing, which are slated to be addressed in future releases of SAP S/4HANA Cloud. These include the following:

- Multiple account assignments on an individual line item are not supported when you create a shopping cart in SAP Ariba guided buying against SAP S/4HANA Cloud.
- Note texts can't be transferred from SAP Ariba guided buying to SAP S/4HANA Cloud.
- Attachments can't be transferred from SAP Ariba guided buying to SAP S/4HANA Cloud.
- Customer-specific fields can't be transferred from SAP Ariba guided buying to SAP S/4HANA Cloud.

SAP S/4HANA for central procurement on-premise is no better with regard to these limitations as of version 1909, and the fixes are planned to come sooner for SAP

S/4HANA Cloud than for on-premise versions since cloud releases and updates occur on a quarterly basis. If you're planning to integrate an SAP S/4HANA 1909 release of central procurement on-premise into your system, first verify the requirements for SAP Ariba guided buying and SAP Ariba in general and determine what integration limitations still apply; you may be better off deploying the SAP S/4HANA for central procurement cloud version to cover these integration areas and newer functionality. Your data situation with multiple backends may also require SAP Master Data Governance to harmonize, especially if you have duplicate supplier records, supplier hierarchies, and partners set up in your backend SAP ERP systems or other duplicate or diverging master data. For more information on the current limitations and on the overall process flow for an SAP Ariba guided buying to SAP S/4HANA for central procurement integration, visit *http://s-prs.co/500316*. For the SAP Best Practices, including automated configuration options, visit *http://s-prs.co/500317*.

13.8   Summary

SAP S/4HANA for central procurement has expanded its functionality greatly since its initial release and represents the future platform for managing procurement activities centrally for multiple ERP systems. The capabilities in central procurement are at some levels much more advanced than what SAP SRM users were able to leverage in the past, while in other areas, such as the integration with SAP Ariba guided buying, work remains to be done to address some of the limitations at a process and functionality level. Now, the next chapter will look further into sourcing and analytics in SAP S/4HANA.

Chapter 14
Sourcing and Procurement Analytics

It's now more possible than ever before to view key procurement reports and conduct drilldown analysis in real time in an SAP S/4HANA environment. The revolution taking place in artificial intelligence and machine learning is also bearing fruit in this regard, as augmented decision-making tools in SAP S/4HANA Sourcing and Procurement arrive via a variety of new functionality and apps.

Procurement analysis and reporting are a necessity for any procurement operation. Procurement analysis and reporting are divided into three distinct areas in SAP S/4HANA Sourcing and Procurement: real-time reporting and monitoring, spend visibility, and reporting and monitoring (Figure 14.1). *Real time reporting and monitoring* is broader in nature and can include general reports pertaining to procurement master data and transaction document status. *Spend visibility* and *reporting* focus on the transactional data in the system, driving reports and insights that allow a procurement organization to better understand in what areas it's spending money and with which suppliers.

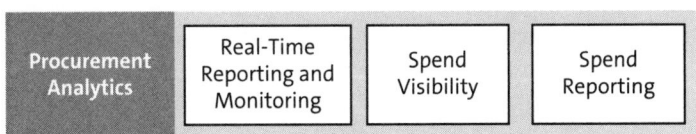

Figure 14.1 Procurement Analytics

This chapter will provide an overview of approaches to reporting and analytics in SAP S/4HANA, as well as the complementary uses and connections available for traditional, business warehouse-based reporting, in which data is offloaded into a business warehouse and used to construct cubes, which then provide analysis drilldown reports for the business user.

14.1   Spend Visibility

Like finance and controlling, a procurement department has a strong focus on spending. Unlike finance, the chief interests of which are cash flow and controlling costs, procurement seeks to understand what is being bought and whether more optimal approaches exist for categorizing and grouping this spend, as well as supporting it via agreements with suppliers. Spend visibility, also called *spend analysis*, provides the procurement team with reporting in this area, combining financial/transactional reporting in which payments are being made to suppliers with the upstream areas, meaning the requisitioning, sourcing, and contracting areas of the transaction. The difference between a classic approach to spend visibility and the approach in SAP S/4HANA is detailed in Figure 14.2.

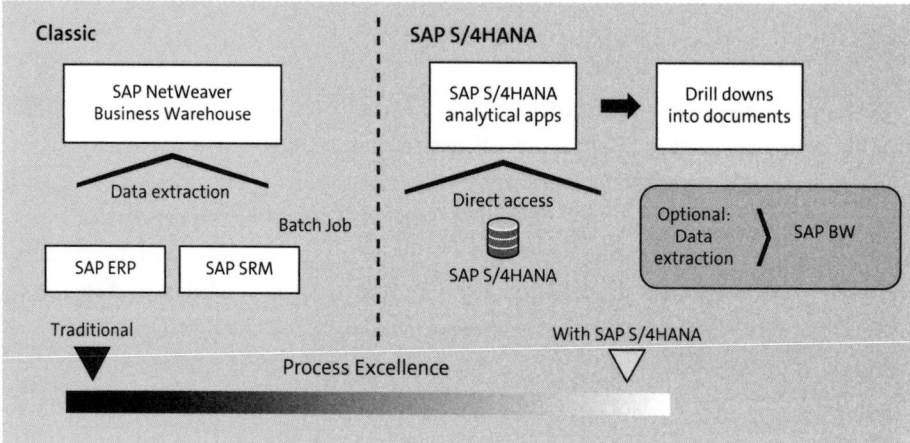

Figure 14.2 Classic versus SAP S/4HANA Sourcing and Procurement Spend Visibility

In a classic approach for spend visibility, the SAP ERP system didn't conduct an extraction in real time, and there were no KPI options. Because the data had been extracted to another environment, drilling down into the minutia of a transaction or supporting financials wasn't always possible, either. For this, you had to return to the transaction system to further query data and/or rebuild your data cubes in your business warehouse to show the sought-after data. SAP S/4HANA still allows for extraction of data to a business warehouse if required, but you can also conduct KPI-based analysis in real time in the transacting system. This makes the view into your spending up-to-date and actionable in an immediate timeframe when required. With its multidimensional spend report, SAP S/4HANA Cloud offers further extensions for spend reporting in later releases (1708 and above), as per the next section.

14.1.1 Multidimensional Spend Reporting in SAP S/4HANA Cloud

The multidimensional purchasing spend report in SAP S/4HANA Cloud allows for purchasing spend to be analyzed dynamically by company code, region, plant, and other variables. The user can drag and drop dimensions, as well as change and adopt filters, dimensions, and measures in rows and columns. Users can flip between a table, bar, or split chart display.

14.1.2 Navigation and Procurement Overview Page

As with multidimensional spend reporting, users can also move between table, bar, or split chart display for monitoring and reporting in SAP S/4HANA Sourcing and Procurement. Buyers and executives can analyze and report on spend, contracts, and suppliers, as well as monitor business-critical situations in the procurement overview page using analytical cards and worklists. *Analytical cards* are screen elements in an overview page. An *overview page* can show many charts and figures on one page, and the user can navigate to further applications by clicking the figures and/or charts contained in the card.

The Procurement Overview Page app provides a graphical dashboard display of key procurement and supplier management reports, as in Figure 14.3.

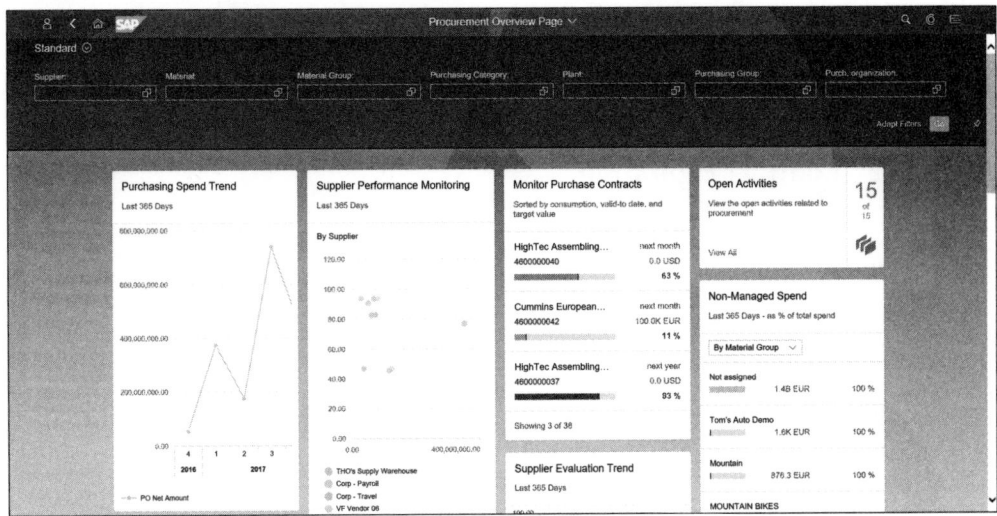

Figure 14.3 Procurement Overview Page App

As of SAP S/4HANA on-premise edition 1909, you can also analyze the efficiency of your approval workflows with the PR Average Approval Time (Flexible Workflow) app, using a KPI to monitor approval time for flexible workflow–based requisitions. A further improvement in 1909 is the availability of the Purchase Order Item Changes app, which allows you analyze what types of changes are being made in the POs, as in Figure 14.4. This insight allows you to further optimize processes to address areas causing frequent updates to POs.

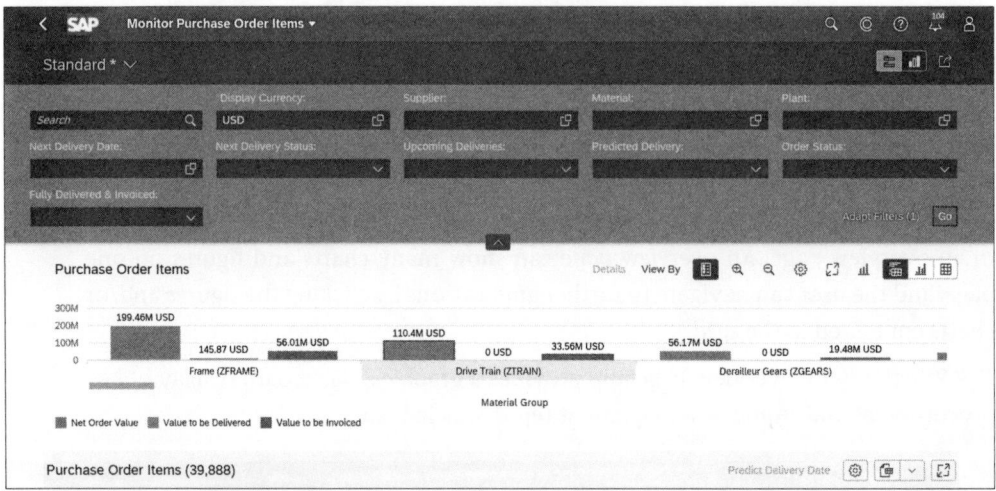

Figure 14.4 Purchase Order Item Changes App

14.2   Contract Expiration

The first step in the evolution of contract reporting is to get contracts out of filing cabinets and into the SAP ERP system. Once contracts are in a system, instead of shuffling through paper files and hoping that you still have enough room and time on a contract to execute another purchase, you can begin to report on these contracts and identify ones that are expiring. Both cloud and on-premise editions of SAP S/4HANA Sourcing and Procurement shipped with this functionality early on, via the Quantity Contract Consumption SAP Fiori app. This app provides a comprehensive overview of all contracts in the system and all data related to them, such as validity timeframe, current released and target amounts, and material group.

Another app is the Contract Expiry app, which shows the target value and consumption, providing a clear visual indicator of the amount left on a contract, as shown in Figure 14.5.

Figure 14.5 Contract Expiry App

SAP S/4HANA has a mandate to raise process intelligence using its new, real-time reporting capabilities. From SAP S/4HANA version 1709 and SAP S/4HANA Cloud version 1705 onward, the Quantity Contract Consumption app not only reports on existing expiration trajectories for contracts but also makes predictions using the predictive analytics algorithm in the system. This algorithm leverages historical consumption data to make predictions about when a contract will be completely consumed.

The algorithm's predictive capability has been further enhanced as of SAP S/4HANA, on-premise edition 1909 to include situational and contextual awareness capabilities, allowing the purchaser to start renewal negotiations at the optimal time and ensure that the purchaser also consumes the existing contract in the most efficient manner possible. To tune the default notifications on contract expirations, you access the Manage Situation Types app. This app notifies designated users of specific situations, such as contract expiry, for which follow-up is required.

14

14.3   Sourcing

The sourcing cockpit and functionality in SAP S/4HANA remains similar to that in previous versions of SAP ERP, and this is by design. For further innovation in sourcing topics, the go-to solution area is SAP Ariba. In SAP Ariba Strategic Sourcing, the collaboration and reporting capabilities are more robust than in SAP S/4HANA. Still, if you're evaluating sourcing from an existing supplier in SAP S/4HANA, you do have several supplier performance reports at your disposal, such as the following SAP S/4HANA apps:

- Manage Sources of Supply
- Operational Supplier Evaluation Last 365 Days
- Overall Supplier Evaluation Last 365 Days
- Supplier Evaluation by Quantity Last 365 Days
- Supplier Evaluation by Price Last 365 Days
- Supplier Evaluation by Time Last 365 Days
- Supplier Evaluation by Questionnaire Last 365 Days

Because these analytics and reports are being generated in real time in the transaction system, they also can be brought to bear on the transactions taking place. For example, beginning in SAP S/4HANA Cloud version 1708, analytical information about the supplier is available at the transaction level. Rather than choosing a name and number for a supplier, by using simple product offerings to determine the supplier eligibility, this approach allows the user to look at the supplier's record holistically and not just at a supplier record. This allows a user to choose a supplier with eyes wide open, rather than grabbing the first eligible supplier off the list. A user now sees scores and other data that differentiates suppliers and can drive purchasing patterns of the organization toward the best-performing suppliers rather than ones that managed to appear at the top of the list based on their name or numerical code.

This new approach toward real-time purchasing analytics can be summarized at functionality, value-proposition, and capabilities levels:

- **Functionality**

  When assigning a source of supply to an open purchase requisition, analytical information is embedded. The user can click the supplier record and review supplier details prior to assigning the supplier the business as in Figure 14.6.

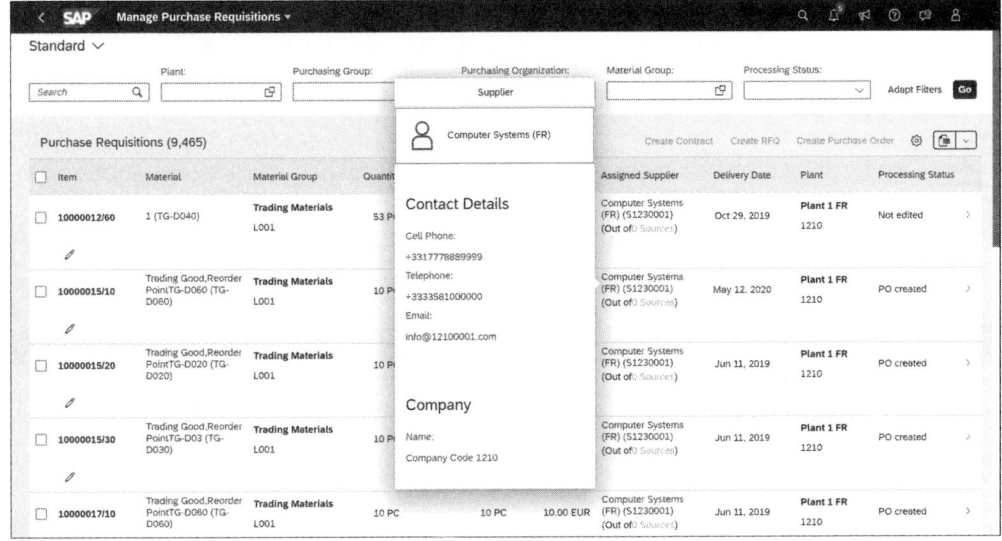

Figure 14.6 Source of Supply Drilldown

- **Value proposition**
  Provides the purchaser additional information (spend by supplier and supplier evaluation score) about available sources of supply to support the decision, as shown in Figure 14.7.

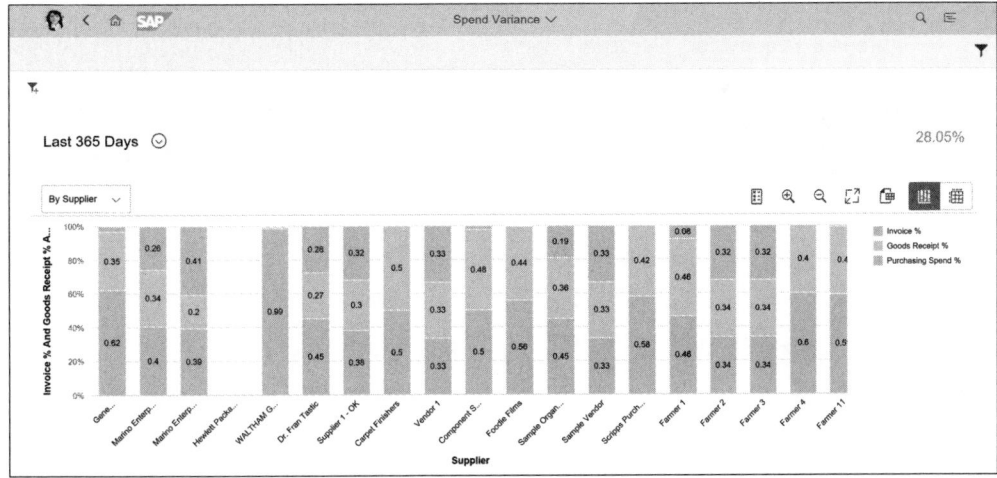

Figure 14.7 Spend by Supplier

- **Capabilities**
  For each valid source of supply, SAP S/4HANA Sourcing and Procurement shows additional information via embedded analytics (price, evaluation score, and spend).

One further enhancement as of SAP S/4HANA 1909 is the analytics capabilities in the Request for Quotation Types app. Here you can leverage real-time analysis about sourcing events and compare different types of sourcing events, such as internal and external ones, as well as external price requests, as in Figure 14.8.

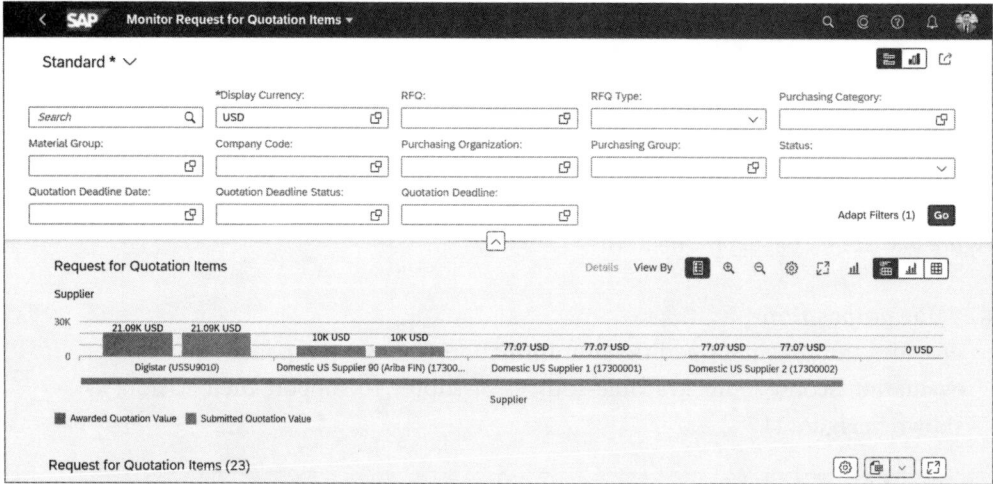

Figure 14.8 Request for Quotation Types

Both the SAP Ariba Strategic Sourcing and SAP Ariba Sourcing for Direct solutions offer additional sourcing and reporting capabilities. The key difference between the two versions is SAP Ariba Sourcing for Direct's support for direct materials sourcing and direct procurement document types, such as scheduling agreements.

14.4   Supplier Performance

Suppliers can also be evaluated in real time, providing instant insight into performance issues or improvements. From these reports, a user can then drill further into individual purchase orders and other documents, including surveys, to obtain a complete, real-time view. Figure 14.9 shows such a performance report for suppliers over time. Suppliers with steep drop-offs in recent performance need to be analyzed further for financial difficulties and supply chain relevance, and transactions correspondingly must be moved to more reliable performers.

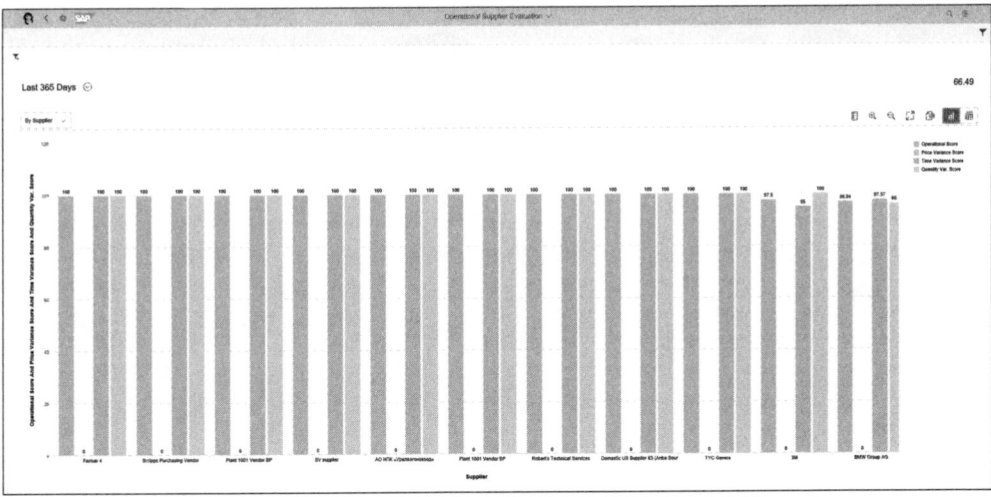

Figure 14.9 Supplier Valuation Scoring

Because these analytics capabilities are now available directly in the SAP ERP environment, they can be embedded at the document level for additional insight at the time of a transaction. This is the subject of the following section.

14.4.1   Purchasing Document Reports and Embedded Analytics

Monitoring purchasing documents in the SAP Business Suite in SAP ERP was done using SAP GUI transactions such as Transaction ME3L or ME4L, among others. With SAP S/4HANA, these legacy reports are transformed and harmonized using the SAP Fiori UX, with additional charts and visual filters to support the user in analyzing specific business situations, such as overdue orders or next-scheduled items on a scheduling agreement. The user can navigate seamlessly from table to object pages or download a report to Excel.

This embedded analytics approach extends to other transactions and documents in SAP S/4HANA Sourcing and Procurement, such as contracts. In the Monitor Purchase Contracts Items app, a user can navigate from line items in the contract to their release history and to an option to renew the contract. Without having to go into another app, the user can review the contract consumption and extend the validity or increase the value of the contract where required, as in Figure 14.10. In this app, a user also can see an overview of all of the contracts by spend type, select an individual contract to see how much remains of it, and then review consumption patterns over time to get an idea of fluctuations in spending on this contract.

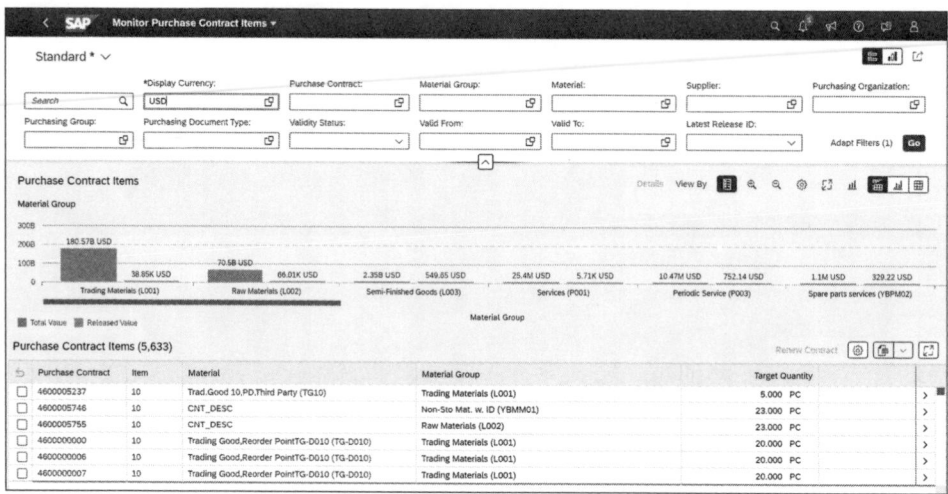

Figure 14.10 Monitor Purchase Contract Items App

As of SAP S/4HANA, on-premise version 1909, you can also schedule a job and store supplier evaluation scores on a specific date for reporting purposes in the Supplier Evaluation Score History app, as in Figure 14.11.

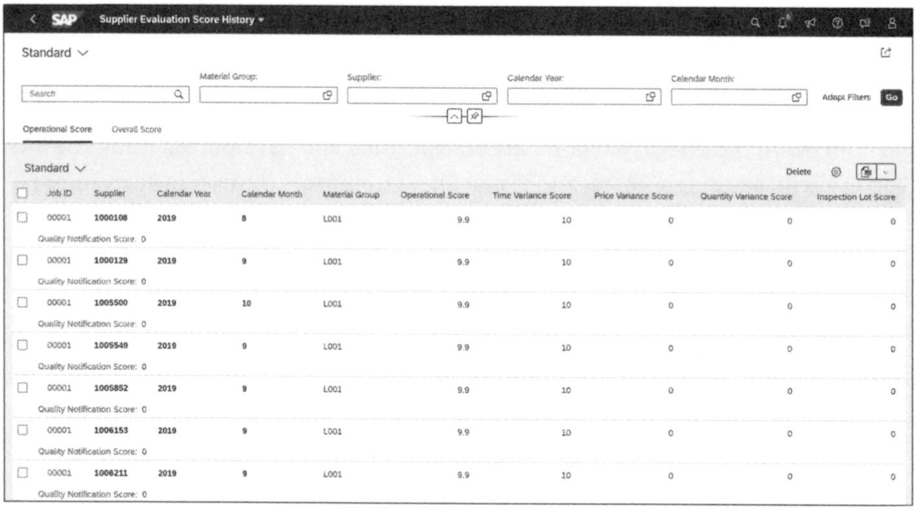

Figure 14.11 Supplier Evaluation Score History

In the Operational Supplier Evaluation KPI, there are two new views to visualize the top and bottom 10 suppliers and their corresponding purchase order net amounts.

14.4.2 Predictive Analytics

As mentioned earlier in this chapter, contract reporting uses predictive analytics capabilities in recent releases of SAP S/4HANA. Predictive analytics is an exciting new area, combining traditional historical data and AI-driven, algorithm-based analysis to drive further accuracy in forecasting.

In later releases of SAP S/4HANA Cloud (1705 onward) and SAP S/4HANA, SAP S/4HANA Sourcing and Procurement reporting also boasts predictive capabilities on top of providing the historical reporting, with capabilities to predict the following:

- Purchase order spend based on open purchase requisitions
- Predictive analytics for contract consumption

The next section looks at other reporting apps available in SAP S/4HANA.

14.5 Reporting

The UI platform for analytics and reporting in SAP S/4HANA is app-centric. The core dashboard apps for a typical buyer are shown in Figure 14.12.

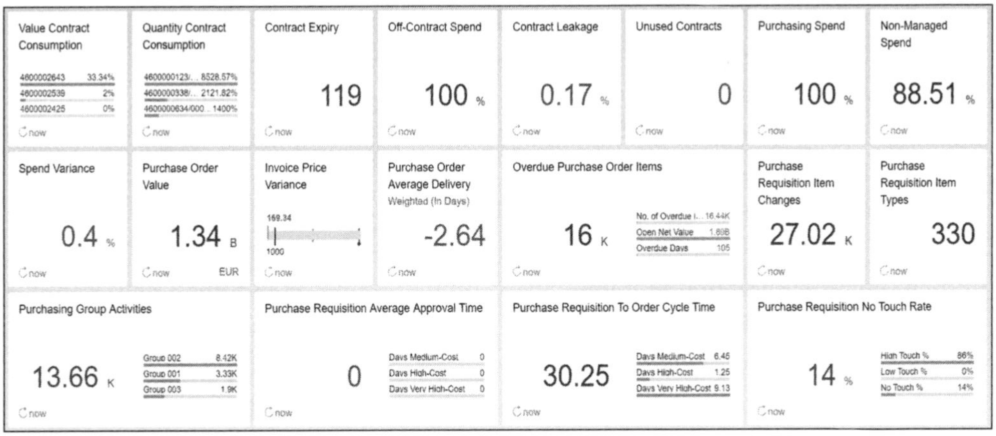

Value Contract Consumption	Quantity Contract Consumption	Contract Expiry	Off-Contract Spend	Contract Leakage	Unused Contracts	Purchasing Spend	Non-Managed Spend
4600002643 33.34% 4600002538 2% 4600002425 0%	4600000123/.. 8528.57% 4600000338/.. 2121.82% 4600000634/000 . 1400%	119	100 %	0.17 %	0	100 %	88.51 %

Spend Variance	Purchase Order Value	Invoice Price Variance	Purchase Order Average Delivery Weighted (in Days)	Overdue Purchase Order Items		Purchase Requisition Item Changes	Purchase Requisition Item Types
0.4 %	1.34 B EUR	168.34 ⊢———⊣ 1000 -2.64	-2.64	16 K	No. of Overdue i.. 16.44K Open Net Value 1.60B Overdue Days 105	27.02 K	330

Purchasing Group Activities	Purchase Requisition Average Approval Time	Purchase Requisition To Order Cycle Time	Purchase Requisition No Touch Rate
13.66 K Group 002 6.42K Group 001 3.33K Group 003 1.9K	0 Days Medium-Cost 0 Days High-Cost 0 Days Very High-Cost 0	30.25 Days Medium-Cost 6.46 Days High-Cost 1.25 Days Very High-Cost 9.13	14 % High Touch % 86% Low Touch % 0% No Touch % 14%

Figure 14.12 SAP S/4HANA Sourcing and Procurement Dashboard

These apps show actionable values on their respective tiles, whether for contract consumption, leakage, volumes, PO values, price variance, or order cycles. The user can set KPIs, and the apps refresh their data automatically. These analytics apps also can be refreshed manually without going into the app itself by clicking the **Now** icon in the lower-left-hand corner. Note that some measures appear in green and others in red. The red measures indicate that the KPI threshold set has been exceeded. A user thus is notified instantly in a simplified manner if something is going off target, without needing to enter the report itself.

SAP S/4HANA analytics and reporting apps extend the entire process flow for procure-to-pay. On the payment side, there are a comparable number of analytic options and reports, to provide accounts payable and invoice users with up-to-the-second insight into payables and cash flow position.

There is a variety of analytic apps for use by accounts payable roles in the SAP S/4HANA system. These apps include the following:

- **Aging Analysis**
  View payables across the organization by net due and overdue amounts

- **Overdue Payables**
  Check overdue amounts to your suppliers by company code, supplier group, supplier, and reason for payment block

- **Future Payables**
  Analyze payables for predefined due periods

- **Cash Discount Forecast**
  Predicts all available cash discounts in the short-term future period

- **Cash Discount Utilization**
  Allows for monitoring of cash discount utilization in real time

- **Days Payable Outstanding**
  Provides information to analyze and understand the accounts payable key performance indicator (KPI)

- **Invoice Processing Analysis**
  Reports on invoices processed in a period, such as the total number of posted invoices and posted line items

- **Supplier Payment Analysis (Manual and Automatic Payments)**
  Used to get insight into payments made in the last 365 days

- **Supplier Payment Analysis (Open Payments)**
  Used to get insight into open payments

Accounts payable apps provide up-to-the-second information and analysis in a consumable format to optimize account payable's understanding of key metrics and cash position. As with procurement apps, SAP S/4HANA boasts a wide array of analytics apps and approaches for AP that weren't available, or in some cases even possible, in previous versions of SAP ERP. If a user requires an app that isn't available as a standard part of SAP S/4HANA, there's an option to build your own app or extend the existing standard ones. The next section looks at the extensibility of the analytics apps.

14.6   Machine Learning

As detailed in Chapter 5, augmented decision-making is the latest type of analytics toolset to be provided in SAP S/4HANA. For operational procurement, these additions in the 1909 version include predicted delivery in the Monitor Purchase Order Items app. Here you can show orders that are likely to experience delays by using the **Predicted Delivery** field as shown in Figure 14.13.

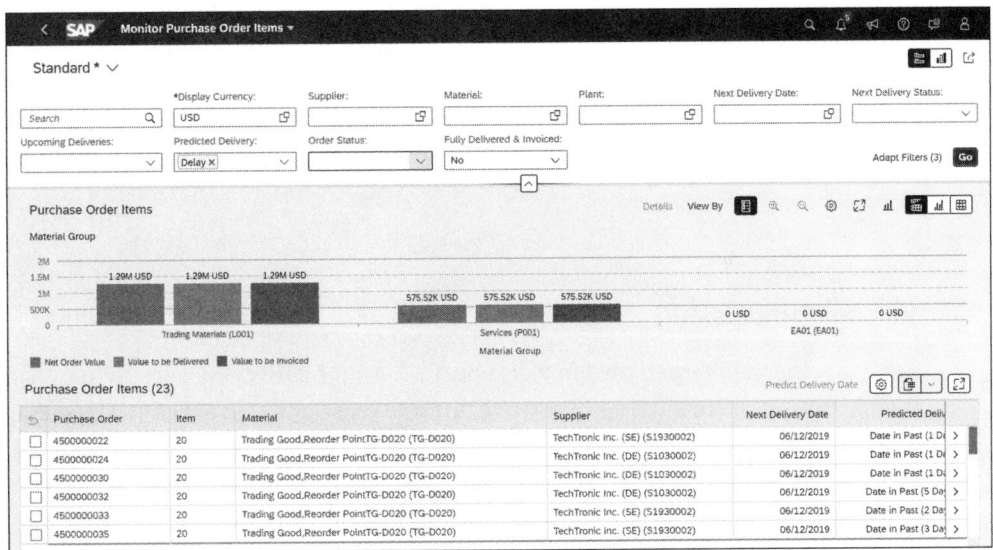

Figure 14.13 Monitor Purchase Order Items

In the My Inbox app, machine learning helps identify workflow items that can be approved with little risk, as in Figure 14.14, accelerating workflow efficiencies and saving time.

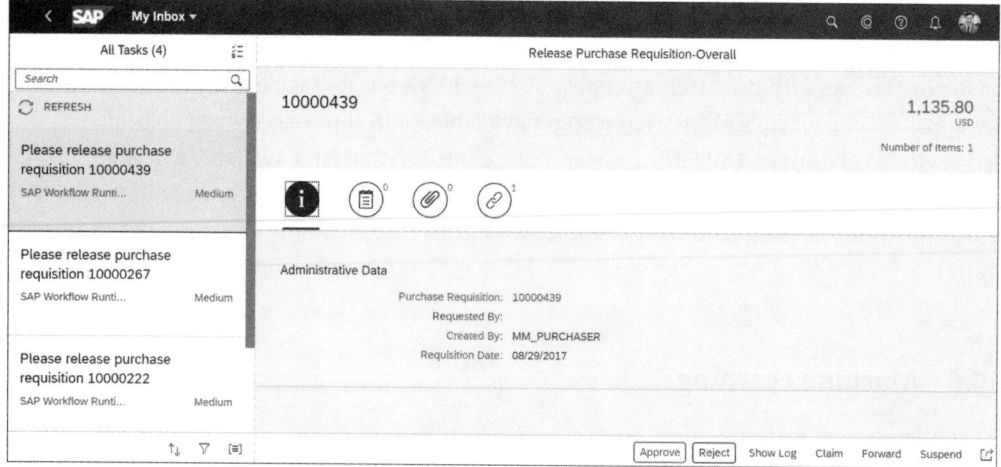

Figure 14.14 My Inbox App with Confidence Level

Much of this augmented-decision-making, machine-learning-based functionality relies on integration of SAP S/4HANA Sourcing and Procurement with SAP Leonardo. You can think of SAP Leonardo as a neural network, a system that mimics an animal brain by learning from examples and patterns, rather than using preprogramed rules and execution statements. This is an exploding area in technology at the moment. General neural network capabilities are growing at a speed 5-10 times faster than proposed by Moore's law, which stipulated that computing power doubles every two years.

14.7   Configuration

Analytics apps can be assigned in a dashboard form for a user or a general role that then gets assigned to a user group. Once this role is assigned, you then have several options for the reporting app for display and further analysis. The **Legend** button in analytics apps allows you to display or hide the legend. You can also zoom in and out and display the report in full screen mode. This is especially useful when communicating reports during meetings, akin to putting a PowerPoint deck in display mode and removing the extraneous control icons to show the audience the essential report. You can also display graphs as tables and export to Excel using these buttons.

14.7.1 Creating a Key Performance Indicator

You can set KPIs to allow dashboard tiles to visually alert business users that their KPI thresholds have been crossed (indicated with red). Green displays mean the KPI hasn't been crossed and the business metric/area is operating as per budget/plan. To set a KPI, you must have the analytics specialist role assigned.

With this role, you now have multiple tiles available and corresponding options for working with KPIs.

Using this role, complete the following steps to set up a KPI:

1. **Create a KPI**
   Define the data source and measure.

2. **Create an evaluation**
   Set evaluation criterion, prompt, values, and so on.

3. **Create a tile**
   Choose the drilldown type and catalog to be saved.

4. **Configure a drilldown**
   Set the dimensions/measures and visualization type.

14.7.2 Configuring Real-Time Reporting/Queries

There are a multitude of procurement-centric analytics apps available in stock SAP S/4HANA. There are also nonstandard, custom reports you can build, as well as other analytics tools in the deep and wide analytics tools portfolio from SAP that you can use for procurement reporting and analytics. There is also an SAP Fiori–based set of apps called Report Design Modeler apps available in SAP S/4HANA Cloud from version 1702 onward. These apps allow users of SAP S/4HANA Cloud to create and manage reports.

For SAP S/4HANA and SAP S/4HANA Cloud, there are two main types of users: key users, or IT users creating reports; and business users, who consume the reports. In some instances, business users also create the reports they're consuming, thereby playing both roles. Key users aren't quite technology users, but they aren't business users either. Key users build reports for business users with various tools and may span multiple departments and divisions of business users with their reports and analysis. To build reports, key users leverage the tools outlined in the following sections.

14.7.3   Exploring Virtual Data Model and Core Data Services in SAP S/4HANA

There are two SAP Fiori app browsers available for understanding and exploring the virtual data model (VDM) and core data services (CDS). The VDM is a structured representation of SAP S/4HANA database views. The VDM follows consistent modeling rules and provides direct access to SAP data via SQL and OData requests.

With an SAP HANA database, a paradigm for application development shifts from the app server directly to the database. To take advantage of this shift, SAP has introduced CDS, a data-modeling architecture that allows database models to be defined and consumed at the database level instead of the app server level, taking advantage of SAP HANA's speed. CDS views aren't persistent, as they are defined as the projection of other entities.

The query browser is part of a toolset aimed at business users, and the view browser is part of the kit for key users. Drilling into the query browser shows possible fields for query and details for running a selected analytical query with SAP Lumira, designer edition for multidimensional analysis. Once on the overview screen, you can select which query you want to review. On the detailed screen of the query, you can review the details of the selected analytic view, including its attributes and measures.

The view browser shows input fields and output of CDS views and can display the data of the selected CDS views. SAP Lumira, designer edition is part of the view browser app and supports analytic queries and multidimensional analysis.

The Custom CDS Views app allows you to take the following actions:

- Display a list of all predelivered data sources and existing custom CDS views.
- Preview details of available data sources and custom CDS views.
- Create a CDS view.

Similar to the Custom CDS Views app, you can also create custom analytical queries in the Custom Analytical Queries app, shown in Figure 14.15. In this app, you can take the following actions:

- Create and manage analytical queries.
- Create calculated or restricted measures.
- Create additional parameters.
- Define which dimensions will be shown in rows and columns or as free dimensions.

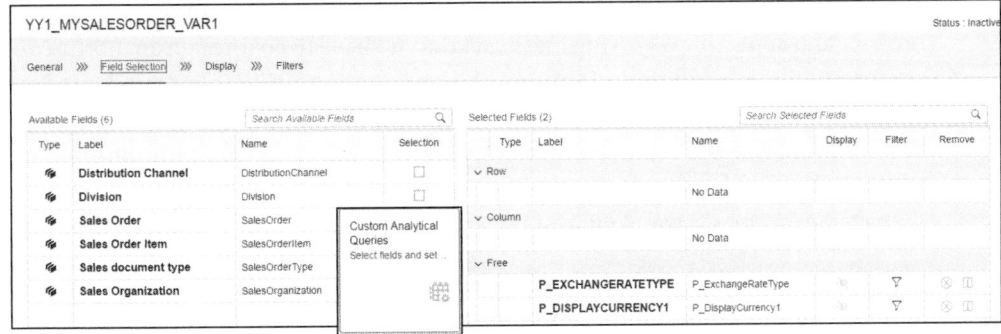

Figure 14.15 Custom Analytical Queries App

14.7.4   Integration of SAP S/4HANA with SAP Analytics Tools

There is also a portfolio of analytics solutions under the SAP BusinessObjects banner. Figure 14.16 outlines the various tools on offer for each type of user.

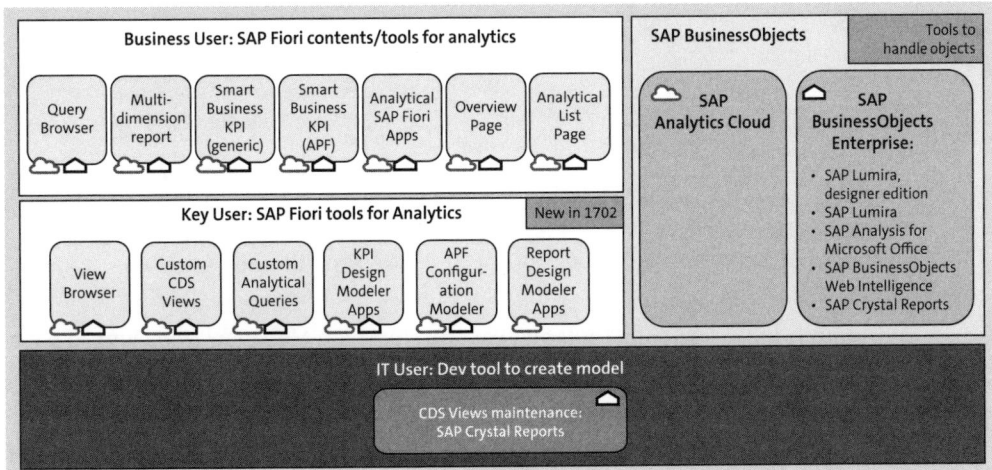

Figure 14.16 User Types for SAP BusinessObjects Tool Offerings

For further build-out of reports, key user tools such as custom CDS views and the view browser are provided to go spelunking down to the database level for wisdom nuggets and views, as well as custom report creation. The resulting reports can then be consumed by the business user.

The business user can set KPIs directly and also has direct control over the query browser and apps. This way, a business user doesn't have to go through an intermediary for day-to-day analysis. In Table 14.1, the key user and business user tools are further explained. SAP Analysis for Microsoft Office, for example, allows business users to directly analyze and report on data, whereas SAP Lumira, designer edition and SAP Lumira require a degree of expertise and specialization on the key user's part, who then creates reports for general business users.

SAP Analytics Solution	Description/Application
SAP Lumira, designer edition	SAP Lumira, designer edition supports IT users creating SAP Lumira, designer edition applications to be consumed by business users.
SAP Lumira	Key users leverage SAP Lumira to create analytic *stories* used by business users.
SAP Analysis for Microsoft Office	Business users analyze CDS views with SAP Analysis for Microsoft Office.
SAP BusinessObjects Web Intelligence	Key users and/or IT users leverage SAP BusinessObjects Web Intelligence to create reports using Query Panel and SAP BusinessObjects Web Intelligence document definition for business user consumption.
SAP Crystal Reports	IT users leverage SAP Crystal Reports to create reports for business users.

Table 14.1 SAP BusinessObjects Tools for SAP S/4HANA Reporting and Analytics

Multidimensional reporting tools such as the Floorplan Manager/Web Dynpro have the following characteristics in SAP S/4HANA:

- Dynamic analysis is possible—that is, slicing, dicing, and drilling down with many attributes.
- Analytical queries based on CDS views are used as a source.
- Web Dynpro objects are used in the backend system.
- No SAP Fiori app is available as a tool to create such reports directly.

The direction for these SAP Analytics reporting tools is to make them interoperable. For example, SAP Lumira and SAP BusinessObjects Explorer, both data-visualization tools, are being integrated, and you can export data from SAP Lumira, designer edition, a tool for building custom dashboards, into SAP Lumira. SAP Analysis for

Microsoft Office, a Microsoft-focused tool for enterprise performance management, is another analytics tool used in conjunction with Microsoft software.

> **Note**
>
> For the most recent interoperability updates for SAP Lumira and SAP Lumira, designer edition, visit *http://s-prs.co/500318*.

14.7.5   Integration with Cloud Applications

Especially for hybrid environments, in which you're leveraging both SAP S/4HANA as the digital core and SAP Ariba and/or SAP Fieldglass to drive your procurement transformation, you'll need to look at analytics and at where data is stored and analyzed.

SAP Fieldglass

SAP S/4HANA natively integrates with SAP Fieldglass. This integration can be activated via guided configuration; middleware is not required. If you do require mediated connectivity for technical or policy reasons, you can leverage the SAP Cloud Platform to mediate the data transfers. Master data can be transferred, including purchasing organizations and plants, as well as transactional data such as supplier-initiated invoices. As such, you can integrate and incorporate the supplier-initiated invoices in SAP Fieldglass into overall spend reporting and analysis apps found in the accounts payable and purchasing areas of SAP S/4HANA, outlined earlier in this chapter.

SAP Ariba

For SAP Ariba, you can integrate the spend management solutions bidirectionally, transferring data between SAP Ariba and SAP S/4HANA. The main mechanisms for this are as follows:

- Direct connectivity or mediated connectivity with SAP. Here, you implement SAP ABAP transports to send and receive SOAP-based data files directly to and from the SAP Ariba system. The mediated connectivity approach makes use of SAP Process Orchestration (SAP PO) to broker the transaction.

- Manual import and export of files from the spend management UI. This approach entails identifying what data you wish to export from SAP Ariba, locating the source using SAP Ariba resources and documentation, and exporting and importing the data manually into SAP S/4HANA's reporting tools and data structures.

14

- Automated file transfer using the SAP Ariba data transfer tool. You can automate the transfer of CSV files between spend management and external systems. The data transfer tool includes a command-line utility that facilitates CSV transfer in batch mode to SAP S/4HANA, as well as a DB connector, a command-line utility that connects the SAP Ariba data transfer tool with a JDBC-based ERP system.
- Real-time transfer using SOAP APIs. You can create webservices to transfer data between systems using SOAP-based protocols.

When deciding where to conduct an analysis, it helps to consolidate the data from all applicable transactions and systems. In the case of SAP Ariba, if your buyers are conducting most of their business in an SAP Ariba area, then it can make the most sense to extract SAP S/4HANA data and perform the comprehensive analysis in the cloud. Conversely, if you're running the procurement operations mostly in SAP S/4HANA, with some SAP Ariba solutions involved and SAP Fieldglass for contingent labor, it may make the most sense to bring the cloud data into SAP S/4HANA, then analyze it comprehensively using the apps and extensibility on offer.

14.8   Summary

The apps-based approach of SAP Fiori in SAP S/4HANA, the topic of the next chapter, extends to analytics, as does the real-time, in-system processing of analytics and reporting in the transacting system. For SAP S/4 HANA Sourcing and Procurement, there are extensive reporting and analytics apps on offer from the initial stage of the process all the way through to accounts payable. In addition, machine learning powers predictive analytics that can aid you in real time for decisions during an individual transaction, such as supplier analysis predicting on-time delivery for an order, and comprehensive analysis, such as workflow analysis for the least risky approvals in an approver's queue. Finally, users can extend their views and analysis via SAP BusinessObjects tools and integrated tools, as well as build customized reports. Integrated tools such as the Report Design Modeler apps in SAP S/4HANA Cloud, browsers, and customization options create a further platform from which to drive real-time insight and, ultimately, better performance in SAP S/4HANA analytics and reporting in general and in SAP S/4HANA Sourcing and Procurement in particular. Next, we'll review SAP S/4HANA integration approaches with SAP Ariba and SAP Fieldglass.

Chapter 15

Integrating SAP S/4HANA with SAP Ariba and SAP Fieldglass

This chapter explains some of the core integration topics for SAP S/4HANA Sourcing and Procurement with SAP Ariba and SAP Fieldglass solutions, providing approach overviews and process definitions.

As discussed in previous chapters, SAP S/4HANA Sourcing and Procurement has expanding integration options with other SAP Cloud solutions—SAP Ariba and SAP Fieldglass in particular. Most large enterprises run "hybrid" models today with SAP S/4HANA. Similar to its meaning in plant terminology, hybrid computing environments have both on-premise and cloud systems grafted together to form a comprehensive solution taking advantage of the strengths of the cloud and core solutions, thus ensuring core master data updates and process integration. For many processes and solution areas in SAP Ariba, financials and master data, such as supplier data, reside in the connected SAP S/4HANA digital core environment. SAP S/4HANA also relies on SAP Ariba and SAP Fieldglass to address supplier collaboration and third-party service provider resource management. To make all of the handoffs and data updates seamless between the two environments, there are multiple integration points and approaches. In addition to indirect procurement areas, SAP Ariba also supports direct procurement via SAP Ariba Supply Chain Collaboration for Buyers. This chapter outlines the various tools available for integrating SAP Ariba and SAP Fieldglass with SAP S/4HANA, as well as the key procurement integration scenarios and processes applicable to these types of environments.

15.1 SAP Ariba Integration Projects and Connectivity Options

Every integration project is different. Like a fingerprint, no two customer datasets are the same. Each integration must take into account its customizations and unique customer landscape. SAP S/4HANA Sourcing and Procurement often will have built-out procurement processes on the planned procurement side for direct procurement in manufacturing and production operations running in SAP S/4HANA. With regard to integration, many standard integrations are now native between SAP S/4HANA and SAP Ariba using prebuilt webservices, whereas others still require a build out using the core integration platforms and technologies available. As in Figure 15.1, the main integration technologies are SAP Process Orchestration/SAP Process Integration (SAP PO/SAP PI), SAP Cloud Platform Integration, and SAP Ariba Cloud Integration Gateway. SAP Ariba Cloud Integration Gateway is the platform-to-be for all future integration approaches and investment at SAP Ariba, whereas SAP Cloud Platform Integration and SAP PO continue to be used at many customers within the integration layer.

> **Note**
>
> Before embarking on an integration effort, please visit the SAP Best Practices area for the latest SAP Ariba integration documentation by scenario and SAP Ariba solution, at *http://s-prs.co/500319*. This link takes you to all available integration packages for SAP Ariba. To visit the general SAP Best Practices area, go to *https://rapid.sap.com/bp/*.

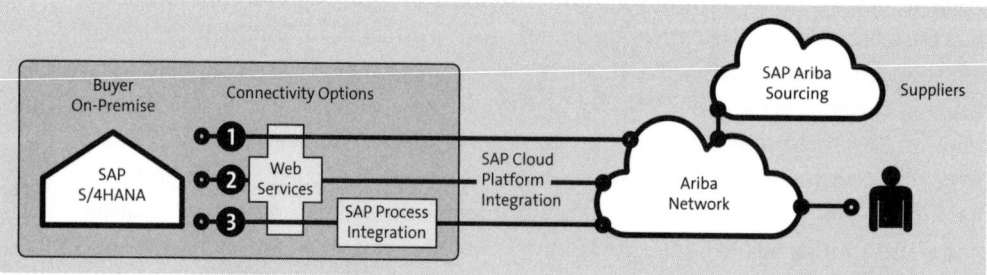

Figure 15.1 SAP S/4HANA Integration with SAP Ariba Solutions: Connectivity Options

The general connectivity options between SAP S/4HANA and SAP Ariba focus on the Ariba Network and SAP Ariba Sourcing. Webservice-based connections exist for the following:

- SAP Ariba Strategic Sourcing
- Purchase order to invoice automation between Ariba Network and SAP S/4HANA
- SAP Ariba Payment and SAP Ariba Discount Collaboration
- SAP Ariba guided buying

In addition to integrating directly via webservices, integration can also support mediation for the webservice via cloud integration or SAP PO (SAP PI mediation is possible for on-premise implementations of SAP S/4HANA). The main supported documents are as follows:

- RFQ and quote
- Purchase order
- Order confirmation
- Advance ship notice
- Goods receipt notice

- Supplier invoice
- Invoice update
- Payment proposal
- Proposal acceptance
- Remittance advice and update

The data flows between SAP S/4HANA and SAP Ariba are thus bidirectional, whether via SAP Ariba Cloud Integration Gateway underpinned by SAP Cloud Platform Integration, SAP PI/SAP PO, or directly via webservices connectivity, as in Figure 15.2.

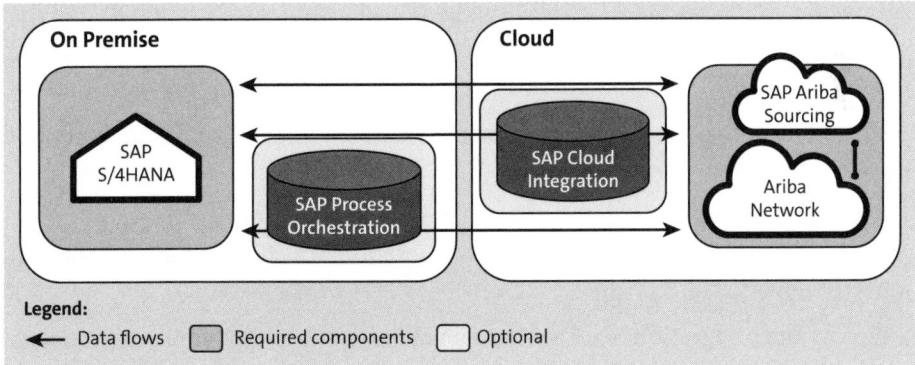

Figure 15.2 System Landscape: Data Flows

There are thus multiple integration scenarios applicable or tangential to the SAP S/4HANA to SAP Ariba integration topic. The deciding factors include the following:

- **Dominant system landscape**
  Is the SAP S/4HANA environment on premise or in the cloud? What are the plans for transforming SAP S/4HANA to a cloud environment?

- **Prepackaged content availability**
  What is the integration path requiring the least amount of custom work?

- **Total cost of ownership (TCO)**
  How much investment will be required to maintain the linkages and integrations going forward? Are there additional upgrades in either SAP Ariba or SAP S/4HANA that can impact the integration and require rework?

- **Go-live timelines**
  Which approach will yield the quickest integration?

- **Connectivity options**
  Are there firewall constraints or a lack thereof, which can influence or impact the options available?

A thorough analysis of the processes/solution areas you wish to integrate between SAP Ariba and SAP S/4HANA also should be conducted. There are four core solution areas in particular to evaluate. First, the PO/IV automation with SAP S/4HANA and the Ariba Network. This scenario is the most common and can yield immediate results and ROI, as transactions are issued out of SAP S/4HANA and processed in the Ariba Network, then finally sent back to SAP S/4HANA.

The second integration area is SAP Ariba Strategic Sourcing connected to SAP S/4HANA. If something needs to be sourced during a transaction in SAP S/4HANA, you can leverage the rich sourcing functionality in SAP Ariba Strategic Sourcing to find the optimal supplier(s) and then revert the item back to SAP S/4HANA for concluding the transaction (or convert to a purchase order in SAP Ariba, depending on your process).

The third integration scenario is linking to SAP S/4HANA for payment processing and discount management in SAP Ariba.

Finally, for direct procurement scenarios between SAP S/4HANA and the Ariba Network, you have SAP Ariba Supply Chain Collaboration, which has additional integration requirements.

Regarding the integration team itself, to underpin a successful implementation, a strong integration lead is required. The integration lead role requires a consultant or subject matter expert with a solid understanding of the master data and transactional integration points and methods, as well as the vernacular of both SAP S/4HANA (ABAP, master data, transaction codes, tables) and SAP Ariba (including topics such as SAP Ariba Cloud Integration Gateway, commerce automation, SAP Ariba Strategic Sourcing, SAP Ariba Buying and Invoicing, SAP Ariba guided buying, SAP Ariba Catalog, SAP Ariba Supply Chain Collaboration, and the Ariba Network). Often an SAP customer will assume that the integration with SAP S/4HANA is included in SAP Ariba's subscription or that it will be handled as part of the delivery of SAP Ariba. Rather than assuming and hoping that the integration will fall into place, this area needs to be defined, scoped, and understood by all of the project participants. Even with a standard, native integration between SAP S/4HANA and SAP Ariba and/or SAP Fieldglass, the customer data fingerprint may be unique enough to require further integration.

The project should eventually reach a cutover stage, in which the newly built integrations are moved to production. Here, a clear strategy for the impacted legacy systems, such as SAP SRM, is required to minimize business disruptions. A poorly planned strategy, or not having a cutover strategy altogether, can cause significant issues on an SAP Ariba integration project, especially a project impacting financials. Some other common issues affecting integration projects include the following:

- Understaffed project teams. Not budgeting adequate resources for both the project team and the customer's IT department (ABAP developers, SAP PI experts, and SAP Basis team members are key participants to have on board). Taking shortcuts and hoping SAP Ariba Support or SAP Ariba Expert Care will bail out the project if there are difficulties will likely cause delays and frustration.

- Not being on the latest SAP Ariba Cloud Integration Gateway or hotfix release. Not being on the latest hotfix release can cause delays when attempting to resolve an error with SAP Ariba Support. SAP Ariba Support expects your organization to be on the latest hotfix release.

Perhaps the most popular integration between SAP Ariba and an SAP S/4HANA environment is for purchasing document exchanges between SAP S/4HANA Sourcing and Procurement and the Ariba Network, as discussed in the next section.

15.2 SAP Ariba

Even prior to being acquired by SAP, SAP Ariba had long been integrating agnostically with backend ERP systems. This tradition of ERP integration continues with the latest, most comprehensive integration platform, called the SAP Ariba Cloud Integration Gateway. You can download SAP Ariba Cloud Integration Gateway via the SAP Service Marketplace as an add-on via *service.sap.com*. Standard documentation and bug fixes are delivered via SAP Notes at *support.sap.com*. SAP Ariba Cloud Integration Gateway provides self-service tools to quickly configure, test, and extend processes, incorporate automated upgrades via Software Update Manager, and monitor with tools such as SAP Solution Manager to provide an integration solution that fits seamlessly in your SAP landscape, thus minimizing TCO expenses and ensuring a smooth transaction flow.

Many of the linkages are also built out directly in SAP S/4HANA. Depending on your approach and requirements, there are numerous options available.

15

15.2.1   Key Integration Technologies

The software required for enabling these integrations is as follows:

- You must have an SAP Ariba Buyer account, which is included in the SAP Ariba Purchase Order/Invoice Automation, SAP Collaborative Commerce, and SAP Ariba Collaborative Finance subscriptions.
- For direct connectivity via the prebuilt webservices, no further software is required.
- For mediated webservice connectivity via SAP Cloud Platform Integration, an SAP Cloud Platform Integration subscription is required.
- For mediated webservice connectivity via SAP Process Orchestration (PI), SAP NetWeaver 7.5 Process Integration (or higher) with Ariba Network Adapter for Ariba Network integration (CI-9 or higher) is required.

In addition to a cloud/on-premise integration, an organization may also need to integrate cloud solutions with other cloud solutions as per Figure 15.3.

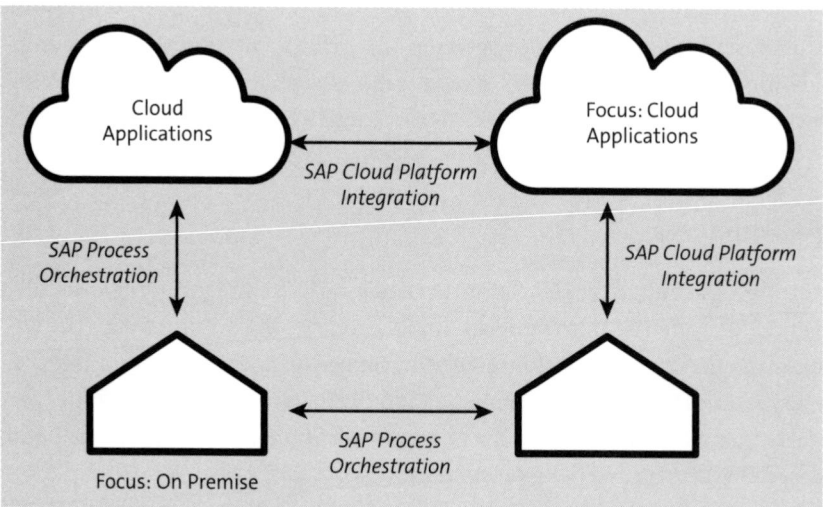

Figure 15.3 SAP Integration Paths

For integrating cloud to cloud, an organization may use the SAP Cloud Platform Integration. In turn, the same can be used to then integrate to an on-premise instance, negating the need for additional middleware such as SAP PI. In this scenario, the organization is better off choosing a single middleware platform if possible, and this would sway the argument towards SAP Cloud Platform Integration over SAP PI.

15.3   SAP Ariba Cloud Integration Gateway

The latest and future go-to integration approach for SAP Ariba is the SAP Ariba Cloud Integration Gateway. Released in 2018, SAP Ariba Cloud Integration Gateway seeks to unify and standardize the various approaches and existing integrations between SAP S/4HANA and SAP Ariba. SAP Ariba Cloud Integration Gateway has a large base upon which to build, with over 200 integrations already in existence between SAP Ariba and SAP ERP. These integrations split roughly down the middle between Ariba Network and SAP Ariba Procurement and Sourcing applications.

15.3.1   SAP Cloud Platform Integration and the SAP Ariba Cloud Integration Gateway

The SAP Ariba Cloud Integration Gateway leveraging SAP Cloud Platform Integration provides a fast, flexible solution to integrate with backend systems, trading partners, and SAP Ariba solutions. SAP Ariba Cloud Integration Gateway is the go-to integration platform for both Ariba Network and SAP Ariba solutions, as well as SAP Cloud applications and on-premise solutions. SAP Ariba Cloud Integration Gateway will serve as the comprehensive linchpin in the future for these preexisting and upcoming integrations between SAP S/4HANA and SAP Ariba, as well as for non-SAP backend systems.

SAP S/4HANA for central procurement is the SAP-recommended and roadmapped approach for connecting and coordinating purchasing activities in multiple ERP systems. However, SAP Ariba Cloud Integration Gateway can also connect a cloud environment to multiple backend ERPs, both SAP S/4HANA and SAP ERP, directly via the SAP Cloud Connector or mediated via your SAP PI or SAP Cloud Platform Integration middleware layer.

There are three main areas in SAP Ariba Cloud Integration Gateway: the backend SAP S/4HANA area, the integration layer, and the SAP Ariba cloud solutions area.

The SAP Ariba Cloud Integration Gateway area provides the following:

- Simple setup supported by configuration wizard
- Mappings for all integration scenarios of SAP Ariba Cloud Integration version 9 including:
  - Ariba Network
  - SAP Ariba Strategic Sourcing Portfolio
  - SAP Ariba Procurement Portfolio

- Multi-ERP setup by system ID/realm ID, meaning multiple backend systems can be connected via the same SAP Ariba Cloud Integration Gateway instance to SAP Ariba Solutions
- Support for conditional routing
- Test central with automation
- One-click deployment to production
- Transaction tracking

On the SAP Ariba solutions side, once you've enabled SAP Ariba Cloud Integration Gateway as an admin and an end point, you can push as well as pull data from the backend systems, leveraging asynchronous webservices and enhanced message contents to avoid having to look up a message in SAP.

Setting up SAP Ariba Cloud Integration Gateway entails three steps. First, you configure the buy-side account for SAP Ariba Cloud Integration Gateway and install and configure the SAP Ariba Cloud Integration add-on for SAP ERP and SAP S/4HANA. Next, you extend it using the extension framework in the add-on interfaces in SAP; the custom eXtensible Stylesheet Language Transformations (XSLTs) can be used for additional data mapping. Finally, you test the integration using the predefined scripts and any customized test cases required. Viewed in more detail in Figure 15.4, the SAP Ariba Cloud Integration Gateway setup can entail five individual steps, with the installation, configuration (both technical and scenario configuration), extensions/enhancements, and test/go-live comprising individual steps.

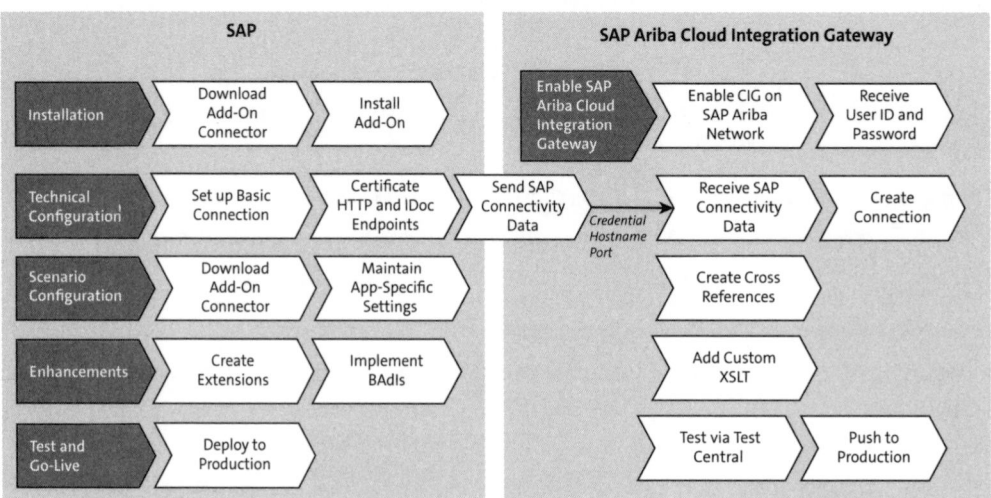

Figure 15.4 SAP Ariba Cloud Integration Gateway Setup

There are multiple systems and steps to consider for integrating SAP S/4HANA. The main systems are the backend, SAP Ariba Cloud Integration Gateway, and the respective solutions within SAP Ariba. Given the robust integration layers available to the user, you are now able to perform a wide variety of integration tasks and permutations in the backend system, SAP Ariba Cloud Integration Gateway, and the receiving SAP Ariba system. This section begins with the configuration of the backend SAP S/4HANA and SAP ERP, moving then to the SAP Ariba Cloud Integration Gateway, and SAP Ariba solution-specific configuration.

15.3.2 Configuring the SAP Ariba Cloud Integration Gateway

The technical and scenario configuration can be accessed in SAP S/4HANA Transaction SPRO under **Integration with Other SAP Components • SAP Ariba Cloud Integration Gateway • Global Settings** for the technical configuration and **Integration with Other mySAP Components • Ariba Cloud Integration • Ariba Network Integration** for scenario configuration, as in Figure 15.5.

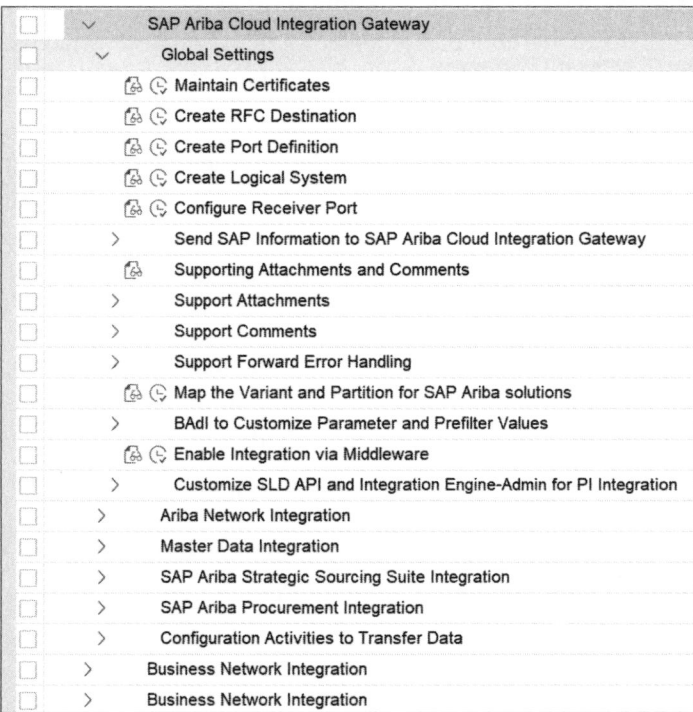

Figure 15.5 SAP Ariba Cloud Integration Gateway Configuration in SAP S/4HANA

Although configuration is not the focus of this chapter, you can leverage this area in the SAP S/4HANA IMG to drive your configuration topics.

15.3.3   SAP Ariba Strategic Sourcing Integration

A key integration option for customers running SAP S/4HANA and looking to take advantage of SAP Ariba cloud solutions to bolster their procurement operations is SAP Ariba Strategic Sourcing integration. Here, a user can generate a request for a quotation, information, purchase or other solicitation type (collectively called an *RFx*) and send this RFx for sourcing in the SAP Ariba Strategic Sourcing tool. SAP Ariba Strategic Sourcing enables the customer suppliers on the Ariba Network to seamlessly collaborate on bidding and identifying the best option for the customer's needs, and then allows for ordering and fulfillment of the item to occur within the SAP ERP and/or SAP Ariba environment. SAP Ariba provides the crucial linkage to and mediation with a huge array of suppliers during this process, which an ERP-based sourcing event would not be able to replicate easily alone, as connecting to suppliers and setting up protocols is simply too laborious to scale.

The integration connects the digital core of SAP S/4HANA with SAP Ariba Strategic Sourcing, with the following key process steps (see Figure 15.6):

1. The purchaser creates an RFQ for SAP S/4HANA purchase requisitions and automatically sends this RFQ to SAP Ariba Strategic Sourcing, triggering a sourcing request.

2. The sourcing manager in SAP Ariba Strategic Sourcing accesses their worklist and converts sourcing requests into sourcing projects, inviting suppliers to bid.

3. Suppliers process the RFQ.

4. The sourcing manager can then monitor sourcing projects and supplier responses, as well as support projects that result in (reverse) auctions or requests for quotations, by adding suppliers to the Ariba Network as required.

5. Finally, once the sourcing process is complete, the sourcing manager can award one or more bids in SAP Ariba Strategic Sourcing. These awarded bids are sent automatically or directly by the sourcing manager to SAP S/4HANA, where purchase orders and/or contracts are created as follow-on documents for the original RFQ.

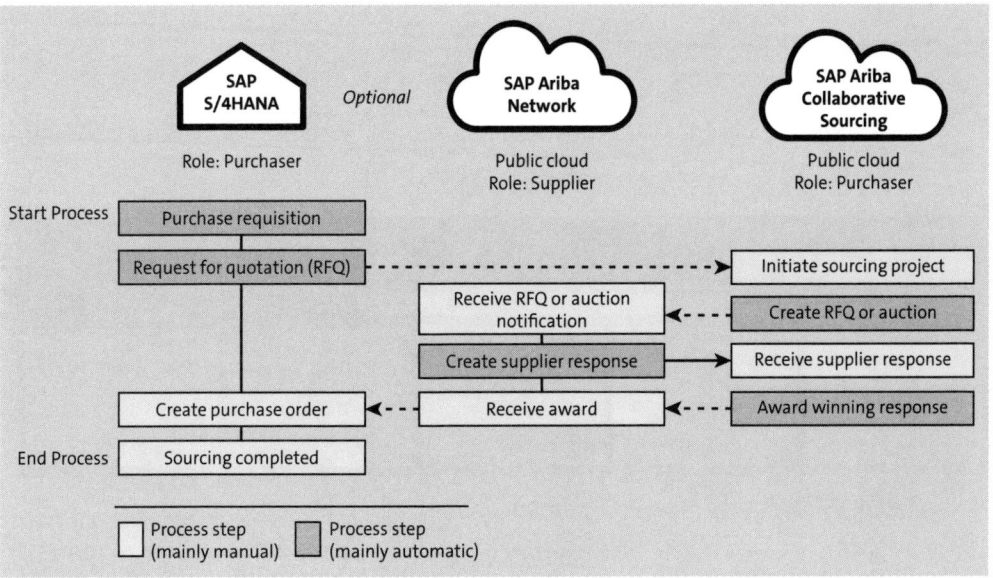

Figure 15.6 Digital Core SAP S/4HANA to SAP Ariba Strategic Sourcing to Ariba Network and Back

The prerequisites for starting the SAP Ariba Strategic Sourcing integration steps in SAP Ariba Cloud Integration Gateway are as follows:

1. You must have an enabled SAP Ariba Strategic Sourcing realm connected to an active buyer account and valid trading buyer/supplier relationship on the Ariba Network.

2. A buyer account must have access to SAP Ariba Cloud Integration Gateway and be set up to send documents back and forth from SAP Ariba Cloud Integration Gateway.

3. You need access to the SAP Marketplace to download the SAP Ariba Cloud Integration Gateway add-on for SAP ERP or SAP S/4HANA.

4. Certificates and add-ons must be configured in SAP ERP or SAP S/4HANA.

5. A sourcing realm needs to be added to a buyer org. under **Feature Availability** by SAP Ariba Customer Support.

Note

For SAP Ariba Strategic Sourcing integration, you only need to enable the SAP Ariba Cloud Integration Gateway through the SAP Ariba Strategic Sourcing realm. For transactions such as quote requests, awards, and contracts, you need to enable the SAP Ariba Cloud Integration Gateway from the Ariba Network as well.

When a buyer logs into SAP Ariba Sourcing, the first area they see is their dashboard, as in Figure 15.7.

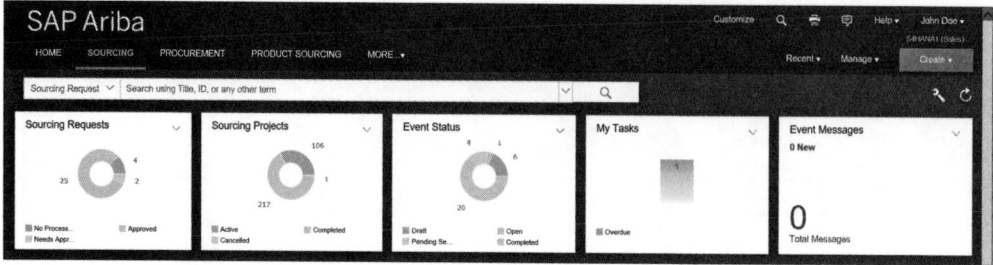

Figure 15.7 SAP Ariba Sourcing Requests

From the dashboard, the buyer can then search for the RFP as in Figure 15.8.

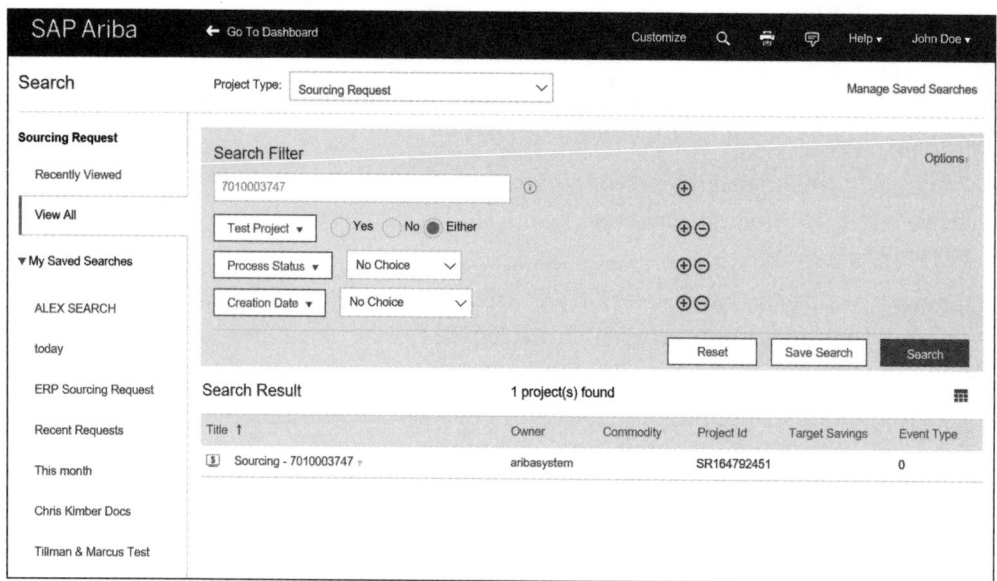

Figure 15.8 SAP Ariba Sourcing: Search

Two actions need to be completed prior to issuing the RFP. The first is preparing the RFP for issuing, and the second is an approval step. You access these steps under **Tasks** as shown in Figure 15.9:

1. In selecting the first task for preparing the sourcing of the request, you mark this step as complete once you've reviewed it. There is also the option to mark this as started as an interim status. Once you've reviewed the two steps and the approvals are completed, your RFP is ready to be converted to an SAP Ariba Sourcing RFP as shown in Figure 15.10.

2. With the tasks complete, you then select **Create** and convert the sourcing request as an SAP Ariba Sourcing RFP as shown in Figure 15.11.

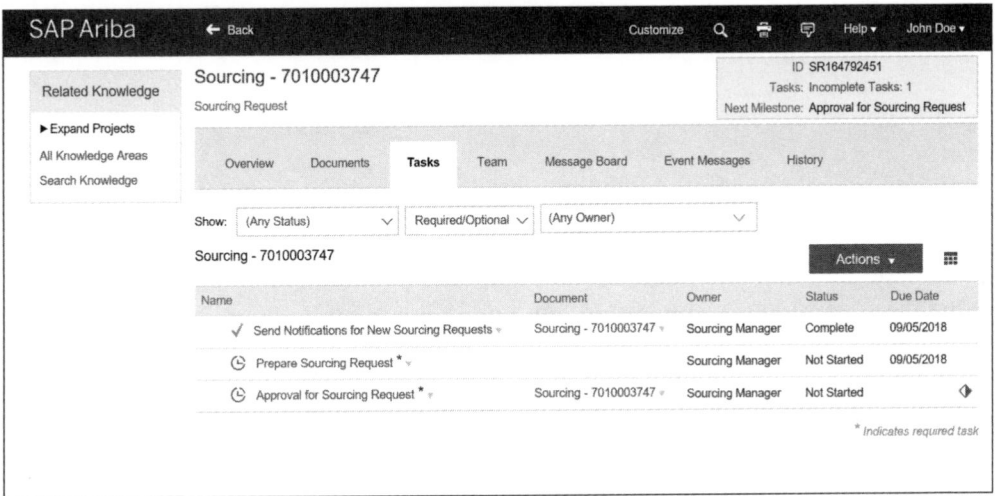

Figure 15.9 SAP Ariba Sourcing: Tasks

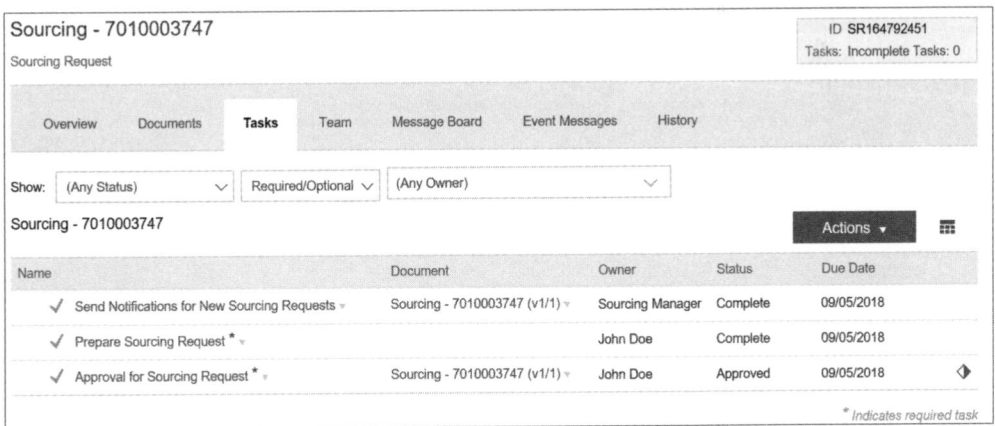

Figure 15.10 SAP Ariba Sourcing Tasks Completed

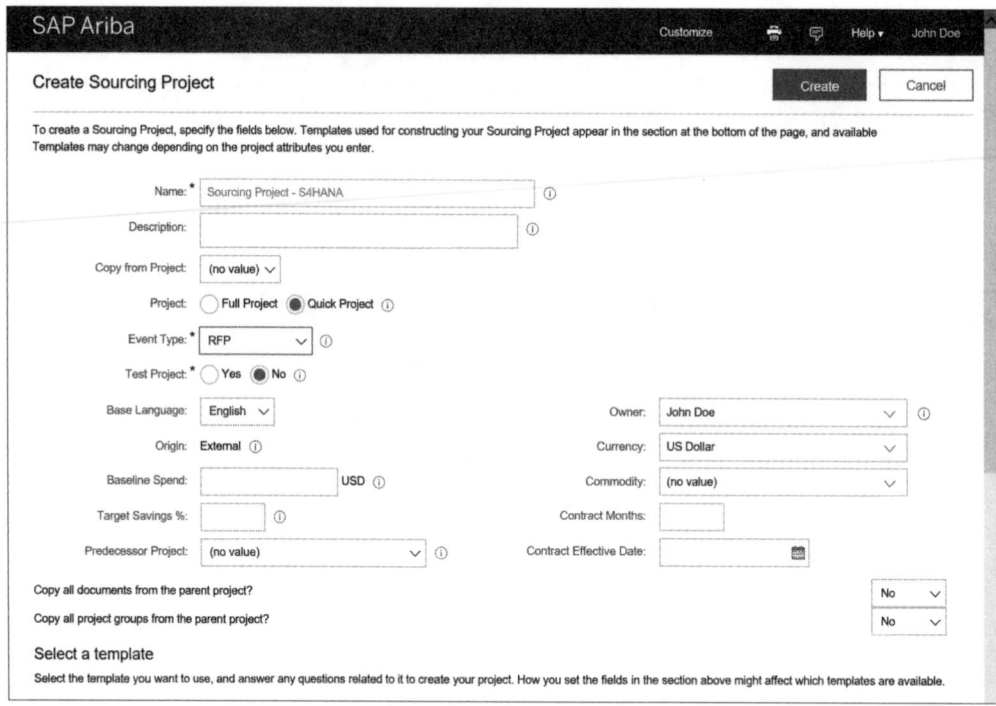

Figure 15.11 Create Sourcing Project

3. The next step is to add bidders to the RFP event as shown in Figure 15.12.

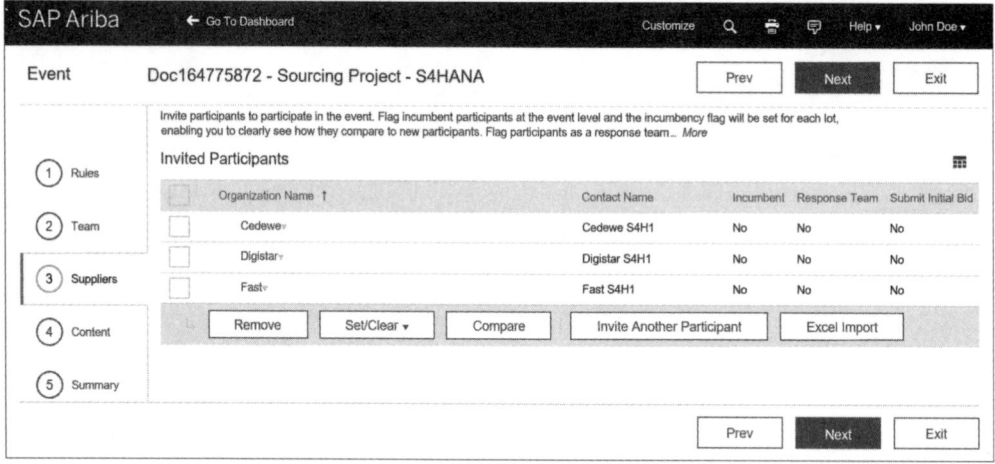

Figure 15.12 Adding Bidders

During these steps for creating an RFP, you also can define and refine the team and the content, finally arriving at the summary page as shown in Figure 15.13.

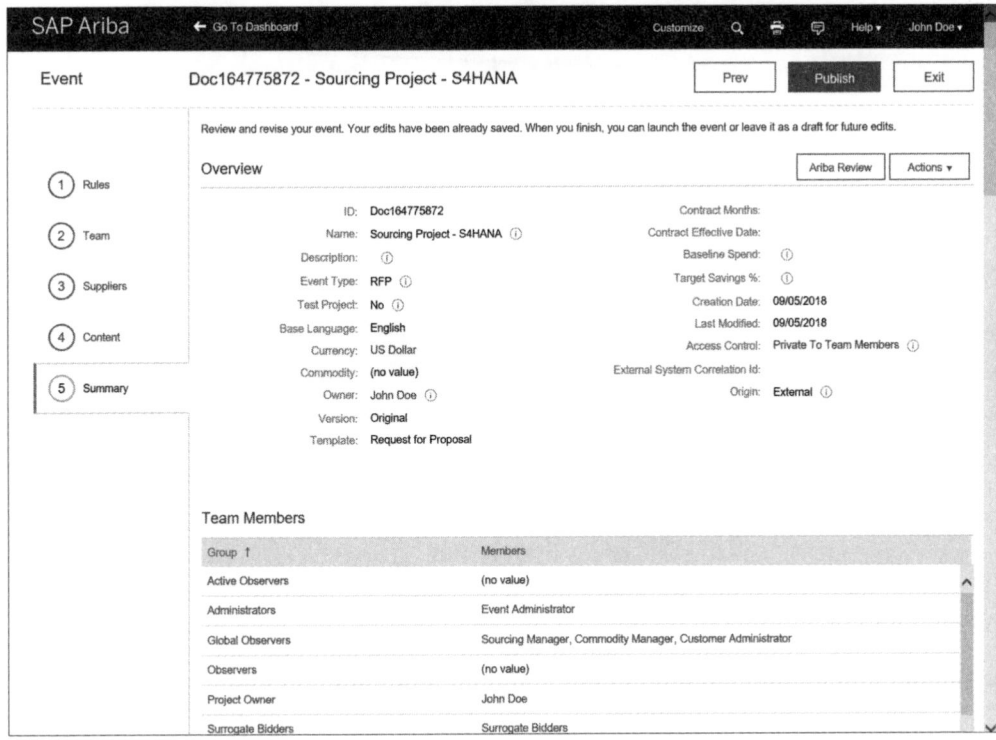

Figure 15.13 Publish RFP

Once you've published the RFP, suppliers can review the request in their Ariba Network area.

The invited supplier is able to review the RFP by logging into their supplier portal on the Ariba Network at supplier.ariba.com. On their home page, a supplier has a dropdown menu that includes their proposals, as shown in Figure 15.14.

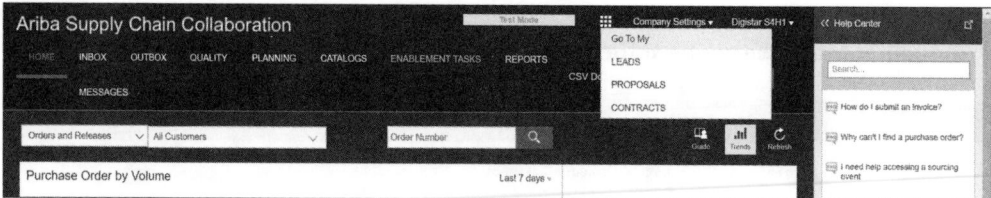

Figure 15.14 SAP Ariba Supplier Bidding

The **Proposals** section lists the bids in **Completed**, **Pending Selection** (where the supplier has already put in a bid), and **Preview** (new RFxs) statuses, as shown in Figure 15.15.

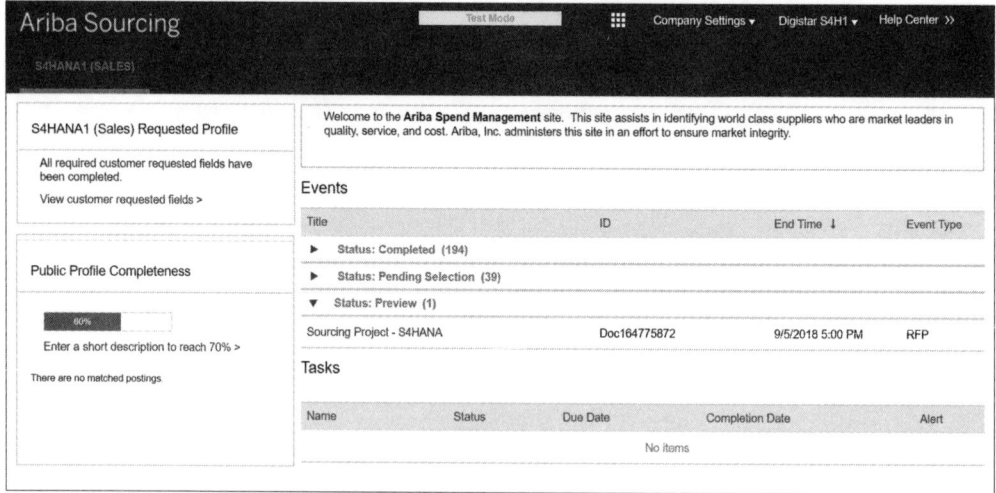

Figure 15.15 Supplier

4. Once the supplier has selected and opened the invitation, the supplier can either decline to participate, or review the prerequisites as shown in Figure 15.16 and accept them as shown in Figure 15.17.

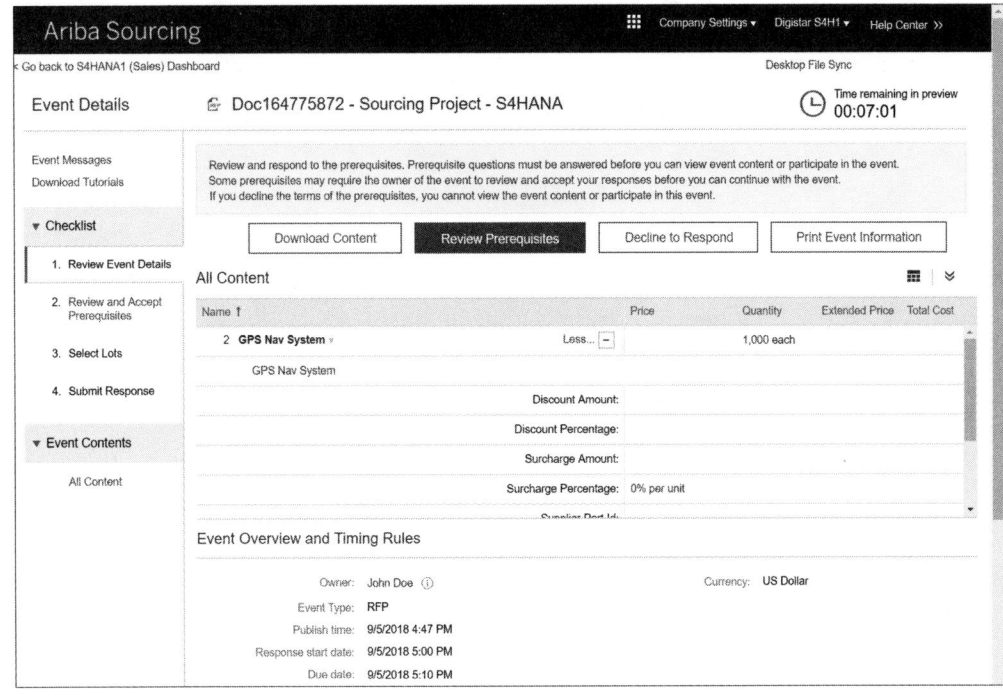

Figure 15.16 Review Prerequisites

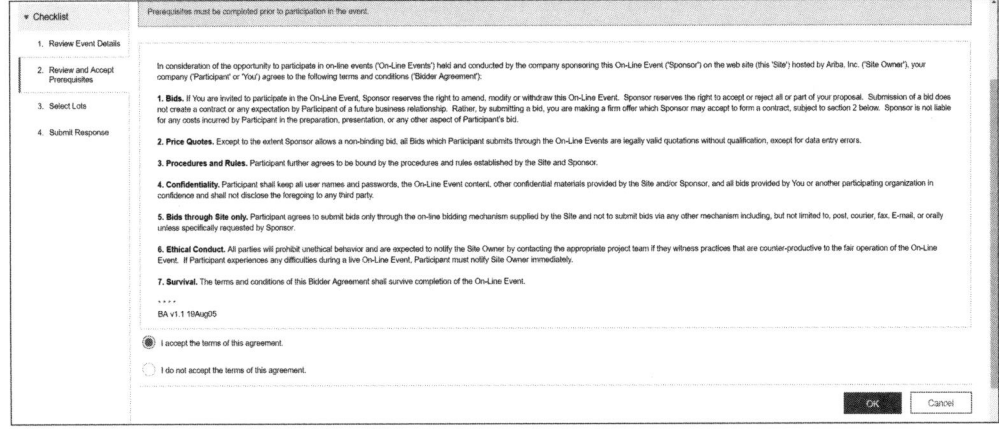

Figure 15.17 Accept Prerequisites Step

5. The next step is to place the bid, which is called *selecting lots* in SAP Ariba. This allows the supplier to select some or all of the items requested in the RFx and

respond as shown in Figure 15.18. During the response, the supplier can also send a message to the customer.

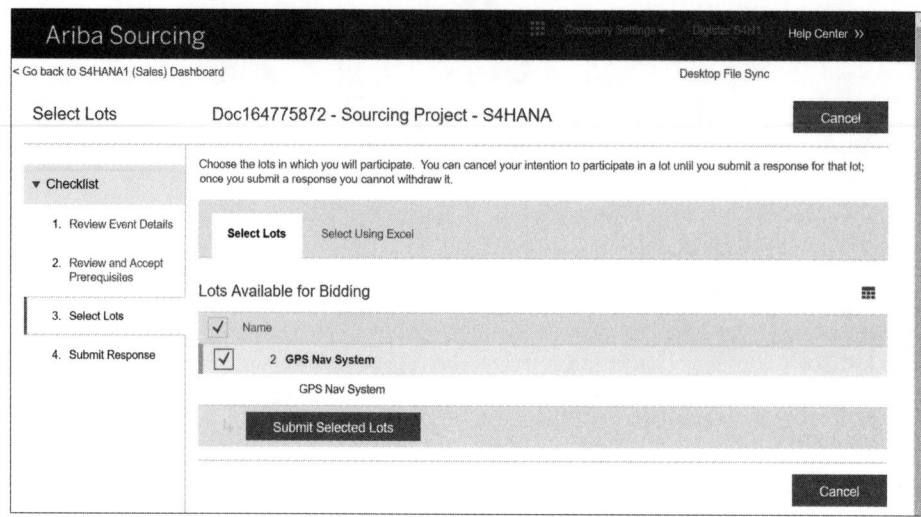

Figure 15.18 Select Lots

6. Next, the buyer maintains the bids as in Figure 15.19.

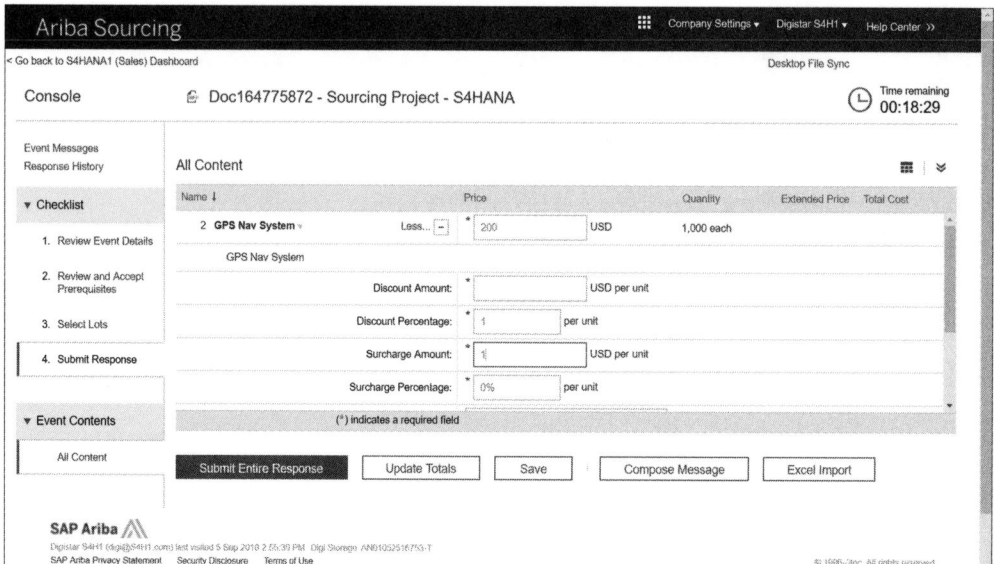

Figure 15.19 Maintain Bid

The buyer then consolidates and compares the bids, selecting, presumably, the best bid that meets their target goals for quality, timing, and price.

Upon submission of the bid by the supplier as shown in Figure 15.19, the bids revert back to the customer for review. As shown in Figure 15.20, it is possible to compare the bids side by side. You can completely or partially award an RFx to a supplier, depending upon what is optimal/preferred. This means a supplier could receive a partial award of the tender, while another supplier could receive the rest of the order.

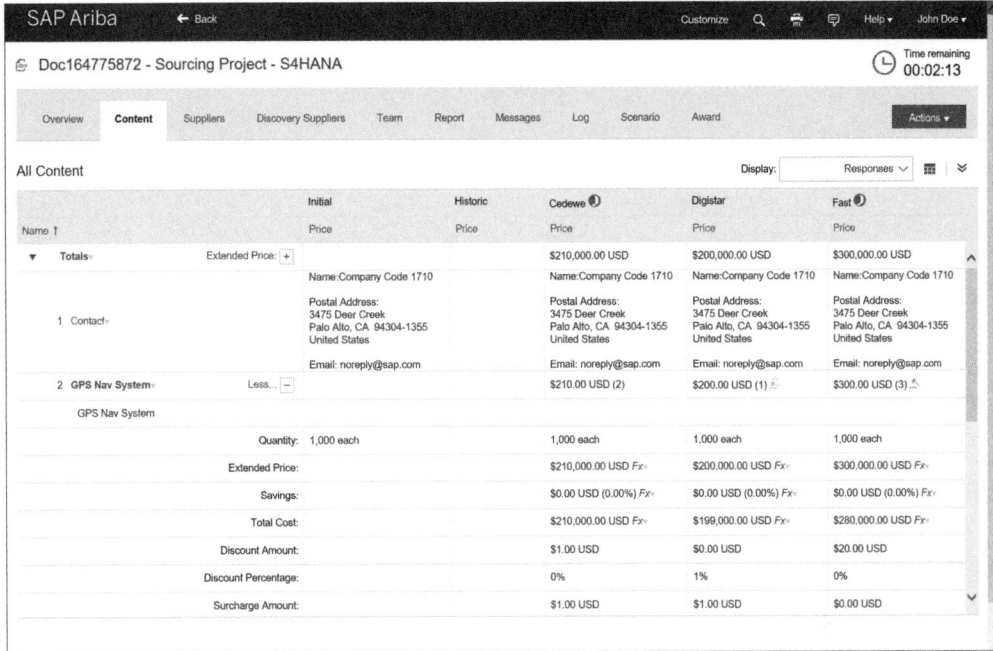

Figure 15.20 Compare Bids

7. In Figure 15.21, you confirm the award(s) for the RFx prior to generating them in the backend SAP S/4HANA environment in Figure 15.22.

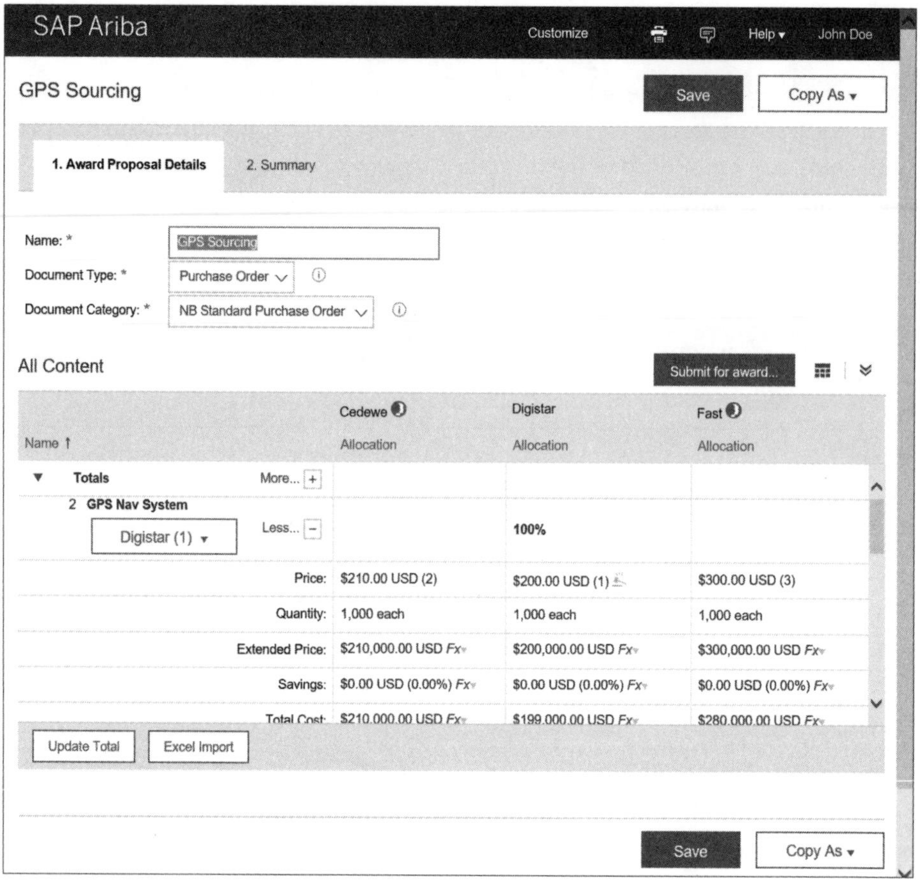

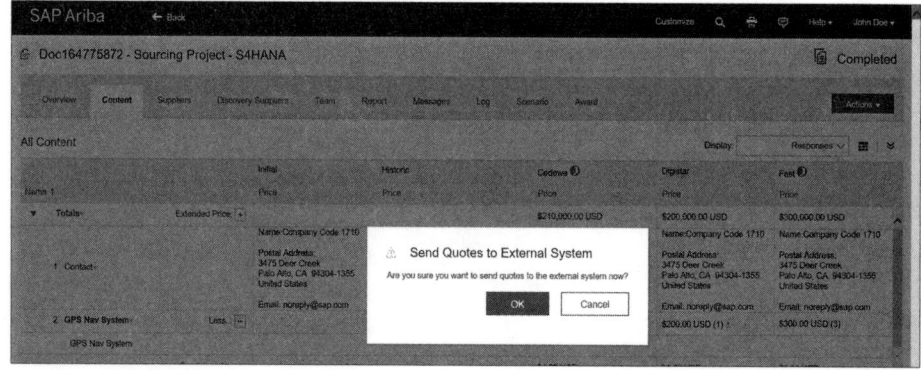

Figure 15.21 SAP Ariba Sourcing: Submit for Award

Figure 15.22 SAP Ariba Sourcing: Send Quotes to External System—SAP S/4HANA

Once the awarded RFP is sent back to SAP S/4HANA, you can generate purchase orders referencing the terms and pricing agreed to in the RFx and issue the purchase orders from SAP S/4HANA.

Depending on the scenario and customer preference, integrating SAP S/4HANA and SAP Ariba Sourcing enables you to address sourcing requirements originating in SAP ERP, with a much larger array of suppliers and functionality than is available in SAP S/4HANA by itself. Many times, a single successful sourcing event can deliver substantial savings to the bottom line of an organization. Integrating SAP S/4HANA with SAP Ariba Sourcing greatly increases the odds of this type of sourcing success occurring. The next section reviews your integration options for SAP Ariba Buying and Invoicing.

15.3.4   SAP Ariba Buying and Invoicing Integration

A typical set of steps for this scenario is as follows:

1. The buyer (either a professional buyer or a casual user) creates a requisition in SAP S/4HANA as per Figure 15.23.

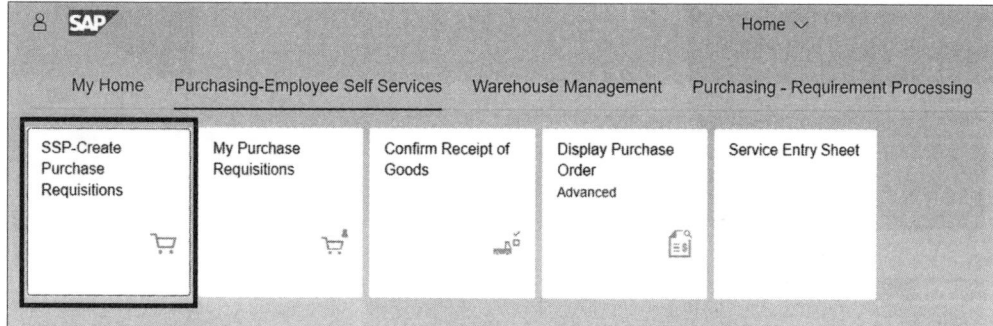

Figure 15.23 Create Requisition via Self-Service Procurement Tile

2. Then the buyer can describe the item, select a material/service master, or shop in a catalog. In Figure 15.24, the buyer punches out to an SAP Ariba Catalog and selects an item from the same.

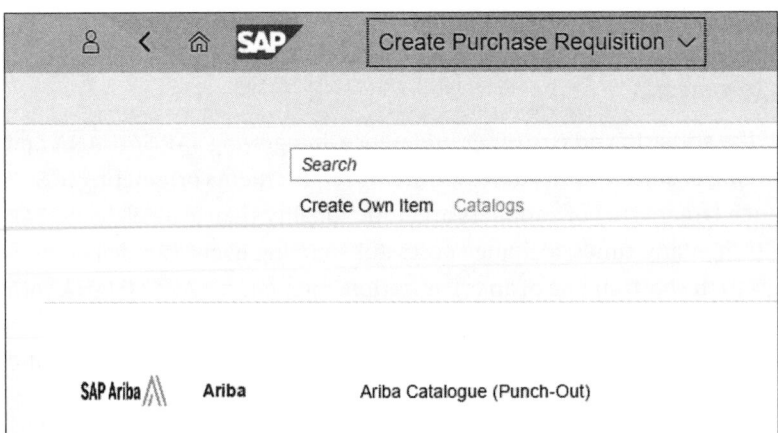

Figure 15.24 SAP Ariba Catalog Punch Out in SAP S/4HANA

3. Then the user searches for and selects the items required as in Figure 15.25 and Figure 15.26.

Figure 15.25 SAP Ariba Catalog Search

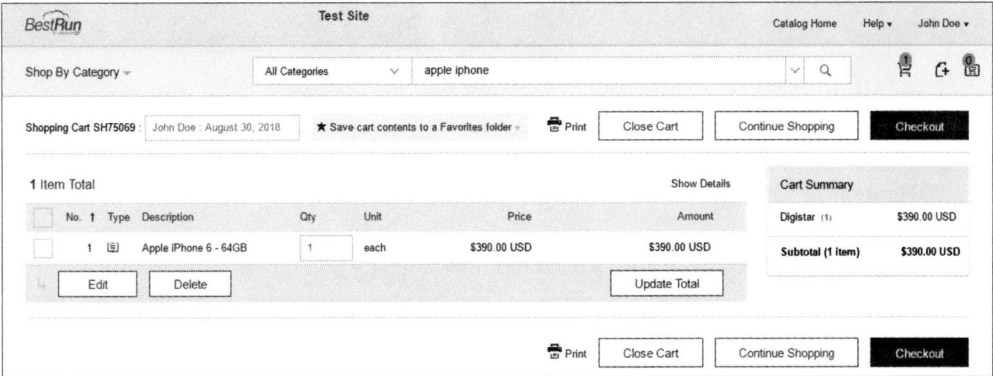

Figure 15.26 SAP Ariba Catalog Item Selection

4. Next, the item is transferred from the SAP Ariba Catalog back to the SAP S/4HANA requisition as in Figure 15.27 and Figure 15.28.

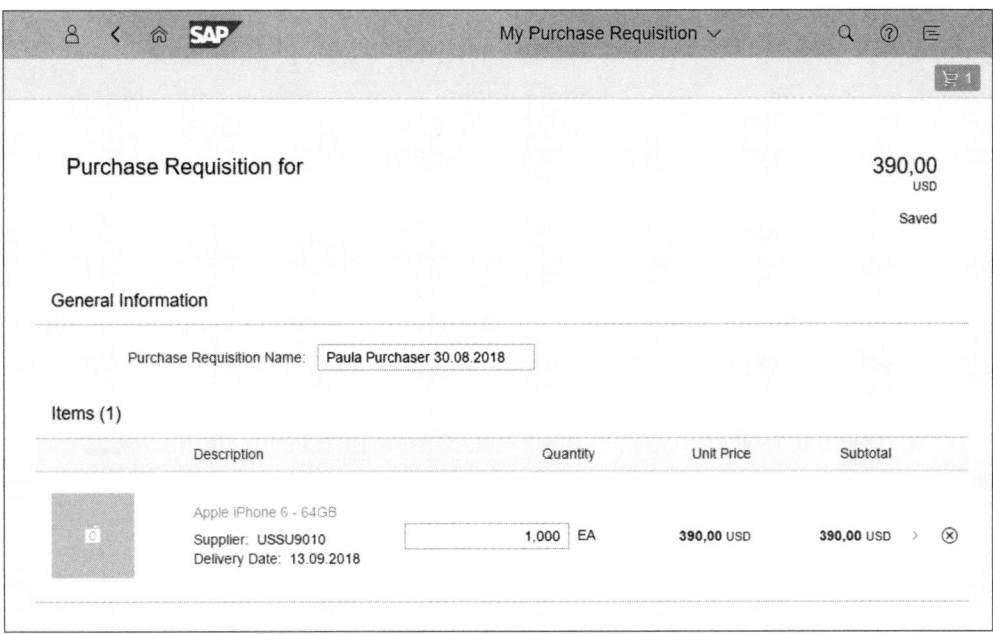

Figure 15.27 SAP S/4HANA Requisition with SAP Ariba Catalog Item

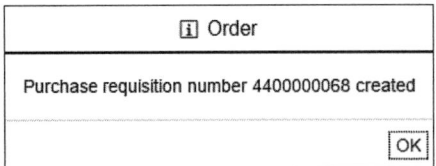

Figure 15.28 Ordered Requisition in SAP S/4HANA

SAP S/4HANA can be configured to automatically convert sourced requisitions to purchase orders, or the requisition can be converted manually. The requisition now shows the corresponding/resulting purchase order number, as in Figure 15.29.

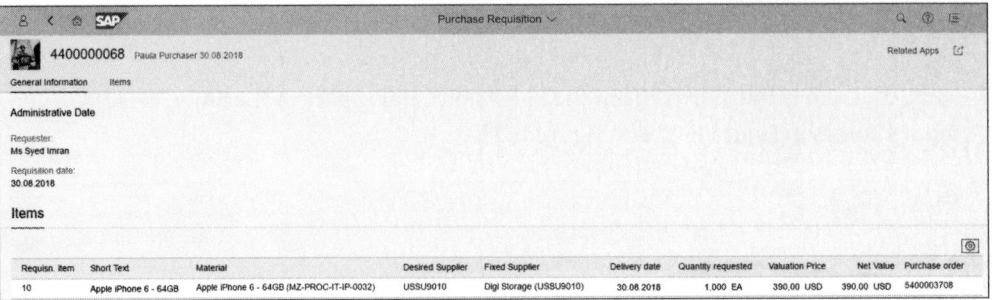

Figure 15.29 PO Number on Requisition: SAP S/4HANA

5. The purchase order is then transmitted to the Ariba Network for processing by the supplier.

Now that the document is up in the Ariba Network, it's time for the supplier to begin collaboration with the customer, reviewing and processing the purchase order as follows:

1. The supplier logs in to the Ariba Network using their login information as shown in Figure 15.30.

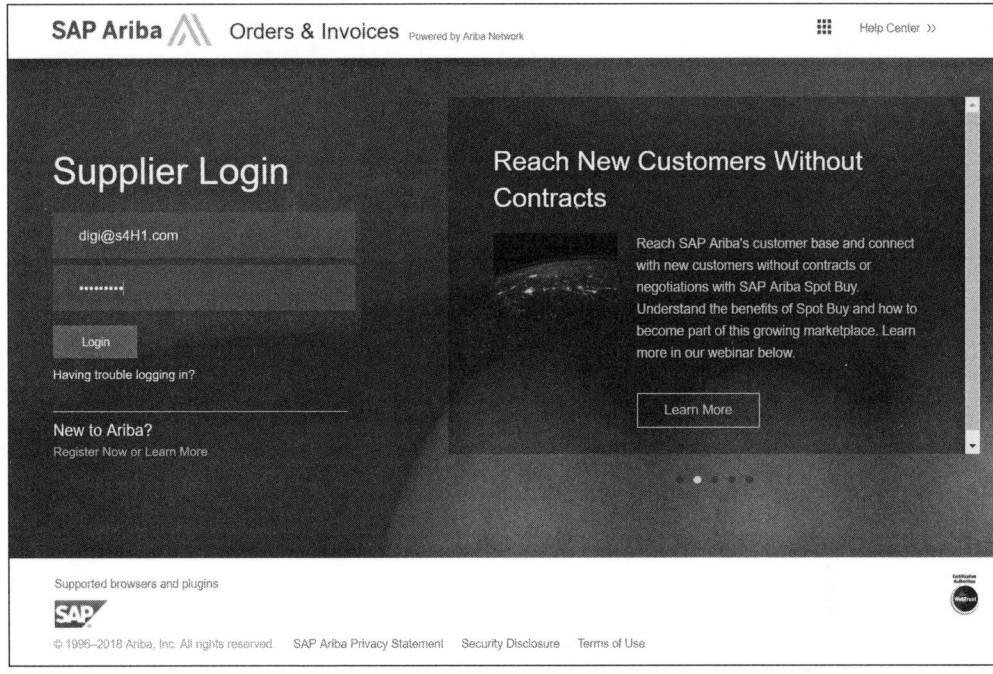

Figure 15.30 Supplier Login Page: Ariba Network

2. From the login page, the supplier then reviews new and existing purchase orders as shown in Figure 15.31.

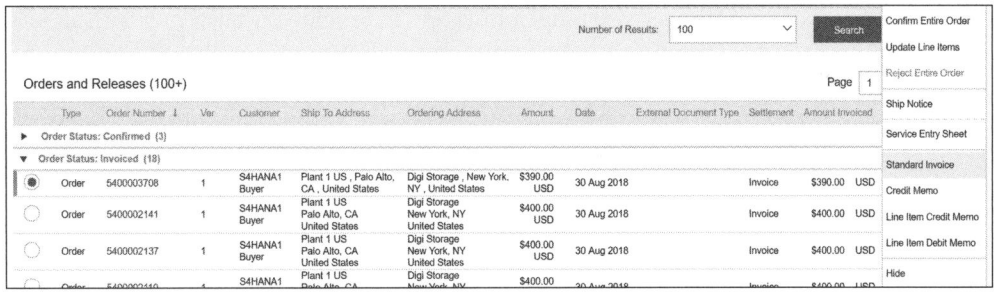

Figure 15.31 Ariba Network: Supplier Orders and Releases

3. To find a purchase order, the supplier user can also enter a partial number or other identifying characteristic as shown in Figure 15.32.

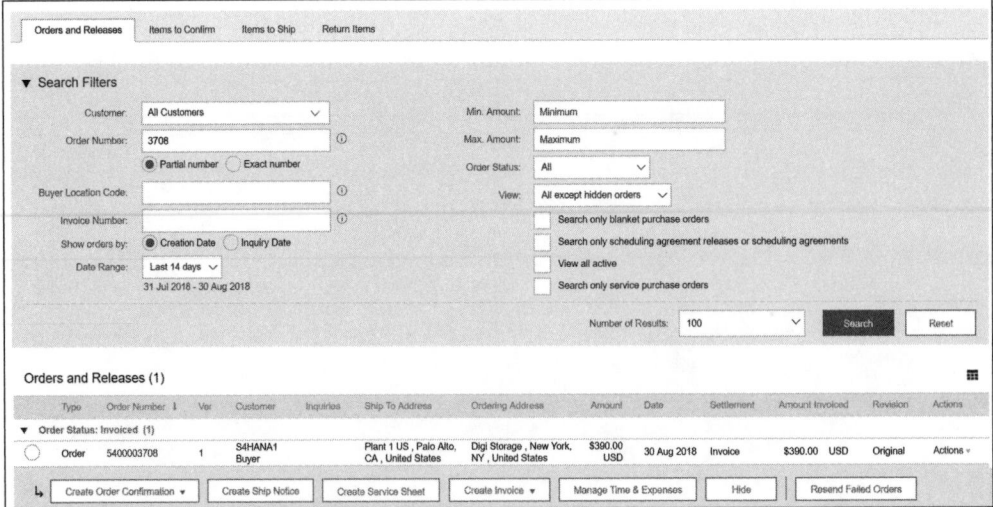

Figure 15.32 Ariba Network: Purchase Order Search

Once the supplier has located the purchase order, the supplier can confirm from their side that they plan to fulfill this order.

The supplier now confirms the order and fulfills it as follows:

1. First they select the correct option for the PO as shown in Figure 15.33 and then confirm it as shown in Figure 15.34 and Figure 15.35.

2. Once the supplier has confirmed that they intend to fulfil the purchase order, they can create an advanced shipping notification to provide the customer with an estimated time of arrival and confirmation that the items have shipped, as in Figure 15.35 and Figure 15.36.

You then confirm the delivery of a good and/or service, which in turn can trigger inventory management processes, as well as provide the grounds for payment for the follow-on invoice document.

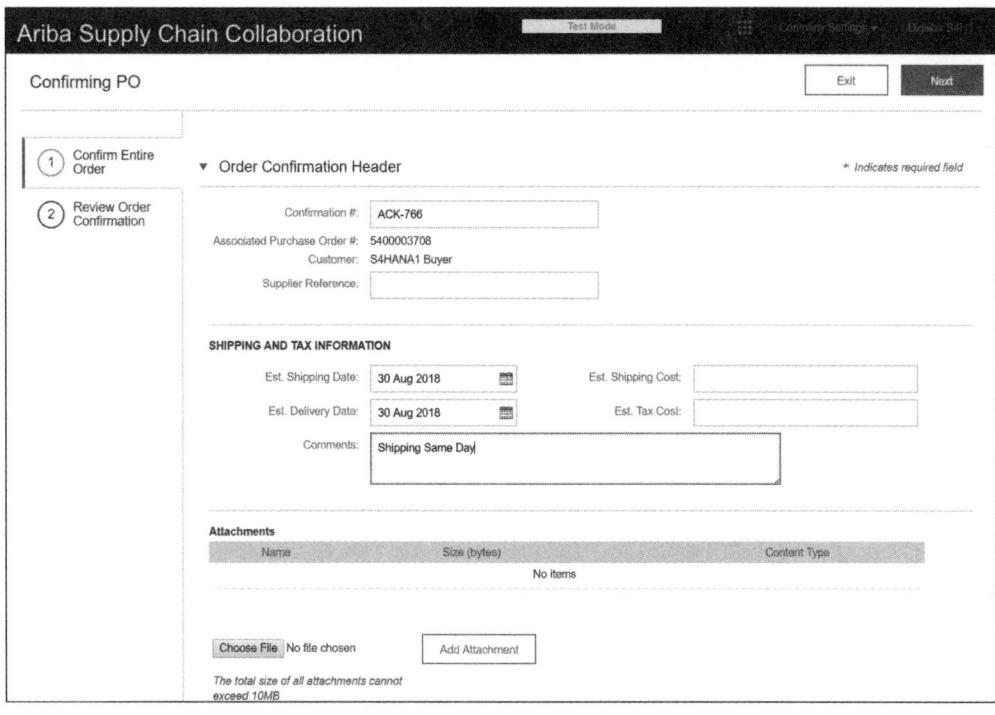

Figure 15.33 Ariba Network: Supplier Confirmation of Purchase Order

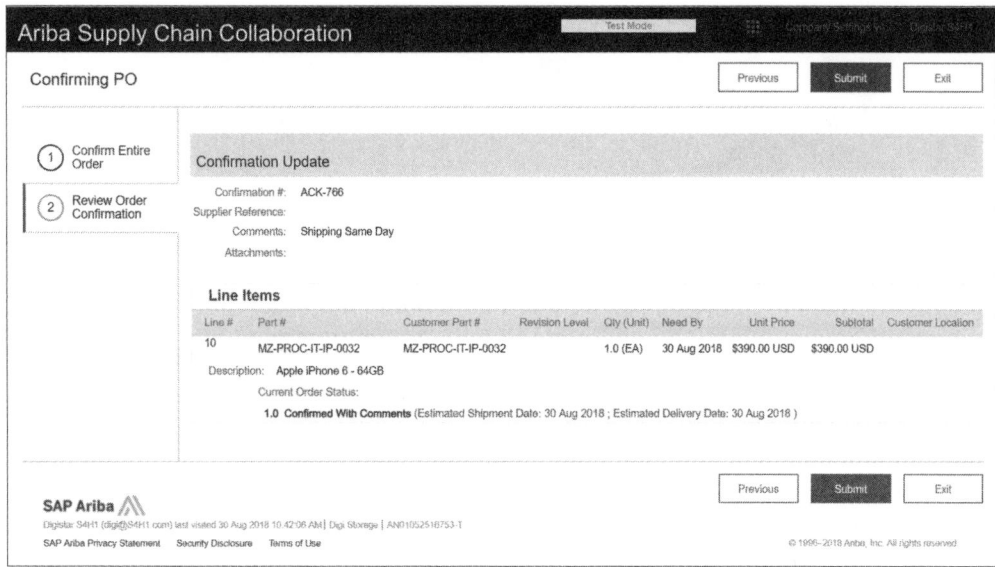

Figure 15.34 Ariba Network: Supplier Confirmation Release

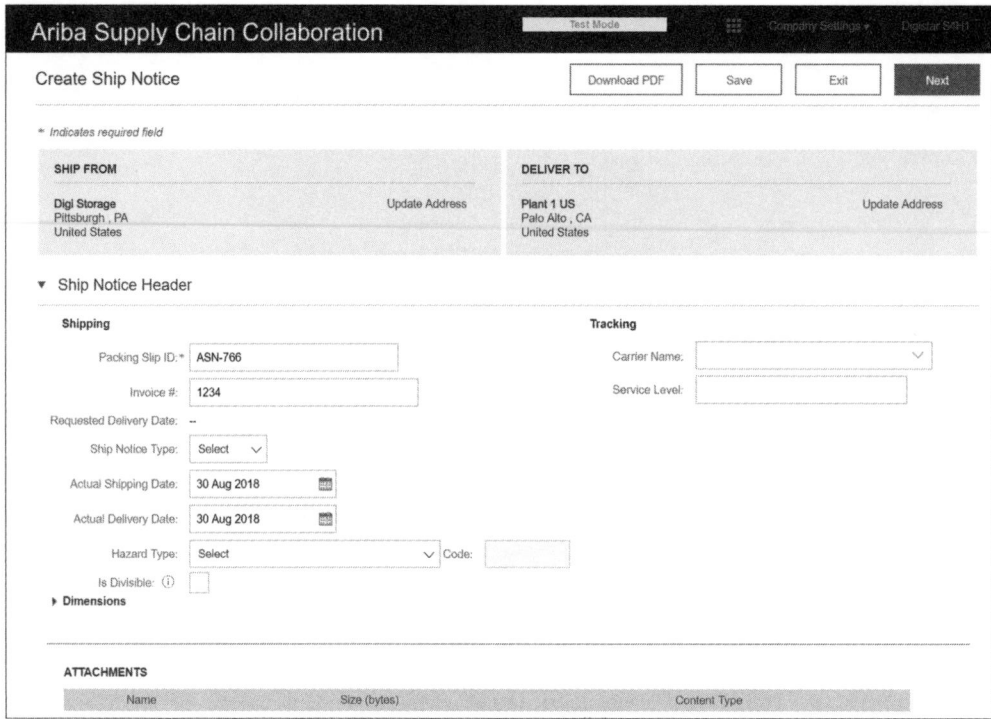

Figure 15.35 Ariba Network: Advanced Shipping Notification: Step 1

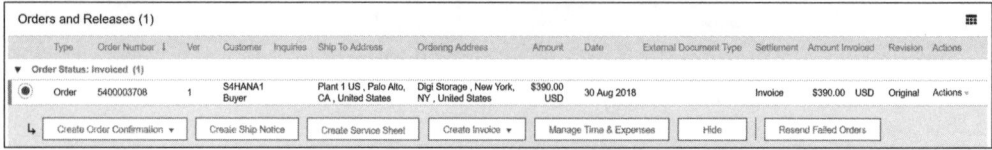

Figure 15.36 Ariba Network: Advanced Shipping Notification: Step 2

When the supplier has delivered the goods/services, the customer can log into SAP S/4HANA and complete the goods receipt as shown in Figure 15.37 and Figure 15.38.

Once these steps are complete, an invoice can be submitted and matched against not only the PO, but also the goods receipt. This is called a *three-way match*, which is more solid than relying on just the PO and the invoice, called a *two-way match*.

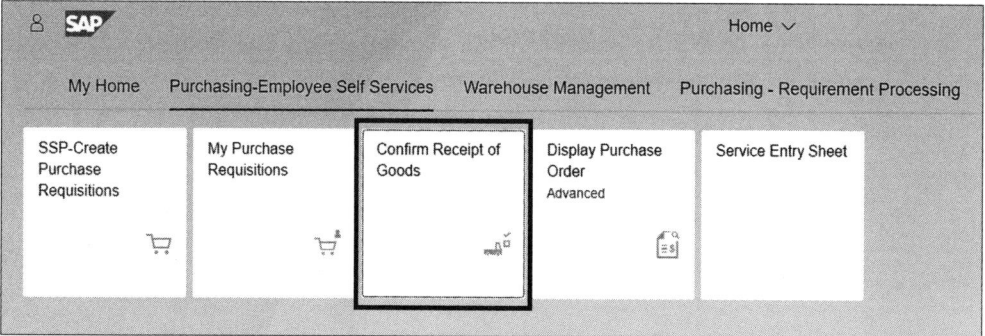

Figure 15.37 SAP S/4HANA: Confirm Receipt of Goods

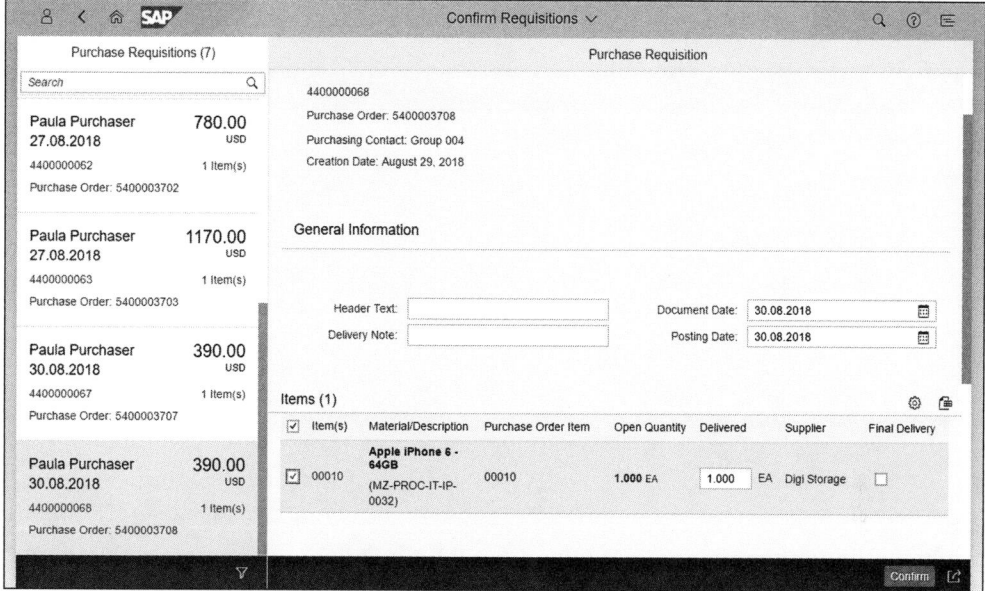

Figure 15.38 SAP S/4HANA: Goods Receipt

Invoices created in a supplier's system—or worse, written out on paper and faxed over to the customer—create all kinds of processing challenges for the customer. By using the Ariba Network to submit an invoice, the supplier and customer save valuable iterations in this process outlined below, making the submission much more accurate and the processing cycles faster. A typical set of steps are as follows:

1. Once the goods receipt has been entered, the supplier can log into the Ariba Network portal and enter their invoice as shown in Figure 15.39. Note that the supplier user can select a PO and then begin creating the invoice using the dropdown options.

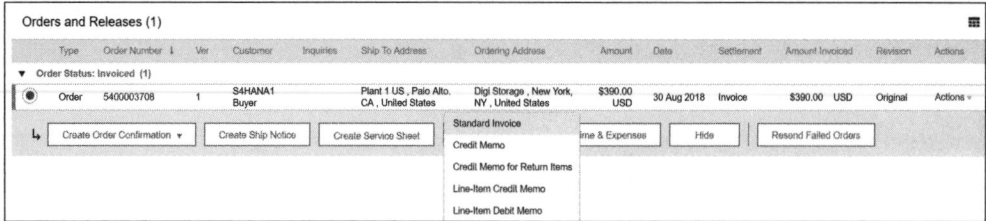

Figure 15.39 Ariba Network: Start Invoice Creation from PO

Once the invoice creation from PO has begun, you enter an invoice as in Figure 15.40.

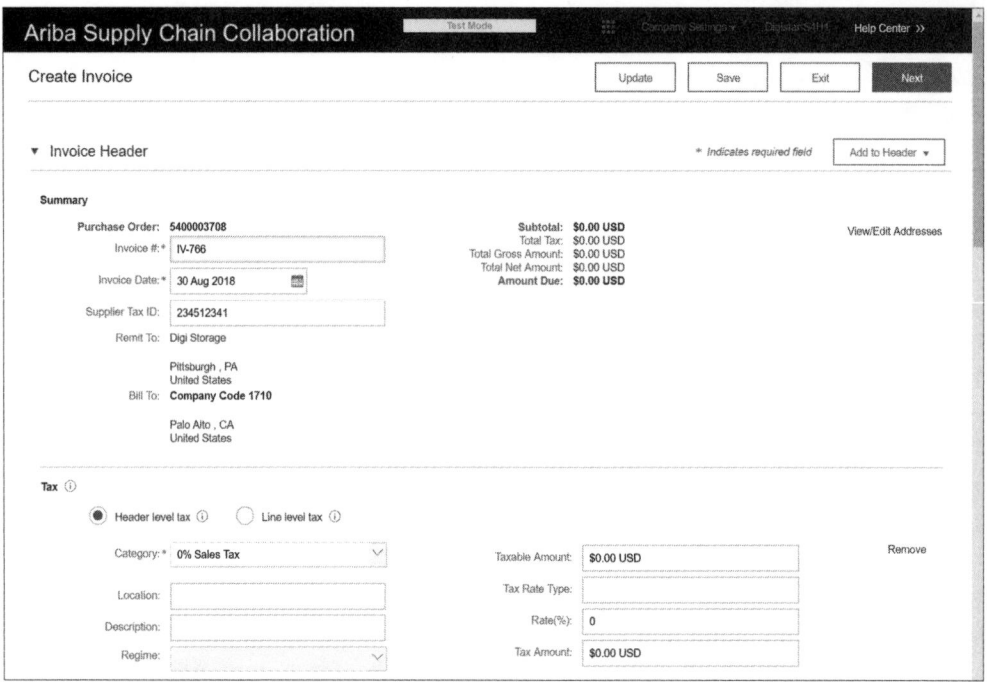

Figure 15.40 SAP Ariba Network: Enter Invoice: Step 1

Next, the supplier user creates an invoice as shown in Figure 15.41.

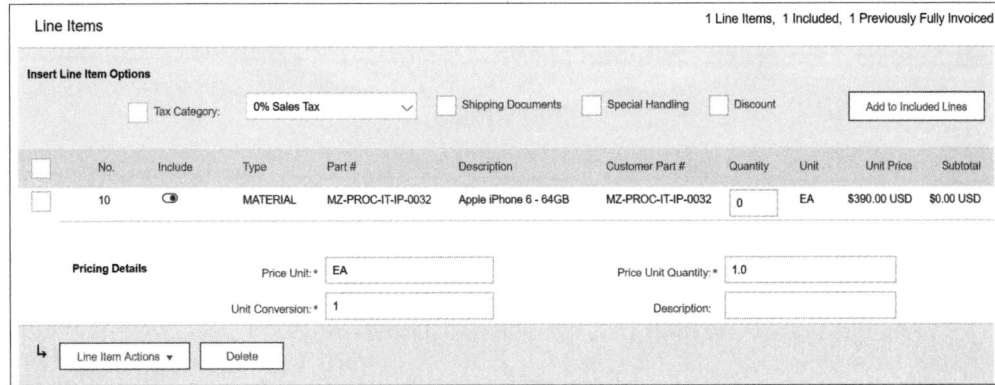

Figure 15.41 Ariba Network: Create Invoice: Step 2

Once the invoice has been entered, you can review in the summary page as per Figure 15.42.

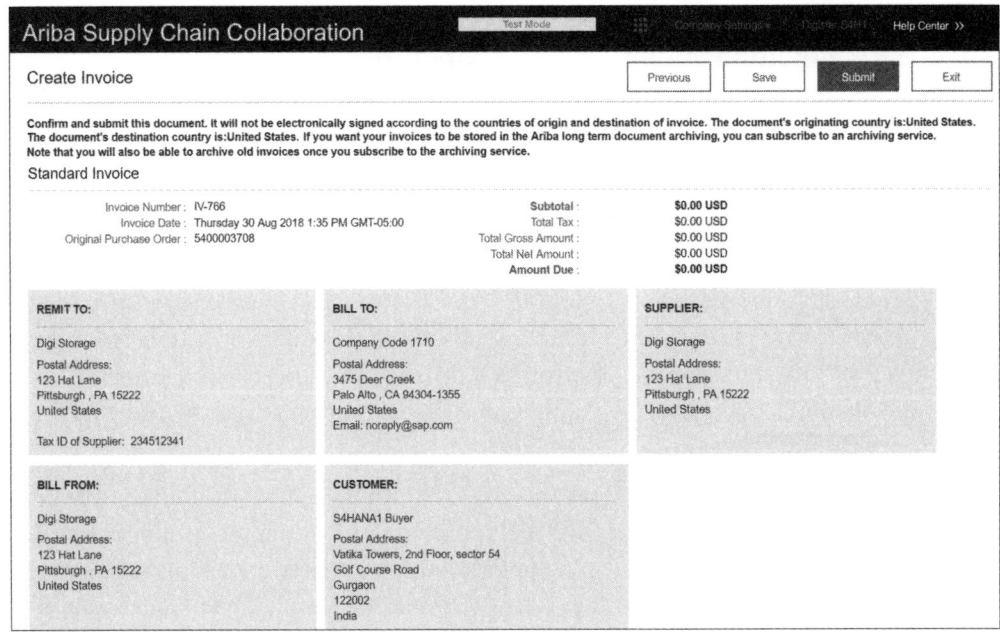

Figure 15.42 Ariba Network: Invoice Summary Page

2. Upon submission of the invoice, the complete document flow is now available in both SAP S/4HANA within the **Follow-On Documents** tab of the purchase order as in Figure 15.43 and in the Ariba Network.

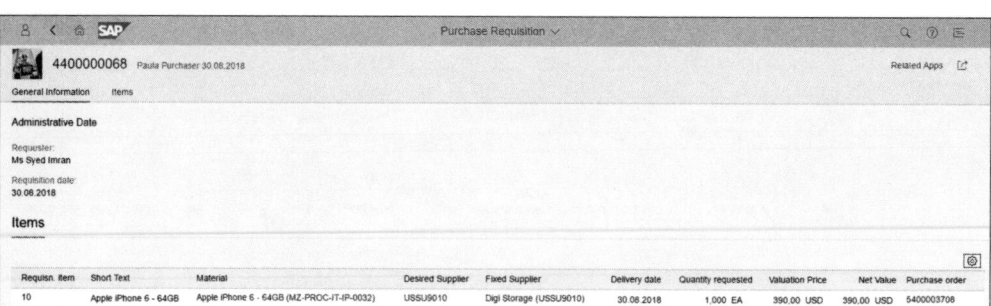

Figure 15.43 Purchase Order Generated from Requisition in SAP S/4HANA

This next section focuses on SAP Ariba Sourcing integration, another native integration available in SAP S/4HANA. For non-native integrations with SAP S/4HANA, such as SAP Ariba Buying, or integrations to previous SAP ERP releases, see the SAP Ariba Cloud Integration Gateway section of this chapter in Section 15.3.1.

15.4 SAP Ariba Supply Chain Collaboration

SAP Ariba Supply Chain Collaboration offers enhanced visibility and efficiency for direct material/merchandise/supply chain collaboration in the Ariba Network. In the past, the SAP Ariba solution platform focused primarily on indirect procurement. With the release of Collaborative Supply Chain (CSC – now called SCC), reviewed in the last edition of this book, SAP Ariba broadened this focus and its solution capabilities to include direct procurement. Expansion of functionality and integration with the Ariba Network was required in order to achieve this. Direct procurement is driven from multiple SAP ERP areas and is typically used to manage and control manufacturing, sales and distribution, production planning, and the ever-present financial aspects.

The latest iteration of this solution is called SAP Ariba Supply Chain Collaboration. Part of the SAP Leonardo umbrella at SAP, as shown in Figure 15.44, SAP Ariba Supply Chain Collaboration connects SAP ERP processes and scenarios in direct procurement and integrated business planning with the Ariba Network and its multitude of suppliers for collaboration. More recently, SAP Ariba Supply Chain Collaboration is also supported by SAP Leonardo. SAP Leonardo enables customers to access intelligent technologies such as machine learning, blockchain, data intelligence, IoT, and analytics via industry innovation kits, open innovation, and embedded intelligence.

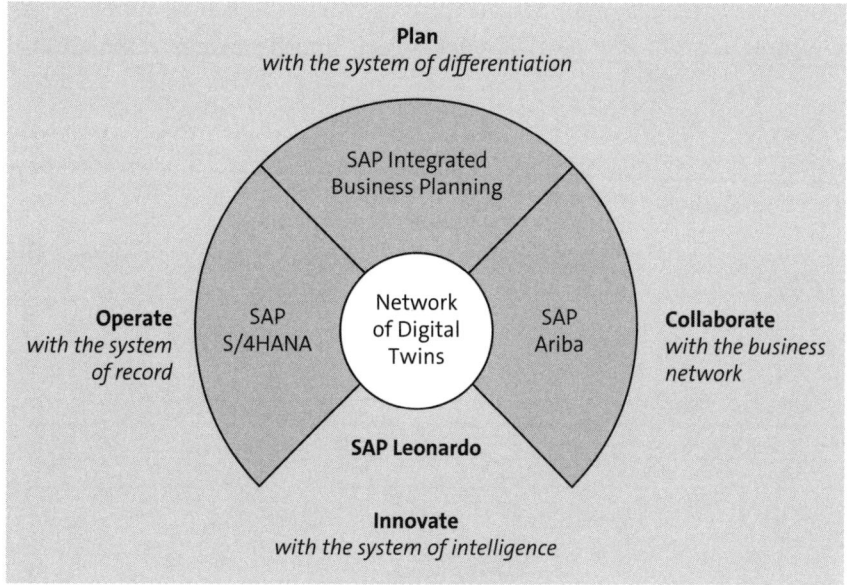

Figure 15.44 SAP Ariba Supply Chain Collaboration

SAP Ariba Supply Chain Collaboration comprises the direct processes of source-to-contract, planning, buy and make, and invoice-to-pay. In each instance, SAP Ariba and the corresponding area in SAP S/4HANA combine to provide complete coverage of the process as detailed in Figure 15.45.

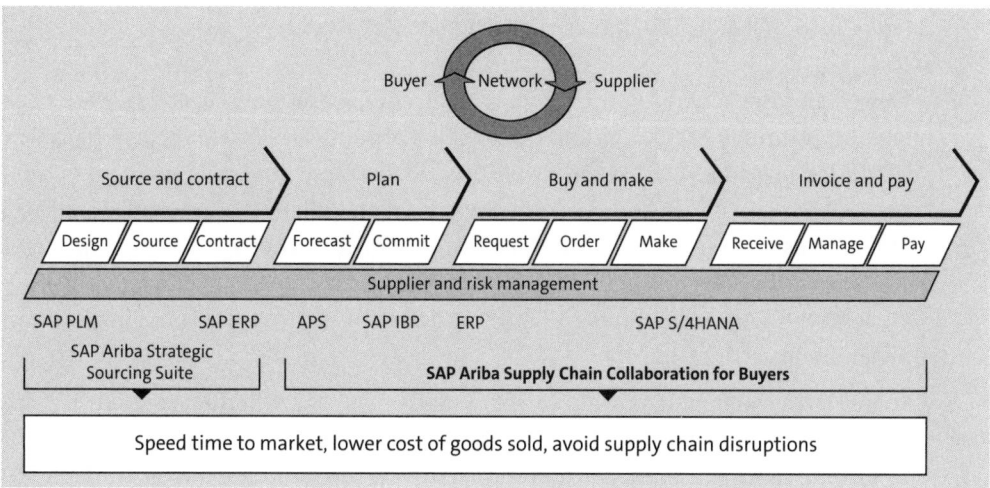

Figure 15.45 Supply Chain Collaboration

In most instances, the demand originates and then is sourced or acquired in SAP Ariba, returning then to SAP S/4HANA for receipt and further processing/usage within the production process.

The processes covered between the buyer and supplier under SAP Ariba Supply Chain Collaboration fall into three categories: planning, buy and make, and invoice/payment processes, as shown in Figure 15.46.

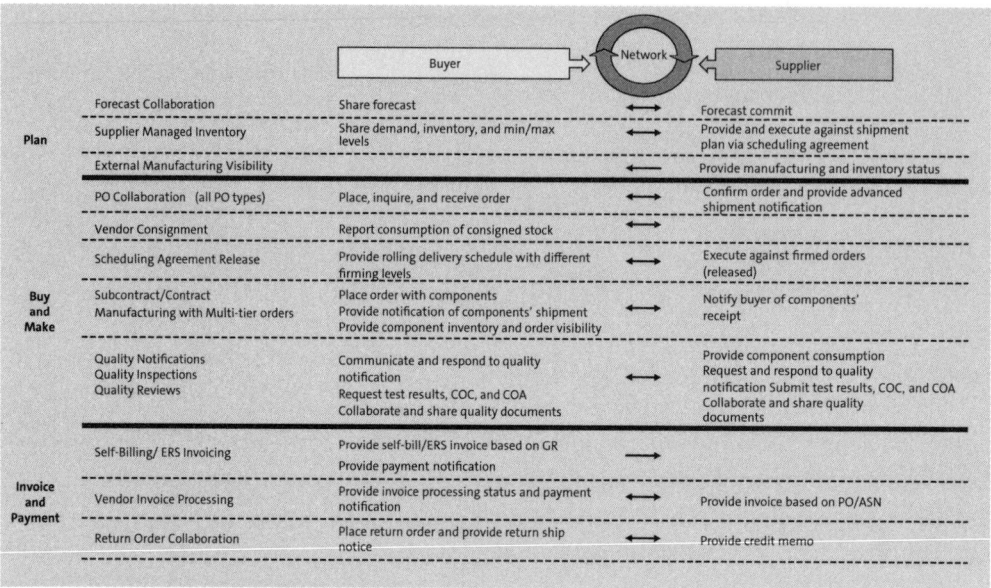

Figure 15.46 SAP Ariba Supply Chain Collaboration Processes

Viewed another way, SAP Ariba Supply Chain Collaboration's capabilities are clustered in planning, execution, and quality. In planning, SAP Ariba Supply Chain Collaboration provides forecast and inventory collaboration. In supply chain execution, the supplier and buyer use SAP Ariba Supply Chain Collaboration to collaborate on direct items and services, multitier items and services, scheduling agreements, and subcontracting and consignment orders. In quality management, suppliers and buyers leverage SAP Ariba Supply Chain Collaboration for notifications, inspections, reviews, and certificates.

Supply chains in manufacturing are particularly complex. Whether a high-tech manufacturer or a life sciences one, each industry has its own nuances and overlay processes, with a core need for collaboration between suppliers and buyers throughout.

Here, the buyer is a manufacturer, and the supplier can be a raw materials supplier, a third-party logistics provider, a subassembly supplier, a contract manufacturer, or a component supplier. SAP Ariba Supply Chain Collaboration provides manufactures and their supply chain stakeholders with the following:

- Collaboration simplicity with a single business network
- Embedded supplier onboarding services
- End-to-end process orchestration across all supplier channels to validate and enforce compliance
- Network intelligence, data, and insights to reduce supply chain risk

Table 15.1 outlines the functionality added in SAP Ariba Supply Chain Collaboration to support the direct procurement processes through the Ariba Network and back.

SAP Ariba Supply Chain Collaboration Function	Description
Forecast	The forecast collaboration component aims to avoid supply shortfalls and reduces and optimizes supply chain stock levels. It compares and displays the buyer's firm or planned net demands and the supplier's firm or planned receipts. The buyer and supplier have the same view of the planning situation and can quickly obtain a quick overview of critical situations. This functionality is integrated with SAP Integrated Business Planning (SAP IBP).
Work order	The work order collaboration component provides a consolidated view of the production demands and the current production progress. It offers customers early insight into changes affecting shipping dates and final quantity.
Replenishment	The replenishment collaboration component offers suppliers a value-added service by performing the replenishment planning task for their business partners. By increasing visibility into actual consumer demand, as well as customer inventory levels, suppliers can make better decisions on how to distribute goods across various customers, which in turn leads to increased customer service levels, lower transportation costs, reduced inventory, and lower sales cost.

Table 15.1 SAP Ariba Supply Chain Collaboration Functionality

15

SAP Ariba Supply Chain Collaboration Function	Description
Inventory	The inventory collaboration component ensures greater visibility of the inventory, as well as the supply-and-demand planning situation in a cross-tier environment.
Quality	Suppliers and customers can use the new quality collaboration component to notify each other of quality problems (or other issues with products or subcontracting components) during the manufacturing process, or after delivery, so that the customer or supplier can quickly react to the complaint.

Table 15.1 SAP Ariba Supply Chain Collaboration Functionality (Cont.)

To keep documents consistent between the SAP Supply Network Collaboration and the Ariba Network, you must perform the business processes for purchase orders and ship notices through the Ariba Network user interface exclusively, and not through the SAP Supply Network Collaboration application.

Not all functions available in SAP supplier collaboration are supported by SAP Supply Network Collaboration integration. Table 15.2 shows the five functions supported and their related SAP Supply Network Collaboration components and starting screens.

Supply Network Collaboration Integration Function	SAP Supply Network Collaboration Component	SAP Supply Network Collaboration Starting Screen
Forecast	Demand	Order Forecast Monitor
Replenishment	Replenishment	Replenishment VMI Monitor
Work Order	Work Order Collaboration	Work Order List
Inventory	Supply Network Inventory	Supply Network Inventory
Quality	Quality Collaboration	Quality Notification Overview

Table 15.2 Comparison Table: SAP Ariba Supply Chain Collaboration Functions with Supply Network Collaboration

SAP Ariba Supply Chain Collaboration 2.0 includes several updated features and functions crucial to many direct procurement processes.

As of the predecessor product, Collaborative Supply Chain 2.0, development for SAP Ariba Supply Chain Collaboration functionality focused on scheduling agreement releases (SARs), ship notices, and order collaboration. In today's SCC, buyers and suppliers now have access to many direct, specific processes and fields that were previously unavailable in the SAP Ariba environment for ship notices, SARs, and order collaboration.

As part of the SAP Ariba Supply Chain Collaboration setup process, suppliers need to be enabled via an adapter in the SAP Ariba cloud integration releases as a prerequisite to support the collaboration processes. This is coordinated via the supplier enablement service. SAP Ariba began providing technical and installation support for adapters in releases as early as 2014 for both SAP ERP and Oracle Fusion.

The steps for deploying the SAP Ariba Supply Chain Collaboration extension start with the buyer:

1. The buyer enables the supplier for particular SAP Ariba Supply Chain Collaboration features.

2. Fields of data supporting enhanced functionality, such as the ordering of direct materials, are passed from the buyer's SAP ERP system to Ariba Network.

3. Through an enhanced Ariba Network user interface, the enabled supplier makes use of the additional fields and enhanced functionality to collaborate with the buyer on documents such as purchase orders, invoices, and ship notices.

To prepare a supplier record in SAP ERP for SAP Ariba Supply Chain Collaboration activities, a relationship flag must be set. This functionality is standard and doesn't require additional installation or configuration. Once the flag is set, industry-specific functionality can be configured. To complete both these activities, your user role must have supplier enablement task management permissions. Buyers do not require further enablement for SAP Ariba Supply Chain Collaboration. As an administrator, you can disable SAP Ariba Supply Chain Collaboration functionality for suppliers.

Once a supplier has been appropriately flagged, they can be directed to the SAP Ariba Supply Chain Collaboration supplier user interface portal. This portal contains all existing Ariba Network supplier functionality, plus SAP Ariba Supply Chain Collaboration and industry-specific SAP Ariba Supply Chain Collaboration functionality. When suppliers are enabled for SAP Ariba Supply Chain Collaboration, they are directed to the supplier portal, where they can access the various SAP Ariba Supply

15

Chain Collaboration features. Previously, the supplier portal was referred to as the Supply Chain Management (SCM) portal.

Suppliers and buyers often collaborate on the creation of purchase orders, invoices, and ship notices for direct material orders. This collaboration requires the exchange of information specific to direct material orders. These features facilitate the collaboration process by allowing more detailed descriptions of materials being procured. These features also allow the supplier to collaborate through the Ariba Network user interface. This is particularly helpful for suppliers that do not have EDI, cXML, or other integrated business-to-business mechanisms in place.

Direct material fields for order and invoice collaboration facilitate the collaboration process for purchase orders, invoices, and ship notices by allowing for more detailed descriptions of materials being procured. This Ariba Network feature is applicable to all supplier users. The buyer's industry type needs to be set as retail to enable this functionality. For buyers using external ERP systems, such as SAP ERP, the adapter is required.

The ship notice business rules feature for order confirmation and ship notice rules supports the direct material collaboration process. This Ariba Network feature is applicable to all supplier users. *Direct material* includes all items, such as raw materials and parts, required to assemble or manufacture a complete product. A rule may be implemented based on customer and market requirements or may be driven by individual needs. A rule can be applied to many suppliers or to a predefined group of suppliers (even if the group only contains one member). Tooltips in the user interface indicate when ship notice rules have been enabled.

Prior to the Collaborative Supply Chain 2.0 release, suppliers could view schedule lines but could not use them in the creation of ship notices through the Ariba Network user interface. With the release of CSC 2.0, scheduling agreement releases become visible in the Ariba Network user interface. This has been further built out in SAP Ariba Supply Chain Collaboration. Buyers can periodically communicate releases to their suppliers, and suppliers can create ship notices for materials requested through scheduling agreement releases. From the new **Items to Ship** tab, a supplier can create a single ship notice containing items from several purchase orders that all are due by the same date.

It is important to note that scheduling agreement releases do not support order confirmations or most invoices. You cannot use scheduling agreement release collaboration for invoices, except for invoices that have been created as carbon copies by direct material buyers. Also, you cannot use scheduling agreement releases for order confirmations. The processing of nonscheduled items is not affected by scheduling agreement releases. These are not restrictions of SAP Ariba Supply Chain Collaboration 2.0 as much as general restrictions in the scheduling agreement process.

Scheduling agreement release collaboration is disabled by default, but the buyer can enable it by following these steps:

1. Log on as a buyer.
2. Click **Manage Profile**.
3. On the **Configuration** page, click **Default Transaction Rules**.
4. Under **Scheduling Agreement Release Setup Rules**, check the box next to **Allow Scheduling Agreement Release Collaboration**.

Suppliers view scheduling agreement releases in the list of documents on the **Orders and Releases** tab and can choose whether to search for only scheduling agreement releases. Suppliers can then create ship notices from scheduling agreement releases.

To support these new functionalities, the following types of messages have been enhanced or added for direct materials buyers and contract manufacturers:

- **Subcontracting purchase order**
  A subcontracting purchase order is a purchase order that is sent from a buyer to a contract manufacturer to request the production and delivery of finished goods.

  The subcontracting purchase order has been enhanced to carry not only item level and schedule line level information, but also subcontracting component information. Subcontracting components are the raw materials that are used for manufacturing the finished goods specified at the item level.

- **Component ship notice**
  A component ship notice is a type of ship notice that informs the contract manufacturer of the shipment of subcontracting components.

- **Component receipt**
  A component receipt is a type of goods receipt that informs the buyer of the receipt of subcontracting components. The contract manufacturer can issue the component receipt against one or more component ship notices.

- **Component consumption (backflush) message**
  The ship notice message has been enhanced to include consumption details in a backflush component message. A backflush component consumption message is a

15

type of ship notice request that informs the buyer of the completion of finished goods from subcontracting components. Unlike real-time component consumption reporting, backflush reporting is done only once, at the end of the production process.

- **Component consumption (real-time) message**
  A real-time component consumption message informs the buyer of consumption of components at any phase of the production cycle.

- **Component inventory message**
  A component inventory message has been added to inform suppliers about quantities of components available for manufacturing.

- **SAP Ariba Supply Chain Collaboration limitation**
  If a subcontracting purchase order has been uploaded or downloaded via a CSV file, a supplier will not see the component level on the downloaded subcontracting purchase order.

15.5   SAP Ariba Supply Chain Collaboration Configuration

To establish basic connectivity between the SAP S/4HANA environment and SAP Ariba Supply Chain Collaboration for Buyers, verify the applicability of these steps in the Configuration Guide for Business Network Collaboration at *http://s-prs.co/500321*. Similar instructions are available for connecting SAP IBP, which replaces SAP Advanced Planning and Optimization, and SAP Ariba Supply Chain Collaboration for Buyers. SAP IBP is the planning tool of choice used in SAP S/4HANA and in conjunction with SAP Ariba Supply Chain Collaboration for Buyers on forecast collaboration topics. Now, execute the (high-level) steps described next.

To begin, verify access to an SAP Ariba Buyer account/SAP Ariba Supply Chain Collaboration for Buyers account by logging in using the credentials provided. If you can't log in, you'll need to request access from SAP Ariba and your account team.

Once verified, invite suppliers to the Ariba Network via the launchpad navigation. These suppliers are those that will be conducting direct procurement transactions and confirmations with your organization. To invite suppliers, navigate to **Business Network • Integration Configuration • Invite Suppliers to Ariba Network**.

The next step requires setting up a *shared secret*. This is a security step to ensure that your suppliers are who they say they are upon login. To maintain a shared secret, proceed as follows:

1. Log in to your SAP Ariba Supply Chain Collaboration for Buyers account.
2. Choose **Administration • Configuration • cXML Setup**.
3. Under **Authentication Method**, select **Shared Secret** and enter your shared secret.

Once you have the security settings in place with the shared secret, it's time to enable your suppliers:

1. Log into your SAP Ariba Buyer account and go to the **Supplier Enablement** tab.
2. Go to the **Active Relationships** tab. If your supplier is in the **Active Relationships** table, jump to the next set of steps and assign a private ID. If the supplier isn't in the **Active Relationships** table, search for the suppler and add it to **Selected Suppliers**. Via **Selected Suppliers**, click the supplier and choose **Request a Relationship**. The supplier must accept the request prior to proceeding to the next instructions.

In the next steps, you'll create a private ID for a supplier so that the supplier can log in:

1. Log on to SAP Ariba Supply Chain Collaboration for Buyers with your SAP Ariba Buyer account.
2. In the **Supplier Enablement Tab**, choose **Supplier Relationships • More Actions • Edit • Edit Preferences for Supplier • Enter Supplier Identifiers for Procurement Application • Add**.
3. If tying the supplier to only one ERP system, enter the supplier ID in the first field.
4. If tying the supplier to multiple ERP backends, choose each system and enter the supplier ID.
5. Save.

You've now set up your suppliers for SAP Ariba Supply Chain Collaboration for Buyers.

> **Note**
>
> An additional setting is available for suppliers in the **Forecast** area to further define whether a supplier can view and forecast data, which is set as a default. In the **Forecast** area, you can override the default forecast rules and determine whether a supplier is allowed to view and commit forecast data. Save your preferences for the supplier by clicking the **Save** button on the screen.

15

15.6   SAP Fieldglass

Founded in Chicago in 1999 and acquired by SAP in 2014, SAP Fieldglass has been providing cloud-based vendor management solutions (VMSs) for over two decades. SAP Fieldglass enables total talent and spend management by answering five key questions about your external supplier of third-party workers:

- Who's working for you?
- What are they doing?
- Where are they located?
- What facilities/systems are they using?
- How much are you paying them?

To properly answer these questions, SAP Fieldglass interfaces with both procurement and HR systems, as shown in Figure 15.47.

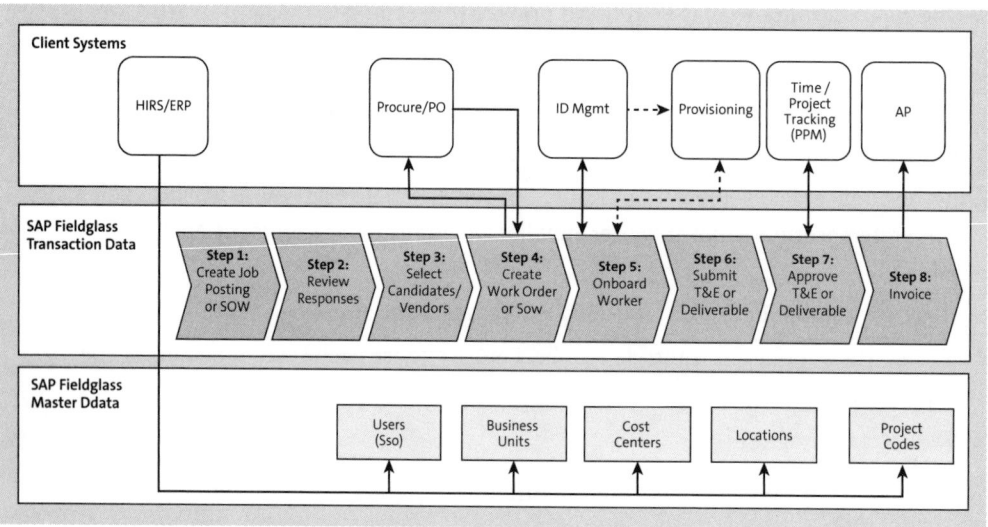

Figure 15.47 SAP Fieldglass Integration Overview

The key areas in SAP Fieldglass are the contingent labor and statement of work (SOW) workflows (Figure 15.48).

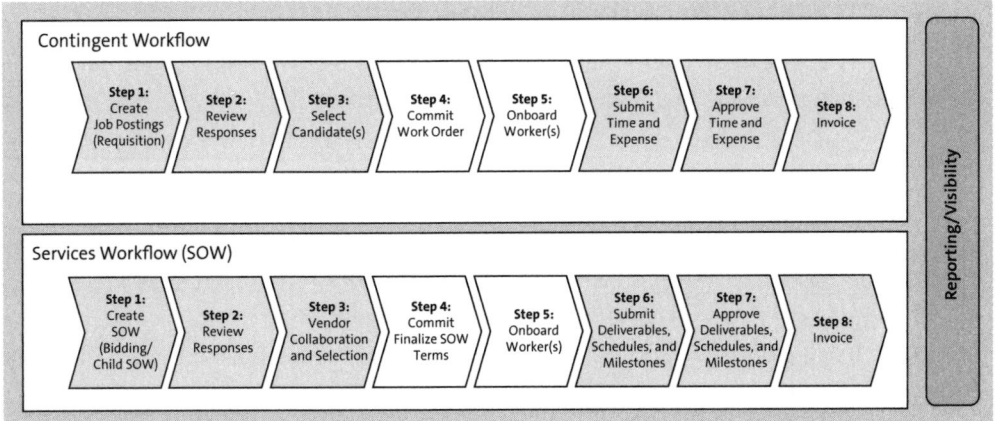

Figure 15.48 SAP Fieldglass Workflow Overview

15.6.1   Key Technologies

In addition to leveraging direct connection linkages between SAP S/4HANA and SAP Ariba and SAP Fieldglass, SAP Fieldglass also supports mediated integration via SAP Cloud Platform Integration.

15.6.2   Integrating SAP Fieldglass Contingent Workforce Management

SAP Fieldglass integrates both directly to SAP S/4HANA and via SAP Ariba. This section provides further overview on both options.

Integrating SAP Fieldglass Via SAP Ariba

SAP Fieldglass integrates with SAP Ariba via the standard SAP Ariba Cloud Integration extractors and loaders. The integration can be mediated via customer middleware or go directly via webservice calls. Nonstandard requirements can be supported using custom-developed SAP Ariba Cloud Integration extractors and loaders. SAP Fieldglass is used to augment SAP Ariba functionality and processes in service procurement in the following ways:

- Managing workers in each SOW engagement by:
  - On/offboarding and provisioning
  - Tenure and performance tracking
  - Tracking and managing expenses

- – Tracking contractor record and related documents
- – Offloading data entry to the services supplier
- Managing engagement-specific supplier performance by:
  - – Tracking deliverables
  - – Rolling up engagement and relationship levels
  - – Providing the supplier with configurable views into performance
  - – Providing the users with drill-down, real-time supplier KPI scorecards
- Downstream SOW authoring and supplier collaboration
- Managing downstream authoring and supplier collaboration by:
  - – Providing self-service, buyer-centric SOW development tools and processes
  - – Offering collaboration options for supplier/buyer on engagement structure and pricing
  - – Ensuring configurability across payment characteristics
- Providing timecard functionality by:
  - – Allocating hours across jobs, project codes, and cost centers
  - – Offering complex rate-management capabilities
  - – Rate benchmarking
  - – Offering mobile capabilities
- Providing a managed service provider (MSP) governance model by:
  - – Native PMO architecture and configurability via workflow changes, reports, custom fields
  - – Single tenant/multi-MSP functionality
  - – Administrative panel for alerts and tactical tracking

SAP Fieldglass can leverage SAP Ariba Buying and Invoicing for a unified UI, a network for distributing POs and invoices (Ariba Network), and approval workflows in both systems. SAP Fieldglass also integrates with SAP Ariba Contracts for managing spend.

Integrating SAP Fieldglass Directly with SAP S/4HANA

The standard integration areas and scenarios for SAP Fieldglass directly with SAP S/4HANA center on the following:

- Replicating business partners. The business partner/supplier is first created and saved in the SAP S/4HANA system, and then pushed via automated direct connectivity integration out to SAP Fieldglass. A passthrough option for the supplier is also available via SAP Cloud Platform Integration. Once the business partner is loaded into SAP Fieldglass, the user manually selects the supplier required to register and initiates an email registration invitation, and the supplier registers/creates their user information.

- Replicating master data. For replicating data from SAP S/4HANA to SAP Fieldglass, you can leverage SAP Fieldglass Web Service Technical Specifications (BusinessPartnerRelationshipPush). Via SOA Manager, SAP S/4HANA can be configured for direct connectivity. Mediated connectivity can be set up via SAP Cloud Platform Integration or SAP PI/SAP PO. Mediated connectivity is the recommended approach as it enables the systems to pass data with additional security controls in place and doesn't expose the URL of SAP S/4HANA to external systems. In either case, you can replicate sales and internal orders, cost centers, work breakdown structure (WBS) elements, company codes, purchasing orgs, and plants. Mapping specifications for import are provided by SAP Fieldglass.

- Creation of transactional data. Here the requester creates a work order or SOW in SAP Fieldglass and passes it along for approval. SAP S/4HANA converts the work order or SOW into a high-level requisition and can drive the approval process using existing workflows in the SAP S/4HANA environment, using the SAP Fieldglass requisition response connector to send a status update to SAP Fieldglass once approved or rejected, along with the purchase requisition ID.

- If rejected, SAP Fieldglass opens up the work order or SOW for editing and resubmission back to SAP S/4HANA. Once approved, the purchase requisition custom field in SAP Fieldglass is updated with this status in the **Posting Information** section of the work order or SOW (**Details** tab). Once any additional workflow steps in SAP Fieldglass are completed, the system issues a work order to the supplier for confirmation in SAP Fieldglass and then consequently issues a PO via SAP S/4HANA.

- SOW processing. The supplier accepts SOWs via a response request in SAP Fieldglass. Once approved by the buyer, the object moves into pending external acceptance status and SAP Fieldglass triggers the creation of a formal purchase order in SAP S/4HANA. SAP S/4HANA runs this request through any approvals required, issues the PO, and then sends a PO ID back to SAP Fieldglass. Applicable worker times and expense sheets can then be submitted back to SAP S/4HANA via a webservice integration task push. Utilizing the SAP Fieldglass entry status upload connector, SAP S/4HANA can send back status updates.

- Regardless of whether service entry sheet functionality integration is enabled between the two systems, any invoiced element in SAP Fieldglass can be integrated

15

with and sent to the SAP S/4HANA system. SAP Fieldglass leverages a download connector called *CXML-formatted invoices* to retrieve all invoices available on the client and process them in SAP S/4HANA. SAP S/4HANA then sends back a final payment status for the invoice to SAP Fieldglass.

- There are two procurement workflows available in the form of lean procurement and standard procurement. Lean includes service entry integrations, but not service hierarchies, and is the go-to integration workflow going forward. Standard procurement is only supported in on-premise SAP S/4HANA environments and does not include service entry integrations.

15.6.3   SAP SuccessFactors

SAP SuccessFactors integration with both SAP S/4HANA and SAP S/4HANA Cloud has a similar integration framework and approach as that for SAP Ariba, based on predefined integration scenarios that you evaluate, activate, and deploy in your environment.

SAP S/4HANA Integration with SAP SuccessFactors Employee Central

SAP S/4HANA integrates with SAP SuccessFactors by leveraging predefined configuration and integration scenarios (see Figure 15.49). This integration is webservice-based and can be scheduled as a middleware job.

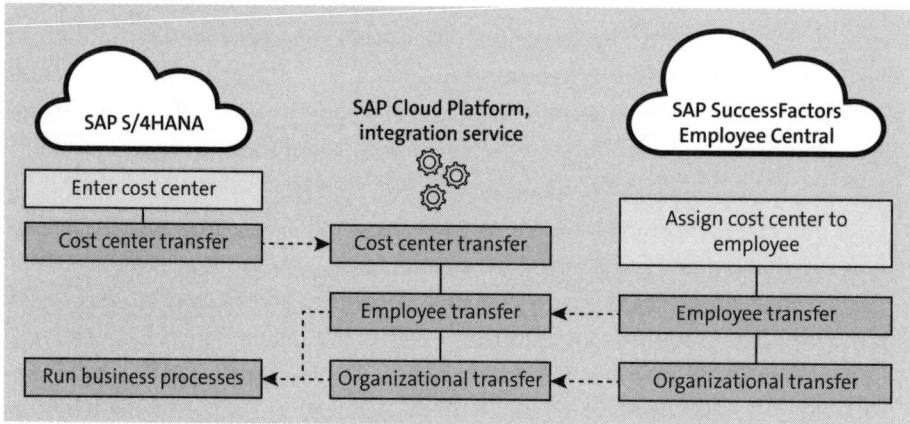

Figure 15.49 Integrating SAP S/4HANA with SAP SuccessFactors Employee Central

The manual process entails creating or identifying a cost center first in SAP S/4HANA. This is a manual step. The cost center is then transferred to SAP SuccessFactors and assigned to the employee. The employee and/or organizational data is transferred back to SAP S/4HANA automatically via batch processing. The configuration is available at *http://s-prs.co/500320*. This includes overview documentation, scope documentation, and the following accelerators:

- Sales supplement, an overview of the package and business value
- Customer presentation, slides on the scope of integration
- Demo script, for communicating the scope and functionality
- Delivery supplement, providing important information about the delivery of the solution
- Service and one-page slides, slides defining the solution and scope (one-pagers)
- Software and delivery requirements, a list of prerequisites for the deployment of the solution
- Solution scope, scope documents
- Project schedule, a schedule for the project including roles/skills required
- SAP Notes, providing additional documentation for the package and implementation

SAP S/4HANA Cloud Integration with SAP SuccessFactors Employee Central

SAP SuccessFactors can also integrate with SAP S/4HANA Cloud using the same approach of best practices, building blocks, and SAP Activate. The required efforts are slightly more varied, and therefore involved, than with the Ariba Network packages. Upon completion of the integration, the employee from SAP SuccessFactors is realized as a business partner (BP) in SAP S/4HANA. Data from SAP SuccessFactors can be used to populate the employee data in SAP S/4HANA, such as the following:

- Basic employee information (person, name, employee)
- Communication information, such as email, phone, and fax
- Payment information with payment method and bank account
- Employee status
- Employment percentage
- Working hours per week
- Job title
- Job information, business unit, division, and department
- Cost center assignment

As with on-premise SAP S/4HANA integrations, from a process standpoint, you first establish or identify the cost center in SAP S/4HANA, then transfer this cost center to SAP SuccessFactors Employee Central and assign an employee, and then transfer the employee record back over to SAP S/4HANA (see Figure 15.50). The transfer processes are automated process steps, whereas the cost center assignment is manual.

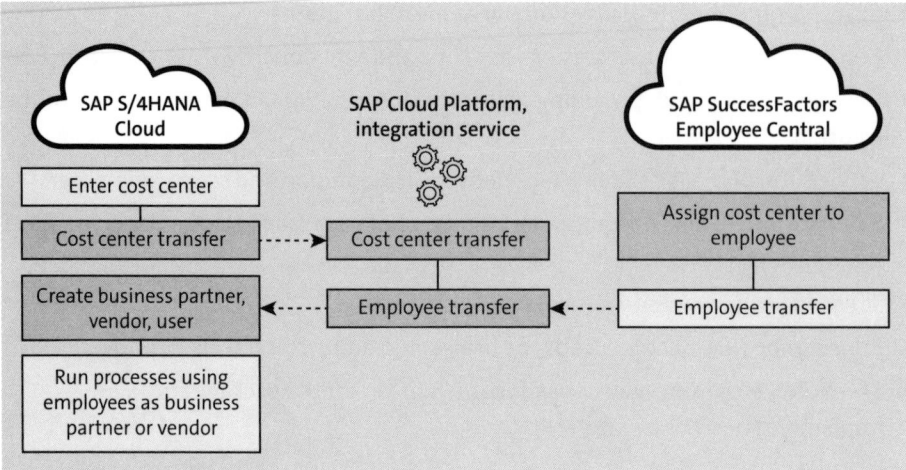

Figure 15.50 Integrating SAP S/4HANA Cloud with SAP SuccessFactors Employee Central

More on SAP SuccessFactors Employee Central integration building blocks and integration information is available at *http://s-prs.co/500320*, where you'll find the latest integration information, as well as the following:

- Process diagram, which outlines the integration approach
- Test script, for verification of implementation
- Process model BPMN2

15.7   Summary

Although cloud solutions offer unprecedented savings in maintenance and ease of use, data and processes from on-premise ERP systems, such as SAP ERP and SAP S/4HANA, are often core for augmenting and completing processes in SAP Ariba. This chapter outlined several integration options for pairing SAP's cloud portfolio solutions for procurement with SAP ERP environments. For SAP Ariba, many of these integrations are here today and accessible via the native integrations in SAP S/4HANA and accessible comprehensively as part of the SAP Cloud Integration Platform.

For integration, more and more of these linkages are being built and will be native out of the box for future releases in all of SAP's cloud and on-premise solutions. However, just because something is an SAP cloud solution doesn't mean that it's completely integrated in all ways with SAP's digital core solutions today. For now, understanding your integration requirements and options for your project are key for successfully realizing the end-to-end processes in SAP's cloud and on-premise solutions. Next, we'll discuss the SAP Fiori UI approach in SAP S/4HANA.

15

Chapter 16
Customizing the UI

This chapter focuses on SAP Fiori, the UI technology underpinning SAP S/4HANA and several future SAP solutions as well. Based on user roles and business processes, SAP Fiori is a design language that underpins the UX in SAP S/4HANA.

One of the biggest challenges for SAP ERP has been UI and design. SAP Fiori focuses on users and design, simplifying and reimagining processes while embracing open standards and service orientation on the technology side. Perhaps equally important for SAP S/4HANA, SAP Fiori is built to run with in-memory and cloud applications. From a business user standpoint, SAP Fiori stands for simplification and reimagined processes, distilling transactions and processes into role-focused apps and easy-to-navigate screens. SAP Fiori is the go-to UI technology for SAP solutions.

16.1 User Interface Options in SAP S/4HANA

The two main UI options in SAP S/4HANA are SAP Fiori and reverting to the SAP GUI transactions familiar to users of older versions of SAP ERP. Many of these transactions are still an option in SAP S/4HANA, but not adopting SAP Fiori and the apps approach in SAP S/4HANA precludes users from leveraging many of the new features of SAP S/4HANA contained only in the apps. First, let's look at SAP Fiori.

16.1.1 SAP Fiori

Many UI approaches of the past created an overwhelming cockpit of controls, buttons, and levers, confounding users looking to accomplish specific tasks in the system. SAP Fiori instead emphasizes role-based interaction while still allowing for adaptability and flexibility to allow users to apply functionality beyond a single path or process. This emphasis on simplicity, rather than feature overload, carries over into the other core tenets of SAP Fiori, which is:

- *Role-based*—that is, designed for you, your needs, and how you work
- *Adaptive*—that is, adapts to multiple use cases and devices
- *Coherent*—that is, provides one fluid, intuitive experience
- *Simple*—that is, includes only what's necessary
- *Delightful*—that is, makes an emotional connection

For example, in SAP Fiori, you can click on a tile such as **Workflow Inbox** and enter the Approvals app (shown in Figure 16.1). Unlike previous workflow approval layouts, you only see the fundamentals: the request list and an expanded window showing the content of a selected request.

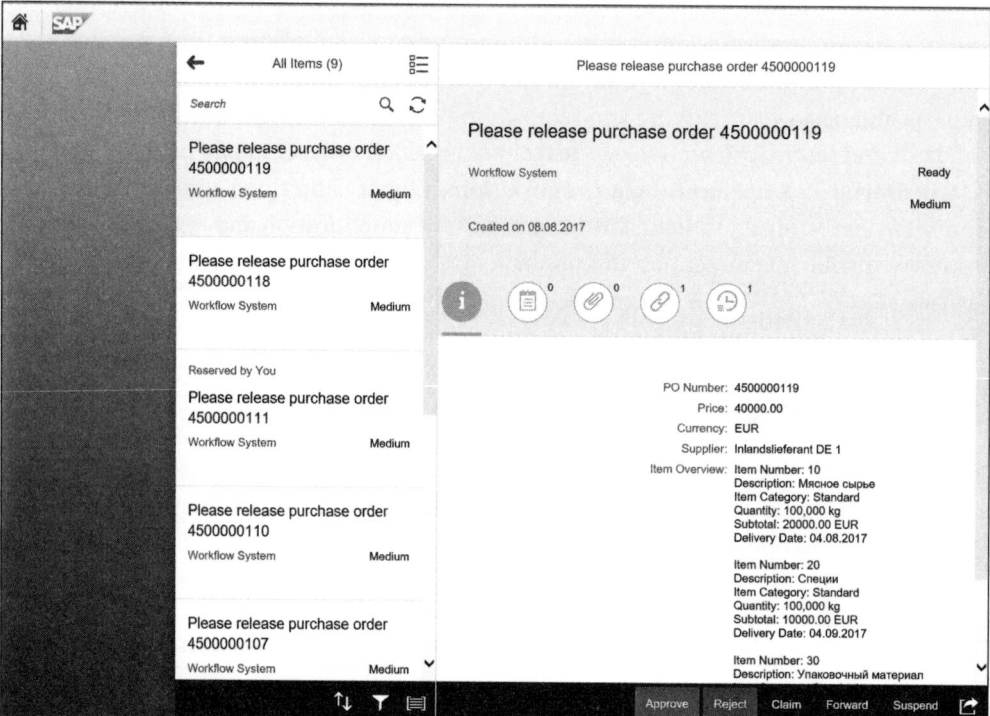

Figure 16.1 SAP Fiori Approvals App

Approvals is quite straightforward from a UI perspective and doesn't need a lot of bells and whistles. Either you approve something or you reject a request, perhaps communicating directly with the user during the process to further refine the order or understand a nuance. Beyond this, there need not be a slew of features. The app is in line with this thinking and with SAP Fiori's approach and principles overall.

There are three types of SAP Fiori apps:

- Transactional apps, which provide task-based access like the ability to change/create documents and data, or entire processes in guided navigation
- SAP Smart Business analytical apps, which display a visual overview of a dedicated topic for KPI-driven analysis
- Fact sheet apps, which offer a view of essential object information and provide contextual navigation between related objects

Both SAP Smart Business analytical and fact sheet apps run on SAP HANA, while the SAP Fiori transactional apps can run on any supported database, including SAP HANA.

SAP Fiori Launchpad

As of SAP S/4HANA 1610, SAP Fiori is the sole UI option. A user can update her profile and access her applications/notifications all via a single landing page called the SAP Fiori launchpad, as shown in Figure 16.2.

By clicking the shell header icons located at the top of the window, a user can navigate to his last activities in the system or to key notifications, as shown in Figure 16.2. The anchor bar at the top replaces the group menu options as in Figure 16.3.

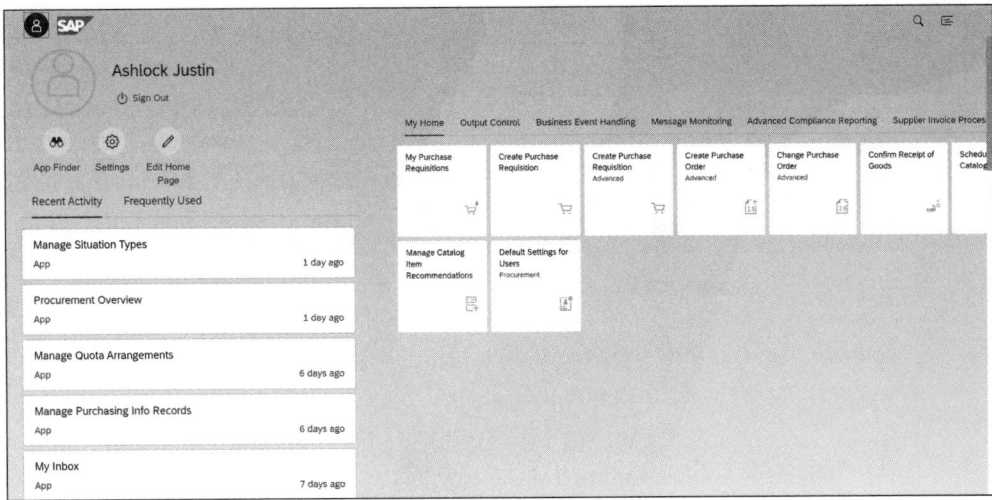

Figure 16.2 SAP Fiori Launchpad Overview

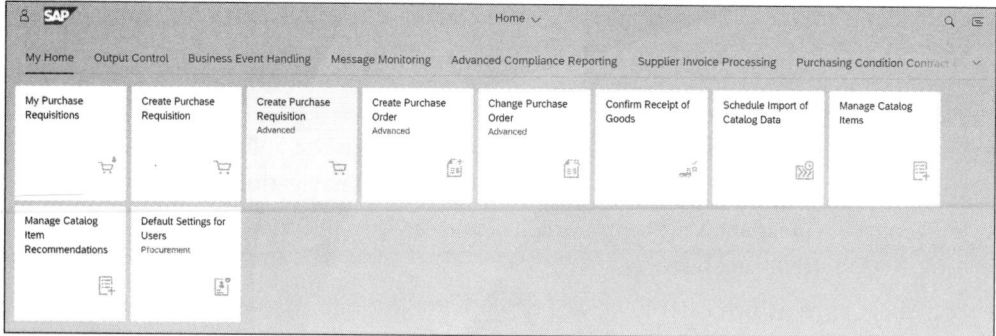

Figure 16.3 SAP Fiori Header Icons and Anchor Bar

Front and center are the apps, which can be made available via tiles or as links. Color-coding and dynamic charts in the tiles are used to update the user about important issues without having to drill into specific areas. A search option shown in Figure 16.4 allows you to search across and within apps, including individual business objects, to find immediate answers.

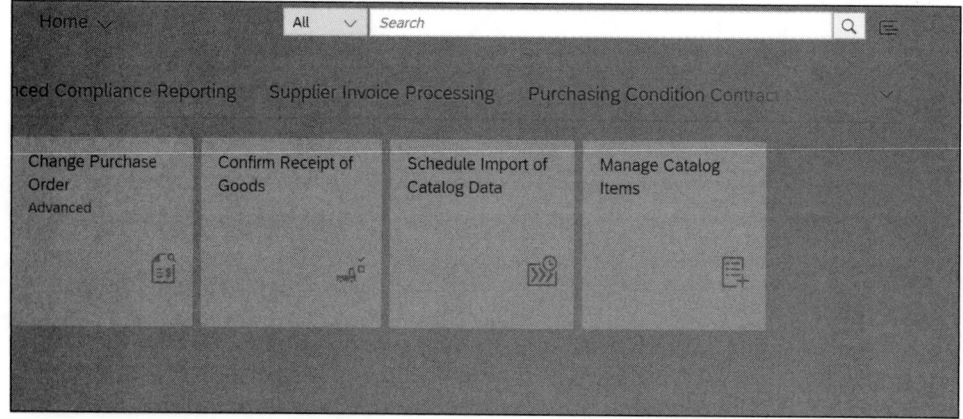

Figure 16.4 SAP Fiori Search Bar

If you need to drill into a business object or app, you can do so directly from the search results, as shown in Figure 16.5.

You also can enter edit mode to personalize groups, tiles, and link menus and to launch into other applications in SAPUI5, in Web Dynpro ABAP, in SAP GUI for HTML, or via URLs. You have to be on a device supporting these UIs for this launch to be successful, however.

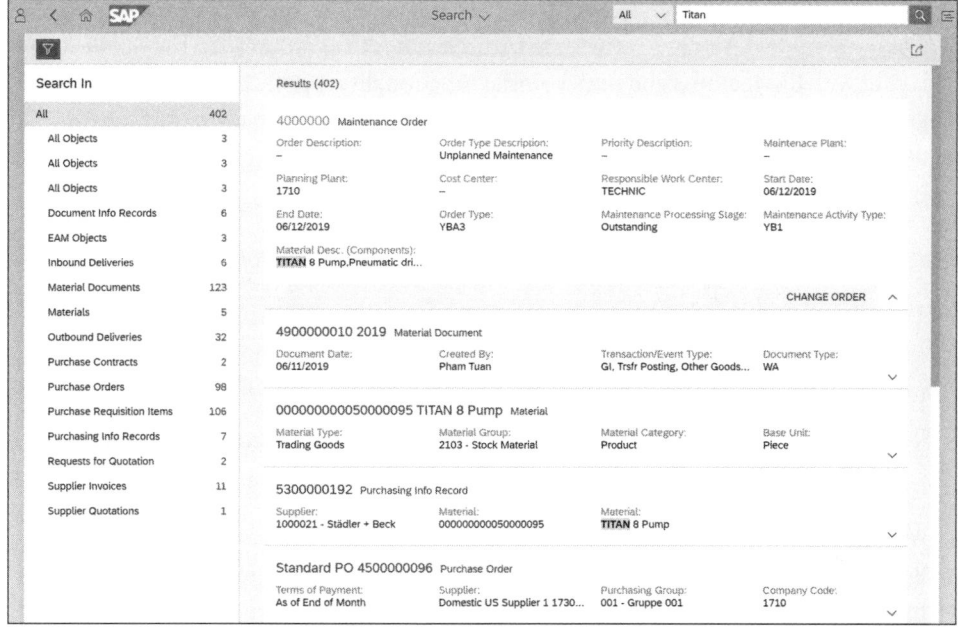

Figure 16.5 SAP Fiori Launchpad Search Results Filter

The supported UI technologies include the following:

- Unified rendering (Web Dynpro, ABAP/Java, HTML GUI, BSP, HTMLB or HTML Business for Java)
- SAPUI5 (SAP Fiori, SAP Fiori launchpad)
- WebClient UIF (SAP CRM)
- SAP Portal Content Management by OpenText (Ajax framework page, SAP Fiori framework page)
- SAP NetWeaver Business Client (for desktop and HTML)

> **Note**
>
> Support is planned for SAPUI5 for custom libraries and SAP GUI for Windows.

SAP Fiori supports the following platforms:

- SAP NetWeaver AS for ABAP
- SAP Portal Content Management by OpenText
- SAP Cloud Platform

16

These changes put all the core information and access at the user's fingertips while leaving some "whitespace" free for a featureless desktop rather than overloading the layout with distractions and nonessential functionality. In the SAP Fiori approach, no general newsfeeds or bulletin boards are found, just the key areas relevant to the user's role.

> **SAP Fiori Design Concept Evolution**
>
> SAP Fiori 2.0 leverages the new Belize theme with light and dark flavors to further refine the SAP Fiori visual language, as well as a clean and consistent layout to convey content and clarity. SAP Fiori 2.0 addressed some of the shortcomings from 1.0, including standardizing screen elements, icons, and color, as well as unifying interactions and adopting application design.

SAP Fiori Architecture

Before you begin implementation or configuration of SAP Fiori for SAP S/4HANA, it's important to understand the underlying SAP Fiori architecture for the different editions of SAP S/4HANA. There are differences between logging into SAP S/4HANA Cloud and SAP S/4HANA.

In SAP S/4HANA Cloud, users log in via the service's web dispatcher and, once authenticated, access the SAP Fiori UI. From there, the user can then access the business logic layer of SAP S/4HANA Cloud via SAP Fiori apps and the general UI.

In an on-premise version of SAP S/4HANA, the user logs into the SAP S/4HANA frontend server either via a browser to access the web dispatcher and system hosted internally or via an on-premise desktop/VPN, as per Figure 16.6. Cloud users go directly to SAP S/4HANA without a mediated connection as in the on-premise version.

For mobile devices, SAP Fiori provides the SAP Mobile Platform, which leverages the SAP Fiori frontend server, as per Figure 16.6.

From an architecture standpoint, the main difference between SAP S/4HANA Cloud and the on-premise version is the frontend server requirement. This is the SAP S/4HANA view with the changed access pattern for the SAP HANA database. From a sizing perspective, the approach stays the same; only the load pattern changes. The desktop's path runs from the web dispatcher directly to the SAP NetWeaver AS for ABAP backend, whereas the mobile devices run through the web dispatcher to the SAP Frontend Server (FES), and then onward to the SAP NetWeaver ABAP backend and SAP S/4HANA database.

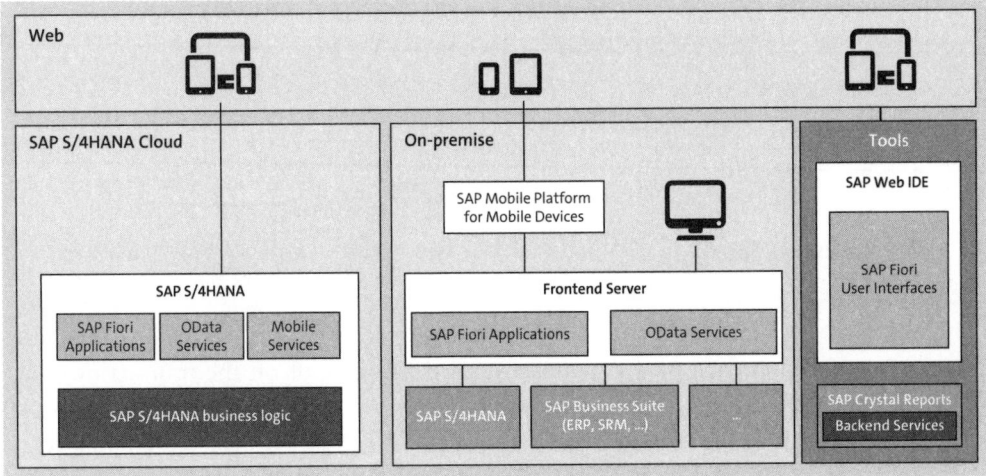

Figure 16.6 SAP Fiori Architecture Overview

As shown in Figure 16.7, the main technical components of SAP Fiori on SAP S/4HANA are the frontend server, including SAP Gateway, SAP NetWeaver/ABAP, including an SAP Gateway add-on, the SAP HANA database, SAP Web Dispatcher, and the SAP Mobile Platform.

16

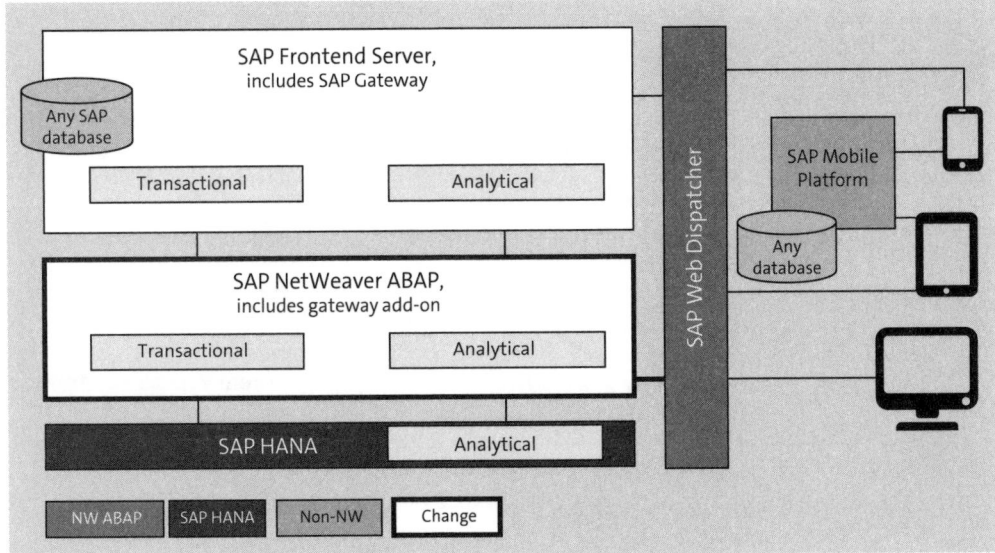

Figure 16.7 SAP Fiori on SAP S/4HANA Architecture: Simplified System View

From SAP S/4HANA, a user can access the SAP Fiori launchpad via a supported web browser and launch the following:

- SAP Fiori apps
- SAP GUI for HTML
- Web Dynpro apps

SAP Business Client

Another way to support SAP Fiori is via the SAP Business Client. The SAP Business Client approach replaces the web browser with a dedicated UI called the SAP Business Client. This approach provides more focused throughput on the transaction side, meaning faster speeds, and it's sometimes favored for desktop users performing specific transactions in the system for this reason. Future support is planned for a Windows SAP GUI in the SAP Business Client UI approach to SAP S/4HANA, as shown in Figure 16.8. The Windows SAP GUI in the SAP Business Client version will initially come in the classic SAP GUI design, with the SAP Fiori theme planned for future releases of this approach.

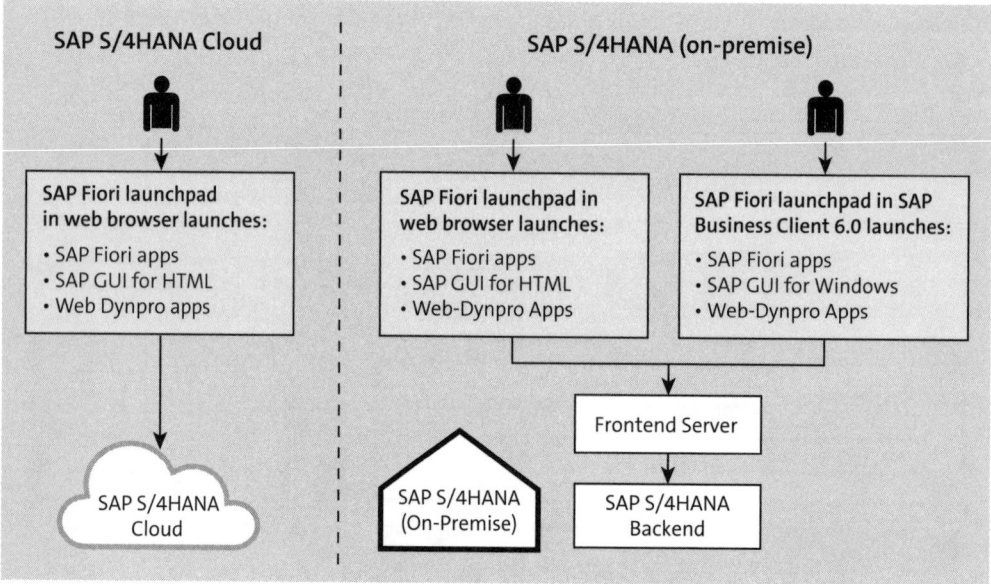

Figure 16.8 SAP Business Client UI Approach for SAP S/4HANA

Central Hub versus Embedded: Deploying SAP Gateway

Further drilling into the general architecture of SAP Fiori for SAP S/4HANA, you can deploy SAP Gateway either in a separate, central hub or in an embedded fashion, as in Figure 16.9 and Figure 16.10. Depending on your role in the project, you may or may not be tasked with deciding on the approach here, as it's typically more of an IT decision. However, knowing the trade-offs, even at a functional level, is helpful for understanding how your SAP Fiori environment works.

Figure 16.9 outlines the components involved for SAP Fiori, principally the Webserver and the ABAP frontend and backend servers. Figure 16.10 dives deeper into the landscape options.

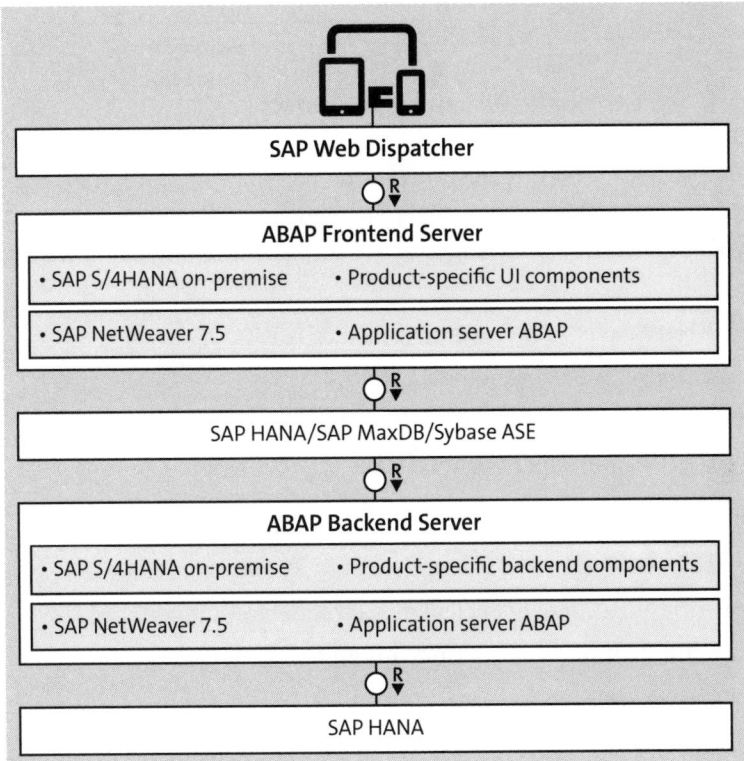

Figure 16.9 SAP Fiori Landscape

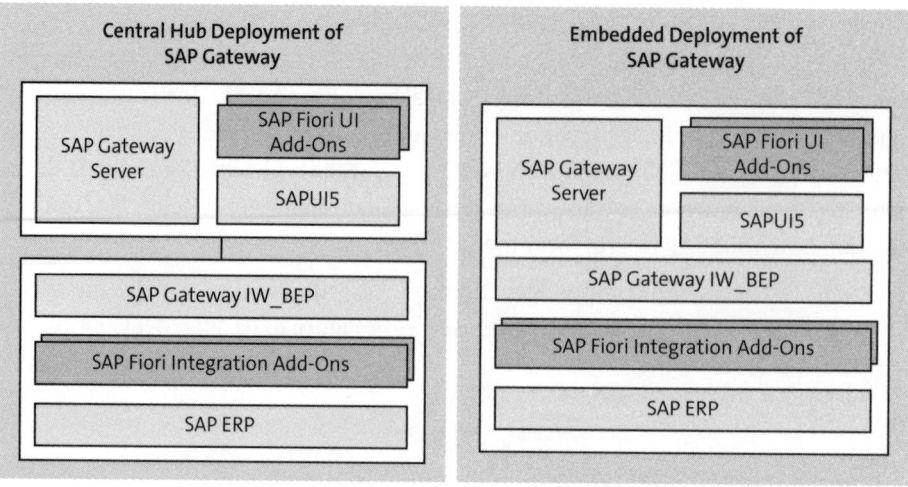

Figure 16.10 Central Hub and Embedded Options for SAP Gateway

The central hub approach is more typical in productive environments than the embedded, though the embedded option is lightweight and allows for speedier setup of test environments. Key advantages of an embedded deployment are as follows:

- No additional SAP NetWeaver ABAP system needed; less TCO
- Less runtime overhead, as well as no remote call
- Direct access to metadata and business data
- Later scale-out to central hub deployment possible

However, some of the concerns for an embedded approach are as follows:

- Innovation speed of SAP Fiori UI and backend must be synchronized
- Update strategy must reflect dependencies between software components
- SAP backend must fulfill minimum system requirements
- Possible scale-up of SAP backend (resizing)

Currently, the majority of customers are on a central hub deployment, which has its own advantages and considerations, as illustrated in Figure 16.11.

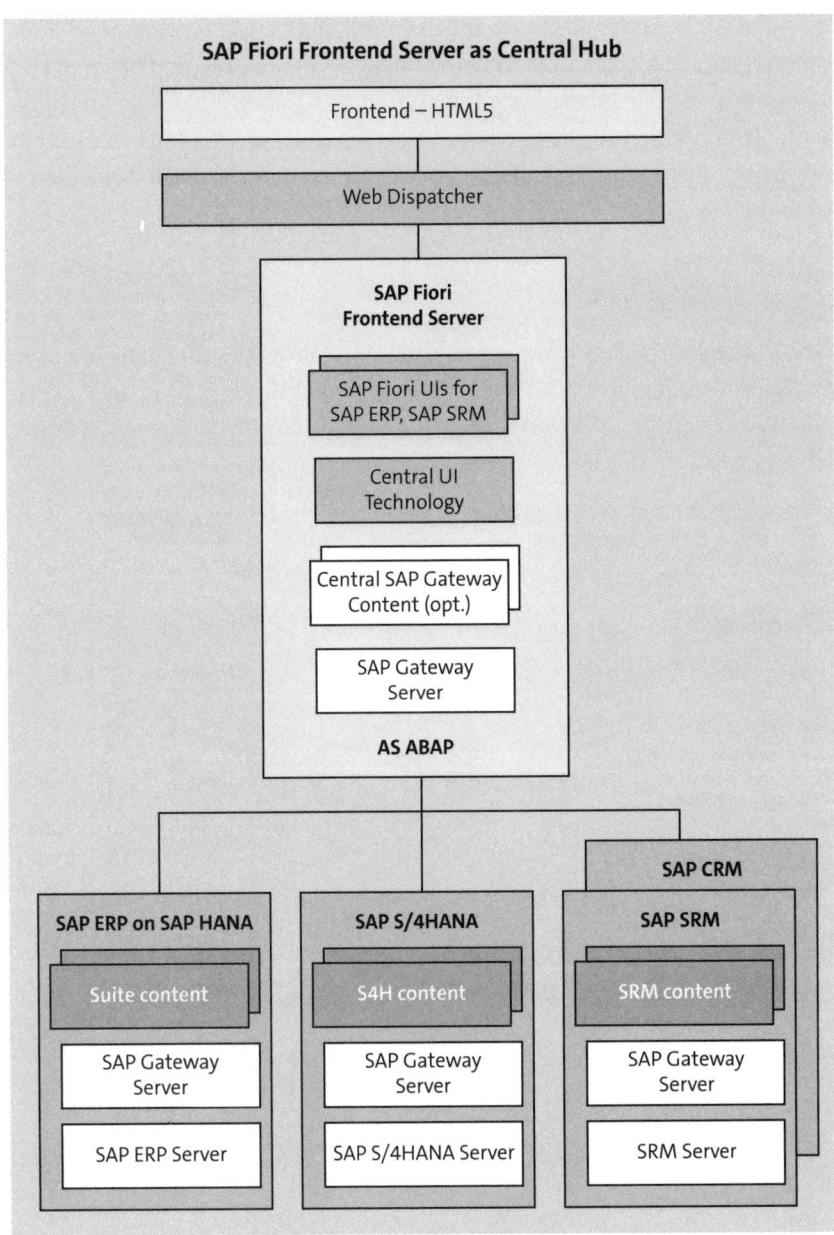

Figure 16.11 Central Hub Deployment for SAP Fiori Frontend Server

16

Regardless of the deployment approach for the SAP Fiori frontend server, SAP Fiori 2.0 is mandatory for all SAP Fiori apps on SAP S/4HANA version 1610 and beyond, and 1610 apps require an SAP database. Existing apps at this 1610 level and beyond currently run on the Belize theme. It's also possible to run older apps on SAP Fiori 2.0 in their respective classic themes. Not all functionality may be accessible for older apps without adjustments.

16.1.2   SAP General User Interface

The SAP GUI has underpinned previous versions of SAP ERP, spanning back decades now. The screenshot in Figure 16.12 may look very familiar to long-time SAP users, even though it's a screenshot of an SAP GUI screen in SAP S/4HANA. Little has changed here, and the transaction code bar still remains in the upper-left-hand corner.

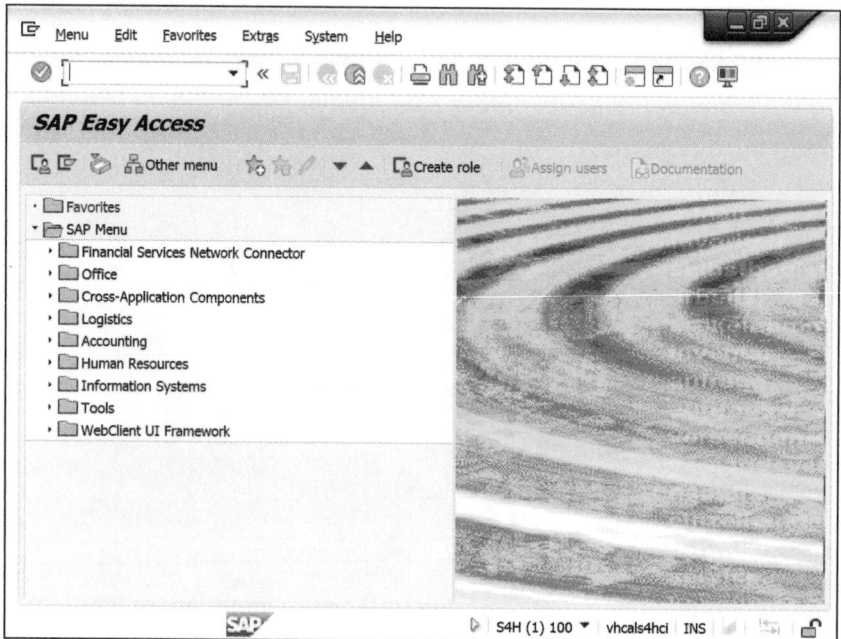

Figure 16.12 SAP GUI

In SAP S/4HANA, you can launch SAP GUI either via HTML or the SAP Business Client approach. There are limitations and advantages to both options. Despite some limitations, SAP GUI HTML is the recommended approach for SAP GUI running the Belize theme. The SAP GUI limitations on the HTML side are as follows:

- Office integration is view-only.

- No bar chart (GANTT), netchart, and supply chain management planning grid controls.

- No new ABAP Editor control (ABAP development needs SAP GUI for Windows).

- Limited support for client interaction (upload/download/execute, etc.), especially in new browsers.

- Limited keyboard navigation.

- Lower performance compared to SAP GUI for Windows.

However, HTML does support SAP Personas features. SAP Personas is the personalization framework integrated into the SAP GUI and multiple operating systems via its browser-based approach. A native Belize theme experience in SAP GUI is available for SAP GUI for Windows 7.5 and SAP Business Client 6.5. As far as using older themes in SAP Fiori, though possible, it isn't recommended, and not all the new features will be enabled using an older theme.

16.2   Configuring SAP Fiori

This section provides a general overview of the installation of and required components for SAP Fiori. You should always check *support.sap.com* prior to installing an SAP system to obtain the latest installation guides and notes.

16.2.1   Installing SAP Fiori

To install SAP Fiori, the technical SAP Basis team on your project will need to complete the following steps:

1. Install SAP NetWeaver 7.5x with the latest service pack stack. The supported databases are SAP HANA, SAP Adaptive Server Enterprise (SAP ASE), and SAP MaxDB.

2. Follow the SAP S/4HANA SAP Fiori foundation configuration guides found at *https://rapid.sap.com/bp/* under **SAP Best Practice for SAP S/4HANA • S/4HANA • UX Best Practice for SAP S/4HANA**.

3. Generate and download the maintenance planner software, which enables planning all changes for your SAP landscape. For more information see *http://s-prs.co/500322*.

4. Perform SAP Gateway basic configuration—that is, the baseline configuration of SAP Gateway.

5. Set up the trusted RFCs/system aliases/SAP Fiori launchpad initial configuration. These are your basic setup steps for enabling the system to communicate with other systems and be configured. Configure your RFCs, define the system alias, and complete baseline configuration for SAP Fiori launchpad.

6. Activate SICF services and OData services. In Transaction SICF, you can activate services and nodes for HTTP communication. Activating OData services allows your RESTful APIs to be extended to support custom needs. *REST* stands for *representational state transfer* and relies on a stateless, client-server-based, and cacheable communication protocol, which typically leverages HTTP.

7. Create and maintain standard SAP Fiori roles.

8. Install and configure SAP Web Dispatcher. SAP Web Dispatcher is required for on-premise installations of SAP S/4HANA and functions as a broker between the user's browser and the SAP S/4HANA system.

9. Activate Enterprise Search (fact sheet applications). SAP Fiori fact sheets provide overview information on a business object. By enabling search, you can identify related fact sheets while searching for an item, such as a material master.

10. Load search indexes. Indexes allow a search to run faster and more comprehensively.

11. Set up the SAP BW client on the SAP S/4HANA system for embedded analytics.

12. Activate the SAP NetWeaver Business Client/WebGUI for HTML/Web Dynpro applications on the backend system.

16.2.2   Embedded and Central Hub Deployment for SAP Fiori

You then either configure a central hub or embedded deployment of SAP Fiori. The central hub and embedded options are the two main ways to set up the system, and each has advantages and concerns. In general, the central hub approach is used for larger production systems and systems required to handle large volumes of users, transactions, and queries. An embedded deployment approach is often used for development and functional testing systems, for which volume requirements are not as pronounced, and sometimes for more modest production systems supporting smaller organizations.

Central hub installation means you install the frontend and backend components on different systems. A central hub deployment requires more effort to set up but allows you to separate your SAP Solution Manager installation from your SAP Fiori apps, making your apps available to business users without having to run SAP Solution Manager. This approach also allows you to consolidate your SAP Fiori apps into one launchpad, even when using multiple systems. You can perform the development either in the SAP Gateway system or directly in SAP Business Suite. Developing directly in SAP Business Suite allows you to reuse data easily because the data is in the system in which the development is taking place. Developing on SAP Gateway allows for a loosely coupled, noninvasive approach to development that can also fulfill security requirements because SAP Gateway can be placed in a separate area from the SAP S/4HANA system.

An embedded approach doesn't require an SAP Gateway system and therefore reduces setup and costs. Development is done directly in the SAP Business Suite system, allowing for similar advantages as found in the central hub option for developing on SAP Business Suite; that is, less intermediation between systems is required. Once you've installed the system with either the embedded or central hub option, you're ready to install SAP Fiori apps.

16.2.3 SAP Fiori App Library

With SAP Fiori installed, go to *www.sap.com/fiori-apps-library* to discover, explore, and implement SAP Fiori apps. In the SAP Fiori app library, you can search for apps, obtain recommendations based on your user profile and transaction code usage, analyze an app both on a functional and technical level, and, finally, implement the app i]n your system. In the library, you can search for and filter apps by business area, product type, and technical specifications. Based on your backend transactions and installed software, the search functionality provides suitable app recommendations as well. You then can explore individual apps, reviewing app details and versions, and finally download the selected apps. Once downloaded, you further review their versions, prerequisites, and dependencies. To implement the selected SAP Fiori apps, you integrate these apps with Maintenance Planner, SAP Solution Manager's cloud-based interface for planning all changes in your system landscape. Finally, you can export SAP Fiori configuration steps to task lists for automatic configuration.

Implementing Procurement-Specific SAP Fiori Apps

Let's now explore the process of implementing an app from the SAP Fiori app library. For procurement-specific apps, you can search for and filter over 460 apps (and growing) for SAP S/4HANA Sourcing and Procurement, as shown in Figure 16.13.

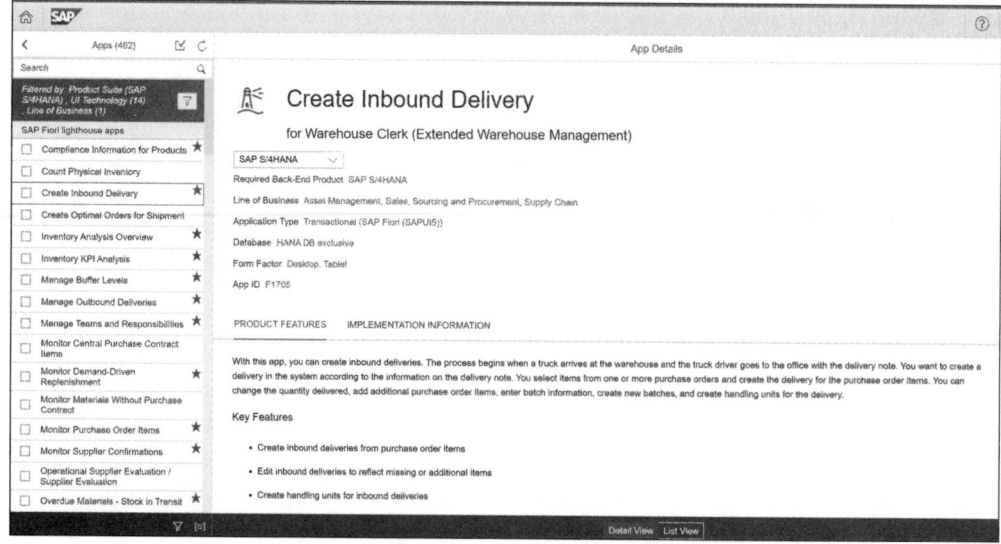

Figure 16.13 SAP Fiori App Library: Procurement Apps

One popular app for procurement is the Create Purchase Requisitions app (see Figure 16.14). Let's walk through how to install or evaluate this app.

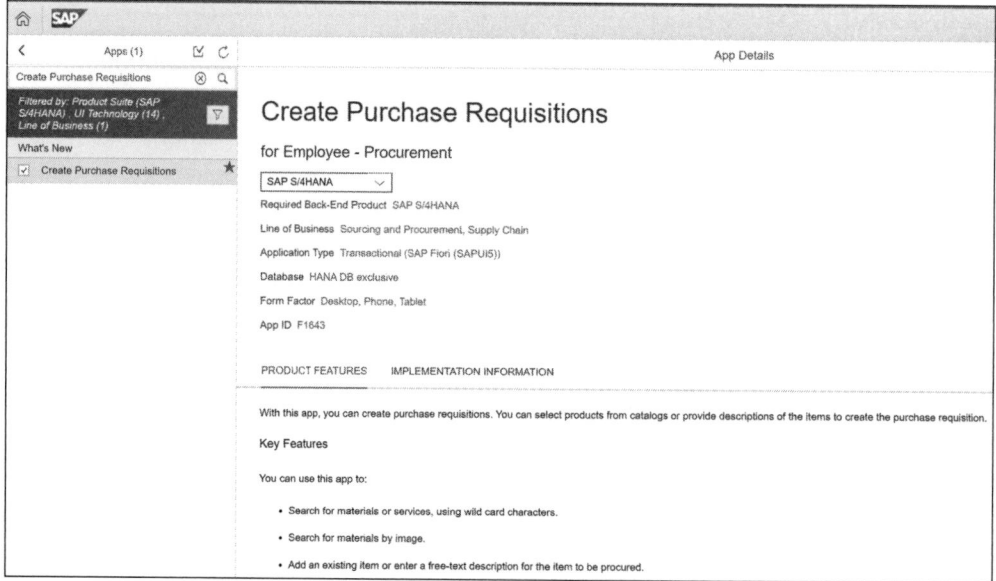

Figure 16.14 Create Purchase Requisitions App

To begin, select whether the system for the installation is in the cloud (**SAP S/4HANA Cloud**) or on-premise (**SAP S/4HANA**), as shown in Figure 16.15.

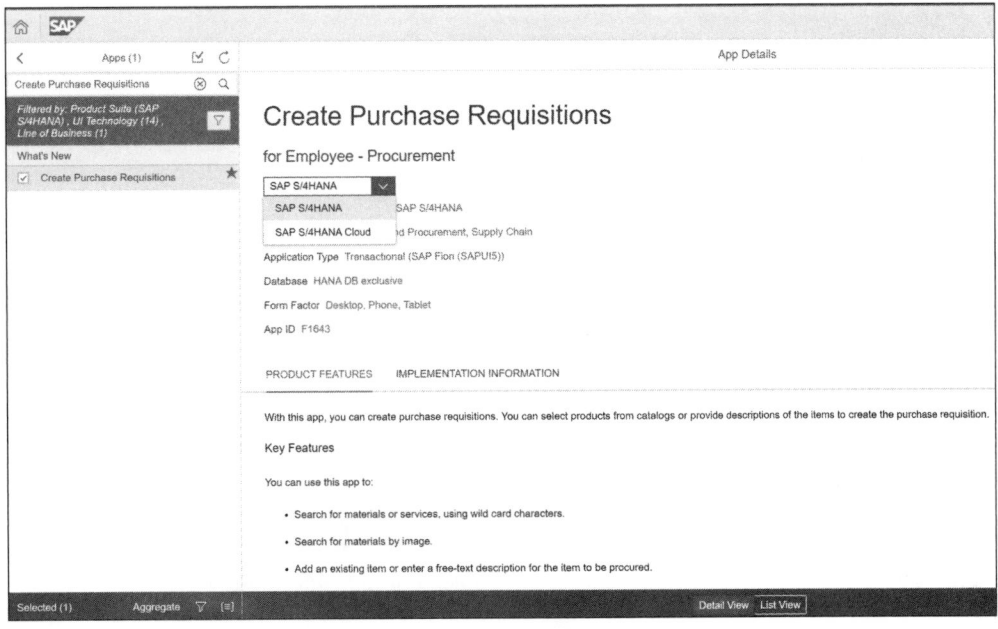

Figure 16.15 Create Purchase Requisitions App: Cloud or On-Premise

Once you've selected your system, you'll need to verify whether your system can support this app. Under **Implementation Information**, you can select your desired SAP S/4HANA version and access all of the implementation information available to install and use this app in your system, as shown in Figure 16.16.

The **Installation** section reviews the required components for this app and reiterates the guidance for the using Maintenance Planner via SAP Solution Manager to determine whether your system landscape will support the app, as shown in Figure 16.17.

In the **Configuration** section, each app may have different areas requiring configuration. For the Create Purchase Requisitions app, ICF nodes, OData services, target mapping, a business catalog, a group, a role, and search connectors all must be activated.

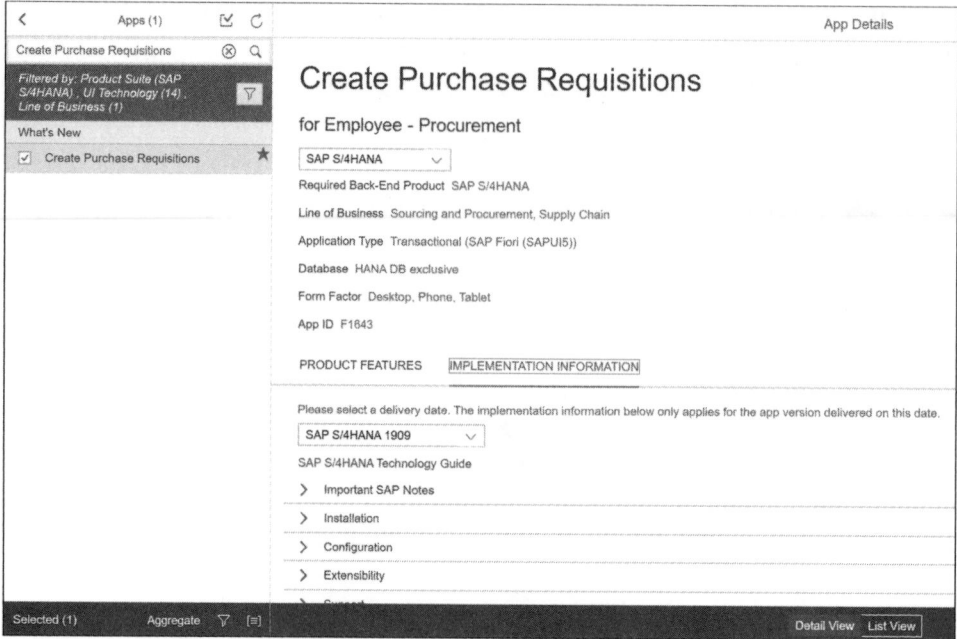

Figure 16.16 Create Purchase Requisitions Implementation Information

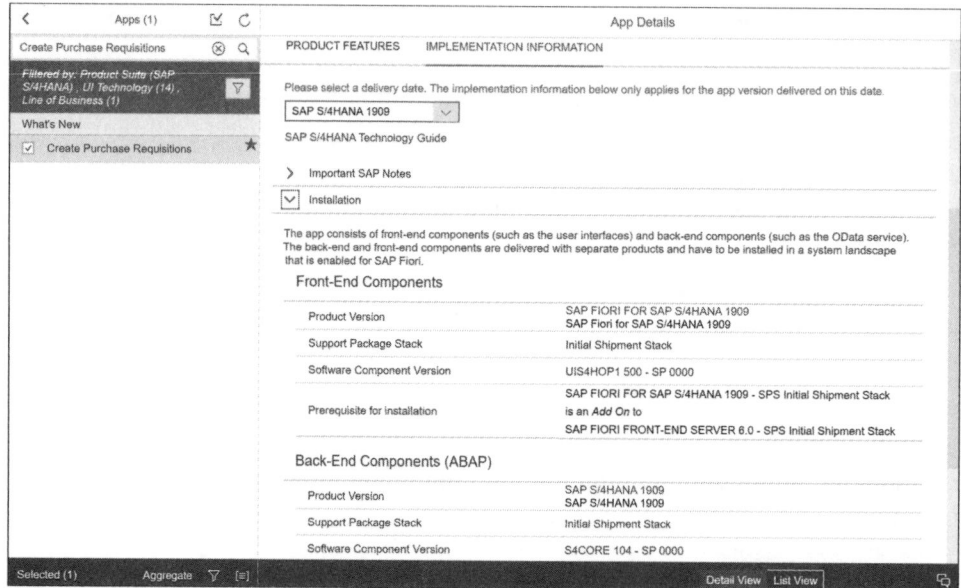

Figure 16.17 Installation Section for Create Purchase Requisitions App

Upon completing the configuration, you can review the **Extensibility** section to identify areas of the app that are extensible, the **Support** section to determine areas to reference for support, and the **Related Apps** section to see groups of apps with similar functionality if required.

Unlike the SAP Fiori settings and the SAP CoPilot features, to which every user may have access, very few users will have authorization to install and/or configure additional apps in the system. The installation of apps is usually managed by a core system team in coordination with technical resources and an SAP Basis team. Each installation, depending on the app, may vary in its steps and areas of review. The SAP Fiori app library also provides recommendation functionality to aid in identifying new relevant apps for your user community, as discussed in the following section.

Recommendations in SAP Fiori App Library Search

You can obtain app recommendations based on your system usage, which allows for further apps to be proposed. The recommendations are driven in part by the transaction codes you currently use in the backend system, highlighting the applicability as shown in Figure 16.18. Here, the search has yielded several relevant results, but from a system-readiness standpoint, only some of the required components for these recommended apps have been installed.

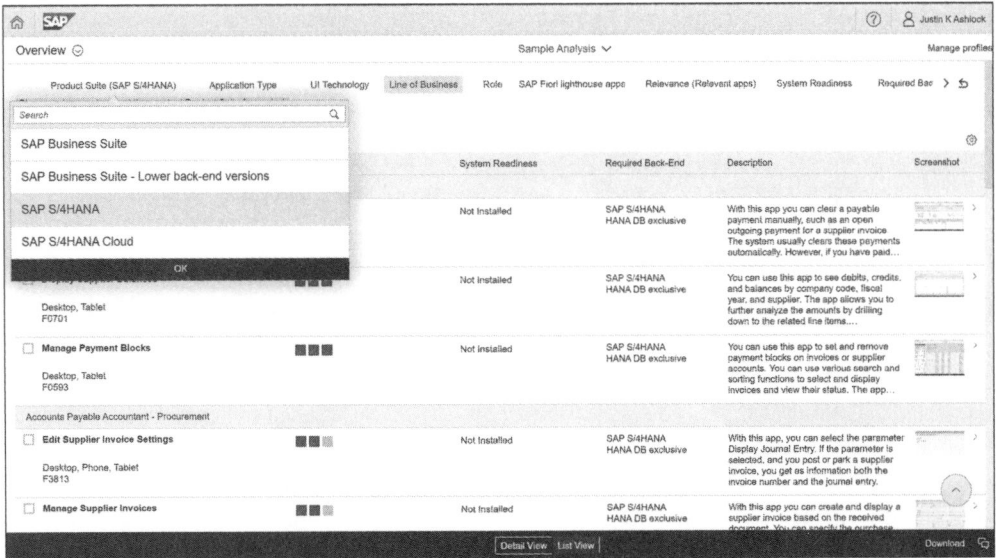

Figure 16.18 SAP Fiori App Recommendations Analysis

To get recommendations, you first select your profile. You can then upload profiles via CSV files to tune the search recommendations still further.

16.3   Customizing SAP Fiori

In SAP S/4HANA Sourcing and Procurement, as in other areas in SAP S/4HANA Enterprise Management, the first thing a user sees at login is the SAP Fiori launchpad, shown in Figure 16.19. The SAP Fiori launchpad displays tiles for apps, as well as other information, serving as the main entry point to SAP Fiori apps on mobile and desktop devices.

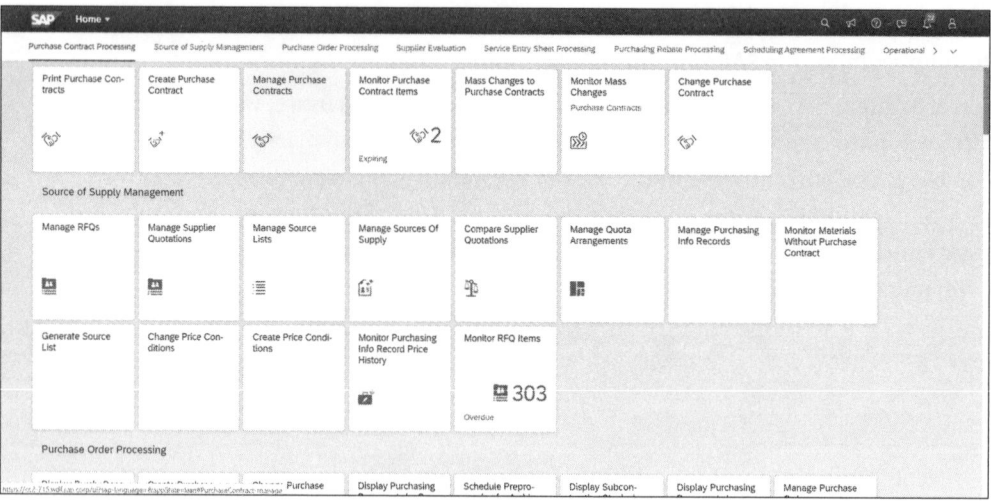

Figure 16.19 SAP Fiori Launchpad for SAP S/4HANA Sourcing and Procurement Users

A user can add, remove, and bundle tiles in the SAP Fiori launchpad and tailor the launchpad to serve as a starting point for all work in the system. The SAP Fiori launchpad automatically adjusts the screen and apps to the type of device being used.

16.3.1   SAP Fiori Edit Mode

You can arrange the dashboard and other apps by going into edit mode, as shown in Figure 16.20. Here, you can move the app tiles and even delete tiles that aren't relevant to/desired for your dashboard. You can also add groups to group relevant apps together and allow for easier navigation.

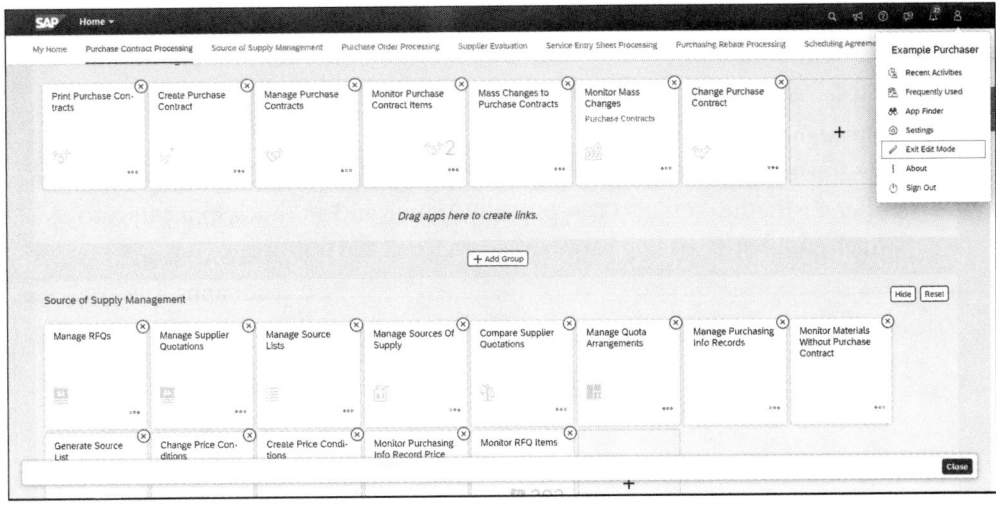

Figure 16.20 SAP Fiori Launchpad in Edit Mode

16.3.2   SAP Fiori User Settings

To tune and adjust the UI, you don't need to have configuration access. By going into the **Settings** area, as shown in Figure 16.21, you can tune several areas in SAP Fiori.

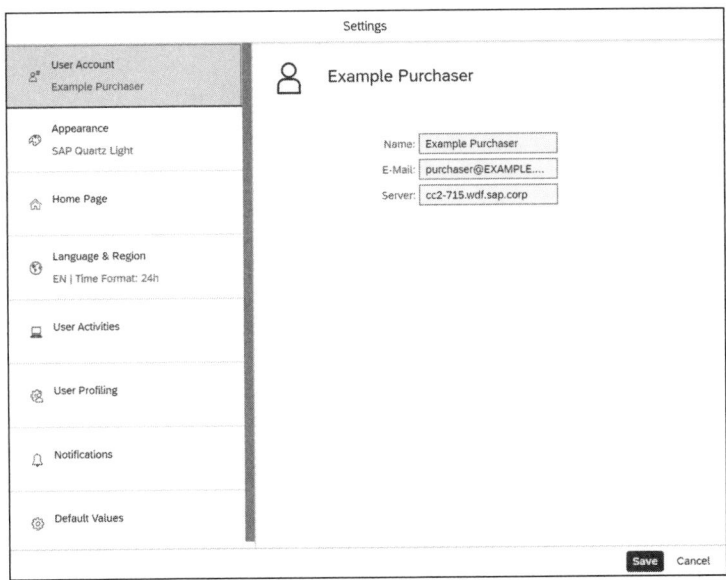

Figure 16.21 User Settings in SAP Fiori

The areas you can change include the following:

- **User Account**
  You can change the user account.

- **Appearance**
  The appearance of the screen can be changed from the standard Belize setting to a different theme. You also can activate **Optimized For Touch Input** (Figure 16.22) which eliminates spacing between screen icons and buttons.

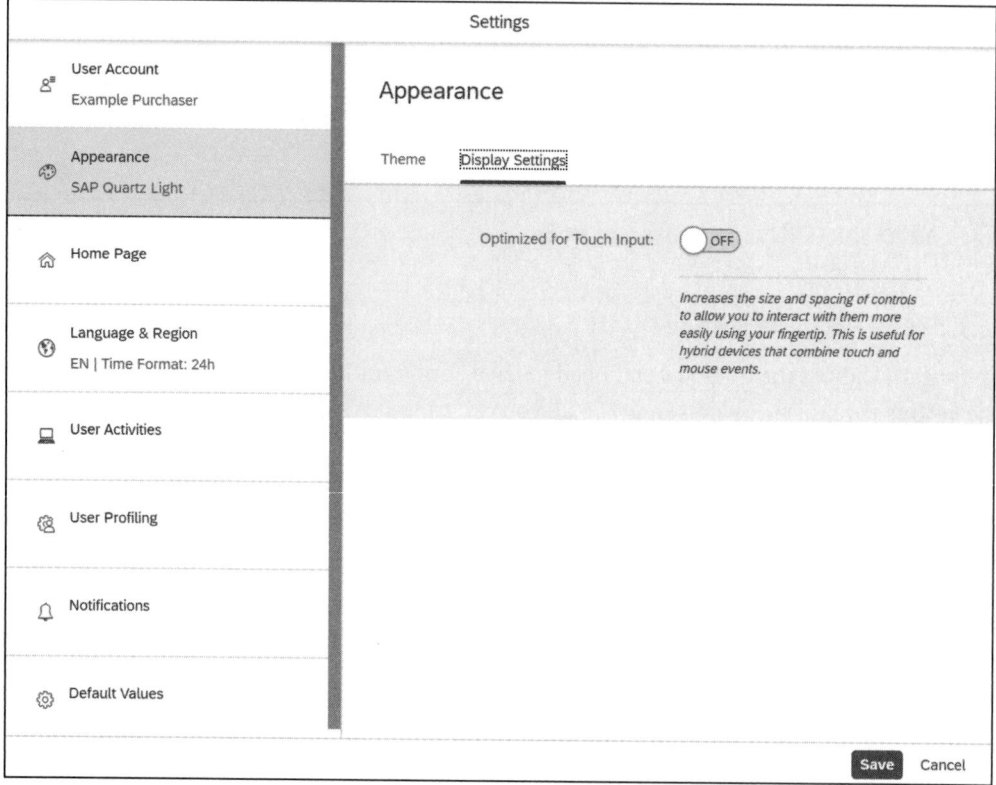

Figure 16.22 Optimized for Touch Input

- **Home Page**
  Here, you have the option of showing all of the content or one group at a time.

- **Language & Region**
  Here, you can set the language, date, and time settings.

- **User Profiling**

  If this feature is turned on, SAP Fiori logs searches and other selections during usage to enable smart searching in the system. For example, if you search for the same thing often and select similar items from the search results, these items will be displayed more prominently. You can also turn this feature off, as shown in Figure 16.23. For cloud instances, there is a tracking switch as well.

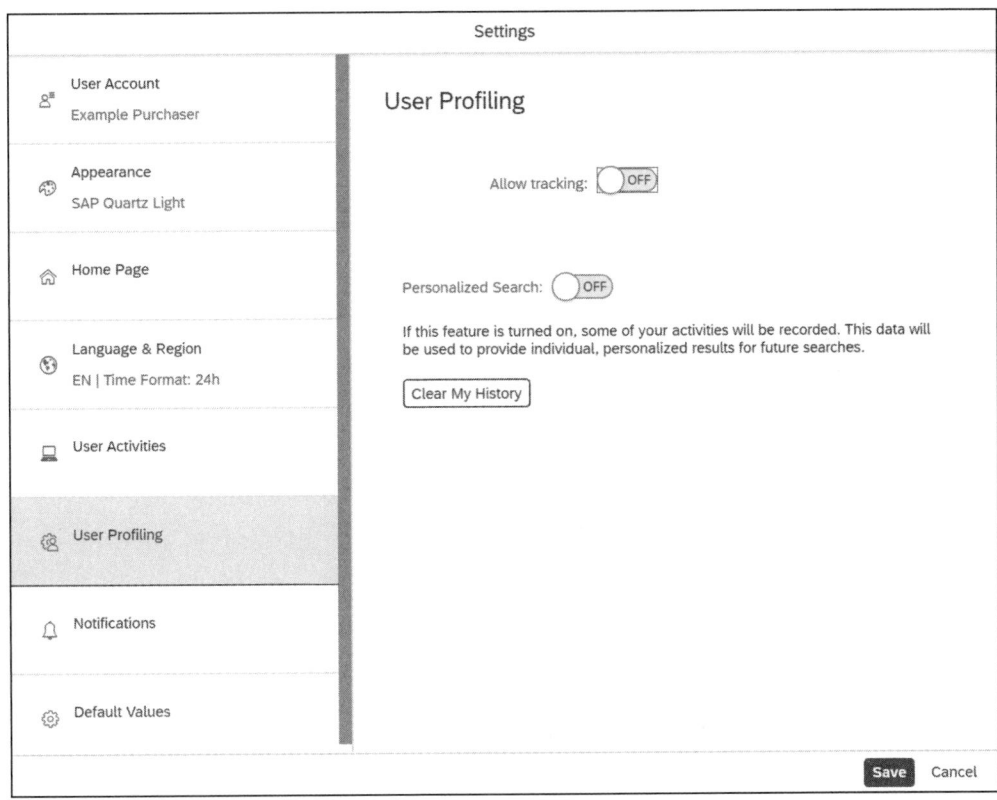

Figure 16.23 SAP Fiori Personalized Search and Tracking

- **Notifications**

  If notifications are enabled in your apps, this is where you'll see app notifications. Otherwise, a message will appear that notifications aren't activated for your apps.

- **Default Values**

  This is a very useful area, especially for users conducting routine transactions in the system. Here, you can set financial defaults for controlling, such as controlling area and cost center. You can also set accounting defaults, such as company code, business area, and/or general ledger account. Finally, you can set defaults for supply chain management, such as bank information, supplier, plant, and customer.

16.3.3   SAP CoPilot

Another usability feature is SAP CoPilot, a digital assistant for enterprises, available as of SAP S/4HANA 1705. You can turn SAP CoPilot on via an icon in the upper-left-hand corner of an SAP Fiori screen if enabled. The icon is circled in green in Figure 16.24.

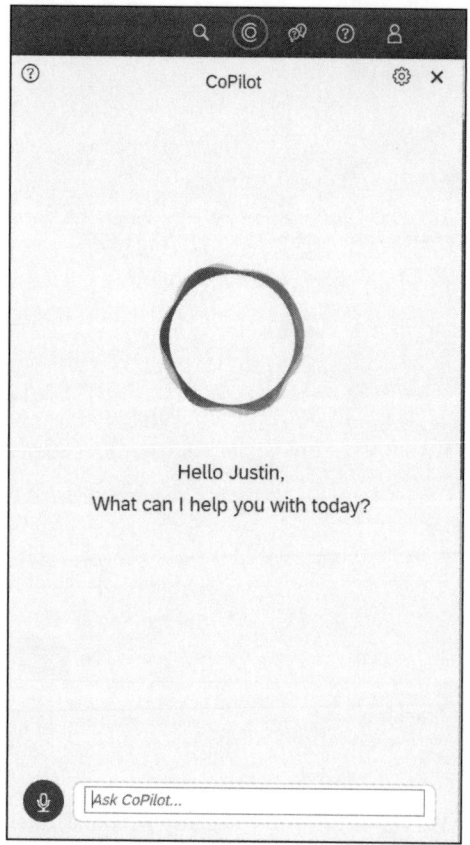

Figure 16.24 SAP CoPilot Icon

After turning on SAP CoPilot, a user can perform the following actions:

- Create notes when working with apps and have these notes linked to the apps.

- Create intelligent screenshots that allow you to navigate in the app to where the screenshot was taken. Colleagues can follow the screenshots to the particular place in the app that they were taken, provided they have access to the app. This allows for faster collaboration and issue resolution when using screenshots in support cases.

- SAP CoPilot recognizes business objects mentioned in chats, notes, or on the screen in general, allowing you to add business objects as such in screenshots, notes, and chats.

- The context extends to the chat feature in SAP S/4HANA, so there's no need to send emails and attach screenshots if you prefer chat. You can also save the chats, along with the attachments, for later use.

- Quick actions allow you to create business objects via *quick create* UIs, which simplify the process by defaulting content from SAP CoPilot.

Classic transactions in SAP, even if they retain essentially the same fields, receive an overhaul in SAP Fiori in terms of appearance. These transactions are usually a couple of layers deeper into the process, rather than on the opening page. A key one for SAP S/4HANA Sourcing and Procurement is the well-known Transaction ME21N for POs. This is now the "advanced" version for creating a PO in SAP S/4HANA (see Figure 16.25), in which, as discussed in Chapter 4, a user can create a framework order and other more involved types of purchase orders.

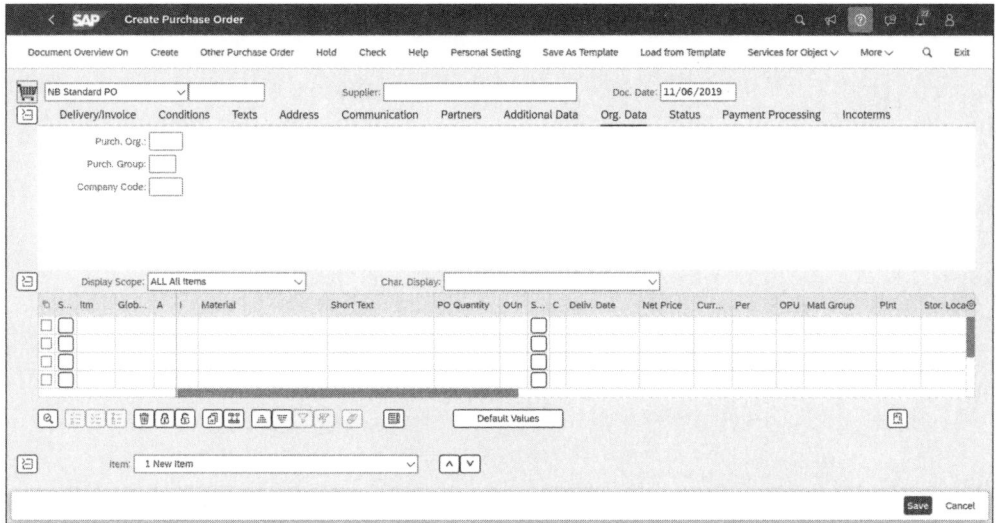

Figure 16.25 SAP Fiori: Create Purchase Order—Advanced

In this transaction, the fields are mostly the same as in an SAP ERP environment, but the look and feel has been updated to align with SAP Fiori principles and approaches. This is the general approach taken by SAP for all classic transactions remaining in SAP Fiori and SAP S/4HANA.

16.4   Summary

SAP Fiori is the de facto UI platform and technology for SAP solutions, and for SAP S/4HANA in particular. In this chapter, we explored the SAP Fiori UI, including the SAP Fiori launchpad, the SAP Fiori architecture, and SAP Fiori configuration. In the next chapter, we'll conclude with a summary of this book and of SAP S/4HANA Sourcing and Procurement.

Chapter 17
Conclusion

As reviewed in this book and in Figure 17.1, SAP S/4HANA covers a host of procurement processes both natively and in concert with SAP Cloud solutions, including central procurement, procurement analytics, supplier management, sourcing and contract management, operational purchasing, and invoice/payables management.

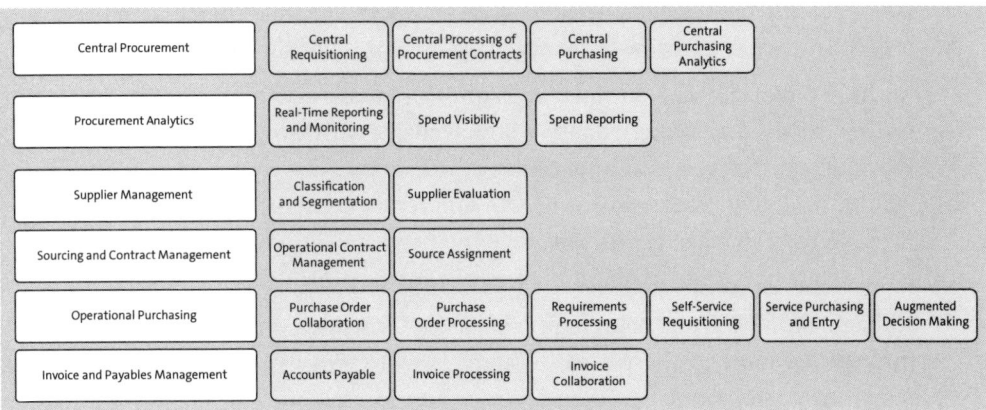

Figure 17.1 SAP S/4HANA Sourcing and Procurement Processes

Underpinning all of these areas is a layer of organizational and transactional master data, which is either defined during the project or at the inception of the original system. Many SAP S/4HANA implementations are greenfield or re-implementations today, requiring a strategy, design, and definition for master data; a refresher on this topic was provided in Chapters 3 and 4. We say a *refresher* because many of the concepts remained the same from previous versions of SAP. One major change for procurement topics in particular is the vendor master. The vendor and customer masters are consolidated in SAP S/4HANA into a unified business partner record. There are several steps prior to a system conversion that need to be performed to convert supplier data to this new model and format.

As covered in Chapter 5, operational procurement in SAP S/4HANA is similar to the previous iterations of self-service procurement in SAP ERP, with a larger emphasis on content management in the form of extensibility with the SAP Ariba Catalog and SAP Ariba Guided Buying areas in the cloud, as well as native catalog indexing/management functionality. Operational purchasing in SAP S/4HANA also leverages the SAP Ariba Network for purchase order and invoice collaboration. As of SAP S/4HANA Cloud release 1911, the integration for SAP Ariba Guided Buying and supplier collaboration SAP Ariba Network are included in the release.

A core procurement area that continues to be covered by SAP ERP is direct procurement and automated processes driven by MRP. Chapter 6 outlined significant changes to MRP and other direct procurement areas in SAP S/4HANA, as well as key integration points via SAP Ariba Supply Chain Collaboration for Buyers and SAP Ariba Network. Direct procurement documents and processes, from scheduling agreements to inventory collaboration, can now be managed via these solutions.

Inventory management, outlined in Chapter 7, remains a core area for SAP S/4HANA; further expansion of functionality is now available with the embedding of SAP EWM. Previously run as a sidecar application, it is now possible to run SAP EWM directly within the digital core of SAP S/4HANA and remove some of the redundant movement steps to manage goods. Resource-intensive inventory management analytics are also much more accessible and timely in SAP S/4HANA.

Managing contracts and sourcing events in SAP S/4HANA was detailed in Chapters 8 through 10. Some of these areas, such as the RFX process in SAP S/4HANA, have remained largely similar to their counterparts in previous SAP ERP iterations. For more robust RFX capabilities, SAP S/4HANA's integration with SAP Ariba Strategic Sourcing provides extensibility in the cloud and turnkey collaboration with suppliers on the SAP Ariba Network.

Other areas, such as contract management, have been bolstered by a host of new functionality contained in enterprise contract management, formerly known as legal content management. Contracts continue to be a core area for managing spend, and SAP S/4HANA offers more clause management and presignature tools for crafting optimal terms and language within an operational contract.

Accounts payable bookends the source-to-pay process covered in SAP S/4HANA and SAP Ariba, but it's a core area for savings realization and efficiency gains. Chapter 11 explained the recent developments in accounts payable for SAP S/4HANA and integration points with OpenText VIM and SAP Ariba Invoicing products.

Chapter 12 on supplier management showcased the power of SAP S/4HANA for analytics. Supplier reports can be driven by KPIs and real-time indicators to provide insight and performance readings in real time. Dashboard and survey functionality allows for SAP ERP users to include subjective feedback in addition to the objective feedback they typically provide on a transaction level, creating a holistic view of supplier performance. Expect more integrated survey capabilities from the Qualtrics acquisition to be applied in future releases in this area, including in the current SAP S/4HANA Cloud release 1911.

SAP S/4HANA for central procurement, as discussed in Chapter 13, represents the go-to platform for consolidating a disparate ERP environment with a centralized procurement operation, much like SAP SRM's approach of yore, but with nuances as well. No longer is a large data load and update required to support the cross-ERP-system management of procurement documents. Instead, central procurement leverages what's already there in the individual ERP systems directly.

Procurement analytics in general has greatly evolved in SAP S/4HANA, and Chapter 14 laid out the major changes and improvements to this area and analytics/reporting in general. The main areas include all of the new reports and apps on offer, capable of providing insight in real time as the transactions occur, as well as the continued extensibility and integration with further reporting tools from SAP BusinessObjects. For reporting areas continuing to require a business warehouse for data, SAP S/4HANA leverages a robust set of SAP BusinessObjects tools, such as SAP Crystal Reports, SAP Lumira, SAP Lumira, designer edition, and SAP Analysis for Microsoft Office. Future releases of SAP S/4HANA will continue down this path of convergence, offering deeper integration and cross-functionality with the SAP BusinessObjects toolsets. Machine-learning functionality driven by SAP Leonardo on the SAP Cloud Platform will also grow in importance as the areas of augmented decision-making and automation evolve.

The discussion of UI in SAP S/4HANA is driven by SAP Fiori. SAP Fiori represents a comprehensive platform and roadmap for SAP S/4HANA, with the goal of making system interaction intuitive on all devices, especially mobile, as well as providing app-based decision-making support and transaction simplification. Chapter 16 outlined the strategy for SAP Fiori, discussed purchasing apps, and covered the extensibility and customization options available today and planned for tomorrow.

The final section of this last chapter will now look to the future of procurement in SAP S/4HANA and procurement technology in general.

17.1 Future State of Procurement Solutions

SAP S/4HANA represents a significant step in reunifying transactions with analytics in one enterprise-grade environment, while applying neural network-approaches in SAP Leonardo and enhanced survey capabilities via SAP Qualtrics to augment and help automate the process of fostering insight for smart decision-making in procurement. Corporate procurement processes have yet to take full advantage of the new level of speed, intelligence, and integration with SAP's various cloud solutions, such as SAP Ariba, SAP Fieldglass, and Concur. SAP S/4HANA introduces a further reunification in the procurement area, unifying the customer and supplier in the form of a holistic business partner record. This is also being mirrored in SAP Ariba and other cloud solutions for procurement; customer and supplier contracts are maintained in the same area, and organizations play dual roles in the SAP Ariba Network as both customer and supplier.

Consumer-level UX is a much-used term these days in procurement systems. As consumers experience simplified processes in purchasing in their everyday lives, they begin to expect similar experiences in their workplaces. Rather than a corporation dictating a process and experience, current and future procurement processes and systems will need to innovate continuously and upgrade often just to keep pace with the relentless momentum in the consumer marketplace while maintaining seamless process integration with other areas of the business necessary for cash flow management, compliance, and production targets. By separating the UI-layer from the underlying logic and applying increased focus in this area, SAP looks to help customers "run simple," beyond the slogan, to address the continual need for simplification and usability.

An enormous amount of structured and unstructured information is generated each day in the digital world, which is often referred to as *big data*. SAP S/4HANA already allows for predictive modeling and analysis. Having been architected from the beginning to manage large datasets in a more efficient, compressed manner allows SAP S/4HANA to incorporate and monitor external factors as well as internal ones and drive this insight into the transactions being conducted.

With real-time analytics in a transacting system comes the possibility of AI-based learning and machine-to-machine transactions. Already there are solutions that leverage these approaches, such as SAP Supply Base Optimization, which leverages predictive analytics libraries and linear programming to negotiate target prices and define award splits. Augmented decision-making capabilities in the later releases of SAP S/4HANA connected to SAP Leonardo allow for predictive analysis and system recommendations in key areas such as contract expiration and management, as well as workflow approval groupings. There are current predictions that more than 60 to 70 percent of procurement tasks could be automated in the coming years, and these types of technologies and solutions will underpin these bold claims.

Automation of labor-intensive areas of the procure-to-pay process has already gone into general availability in SAP S/4HANA. Further machine-based learning approaches for procurement, under the overall SAP Leonardo initiative, can be found on the invoice-processing side in SAP Cash Application. Here, labor-intensive invoice-matching processes are automated, using machine learning to match criteria from historical processing and thus automatically match and clear payments. It is safe to say, without hyperbole, that this area is still very much in its early years of growth and development. Another fast-growing area for procurement and automation is the Internet of Things (IoT). IoT and the Industrial Internet of Things (IIoT) refer to vast networks of devices connected to the internet, from phones to machines to appliances. All of these connection points represent an opportunity to drive and automate procurement activities to support continued operations and avoid unexpected maintenance issues or failures. Already these connected devices communicate large amounts of information with SAP systems, from location to wear and tear. Machines on the shop floor and elsewhere can be set up to notify users of pending maintenance or parts needing replacement, and then order services and replacement parts.

17

17.2   Future State of the Procurement Supply Chain

As global supply chains come under increasing strain, from both natural and man-made headwinds in the form of climate change and trade wars, systems of procurement and supply will increasingly rely on flexibility and intelligence to navigate the terrain and even build competitive advantages with logistics and procurement operations. Indeed, some of the most successful corporations today are weaponizing logistics and procurement to drive costs out of their operations and dramatically increase speed, with game-changing effects on their competition. With the need for speed and agility, the old model for shipping 40-foot-container loads on a slow boat from China to distribution centers around the world may no longer cut it, even without the growing threat of tariffs and retaliation cycles. New supply chains, models, and tools, as well as suppliers, go-to-market strategies, and mitigation planning, are more relevant than ever before.

Having technologies and solutions that simultaneously take advantage of cloud efficiencies in computing while providing an integrated, cross-line-of-business environment to coordinate these activities in real time is paramount to an organization's success. Procurement is growing in importance in these choppy seas and will continue to grow during the coming waves of change as a competitive differentiator. With SAP Ariba, SAP Fieldglass, Concur, and SAP S/4HANA Sourcing and Procurement, SAP intends to remain firmly at the tiller.

The Author

Justin Ashlock has spent over half of his 20-year-plus career in technology at SAP America, serving as the lead consultant for hundreds of global SAP customer projects and engagements supporting over $100 billion in procurement and logistics activities worldwide. Justin is a the vice president of procurement services delivery within SAP's CX success and services organization. In this role, he provides general management for the North American procurement services practice, while also providing global delivery strategy and consistency to MEE and CIS regions. Justin holds a bachelor's degree from the University of California, Berkeley, and a master's degree in business administration from the University of Notre Dame.

Contributors

Chelliah Soundar started his career as an electrical engineer at a leading automobile manufacturing company in India after graduating from a highly ranked engineering school, National Institute of Technology, in Tiruchirappalli, India. He transitioned to the technology sector and began implementing SAP ERP solutions for various customers. He has more than 12 years of experience in SAP customer projects in the areas of sourcing and procurement and materials management. Currently, Soundar is supporting SAP S/4HANA implementation projects globally as an SAP S/4HANA product expert in SAP's elite team, the regional implementation group. He provides SAP S/4HANA training and enablement sessions for SAP customers, implementation partners, and colleagues within SAP from both product and project perspective. He also has an MBA degree from Texas A&M University.

Robert (Bob) Gotschall works as a solutions consultant at Venetia Partners. He was formerly a Platinum Consultant in sourcing and procurement and in materials management and operations at SAP Americas. He's had 21 years of full lifecycle SAP implementation experience, and 37 years of information systems design and implementation experience in total.

He is an expert in the design and implementation of procure-to-pay and logistics execution business processes using SAP capabilities, including SAP S/4HANA. He has process expertise in sourcing, procurement, inventory management, logistics invoice verification, inbound and outbound logistics, warehouse management, batch management and handling unit management. Bob has earned a bachelor's degree in Computer Science from Purdue University.

Index

Q

R

- Configure embedded PP-DS in SAP S/4HANA for advanced manufacturing

- Run production planning and detailed scheduling step by step

- Master planning, service, and scheduling heuristics

Mahesh MG

PP-DS with SAP S/4HANA

Are you ready for embedded PP-DS? Advance your production planning and detailed scheduling with this comprehensive guide! Discover how the PP-DS integration model has been simplified with SAP S/4HANA. Then follow step-by-step instructions for configuring and running PP-DS in your system, from determining your requirements to monitoring your results. With details on advanced features, troubleshooting, and migration, this is your all-in-one PP-DS resource.

476 pages, pub. 02/2020
E-Book: $79.99 | **Print:** $89.95 | **Bundle:** $99.99

www.sap-press.com/4951

- Configure SAP S/4HANA for your materials management requirements

- Maintain critical material and business partner records

- Walk through MRP, inventory management, purchasing, and quotation management

Jawad Akhtar, Martin Murray

Materials Management with SAP S/4HANA

Business Processes and Configuration

Materials management has transitioned to SAP S/4HANA—let us help you do the same! Whether your focus is on materials planning, procurement, or inventory, this guide will teach you to configure and manage your critical processes in SAP S/4HANA. Start by creating your organizational structure and defining business partners and material master data. Then get step-by-step instructions for defining the processes you need, from creating purchase orders and receiving goods to running MRP and using batch management. The new MM is here!

946 pages, pub. 10/2018
E-Book: $79.99 | **Print:** $89.95 | **Bundle:** $99.99

www.sap-press.com/4711

- Implement production planning for discrete, process, and repetitive manufacturing with SAP S/4HANA

- Configure and run MRP, batch management, capacity planning, and more

- Analyze your data with standard analytics and SAP Fiori apps

Jawad Akhtar

Production Planning with SAP S/4HANA

Allocate your materials, personnel, and machinery with SAP S/4HANA! This comprehensive guide will show you how to configure production planning in SAP S/4HANA for discrete, process, and repetitive manufacturing. Next, you'll learn to run those processes using step-by-step instructions. Master production workflows, like batch management, S&OP, demand management, PP-DS, and MRP. With industry examples throughout, this guide is your one-stop shop for PP with SAP S/4HANA!

1010 pages, pub. 03/2019

E-Book: $79.99 | **Print:** $89.95 | **Bundle:** $99.99

www.sap-press.com/4821

Interested in reading more?

Please visit our website for all new book
and e-book releases from SAP PRESS.

www.sap-press.com